SOCIAL DEVIANCE

Library of Congress Cataloging-in-Publication Data

Social deviance : readings in theory and research / edited by Henry N. Pontell. — 4th ed.
  p.   cm.
  Includes bibliographical references.
  ISBN 0–13–040774–7
  1. Deviant behavior.   I. Pontell, Henry N.

HM811.S58835 2002
302.5′42—dc21   2001045947
                                           CIP

Publisher: *Nancy Roberts*
Managing Editor (editorial): *Sharon Chambliss*
Managing Editor (production): *Ann Marie McCarthy*
Production Liaison: *Fran Russello*
Project Manager: *Patty Donovan/Pine Tree Composition*
Prepress and Manufacturing Buyer: *Mary Ann Gloriande*
Art Director: *Jayne Conte*
Cover Designer: *Bruce Kenselaar*
Marketing Manager: *Chris Barker*

This book was set in 10/12 Times Roman by *Pine Tree Composition, Inc.*
and was printed and bound by *Hamilton Printing Company.*
The cover was printed by *Jaguar Graphics*

 © 2002, 1999, 1996, 1993 by Pearson Education, Inc.
Upper Saddle River, New Jersey 07458

Printed in the United States of America
10 9 8 7 6 5 4 3 2 1

ISBN: 0-13-040774-7

Pearson Education Ltd., *London*
Pearson Education Australia Pte, Limited, *Sydney*
Pearson Education Singapore, Pte. Ltd.
Pearson Education North Asia Ltd., *Hong Kong*
Pearson Education Canada Ltd., *Toronto*
Pearson Educación de Mexico, S.A. de C.V.
Pearson Education—Japan, *Tokyo*
Pearson Education Malaysia, Pte. Ltd.
Pearson Education, Upper Saddle River, New Jersey

FOURTH EDITION

SOCIAL DEVIANCE
Readings
in
Theory and Research

Edited

by

HENRY N. PONTELL
University of California, Irvine

Upper Saddle River, New Jersey 07458

For my family and friends

and in memory of
Edwin M. Lemert

Note to the Reader

The language used in some of these pieces may be offensive to some readers in that it may reflect insensitivity towards certain social groups. Neither the text author, the publisher nor, for that matter, any of the individual authors to our knowledge, condone or agree with language that could be construed as being racist, sexist, homophobic, or insensitive to the handicapped or other groups. It is the intention of the author and publisher that the chapters be read in the context of the era and theoretical perspective within which they were produced, and valued for their main contributions to the historical development of the field of social deviance.

Contents

Mental Disorder 449

*add something
on marijuana
to drugs*

PREFACE

In this fourth edition of *Social Deviance*, I have built on the strengths of previous editions. While the organization of topics remains the same, I have added new works and deleted others at the suggestion of colleagues and students. My objectives in this fourth edition were to: (1) present both classic theoretical works as well as contemporary substantive research, (2) provide a broad array of readings representing different perspectives in the field of deviance, and (3) include readings that would be suitable for undergraduates.

Although some of the older theoretical selections are occasionally more difficult for students to comprehend, they represent major influences in the development of the field of deviance and deserve attention and understanding. The section of this edition presenting theoretical perspectives has been modified with the addition of new pieces representing developments in both feminist scholarship (sex tourism in Thailand), and the labeling perspective (whiteness as stigma). In the section on deviant behaviors, I have added new readings on professional misconduct by psychotherapists and on statutory rape.

This edition has greatly benefited from the work and dedication of my research assistants who helped secure articles and permissions and who sat through meetings where the merits of all potential articles were discussed. I extend my greatest thanks to Helena Rene, Veronica Gerth, and Natasha Nichols, all of whom provided excellent assistance for this edition. I also thank Marilyn Wahlert and Judy Omiya in the Department of Criminology, Law and Society at UC, Irvine for their superb support in preparing materials for the final manuscript. As always, Sharon Chambliss and Nancy Roberts at Prentice Hall have been ideal editors, and I greatly appreciate their help with this new edition. Finally, I would like to acknowledge and thank the students in my deviance courses for their valuable comments and suggestions regarding past editions that should result in continued improvements of this reader.

Henry N. Pontell
University of California, Irvine

SOCIAL DEVIANCE

PART I

INTRODUCTION

What is deviance? This is a difficult question to answer simply, as the term conjures up many disparate images and may mean different things to different people. Prostitutes, alcoholics, burglars, drug addicts, and transvestites may come to mind. Or, at the other end of the spectrum of respectability, one might think of Charles Keating and Michael Milken, who were convicted of major financial crimes. While it may appear that these examples have nothing in common, they all represent examples of deviant behavior, in that they involve actions and characteristics that have elicited negative reactions from relatively large or powerful audiences. This is not meant to imply that there is one simplistic definition of deviance agreed upon by social scientists. In fact, to the contrary, social scientists are still not in full agreement regarding a precise definition. The chapters that follow will present these different theoretical concerns and research approaches regarding the study of deviance.

The three introductory pieces provide clear examples of this diversity of thought and represent important and interesting works in the field of deviance. Howard Becker's classic piece on "Moral Entrepreneurs" examines how deviant categories are created and how enforcement of these categories is socially structured. The moral crusader or "rule creator" has a personal stake in

the content of social rules and works to change them to fit his and her own world view. The "rule enforcer," on the other hand, takes a detached view of the rule itself and is more interested in work situations involving enforcement. This detachment and concern over job responsibilities leads enforcers to label deviance in a selective manner. Thus, Becker concludes that whether one is actually labeled a deviant depends on factors extraneous to the behavior itself. This idea is central to the labeling perspective on deviance.

Gary Marx's article, "Ironies of Social Control," focuses on a relatively neglected area of study: the interactive context within which deviance occurs. In this important piece, Marx argues that authorities themselves may in fact help deviance and law breaking to occur. He classifies those instances where authorities contribute to, or even generate, deviant behavior as including three ideal types. "Escalation" refers to enforcement action that may unintentionally encourage rule breaking. "Nonenforcement" refers to the idea that by not taking action authorities intentionally permit rule breaking. "Covert facilitation" occurs when authorities take deceptive or hidden action that intentionally encourages rule breaking. Marx presents examples of each type of action and shows how more than one may be involved in a given example of rule breaking.

The study provides ample evidence that police efforts can positively influence the commission of offenses; a novel idea that appears to fly in the face of both popular and scholarly understandings of deviance and formal social control.

In the "Discovery of Child Abuse" Stephen Pfohl examines the social forces that promoted the labeling of child beating as deviant and that produced universal criminal legislation in the 1960s. This is an important work that illustrates how deviant categories are created. Using a historical framework, Pfohl considers the social reaction to child abuse before the formulation of a fixed label and finds that such reactions were sporadic. He shows that the perception of abuse as deviance was not due to any escalation in the behavior itself, but rather to the organizational structure of the medical profession, which led to the "discovery" by pediatric radiologists, who saw x-rays of broken bones. A new "illness" was created, and the clinical term of "battered child syndrome" was used so that medical practitioners could control the consequences of their diagnoses and prevent management of such cases by extramedical formal social control agents. Pfohl discusses the consequences of this definition for both child abuse legislation and the prosecution of abusers.

MORAL ENTREPRENEURS
THE CREATION AND ENFORCEMENT OF DEVIANT CATEGORIES*

Howard S. Becker

RULE CREATORS

The prototype of the rule creator, but not the only variety, as we shall see, is the crusading reformer. He is interested in the content of rules. The existing rules do not satisfy him because there is some evil which profoundly disturbs him. He feels that nothing can be right in the world until rules are made to correct it. He operates with an absolute ethic; what he sees is truly and totally evil with no qualification. Any means is justified to do away with it. The crusader is fervent and righteous, often self-righteous.

It is appropriate to think of reformers as crusaders because they typically believe that their mission is a holy one. The prohibitionist serves as an excellent example, as does the person who wants to suppress vice and sexual delinquency or the person who wants to do away with gambling.

*Reprinted with the permission of The Free Press, a Division of Simon & Schuster Inc. from *Outsiders: Studies in the Sociology of Deviance* by Howard S. Becker. Copyright © 1963 by The Free Press.

These examples suggest that the moral crusader is a meddling busybody, interested in forcing his own morals on others. But this is a one-sided view. Many moral crusades have strong humanitarian overtones. The crusader is not only interested in seeing to it that other people do what he thinks [is] right. He believes that if they do what is right it will be good for them. Or he may feel that his reform will prevent certain kinds of exploitation of one person by another. Prohibitionists felt that they were not simply forcing their morals on others, but attempting to provide the conditions for a better way of life for people prevented by drink from realizing a truly good life. Abolitionists were not simply trying to prevent slave owners from doing the wrong thing; they were trying to help slaves achieve a better life. Because of the importance of the humanitarian motive, moral crusaders (despite their relatively single-minded devotion to their particular cause) often lend their support to other humanitarian crusades. Joseph Gusfield has pointed out that:

The American temperance movement during the 19th century was part of a general effort toward the improvement of the worth of the human being through improved morality as well as economic conditions. The mixture of the religious, the equalitarian, and the humanitarian was an outstanding facet of the moral reformism of many movements. Temperance supporters formed a large segment of movements such as sabbatarianism, abolition, woman's rights, agrarianism, and humanitarian attempts to improve the lot of the poor. . . .

In its auxiliary interests the WCTU revealed a great concern for the improvement of the welfare of the lower classes. It was active in campaigns to secure penal reform, to shorten working hours and raise wages for workers, and to abolish child labor and in a number of other humanitarian and equalitarian activities. In the 1880's the WCTU worked to bring about legislation for the protection of working girls against the exploitation by men.[1]

As Gusfield says,[2] "Moral reformism of this type suggests the approach of a dominant class toward those less favorably situated in the economic and social structure." Moral crusaders typically want to help those beneath them to achieve a better status. That those beneath them do not always like the means proposed for their salvation is another matter. But this fact—that moral crusades are typically dominated by those in the upper levels of the social structure—means that they add to the power they derive from the legitimacy of their moral position, the power they derive from their superior position in society.

Naturally, many moral crusades draw support from people whose motives are less pure than those of the crusader. Thus, some industrialists supported Prohibition because they felt it would provide them with a more manageable labor force.[3] Similarly, it is sometimes rumored that Nevada gambling interests support the opposition to attempts to legalize gambling in California because it would cut so heavily into their business, which depends in substantial measure on the population of Southern California.[4]

The moral crusader, however, is more concerned with ends than with means. When it comes to drawing up specific rules (typically in the form of legislation to be proposed to a state legislature or the federal Congress), he frequently relies on the advice of experts. Lawyers, expert in the drawing of acceptable legislation, often play this role. Government bureaus in whose jurisdiction the problem falls may also have the necessary expertise, as did the Federal Bureau of Narcotics in the case of the marihuana problem.

As psychiatric ideology, however, becomes increasingly acceptable, a new expert has appeared—the psychiatrist. Sutherland, in his discussion of the natural history of sexual psychopath laws, pointed to the psychiatrist's influence.[5] He suggests the following as the conditions under which the sexual psychopath law, which provides that a person "who is diagnosed as a sexual psychopath may be confined for an indefinite period in a state hospital for the insane,"[6] will be passed.

First, these laws are customarily enacted after a state of fear has been aroused in a community by a few serious sex crimes committed in quick succession. This is illustrated in Indiana, where a law was passed following three or four sexual attacks in Indianapolis, with murder in two. Heads of families bought guns and watch dogs, and the supply of locks and chains in the hardware stores of the city was completely exhausted. . . .

A second element in the process of developing sexual psychopath laws is the agitated activity of the community in connection with the fear. The attention of the community is focused on sex crimes, and people in the most varied situations envisage dangers and see the need of and possibility for their control. . . .

The third phase in the development of those sexual psychopath laws has been the appointment of a committee. The committee gathers the many conflicting recommendations of persons and groups of persons, attempts to determine "facts," studies procedures in other states, and makes recommendations, which generally include bills for the legislature. Although the general fear usually subsides within a few days, a committee has the formal duty of following through until positive action is taken. Terror which does not result in a committee is much less likely to result in a law.[7]

In the case of sexual psychopath laws, there usually is no government agency charged with dealing in a specialized way with sexual deviations. Therefore, when the need for expert advice in drawing up legislation arises, people frequently turn to the professional group most closely associated with such problems:

In some states, at the committee stage of the development of a sexual psychopath law, psychiatrists have played an important part. The psychiatrists, more than any others, have been the interest group back of the laws. A committee of psychiatrists and neurologists in Chicago wrote the bill which became the sexual psychopath law of Illinois; the bill was sponsored by the Chicago Bar Association and by the state's attorney of Cook County and was enacted with little opposition in the next session of the State Legislature. In Minnesota all the members of the governor's committee except one were psychiatrists. In Wisconsin the Milwaukee Neuropsychiatric Society shared in pressing the Milwaukee Crime Commission for the enactment of a law. In Indiana the attorney-general's committee received from the American Psychiatric Association copies of all the sexual psychopath laws which had been enacted in other states.[8]

The influence of psychiatrists in other realms of the criminal law has increased in recent years.

In any case, what is important about this example is not that psychiatrists are becoming increasingly influential, but that the moral crusader, at some point in the development of his crusade, often requires the services of a professional who can draw up the appropriate rules in an appropriate form. The crusader himself is often not concerned with such details. Enough for him that the main point has been won; he leaves its implementation to others.

By leaving the drafting of the specific rule in the hands of others, the crusader opens the door for many unforeseen influences. For those who draft legislation for crusaders have their own interest, which may affect the legislation they prepare. It is likely that the sexual psychopath laws drawn by psychiatrists contain many features never intended by the citizens who spearheaded the drives to "do something about sex crimes," features which do however reflect the professional interests of organized psychiatry.

RULE ENFORCERS

The most obvious consequence of a successful crusade is the creation of a new set of rules. With the creation of a new set of rules we often find that a new set of enforcement agencies and officials is established. Sometimes, of course, existing agencies take over the administration of the new rule, but more frequently a new set of rule enforcers is created. The passage of the Harrison Act presaged the creation of the Federal Narcotics Bureau, just as the passage of the Eighteenth Amendment led to the creation of police agencies charged with enforcing the Prohibition Laws.

With the establishment of organizations of rule enforcers, the crusade becomes institutionalized. What started out as a drive to convince the world of the moral necessity of a new rule finally becomes an organization devoted to the enforcement of the rule. Just as radical political movements turn into organized political parties and lusty evangelical sects become staid religious denominations, the final outcome of the moral crusade is a police force. To understand, therefore, how the rules creating a new class of outsiders are applied to particular people we must understand the motives and interests of police, the rule enforcers.

Although some policemen undoubtedly have a kind of crusading interest in stamping out evil, it is probably much more typical for the policeman to have a certain detached and objective view of his job. He is not so much concerned with the content of any particular rule as he is with the fact that it is his job to enforce the rule. When the rules are changed, he punishes what was once acceptable behavior just as he ceases to punish behavior that has been made legitimate by a change in the rules. The enforcer, then, may not be interested in the content of the rule as such, but only in the fact that the existence of the rule provides him with a job, a profession, and a raison d'être.

Since the enforcement of certain rules provides justification for his way of life, the enforcer has two interests which condition his enforcement activity: first, he must justify the existence of his position and, second, he must win the respect of those he deals with.

These interests are not peculiar to rule enforcer. Members of all occupations feel the need to justify their work and win the respect of others. Musicians would like to do this but have difficulty finding ways of successfully impressing their worth on customers. Janitors fail to win their tenants' respect, but develop an ideology which stresses the quasi-professional responsibility they have to keep confidential the intimate knowledge of tenants they acquire in the course of their work.[9] Physicians, lawyers, and other professionals, more successful in winning the respect of clients, develop elaborate mechanisms for maintaining a properly respectful relationship.

In justifying the existence of his position, the rule enforcer faces a double problem. On the one hand, he must demonstrate to others that the problem still exists: The rules he is supposed to enforce have some point, because infractions occur. On the other hand, he must show that his attempts at enforcement are effective and worthwhile, that the evil he is supposed to deal with is in fact being dealt with adequately. Therefore, enforcement organizations, particularly when they are seeking funds, typically oscillate between two kinds of claims. First, they say that by reason of their efforts the problem they deal with is approaching solution. But, in the same breath, they say the problem is perhaps worse than ever (though through no fault of their own) and requires renewed and increased effort to keep it under control. Enforcement officials can be more vehement than anyone else in their insistence that the problem they are supposed to deal with is still with us, in fact is more with us than ever before. In making these claims, enforcement officials provide good reason for continuing the existence of the position they occupy.

We may also note that enforcement officials and agencies are inclined to take a pessimistic view of human nature. If they do not actually believe in original sin, they at least like to dwell on the difficulties in getting people to abide by rules, on the characteristics of human nature that lead people toward evil. They are skeptical of attempts to reform rule-breakers.

The skeptical and pessimistic outlook of the rule enforcer, of course, is reinforced by his daily experience. He sees, as he goes about his work, the evidence that the problem is still with us. He sees the people who continually repeat offenses, thus definitely branding themselves in his eyes as outsiders. Yet it is not too great a stretch of the imagination to suppose that one of the underlying reasons for the enforcer's pessimism about human nature and the possibilities of reform is

that fact that if human nature were perfectible and people could be permanently reformed, his job would come to an end.

In the same way, a rule enforcer is likely to believe that it is necessary for the people he deals with to respect him. If they do not, it will be very difficult to do his job; his feeling of security in his work will be lost. Therefore, a good deal of enforcement activity is devoted not to the actual enforcement of rules, but to coercing respect from the people the enforcer deals with. This means that one may be labeled as a deviant not because he has actually broken a rule, but because he has shown disrespect to the enforcer of the rule.

Westley's study of policemen in a small industrial city furnishes a good example of this phenomenon. In his interview, he asked policemen, "When do you think a policeman is justified in roughing a man up?" He found that "at least 37% of the men believed that it was legitimate to use violence to coerce respect."[10] He gives some illuminating quotations from his interviews:

Well, there are cases. For example, when you stop a fellow for a routine questioning, say a wise guy, and he starts talking back to you and telling you you are no good and that sort of thing. You know you can take a man in on a disorderly conduct charge, but you can practically never make it stick. So what you do in a case like that is to egg the guy on until he makes a remark where you can justifiably slap him and, then, if he fights back, you can call it resisting arrest.

Well, a prisoner deserves to be hit when he goes to the point where he tries to put you below him.

You've gotta get rough when a man's language becomes very bad, when he is trying to make a fool of you in front of everybody else. I think most policemen try to treat people in a nice way, but usually you have to talk pretty rough. That's the only way to set a man down, to make him show a little respect.[11]

What Westley describes is the use of an illegal means of coercing respect from others. Clearly, when a rule enforcer has the option of enforcing a rule or not, the difference in what he does may be caused by the attitude of the offender toward him. If the offender is properly respectful, the enforcer may smooth the situation over. If the offender is disrespectful, then sanctions may be visited on him. Westley has shown that this differential tends to operate in the case of traffic offenses, where the policeman's discretion is perhaps at a maximum.[12] But it probably operates in other areas as well.

Ordinarily, the rule enforcer has a great deal of discretion in many areas, if only because his resources are not sufficient to cope with the volume of rule-breaking he is supposed to deal with. This means that he cannot tackle everything at once and to this extent must temporize with evil. He cannot do the whole job and knows it. He takes his time, on the assumption that the problems he deals with will be around for a long while. He establishes priorities, dealing with things in their turn, handling the most pressing problems immediately and leaving others for later. His attitude toward his work, in short, is professional. He lacks the naive moral fervor characteristic of the rule creator.

If the enforcer is not going to tackle every case he knows of at once, he must have a basis for deciding when to enforce the rule, which persons committing which acts to label as deviant. One criterion for selecting people is the "fix." Some people have sufficient political influence or know-how to be able to ward off attempts at enforcement, if not at the time of apprehension then at a later stage in the process. Very often, this function is professionalized; someone performs the job on a full-time basis, available to anyone who wants to hire him. A professional thief described fixers this way:

There is in every large city a regular fixer for professional thieves. He has no agents and does not solicit and seldom takes any case except that of a professional thief, just as they seldom go to anyone except him. This centralized and monopolized system of fixing for professional thieves is found in practically all of the large cities and many of the small ones.[13]

Since it is mainly professional thieves who know about the fixer and his operations, the consequence of this criterion for selecting people to apply the rules to is that amateurs tend to be caught, convicted, and labeled deviant much more frequently than professionals. As the professional thief notes:

You can tell by the way the case is handled in court when the fix is in. When the copper is not very certain he has the right man, or the testimony of the copper and the complainant does not agree, or the prosecutor goes easy on the defendant, or the judge is arrogant in his decisions, you can always be sure that someone has got the word in. This does not happen in many cases of theft, for there is one case of a professional to twenty-five or thirty amateurs who know nothing about the fix. These amateurs get the hard end of the deal every time. The coppers bawl out about the thieves, no one holds up his testimony, the judge delivers an oration, and all of them get credit for stopping a crime wave. When the professional hears the case immediately preceding his own, he will think, "He should have got ninety years. It's the damn amateurs who cause all the heat in the stores." Or else he thinks, "Isn't it a damn shame for that copper to send that kid away for a pair of hose, and in a few minutes he will agree to a small fine for me for stealing a fur coat?" But if the coppers did not send the amateurs away to strengthen their records of convictions, they could not sandwich in the professionals whom they turn loose.[14]

Enforcers of rules, since they have no stake in the content of particular rules themselves, often develop their own private evaluation of the importance of various kinds of rules and infractions of them. This set of priorities may differ considerably from those held by the general public. For instance, drug users typically believe (and a few policemen have personally confirmed it to me) that police do not consider the use of marihuana to be as important a problem or as dangerous a practice as the use of opiate drugs. Police base this conclusion on the fact that, in their experience, opiate users commit other crimes (such as theft or prostitution) in order to get drugs, while marihuana users do not.

Enforcers then, responding to the pressures of their own work situation, enforce rules and create outsiders in a selective way. Whether a person who commits a deviant act is in fact labeled a deviant depends on many things extraneous to his actual behavior: whether the enforcement official feels that at this time he must make some show of doing his job in order to justify his position, whether the misbehaver shows proper deference to the enforcer, whether the "fix" has been put in, and where the kind of act he has committed stands on the enforcer's list of priorities.

The professional enforcer's lack of fervor and routine approach to dealing with evil may get him into trouble with the rule creator. The rule creator, as we have said, is concerned with the content of the rules that interest him. He sees them as the means by which evil can be stamped out. He does not understand the enforcer's long-range approach to the same problems and cannot see why all the evil that is apparent cannot be stamped out at once.

When the person interested in the content of a rule realizes or has called to his attention the fact that enforcers are dealing selectively with the evil that concerns him, his righteous wrath may be aroused. The professional is denounced for viewing the evil too lightly, for failing to do his duty. The moral entrepreneur, at whose instance the rule was made, arises again to say that the outcome of the last crusade has not been satisfactory or that the gains once made have been whittled away and lost.

NOTES

1. Joseph R. Gusfield, "Social Structure and Moral Reform: A Study of the Woman's Christian Temperance Union," *American Journal of Sociology,* LXI (November, 1955), 223.

2. *Ibid.*

3. See Raymond G. McCarthy, editor, *Drinking and Intoxication* (New Haven and New York: Yale Center of Alcohol Studies and The Free Press of Glencoe, 1959), pp. 395–396.

4. This is suggested in Oscar Lewis, *Sagebrush Casinos: The Story of Legal Gambling in Nevada* (New York: Doubleday and Co., 1953), pp. 223–234.

5. Edwin H. Sutherland, "The Diffusion of Sexual Psychopath Laws," *American Journal of Sociology,* LVI (September, 1950), 142–148.

6. *Ibid.*, p. 142.

7. *Ibid.*, pp. 143–145.

8. *Ibid.*, pp. 145–146.

9. See Ray Gold, "Janitors Versus Tenants: A Status-Income Dilemma," *American Journal of Sociology,* LVII (March, 1952), 486–493.

10. William A. Westley, "Violence and the Police," *American Journal of Sociology,* LIX (July, 1953), 39.

11. *Ibid.*

12. See William A. Westley, "The Police: A Sociological Study of Law, Custom, and Morality" (unpublished Ph.D. dissertation, University of Chicago, Department of Sociology, 1951).

13. Edwin H. Sutherland (editor), *The Professional Thief* (Chicago: University of Chicago Press, 1937), pp. 87–88.

14. *Ibid.*, pp. 91–92.

Ironies of Social Control
Authorities as Contributors to Deviance Through Escalation, Nonenforcement, and Covert Facilitation*

Gary T. Marx

Many current theoretical approaches to deviance causation tend to neglect a crucial level of analysis: the specific interactive context within which

*© 1981 by the Society for the Study of Social Problems. Reprinted from *Social Problems* 28:3 (Feb. 1981), pp. 221–233, by permission of the author and the publisher.

rule breaking occurs. Anomie (Merton, 1957) and subcultural theorists (Sutherland and Cressey, 1974) and combinations of these approaches (Cloward and Ohlin, 1960) tend to focus on rather abstract initial group properties such as opportunity structures and norms, rather than on the interactive group processes out of which behavior emerges. Those questioning the mechanistic force of such variables nevertheless stress the independence of the deviant as a maker of choices (Matza, 1966).

Even when attention is given to situational aspects of rule breaking, as with some functionalists, the focus tends to be too mechanistic. In what can be called the trampoline model of social control (Homans, 1950; Parsons, 1951), norm violations lead to reparative social control responses. Social controllers are thought to be in a relentless struggle with autonomous criminals, who freely choose to violate the law, and who always do what they are charged with having done. The systemic and reciprocal effects become most apparent *after* the deviance appears. In contrast (and closer to the perspective to be developed here), theorists such as Reiss (1951) and Hirschi (1969) see social control as an important variable in the production of deviance. However, they argue that it is the absence of social control that helps to explain deviance. I shall argue that its *presence* does too.

Whatever merit the above approaches have for dealing with various aspects of deviance, they must be supplemented by a theoretical perspective which focuses on the immediate context of the rule infraction. Such a perspective must at least take as an empirical question the degree of autonomy in the actions of the rule violator, and whether people actually do what they are charged with having done.

In current theories the deviant is seen either as autonomous or as a pawn of broad social and cultural forces. Most interpretations tend to reify the categories of authority and "criminal" and to draw the line between them too sharply. They miss the interdependence that may exist between these groups and the extent to which authorities may induce or help others to break the law, be involved in law breaking themselves, or create false records about others' supposed law breaking. Conversely, the extent to which those engaged in illegal activities may be contributing to social order is also ignored. Here I focus on some neglected aspects of the role of authorities in law violations.

The idea that authorities may play a role in generating deviance is not new. Clearly, the labeling perspective has focused attention on the role of authorities—for example, the work of Tannenbaum (1938), Kitsuse (1962), Becker (1963), Wilkins (1965), Scheff (1966), Lemert (1951, 1972), and Hawkins and Tiedeman (1975). In such work, authorities have been seen to "create" deviance by defining some of a wide range of behavior as illegal, using their discretion about which laws will then be most actively enforced, and singling out some of those who violate these laws for processing by the criminal justice system. Subsequent restrictions on the behavior of those processed as deviants, such as their being singled out for special attention by authorities, and subsequent changes in their self-images, are thought to result in their becoming even more involved in deviant activities.

These are not, however, the roles that authorities play in creating deviance on which I wish to focus. Much of the labeling argument is true by definition; that which isn't seems plausible enough and has the easy virtue of overlapping with the underdog worldview of many who hold it, though systematic research in its support cannot be said to be overwhelming (Manning, 1973; Wellford, 1975; Gove, 1980). Yet if subsequent evidence suggests that labeling as such does not, on balance, amplify deviance and even deters it, I think a strong case can still be made for the important role of authorities.

I do begin at an abstract level with what I see to be a fundamental insight of the labeling perspective: the possible irony of social controllers creating what they set out to control. But then I emphasize a different set of factors. In spite of its calling attention to the role of authorities, the emphasis in the labeling approach is usually placed on what authorities do to others already known or thought to be deviant. Its main concern is with the secondary rather than primary deviance. Its usual focus is not on the behavior of control agents before or during the rule breaking, nor on the degree of autonomy in the actions of the rule breaker. Nor is its usual focus even on whether the deviance actually occurred, preferring instead, in Rains's (1975:10) words, "to describe the full process of imputation without regard for warrant." But here I will deliberately focus on infraction—on some of the ways in which it is shaped or induced by prior or concomitant actions of authorities, and on some of the causes involved.[1]

Situations where social control contributes to, or even generates, rule-breaking behavior include these three ideal types:

A. Escalation (by taking enforcement action, authorities unintentionally encourage rule breaking).
B. Nonenforcement (by strategically taking *no enforcement action*, authorities intentionally permit rule breaking).
C. Covert facilitation (by taking *hidden or deceptive enforcement action*, authorities intentionally encourage rule breaking).

These are analytic distinctions. In a given empirical instance all may be present.

In much of the rest of the paper I discuss these types of social control. I use examples from criminal justice situations primarily, but believe the processes are also evident in other social settings, such as the school, family, and work.

Documents and published accounts are major sources. However, I have also drawn on interviews and observations made over a seven-year period in 18 U.S. police departments while studying community police patrols, community service officers, civilian police planners, and performance measures, plus those made during a year spent studying English and French police. My initial interest in the topic grew out of work done for the Kerner Commission in 1968 on police behavior in civil disorders.

ESCALATION

The clearest cases of authorities contributing to rule breaking involve escalation. As with facilitation, authorities' intervention is conducive to deviance. However, secrecy need not be involved (the facilitation can be overt), and the final consequence is generally not consciously, or at best publicly, sought by controllers when they initially enter the situation.[2] It is not simply that social control has no effect, rather that it can amplify. (In the language of cybernetics, this is a case of deviation amplifying feedback [Cf. Maruyama, 1963]—in everyday language, snow-balling or mushrooming). In escalation the very process of social control directly triggers violations. In urging that attention be focused on the deviant act as such, Cohen has written:

The history of a deviant act is a history of an interaction process. The antecedents of the act are an unfolding sequence of acts contributed by a set of actors (1965:9).

Nowhere is this logic clearer than in the case of escalation. Five major analytic elements of escalation are:

1. An increase in the *frequency* of the original violations.
2. An increase in the *seriousness* of violations, including the greater use of violence.
3. The appearance of *new* categories of violators and/or victims (without a net diminution of those previously present).
4. An increase in the commitment and/or skill and effectiveness of those engaged in the violation.
5. The appearance of violations whose very definition is tied to social control intervention.

Escalation may stem from initial or postapprehension enforcement efforts.

Police involvement in family conflict, crowd, and automobile chase situations can contribute to violations when none were imminent, or it can increase the seriousness of these situations. In responding to challenges to their authority or to interpersonal conflict situations, preemptive police actions (euphemistically called by some with a sardonic smile, "constructive coercion" and "preventive violence") may lead to further violence.

A three-year study of police-citizen incidents in New York City notes "the extent to which the handling of relatively minor incidents such as traffic violations or disorderly disputes between husbands and wives seemed to create a more serious situation than existed prior to the police attempt to control the situation" (McNamara, 1967). Family disturbance calls are an important source of police injuries to citizens and vice versa. Bard has similarly observed that "there is more than ample evidence that insensitive, untrained, and inept police management of human problems is a significant breeding ground for violence" (1971:3). Certain styles of intervention are likely to provoke aggressive responses.

An English policeman characterized the 1960s' riot control behavior of American police in some cities as "oilin' the fire." Police responses to crowd situations offer many examples of escalation (Marx, 1970; Stark, 1972). Provocative overreaction (referred to by another English policeman as "cracking a nut with a sledgehammer") can turn a peaceful crowd into a disorderly one. In the 1967 riot in New Haven, for example, a small group of angry but as yet law-abiding blacks marched in the street—to be met by police tear gas; this then provoked a small riot. Or in Detroit a small riot emerged during the Poor People's March when, during a meeting in a large hall, police inside the building tried to push people outside, at the same time that mounted police outside were trying to push people back inside. Such police reactions and subsequent arrests may occur in the most benign of circumstances, such as at sporting events or concerts.

High-speed chases offer another all too tragic example. They result in injuries, in death, and often in manslaughter charges against persons who, in the absence of the chase, might have faced minimal or no charges. For example, in a Boston suburb, a car being chased by two police cruisers at speeds of 95 miles an hour killed a footpatrolman. The young driver of the car was subsequently charged not only with speeding but with manslaughter. The same day a 15-year-old youth facing manslaughter charges hung himself in a jail in a nearby town. He was arrested the week before, following a high-speed chase in which his car killed two people (*Boston Globe*, November 21, 1975). The high-speed chase, perhaps because of the risks and emotions involved and the denial of police authority, also figures disproportionately in situations where prisoners are abused. The escalation here has second-order effects, coming to involve new offenders (police themselves) as well as new offenses (e.g., assault and denial of civil rights).

One consequence of strong enforcement actions can be to change the personnel and social organization of those involved in illegal activities. For example, stepped-up enforcement efforts with respect to heroin and cocaine appear to have moved the drug traffic away from less sophisticated and skilled local, often amateur, groups to more highly skilled, centralized, better organized criminal groups (Young, 1971; Sabbag, 1976; Adler *et al.*, forthcoming). The greater skill and sophistication of those now drawn into the activity may mean the development of new markets. Increased risks may mean greater profits, as well as incentives to develop new consumers and markets. The more professional criminals are more likely to be able to avoid prosecution and are in a better position to induce police corruption.

Increased corruption, a frequent escalatory consequence of stepped-up enforcement efforts, is one of a number of second-order forms of illegality which may indirectly appear. Even attacking corruption may generate other problems. Thus, following reform efforts in one city (Sherman, 1978:257), police morale declined and citizen complaints went up sharply, as did police use of firearms. In Boston a recent increase in high-speed chases and attendant offenses and injuries is directly traceable to an order to enforce traffic laws more stringently. Another second-order effect can be seen in the monopoly profits which may accrue to those who provide vice in a context of strong enforcement pressures. These profits can be invested in still other illegal activities. Thus, some of the tremendous profits earned by organized crime groups that emerged during prohibition, and the skills developed then, went into gambling, labor racketeering, and narcotics. Violence may increase among criminal groups contending for new monopoly profits. Their monopoly may also have been aided by informing on competitors. The increased cost of the product they provide may mean increased illegality on the part of customers facing higher prices (Schur, 1965). A link between drug addiction and street crime, for example, has often been argued.

Authorities may directly provide new resources which have unintended effects. Part of the increased homicide rates in the 1970s, for example, particularly among minority youths, has been attributed to vastly augmented amounts of federal "buy" money for drugs. This increased the opportunity for youths to become informers, and some of them were subsequently killed. The drugs, stolen goods, money, weapons, and tips sometimes given to informers and others who aid police may be used in subsequent crimes. A more benign resource may be the youth workers sent to work with gangs in their environment. Some of the detached street-worker programs, aimed at reducing gang delinquency, may have actually increased it: By strengthening identification with the gang, they made it more cohesive and encouraged new recruits (Klein, 1969). Klein observes that the assumed advantages of group work with gangs are "mythical," and he advocates abandoning standard detached worker programs. In Chicago, anti-poverty funds for self-help programs among gangs offered resources, opportunities and incentives which created a context for fraud, extortion and violence (Short, 1974).

Contemporary American law has evolved an increasing number of crimes which emerge solely as an artifact of social control intervention. These emerge incidentally to efforts to enforce other laws. If authorities had not taken action, the offense would not have been committed. Resisting arrest or assaulting an officer are familiar examples. The prosecution of white-collar crimes offers a different example.

Prosecutors who initially set out to make cases of corruption, fraud, or food and drug violations may be unable to prove the targeted crime, yet still be able to prosecute for perjury or obstruction of justice. The latter violations become possible only after an investigation begins and can exist regardless of the quality of evidence for the case the prosecutor originally hoped to make.

More routine are white-collar offenses involving the violation of requirements imposed on citizens to aid in the investigation of still other crimes. In and of themselves the violations need not produce social harm. In the effort to detect and sanction infractions the criminal justice system can promote crimes because of its own need for information. Failing to file reports or filing a false statement to the U.S. government are examples. Failure to file an income tax form is a crime even if one owes no taxes.[3]

Most of the escalation examples considered here have involved the initial enforcement effort and one point in time. The work of Wilkins (1965) and that of Lemert (1951, 1972) calls attention to postapprehension escalation and a person's "career" as a deviant. Wilkins sees a spiraling interactive process whereby rule breaking leads to sanctioning, which then leads to more serious rule breaking, which in turn leads to more serious sanctioning and so on. Lemert focuses on how people may change their lives and self-conceptions in response to being formally processed, punished, stigmatized, segregated, or isolated. To the extent that their lives and identities come to be organized around the facts of their publicly labeled deviance, they are secondary deviants.

However, postapprehension escalation can occur without an accelerating spiral or changes in self-image. Having been apprehended for one offense, or identified as a rule violator, can set in motion actions by authorities that make additional violations more likely. For one thing, contact with the criminal justice system may alter one's status (e.g., to probationer, inmate, or parolee) so that one is guilty of a misdemeanor or felony for acts that would be legally inoffensive if committed by others. In addition, being placed in such statuses may provide actors with inducements to the commission of a crime, either by way of opportunity or pressure, to which others are not exposed.

Among the most poignant and tragic examples of escalation are those that emerge from the application of the initial sanction. Prisoners, such as George Jackson, who are sent up at a young age for a short term, then who find their sentences continually lengthened because of their behavior in prison, are clear examples. According to one study, only 6 to 40 offenses punishable in one state prison would be misdemeanors or felonies if done outside (Barnes and Teeters, 1959, as cited in Lemert, 1972:81). Similarly, violation of some of the regulations faced by those on parole or probation can send them to prison, but the same acts are not illegal when done by others.

For those not yet in prison, the need to meet bail and expensive legal fees can exert pressure to obtain such funds illegally. Clarence Darrow reported the case of a young thief who wanted the famous lawyer to defend him. Darrow asked if he had any money. The young man said, "No," and then with a smile said he thought he could raise some by that evening. An undercover narcotics detective (more taken by the seeming stupidity of those he arrests than of the system that generates their behavior) reports, "I even make buys again from guys who I've arrested and come right back out to make some fast bread for their expenses in court" (Schiano and Burton, 1974:93). There seems to be the possibility of infinite regress here.

Escalation is of course only one form that the interdependence and reciprocal influences among rule breakers and enforcers can take. It is treated here because of its irony. A more common form is probably displacement (without a significant increase or decrease in infractions). Displacement may occur with respect to other types of rule breaking, rule breakers, victims, place, and procedure (Reppetto, 1976a).

Social control actions may unintentionally generate functional alternatives. The relationship between controllers and controlled may often be characterized as a movable equilibrium. As in sports or any competitive endeavor, new strategies, techniques and resources may give one side a temporary advantage, but the other side tends to find ways to neutralize, avoid, or counter them. The action may become more sophisticated, practitioners more skilled, and the nature of the game may be altered—but the game does not stop. A saying among Hong Kong drug dealers in response to periodic clampdowns captures this nicely: "Shooting the singer is no way to stop the opera."

NONENFORCEMENT

In nonenforcement, the contribution of authorities to deviance is more indirect than with escalation or covert facilitation. Rule breaking does not expand unintentionally and authorities do not set people up and covertly facilitate it. Instead, those involved in nonenforcement relationships (e.g., with police) may break rules partly because they believe they will not be appropriately sanctioned. Here we have an exchange relationship between police and offenders. Offenders perform services for police; in return they are allowed to break rules and may receive other benefits.

When it is organized and specialized, non-enforcement is the most difficult of the three forms of interdependence to identify empirically. As a strategy it is often illegal and is more likely to be hidden. One does not find conditions for its use spelled out in policy manuals. Indeed the opposite is more apt to be true. In prohibiting nonenforcement, training and policy guidelines often go to great lengths to point out its dangers. Police are sworn to uphold the law: Not to do so may involve them in malfeasance, aiding and abetting a felon, compounding a felony, perjury, and a host of other violations. Some anticorruption policies are from one perspective antinonenforcement policies. They seek to create conditions that will work against collusive nonenforcement relations; at the same time the realities of the police job are such that it emerges as a major fact of police life.

Obtaining reliable information on this process is difficult. Police sometimes deny its existence and almost always deny its possible criminogenic implications, while their critics may exaggerate them. The existence of nonenforcement cannot be denied, although given the absence of systematic research, there is much room for disagreement about its extensiveness and its net consequences.[4] My purpose here is to analyze it as an ideal-typical category which sometimes has crime-generative effects.

Nonenforcement may literally involve taking no enforcement action, passing on information regarding police and criminal activities (including tips on raids), using improper procedures that will not stand up in court, offering ineffective testimony, helping a person facing charges to obtain leniency, giving gifts of contraband, and taking enforcement action against competitors. While there is sometimes overlap, we can differentiate "self-interested nonenforcement" involving traditional police corruption from "principled nonenforcement"—of most interest here—where police actions are thought to serve broader organizational goals.[5] Nonenforcement or leniency can be an important resource that authorities offer to those engaged in rule breaking whose cooperation they need. It is protected by the legitimate discretion in the police role and the United States' comparatively high standards of proof and rules of evidence required for conviction.

Police may adopt a policy of nonenforcement with respect to (1) informants who give them information about the law breaking of others and/or help in facilitating the controlled commission of a crime; (2) vice entrepreneurs who agree to keep their own illegal behavior within agreed upon bounds; (3) individuals who either directly regulate the behavior of others using resources police lack or means they are denied, or who take actions desired by authorities but considered too politically risky for them to undertake.

A former director of the FBI states, "Without informants we're nothing" (*New York Times*, April 16, 1974). The informant system, central to many types of law enforcement, is a major source of nonenforcement. Informants can offer police a means of getting information and making arrests that cannot come from other sources, given strictures against electronic surveillance, search and seizure, coercion, and the difficulty of infiltration. In return the system can work to the advantage of rule breakers. In the words of an FBI agent known for his ability to cultivate informants among those in organized crime:

They [informants] worked with agents because it was profitable for them: They avoided prison, got reduced sentences or parole for friends and relatives, maybe enjoyed some revenge against guys who had betrayed them, and picked up informer fees and some very substantial sums in the way of rewards paid by insurance companies delighted to refund five percent in return for saving the ninety-five percent liability (Villano, 1977:103).

The system can be used by both police and informants as a form of institutionalized blackmail. Potentially damaging action such as arrest or denouncement of someone as an informant or offender is withheld as long as the cooperation sought is forthcoming.

The tables can also get turned, as the informant manipulates the control agent into corrupt activities (or merely acquiesces in the agent's desire for these). For example, in the case of drugs, the exchange of immunity or drugs for information can, in a series of incremental changes, lead to joint marketing and other criminal ventures (Commission, 1972). The nonenforcement may become mutual and the balance of power shift.

The informant not only controls the flow of information but could even threaten exposure, which may entail greater risk for the police officer than for the drug dealer (Moore, 1977; Karchmer, 1979).

Where the informant is involved in the controlled commission of a crime, social control actions may generate rule breaking in two ways. Criminogenic effects may be present because police ignore illegal activities of the informant. But they may also be present because informants covertly facilitate the rule breaking of others. Informants facing charges or desiring drugs, for example, may have strong incentives to facilitate others' deviance.[6]

Louis Tackwood, an informant for the Los Angeles Police Department for ten years, worked first in traditional crime and later in radical politics. He appears to have committed numerous crimes, yet never to have been sentenced. He recalls:

I never worried about getting caught. It was the idea of the money, the free crime. Here's a cat, a person, who like me has been successful in forming several organizations for crime. Here are the police officers telling me, hey, we want you to work for us. Two things went through my mind then—money and I got a free hand to do anything I want to do (Citizens Committee and Tackwood, 1973:24).

In more muted terms, a former commander of detectives in Chicago hints at how the informant system in a context of secrecy and specialization may work at cross-purposes:

The burglary detectives may be inclined to "pass" a junkie with a small amount of drugs if he can turn up stolen property, while the narco squad will forget a few nickel and dime burglaries in return for cooperation in apprehending a major peddler. Homicide investigators looking for information on a murder will view a busy prostitute only as a source of information (Reppetto, 1976b).

People often become informants while in jail, or facing arrest. Sentencing may be deferred for a period of time while the informant "works off" the charges (for example, see Cloyd, 1979). In some police circles this is known as "flipping" or "turning" a man. With respect to drug enforcement, in some cities a point system is used whereby the informant receives one point for each marijuana purchase and two points for the purchase of harder drugs. If the informant earns a fixed number of points, such as ten, charges will be dropped. There is no doubt considerable variation among departments and within. Accounts such as that offered by Tackwood are perhaps best treated as ideal-typical illustrations.

The practice of police foregoing prosecution in return for information is more common than granting the informant a wild license to burglarize. Even here, the prior knowledge that one may be able to trade information for leniency can be conducive to law violations. Individuals sometimes manage to avoid arrest by falsely claiming that they are informants.

The exchange system is most highly developed for drugs. Something of a *de facto* license to deal may be offered ("you don't look too close at him"). To be useful the informant must be close to or involved in capering. In commenting on large transactions a detective observes, "Any junk dealer that you work with as an informant is moving junk when you're working with him. It has to be. You can't waste time chasing after some churchgoing Mary. If he's selling onions, what's he gonna tell you? The only way he can know what's coming down is if he's doing business." In this case the arrangement was "one for three." "For every load he gives you, he moves three." The rationale is clearly stated (Grosso and Rosenberg, 1979:55): "If he gives us one, it's one we wouldn't have had otherwise, right?"

The system occasionally is reproduced as a means of internal control. The Knapp Commission (1972) in New York offered leniency to corrupt police in return for their cooperation in catching other police. See Shecter and Phillips (1974), Daley (1978), and Grosso and Rosenberg (1979) for some of the ambiguities surrounding this procedure.

Certain occupational categories such as the fence have historically involved the informant's role (Klockars, 1974). The fence may offer information to the police, can return stolen goods— and in the case of thief takers, such as Jonathan Wild, even directly apprehend thieves, while receiving a degree of immunity and police help in regulating their clientele and employees.

The major vice control strategy at the turn of the century was one of containment, and it is still important. In what would only seem a contradiction to the outside observer, late nineteenth century police in many cities had written rules governing how houses of prostitution and gambling were to be run, though these were clearly illegal. Some vice entrepreneurs took pride in the honest quality of the services they provided. The very extensive Lexow hearings (Senate Committee, 1895) on the New York police show how they systematically licensed gambling, prostitution and police activities (Steffens, 1957, offers a classic discussion).

In return for noninterference from police (often further bought by the payment of bribes), vice entrepreneurs may agree to engage in self-policing and operate with relative honesty (i.e., run orderly disorderly houses), restrict their activities to one type of vice, stay in a given geographical area, and run low-visibility operations. By favoring certain vice operators and cooperating with them to keep others out, police may introduce a degree of control and stability into what would otherwise be a chaotic cutthroat situation. Establishing a peaceful racket organization may also be seen as a way of not alienating a local community that demands vice activities (Whyte, 1967). The goal becomes compromises reached through negotiation and regulation, rather than elimination of the activity.

Instead of being offered as a reward for self-regulation, nonenforcement may also be extended for regulating others. The literature on prisons gives many examples of the role selected prisoners play in maintaining order. Concessions, some clearly illegal, may be given to key prisoners in return for their regulating the behavior of others through questionable means (Sykes, 1958; Cloward *et al.*, 1960).

These represent cases where full control is technically impossible. Authorities need the continuing support of at least some of those they wish to control, and they are willing to pay a price for it. In other cases authorities may be capable of repressive action but prefer to delegate it because it is seen as too risky for them to undertake directly. For example, in 1963 the FBI experienced strong pressure to find the killer of civil rights leader Medgar Evers. They had learned the names of some of those involved and had the murder weapon, but could not obtain evidence on who fired the shot. Under FBI direction, an active burglar and fence kidnapped and threatened to kill a key figure in the plot and was able to obtain a signed statement identifying the murderer. In return, the cooperative burglar was "the beneficiary of the best the Bureau could do for him"—he avoided a long prison sentence for armed robbery and kept $800 in cash stolen from the man's wallet (Villano, 1977).

Vigilante-type groups offer another example. Police may look the other way and essentially delegate certain enforcement rights to a group that wishes to take action that police might like to take but are unwilling to. The summary justice of the southern lynch mob, and group violence against blacks, were often conspicuous because of the lack of a restraining police presence. Until recently in many areas of the South, police (when not themselves members) ignored or gave encouragement to the Klan. The weak, if not openly supportive, attitude of many southern leaders in the face of discrimination and white violence significantly encouraged the Klan. This greatly hampered the federal effort to enforce civil rights laws and protect civil rights workers. With respect to traditional offenses, it has been claimed that in some urban minority areas police have been less than diligent in investigating the murders of drug pushers supposedly carried out by vigilantes seeking to rid their communities of pushers.

Still another type of nonenforcement can originate in some criminals' possession of unique skills, or even in their having the same enemies as authorities do. The fact that organized crime and the United States government have had some common enemies (Mussolini in Italy and Castro in Cuba) has sometimes led to cooperation between them. In Italy local mafiosi were active in the underground and provided the Allies with intelligence for the invasion of Sicily. As the Allies then moved on to the Italian mainland, anti-Fascist mafia were appointed to important positions in many towns and villages. The French liner *Normandie* was burned in New York, just before it was to become an Allied troop ship.

Following this incident, the government sought the aid of mob-controlled longshoremen, truckers, and guards as help against waterfront sabotage and infiltration during World War II.[7] Help was received from Joe (Socks) Lanza on the East Side and Lucky Luciano on the West Side. Just what the government offered in return is less clear, although Luciano's cooperation won him, at least, a transfer to more comfortable prison quarters near Albany (Talese, 1972:206).

Recent reports of connections between the CIA and the underworld may simply be the continuation of an old American tradition. The CIA with its "executive action program" designed to "eliminate the effectiveness of foreign leaders" also delegated some of its dirty work (such as assassination efforts directed against Castro and Lumumba) to underworld figures. In Castro's case organized crime figures were thought to have "expertise and contacts not available to law-abiding citizens." They also had a motive which it was thought would take attention away from sponsorship of the U.S. government. According to one estimate (Schlesinger, 1978), Castro's coming to power cost organized crime $100 million a year. Outsiders were used by the CIA to avoid having "an Agency person or government person get caught" (Select Committee, 1975:74).

A former bank robber and forger involved in the unsuccessful plot to assassinate Lumumba was given plastic surgery and a toupee by the CIA before being sent to the Congo. This man was recommended by the Chief of the CIA's Africa Division as a "field operative" because "if he is given an assignment which may be morally wrong in the eyes of the world, but necessary because his case officer ordered him to carry it out, then it is right, and he will dutifully undertake appropriate action for its execution without pangs of conscience. In a word, he can rationalize all actions" (Select Committee, 1975:46). It appears that in extreme cases one crucial element which agents of social control may obtain in such exchange relationships is a psychopathic personality not inhibited by conventional moral restraints.

In a related example in Indochina, the United States took over the French policy of ignoring (or even encouraging) the growing of and trafficking in opium in return for anticommunist activities. According to McCoy (1972), the CIA provided planes and military equipment used by Laotian Hill tribes to ship opium to Saigon, where it was then processed into heroin (see also Chambliss, 1977).

Still another type of strategic nonenforcement, one not involving exchanges, happens when authorities fail to take action about a violation they know is planned, or in progress, until the violation is carried out. This permits arrest quotas to be met and can lead to heavier charges, greater leverage in negotiations, better evidence, and a higher level of offender arrest. For example, an experienced cocaine smuggler, who could easily identify "amateurs" in the business, argues that federal agents always waited for such persons to be arrested before talking to them. He notes:

Rather than walk up to someone obviously headed for trouble—where they might flash a badge and say, "Get smart, kid, it's not going to work"—they will, as a matter of policy, allow him to risk his life with the local heavies, get a few snorts of pure, and walk into jail at the airport back home. Why prevent smuggling when you can punish it—isn't that what jails are for (Sabbag, 1976:120)?

COVERT FACILITATION

The passive nonenforcement involving exchange relationships described above can be differentiated from a more active surreptitious role authorities may play as they (or their agents) directly enter into situations in order to facilitate rule breaking by others. The rule breaking that emerges from nonenforcement may be seen by authorities as an undesirable if perhaps necessary side effect. In the case of covert facilitation, authorities consciously seek to encourage rule breaking: Getting someone to break the rule is the major goal. Both law and internal policy are often favorable to police facilitation of crime. This is a very old phenomenon. Eve, after all, was set up by the serpent. In the Bible she says, "The serpent beguiled me and I did eat." Indicating awareness of the paradoxical (provocative yet lawful) nature of the tactic, some police describe it as *lawful* entrapment. A not atypical pol-

icy manual of one police department contains a section on "permissible tactics for arranging the controlled commission of an offense." Police are told that they or their agents under appropriate conditions may:

A. affirmatively suggest the commission of the offense to the subject;
B. attempt to form a relationship with the subject of sufficient closeness to overcome the subject's possible apprehension over his trustworthiness;
C. offer the subject more than one opportunity to commit the offense;
D. create a continuing opportunity for the subject to commit the offense;
E. minimize the possibility of being apprehended for committing the offense.

For the purposes of this paper we identify at least three types of covert facilitation:

1. disguised police or their agents cooperating with others in illegal actions;
2. police secretly generating opportunities for rule breaking without being coconspirators;
3. police secretly generating motives for rule breaking without being coconspirators.

With respect to the "controlled commission of an offense," police or their agents may enter into relationships with those who don't know that they are police, to buy or sell illegal goods and services or to victimize others. The former is the most common. Agents of social control may purchase or sell drugs, pose as tourists seeking prostitutes, as prostitutes seeking customers, or as homosexuals seeking partners. They may pose as fences buying or selling stolen goods, as hit men taking a contract, as criminals trying to bribe prosecutors, and as entrepreneurs running pornographic bookstores. They may join groups that are (or become) involved in car theft, burglary, or robbery. They may infiltrate political groups thought to be dangerous. The last decade reveals many examples of covert facilitation as authorities responded to widespread protest (Marx, 1974).

Both of the two other types of covert facilitation (deceptively creating opportunity structures or motives but without collusion) have a "give-them-enough-rope" quality. Police activity here is more passive and the deception is of a greater order from that involved in the "controlled commission of an offense." Police do not directly enter into criminal conspiracies with their targets, and charges of entrapment would not be supported—but they do attempt to structure the world in such a way that violations are made more likely.

The use of decoys to draw street crime is a major form of police creation of opportunity structures. Police anticrime squads, increasingly in vogue, may disguise their members as old women, clerics, derelicts, tennis players, and bike riders; they may use attractive police women in civilian clothes to induce robbery and assault, with other police watching from close by (Halper and Ku, 1976). Private guards posing as inattentive customers paying for small purchases with large bills routinely test cashier honesty. Plain-clothed "security inspectors" may test employee vigilance by seeing if they can get away with shoplifting. There is almost no limit to the variety of attractive opportunities for property theft that can be generated. Other examples include leaving packages in a watched unmarked decoy car with its windows open, leaving expensive skis (which, when moved, emit an electronic signal audible only to guards) in a conspicuous place at ski resorts, and opening crates of expensive merchandise at airport storage terminals and dusting it with an invisible powder that can be seen only by an ultraviolet light machine that employees pass as they leave work (Marx, 1980).

Covert facilitation involving the creation of motives can be seen in many counterintelligence activities. Here the goal may be disruption and subversion (rather than strictly law enforcement). In "dirty tricks" campaigns, police may take clandestine actions in the hope of provoking factionalism and violence. In one extreme example, an FBI agent in Tucson, Arizona, instigated a series of bombings of a Mafia home and a business to encourage fighting among rival organized crime groups (Talese, 1972). In one of the more bizarre cases of the last decade, the FBI, in "Operation Hoodwink," sought to encourage conflict between the Communist Party and elements in organized crime (Donner, 1976). The FBI was also responsible for burning cars of leftist activists so that it appeared to be done by rival political groups (*New York Times*, July 11, 1976). Undercover agents operating on opposing sides apparently played an important role in the violent split that occurred between the Huey Newton and Eldridge Cleaver factions of the Black Panthers. Perhaps more common are efforts to make it appear that an individual involved in criminal or radical politics is an informant, by planting information or contriving leaks. The "informant" may then be subject to possible retaliatory violence. This may be done by a genuine informant as part of a strategy of subversion or to cast blame elsewhere if arrests are to be made where it will be obvious that an informant was present (Schiano and Burton, 1974; Villano, 1977).

Some of the trickery of uniformed police might also be classified here. In the following extreme example from Wambaugh (1975:47), the power of the police office is used to generate a motive. A black bar known for heavy-drinking patrons is staked out. The plan is:

. . . to find a drunk sleeping in his car in the parking lot at the rear and wake him gently telling him that he had better go home and sleep it off. Then they would wait down the street in the darkness and arrest the grateful motorist for drunk driving as he passed by.[8]

In a version of turnabout as fair play (at least to reform police executives), covert facilitation may also be turned inward in efforts to deal with corrupt police and assess police honesty. Tactics recently used by the New York City police include: planting illegally parked cars with money in them to see if police tow truck operators would steal it; planting "lost" wallets near randomly selected police to see if they would be turned in intact; offering bribes to arresting officers; putting through a contrived "open door" call to an apartment where marked money was prominently displayed to see if two officers under suspicion would steal it (they did); establishing phony gambling operations to see if police sought protection money; and having an undercover officer pose as a pusher to see if other undercover narcotics agents paid out the full amount of "buy" money they claimed (*New York Times*, November 29, 1972 and December 28, 1973; Sherman, 1978).

Government lawyers, judges, and congressmen may also be targets of such tactics. Thus Sante A. Bario, a federal drug agent, posed as Salvatore Barone, a Las Vegas underworld figure, and was "arrested" in a Queens bar for carrying two loaded pistols. He then offered an assistant district attorney under suspicion $15,000 and the "charges" were dismissed (as was the assistant D.A.; Lardner, 1977); Operation Abscam, part of a federal bribery investigation, involved undercover agents posing as Arab sheiks who offered money to congressmen in return for favors (*New York Times*, February 4, 1980).

For convenience we have thus far treated three types of interdependence as if they were distinct empirically as well as analytically. However, there are deviance and social control situations in which each or several are present—or where they merge or may be temporally linked. One of the things rule breakers may offer to police in return for nonenforcement is aid in covertly facilitating someone else's rule breaking. The arrest that emerges out of this can involve escalation. For example, a drug informant's petty theft may be ignored (nonenforcement) in return for his making controlled buys (covert facilitation). The arrest growing out of this may lead to additional charges if the suspect is involved in a high-speed chase and fights with the arresting officers after they call him a name. Escalation may lead to a later policy of nonenforcement in those situations where authorities perceive that their intervention would in fact only make matters worse.[9] Stepped-up enforcement may also lead to nonenforcement by increasing opportunities for police corruption.

NOTES

1. Other forms of interdependence treated in the larger work from which this article is drawn, but ignored here, include: (a) "cops as robbers," where authorities are self-interested rule breakers; (b) the falsely accused; (c) the efforts of citizens to provoke, bribe, or otherwise implicate police in their rule breaking.

2. Because of their intentionality, nonenforcement and covert facilitation are social control strategies; this cannot be said of escalation which is defined by its unintended consequences, though these may be present with the former as well. Sometimes, of course, police may follow a policy of deliberate provocation in the

hope of encouraging escalation so that they can legally use force, bring heavier charges, or dispense "alley justice."

3. As Jack Katz has pointed out in a private communication, "Such laws reflect the fact that in a way large sections of our society are always under investigation for a crime."

4. Estimates of how widespread this is vary. A knowledgeable crime reporter (Plate, 1975:103) observes, "the number of criminals actually licensed by police to make a living in this way is quite extraordinary." According to one estimate, 50 percent of those arrested by the old Federal Bureau of Narcotics were converted into "specialized employees" (McIntyre, 1967:10–13).

5. Here we ignore the many other sources of nonenforcement such as lack of resources, intimidation, bureaucratic timidity, lack of belief in the rule, or compassion, as well as the suspension of law enforcement in order to have something to hold over a person should the need arise later.

6. A narcotics agent critical of this practice notes: "They put such pressure on the informant that, in effect, you've got him by the nuts. That's even what they call it, 'the nut,' working off the nut, or the violation. The pressure is so great he'll manufacture information, make up some to get off the hook. It's just a perfect example of how law enforcement is maintaining the problem" (Browning, 1976).

7. A more cynical interpretation is that Luciano actually arranged for the destruction of the *Normandie* as the prelude for his subsequently exchanging mob protection against future "foreign" sabotage (Gosch and Hammer, 1975).

8. This is mentioned because of its analytic significance. Far more common is the reverse: monitoring bars as they close and encouraging drunks not to drive, or even arranging transportation for them.

9. In the case of civil disorders, however, underreaction as part of a policy of nonenforcement can have the unintended consequence of encouraging the spread of disorder. The three largest civil disorders of the 1960s (Watts, Newark, and Detroit) were all characterized by the initial period of police underreaction. Given the infraction-generating potential of both over- and underreaction, police often find themselves criticized no matter how they respond, and policies are cyclical.

REFERENCES

ADLER, P. A., P. ADLER and J. DOUGLAS. Forthcoming "Organized crime: Drug dealing for pleasure and profit." In J. Douglas, *Observations of Deviance*, second edition. New York: Random House.

BARD, M. 1971. "Iatrogenic violence." *The Police Chief* (January):16–17.

BARNES, H. and N. TEETERS. 1959. *New Horizons in Criminology*. Englewood Cliffs, N.J.: Prentice Hall.

BECKER, H. 1963. *Outsiders*. Glencoe, Ill.: Free Press.

BROWNING, F. 1976. "An American gestapo." *Playboy*, February.

CHAMBLISS, W. 1977. "Markets, profits, labor and smack." *Contemporary Crises* I:53–76.

Citizens Research and Investigation Committee and Louis F. Tackwood. 1973. *The Glass House Tapes*. New York: Avon Books.

CLOWARD, R. and L. OHLIN. 1960. *Delinquency and Opportunity: A Theory of Delinquent Groups*. Glencoe, Ill.: Free Press.

CLOWARD, R. *et al.* 1960. *Theoretical Studies in Social Organization of the Prison*. New York: Social Science Research Council.

CLOYD, J. 1979. "Prosecution's power, procedural rights, and pleading guilty: The problem of coercion in plea bargaining cases." *Social Problems* 26(4):452–466.

COHEN, A. 1965. "The sociology of the deviant act." *American Sociological Review* 30:5–14.

Commission to Investigate Allegations of Police Corruption and the City's Anti-Corruption Procedures (1972). *The Knapp Commission Report on Police Corruption*. New York: Braziller.

DALEY, R. 1978. *The Prince of the City*. Boston: Houghton Mifflin.

DONNER, F. 1976. "Let him wear a wolf's head: What the FBI did to William Albertson." *Civil Liberties Review* 3 (April–May):12–22.

GOSCH, M. and R. HAMMER. 1975. *The Last Testament of Lucky Luciano*. Boston: Little, Brown.

GOVE, W. R. (ed.). 1980. *The Labeling of Deviance*. Beverly Hills, Calif.: Sage.

GROSSO, S. and P. ROSENBERG. 1979. *Point Blank*. New York: Avon Books.

HALPER, A. and R. KU. 1976. *New York City Police Department Street Crime Unit*. Washington, D.C.: U.S. Government Printing Office.

HAWKINS, R. and G. TIEDEMAN. 1975. *The Creation of Deviance*. Columbus, Ohio: C. Merrill.

HIRSCHI, T. 1969. *Causes of Delinquency*. Berkeley: University of California Press.

HOMANS, G. 1950. *The Human Group*. New York: Harcourt, Brace and World.

KARCHMER, C. 1979. "Corruption towards performance: Goals and operations in proactive law enforcement." Paper presented to Western Political Science Association, Portland, Oregon.

KITSUSE, J. 1962. "Societal reactions to deviant behavior: Problems of theory and method." *Social Problems* 9 (Spring):247–256.

KLEIN, M. 1969. "Gang cohesiveness, delinquency and a street work program." *Journal of Research in Crime and Delinquency* 6(1):135–166.

KLOCKARS, C. 1974. *The Professional Fence*. New York: Free Press.

LARDNER, J. 1977. "How prosecutors get nabbed." *New Republic*, January 29:22–25.

LEMERT, E. 1951. *Social Pathology*. New York: McGraw-Hill.

1972. *Human Deviance, Social Problems and Social Control*. Englewood Cliffs, N.J.: Prentice Hall.

MANNING, P. 1973. "On deviance." *Contemporary Sociology: A Journal of Reviews* 2:123–128.

MARUYAMA, M. 1963. "The second cybernetics: Deviation-amplifying mutual causative processes." *American Scientist* 51:164–179.

MARX, G. 1970. "Civil disorder and the agents of social control." *Journal of Social Issues* 26(1): 19–57.

1974. "Thoughts on a neglected category of social movement participant: Agents provocateurs and informants." *American Journal of Sociology* 80 (2):402–442.

1980. "The new police undercover work." *Journal of Urban Life* 8 (4):400–446.

MATZA, D. 1966. *Delinquency and Drift*. New York: Wiley.

MCCOY, A. 1972. *The Politics of Heroin in Southeast Asia*. New York: Harper and Row.

MCINTYRE, D., JR. 1967. *Law Enforcement in the Metropolis*. Chicago: American Bar Foundation.

MCNAMARA, J. H. 1967. "Uncertainty in police work: The relevance of police recruits' background and training." Pp. 163–252 in D. Bordua (ed.). *The Police*. New York: Wiley.

MERTON, R. 1957. *Social Theory and Social Structure*. Glencoe, Ill.: Free Press.

Moore, M. 1977. *Buy and Bust*. Lexington, Mass.: Lexington Press.

PARSONS, T. 1951. *The Social System*. New York: Free Press.

PLATE, N. 1975. *Crime Pays: The Theory and Practice of Professional Crime in the United States*. New York: Simon and Schuster.

RAINS, P. 1975. "Imputations of deviance: A retrospective essay on the labeling perspective." *Social Problems* 23 (1):1–11.

REISS, A. 1951. "Delinquency as the failure of personal and social control." *American Sociological Review* 16 (April):196-207.

REPPETTO, T. A. 1976a. "Crime prevention and the displacement phenomenon." *Crime and Delinquency* (April):166–177.

———. 1976b. "The uneasy milieu of the detective." Pp. 130–136 in A. Niederhoffer and A. Blumberg (eds.), *The Ambivalent Force*, 2nd edition. Hindsdale, Ill.: Dryden.

SABBAG, R. 1976. *Snow Blind.* New York: Avon.

SCHEFF, T. 1966. *Being Mentally Ill: A Sociological Theory.* Chicago: Aldine.

SCHIANO, A. and A. BURTON. 1974. *Solo.* New York: Warner.

SCHLESINGER, A. 1978. *Robert Kennedy and His Times.* Boston: Houghton Mifflin.

SCHUR, E. 1965. *Crimes Without Victims.* Englewood Cliffs, N.J.: Prentice Hall.

Select Committee to Study Governmental Operations With Respect to Intelligence Activities.

1975 Alleged Assassination Plots Involving Foreign Leaders. Washington, D.C.: U.S. Government Printing Office.

Senate Committee Appointed to Investigate the Police Dept. of New York City 1895. Report and Proceedings. Albany, New York.

SHECTER, L. and W. PHILLIPS. 1974. *On the Pad.* New York: G. P. Putnam.

SHERMAN, L. 1978. *Scandal and Reform.* Berkeley: University of California Press.

SHORT, J. F. 1974. "Youth, gangs, and society: Micro- and macrosociological processes." *Sociological Quarterly* 15 (Winter):3–19.

STARK, R. 1972. *Police Riots: Collective Violence and Law Enforcement.* Belmont, Calif.: Wadsworth.

STEFFENS, L. 1957. *Shame of the Cities.* New York: Hill and Wang.

SUTHERLAND, E. H. and D. CRESSEY. 1974. *Criminology.* Philadelphia: Lippincott.

SYKES, G. 1958. *The Society of Captives.* Princeton, N.J.: Princeton University Press.

TALESE, G. 1972. *Honor Thy Father.* Greenwich, Conn.: Fawcett Crest.

TANNENBAUM, F. 1938. *Crime and the Community.* Boston: Ginn.

VILLANO, A. with G. ASTOR. 1977. *Brick Agent.* New York: Quadrangle.

WAMBAUGH, J. 1975. *The Choirboys.* New York: Dell.

WELLFORD, C. 1975. "Labeling theory and criminology: An assessment." *Social Problems* 22 (3):332–345.

WHYTE, W. F. 1967. *Street Corner Society.* Chicago: University of Chicago Press.

WILKINS, L. 1965. *Social Deviance.* Englewood Cliffs, N.J.: Prentice Hall.

YOUNG, J. 1971. "The roles of the police as amplifiers of deviancy." Pp. 27–61 in S. Cohen (ed.), *Images of Deviance.* London: Penguin Books.

THE "DISCOVERY" OF CHILD ABUSE*

Stephen J. Pfohl**

Despite documentary evidence of child beating throughout the ages, the "discovery" of child abuse as deviance and its subsequent criminaliza-

*© 1977 by the Society for the Study of Social Problems. reprinted from *Social Problems*, 24:3 (Feb., 1977), pp. 310–323, by permission of the author and publisher.

**The author acknowledges the invaluable collaboration of Judith Dilorio of The Ohio State University in bringing this manuscript to its final form. Also acknowledged are the critical comments of John Conrad, Raymond Michalowski, and Dee Roth. Consultation with Simon Dinitz, Gideon Fishman, and Andrew Rutherford on an earlier draft of this paper is likewise appreciated. Gratitude is also expressed to Kathy Delgarn for the preparation of the manuscript.

tion are recent phenomena. In a four-year period beginning in 1962, the legislatures of all fifty states passed statutes against the caretaker's abuse of children. This paper is a study of the organization of social forces which gave rise to the deviant labeling of child beating and which promoted speedy and universal enactment of criminal legislation. It is an examination of certain organized medical interests, whose concern in the discovery of the "battered child syndrome" manifestly contributed to the advance of humanitarian pursuits while covertly rewarding the groups themselves.

The structure of the present analysis is four-fold: First, a historical survey of social reaction to abusive behavior prior to the formulation of fixed labels during the early sixties, focussing on the impact of three previous reform movements. These include the nineteenth-century "house-of-refuge" movement, early twentieth century crusades by the Society for the Prevention of Cruelty to Children, and the rise of juvenile courts. The second section concentrates on the web of cultural values related to the protection of children at the time of the "discovery" of abuse as deviance. A third section examines factors associated with the organizational structure of the medical profession conducive to the "discovery" of a particular type of deviant label. The fourth segment discusses social reaction. Finally, the paper provides a sociological interpretation of a particular social-legal development. Generically it gives support for a synthesis of conflict and labeling perspectives in the sociology of deviance and law.

THE HISTORY OF SOCIAL REACTION: PREVENTIVE PENOLOGY AND "SOCIETY SAVING"

The purposeful beating of the young has for centuries found legitimacy in beliefs of its necessity for achieving disciplinary, educational, or religious obedience (Radbill, 1968). Both the Roman legal code of "Patria Patistas" (Shepard, 1965) and the English common law (Thomas, 1973) gave guardians limitless power over their children who, with chattel-like status, had no legal right to protection.

The common law heritage of America similarly gave rise to a tradition of legitimized violence toward children. Legal guardians had the right to impose any punishment deemed necessary for the child's upbringing. In the seventeenth century, a period dominated by religious values and institutions, severe punishments were considered essential to the "sacred" trust of child-rearing (Earle, 1926: 119–126). Even in the late eighteenth and early nineteenth centuries, a period marked by the decline of religious domination and the rise of rationalism and a proliferation of statutes aimed at codifying unacceptable

human behavior, there were no attempts to prevent caretaker abuse of children. A major court in the state of North Carolina declared that the parent's judgment of need for a child's punishment was presumed to be correct. Criminal liability was said to exist only in cases resulting in "permanent injury" (*State v. Pendergass*, in Paulsen, 1966:686).

I am not suggesting that the American legal tradition failed to recognize any abuse of discipline as something to be negatively sanctioned. A few cases resulting in the legal punishment of parents who murdered their children have been recorded. But prior to the 1960s socio-legal reactions were sporadic and atypical of sustained reactions against firmly labeled deviance.

Beginning in the early nineteenth century, a series of three reform movements directed attention to the plight of beaten, neglected, and delinquent children. These included the nineteenth century "House of Refuge" movement, the turn of the century crusades by the Society for the Prevention of Cruelty to Children, and the early twentieth century rise of juvenile courts. Social response, however, seldom aimed measures at ameliorating abuse or correcting abusive parents. Instead, the child, rather than his or her guardians, became the object of humanitarian reform.

In each case the primary objective was not to save children from cruel or abusive parents, but to save society from future delinquents. Believing that wicked and irresponsible behavior was engendered by the evils of poverty and city life, these movements sought to curb criminal tendencies in poor, urban youths by removing them from corrupt environments and placing them in institutional settings. There they could learn order, regularity, and obedience (Rothman, 1971). Thus, it was children, not their abusive guardians, who felt the weight of the moral crusade. They, not their parents, were institutionalized.

The "House of Refuge" Movement

Originating in the reformist dreams of the Jacksonian era, the so-called "House of Refuge Movement" sought to stem the social pathologies of an industrializing nation by removing young people endangered by "corrupt urban environments" to institutional settings. Neglect statutes providing for the removal of the young from bad home lives were originally enacted to prevent children from mingling freely with society's dregs in alms houses or on the streets. In 1825, the first statute was passed and the first juvenile institution, the New York House of Refuge, was opened. Originally privately endowed, the institution soon received public funds to intervene in neglectful home situations and transplant children to a controlled environment, where they shared a "proper growing up" with other vagrant, abandoned, and neglected youths as well as with delinquents who had violated criminal statutes. Similar institutions were established in Philadelphia and Boston a year later, in New Orleans in 1845, and in Rochester and Baltimore in 1849.

The constitutionality of the neglect statutes, which formed the basis for the House of Refuge movement, was repeatedly challenged on the grounds that it was really imprisonment without due process. With few exceptions court case after court case upheld the policy of social intervention on the Aristotelian principle of "parens patriae." This principle maintained that the State has the responsibility to defend those who cannot defend themselves, as well as to assert its privilege in compelling infants and their guardians to act in ways most beneficial to the State.

The concept of preventive penology emerged in the wording of these court decisions. A distinction between "deliquency" (the actual violation of criminal codes) and "dependency" (being born into a poor home with neglectful or abusive parents) was considered irrelevant for "child saving." The two were believed to be intertwined in poverty and desolation. If not stopped, both would perpetuate themselves. For the future good of both child and society, "parens patriae" justified the removal of the young before they became irreparably tainted (Thomas, 1972:322–323).

The underlying concept of the House of Refuge movement was that of preventive penology, not child protection. This crusade registered no real reaction against child beating. The virtue of removing children from their homes was not to point up abuse or neglect and protect its victims, it was to decrease the likelihood that

parental inadequacies, the "cause of poverty," would transfer themselves to the child and hence to the next generation of society (Giovannoni, 1971:652). Thus, as indicated by Zalba (1966), the whole nineteenth century movement toward institutionalization actually failed to differentiate between abuse and poverty and therefore registered no social reaction against beating as a form of deviance.

Mary Ellen, the SPCC, and a Short-Lived Social Reaction

The first period when public interest focussed on child abuse occurred in the last quarter of the nineteenth century. In 1875, the Society for the Prevention of Cruelty to Animals intervened in the abuse case of a nine-year-old girl named Mary Ellen who had been treated viciously by foster parents. The case of Mary Ellen was splashed across the front pages of the nation's papers with dramatic results. As an outgrowth of the journalistic clamor, the New York Society for the Prevention of Cruelty to Children was formed. Soon incorporated under legislation that required law enforcement and court officials to aid agents of authorized cruelty societies, the NYSPCC and other societies modeled after it undertook to prevent abuse.

Though the police functions of the anti-cruelty societies represented a new reaction to abuse, their activities did not signify a total break with the society-saving emphasis of the House of Refuge Movement. In fact, three lines of evidence suggest that the SPCC enforcement efforts actually withheld a fixed label of deviancy from the perpetrators of abuse, in much the same manner as had the House of Refuge reforms. First, the "saving" of the child actually boosted the number of children placed in institutions, consequently supporting House of Refuge activities (Thomas, 1972:311). Second, according to Falks (1970:176), interorganizational dependency grew between the two reform movements, best evidenced by the success of SPCC efforts in increasing public support to childcare institutions under the auspices of House of Refuge groups. Finally, and perhaps most convincingly, natural parents were not classified as abusers of the great majority of the so-called "rescued children." In fact, the targets of these savings missions were cruel employers and foster or adopted parents (Giovannoni, 1971:653). Rarely did an SPCC intervene against the "natural" balance of power between parents and children. The firmness of the SPCC's alleged social action against abuse appears significantly dampened by its reluctance to shed identification with the refuge house emphasis on the "industrial sins of the city" and to replace it with a reaction against individuals.

The decline of the SPCC movement is often attributed to lack of public interest, funding problems, mergers with other organizations, and the assumption of protection services by public agencies (Felder, 1971:187). Its identification with the House of Refuge Movement also contributed to its eventual demise. More specifically, the House of Refuge emphasis on the separation of child from family, a position adopted and reinforced by the SPCC's activities, came into conflict with perspectives advocated by the newly emerging professions of social work and child psychology (Kadushin, 1967:202f). Instead of removing the child from the home, these new interests emphasized efforts to unite the family (Thomas, 1972). This latter position, backed by the power of professional expertise, eventually undercut the SPCC's policy of preventive policing by emphasizing the protection of the home.

The erosion of the SPCC position was foreshadowed by the 1909 White House Conference on Children. This Conference proclaimed that a child should not be removed from his or her home for reasons of poverty alone and called for service programs and financial aid to protect the home environment. Yet, the practice of preventive policing and institutionalization did not vanish, due, in part, to the development of the juvenile court system. The philosophy and practice of this system continued to identify abuse and neglect with poverty and social disorganization.

The Juvenile Court and the Continued Shadow of Abuse

The founding of the first juvenile court in Illinois in 1899 was originally heralded as a major landmark in the legal protection of juveniles. By 1920, courts were established in all but three states. Nonetheless, it is debatable that much reform was accomplished by juvenile court legislation. Coalitions of would-be reformers (headed by various female crusaders and the commissioners of several large public reformatories) argued for the removal of youthful offenders from adult institutions and advocated alteration of the punitive, entrepreneurial, and sectarian "House of Refuge" institutions (Fox, 1970:1225–29). More institutions and improved conditions were demanded (Thomas, 1972:323). An analysis of the politics of juvenile court legislation suggests, however, that successful maneuvering by influential sectarian entrepreneurs resulted in only a partial achievement of reformist goals (Fox, 1970:1225–26). Legislation did remove juveniles from adult institutions. It did not reduce the House of Refuge movement's control of juvenile institutions. Instead, legislation philosophically supported and financial reinforced the movement's "society-saving" operation of sectarian industrial schools (Fox, 1970:1226–27).

The channeling of juvenile court legislation into the "society-saving" mold of the House of Refuge movement actually withheld a deviant label from abusive parents. Even the reformers, who envisioned it as a revolution in child protection, did not see the court as protection from unfit parents. It was meant instead to prevent the development of "lower class" delinquency (Platt, 1969) and to rescue "those less fortunate in the social order" (Thomas, 1972:326). Again, the victims of child battering were characterized as predelinquents, as part of the general "problem" of poverty. These children, not their guardians, were the targets of court action and preventive policies. The courts, like the House of Refuge and SPCC movements before them, constrained any social reaction which would apply the label of deviant to parents who abused their children.

SOCIAL REACTION AT MID-CENTURY: THE CULTURAL SETTING FOR THE "DISCOVERY" OF ABUSE

The Decline of Preventive Penology

As noted, preventive penology represented the philosophical basis for various voluntary associations and legislative reform efforts resulting in the institutionalization of neglected or abused children. Its primary emphasis was on the protection of society. The decline of preventive penology is partially attributed to three variables: the perceived failure of "institutionalization," the impact of the "Great Depression" of the 1930s, and a change in the cultural meaning of "adult vices."

In the several decades prior to the discovery of abuse, the failure of institutionalization to "reorder" individuals became increasingly apparent. This realization undermined the juvenile courts' role in administering a predelinquency system of crime prevention. Since the rise of juvenile courts historically represented a major structural support for the notion of preventive penology, the lessening of its role removed a significant barrier to concern with abuse as an act of individual victimization. Similarly, the widespread experience of poverty during the Great Depression weakened other beliefs in preventive penology. As impersonal economic factors impoverished a great number of citizens of good moral credentials, the link between poverty and immorality began to weaken.

Another characteristic of the period immediately prior to the discovery of abuse was a changing cultural awareness of the meaning of adult vice as indices of the future character of children. "Parental immoralities that used to be seen as warnings of oncoming criminality in children [became] acceptable factors in a child's home-life" (Fox, 1970:1234). Parental behavior such as drinking, failing to provide a Christian education, and refusing to keep a child busy with useful labor were no longer classified as nonacceptable nor deemed symptoms of immorality transmitted to the young. Hence, the saving of society from the tainted young became less of a mandate, aiding the perception of social harm against children as "beings" in themselves.

Advance of Child Protection

Concurrent with the demise of "society-saving" in the legal sphere, developments in the fields of child welfare and public policy heightened interest in the problems of the child as an individual. The 1909 White House Conference on Children spawned both the "Mother's Aid"

movement and the American Association for the Study and Prevention of Infant Mortality. The former group, from 1910 to 1930, drew attention to the benefits of keeping children in the family while pointing out the detrimental effects of dehumanizing institutions. The latter group then, as now, registered concern over the rate of infant deaths.

During the first half of the twentieth century, the Federal Government also met the issue of child protection with legislation that regulated child labor, called for the removal of delinquent youths from adult institutions, and established, in 1930, a bureaucratic structure whose purpose revolved around child protection. The Children's Bureau of HEW immediately adopted a "Children's Charter" promising every child a home with love and security plus full-time public services for protection from abuse, neglect, exploitation or moral hazard (Radbill, 1968:15).

Despite the growth of cultural and structural dispositions favoring the protection and increased rights of children, there was still no significant attention given to perpetrators of abuse, in the courts (Paulsen, 1966:710), in the legislature (DeFrancis, 1967:3), or by child welfare agencies (Zalba, 1966). While this inactivity may have been partly caused by the lack of effective mechanisms for obtaining data on abuse (Paulsen, 1966:710), these agencies had little social incentive for interfering with an established power set—the parent over the child. As a minority group possessing neither the collective awareness nor the elementary organizational skills necessary to address their grievances to either the courts or to the legislators, abused and neglected children awaited the advocacy of some other organized interest. This outside intervention would not, however, be generated by that sector of "organized helping" most closely associated with the protective needs of children—the growing web of child welfare bureaucracies at state and federal levels. Social work had identified its professional advance with the adoption of the psychoanalytic model of casework (Zalba, 1966). This perspective, rather than generating a concern with political inequities internal to the family, focused instead on psychic disturbances internal to its members. Rather than challenging the strength of parents, this served to reinforce the role of powerful guardians in the rearing of young.

Nor would advocacy come from the public at large. Without organized labeling interests at mid-century, child abuse had not become an issue publicly regarded as a major social problem. In fact, a fairly general tolerance for abuse appeared to exist. This contention is supported by the findings of a nationwide study conducted by NORC during the period in which laws against abuse were actually being adopted (Gil & Nobel, 1969). Despite the wide-scale publicizing of abuse in this "post-discovery" period, public attitudes remained lenient. Data revealed a high degree of empathy with convicted or suspected perpetrators (Gil, 1970:63–67). These findings are understandable in light of cultural views accepting physical force against children as a nearly universally applied precept of intrafamilial organization (Goode, 1971). According to the coordinator of the national survey, "Culturally determined permissive attitudes toward the use of physical force in child rearing seem to constitute the common core of all physical abuse of children in American society" (Gil, 1970:141).

While the first half of the twentieth century is characterized by an increasing concern for child welfare, it developed with neither an organizational nor attitudinal reaction against child battering as a specific form of deviance. The "discovery" of abuse, its definition as a social problem and the socio-legal reaction against it, awaited the coalition of organized interests.

THE ORGANIZATION OF SOCIAL REACTION AGAINST THE "BATTERED CHILD SYNDROME"

What organization of social forces gave rise to the discovery of abuse as deviance? The discovery is not attributable to any escalation of abuse itself. Although some authors have recently suggested that the increasing nuclearization of the family may increase the victimization of its offspring (Skolnick & Skolnick, 1971), there has never been any evidence that, aside from reporting inflation due to the impact of new laws, battering behavior was actually increasing (Eads,

1972). The attention here is on the organizational matrix encouraging a recognition of abuse as a social problem. In addressing this issue I will examine factors associated with the organizational structure of the medical profession leading to the discovery of abuse by pediatric radiologists rather than by other medical practitioners.

The "discovery" of abuse by pediatric radiology has often been described chronologically (Radbill, 1968:15; McCoid, 1966:2–5; Thomas, 1972:330). John Caffey (1946) first linked observed series of long bone fractures in children with what he termed some "unspecific origin." Although his assumption was that some physical disturbance would be discovered as the cause of this pattern of "subdural hematoma," Coffey's work prompted a series of further investigations into various bone injuries, skeletal trauma, and multiple fractures in young children. These research efforts lead pediatric radiology gradually to shift its diagnosis away from an internal medical explication toward the ascription of social cause.

In subsequent years it was suggested that what was showing up on x-rays might be the results of various childhood accidents (Barmeyer, *et al.*, 1951), of "parental carelessness" (Silverman, 1953), of "parental conduct" (Bakwin, 1956), and most dramatically, of the "indifference, immaturity and irresponsibility of parents" (Wooley & Evans, 1955). Surveying the progression of this research and reviewing his own investigations, Coffey (1957) later specified "misconduct and deliberate injury" as the primary etiological factors associated with what he had previously labelled "unspecific trauma." The discovery of abuse was on its way. Both in scholarly research (McCoid, 1966:7) and journalist outcry (Radbill, 1968:16), the last years of the fifties showed dramatically increased concern for the beaten child.

Why did pediatric radiologists and not some other group "see" abuse first? Legal and social welfare agents were either outside the scene of abusive behavior or inside the constraining vision of psychoanalytically committed casework. But clinicians, particularly hospital physicians and pediatricians, who encountered abused children more immediately, should have discovered "abuse" before the radiologists.

Four factors impeded the recognition of abuse (as it was later labeled). First, some early research maintained that doctors in emergency room settings were simply unaware of the possibilities of "abuse" as a diagnosis (Bain, 1963; Boardman, 1962). While this may be true, the massive symptoms (blood, burns, bruises) emergency room doctors faced far outweighed the lines appearing on the x-ray screens of radiologic specialists. A second line of evidence contends that many doctors were simply psychologically unwilling to believe that parents would inflict such atrocities on their own children (Elmer, 1960; Fontana, Donovan, Wong, 1963; Kempe *et al.*, 1963). This position is consistent with the existing cultural assumptions pairing parental power with parental wisdom and benevolence. Nonetheless, certain normative and structural elements within professional medicine appear of greater significance in reinforcing the physician's reluctance to get involved, even diagnostically. These factors are the "norm of confidentiality between doctor and client" and the goal of professional autonomy.

The "norm of confidentiality" gives rise to the third obstacle to a diagnosis of abuse: the possibility of legal liability for violating the confidentiality of the physician-patient relationship (Boardman, 1962). Interestingly, although some research connotes doctors' concern over erroneous diagnosis (Braun, Braun & Simonds, 1963), physicians primarily view the parent, rather than the child, as their real patient. On a strictly monetary level, of course, it is the parent who contracts with the doctor. Additional research has indicated that, particularly in the case of pediatricians, the whole family is viewed as one's clinical domain (Bucher & Strauss, 1961:329). It is from this vantage point that the impact of possible liability for a diagnostic disclosure is experienced. Although legal liability for a diagnosis of abuse may or may not have been the risk (Paulsen, 1967b:32), the belief in such liability could itself have contributed to the narrowness of a doctor's diagnostic perceptions (McCoid, 1966:37).

A final deterrent to the physician's "seeing" abuse is the reluctance of doctors to become involved in a criminal justice process that would take both their time (Bain, 1963:895) and ability to guide the consequences of a particular diagnosis (Boardman, 1962:46). This deterrent is particularly related to the traditional success of organized medicine in politically controlling the consequences of its own performance, not just for medical practitioners but for all who come in contact with a medical problem (Freidson, 1969:106; Hyde, *et al.*, 1954).

The political control over the consequences of one's profession would be jeopardized by the medical diagnosis of child abuse. Doctors would be drawn into judicial proceedings and subordinated to a role as witnesses. The outcome of this process would be decided by criminal justice standards rather than those set forth by the medical profession. Combining this relatively unattractive alternative with the obvious and unavoidable drain on a doctor's financial earning time, this fourth obstacle to the clinician's discovery of abuse is substantial.

Factors Conducive to the Discovery of Abuse by Pediatric Radiology

Why didn't the above factors inhibit the discovery of abuse by pediatric radiologists as well as by clinicians? First it must be recognized that the radiologists in question (Caffey, Barmeyer, Silverman, Wooley and Evans) were all researchers of children's x-rays. As such, the initial barrier becomes irrelevant. The development of diagnostic categories was a consequence rather than a precondition of the medical mission. Regarding the psychological denial of parental responsibility for atrocities, it must be remembered that the dramatic character of a beating is greatly reduced by the time it reaches an x-ray laboratory. Taken by technicians and developed as black and white prints, the radiologic remnants of abuse carry with them little of the horror of the bloody assault.

With a considerable distance from the patient and his or her family, radiologists are removed from the third obstacle concerning legal liabilities entailed in violating the doctor-patient relationship. Unlike pediatricians, radiologists do not routinely regard the whole family as their clinical domain. Of primary importance is the individual whose name or number is imprinted on the x-ray frames. As such, fears about legal sanctions instigated by a parent whom one has never seen are less likely to deter the recognition of abuse.

Given the irrelevance of the first three obstacles, what about the last? Pediatric radiologists are physicians and as such would be expected to participate in the "professional control of consequences" ethos. How is it that they negotiate this obstacle in favor of public recognition and labelling of abuse?

The Discovery: An Opportunity for Advancement Within the Medical Community

To ask why the general norm of "professional control of consequences" does not apply equally to radiologists as to their clinical counterparts is to confuse the reality of organized medicine with its image. Although the medical profession often appears to outsiders as a separate and unified community within a community (Goode, 1957), and although medical professionals generally favor the maintenance of this image (Glaser, 1960), it is nonetheless more adequately described as an organization of internally competing segments, each striving to advance its own historically derived mission and future importance (Bucher & Strauss, 1961). In analyzing pediatric radiology as one such segment, several key variables facilitated its temporary parting with the dominant norms of the larger medical community. This parting promoted the elevation of its overall status within that community.

The first crucial element is that pediatric radiology was a marginal specialty within organized medicine. It was a research-oriented subfield in a profession that emphasized face-to-face clinical interaction. It was a safe intellectual endeavor within an overall organization which placed a premium on risky pragmatic enterprise. Studies of value orientations among medical students at the time of the "discovery" of abuse have suggested that those specialties which stress "helping others," "being of service," "being useful," and "working with people" were ranked above those which work "at medical problems that do not require frequent contact with patients" (Cahalan,

1957). On the other hand, intellectual stimulation afforded very little prestige. Supporting this conclusion was research indicating that although forty-three percent of practicing physicians selected "close patient relations" as a mandate of their profession, only twenty-four percent chose "research" as worthy of such an evaluation (Philips, 1964). Pairing this ranking system with the profession's close-knit, "fraternity-like" communication network (Hall, 1946), one would expect research-oriented radiologists to be quite sensitive about their marginal evaluation by colleagues.

Intramedical organizational rankings extend along the lines of risk-taking as well as patient-encounters. Here, too, pediatric radiologists have traditionally ranked lower than other medical specialties. Becker's (1961) study of medical student culture suggests that the most valued specialties are those which combine wide experiences with risk and responsibility. These are most readily "symbolized by the possibility of killing or disabling patients in the course of making a mistake" (Freidson, 1969:107). From this perspective, it is easy to understand why surgery and internal medicine head the list of the most esteemed specialties. Other research has similarly noted the predominance of surgeons among high elected officials of the American Medical Association (Hall, 1946). Devoid of most risk taking, little involved in life or death decisions, pediatric radiologists are again marginal to this ethos of medical culture.

The "discovery" of child abuse offered pediatric radiologists an alternative to their marginal medical status. By linking themselves to the problem of abuse, radiologists became indirectly tied into the crucial clinical task of patient diagnosis. In addition, they became a direct source of input concerning the risky "life or death" consequences of child beating. This could represent an advance in status, a new basis for recognition within the medical profession. Indeed, after initial documentation of abuse, literature in various journals of radiology, roentgenology, and pediatrics, articles on this topic by Wooley and Evans (1955) and Gwinn, Lewin and Peterson (1961) appeared in the *Journal of the American Medical Association*. These were among the very few radiologic research reports published by that prestigious journal during the time period. Hence, the first factor conducive to the radiological discovery of abuse was a potential for intraorganizational advance in prestige.

The Discovery: An Opportunity for Coalition Within the Medical Community

A second factor encouraging the discovery of abuse by relatively low-status pediatric radiologists concerns the opportunity for a coalition of interests with other more prestigious segments within organized medicine. The two other segments radiologists joined in alliance were pediatrics and psychodynamically oriented psychiatry. By virtue of face-to-face clinical involvements, these specialties were higher ranking than pediatric radiology. Nevertheless each contained a dimension of marginality. Pediatrics had attained valued organizational status several decades prior to the discovery of abuse. Yet, in an age characterized by preventive drugs and treatments for previously dangerous or deadly infant diseases, it was again sliding toward the margins of the profession (Bucher & Strauss, 1961). Psychodynamic psychiatry (as opposed to its psychosomatic cousin) experienced marginality in dealing with non-physical problems.

For both pediatrics and psychodynamic psychiatry, links with the problem of abuse could partially dissipate the respective marginality of each. Assuming a role in combating the "deadly" forces of abuse could enlarge the "risky" part of the pediatric mission. A symbolic alliance of psychodynamic psychiatry with other bodily diagnostic and treatment specialties could also function to advance its status. Neither of these specialties was in a position to "see" abuse before the radiologists. Pediatricians were impeded by the obstacles discussed above. Psychiatrists were blocked by the reluctance of abusive parents to admit their behavior as problematic (Steele & Pollock, 1968). Nonetheless, the interests of both could perceivably be advanced by a coalition with the efforts of pediatric radiologists. As such, each represented a source of potential support for pediatric radiologists in their discovery of abuse. This potential for coalition served

to reinforce pediatric radiology in its movement toward the discovery of abuse.

The Discovery: An Opportunity for the Application of an Acceptable Label

A crucial impediment to the discovery of abuse by the predominant interests in organized medicine was the norm of controlling the consequences of a particular diagnosis. To diagnose abuse as social deviance might curtail the power of organized medicine. The management of its consequences would fall to the extramedical interests of formal agents of social control. How is it then, that such a diagnosis by pediatric radiology and its endorsement by pediatric and psychiatric specialties is said to have advanced these specialties within the organization of medicine? Wasn't it more likely that they should have received criticism rather than acclaim from the medical profession?

By employing a rather unique labelling process the coalition of discovery interests was able to convert the possible liability into a discernible advantage. The opportunity of generating a medical, rather than socio-legal label for abuse provided the radiologists and their allies with a situation in which they could both reap the rewards associated with the diagnosis and avoid the infringement of extra-medical controls. What was discovered was no ordinary behavior form but a "syndrome." Instead of departing from the tradition of organized medicine, they were able to idealize its most profound mission. Possessing a repertoire of scientific credibility, they were presented with the opportunity "to label as illness what was not previously labeled at all or what was labeled in some other fashion, under some other institutional jurisdiction" (Freidson, 1969:261).

The symbolic focal point for the acceptable labeling of abuse was the 1962 publication of an article entitled "The Battered Child Syndrome" in the *Journal of the American Medical Association* (Kempe *et al.*, 1962). This report, representing the joint research efforts of a group of radiologic, pediatric, and psychiatric specialists, labelled abuse as a "clinical condition" existing as an "unrecognized trauma" (Kempe *et al.*,

1962:17). It defined the deviance of its "psycho-pathic" perpetrators as a product of "psychiatric factors" representing "some defect in character structure" (Kempe *et al.,* 1962:24). As an indicator of prestige within organized medicine, it is interesting to note that the position articulated by those labellers was endorsed by the editorial board of the AMA in that same issue of *JAMA.*

As evidenced by the AMA editorial, the discovery of abuse as a new "illness" reduced drastically the intra-organizational constraints on doctors "seeing" abuse. A diagnostic category had been invented and publicized. Psychological obstacles in recognizing parents as capable of abuse were eased by the separation of normatively powerful parents from non-normatively pathological individuals. Problems associated with perceiving parents as patients whose confidentiality must be protected were reconstructed by typifying them as patients who needed help. Moreover, the maintenance of professional autonomy was assured by pairing deviance with sickness. This last statement is testimony to the power of medical nomenclature. It was evidenced by the fact that (prior to its publication) the report which coined the label "battered child syndrome" was endorsed by a Children's Bureau conference which included social workers and law enforcement officials as well as doctors (McCoid, 1965:12).

The Generation of the Reporting Movement

The discovery of the "battered child syndrome" was facilitated by the opportunities for various pediatric radiologists to advance in medical prestige, form coalitions with other interests, and invent a professionally acceptable deviant label. The application of this label has been called the child abuse reporting movement. This movement was well underway by the time the 1962 Children's Bureau Conference confirmed the radiological diagnosis of abuse. Besides foreshadowing the acceptance of the sickness label, this meeting was also the basis for a series of articles to be published in *Pediatrics* which would further substantiate the diagnosis of abuse. Soon, however, the reporting movement spread beyond

intra-organizational medical maneuvering to incorporate contributions from various voluntary associations, governmental agencies, as well as the media.

Extramedical responses to the newly discovered deviance confirmed the recognition of abuse as an illness. These included reports by various social welfare agencies which underscored the medical roots of the problem. For instance, the earliest investigations of the problem by social service agents resulted in a call for cooperation with the findings of radiologists in deciding the fate of abusers (Elmer, 1960:100). Other studies called for "more comprehensive radiological examinations" (Boardman, 1962:43). That the problem was medical in its roots as well as consequences was reinforced by the frequent referral of caseworkers to themselves as "battered child therapists" whose mission was the "curing" of "patients" (Davoren, 1968). Social welfare organizations, including the Children's Division of the American Humane Association, the Public Welfare Association, and the Child Welfare League, echoed similar concerns in sponsoring research (Children's Division, 1963; De Francis, 1963) and lobbying for "treatment based" legislative provisions (McCoid, 1965).

Not all extramedical interests concurred with treatment of abusers as "sick." Various law enforcement voices argued that the abuse of children was a crime and should be prosecuted. On the other hand, a survey of thirty-one publications in major law journals between 1962–1972 revealed that nearly all legal scholars endorsed treatment rather than punishment to manage abusers. Lawyers disagreed, however, as to whether reports should be mandatory and registered concern over who should report to whom. Yet, all concurred that various forms of immunity should be granted reporters (Paulsen, 1967a; De Francis, 1967). These are all procedural issues. Neither law enforcers nor legal scholars parted from labelling abuse as a problem to be managed. The impact of the acceptable discovery of abuse by a respected knowledge sector (the medical profession) had generated a stigmatizing scrutiny bypassed in previous eras.

The proliferation of the idea of abuse by the media cannot be underestimated. Though its stories were sensational, its credibility went unchallenged. What was publicized was not some amorphous set of muggings but a "syndrome." Titles such as "Cry rises from beaten babies" (*Life*, June 1963), "Parents who beat children" (*Saturday Evening Post*, October 1962), "The shocking price of parental anger" (*Good Housekeeping*, March 1964), and "Terror struck children" (*New Republic*, May 1964) were all buttressed by an awe of scientific objectivity. The problem had become "real" in the imaginations of professionals and laymen alike. It was rediscovered visually by ABC's "Ben Casey," NBC's "Dr. Kildare," and CBS's "The Nurses," as well as in several other television scripts and documentaries (Paulsen, 1967b:488–489).

Discovered by the radiologists, substantiated by their colleagues, and distributed by the media, the label was becoming widespread. Despite this fact, actual reporting laws were said to be the cooperative accomplishments of zealous individuals and voluntary associations (Paulsen, 1967b:491). Who exactly were these "zealous individuals"?

Data on legislative lobbyists reveal that, in almost every state, the civic committee concerned with abuse legislation was chaired by a doctor who "just happened" to be a pediatrician (Paulsen, 1967b:491). Moreover, "the medical doctors who most influenced the legislation frequently were associated with academic medicine" (Paulsen, 1967b:491). This information provides additional evidence of the collaborative role of pediatricians in guiding social reaction to the deviance discovered by their radiological colleagues.

Lack of Resistance to the Label

In addition to the medical interests discussed above, numerous voluntary associations provided support for the movement against child abuse. These included the League of Women Voters, Veterans of Foreign Wars, the Daughters of the American Republic, the District Attorneys Association, Council of Jewish Women, State Federation of Women's Clubs, Public Health Associations, plus various national chapters of social workers (Paulsen, 1967b:495). Two characteristics emerge from an examination of these interests. They either have a professional stake in the problem or represent the civic concerns of certain upper-middle class factions. In either case the labelers were socially and politically removed from the abusers, who in all but one early study (Steele and Pollock), were characterized as lower class and minority group members.

The existence of a wide social distance between those who abuse and those who label facilitates not only the likelihood of labelling but nullifies any organized resistance to the label by the "deviant" group itself. Research findings which describe abusers as belonging to no outside-the-family associations or clubs (Young, 1964) or which portray them as isolates in the community (Giovannoni, 1971) reinforce the conclusion. Labelling was generated by powerful medical interests and perpetuated by organized media, professional and upper-middle class concerns. Its success was enlarged by the relative powerlessness and isolation of abusers, which prevented the possibility of organized resistance to the labelling.

THE SHAPE OF SOCIAL REACTION

I have argued that the organizational advantages surrounding the discovery of abuse by pediatric radiology set in motion a process of labelling abuse as deviance and legislating against it. The actual shape of legislative enactments has been discussed elsewhere (De Francis, 1967; Paulsen, 1967a). The passage of the reporting laws encountered virtually no opposition. In Kentucky, for example, no one even appeared to testify for or against the measure (Paulsen, 1967b:502). Any potential opposition from the American Medical Association, whose interests in autonomous control of the consequences of a medical diagnosis might have been threatened, had been undercut by the radiologists' success in defining abuse as a new medical problem. The AMA, unlikely to argue against conquering illness, shifted to support reporting legislation which would maximize a physician's diagnostic options.

The consequences of adopting a "sick" label for abusers is mirrored in two findings: the low rate of prosecution afforded offenders and the modification of reporting statutes so as exclusively to channel reporting toward "helping services." Regarding the first factor, Grumet

(1970:306) suggests that despite existing laws and reporting statutes, actual prosecution has not increased since the time of abuse's "discovery." In support is Thomas (1972) who contends that the actual percentage of cases processed by family courts has remained constant during the same period. Even when prosecution does occur, convictions are obtained in only five to ten percent of the cases (Paulsen, 1966b). And even in these cases, sentences are shorter for abusers than for other offenders convicted under the same law of aggravated assault (Grumet, 1970:307).

State statutes have shifted on reporting from an initial adoption of the Children's Bureau model of reporting to law enforcement agents, toward one geared at reporting to child welfare or child protection agencies (De Francis, 1970). In fact, the attention to abuse in the early sixties has been attributed as a factor in the development of specialized "protective interests" in states which had none since the days of the SPCC crusades (Eads, 1969). This event, like the emphasis on abuser treatment, is evidence of the impact of labelling of abuse as an "illness."

REFERENCES

BAIN, KATHERINE. 1963. "The physically abused child." *Pediatrics* 31 (June): 895–897.

BAKWIN, HARRY. 1956. "Multiple skeletal lesions in young children due to trauma." *Journal of Pediatrics* 49 (July): 7–15.

BARMEYER, G. H., L. R. ANDERSON and W. B. COX. 1951. "Traumatic periostitis in young children." *Journal of Pediatrics* 38 (Feb): 184–190.

BECKER, HOWARD S. 1963. *The Outsiders.* New York: The Free Press.

BECKER, HOWARD S. et al. 1961. *Boys in White.* Chicago: University of Chicago Press.

BOARDMAN, HELEN. 1962. "A project to rescue children from inflicted injuries." *Journal of Social Work* 7 (January): 43–51.

BRAUN, IDA G., EDGAR J. BRAUN and CHARLOTTE SIMONDS. 1963. "The mistreated child." *California Medicine* 99 (August): 98–103.

BREMNER, R. 1970. *Children and Youth in America: A Documentary History. Vol. 1.* Cambridge, Mass.: Harvard University Press.

BUCHER, RUE and ANSELM STRAUSS. 1961. "Professions in process." *American Journal of Sociology* 66 (January): 325–334.

CAFFEY, JOHN. 1946. "Multiple fractures in the long bones of infants suffering from chronic subdural hematoma." *American Journal of Roentgenology* 56(August): 163–173.

1957. "Traumatic lesions in growing bones other than fractures and lesions: clinical and radiological features." *British Journal of Radiology* 30(May): 225–238.

CAHALAN, DON. 1957. "Career interests and expectations of U.S. medical students." 32: 557–563.

CHAMBLISS, WILLIAM J. 1964. "A sociological analysis of the law of vagrancy." *Social Problems* 12(Summer): 67–77.

Children's Division. 1963. *Child Abuse—Preview of a Nationwide Survey.* Denver: American Humane Association (Children's Division).

DAVOREN, ELIZABETH. 1968. "The role of the social worker." Pp. 153–168 in Ray E. Helfer and Henry C. Kempe (eds.), *The Battered Child.* Chicago: University of Chicago Press.

DE FRANCIS, VINCENT. 1963. "Parents who abuse children." *PTA Magazine* 58(November): 16–18.

1967. "Child abuse—the legislative response." *Denver Law Journal* 44(Winter): 3–41.

1970. *Child Abuse Legislation in the 1970's.* Denver: American Humane Association.

EADS, WILLIAM E. 1969. "Observations on the establishment of child protection services in California." *Stanford Law Review* 21(May): 1129–1155.

EARLE, ALICE MORSE. 1926. *Child Life in Colonial Days.* New York: Macmillan.

ELMER, ELIZABETH. 1960. "Abused young children seen in hospitals." *Journal of Social Work* 3(October): 98–102.

FELDER, SAMUEL. 1971. "A lawyer's view of child abuse." *Public Welfare* 29: 181–188.

FOLKS, HOMER. 1902. *The Case of the Destitute, Neglected and Delinquent Children.* New York: Macmillan.

FONTANA, V., D. DONOVAN and R. WONG. 1963. "The maltreatment syndrome in children." *New England Journal of Medicine* 269(December): 1389–1394.

FOX, SANFORD J. 1970. "Juvenile justice reform: an historical perspective." *Stanford Law Review* 22(June): 1187–1239.

FREIDSON, ELIOT J. 1969. "Medical personnel: physicians." Pp. 105–114 in David L. Sills (ed.), *International Encyclopedia of the Social Sciences.* Vol. 10. New York: Macmillan.

1971. The Profession of Medicine: *A Study in the Sociology of Applied Knowledge.* New York: Dodd, Mead and Co.

GIL, DAVID. 1970. *Violence Against Children.* Cambridge, Mass.: Harvard University Press.

GIL, DAVID and JOHN H. NOBLE. 1969. "Public knowledge, attitudes and opinions about physical child abuse." *Child welfare* 49(July): 395–401.

GIOVANNONI, JEANNE. 1971. "Parental mistreatment." *Journal of Marriage and the Family* 33(November): 649–657.

GLASER, WILLIAM A. 1960. "Doctors and politics." *American Journal of Sociology* 66(November): 230–245.

GOODE, WILLIAM J. 1957. "Community within a community: the profession." *American Sociological Review* 22(April): 194–200.

———. 1971. "Force and violence in the family." *Journal of Marriage and the Family* 33(November): 424–436.

GRUMET, BARBARA R. 1970. "The plaintive plaintiffs: victims of the battered child syndrome." *Family Law Quarterly* 4(September): 296–317.

GUSFIELD, JOSEPH R. 1963. *Symbolic Crusades.* Urbana, Ill.: University of Illinois Press.

GWINN, J.J., K.W. LEWIN and H.G. PETERSON. 1961. "Roentgenographic manifestations of unsuspected trauma in infancy." *Journal of the American Medical Association* 181(June): 17–24.

HALL, JEROME. 1952. *Theft, Law and Society.* Indianapolis: Bobbs-Merrill Co.

HALL, OSWALD. 1946. "The informal organization of medicine." *Canadian Journal of Economics and Political Science* 12(February): 30–41.

HYDE, D.R., P. WOLFF, A. GROSS and E.L. HOFFMAN. 1954. "The American Medical Association: power, purpose and politics in organized medicine." *Yale Law Journal* 63(May): 938–1022.

KADUSHIN, ALFRED. 1967. *Child Welfare Services.* New York: Macmillan.

KEMPE, C.H., F.N. SILVERMAN, B.F. STEELE, W. DROEGEMULLER and H.K. SILVER. 1963. "The battered-child syndrome." *Journal of the American Medical Association* 181(July): 17–24.

LEMERT, EDWIN M. 1974. "Beyond Mead: the societal reaction to deviance." *Social Problems* 21(April): 457–467.

McCOID, A.H. 1966. "The battered child syndrome and other assaults upon the family." *Minnesota Law Review* 50(November): 1–58.

PAULSEN, MONRAD G. 1966. "The legal framework for child protection." *Columbia Law Review* 66(April): 679–717.

———. 1967. "Child abuse reporting laws: the shape of the legislation." *Columbia Law Review* 67(January): 1–49.

PHILIPS, BERNARD S. 1964. "Expected value deprivation and occupational preference." *Sociometry* 27(June): 15–160.

PLATT, ANTHONY M. 1969. *The Child Savers: The Invention of Juvenile Delinquency.* Chicago: University of Chicago Press.

QUINNEY, RICHARD. 1970. *The Social Reality of Crime.* Boston: Little, Brown.

RADBILL, SAMUEL X. 1968. "A history of child abuse and infanticide." Pp. 3–17 in Ray E. Helfer and Henry C. Kempe (eds.), *The Battered Child.* Chicago: University of Chicago Press.

ROTHMAN, DAVID J. 1971. *The Discovery of the Asylum: Social Order and Disorder in the New Republic.* Boston: Little, Brown.

SHEPARD, ROBERT E. 1965. "The abused child and the law." *Washington and Lee Law Review* 22(Spring): 182–195.

SILVERMAN, F.N. 1965. "The roentgen manifestations of unrecognized skeletal trauma in infants." *American Journal of Roentgenology, Radium and Nuclear Medicine* 69(March): 413–426.

SKOLNICK, ARLENE and JEROME H. SKOLNICK. 1971. *The Family in Transition.* Boston: Little, Brown.

STEELE, BRANDT and CARL F. POLLOCK. 1968. "A psychiatric study of parents who abuse infants and small children." Pp. 103–147 in Ray E. Helfer and Henry C. Kempe (eds.), *The Battered Child.* Chicago: University of Chicago Press.

SUTHERLAND, EDWIN H. 1950. "The diffusion of sexual psychopath laws." *American Journal of Sociology* 56(September): 142–148.

THOMAS, MASON P. 1972. "Child abuse and neglect: historical overview, legal matrix and social perspectives." *North Carolina Law Review* 50(February): 239–249.

WOOLEY, P.V. and W.A. EVANS JR. 1955. "Significance of skeletal lesions in infants resembling those of traumatic origin." *Journal of the American Medical Association* 158(June): 539–543.

YOUNG, LEONTINE. 1964. *Wednesday's Children: A Study of Child Neglect and Abuse.* New York: McGraw-Hill.

ZALBA, SERAPIO R. 1966. "The abused child. I. A survey of the problems." *Social Work* 11(October): 3–16.

PART II

THEORIES

Functionalism and Anomie

While it would strike most casual observers as odd, social scientists have noted that deviance can serve positive functions for groups and for society as a whole. Drawing from the classic work of Emile Durkheim, one of the founders of modern sociology, functionalists view deviance as an integral part of healthy societies. Deviance serves to establish group boundaries for acceptable behavior. Punishing violators of group norms can serve to strengthen social rules and sharpen social boundaries by bringing these matters to public attention. Rather than seeing deviance merely as pathological, functionalists focus on the purposes it serves as a normal phenomenon of healthy societies. In fact, they believe that deviance is universal, that it exists in all societies, and that it serves an important role in social life. This position is formulated in Emile Durkheim's classic statement in "The Normal and the Pathological." Durkheim identifies the positive aspects of crime and claims that it is a normal part of society, "a factor in public health, an integral part of all healthy societies."

Anomie is a term used by Durkheim to describe a "lack of norms" in society. This lack of clear rules for behavior can exist at both the societal and individual levels. Rapid social change, for example, may bring new norms to the fore that are either not fully clear or not internalized by all segments of the population. Deviance may arise as persons attempt to adapt to these new situations.

Drawing from this tradition, Robert Merton, one of the most famous modern sociologists in the world, formulated his classic work, "Social Structure and Anomie." Merton extended Durkheim's insight that deviance arises from social organization, and seeks to examine what processes account for deviance other than biological mechanisms and impulses. His theory centers on the notion that deviance arises from the incongruence between two major elements of social structure—cultural goals and institutionalized norms or means. When these elements are discordant, deviance may result, as part of a normal process of individual adaptation. The typology of adaptations he presents is one of the more famous examples of modern sociology.

Richard Cloward and Lloyd Ohlin's piece extends Merton's formulation by highlighting the notion that adapting in a deviant manner to social strain entails differential access to illegitimate means. In other words, to enact deviance, one must have access to illegitimate groups and structures from which to learn such behavior. Cloward and Ohlin believe that persons have differential opportunities for rule breaking depending on their location in the social structure. When legitimate opportunities are blocked, the extent of deviant behavior will vary according to the availability of illegitimate means.

THE NORMAL AND THE PATHOLOGICAL*

Emile Durkheim

If there is any fact whose pathological character appears incontestable, that fact is crime. All criminologists are agreed on this point. Although they explain this pathology differently, they are unanimous in recognizing it. But let us see if this problem does not demand a more extended consideration.

We shall apply the foregoing rules. Crime is present not only in the majority of societies of one particular species but in all societies of all types. There is no society that is not confronted with the problem of criminality. Its form changes; the acts thus characterized are not the same everywhere; but, everywhere and always, there have been men who have behaved in such a way as to draw upon themselves penal repression. If, in proportion as societies pass from the lower to the higher types, the rate of criminality, i.e., the relation between the yearly number of crimes and the population, tended to decline, it might be believed that crime, while still normal, is tending to lose this character of normality. But we have no reason to believe that such a regression is substantiated. Many facts would seem rather to indicate a movement in the opposite direction. From the beginning of the [nineteenth] century, statistics enable us to follow the course of criminality. It has everywhere increased. In France the increase is nearly 300 percent. There is, then, no phenomenon that presents more indisputably all the symptoms of normality, since it appears closely connected with the conditions of all collective life. To make of crime a form of social morbidity would be to admit that morbidity is not something accidental, but, on the contrary, that in certain cases it grows out of the fundamental constitution of the living organism; it would result in wiping out all distinction between the physiological and the pathological. No doubt it is possible that crime itself will have abnormal forms, as, for example, when its rate is unusually high. This excess is, indeed, undoubtedly morbid in nature. What is normal, simply, is the existence of criminality, provided that it attains and does not exceed, for each social type, a certain level, which it is perhaps not impossible to fix in conformity with the preceding rules.[1]

Here we are, then, in the presence of a conclusion in appearance quite paradoxical. Let us make no mistake. To classify crime among the phenomena of normal sociology is not to say merely that it is an inevitable, although regrettable phenomenon, due to the incorrigible wickedness of men; it is to affirm that it is a factor in public health, an integral part of all healthy societies. This result is, at first glance, surprising enough to have puzzled even ourselves for a long time. Once this first surprise has been overcome, however, it is not difficult to find reasons explaining this normality and at the same time confirming it.

In the first place crime is normal because a society exempt from it is utterly impossible. Crime . . . consists of an act that offends certain very strong collective sentiments. In a society in which criminal acts are no longer committed, the sentiments they offend would have to be found without exception in all individual consciousnesses, and they must be found to exist with the same degree as sentiments contrary to them. Assuming that this condition could actually be realized, crime would not thereby disappear; it would only change its form, for the very cause which would thus dry up the sources of criminality would immediately open up new ones.

Indeed, for the collective sentiments which are protected by the penal law of a people at a specified moment of its history to take possession of the public conscience or for them to acquire a stronger hold where they have an insufficient grip, they must acquire an intensity greater than that which they had hitherto had. The community as a whole must experience them more vividly, for it can acquire from no other source the greater force necessary to control these individuals who formerly were the most refractory. For murderers to disappear, the horror of bloodshed must become greater in those social strata from which murderers are recruited; but, first it must become greater throughout the entire society. Moreover, the very absence of crime would directly contribute to produce this horror; because any sentiment seems much more respectable when it is always and uniformly respected.

One easily overlooks the consideration that these strong states of the common consciousness cannot be thus reinforced without reinforcing at the same time the more feeble states, whose violation previously gave birth to mere infraction of convention—since the weaker ones are only the prolongation, the attenuated form, of the stronger. Thus robbery and simple bad taste injure the same single altruistic sentiment, the respect for that which is another's. However, this same sentiment is less grievously offended by bad taste than by robbery; and since, in addition, the average consciousness has not sufficient intensity to react keenly to the bad taste, it is treated with greater tolerance. That is why the person guilty of bad taste is merely blamed, whereas the thief is punished. But, if this sentiment grows stronger, to the point of silencing in all consciousnesses the inclination which disposes man to steal, he will become more sensitive to the offenses which, until then, touched him but lightly. He will react against them, then, with more energy; they will be the object of greater opprobrium, which will transform certain of them from the simple moral faults that they were and give them the quality of crimes. For example, improper contracts, or contracts improperly executed, which only incur public blame or civil damages, will become offenses in law.

Imagine a society of saints, a perfect cloister of exemplary individuals. Crimes, properly so called, will there be unknown; but faults which appear venial to the layman will create there the same scandal that the ordinary offense does in ordinary consciousnesses. If, then, this society has the power to judge and punish, it will define these acts as criminal and will treat them as such. For the same reason, the perfect and upright man judges his smallest failings with a severity that the majority reserve for acts more truly in the nature of an offense. Formerly, acts of violence against persons were more frequent than they are today, because respect for individual dignity was less strong. As this has increased, these crimes have become more rare; and also, many acts violating this sentiment have been introduced into the penal law which were not included there in primitive times.[2]

In order to exhaust all the hypotheses logically possible, it will perhaps be asked why this unanimity does not extend to all collective sentiments without exception. Why should not even the most feeble sentiment gather enough energy to prevent all dissent? The moral consciousness of the society would be present in its entirety in all the individuals, with a vitality sufficient to prevent all acts offending it—the purely conventional faults as well as the crimes. But a uniformity so universal and absolute is utterly impossible; for the immediate physical milieu in which each one of us is placed, the hereditary antecedents, and the social influences vary from one individual to the next, and consequently diversify consciousnesses. It is impossible for all to be alike, if only because each one has his own organism and that these organisms occupy different areas in space. That is why, even among the lower peoples, where individual originality is very little developed, it nevertheless does exist.

Thus, since there cannot be a society in which the individuals do not differ more or less from the collective type, it is also inevitable that, among these divergences, there are some with a criminal character. What confers this character upon them is not the intrinsic quality of a given act but that definition which the collective conscience lends them. If the collective conscience is stronger, if it has enough authority practically to suppress these divergences, it will also be more sensitive, more exacting; and, reacting against the slightest deviations with the energy it otherwise displays only against more considerable infractions, it will attribute to them the same gravity as formerly to crimes. In other words, it will designate them as criminal.

Crime is, then, necessary; it is bound up with the fundamental conditions of all social life, and by that very fact it is useful, because these conditions of which it is a part are themselves indispensable to the normal evolution of morality and law.

Indeed, it is no longer possible today to dispute the fact that law and morality vary from one social type to the next, nor that they change within the same type if the conditions of life are modified. But, in order that these transformations may be possible, the collective sentiments at the basis of morality must not be hostile to change, and consequently must have but moderate energy. If they were too strong, they would no longer be plastic. Every pattern is an obstacle to new patterns, to the extent that the first pattern is inflexible. The better a structure is articulated, the more it offers a healthy resistance to all modification; and this is equally true of functional, as of anatomical, organization. If there were no crimes, this condition could not have been fulfilled; for such a hypothesis presupposes that collective sentiments have arrived at a degree of intensity unexampled in history. Nothing is good indefinitely and to an unlimited extent. The authority which the moral conscience enjoys must not be excessive; otherwise no one would dare criticize it, and it would too easily congeal into an immutable form. To make progress, individual originality must be able to express itself. In order that the originality of the idealist whose dreams transcend his century may find expression, it is necessary that the originality of the criminal, who is below the level of his time, shall also be possible. One does not occur without the other.

Nor is this all. Aside from this indirect utility, it happens that crime itself plays a useful role in this evolution. Crime implies not only that the way remains open to necessary changes but that in certain cases it directly prepares these changes. Where crime exists, collective sentiments are sufficiently flexible to take on a new form, and

crime sometimes helps to determine the form they will take. How many times, indeed, it is only an anticipation of future morality—a step toward what will be! According to Athenian law, Socrates was a criminal, and his condemnation was no more than just. However, his crime, namely, the independence of his thought, rendered a service not only to humanity but to his country. It served to prepare a new morality and faith which the Athenians needed, since the traditions by which they had lived until then were no longer in harmony with the current conditions of life. Nor is the case of Socrates unique; it is reproduced periodically in history. It would never have been possible to establish the freedom of thought we now enjoy if the regulations prohibiting it had not been violated before being solemnly abrogated. At that time, however, the violation was a crime, since it was an offense against sentiments still very keen in the average conscience. And yet this crime was useful as a prelude to reforms which daily became more necessary. Liberal philosophy had as its precursors the heretics of all kinds who were justly punished by secular authorities during the entire course of the Middle Ages and until the eve of modern times.

From this point of view the fundamental facts of criminality present themselves to us in an entirely new light. Contrary to current ideas, the criminal no longer seems a totally unsociable being, a sort of parasitic element, a strange and unassimilable body, introduced into the midst of society.[3] On the contrary, he plays a definite role in social life. Crime, for its part, must no longer be conceived as an evil that cannot be too much suppressed. There is no occasion for self-congratulation when the crime rate drops noticeably below the average level, for we may be certain that this apparent progress is associated with some social disorder. Thus, the number of assault cases never falls so low as in times of want.[4] With the drop in crime rate, and as a reaction to it, comes a revision, or the need of a revision in the theory of punishment. If, indeed, crime is a disease, its punishment is its remedy and cannot be otherwise conceived; thus, all the discussions it arouses bear on the point of determining what the punishment must be in order to fulfill this role of remedy. If crime is not pathological at all, the objects of punishment cannot be to cure it, and its true function must be sought elsewhere. . . .

NOTES

1. From the fact that crime is a phenomenon of normal sociology, it does not follow that the criminal is an individual normally constituted from the biological and psychological points of view. The two questions are independent of each other. This independence will be better understood when we have shown, later on, the difference between psychological and sociological facts.

2. Calumny, insults, slander, fraud, etc.

3. We have ourselves committed the error of speaking thus of the criminal, because of a failure to apply our rule (*Division du travail social*, pp. 395–96).

4. Although crime is a fact of normal sociology, it does not follow that we must not abhor it. Pain itself has nothing desirable about it; the individual dislikes it as society does crime, and yet it is a function of normal physiology. Not only is it necessarily derived from the very constitution of every living organism, but it plays a useful role in life, for which reason it cannot be replaced. It would, then, be a singular distortion of our thought to present it as an apology for crime. We would not even think of protesting against such an interpretation, did we not know to what strange accusations and misunderstandings one exposes oneself when one undertakes to study moral facts objectively and to speak of them in a different language from that of the layman.

SOCIAL STRUCTURE AND ANOMIE*

Robert K. Merton

There persists a notable tendency in sociological theory to attribute the malfunctioning of social structure primarily to those of man's imperious biological drives which are not adequately restrained by social control. In this view, the social order is solely a device for "impulse management" and the "social processing" of tensions. These impulses which break through social control, be it noted, are held to be biologically derived. Nonconformity is assumed to be rooted in original nature.[1] Conformity is by implication the result of a utilitarian calculus or unreasoned conditioning. This point of view, whatever its other deficiencies, clearly begs one question. It provides no basis for determining the nonbiological conditions which induce deviations from prescribed patterns of conduct. In this paper, it will

*"Social Structure and Anomie," by Robert K. Merton. *American Sociological Review*, 3 (1938), pp. 672–682. By permission of the author and The American Sociological Association.

be suggested that certain phases of social structure generate the circumstances in which infringement of social codes constitutes a "normal" response.[2]

The conceptual scheme to be outlined is designed to provide a coherent, systematic approach to the study of sociocultural sources of deviate behavior. Our primary aim lies in discovering how some social structures *exert a definite pressure* upon certain persons in the society to engage in nonconformist rather than conformist conduct. The many ramifications of the scheme cannot all be discussed; the problems mentioned outnumber those explicitly treated.

Among the elements of social and cultural structure, two are important for our purposes. These are analytically separable although they merge imperceptibly in concrete situations. The first consists of culturally defined goals, purposes, and interests. It comprises a frame of aspirational reference. These goals are more or less integrated and involve varying degrees of prestige and sentiment. They constitute a basic, but not the exclusive, component of what Linton aptly has called "designs for group living." Some of these cultural aspirations are related to the original drives of man, but they are not determined by them. The second phase of the social structure defines, regulates, and controls the acceptable modes of achieving these goals. Every social group invariably couples its scale of desired ends with moral or institutional regulation of permissible and required procedures for attaining these ends. These regulatory norms and moral imperatives do not necessarily coincide with technical or efficiency norms. Many procedures which from the standpoint of particular individuals would be most efficient in securing desired values, e.g., illicit oil-stock schemes, theft, fraud, are ruled out of the institutional area of permitted conduct. The choice of expedients is limited by the institutional norms.

To say that these two elements, culture goals and institutional norms, operate jointly is not to say that the ranges of alternative behaviors and aims bear some constant relation to one another. The emphasis upon certain goals may vary independently of the degree of emphasis upon institutional means. There may develop a disproportionate, at times, a virtually exclusive, stress upon the value of specific goals, involving relatively slight concern with the institutionally appropriate modes of attaining these goals. The limiting case in this direction is reached when the range of alternative procedures is limited only by technical rather than institutional considerations. Any and all devices which promise attainment of the all important goal would be permitted in this hypothetical polar case.[3] This constitutes one type of cultural malintegration. A second polar type is found in groups where activities originally conceived as instrumental are transmuted into ends in themselves. The original purposes are forgotten and ritualistic adherence to institutionally prescribed conduct becomes virtually obsessive.[4] Stability is largely ensured while change is flouted. The range of alternative behaviors is severely limited. There develops a tradition-bound, sacred society characterized by neophobia. The occupational psychosis of the bureaucrat may be cited as a case in point. Finally,

there are the intermediate types of groups where a balance between culture goals and institutional means is maintained. These are the significantly integrated and relatively stable, though changing, groups.

An effective equilibrium between the two phases of the social structure is maintained as long as satisfactions accrue to individuals who conform to both constraints, viz., satisfactions from the achievement of the goals and satisfactions emerging directly from the institutionally canalized modes of striving to attain these ends. Success, in such equilibrated cases, is twofold. Success is reckoned in terms of the product and in terms of the process, in terms of the outcome and in terms of activities. Continuing satisfactions must derive from sheer *participation* in a competitive order as well as from eclipsing one's competitors if the order itself is to be sustained. The occasional sacrifices involved in institutionalized conduct must be compensated by socialized rewards. The distribution of statuses and roles through competition must be so organized that positive incentives for conformity to roles and adherence to status obligations are provided *for every position* within the distributive order. Aberrant conduct, therefore, may be viewed as a symptom of dissociation between culturally defined aspirations and socially structured means.

Of the types of groups which result from the independent variation of the two phases of the social structure, we shall be primarily concerned with the first, namely, that involving a disproportionate accent on goals. This statement must be recast in a proper perspective. In no group is there an absence of regulatory codes governing conduct, yet groups do vary in the degree to which these folkways, mores, and institutional controls are effectively integrated with the more diffuse goals which are part of the culture matrix. Emotional convictions may cluster about the complex of socially acclaimed ends, meanwhile shifting their support from the culturally defined implementation of these ends. As we shall see, certain aspects of the social structure may generate countermores and antisocial behavior precisely because of differential emphases on goals and regulations. In the extreme case, the latter may be so vitiated by the goal-emphasis that the

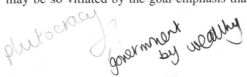

range of behavior is limited only by considerations of technical expediency. The sole significant question then becomes, Which available means is most efficient in netting the socially approved value?[5] The technically most feasible procedure, whether legitimate or not, is preferred to the institutionally prescribed conduct. As this process continues, the integration of the society becomes tenuous and anomie ensues.

Thus, in competitive athletics, when the aim of victory is shorn of its institutional trappings, and success in contests becomes construed as "winning the game" rather than "winning through circumscribed modes of activity," a premium is implicitly set upon the use of illegitimate but technically efficient means. The star of the opposing football team is surreptitiously slugged; the wrestler furtively incapacitates his opponent through ingenious but illicit techniques; university alumni covertly subsidize "students" whose talents are largely confined to the athletic field. The emphasis on the goal has so attenuated the satisfactions deriving from sheer participation in the competitive activity that these satisfactions are virtually confined to a successful outcome. Through the same process, tension generated by the desire to win in a poker game is relieved by successfully dealing oneself four aces, or, when the cult of success has become completely dominant, by sagaciously shuffling the cards in a game of solitaire. The faint twinge of uneasiness in the last instance and the surreptitious nature of public derelicts indicate clearly that the institutional rules of the game *are known* to those who evade them, but that the emotional supports of these rules are largely vitiated by cultural exaggeration of the success-goal.[6] They are microcosmic images of the social macrocosm.

Of course, this process is not restricted to the realm of sport. The process whereby exaltation of the end generates a *literal demoralization*, i.e., a deinstitutionalization, of the means is one which characterizes many[7] groups in which the two phases of the social structure are not highly integrated. The extreme emphasis upon the accumulation of wealth as a symbol of success[8] in our own society militates against the completely effective control of institutionally regulated modes of acquiring a fortune.[9] Fraud, corruption, vice,

crime, in short, the entire catalogue of proscribed behavior becomes increasingly common when the emphasis on the *culturally induced* success-goal becomes divorced from a coordinated institutional emphasis. This observation is of crucial theoretical importance in examining the doctrine that antisocial behavior most frequently derives from biological drives breaking through the restraints imposed by society. The difference is one between a strictly utilitarian interpretation which conceives man's ends as random and an analysis which finds these ends deriving from the basic values of the culture.[10]

Our analysis can scarcely stop at this juncture. We must turn to other aspects of the social structure if we are to deal with the social genesis of the varying rates and types of deviate behavior characteristic of different societies. Thus far, we have sketched three ideal types of social orders constituted by distinctive patterns of relations between culture ends and means. Turning from these types of *culture patterning*, we find five logically possible, alternative modes of adjustment or adaptation *by individuals* within the culture-bearing society or group.[11] These are schematically presented in the following table, where (+) signifies "acceptance," (−) signifies "elimination," and (±) signifies "rejection and substitution of new goals and standards."

		Culture Goals	Institutionalized Means
I.	Conformity	+	+
II.	Innovation	+	−
III.	Ritualism	−	+
IV.	Retreatism	−	−
V.	Rebellion[12]	±	±

Our discussion of the relation between these alternative responses and other phases of the social structure must be prefaced by the observation that persons may shift from one alternative to another as they engage in different social activities. These categories refer to role adjustments in specific situations, not to personality in toto. To treat the development of this process in various spheres of conduct would introduce a complexity unmanageable within the confines of this paper. For this reason, we shall be concerned primarily with economic activity in the broad sense, "the production, exchange, distribution, and consumption of goods and services" in our competitive society, wherein wealth has taken on a highly symbolic cast. Our task is to search out some of the factors which exert pressure upon individuals to engage in certain of these logically possible alternative responses. This choice, as we shall see, is far from random.

In every society, Adaptation I (conformity to both culture goals and means) is the most common and widely diffused. Were this not so, the stability and continuity of the society could not be maintained. The mesh of expectancies which constitutes every social order is sustained by the modal behavior of its members falling within the first category. Conventional role behavior oriented toward the basic values of the group is the rule rather than the exception. It is this fact alone which permits us to speak of a human aggregate as comprising a group or society.

Conversely, Adaptation IV (rejection of goals and means) is the least common. Persons who "adjust" (or maladjust) in this fashion are, strictly speaking, *in* the society but not *of* it. Sociologically, these constitute the true "aliens." Not sharing the common frame of orientation, they can be included within the societal population merely in a fictional sense. In this category are *some* of the activities of psychotics, psychoneurotics, chronic autists, pariahs, outcasts, vagrants, vagabonds, tramps, chronic drunkards, and drug addicts.[13] These have relinquished, in certain spheres of activity, the culturally defined goals, involving complete aim-inhibition in the polar case, and their adjustments are not in accord with institutional norms. This is not to say that in some cases the source of their behavioral adjustments is not in part the very social structure which they have in effect repudiated nor that their very existence within a social area does not constitute a problem for the socialized population.

This mode of "adjustment" occurs, as far as structural sources are concerned, when both the culture goals and institutionalized procedures have been assimilated thoroughly by the individual and imbued with affect and high positive value, but where those institutional procedures which promise a measure of successful attainment of the goals are not available to the individual. In such instances, there results a twofold mental conflict insofar as the moral obligation for adopting institutional means conflicts with the pressure to resort to illegitimate means (which may attain the goal) and inasmuch as the individual is shut off from means which are both legitimate *and* effective. The competitive order is maintained, but the frustrated and handicapped individual who cannot cope with this order drops out. Defeatism, quietism, and resignation are manifested in escape mechanisms which ultimately lead the individual to "escape" from the requirements of the society. It is an expedient which arises from continued failure to attain the goal by legitimate measures and from an inability to adopt the illegitimate route because of internalized prohibitions and institutionalized compulsives, *during which process the supreme value of the success-goal has as yet not been renounced.* The conflict is resolved by eliminating *both* precipitating elements, the goals and means. The escape is complete, the conflict is eliminated, and the individual is asocialized.

Be it noted that where frustration derives from the inaccessibility of effective institutional means for attaining economic or any other type of highly valued "success," that Adaptations II, III and V (innovation, ritualism, and rebellion) are also possible. The result will be determined by the particular personality, and thus, the *particular* cultural background, involved. Inadequate socialization will result in the innovation response, whereby the conflict and frustration are eliminated by relinquishing the institutional means and retaining the success-aspiration; an extreme assimilation of institutional demands will lead to ritualism, wherein the goal is dropped as beyond one's reach but conformity to the mores persists; and rebellion occurs when emancipation from the reigning standards, due to frustration or to marginalist perspectives, leads to the attempt to introduce a "new social order."

Our major concern is with the illegitimacy adjustment. This involves the use of conventionally proscribed but frequently effective means of attaining at least the simulacrum of culturally defined success—wealth, power, and the like. As we have seen, this adjustment occurs when the individual has assimilated the cultural emphasis on success without equally internalizing the morally prescribed norms governing means for its attainment. The question arises, Which phases of our social structure predispose toward this mode of adjustment? We may examine a concrete instance, effectively analyzed by Lohman,[14] which provides a clue to the answer. Lohman has shown that specialized areas of vice in the near north side of Chicago constitute a "normal" response to a situation where the cultural emphasis upon pecuniary success has been absorbed, but where there is little access to conventional and legitimate means for attaining such success. The conventional occupational opportunities of persons in this area are almost completely limited to manual labor. Given our cultural stigmatization of manual labor, and its correlate, the prestige of white collar work, it is clear that the result is a strain toward innovational practices. The limitation of opportunity to unskilled labor and the resultant low income cannot compete *in terms of conventional standards of achivement* with the high income from organized vice.

For our purposes, this situation involves two important features. First, such antisocial behavior is in a sense "called forth" by certain conventional values of the culture *and* by the class structure involving differential access to the approved opportunities for legitimate, prestige-bearing pursuit of the culture goals. The lack of high integration between the means-and-end elements of the cultural pattern and the particular class structure combine to favor a heightened frequency of antisocial conduct in such groups. The second consideration is of equal significance. Recourse to the first of the alternative responses, legitimate effort, is limited by the fact that actual advance toward desired success-symbols through conventional channels is, despite our persisting open-class ideology,[15] relatively rare and difficult for those handicapped by little formal education and few economic resources. The dominant pressure of group standards of success is, therefore, on the gradual attenuation of legitimate, but by and large ineffective, strivings and the increasing use of illegitimate, but more or less effective, expedients of vice and crime. The cultural demands made on persons in this situation are incompati-

ble. On the one hand, they are asked to orient their conduct toward the prospect of accumulating wealth, and on the other, they are largely denied effective opportunities to do so institutionally. The consequences of such structural inconsistency are psychopathological personality, and/or antisocial conduct, and/or revolutionary activities. The equilibrium between culturally designated means and ends becomes highly unstable with the progressive emphasis on attaining the prestige-laden ends by any means whatsoever. Within this context, Capone represents the triumph of amoral intelligence over morally prescribed "failure," when the channels of vertical mobility are closed or narrowed[16] *in a society which places a high premium on economic affluence and social ascent for all its members.*[17]

This last qualification is of primary importance. It suggests that other phases of the social structure besides the extreme emphasis on pecuniary success must be considered if we are to understand the social sources of antisocial behavior. A high frequency of deviate behavior is not generated simply by "lack of opportunity" or by this exaggerated pecuniary emphasis. A comparatively rigidified class structure, a feudalistic or caste order, may limit such opportunities far beyond the point which obtains in our society today. It is only when a system of cultural values extols, virtually above all else, certain *common* symbols of success *for the population at large* while its social structure rigorously restricts or completely eliminates access to approved modes of acquiring these symbols *for a considerable part of the same population* that antisocial behavior ensues on a considerable scale. In other words, our egalitarian ideology denies by implication the existence of noncompeting groups and individuals in the pursuit of pecuniary success. The same body of success-symbols is held to be desirable for all. These goals are held to *transcend class lines,* not to be bounded by them, yet the actual social organization is such that there exist class differentials in the accessibility of these *common* success-symbols. Frustration and thwarted aspiration lead to the search for avenues of escape from a culturally induced intolerable situation; or unrelieved ambition may eventuate in illicit attempts to acquire the dominant values.[18] The American stress on pecuniary success and ambitiousness for all thus invites exaggerated anxieties, hostilities, neuroses, and antisocial behavior.

This theoretical analysis may go far toward explaining the varying correlations between crime and poverty.[19] Poverty is not an isolated variable. It is one in a complex of interdependent social and cultural variables. When viewed in such a context, it represents quite different states of affairs. Poverty as such, and consequent limitation of opportunity, are not sufficient to induce a conspicuously high rate of criminal behavior. Even the often mentioned "poverty in the midst of plenty" will not necessarily lead to this result. Only insofar as poverty and associated disadvantages in competition for the culture values approved for *all* members of the society are linked with the assimilation of a cultural emphasis on monetary accumulation as a symbol of success is antisocial conduct a "normal" outcome. Thus, poverty is less highly correlated with crime in southeastern Europe than in the United States. The possibilities of vertical mobility in these European areas would seem to be fewer than in this country, so that neither poverty per se nor its association with limited opportunity is sufficient to account for the varying correlations. It is only when the full configuration is considered, poverty, limited opportunity, and a commonly shared system of success symbols, that we can explain the higher association between poverty and crime in our society than in others where rigidified class structure is coupled with *differential class symbols of achievement.*

In societies such as our own, then, the pressure of prestige-bearing success tends to eliminate the effective social constraint over means employed to this end. The "end-justifies-the-means" doctrine becomes a guiding tenet for action when the cultural structure unduly exalts the end and the social organization unduly limits possible recourse to approved means. Otherwise put, this notion and associated behavior reflect a lack of cultural coordination. In international relations, the effects of this lack of integration are notoriously apparent. An emphasis upon national power is not readily coordinated with an inept organization of legitimate, i.e., internationally defined and accepted, means for attaining this goal. The result is a tendency toward the abrogation of international law, treaties become scraps of paper, "undeclared warfare" serves as a technical evasion, the bombing of civilian populations is rationalized,[20] just as the same societal situation induces the same sway of illegitimacy among individuals.

The social order we have described necessarily produces this "strain toward dissolution." The pressure of such an order is upon outdoing one's competitors. The choice of means within the ambit of institutional control will persist as long as the sentiments supporting a competitive system, i.e., deriving from the possibility of outranking competitors and hence enjoying the favorable response of others, are distributed throughout the entire system of activities and are not confined merely to the final result. A stable social structure demands a balanced distribution of affect among its various segments. When there occurs a shift of emphasis from the satisfactions deriving from competition itself to almost exclusive concern with successful competition, the resultant stress leads to the breakdown of the regulatory structure.[21] With the resulting attenuation of the institutional imperatives, there occurs an approximation of the situation erroneously held by utilitarians to be typical of society generally wherein calculations of advantage and fear of punishment are the sole regulating agencies. In such situations, as Hobbes observed, force and fraud come to constitute the sole virtues in view of their relative efficiency in attaining goals—which were for him, of course, not culturally derived.

It should be apparent that the foregoing discussion is not pitched on a moralistic plane. Whatever the sentiments of the writer or reader concerning the ethical desirability of coordinating the means-and-goals phases of the social structure, one must agree that lack of such coordination leads to anomie. Insofar as one of the most general functions of social organization is to provide a basis for calculability and regularity of behavior, it is increasingly limited in effectiveness as these elements of the structure become dissociated. At the extreme, predictability virtually disappears, and what may be properly termed cultural chaos or anomie intervenes.

This statement, being brief, is also incomplete. It has not included an exhaustive treatment of the various structural elements which predispose toward one rather than another of the alternative responses open to individuals; it has neglected, but not denied the relevance of, the factors determining the specific incidence of these responses; it has not enumerated the various concrete responses which are constituted by combinations of specific values of the analytical variables; it has omitted, or included only by implication, any consideration of the social functions performed by illicit responses; it has not tested the full explanatory power of the analytical scheme by examining a large number of group variations in the frequency of deviate and conformist behavior; it has not adequately dealt with rebellious conduct which seeks to refashion the social framework radically; it has not examined the relevance of cultural conflict for an analysis of culture–goal and institutional–means malintegration. It is suggested that these and related problems may be profitably analyzed by this scheme.

NOTES

1. E.g., Ernest Jones, *Social Aspects of Psychoanalysis*, 28, London, 1924. If the Freudian notion is a variety of the "original sin" dogma, then the interpretation advanced in this paper may be called the doctrine of "socially derived sin."

2. "Normal" in the sense of a culturally oriented, if not approved, response. This statement does not deny the relevance of biological and personality differences which may be significantly involved in the *incidence* of deviate conduct. Our focus of interest is the social and cultural matrix; hence we abstract from other factors. It is in this sense, I take it, that James S. Plant speaks of the "normal reaction of normal people to abnormal conditions." See his *Personality and the Cultural Pattern*, 248, New York, 1937.

3. Contemporary American culture has been said to tend in this direction. See André Siegfried, *America Comes of Age*, 26–37, New York, 1927. The alleged extreme(?) emphasis on the goals of monetary success and material prosperity leads to dominant concern with technological and social instruments designed to produce the desired result, inasmuch as institutional controls become of secondary importance. In such a situation, innovation flourishes as the *range of means*

employed is broadened. In a sense, then, there occurs the paradoxical emergence of "materialists" from an "idealistic" orientation. Cf. Durkheim's analysis of the cultural conditions which predispose toward crime and innovation, both of which are aimed toward efficiency, not moral norms. Durkheim was one of the first to see that "contrairement aux idées courantes le criminel n'apparait plus comme un etre radicalement insociable, comme une sort d'element parasitaire, de corps etranger et inassimilable, introduit au sein de la societe; c'est un agent regulier de la vie sociale" (Contrary to common thinking, the criminal no longer appears as a totally unsociable human being, as a sort of parasite, alien and unassimilable, introduced in the midst of society; he is a regular member of social life). See *Les Regles de la Methode Sociologique*, 86–89, Paris, 1927.

4. Such ritualism may be associated with a mythology which rationalizes these actions so that they appear to retain their status as means, but the dominant pressure is in the direction of strict ritualistic conformity, irrespective of such rationalizations. In this sense, ritual has proceeded farthest when such rationalizations are not even called forth.

5. In this connection, one may see the relevance of Elton Mayo's paraphrase of the title of Tawney's well-known book. "Actually the problem *is not that of the sickness of an acquisitive society; it is that of the acquisitiveness of a sick society.*" *Human Problems of an Industrial Civilization*, 153, New York, 1933. Mayo deals with the process through which wealth comes to be a symbol of social achievement. He sees this as arising from a state of anomie. We are considering the unintegrated monetary success goal as an element in producing anomie. A complete analysis would involve both phases of this system of interdependent variables.

6. It is unlikely that interiorized norms are completely eliminated. Whatever residuum persists will induce personality tensions and conflict. The process involves a certain degree of ambivalence. A manifest rejection of the institutional norms is coupled with some latent retention of their emotional correlates. "Guilt feelings," "sense of sin," "pangs of conscience" are obvious manifestations of this unrelieved tension; symbolic adherence to the nominally repudiated values or rationalizations constitute a more subtle variety of tensional release.

7. "Many," and not all, unintegrated groups, for the reason already mentioned. In groups where the primary emphasis shifts to institutional means, i.e., when the range of alternatives is very limited, the outcome is a type of ritualism rather than anomie.

8. Money has several peculiarities which render it particularly apt to become a symbol of prestige

divorced from institutional controls. As Simmel emphasized, money is highly abstract and impersonal. However acquired, through fraud or institutionally, it can be used to purchase the same goods and services. The anonymity of metropolitan culture, in conjunction with this peculiarity of money, permits wealth, the sources of which may be unknown to the community in which the plutocrat lives, to serve as a symbol of status.

9. The emphasis upon wealth as a success-symbol is possibly reflected in the use of the term "fortune" to refer to a stock of accumulated wealth. This meaning becomes common in the late sixteenth century (Spenser and Shakespeare). A similar usage of the Latin *fortuna* comes into prominence during the first century B.C. Both these periods were marked by the rise to prestige and power of the "bourgeoisie."

10. See Kingsley Davis, "Mental Hygiene and the Class Structure," *Psychiatry*, 1928, I, esp. 62–63; Talcott Parsons, *The Structure of Social Action*, 59–60, New York, 1937.

11. This is a level intermediate between the two planes distinguished by Edward Sapir, namely, culture patterns and personal habit systems. See his "Contribution of Psychiatry to an Understanding of Behavior in Society," *American Journal of Sociology*, 1937, 42:862–70.

12. This fifth alternative is on a plane clearly different from that of the others. It represents a *transitional* response which seeks to *institutionalize* new procedures oriented toward revamped cultural goals shared by the members of the society. It thus involves efforts to *change* the existing structure rather than to perform accommodative actions *within* this structure, and introduces additional problems with which we are not at the moment concerned.

13. Obviously, this is an elliptical statement. These individuals may maintain some orientation to the values of their particular differentiated groupings within the larger society or, in part, of the conventional society itself. Insofar as they do so, their conduct cannot be classified in the "passive rejection" category (IV). Nels Anderson's description of the behavior and attitudes of the bum, for example, can readily be recast in terms of our analytical scheme. See *The Hobo*, 93–98, et passim, Chicago, 1923.

14. Joseph D. Lohman, "The Participant Observer in Community Studies," *American Sociological Review*, 1937, 2:890-98.

15. The shifting historical role of this ideology is a profitable subject for exploration. The "office-boy-to-president" stereotype was once in approximate accord with the facts. Such vertical mobility was probably more common then than now, when the class structure is more rigid. (See the following note.) The ideology largely persists, however, possibly because it still performs a useful function for maintaining the status quo. For insofar as it is accepted by the "masses," it constitutes a useful sop for those who might rebel against the entire structure, were this consoling hope removed. This ideology now serves to lessen the probability of Adaptation V. In short, the role of this notion has changed from that of an approximately valid empirical theorem to that of an ideology, in Mannheim's sense.

16. There is a growing body of evidence, though none of it is clearly conclusive, to the effect that our class structure is becoming rigidified and that vertical mobility is declining. Taussig and Joslyn found that American business leaders are being *increasingly* recruited from the upper ranks of our society. The Lynds have also found a "diminished chance to get ahead" for the working classes in Middletown. Manifestly, these objective changes are not alone significant; the individual's subjective evaluation of the situation is a major determinant of the response. The extent to which this change in opportunity for social mobility has been recognized by the least advantaged classes is still conjectural, although the Lynds present some suggestive materials. The writer suggests that a case in point is the increasing frequency of cartoons which observe in a tragi-comic vein that "my old man says everybody can't be President. He says if ya can get three days a week steady on W.P.A. work ya ain't doin' so bad either." See F. W. Taussig and C. S. Joslyn, *American Business Leaders*, New York, 1932; R. S. and H. M. Lynd, *Middletown in Transition*, 67ff., chap. 12, New York, 1937.

17. The role of the Negro in this respect is of considerable theoretical interest. Certain elements of the Negro population have assimilated the dominant caste's values of pecuniary success and social advancement, but they also recognize that social ascent is at present restricted to their own caste almost exclusively. The pressures upon the Negro which would otherwise derive from the structural inconsistencies we have noticed are hence not identical with those upon lower class whites. See Kingsley Davis, op. cit., 63; John Dollard, *Caste and Class in a Southern Town*, 66 ff., New Haven, 1936; Donald Young, *American Minority Peoples*, 581, New York, 1932.

18. The psychical coordinates of these processes have been partly established by the experimental evidence concerning *Anspruchsniveaus* and levels of performance. See Kurt Lewin, *Vorsatz, Willie und Bedurfnis*, Berlin, 1926; N. F. Hoppe, "Erfolg und Misserfolg," *Psycholische Forschung*, 1930, 14:1–63; Jerome D. Frank, "Individual Differences in Certain Aspects of the Level of Aspiration," *American Journal of Psychology*, 1935, 47:119–28.

19. Standard criminology texts summarize the data in this field. Our scheme of analysis may serve to resolve some of the theoretical contradictions which P. A. Sorokin indicates. For example, "not everywhere nor always do the poor show a greater proportion of crime . . . many poorer countries have had less crime than the richer countries . . . The [economic] improvement in the second half of the nineteenth century, and the beginning of the twentieth, has not been followed by a decrease of crime." See his *Contemporary Sociological Theories*, 560–61, New York, 1928. The cru-

cial point is, however, that poverty has varying social significance in different social structures, as we shall see. Hence, one would not expect a linear correlation between crime and poverty.

20. See M. W. Royse, *Aerial Bombardment and the International Regulation of War*, New York, 1928.

21. Since our primary concern is with the sociocultural aspects of this problem, the psychological correlates have been only implicitly considered. See Karen Horney, *The Neurotic Personality of Our Time*, New York, 1937, for a psychological discussion of this process.

ILLEGITIMATE MEANS AND DELINQUENT SUBCULTURES*

Richard A. Cloward AND Lloyd E. Ohlin

THE AVAILABILITY OF ILLEGITIMATE MEANS

Social norms are two-sided. A prescription implies the existence of a prohibition, and vice versa. To advocate honesty is to demarcate and condemn a set of actions which are dishonest. In other words, norms that define legitimate practices also implicitly define illegitimate practices. One purpose of norms, in fact, is to delineate the boundary between legitimate and illegitimate practices. In setting this boundary, in segregating and classifying various types of behavior, they make us aware not only of behavior that is regarded as right and proper but also of behavior that is said to be wrong and improper. Thus the criminal who engages in theft or fraud does not invent a new way of life; the possibility of employing alternative means is acknowledged, tacitly at least, by the norms of the culture.

This tendency for proscribed alternatives to be implicit in every prescription, and vice versa, al-

though widely recognized, is nevertheless a reef upon which many a theory of delinquency has foundered. Much of the criminological literature assumes, for example, that one may explain a criminal act simply by accounting for the individual's readiness to employ illegal alternatives of which his culture, through its norms, has already made him generally aware. Such explanations are quite unsatisfactory, however, for they ignore a host of questions regarding the *relative availability* of illegal alternatives to various potential criminals. The aspiration to be a physician is hardly enough to explain the fact of becoming a physician; there is much that transpires between the aspiration and the achievement. This is no less true of the person who wants to be a successful criminal. Having decided that he "can't make it legitimately," he cannot simply choose among an array of illegitimate means, all equally available to him. . . . It is assumed in the theory of anomie that access to conventional means is differentially distributed, that some individuals, because of their social class, enjoy certain advantages that are denied to those elsewhere in the class structure. For example, there are variations in the degree to which members of various classes are fully exposed to and thus acquire the values, knowledge, and skills that facilitate upward mobility. It should not be starting, therefore, to suggest that there are socially structured variations in the availability of illegitimate means as well. In connection with delinquent subcultures, we shall be concerned principally with differentials in access to illegitimate means within the lower class.

Many sociologists have alluded to differentials in access to illegitimate means without explicitly incorporating this variable into a theory of deviant behavior. This is particularly true of scholars in the "Chicago tradition" of criminology. Two closely related theoretical perspectives emerged from this school. The theory of "cultural transmission," advanced by Clifford R. Shaw and Henry D. McKay, focuses on the development in some urban neighborhoods of a criminal tradition that persists from one generation to another despite constant changes in population.[1] In the theory of "differential association," Edwin H. Sutherland described the processes by which criminal values are taken over by the individual.[2] He asserted that criminal behavior is learned, and that it is learned in interaction with others who have already incorporated criminal values. Thus the first theory stresses the value systems of different areas; the second, the systems of social relationships that facilitate or impede the acquisition of these values.

Scholars in the Chicago tradition, who emphasized the processes involved in learning to be criminal, were actually pointing to differentials in the availability of illegal means—although they did not explicitly recognize this variable in their analysis. This can perhaps best be seen by examining Sutherland's classic work, *The Professional Thief*. "An inclination to steal," according to Sutherland, "is not a sufficient explanation of the genesis of the professional thief."[3] The "self-made" thief, lacking knowledge of the ways of securing immunity from prosecution and similar techniques of defense, "would quickly land in prison; . . . a person can be a professional thief only if he is recognized and received as such by other professional thieves." But recognition is not freely accorded: "Selection and tutelage are the two necessary elements in the process of acquiring recognition as a professional thief . . . A person cannot acquire recognition as a professional thief until he has had tutelage in professional theft, *and tutelage is given only to a few persons selected from the total population.*" For one thing, "the person must be appreciated by the professional thieves. He must be appraised as having an adequate equipment of wits, front, talking-ability, honesty, reliability, nerve, and determination." Furthermore, the aspirant is judged by high standards of performance, for only "a very small percentage of those who start on this process ever reach the stage of professional thief. . . ." Thus motivation and pressures toward deviance do not fully account for deviant behavior any more than motivation and pressures toward conformity account for conforming behavior. The individual must have access to a learning environment and, once having been trained, must be allowed to perform his role. Roles, whether conforming or deviant in content, are not necessarily freely available; access to them depends on a variety of factors, such as one's socioeconomic position, age, sex, ethnic affiliation, personality characteristics, and the like. The potential thief, like the potential physician, finds that access to his goal is governed by many criteria other than merit and motivation.

What we are asserting is that access to illegitimate roles is not freely available to all, as is commonly assumed. Only those neighborhoods in which crime flourishes as a stable, indigenous institution are fertile criminal learning environments for the young. Because these environments afford integration of different age-levels of offender, selected young people are exposed to "differential association" through which tutelage is provided and criminal values and skills are acquired. To be prepared for the role may not, however, ensure that the individual will ever discharge it. One important limitation is that more youngsters are recruited into these patterns of differential associations than the adult criminal structure can possibly absorb. Since there is a surplus of contenders for these elite positions, criteria and mechanisms of selection must be evolved. Hence a certain proportion of those who aspire may not be permitted to engage in the behavior for which they have prepared themselves.

Thus we conclude that access to illegitimate roles, no less than access to legitimate roles, is limited by both social and psychological factors.

We shall here be concerned primarily with socially structured differentials in illegitimate opportunities. Such differentials, we contend, have much to do with the type of delinquent subculture that develops.

LEARNING AND PERFORMANCE STRUCTURES

Our use of the term "opportunities," legitimate or illegitimate, implies access to both learning and performance structures. That is, the individual must have access to appropriate environments for the acquisition of the values and skills associated with the performance of a particular role, and he must be supported in the performance of the role once he has learned it.

Tannenbaum, several decades ago, vividly expressed the point that criminal role performance, no less than conventional role performance, presupposes a patterned set of relationships through which the requisite values and skills are transmitted by established practitioners to aspiring youth:

It takes a long time to make a good criminal, many years of specialized training and much preparation. But training is something that is given to people. People learn in a community where the materials and the knowledge are to be had. A craft needs an atmosphere saturated with purpose and promise. The community provides the attitudes, the point of view, the philosophy of life, the example, the motive, the contacts, the friendships, the incentives. No child brings those into the world. He finds them here and available for use and elaboration. The community gives the criminal his materials and habits, just as it gives the doctor, the lawyer, the teacher, and the candlestick-maker theirs.[4]

Sutherland systematized this general point of view, asserting that opportunity consists, at least in part, of learning structures. Thus "criminal behavior is learned" and, furthermore, it is learned "in interaction with other persons in a process of communication." However, he conceded that the differential-association theory does not constitute a full explanation of criminal behavior. In a paper circulated in 1944, he noted that "criminal behavior is partially a function of opportunities to commit specific classes of crime, such as embezzlement, bank burglary, or illicit heterosexual intercourse." Therefore, "while opportunity may

be partially a function of association with criminal patterns and of the specialized techniques thus acquired, it is not determined entirely in that manner, and consequently differential association is not the sufficient cause of criminal behavior."[5]

To Sutherland, then, illegitimate opportunity included conditions favorable to the performance of a criminal role as well as conditions favorable to the learning of such a role (differential associations). These conditions, we suggest, depend upon certain features of the social structure of the community in which delinquency arises.

DIFFERENTIAL OPPORTUNITY: A HYPOTHESIS

We believe that each individual occupies a position in both legitimate and illegitimate opportunity structures. This is a new way of defining the situation. The theory of anomie views the individual primarily in terms of the legitimate opportunity structure. It poses questions regarding differentials in access to legitimate routes to success-goals; at the same time it assumes either that illegitimate avenues to success-goals are freely available or that differentials in their availability are of little significance. This tendency may be seen in the following statement by Merton:

Several researches have shown that specialized areas of vice and crime constitute a "normal" response to a situation where the cultural emphasis upon pecuniary success has been absorbed, but where there is little access to conventional and legitimate means for becoming successful. The occupational opportunities of people in these areas are largely confined to manual labor and the lesser white-collar jobs. Given the American stigmatization of manual labor *which has been found to hold rather uniformly for all social classes*, and the absence of realistic opportunities for advancement beyond this level, the result is a marked tendency toward deviant behavior. The status of unskilled labor and the consequent low income cannot readily compete *in terms of established standards of worth* with the promises of power and high income from organized vice, rackets, and crime. . . . [Such a situation] leads toward the gradual attenuation of legitimate, but by and large ineffectual, strivings and the increasing use of illegitimate, but more or less effective, expedients.[6]

The cultural-transmission and differential-association tradition, on the other hand, assumes that access to illegitimate means is variable, but it does not recognize the significance of comparable differentials in access to legitimate means. Sutherland's "ninth proposition" in the theory of differential association states:

Though criminal behavior is an expression of general needs and values, it is not explained by those general needs and values since non-criminal behavior is an expression of the same needs and values. Thieves generally steal in order to secure money, but likewise honest laborers work in order to secure money. The attempts by many scholars to explain criminal behavior by general drives and values, such as the happiness principle, striving for social status, the money motive, or frustration, have been and must continue to be futile since they explain lawful behavior as completely as they explain criminal behavior.[7]

In this statement, Sutherland appears to assume that people have equal and free access to legitimate means regardless of their social position. At the very least, he does not treat access to legitimate means as variable. It is, of course, perfectly true that "striving for social status," "the money motive," and other socially approved drives do not fully account for either deviant or conforming behavior. But if goal-oriented behavior occurs under conditions in which there are socially structured obstacles to the satisfaction of these drives by legitimate means, the resulting pressures, we contend, might lead to deviance.

The concept of differential opportunity structures permits us to unite the theory of anomie, which recognizes the concept of differentials in access to legitimate means, and the "Chicago tradition," in which the concept of differentials in access to illegitimate means is implicit. We can now look at the individual, not simply in relation to one or the other system of means, but in relation to both legitimate and illegitimate systems. This approach permits us to ask, for example, how the relative availability of illegitimate opportunities affects the resolution of adjustment problems leading to deviant behavior. We believe that the way in which these problems are resolved may depend upon the kind of support for one or another type of illegitimate activity that is given at different points in the social structure. If,

in a given social location, illegal or criminal means are not readily available, then we should not expect a criminal subculture to develop among adolescents. By the same logic, we should expect the manipulation of violence to become a primary avenue to higher status only in areas where the means of violence are not denied to the young. To give a third example, drug addiction and participation in subcultures organized around the consumption of drugs presuppose that persons can secure access to drugs and knowledge about how to use them. In some parts of the social structure, this would be very difficult; in others, very easy. In short, there are marked differences from one part of the social structure to another in the types of illegitimate adaptation that are available to persons in search of solutions to problems of adjustment arising from the restricted availability of legitimate means.[8] In this sense, then, we can think of individuals as being located in two opportunity structures—one legitimate, the other illegitimate. Given limited access to success-goals by legitimate means, the nature of the delinquent response that may result will vary according to the availability of various illegitimate means.[9]

NOTES

1. See esp. C. R. Shaw, *The Jack-Roller* (Chicago: University of Chicago Press, 1930); Shaw, *The Natural History of a Delinquent Career* (Chicago: University of Chicago Press, 1931); Shaw *et al., Delinquency Areas* (Chicago: University of Chicago Press, 1940); and Shaw and H. D. McKay, *Juvenile Delinquency and Urban Areas* (Chicago: University of Chicago Press, 1942).

2. E. H. Sutherland, ed., *The Professional Thief* (Chicago: University of Chicago Press, 1937); and Sutherland, *Principles of Criminology*, 4th Ed. (Philadelphia: Lippincott, 1947).

3. All quotations on this page are from *The Professional Thief*, pp. 211–13. Emphasis added.

4. Frank Tannenbaum, "The Professional Criminal," *The Century*, Vol. 110 (May–Oct. 1925): p. 577.

5. See A. K. Cohen, Alfred Lindesmith, and Karl Schussler, eds., *The Sutherland Papers* (Bloomington, Ind.: Indiana University Press, 1956), pp. 31–35.

6. R. K. Merton, *Social Theory and Social Structure*, Rev. and Enl. Ed. (Glencoe, Ill.: Free Press, 1957), pp. 145–46.

7. *Principles of Criminology, op. cit.*, pp. 7–8.

8. For an example of restrictions on access to illegitimate roles, note the impact of racial definitions in the following case: "I was greeted by two prisoners who were to be my cell buddies. Ernest was a first offender, charged with being a 'hold-up' man. Bill, the other buddy, was an old offender, going through the machinery of becoming a habitual criminal, in and out of jail. . . . The first thing they asked me was, 'What are you in for?' I said, 'Jack-rolling.' The hardened one (Bill) looked at me with a superior air and said, 'A hoodlum, eh? An ordinary sneak thief. Not willing to leave jack-rolling to the niggers, eh? That's all they're good for. Kid, jack-rolling's not a white man's job.' I could see that he was disgusted with me, and I was too scared to say anything" (Shaw, *The Jack-Roller, op. cit.*, p. 101).

9. For a discussion of the way in which the availability of illegitimate means influences the adaptations of inmates to prison life, see R. A. Cloward, "Social Control in the Prison," *Theoretical Studies of the Social Organization of the Prison*, Bulletin No. 15 (New York: Social Science Research Council, March 1960), pp. 20–48.

Symbolic Interactionism/Labeling

Labeling theory or the "interactionist approach" to deviance does not focus on the causes of deviance per se, but rather on how certain behaviors come to be labeled as deviant in the first place and how such designations influence future behavior. Whether labeling is actually a "theory" has been debated by sociologists since the term was created. Some have argued that it really isn't a theory since it does not explain the causes of deviance. Rather, it posits a reactive view of deviance, where audience responses are viewed as just as important as the behavior itself. Influenced heavily by the writings of Edwin Lemert, whose initial insights into symbolic interactionism paved the way for future thinking in this area, the labeling approach represents a social-psychological perspective on deviance. A central concept involves the "social self." Charles Horton Cooley's piece, "The Social Self," defines the social aspects of the self through his central concept of the "looking-glass self." Our individual identities revolve around the ways we perceive ourselves. How we perceive ourselves (as in a mirror, or looking-glass) in large part depends upon how we think others see us. Our self feelings arise from this process, and they are important in understanding how deviant identities are formed.

Edwin Lemert, a preeminent twentieth century sociologist, had a profound influence on the de-

velopment of the labeling perspective. In his classic formulation regarding "Primary and Secondary Deviation," Lemert argues that the initial or "primary" causes of deviance were not that important. Of more consequence were the reactions by others to such behaviors. Secondary deviation occurs when the person enacting the deviant behavior organizes his or her identity around these reactions by others.

Stigmatization is a major concept in the sociological study of deviance and refers to a process by which individuals are forced to reconsider their self-identities. In the selection, "Stigma and Social Identity," Erving Goffman describes the concept of stigma and its relevance to the study of deviance. Referring to "an attribute that is deeply discrediting," stigma is a central concept in the labeling approach to deviance. Goffman discusses the different types of stigma and how individuals attempt to manage it in everyday life.

In the piece, "Whiteness as Stigma," Debbie Storr's uses Goffman's classic conceptualization to examine racial mixing. She argues that while such mixing of different races has generally been stigmatized by the public, that historically stigmatized mixed-race women reject these patterns of stigma by reassigning them to their white European ancestry. This reversal is explained by women who embrace and articulate their non-white identities, and highlights a new perspective on the meanings of race and racial belonging.

Leslie Margolin's article, "Deviance on Record," examines how written documents are used by social control agents to piece together a deviant identity for those accused of child abuse. Using official records and focusing on the power imbalance between investigators and suspects, she shows how social workers "prove" that someone committed abuse and the means by which they impose their version of reality upon the accused. Following a well established tradition of research on how officials process deviants, she finds that bureaucrats devise ways of imputing intentionality in these cases that largely ignore suspects' accounts.

In the article, "On Behalf of Labeling Theory," Erich Goode defends the perspective from critics both within and outside its ranks. Citing the major objections to labeling as a useful perspective in the study of deviance, Goode argues that labeling is important for understanding such behavior even if it isn't a bona fide theory. It is useful, he claims, for examining specific features of deviance, through the introduction of what he identifies as "sensitizing concepts." These ideas can then be used for analyzing the social processes that take place between the commission of a deviant act and the acquisition of a deviant identity.

THE SOCIAL SELF*

Charles Horton Cooley

The social self is simply any idea, or system of ideas, drawn from the communicative life, that the mind cherishes as its own. Self-feeling has its chief scope *within* the general life, not outside of it. . . .

That the "I" of common speech has a meaning which includes some sort of reference to other persons is involved in the very fact that the word and the ideas it stands for are phenomena of language and the communicative life. It is doubtful whether it is possible to use language at all without thinking more or less distinctly of someone else, and certainly the things to which we give names and which have a large place in reflective thought are almost always those which are impressed upon us by our contact with other people. Where there is no communication there can be no nomenclature and no developed thought. What we call "me," "mine," or "myself" is, then, not something separate from the general life, but the most interesting part of it, a part whose interest arises from the very fact that it is both general and individual. That is, we care for it just because it is that phase of the mind that is living and striving in the common life, trying to impress itself upon the minds of others. "I" is a militant social tendency, working to hold and enlarge its place in the general current of tendencies. So far as it can it waxes, as all life does. To think of it as apart from society is a palpable absurdity of which no one could be guilty who really *saw* it as a fact of life. . . .

The reference to other persons involved in the sense of self may be distinct and particular, as when a boy is ashamed to have his mother catch him at something she has forbidden, or it may be vague and general, as when one is ashamed to do something which only his conscience, expressing his sense of social responsibility, detects and disapproves; but it is always there. There is no sense of "I," as in pride or shame, without its

*"The Social Self" by Charles H. Cooley, *Human Nature and the Social Order* (New York: Charles Scribner's Sons), 1902, pp. 179–185, 259–260.

correlative sense of you, or he, or they. Even the miser gloating over his hidden gold can feel the "mine" only as he is aware of the world of men over whom he has secret power; and the case is very similar with all kinds of hidden treasure. Many painters, sculptors, and writers have loved to withhold their work from the world, fondling it in seclusion until they were quite done with it; but the delight in this, as in all secrets, depends upon a sense of the value of what is concealed.

. . . We think of the body as "I" when it comes to have social function or significance, as when we say "I am looking well today," or "I am taller than you are." We bring it into the social world, for the time being, and for that reason, put our self-consciousness into it. Now it is curious, though natural, that in precisely the same way we may call any inanimate object "I" with which we are identifying our will and purpose. This is notable in games, like golf or croquet, where the ball is the embodiment of the player's fortunes. You will hear a man say, "I am in the long grass down by the third tee," or "I am in position for the middle arch." So a boy flying a kite will say, "I am higher than you," or one shooting at a mark will declare that he is just below the bullseye.

In a very large and interesting class of cases the social reference takes the form of a somewhat definite imagination of how one's self—that is any idea he appropriates—appears in a particular mind, and the kind of self-feeling one has is determined by the attitude toward this attributed to that other mind. A social self of this sort might be called the reflected or looking-glass self:

> *"Each to each a looking-glass*
> *Reflects the other that doth pass."*

As we see our face, figure, and dress in the glass, and are interested in them because they are ours, and pleased or otherwise with them according as they do or do not answer to what we should like them to be, so in imagination we perceive in another's mind some thought of our appearance, manners, aims, deeds, character, friends, and so on, and are variously affected by it.

A self-idea of this sort seems to have three principal elements: the imagination of our appearance to the other person; the imagination of his judgment of that appearance, and some sort of self-feeling, such as pride or mortification. The comparison with a looking-glass hardly suggests the second element, the imagined judgment, which is quite essential. The thing that moves us to pride or shame is not the mere mechanical reflection of ourselves, but an imputed sentiment, the imagined effect of this reflection upon another's mind. This is evident from the fact that the character and weight of that other, in whose mind we see ourselves, makes all the difference with our feeling. We are ashamed to seem evasive in the presence of a straightforward man, cowardly in the presence of a brave one, gross in the eyes of a refined one, and so on. We always imagine, and in imagining share, the judgments of the other mind. A man will boast to one person of an action—say some sharp transaction in trade—which he would be ashamed to own to another.

It should be evident that the ideas that are associated with self-feeling and form the intellectual content of the self cannot be covered by any simple description, as by saying that the body has such a part in it, friends such a part, plans so much, etc., but will vary indefinitely with particular temperaments and environments. The tendency of the self, like every aspect of personality, is expressive of far-reaching hereditary and social factors, and is not to be understood or predicted except in connection with the general life. Although special, it is in no way separate—speciality and separateness are not only different but contradictory, since the former implies connection with a whole. The object of self-feeling is affected by the general course of history, by the particular development of nations, classes, and professions, and other conditions of this sort.

The truth of this is perhaps most decisively shown in the fact that even those ideas that are most generally associated or colored with the "my" feeling, such as one's idea of his visible person, of his name, his family, his intimate friends, his property, and so on, are not universally so associated, but may be separated from the self by peculiar social conditions. . . .

The peculiar relations to other persons attending any marked personal deficiency or peculiarity are likely to aggravate, if not to produce, abnormal manifestations of self-feeling. Any such trait sufficiently noticeable to interrupt easy and familiar intercourse with others, and make people talk and think *about* a person or *to* him rather than *with* him, can hardly fail to have this effect. If he is naturally inclined to pride or irritability, these tendencies, which depend for correction upon the flow of sympathy, are likely to be increased. One who shows signs of mental aberration is, inevitably perhaps, but cruelly, shut off from familiar, thoughtless intercourse, partly excommunicated; his isolation is unwittingly proclaimed to him on every countenance by curiosity, indifference, aversion, or pity, and in so far as he is human enough to need free and equal communication and feel the lack of it, he suffers pain and loss of a kind and degree which others can only faintly imagine, and for the most part ignore. He finds himself apart, "not in it," and feels chilled, fearful, and suspicious. Thus "queerness" is no sooner perceived than it is multiplied by reflection from other minds. The same is true in some degree of dwarfs, deformed or disfigured persons, even the deaf and those suffering from the infirmities of old age.

PRIMARY AND SECONDARY DEVIATION*

Edwin M. Lemert

SOCIOPATHIC INDIVIDUATION

The deviant person is a product of differentiating and isolating processes. Some persons are individually differentiated from others from the time of birth onward, as in the case of a child born with a congenital physical defect or repulsive appearance, and as in the case of a child born into a minority racial or cultural group. Other persons grow to maturity in a family or in a social class where pauperism, begging, or crime are more or less institutionalized ways of life for the entire group. In these latter instances the person's sociopsychological growth may be normal in every way, his status as a deviant being entirely caused by his maturation within the framework of social organization and culture designated as "pathological" by the larger society. This is true of many delinquent children in our society.[1]

It is a matter of great significance that the delinquent child, growing up in the delinquency areas of the city, has very little access to the cultural heritages of the larger conventional society. His infrequent contacts with this larger society are for the most part formal and external. Quite naturally his conception of moral values is shaped and molded by the moral code prevailing in his play groups and the local community in which he lives . . . the young delinquent has very little appreciation of the meaning of the traditions and formal laws of society. . . . Hence the conflict between the delinquent and the agencies of society is, in its broader aspects, a conflict of divergent cultures.

The same sort of gradual, unconscious process which operates in the socialization of the deviant child may also be recognized in the acquisition of socially unacceptable behavior by persons after having reached adulthood. However, with more verbal and sophisticated adults, step-by-step violations of societal norms tend to be progressively rationalized in the light of what is socially acceptable. Changes of this nature can take place at the level of either overt or covert behavior, but with a greater likelihood that adults will preface overt behavior changes with projective symbolic departures from society's norms. When the latter occur, the subsequent overt changes may appear to be "sudden" personality modifications. However, whether these changes are completely radical ones is to some extent a moot point. One writer holds strongly to the opinion that sudden and dramatic shifts in behavior from normal to abnormal are seldom the case, that a sequence of small preparatory transformations must be the prelude to such apparently sudden behavior changes. This writer is impressed by the day-by-day growth of "reserve potentialities" within personalities of all individuals, and he contends that many normal persons carry potentialities for abnormal behavior, which, given proper conditions, can easily be called into play.[2]

Personality Changes Not Always Gradual

This argument is admittedly sound for most cases, but it must be taken into consideration that traumatic experiences often speed up changes in personality.[3] Nor can the "trauma" in these experiences universally be attributed to the unique way in which the person conceives of the experience subjectively. Cases exist to show that personality modifications can be telescoped or that there can be an acceleration of such changes caused largely by the intensity and variety of the social stimulation. Most soldiers undoubtedly have entirely different conceptions of their roles after intensive combat experience. Many admit to having "lived a lifetime" in a relatively short period of time after they have been under heavy fire in battle for the first time. Many generals have remarked that their men have to be a little "shooted" or "blooded" in order to become good soldiers. In the process of group formation, crises and interactional amplification are vital requisites to forging true, role-oriented group behavior out of individuated behavior.[4]

The importance of the person's conscious symbolic reactions to his or her own behavior cannot be overstressed in explaining the shift from normal to abnormal behavior or from one type of pathological behavior to another, particularly where behavior variations become systematized or structured into pathological roles. This is not to say that conscious choice is a determining factor in the differentiating process. Nor does it mean that the awareness of the self is a purely

conscious perception. Much of the process of self-perception is doubtless marginal from the point of view of consciousness.[5] But however it may be perceived, the individual's self-definition is closely connected with such things as self-acceptance, the subordination of minor to major roles, and with the motivation involved in learning the skills, techniques, and values of a new role. *Self-definitions or self-realizations are likely to be the result of sudden perceptions and they are especially significant when they are followed immediately by overt demonstrations of the new role they symbolize.* The self-defining junctures are critical points of personality genesis and in the special case of the atypical person they mark a division between two different types of deviation.

Primary and Secondary Deviation

There has been an embarrassingly large number of theories, often without any relationship to a general theory, advanced to account for various specific pathologies in human behavior. For certain types of pathology, such as alcoholism, crime, or stuttering, there are almost as many theories as there are writers on these subjects. This has been occasioned in no small way by the preoccupation with the origins of pathological behavior and by the fallacy of confusing *original* causes with *effective* causes. All such theories have elements of truth, and the divergent viewpoints they contain can be reconciled with the general theory here if it is granted that original causes or antecedents of deviant behaviors are many and diversified. This holds especially for the psychological processes leading to similar pathological behavior, but it also holds for the situational concomitants of the initial aberrant conduct. A person may come to use excessive alcohol not only for a wide variety of subjective reasons but also because of diversified situational influences, such as the death of a loved one, business failure, or participating in some sort of organized group activity calling for heavy drinking of liquor. Whatever the original reasons for violating the norms of the community, they are important only for certain research purposes, such as assessing the extent of the "social problem" at a given time or determining the requirements for a rational program of social control. From a narrower sociological viewpoint the deviations are not significant until they are organized subjectively and transformed into active roles and become the social criteria for assigning status. The deviant individuals must react symbolically to their own behavior aberrations and fix them in their socio-psychological patterns. The deviations remain primary deviations or symptomatic and situational as long as they are rationalized or otherwise dealt with as functions of a socially acceptable role. Under such conditions normal and pathological behaviors remain strange and somewhat tensional bedfellows in the same person. Undeniably a vast amount of such segmental and partially integrated pathological behavior exists in our society and has impressed many writers in the field of social pathology.

Just how far and for how long a person may go in dissociating his sociopathic tendencies so that they are merely troublesome adjuncts of normally conceived roles is not known. Perhaps it depends upon the number of alternative definitions of the same overt behavior that he can develop; perhaps certain physiological factors (limits) are also involved. However, if the deviant acts are repetitive and have a high visibility, and if there is a severe societal reaction, which, through a process of identification is incorporated as part of the "me" of the individual, the probability is greatly increased that the integration of existing roles will be disrupted and that reorganization based upon a new role or roles will occur. (The "me" in this context is simply the subjective aspect of the societal reaction.) Reorganization may be the adoption of another normal role in which the tendencies previously defined as "pathological" are given a more acceptable social expression. The other general possibility is the assumption of a deviant role, if such exists; or, more rarely, the person may organize an aberrant sect or group in which he creates a special role of his own. *When a person begins to employ his deviant behavior or a role based upon it as a means of defense, attack, or adjustment to the overt and covert problems created by the consequent societal reaction to him, his deviation is secondary.* Objective evidences of this change will be found in the symbolic appurtenances of the new role, in clothes, speech, posture, and mannerisms, which in some cases heighten social visibility, and which in some cases serve as symbolic cues to professionalization.

Role Conceptions of the Individual Must Be Reinforced by Reactions of Others

It is seldom that one deviant act will provoke a sufficiently strong societal reaction to bring about secondary deviation, unless in the process of introjection the individual imputes or projects meanings into the social situation which are not present. In this case anticipatory fears are involved. For example, in a culture where a child is taught sharp distinctions between "good" women and "bad" women, a single act of questionable morality might conceivably have a profound meaning for the girl so indulging. However, in the absence of reactions by the person's family, neighbors, or the larger community, reinforcing the tentative "bad-girl" self-definition, it is questionable whether a transition to secondary deviation would take place. It is also doubtful whether a temporary exposure to a severe punitive reaction by the community will lead a person to identify himself with a pathological role, unless, as we have said, the experience is highly traumatic. Most frequently there is a progressive reciprocal relationship between the deviation of the individual and the societal reaction, with a compounding of the societal reaction out of the minute accretions in the deviant behavior, until a point is reached where in-grouping and outgrouping between society and the deviant is manifest.[6] At this point a stigmatizing of the deviant occurs in the form of name calling, labeling, or stereotyping.

The sequence of interaction leading to secondary deviation is roughly as follows: (1) primary deviation; (2) social penalties; (3) further primary deviation; (4) stronger penalties and rejections; (5) further deviation, perhaps with hostilities and resentment beginning to focus upon those doing the penalizing; (6) crisis reached in the tolerance quotient, expressed in formal action by the community stigmatizing of the deviant;

(7) strengthening of the deviant conduct as a reaction to the stigmatizing and penalties; (8) ultimate acceptance of deviant social status and efforts at adjustment on the basis of the associated role.

As an illustration of this sequence the behavior of an errant schoolboy can be cited. For one reason or another, let us say excessive energy, the schoolboy engages in a classroom prank. He is penalized for it by the teacher. Later, due to clumsiness, he creates another disturbance and again he is reprimanded. Then, as something happens, the boy is blamed for something he did not do. When the teacher uses the tag "bad boy" or "mischief maker" or other invidious terms, hostility and resentment are excited in the boy, and he may feel that he is blocked in playing the role expected of him. Thereafter, there may be a strong temptation to assume his role in the class as defined by the teacher, particularly when he discovers that there are rewards as well as penalties deriving from such a role. There is, of course, no implication here that such boys go on to become delinquents or criminals, for the mischief-maker role may later become integrated with or retrospectively rationalized as part of a role more acceptable to school authorities.[7] If such a boy continues this unacceptable role and becomes delinquent, the process must be accounted for in the light of the general theory of this volume. There must be a spreading corroboration of a sociopathic self-conception and societal reinforcement at each step in the process.

The most significant personality changes are manifest when societal definitions and their subjective counterpart become generalized. When this happens, the range of major role choices becomes narrowed to one general class.[8] This was very obvious in the case of a young girl who was the daughter of a paroled convict and who was attending a small Middle Western college. She continually argued with herself and with the author, in whom she had confided, that in reality she belonged on the "other side of the railroad tracks" and that her life could be enormously simplified by acquiescing in this verdict and living accordingly. While in her case there was a tendency to dramatize her conflicts, nevertheless there was enough societal reinforcement of her self-conception by the treatment she received in her relationship with her father and on dates with college boys to lend it a painful reality. Once these boys took her home to the shoddy dwelling in a slum area where she lived with her father, who was often in a drunken condition, they abruptly stopped seeing her again or else became sexually presumptive.

NOTES

1. Shaw, C., *The Natural History of a Delinquent Career*, Chicago, 1941, pp. 75–76. Quoted by permission of the University of Chicago Press, Chicago.

2. Brown, L. Guy, *Social Pathology*, 1942, pp. 44–45.

3. Allport, G., *Personality, A Psychological Interpretation*, 1947, p. 57.

4. Slavson, S. R., *An Introduction to Group Psychotherapy*, 1943, pp. 10, 229*ff*.

5. Murphy, G., *Personality*, 1947, p. 482.

6. Mead, G., "The Psychology of Punitive Justice," *American Journal of Sociology*, 23 March, 1918, pp. 577–602.

7. Evidence for fixed or inevitable sequences from predelinquency to crime is absent. Sutherland, E. H., *Principles of Criminology*, 1939, 4th ed., p. 202.

8. Sutherland seems to say something of this sort in connection with the development of criminal behavior. *Ibid.*, p. 86.

STIGMA AND SOCIAL IDENTITY*

Erving Goffman

The Greeks, who were apparently strong on visual aids, originated the term *stigma* to refer to bodily signs designed to expose something unusual and bad about the moral status of the signifier. The signs were cut or burnt into the body and advertised that the bearer was a slave, a criminal, or a traitor—a blemished person, ritually polluted, to be avoided, especially in public places. Later, in Christian times, two layers of metaphor were added to the term: the first referred to bodily signs of holy grace that took the form of eruptive blossoms on the skin; the second, a medical allusion to this religious allusion, referred to bodily signs of physical disorder. Today the term is widely used in something like the original literal sense, but is applied more to the disgrace itself than to the bodily evidence of it. Furthermore, shifts have occurred in the kinds of disgrace that arouse concern. Students, however, have made little effort to describe the structural preconditions of stigma, or even to provide a definition of the concept itself. It seems necessary, therefore, to try at the beginning to sketch in some very general assumptions and definitions.

PRELIMINARY CONCEPTIONS

Society establishes the means of categorizing persons and the complement of attributes felt to be ordinary and natural for members of each of these categories. Social settings establish the categories of persons likely to be encountered there. The routines of social intercourse in established settings allow us to deal with anticipated others without special attention or thought. When a stranger comes into our presence, then, first appearances are likely to enable us to anticipate his category and attributes, his "social identity"—to use a term that is better than "social status" because personal attributes such as "honesty" are involved, as well as structural ones, like "occupation."

We lean on these anticipations that we have, transforming them into normative expectations into righteously presented demands.

Typically, we do not become aware that we have made these demands or aware of what they are until an active question arises as to whether or not they will be fulfilled. It is then that we are likely to realize that all along we had been making certain assumptions as to what the individual before us ought to be. Thus, the demands we make might better be called demands made "in effect," and the character we impute to the individual might better be seen as an imputation made in potential retrospect—a characterization "in effect," a *virtual social identity*. The category and attributes he could in fact be proved to possess will be called his *actual social identity*.

While the stranger is present before us, evidence can arise of his possessing an attribute that makes him different from others in the category of persons available for him to be, and of a less desirable kind—in the extreme, a person who is quite thoroughly bad, or dangerous, or weak. He is thus reduced in our minds from a whole and usual person to a tainted, discounted one. Such an attribute is a stigma, especially when its discrediting effect is very extensive; sometimes it is also called a failing, a shortcoming, a handicap. It constitutes a special discrepancy between virtual and actual social identity. Note that there are other types of discrepancy between virtual and actual social identity, for example the kind that causes us to reclassify an individual from one socially anticipated category to a different but equally well-anticipated one, and the kind that causes us to alter our estimation of the individual upward. Note, too, that not all undesirable attributes are at issue, but only those which are

*From *Stigma: Notes on the Management of Spoiled Identity* by Erving Goffman, pp. 2–9. Copyright © 1963 by Simon & Schuster, Inc. Copyright renewed © 1991 by Simon & Schuster, Inc. Reprinted by permission of Simon & Schuster, Inc.

incongruous with our stereotype of what a given type of individual should be.

The term stigma, then, will be used to refer to an attribute that is deeply discrediting, but it should be seen that a language of relationships, not attributes, is really needed. An attribute that stigmatizes one type of possessor can confirm the usualness of another, and therefore is neither creditable nor discreditable as a thing in itself. For example, some jobs in America cause holders without the expected college education to conceal this fact; other jobs, however, can lead the few of their holders who have a higher education to keep this a secret, lest they be marked as failures and outsiders. Similarly, a middle class boy may feel no compunction in being seen going to the library; a professional criminal, however, writes:

I can remember before now on more than one occasion, for instance, going into a public library near where I was living, and looking over my shoulder a couple of times before I actually went in just to make sure no one who knew me was standing about and seeing me do it.[1]

So, too, an individual who desires to fight for his country may conceal a physical defect, lest his claimed physical status be discredited; later, the same individual, embittered and trying to get out of the army, may succeed in gaining admission to the army hospital, where he would be discredited if discovered in not really having an acute sickness.[2] A stigma, then, is really a special kind of relationship between attribute and stereotype, although I don't propose to continue to say so, in part because there are important attributes that almost everywhere in our society are discrediting.

The term stigma and its synonyms conceal a double perspective: Does the stigmatized individual assume his differentness is known about already or is evident on the spot, or does he assume it is neither known about by those present nor immediately perceivable by them? In the first case one deals with the plight of the *discredited*, in the second with that of the *discreditable*. This is an important difference, even though a particular stigmatized individual is likely to have experi-

ence with both situations. I will begin with the situation of the discredited and move on to the discreditable but not always separate the two.

Three grossly different types of stigma may be mentioned. First there are abominations of the body—the various physical deformities. Next there are blemishes of individual character perceived as weak will, domineering or unnatural passions, treacherous and rigid beliefs, and dishonesty, these being inferred from a known record of, for example, mental disorder, imprisonment, addiction, alcoholism, homosexuality, unemployment, suicidal attempts, and radical political behavior. Finally there are the tribal stigma of race, nation, and religion, these being stigma that can be transmitted through lineages and equally contaminate all members of a family.[3] In all of these various instances of stigma, however, including those the Greeks had in mind, the same sociological features are found: An individual who might have been received easily in ordinary social intercourse possesses a trait that can obtrude itself upon attention and turn those of us whom he meets away from him, breaking the claim that his other attributes have on us. He possesses a stigma, an undesired differentness from what we had anticipated. We and those who do not depart negatively from the particular expectations at issue I shall call the *normals*.

The attitudes we normals have toward a person with a stigma, and the actions we take in regard to him, are well known, since these responses are what benevolent social action is designed to soften and ameliorate. By definition, of course, we believe the person with a stigma is not quite human. On this assumption we exercise varieties of discrimination, through which we effectively, if often unthinkingly, reduce his life chances. We construct a stigma-theory, an ideology to explain his inferiority and account for the danger he represents, sometimes rationalizing an animosity based on other differences, such as those of social class.[4] We use specific stigma terms such as cripple, bastard, moron in our daily discourse as a source of metaphor and imagery, typically without giving thought to the original meaning.[5] We tend to impute a wide range of imperfections on the basis of the original one,[6] and at the same time to impute some desirable but un-desired attributes, often of a supernatural cast, such as "sixth sense," or "understanding":[7]

For some, there may be a hesitancy about touching or steering the blind, while for others, the perceived fail-ure to see may be generalized into a gestalt of disabil-ity, so that the individual shouts at the blind as if they were deaf or attempts to lift them as if they were crip-pled. Those confronting the blind may have a whole range of belief that is anchored in the stereotype. For instance, they may think they are subject to unique judgment, assuming the blinded individual draws on special channels of information unavailable to others.[8]

Further, we may perceive his defensive response to his situation as a direct expression of his de-fect, and then see both defect and response as just retribution for something he or his parents or his tribe did, and hence a justification of the way we treat him.[9]

Now turn from the normal to the person he is normal against. It seems generally true that mem-bers of a social category may strongly support a standard of judgment that they and others agree does not directly apply to them. Thus it is that a businessman may demand womanly behavior from females or ascetic behavior from monks, and not construe himself as someone who ought to realize either of these styles of conduct. The distinction is between realizing a norm and merely supporting it. The issue of stigma does not arise here, but only where there is some ex-pectation on all sides that those in a given cate-gory should not only support a particular norm but also realize it.

Also, it seems possible for an individual to fail to live up to what we effectively demand of him, and yet be relatively untouched by this failure; insulated by his alienation, protected by identity beliefs of his own, *he feels that he is a full-fledged normal human being, and that we are the ones who are not quite human.* He bears a stigma but does not seem to be impressed or repentant about doing so. This possibility is celebrated in exemplary tales about Mennonites, Gypsies, shameless scoundrels, and very orthodox Jews.

In America at present, however, separate sys-tems of honor seem to be on the decline. The stigmatized individual tends to hold the same be-liefs about identity that we do; this is a pivotal fact. His deepest feelings about what he is may be his sense of being a "normal person," a human being like anyone else, a person, therefore, who deserves a fair chance and a fair break.[10] (Actu-ally, however phrased, he bases his claims not on what he thinks is due *everyone*, but only every-one of a selected social category into which he unquestionably fits, for example, anyone of his age, sex, profession, and so forth.) Yet he may perceive, usually quite correctly, that whatever others profess, they do not really "accept" him and are not ready to make contact with him on "equal grounds."[11] Further, the standards he has incorporated from the wider society equip him to be intimately alive to what others see as his fail-ing, inevitably causing him, if only for moments, to agree that he does indeed fall short of what he really ought to be. Shame becomes a central pos-sibility, arising from the individual's perception of one of his own attributes as being a defiling thing to possess, and one he can readily see him-self as not possessing.

The immediate presence of normals is likely to reinforce this split between self-demands and self, but in fact self-hate and self-derogation can also occur when only he and a mirror are about:

When I got up at last . . . and had learned to walk again, one day I took a hand glass and went to a long mirror to look at myself, and I went alone. I didn't want anyone . . . to know how I felt when I saw myself for the first time. But there was no noise, no outcry; I didn't scream with rage when I saw myself. I just felt numb. That person in the mirror *couldn't* be me. I felt inside like a healthy, ordinary, lucky person—oh, not like the one in the mirror! Yet when I turned my face to the mirror there were my own eyes looking back, hot with shame . . . when I did not cry or make any sound, it became impossible that I should speak of it to anyone, and the confusion and the panic of my discov-ery were locked inside me then and there, to be faced alone, for a very long time to come.[12]

Over and over I forgot what I had seen in the mir-ror. It could not penetrate into the interior of my mind and become an integral part of me. I felt as if it had nothing to do with me; it was only a disguise. But it was not the kind of disguise which is put on voluntar-ily by the person who wears it, and which is intended to confuse other people as to one's identity. My disguise had been put on me without my consent or knowledge like the ones in fairy tales, and it was I myself who was confused by it, as to my own identity. I looked in the mirror, and was horror-struck because I did not recognize myself. In the place where I was standing, with that persistent romantic elation in me, as if I were a favored fortunate person to whom everything was possible, I saw a stranger, a little, pitiable, hideous figure, and a face that became, as I stared at it, painful and blushing with shame. It was only a disguise, but it was on me, for life. It was there, it was there, it was real. Every one of those encounters was like a blow on the head. They left me dazed and dumb and senseless everytime, until slowly and stubbornly my robust persistent illusion of well-being and of personal beauty spread all through me again, and I forgot the irrelevant reality and was all unprepared and vulnerable again.[13]

The central feature of the stigmatized individual's situation in life can now be stated. It is a question of what is often, if vaguely, called "acceptance." Those who have dealings with him fail to accord him the respect and regard which the uncontaminated aspects of his social identity have led them to anticipate extending, and have led him to anticipate receiving; he echoes this denial by finding that some of his own attributes warrant it.

How does the stigmatized person respond to his situation? In some cases it will be possible for him to make a direct attempt to correct what he sees as the objective basis of his failing, as when a physically deformed person undergoes plastic surgery, a blind person eye treatment, an illiterate remedial education, a homosexual psychotherapy. (Where such repair is possible, what often results is not the acquisition of fully normal status, but a transformation of self from someone with a particular blemish into someone with a record of having corrected a particular blemish.) Here proneness to "victimization" is to be cited, a result of the stigmatized person's exposure to fraudulent servers selling speech correction, skin lighteners, body stretchers, youth restorers (as in rejuvenation through fertilized egg yolk treatment), cures, through faith, and poise in conversation. Whether a practical technique or fraud is involved, the quest, often secret, that results provides a special indication of the extremes to

which the stigmatized can be willing to go, and hence the painfulness of the situation that leads them to these extremes. One illustration may be cited:

Miss Peck [a pioneer New York social worker for the hard of hearing] said that in the early days the quacks and get-rich-quick medicine men who abounded saw the League [for the hard of hearing] as their happy hunting ground, ideal for the promotion of magnetic head caps, miraculous vibrating machines, artificial eardrums, blowers, inhalers, massagers, magic oils, balsams, and other guaranteed, sure-fire, positive, and permanent cure-alls for incurable deafness. Advertisements for such hokum (until the 1920s when the American Medical Association moved in with an investigation campaign) beset the hard of hearing in the pages of the daily press, even in reputable magazines.[14]

The stigmatized individual can also attempt to correct his condition indirectly by devoting much private effort to the mastery of areas of activity ordinarily felt to be closed on incidental and physical grounds to one with his shortcoming. This is illustrated by the lame person who learns or relearns to swim, ride, play tennis, or fly an airplane, or the blind person who becomes expert at skiing and mountain climbing.[15] Tortured learning may be associated, of course, with the tortured performance of what is learned, as when an individual, confined to a wheelchair, manages to take to the dance floor with a girl in some kind of mimicry of dancing.[16] Finally, the person with a shameful differentness can break with what is called reality, and obstinately attempt to employ an unconventional interpretation of the character of his social identity.

The stigmatized individual is likely to use his stigma for "secondary gains," as an excuse for ill success that has come his way for other reasons:

For years the scar, harelip or misshapen nose has been looked on as a handicap, and its importance in the social and emotional adjustment is unconsciously all embracing. It is the "hook" on which the patient has hung all inadequacies, all dissatisfactions, all procrastinations and all unpleasant duties of social life, and he has come to depend on it not only as a reasonable escape from competition but as a protection from social responsibility.

When one removes this factor by surgical repair, the patient is cast adrift from the more or less acceptable emotional protection it has offered and soon he finds, to his surprise and discomfort, that life is not all smooth sailing even for those with unblemished, "ordinary" faces. He is unprepared to cope with this situation without the support of a "handicap," and he may turn to the less simple, but similar, protection of the behavior patterns of neurasthenia, hysterical conversion, hypochondriasis or the acute anxiety states.[17]

He may also see the trials he has suffered as a blessing in disguise, especially because of what it is felt that suffering can teach one about life and people:

But now, far away from the hospital experience, I can evaluate what I have learned. [A mother permanently disabled by polio writes.] For it wasn't only suffering: it was also learning through suffering. I know my awareness of people has deepened and increased, that those who are close to me can count on me to turn all my mind and heart and attention to their problems. I could not have learned *that* dashing all over a tennis court.[18]

Correspondingly, he can come to reassess the limitations of normals, as a multiple sclerotic suggests:

Both healthy minds and healthy bodies may be crippled. The fact that "normal" people can get around, can see, can hear, doesn't mean that they are seeing or hearing. They can be very blind to the things that spoil their happiness, very deaf to the pleas of others for kindness; when I think of them I do not feel any more crippled or disabled than they. Perhaps in some small way I can be the means of opening their eyes to the beauties around us: things like a warm handclasp, a voice that is anxious to cheer, a spring breeze, music to listen to, a friendly nod. These people are important to me, and I like to feel that I can help them.[19]

And a blind writer:

That would lead immediately to the thought that there are many occurrences which can diminish satisfaction in living far more effectively than blindness, and that lead would be an entirely healthy one to take. In this light, we can perceive, for instance, that some inadequacy like the inability to accept human love, which can effectively diminish satisfaction of living almost to the vanishing point, is far more a tragedy than blindness. But it is unusual for the man who suffers from

such a malady even to know he has it and self pity is, therefore, impossible for him.[20]

And a cripple:

As life went on, I learned of many, many different kinds of handicap, not only the physical ones, and I began to realize that the words of the crippled girl in the extract above [words of bitterness] could just as well have been spoken by young women who had never needed crutches, women who felt inferior and different because of ugliness, or inability to bear children, or helplessness in contacting people, or many other reasons.[21]

The responses of the normal and of the stigmatized that have been considered so far are ones which can occur over protracted periods of time and in isolation from current contact between normals and stigmatized.[22] This book, however, is specifically concerned with the issue of "mixed contacts"—the moments when stigmatized and normals are in the same "social situation," that is, in one another's immediate physical presence, whether in a conversation-like encounter or in the mere co-presence of an unfocused gathering.

The very anticipation of such contacts can of course lead normals and the stigmatized to arrange life so as to avoid them. Presumably this will have larger consequences for the stigmatized, since more arranging will usually be necessary on their part:

Before her disfigurement [amputation of the distal half of her nose] Mrs. Dover, who lived with one of her two married daughters, had been an independent, warm and friendly woman who enjoyed traveling, shopping, and visiting her many relatives. The disfigurement of her face, however, resulted in a definite alteration in her way of living. The first two or three years she seldom left her daughter's home, preferring to remain in her room or to sit in the backyard. "I was heartsick," she said; "the door had been shut on my life."[23]

Lacking the salutary feed-back of daily social intercourse with others, the self-isolate can become suspicious, depressed, hostile, anxious, and bewildered. Sullivan's version may be cited:

The awareness of inferiority means that one is unable to keep out of consciousness the formulation of some chronic feeling of the worst sort of insecurity, and this means that one suffers anxiety and perhaps even something worse, if jealousy is really worse than anxiety.

The fear that others can disrespect a person because of something he shows means that he is always insecure in his contact with other people; and this insecurity arises, not from mysterious and somewhat disguised sources, as a great deal of our anxiety does, but from something which he knows he cannot fix. Now that represents an almost fatal deficiency of the self-system, since the self is unable to disguise or exclude a definite formulation that reads, "I am inferior. Therefore people will dislike me and I cannot be secure with them."[24]

When normals and stigmatized do in fact enter one another's immediate presence, especially when they there attempt to sustain a joint conversational encounter, there occurs one of the primal scenes of sociology; for, in many cases, these moments will be the ones when the causes and effects of stigma must be directly confronted by both sides.

The stigmatized individual may find that he feels unsure of how we normals will identify him and receive him.[25] An illustration may be cited from a student of physical disability:

Uncertainty of status for the disabled person obtains over a wide range of social interactions in addition to that of employment. The blind, the ill, the deaf, the crippled can never be sure what the attitude of a new acquaintance will be, whether it will be rejective or accepting, until the contact has been made. This is exactly the position of the adolescent, the light-skinned Negro, the second generation immigrant, the socially mobile person and the woman who has entered a predominantly masculine occupation.[26]

This uncertainty arises not merely from the stigmatized individual's not knowing which of several categories he will be placed in, but also, where the placement is favorable, from his knowing that in their hearts the others may be defining him in terms of his stigma:

And I always feel this with straight people—that whenever they're being nice to me, pleasant to me, all the time really, underneath they're only assessing me as a criminal and nothing else. It's too late for me to be any different now to what I am, but I still feel this keenly, that that's their only approach, and they're quite incapable of accepting me as anything else.[27]

Thus in the stigmatized arises the sense of not knowing what the others present are "really" thinking about him.

Further, during mixed contacts, the stigmatized individual is likely to feel that he is "on,"[28] having to be self-conscious and calculating about the impression he is making, to a degree and in areas of conduct which he assumes others are not.

Also, he is likely to feel that the usual scheme of interpretation for everyday events has been undermined. His minor accomplishments, he feels, may be assessed as signs of remarkable and noteworthy capacities in the circumstances. A professional criminal provides an illustration:

"You know, it's really amazing you should read books like this, I'm staggered I am. I should've thought you'd read paper-backed thrillers, things with lurid covers, books like that. And here you are with Claud Cockburn, Hugh Klare, Simone de Beauvoir, and Lawrence Durrell!"

You know, he didn't see this as an insulting remark at all: In fact, I think he thought he was being honest in telling me how mistaken he was. And that's exactly the sort of patronizing you get from straight people if you're a criminal. "Fancy that!" they say. "In some ways you're just like a human being!" I'm not kidding, it makes me want to choke the bleeding life out of them.[29]

A blind person provides another illustration:

His once most ordinary deeds—walking nonchalantly up the street, locating the peas on his plate, lighting a cigarette—are no longer ordinary. He becomes an unusual person. If he performs them with finesse and assurance they excite the same kind of wonderment inspired by a magician who pulls rabbits out of hats.[30]

At the same time, minor failings or incidental impropriety may, he feels, be interpreted as a direct expression of his stigmatized differentness. Ex-mental patients, for example, are sometimes afraid to engage in sharp interchanges with spouse or employer because of what a show of emotion might be taken as a sign of. Mental defectives face a similar contingency:

It also happens that if a person of low intellectual ability gets into some sort of trouble the difficulty is more or less automatically attributed to "mental defect" whereas if a person of "normal intelligence" gets into a similar difficulty, it is not regarded as symptomatic of anything in particular.[31]

A one-legged girl, recalling her experience with sports, provides other illustrations:

Whenever I fell, out swarmed the women in droves, clucking and fretting like a bunch of bereft mother hens. It was kind of them, and in retrospect I appreciate their solicitude, but at the time I resented and was greatly embarrassed by their interference. For they assumed that no routine hazard to skating—no stick or stone—upset my flying wheels. It was a foregone-conclusion that *I* fell because I was a poor, helpless cripple.[32]

Not one of them shouted with outrage, "That dangerous wild bronco threw her!"—which, God forgive, he did technically. It was like a horrible ghostly visitation of my old roller-skating days. All the good people lamented in chorus, "That poor, poor girl fell off!"[33]

When the stigmatized person's failing can be perceived by our merely directing attention (typically, visual) to him—when, in short, he is a discredited, not discreditable, person—he is likely to feel that to be present among normals nakedly exposes him to invasions of privacy,[34] experienced most pointedly perhaps when children simply stare at him.[35] This displeasure in being exposed can be increased by the conversations strangers may feel free to strike up with him, conversations in which they express what he takes to be morbid curiosity about his condition, or in which they proffer help that he does not need or want.[36] One might add that there are certain classic formulae for these kinds of conversations: "My dear girl, how did you get your quiggle"; "My great uncle had a quiggle, so I feel I know all about your problem"; "You know I've always said that Quiggles are good family men and look after their own poor"; "Tell me, how do you manage to bathe with a quiggle?" The implication of these overtures is that the stigmatized individual is a person who can be approached by strangers at will, providing only that they are sympathetic to the plight of persons of his kind.

Given what the stigmatized individual may well face upon entering a mixed social situation, he may anticipatorily respond by defensive cowering. This may be illustrated from an early study of some German unemployed during the Depression, the words being those of a 43-year-old mason:

How hard and humiliating it is to bear the name of an unemployed man. When I go out, I cast down my eyes because I feel myself wholly inferior. When I go along the street, it seems to me that I can't be compared with an average citizen, that everybody is pointing at me with his finger. I instinctively avoid meeting anyone. Former acquaintances and friends of better times are no longer so cordial. They greet me indifferently when we meet. They no longer offer me a cigarette and their eyes seem to say, "You are not worth it, you don't work."[37]

A crippled girl provides an illustrative analysis:

When . . . I began to walk out alone in the streets of our town . . . I found then that wherever I had to pass three or four children together on the sidewalk, if I happened to be alone, they would shout at me, . . . Sometimes they even ran after me, shouting and jeering. This was something I didn't know how to face, and it seemed as if I couldn't bear it. . . .

For awhile those encounters in the street filled me with a cold dread of all unknown children . . .

One day I suddenly realized that I had become so self-conscious and afraid of all strange children that, like animals, they knew I was afraid, so that even the mildest and most amiable of them were automatically prompted to derision by my own shrinking and dread.[38]

Instead of cowering, the stigmatized individual may attempt to approach mixed contacts with hostile bravado, but this can induce from others its own set of troublesome reciprocations. It may be added that the stigmatized person sometimes vacillates between cowering and bravado, racing from one to the other, thus demonstrating one central way in which ordinary face-to-face interaction can run wild.

I am suggesting, then, that the stigmatized individual—at least the "visibly" stigmatized one—will have special reasons for feeling that mixed social situations make for anxious unanchored interaction. But if this is so, then it is to be suspected that we normals will find these situations shaky too. We will feel that the stigmatized individual is either too aggressive or too shame-faced, and in either case too ready to read unintended meanings into our actions. We ourselves may feel that if we show direct sympathetic concern for his condition, we may be over-stepping ourselves; and yet if we actually forget that he has a failing we are likely to make impossible demands of him or unthinkingly slight his fellow-sufferers. Each potential source of discomfort for him when we are with him can become something we sense he is aware of, aware that we are aware of, and even aware of our state of awareness about his awareness; the stage is then set for the infinite regress of mutual consideration that Meadian social psychology tells us how to begin but not how to terminate.

Given what both the stigmatized and we normals introduce into mixed social situations, it is understandable that all will not go smoothly. We are likely to attempt to carry on as though in fact he wholly fitted one of the types of person naturally available to us in the situation, whether this means treating him as someone better than we feel he might be or someone worse than we feel he probably is. If neither of these tacks is possible, then we may try to act as if he were a "nonperson," and not present at all as someone of whom ritual notice is to be taken. He, in turn, is likely to go along with these strategies, at least initially.

In consequence, attention is furtively withdrawn from its obligatory targets, and self-consciousness and "other-consciousness" occurs, expressed in the pathology of interaction—uneasiness.[39] As described in the case of the physically handicapped:

Whether the handicap is overtly and tactlessly responded to as such or, as is more commonly the case, no explicit reference is made to it, the underlying condition of heightened, narrowed, awareness causes the interaction to be articulated too exclusively in terms of it. This, as my informants described it, is usually accompanied by one or more of the familiar signs of discomfort and stickiness: the guarded references, the common everyday words suddenly made taboo, the fixed stare elsewhere, the artificial levity, the compulsive loquaciousness, the awkward solemnity.[40]

In social situations with an individual known or perceived to have a stigma, we are likely, then, to employ categorizations that do not fit, and we and he are likely to experience uneasiness. Of course, there is often significant movement from this starting point. And since the stigmatized person is likely to be more often faced with these situations than are we, he is likely to become the more adept at managing them.

THE OWN AND THE WISE

Earlier it was suggested that a discrepancy may exist between an individual's virtual and actual identity. This discrepancy, when known about or apparent, spoils his social identity; it has the effect of cutting him off from society and from himself so that he stands a discredited person facing an unaccepting world. In some cases, as with the individual who is born without a nose, he may continue through life to find that he is the only one of his kind and that all the world is against him. In most cases, however, he will find that there are sympathetic others who are ready to adopt his standpoint in the world and to share with him the feeling that he is human and "essentially" normal in spite of appearances and in spite of his own self-doubts. Two such categories will be considered.

The first set of sympathetic others is of course those who share his stigma. Knowing from their own experience what it is like to have this particular stigma, some of them can provide the individual with instruction in the tricks of the trade and with a circle of lament to which he can withdraw for moral support and for the comfort of feeling at home, at ease, accepted as a person who really is like any other normal person. One example may be cited from a study of illiterates:

The existence of a different value system among these persons is evinced by the communality of behavior which occurs when illiterates interact among themselves. Not only do they change from unexpressive and confused individuals, as they frequently appear in larger society, to expressive and understanding persons with their own group, but moreover they express themselves in institutional terms. Among themselves they have a universe of response. They form and recognize symbols of prestige and disgrace; evaluate relevant situations in terms of their own norms and in their own idiom: and in their interrelations with one another, the mask of accommodative adjustment drops.[41]

Another from the hard of hearing:

I remembered how relaxing it was, at Nitchie School, to be with people who took impaired hearing for granted. Now I wanted to know some people who took hearing aids for granted. How restful it would be to adjust the volume control on my transmitter without caring whether or not anyone was looking. To stop thinking, for awhile, about whether the cord at the back of my neck was showing. What luxury to say out loud to someone, "Ye gods, my battery's dead!"[42]

Among his own, the stigmatized individual can use his disadvantage as a basis for organizing life, but he must resign himself to a half-world to do so. Here he may develop to its fullest his sad tale accounting for his possession of the stigma. The explanations produced by the mentally defective to account for admission to the institution for their kind provide an example:

(1) "I got mixed up with a gang. One night we were robbing a gas station and the cops got me. I don't belong here." (2) "You know, I shouldn't be here at all. I'm epileptic, I don't belong here with these other people." (3) "My parents hate me and put me in here." (4) "They say I'm crazy. I'm not crazy, but even if I was, I don't belong in here with these low-grades."[43]

On the other hand, he may find that the tales of his fellow-sufferers bore him, and that the whole matter of focusing on atrocity tales, on group superiority, on trickster stories, in short, on the "problem," is one of the large penalties for having one. Behind this focus on the problem is, of course, a perspective not so much different from that of the normal as it is specialized in one sector:

We all seem to be inclined to identify people with characteristics which are of important to us, or which we think must be of general importance. If you asked a person who the late Franklin D. Roosevelt was, he would probably answer that Roosevelt was the 32nd president of the United States, not that he was a man suffering from polio, although many persons, of course, would have mentioned his polio as supplementary information, considering it an interesting fact that he managed to fight his way to the White House in spite of this handicap. The cripple, however, would probably think of Mr. Roosevelt's polio when he heard his name mentioned.[44]

In the sociological study of stigmatized persons, one is usually concerned with the kind of corporate life, if any, that is sustained by those of a particular category. Certainly here one finds a fairly full catalogue of types of group formation and types of group function. There are speech defectives whose peculiarity apparently discourages any group formation whatsoever.[45] On the boundaries of a willingness to unite are exmental patients—only a relatively small number are currently willing to support mental health clubs, in spite of innocuous club titles which allow members to come together under a plain wrapper.[46] Then there are the huddle-together self-help clubs formed by the divorced, the aged, the obese, the physically handicapped,[47] the ileostomied and colostomied.[48] There are residential clubs, voluntary to varying degrees, formed for the ex-alcoholic and the ex-addict. There are national associations such as AA which provide a full doctrine and almost a way of life for their members. Often these associations are the culmination of years of effort on the part of variously situated persons and groups, providing exemplary objects of study as social movements.[49] There are mutual-claims networks formed by ex-convicts from the same prison or reformatory, an example of which is the tacit society claimed to exist in South America of escapees from the French penal settlement in French Guiana;[50] more traditionally, there are national networks of acquainted individuals (or acquainted once-removed) to which some criminals and some homosexuals seem to belong. There are also urban milieux containing a nucleus of service institutions which provide a territorial base for prostitutes, drug addicts, homosexuals, alcoholics, and other shamed groups, these establishments being sometimes shared by outcasts of different kinds, sometimes not. Finally, within the city, there are full-fledged residential communities, ethnic, racial, or religious, with a high concentration of tribally stigmatized persons and (in contradistinction to much other group formation among the stigmatized) the family, not the individual, as the basic unit of organization.

Here, of course, there is a common conceptual confusion. The term "category" is perfectly abstract and can be applied to any aggregate, in this case persons with a particular stigma. A good portion of those who fall within a given stigma category may well refer to the total membership by the term "group" or an equivalent, such as "we," or "our people." Those outside the category may similarly designate those within it in group terms. However, often in such cases the full membership will not be part of a single group, in the strictest sense; they will neither have a capacity for collective action, nor a stable and embracing pattern of mutual interaction. What one does find is that the members of a particular stigma category will have a tendency to come together into small social groups whose members all derive from the category, these groups themselves being subject to overarching organization to varying degrees. And one also finds that when one member of the category happens to come into contact with another, both may be disposed to modify their treatment of each other by virtue of believing that they each belong to the same "group." Further, in being a member of the category, an individual may have an increased probability of coming into contact with any other member, and even forming a relationship with him as a result. A category, then, can function to dispose its members to group-formation and relationships, but its total membership does not thereby constitute a group—a conceptual nicety that will hereafter not always be observed in this essay.

Whether or not those with a particular stigma provide the recruitment base for a community that is ecologically consolidated in some way, they are likely to support agents and agencies who represent them. (Interestingly, we have no word to designate accurately the constituents, following, fans, subjects, or supporters of such representatives.) Members may, for example, have an office or lobby to push their case with the press or government, differing here in terms of whether they can have a man of their own kind, a "native" who really knows, as do the deaf, the blind, the alcoholic, and Jews, or someone from the other side, as do ex-cons and the mentally defective.[51] (Action groups which serve the same category of stigmatized person may sometimes be in slight opposition to each other, and this opposition will often reflect a difference between management by natives and management by normals.) A characteristic task of these representatives is to convince the public to use a softer social label for the category in question:

Acting on this conviction, the League [New York League for the Hard of Hearing] staff agreed to use only such terms as hard of hearing, impaired hearing, and hearing loss; to excise the word deaf from their conversation, their correspondence and other writings, their teaching, and their speeches in public. It worked. New York in general gradually began to use the new vocabulary. Straight thinking was on the way.[52]

Another of their usual tasks is to appear as "speakers" before various audiences of normals and of the stigmatized; they present the case for the stigmatized and, when they themselves are natives of the group, provide a living model of fully normal achievement, being heroes of adjustment who are subject to public awards for proving that an individual of this kind can be a good person.

Often those with a particular stigma sponsor a publication of some kind which gives voice to shared feelings, consolidating and stabilizing for the reader his sense of the realness of "his" group and his attachment to it. Here the ideology of the members is formulated—their complaints, their aspirations, their politics. The names of well-known friends and enemies of the "group" are cited, along with information to confirm the goodness or the badness of these people. Success stories are printed, tales of heroes of assimilation who have penetrated new areas of normal acceptance. Atrocity tales are recorded, recent and historic, of extreme mistreatment by normals. Exemplary moral tales are provided in biographical and autobiographical form illustrating a desirable code of conduct for the stigmatized. The publication also serves as a forum for presenting some division of opinion as to how the situation of the stigmatized person ought best to be handled. Should the individual's failing require special equipment, it is here advertised and reviewed. The readership of these publications provides a market for books and pamphlets which present a similar line.

It is important to stress that, in America at least, no matter how small and how badly off a particular stigmatized category is, the viewpoint of its members is likely to be given public presentation of some kind. It can thus be said that Americans who are stigmatized tend to live in a literarily defined world, however uncultured they might be. If they don't read books on the situation of persons like themselves, they at least read magazines and see movies; and where they don't do these, then they listen to local, vocal associates. An intellectually worked-up version of their point of view is thus available to most stigmatized persons.

A commitment is here required about those who come to serve as representatives of a stigmatized category. Starting out as someone who is a little more vocal, a little better known, or a little better connected than his fellow-sufferers, a stigmatized person may find that the "movement" has absorbed his whole day, and that he has become a professional. This end point is illustrated by a hard of hearing:

In 1942 I was spending almost every day at the League. Mondays I sewed with the Red Cross Unit. Tuesdays I worked in the office, typing and filing, operating the switchboard in a pinch. Wednesday afternoons I assisted the doctor at the League's deafness-prevention clinic at Manhattan Eye and Ear Hospital, a job I particularly enjoyed—keeping records on children who, because their head colds, running ears, infections, and potentially deafening after-effects of childhood diseases were getting the benefit of new knowledge, new drugs, and new otological techniques, probably would not be growing up with cotton in their ears. Thursday afternoons I sat in on League adult lip-reading classes and afterwards we all played cards and drank tea. Fridays I worked on the *Bulletin*. Saturdays I made egg-salad sandwiches and cocoa. Once a month I attended the meeting of the Women's Auxiliary, a volunteer group organized in 1921 by Mrs. Wendell Phillips and other interested otologists' wives to raise funds, promote membership, and represent the League socially. I made Halloween favors for the six-year-olds and helped serve the Old Timers' Thanksgiving Dinner. I wrote the Christmas mail appeal for contributions, helped address the envelopes and lick the stamps. I hung the new curtains and mended the old ping-pong table; chaperoned the young people's Valentine Dance and manned a booth at the Easter Bazaar.[53]

It might be added that once a person with a particular stigma attains high occupational, political, or financial position—how high depending on the stigmatized group in question—a new career is likely to be thrust upon him, that of representing his category. He finds himself too eminent to avoid being presented by his own as an instance of them. (The weakness of a stigma can thus be measured by how eminent a member of the category may be and yet manage to avoid these pressures.)

Two points are sometimes made about this kind of professionalism. First, in making a profession of their stigma, native leaders are obliged to have dealings with representatives of other categories, and so find themselves breaking out of the closed circle of their own kind. Instead of leaning on their crutch, they get to play golf with it, ceasing, in terms of social participation, to be representative of the people they represent.[54]

Secondly, those who professionally present the viewpoint of their category may introduce some systematic bias in this presentation simply because they are sufficiently involved in the problem to write about it. Although any particular stigma category is likely to have professionals who take different lines, and may even support publications which advocate different programs, there is uniform tacit agreement that the situation of the individual with this particular stigma is worth attention. Whether a writer takes a stigma very seriously or makes light of it, he must define it as something worth writing about. This minimal agreement, even when there are no others, helps to consolidate belief in the stigma as a basis for self-conception. Here again representatives are not representative, for representation can hardly come from those who give no attention to their stigma, or who are relatively unlettered.

I do not mean to suggest here that professionals provide the stigmatized with the sole public source of reminder as to their situation in life; there are other reminders. Each time someone with a particular stigma makes a spectacle of himself by breaking a law, winning a prize, or becoming a first of his kind, a local community may take gossipy note of this; these events can even make news in the mass media of the wider society. In any case, they who share the noted person's stigma suddenly become accessible to the normals immediately around and become subject to a slight transfer of credit or discredit to themselves. Their situation thus leads them easily into living in a world of publicized heroes and villains of their own stripe, their relation to this world being underlined by immediate associates, both normal and otherwise, who bring them news about how one of their kind has fared.

I have considered one set of individuals from whom the stigmatized person can expect some support: those who share his stigma and by virtue of this are defined and define themselves as his own kind. The second set are—to borrow a term once used by homosexuals—the "wise," namely, persons who are normal but whose special situation has made them intimately privy to the secret life of the stigmatized individual and sympathetic with it, and who find themselves accorded a measure of acceptance, a measure of courtesy membership in the clan. Wise persons are the marginal men before whom the individual with a fault need feel no shame nor exert self-control, knowing that in spite of his failing he will be seen as an ordinary other. An example may be cited from the world of prostitutes:

Although she sneers at respectability, the prostitute, particularly the call girl, is supersensitive in polite society, taking refuge in her off hours with Bohemian artists, writers, actors and would-be intellectuals. There she may be accepted as an off-beat personality, without being a curiosity.[55]

Before taking the standpoint of those with a particular stigma, the normal person who is becoming wise may first have to pass through a heart-changing personal experience, of which there are many literary records.[56] And after the sympathetic normal makes himself available to the stigmatized, he often must wait their validation of him as a courtesy member. The self must not only be offered, it must be accepted. Sometimes, of course, the final step does seem to be initiated by the normal; the following is an example of this.

I don't know whether I can or not, but let me tell of an incident. I was once admitted to a group of Negro boys of about my own age with whom I used to fish. When I first began to join them, they would carefully use the term "Negro" in my presence. Gradually, as we went fishing more and more often, they began to joke with each other in front of me and to call each other "nigger." The real change was in their utilization of the word "nigger" when joking after the previous inability to use the word "nigger" at all.

One day when we were swimming, a boy shoved me with mock violence and I said to him, "Don't give me that nigger talk."

He replied, "You bastard," with a big grin.

From that time on, we could all use the word "nigger" but the old categories had totally changed. Never, as long as I live, will I forget the way my stomach felt after I used the word "nigger" without any reservation.[57]

One type of wise person is he whose wiseness comes from working in an establishment which caters either to the wants of those with a particular stigma or to actions that society takes in regard to these persons. For example, nurses and physical therapists can be wise; they can come to know more about a given type of prosthetic equipment than the patient who must learn to use it so as to minimize his disfigurement. Gentile employees in delicatessens are often wise, as are straight bartenders in homosexual bars, and the maids of Mayfair prostitutes.[58] The police, in constantly having to deal with criminals, may become wise in regard to them, leading a professional to suggest that ". . . in fact the police are the only people apart from other criminals who accept you for what you are."[59]

A second type of wise person is the individual who is related through the social structure to a stigmatized individual—a relationship that leads the wider society to treat both individuals in some respects as one. Thus the loyal spouse of the mental patient, the daughter of the ex-con, the parent of the cripple, the friend of the blind, the family of the hangman,[60] are all obliged to share some of the discredit of the stigmatized person to whom they are related. One response to this fate is to embrace it, and to live within the world of one's stigmatized connection. It should be added that persons who acquire a degree of stigma in this way can themselves have connections who acquire a little of the disease twice-removed. The problems faced by stigmatized persons spread out in waves, but of diminishing intensity. A newspaper advice column provides an illustration:

Dear Ann Landers:

I'm a girl 12 years old who is left out of all social activities because my father is an ex-convict. I try to be nice and friendly to everyone but it's no use. The girls at school have told me that their mothers don't want them to associate with me because it will be bad for their reputations. My father had some bad publicity in the papers and even though he has served his time nobody will forget it.

Is there anything I can do? I am very lonesome because it's no fun to be alone all the time. My mother tries to take me places with her but I want to be with people my own age. Please give me some advice—An OUTCAST.[61]

In general, the tendency for a stigma to spread from the stigmatized individual to his close connections provides a reason why such relations tend either to be avoided or to be terminated, where existing.

Persons with a courtesy stigma provide a model of "normalization,"[62] showing how far normals could go in treating the stigmatized person as if he didn't have a stigma. (Normalization is to be distinguished from "normification," namely, the effort on the part of a stigmatized individual to present himself as an ordinary person, although not necessarily making a secret of his failing.) Further, a cult of the stigmatized can occur, the stigmaphobic response of the normal being countered by the stigmaphile response of the wise. The person with a courtesy stigma can in fact make both the stigmatized and the normal uncomfortable: by always being ready to carry a burden that is not "really" theirs, they can confront everyone else with too much morality; by treating the stigma as a neutral matter to be looked at in a direct, off-hand way, they open themselves and the stigmatized to misunderstanding by normals who may read offensiveness into this behavior.[63]

The relation between the stigmatized and his stand-in can be an uneasy one. The person with a failing may feel that reversion to type may occur at any moment, and at a time when defenses are down and dependency is up. Thus a prostitute:

Well, I want to see what I can do with acting first. I've explained to him that if we were married and had a fight, he'd throw it up to me. He said no, but that's the way men are.[64]

On the other hand, the individual with a courtesy stigma may find that he must suffer many of the standard deprivations of his courtesy group and yet not be able to enjoy the self-elevation which is a common defense against such treatment. Further, much like the stigmatized in regard to him, he can doubt that in the last analysis he is really "accepted" by his courtesy group.[65]

MORAL CAREER

Persons who have a particular stigma tend to have similar learning experiences regarding their plight, and similar changes in conception of self—a similar "moral career" that is both cause and effect of commitment to a similar sequence of personal adjustments. (The natural history of a category of persons with a stigma must be clearly distinguished from the natural history of the stigma itself—the history of the origins, spread, and decline of the capacity of an attribute to serve as a stigma in a particular society, for example, divorce in American upper middle class society.) One phase of this socialization process is that through which the stigmatized person learns and incorporates the standpoint of the normal, acquiring thereby the identity beliefs of the wider society and a general idea of what it would be like to possess a particular stigma. Another phase is that through which he learns that he possesses a particular stigma and, this time in detail, the consequence of possessing it. The timing and interplay of these two initial phases of the moral career form important patterns, establishing the foundation for later development, and providing a means of distinguishing among the moral careers available to the stigmatized. Four such patterns may be mentioned.

One pattern involves those with an inborn stigma who become socialized into their disadvantageous situation even while they are learning and incorporating the standards against which they fall short.[66] For example, an orphan learns that children naturally and normally have parents, even while he is learning what it means not to have any. After spending the first sixteen years of his life in the institution he can later still feel that he naturally knows how to be a father to his son.

A second pattern derives from the capacity of a family, and to a much lesser extent a local neighborhood, to constitute itself a protective capsule for its young. Within such a capsule a congenitally stigmatized child can be carefully sustained by means of information control. Self-belittling definitions of him are prevented from entering the charmed circle, while broad access is given to other conceptions held in the wider society, ones that lead the encapsulated child to see himself as a fully qualified ordinary human being, of normal identity in terms of such basic matters as age and sex.

The point in the protected individual's life when the domestic circle can no longer protect him will vary by social class, place of residence, and type of stigma, but in each case will give rise to a moral experience when it occurs. Thus, public school entrance is often reported as the occasion of stigma learning, the experience sometimes coming very precipitously on the first day of school, with taunts, teasing, ostracism, and fights.[67] Interestingly, the more the child is "handicapped" the more likely he is to be sent to a special school for persons of his kind, and the more abruptly he will have to face the view which the public at large takes of him. He will be told that he will have an easier time of it among "his own," and thus learn that the own he thought he possessed was the wrong one, and that this lesser own is really his. It should be added that where the infantilely stigmatized manages to get through his early school years with some illusions left, the onset of dating or job-getting will often introduce the moment of truth. In some cases, merely an increased likelihood of incidental disclosure is involved:

I think the first realization of my situation, and the first intense grief resulting from this realization, came one day, very casually, when a group of us in our early teens had gone to the beach for the day. I was lying on the sand, and I guess the fellows and girls thought I was asleep. One of the fellows said, "I like Domenica very much, but I would never go out with a blind girl." I cannot think of any prejudice which so completely rejects you.[68]

In other cases, something closer to systematic exposure is involved, as a cerebral palsy victim suggests:

With one extremely painful exception, as long as I was in the protective custody of family life or college schedules and lived without exercising my rights as an adult citizen, the forces of society were kindly and un-ruffling. It was after college, business school, and in-numerable stretches as a volunteer worker on community projects that I was often bogged down by the medieval prejudices and superstitions of the business world. Looking for a job was like standing before a firing squad. Employers were shocked that I had the gall to apply for a job.[69]

A third pattern of socialization is illustrated by one who becomes stigmatized late in life, or learns late in life that he has always been discreditable—the first involving no radical reorganization of his view of his past, the second involving this factor. Such an individual has thoroughly learned about the normal and the stigmatized long before he must see himself as deficient. Presumably he will have a special problem in reidentifying himself, and a special likelihood of developing disapproval of self:

When I smelled an odor on the bus or subway before the colostomy I used to feel very annoyed. I'd think that the people were awful, that they didn't take a bath or that they should have gone to the bathroom before traveling. I used to think that they might have odors from what they ate. I used to be terribly annoyed; to me it seemed that they were filthy, dirty. Of course, at the least opportunity I used to change my seat and if I couldn't it used to go against my grain. So naturally, I believe that the young people feel the same way about me if I smell.[70]

While there are certainly cases of individuals discovering only in adult life that they belong to a stigmatized tribal group or that their parents have a contagious moral blemish, the usual case here is that of physical handicaps that "strike" late in life:

But suddenly I woke up one morning, and found that I could not stand. I had had polio, and polio was as simple as that. I was like a very young child who had been dropped into a big, black hole, and the only thing I was certain of was that I could not get out unless someone helped me. The education, the lectures, and the parental training which I had received for twenty-four years didn't seem to make me the person who could do anything for me now. I was like everyone else—normal, quarrelsome, gay, full of plans, and all of a sudden something happened! Something happened and I became a stranger. I was a greater stranger to myself than to anyone. Even my dreams did not know me.

They did not know what they ought to let me do—and when I went to dances or to parties in them, there was always an odd provision or limitation—not spoken of or mentioned, but there just the same. I suddenly had the very confusing mental and emotional conflict of a lady leading a double life. It was unreal and it puzzled me, and I could not help dwelling on it.[71]

Here the medical profession is likely to have the special job of informing the infirm who he is going to have to be.

A fourth pattern is illustrated by those who are initially socialized in an alien community, whether inside or outside the geographical boundaries of the normal society, and who then must learn a second way of being that is felt by those around them to be the real and valid one.

It should be added that when an individual acquires a new stigmatized self late in life, the uneasiness he feels about new associates may slowly give way to uneasiness felt concerning old ones. Post-stigma acquaintances may see him simply as a faulted person; pre-stigma acquaintances, being attached to a conception of what he once was, may be unable to treat him either with formal tact or with familiar full acceptance:

My task [as a blind writer interviewing prospective clients for his literary product] was to put the men I'd come to see at their ease—the reverse of the usual situation. Curiously, I found it much easier to do with men I'd never met before. Perhaps this was because with strangers there was no body of reminiscences to cover before business could be gotten down to and so there was no unpleasant contrast with the present.[72]

Regardless of which general pattern the moral career of the stigmatized individual illustrates, the phase of experience during which he learns that he possesses a stigma will be especially interesting, for at this time he is likely to be thrown into a new relationship to others who possess the stigma too.

In some cases, the only contact the individual will have with his own is a fleeting one, but sufficient nonetheless to show him that others like himself exist:

When Tommy came to the clinic the first time, there were two other little boys there, each with a congenital absence of an ear. When Tommy saw them, his right hand went slowly to his own defective ear, and he turned with wide eyes to his father and said, "There's another boy with an ear like mine."[73]

In the case of the individual who has recently become physically handicapped, fellow-sufferers more advanced than himself in dealing with the failing are likely to make him a special series of visits to welcome him to the club and to instruct him in how to manage himself physically and psychically:

Almost my first awareness that there are mechanics of adjustment came to me with the comparison of two fellow patients I had at the Eye and Ear Infirmary. They used to visit me as I lay abed and I came to know them fairly well. Both had been blind for seven years. They were about the same age—a little past thirty—and both had college educations.[74]

In the many cases where the individual's stigmatization is associated with his admission to a custodial institution such as a jail, sanatorium, or orphanage, much of what he learns about his stigma will be transmitted to him during prolonged intimate contact with those in the process of being transformed into his fellow-sufferers.

As already suggested, when the individual first learns who it is that he must now accept as his own, he is likely, at the very least, to feel some ambivalence; for these others will not only be patently stigmatized, and thus not like the normal person he knows himself to be, but may also have other attributes with which he finds it difficult to associate himself. What may end up as a freemasonry may begin with a shudder. A newly blind girl on a visit to The Lighthouse directly from leaving the hospital provides an illustration:

My questions about a guide dog were politely turned aside. Another sighted worker took me in tow to show me around. We visited the Braille library; the classrooms; the clubrooms where the blind members of the music and dramatic groups meet; the recreation hall where on festive occasions the blind dance with the blind; the bowling alleys where the blind play together; the cafeteria, where all the blind gather to eat together; the huge workshops where the blind earn a subsistence income by making mops and brooms, weaving rugs, caning chairs. As we moved from room to room, I could hear the shuffling of feet, the muted voices, the tap-tap-tapping of canes. Here was the safe, segregated world of the sightless—a completely different world, I was assured by the social worker, from the one I had just left. . . .

I was expected to join this world. To give up my profession and to earn my living making mops. The Lighthouse would be happy to teach me how to make mops. I was to spend the rest of my life making mops with other blind people, eating with other blind people, dancing with other blind people. I became nauseated with fear, as the picture grew in my mind. Never had I come upon such destructive segregation.[75]

Given the ambivalence built into the individual's attachment to his stigmatized category, it is understandable that oscillations may occur in his support of, identification with, and participation among his own. There will be "affiliation cycles" through which he comes to accept the special opportunities for in-group participation or comes to reject them after having accepted them before.[76] There will be corresponding oscillations in belief about the nature of own group and the nature of normals. For example, adolescence (and the high school peer group) can bring a marked decline in own-group identification and a marked increase in identification with normals.[77] The later phases of the individual's moral career are to be found in these shifts of participation and belief.

The relationship of the stigmatized individual to the informal community and formal organizations of his own kind is, then, crucial. This relationship will, for example, mark a great difference between those whose differentness provides them very little of a new "we," and those, such as minority group members, who find themselves a part of a well-organized community with long-standing traditions—a community that makes appreciable claims on loyalty and income, defining the member as someone who should take pride in his illness and not seek to get well. In any case, whether the stigmatized group is an established one or not, it is largely in relation to this own-group that it is possible to discuss the natural history and the moral career of the stigmatized individual.

In reviewing his own moral career, the stigmatized individual may single out and retrospectively elaborate experiences which serve for him to account for his coming to the beliefs and practices that he now has regarding his own kind and normals. A life event can thus have a double

bearing on moral career, first as immediate objective grounds for an actual turning point, and later (and easier to demonstrate) as a means of accounting for a position currently taken. One experience often selected for this latter purpose is that through which the newly stigmatized individual learns that full-fledged members of the group are quite like ordinary human beings:

When I [a young girl turning to a life of vice and first meeting her madam] turned into Fourth Street my courage again failed me, and I was about to beat a retreat when Mamie came out of a restaurant across the street and warmly greeted me. The porter, who came to the door in response to our ring, said that Miss Laura was in her room, and we were shown in. I saw a woman comely and middle-aged, who bore no resemblance to the horrible creature of my imagination. She greeted me in a soft, well-bred voice, and everything about her so eloquently spoke of her potentialities for motherhood that instinctively I looked around for the children who should have been clinging to her skirts.[78]

Another illustration is provided by a homosexual in regard to his becoming one:

I met a man with whom I had been at school. . . . He was, of course, gay himself, and took it for granted that I was, too. I was surprised and rather impressed. He did not look in the least like the popular idea of a homosexual, being well-built, masculine, and neatly dressed. This was something new to me. Although I was perfectly prepared to admit that love could exist between men, I had always been slightly repelled by the obvious homosexuals whom I had met because of their vanity, their affected manner, and their ceaseless chatter. These, it now appeared, formed only a small part of the homosexual world, although the most noticeable one. . . .[79]

A cripple provides a similar statement:

If I had to choose one group of experiences that finally convinced me of the importance of this problem [of self-image] and that I had to fight my own battles of identification, it would be the incidents that made me realize with my heart that cripples could be identified with characteristics other than their physical handicap. I managed to see that cripples could be comely, charming, ugly, lovely, stupid, brilliant—just like all other people, and I discovered that I was able to hate or love a cripple in spite of his handicap.[80]

It may be added that in looking back to the occasion of discovering that persons with his stigma are human beings like everyone else, the individual may bring to bear a later occasion when his pre-stigma friends imputed un-humanness to those he had by then learned to see as full-fledged persons like himself. Thus, in reviewing her experience as a circus worker, a young girl sees first that she had learned her fellow-workers are not freaks, and second that her pre-circus friends fear for her having to travel in a bus along with other members of the troupe.[81]

Another turning point—retrospectively if not originally—is the isolating, incapacitating experience, often a period of hospitalization, which comes later to be seen as the time when the individual was able to think through his problem, learn about himself, sort out his situation, and arrive at a new understanding of what is important and worth seeking in life.

It should be added that not only are personal experiences retrospectively identified as turning points, but experiences once removed may be employed in this way. For example, a reading of the literature of the group may itself provide an experience felt and claimed as reorganizing:

I do not think it is claiming too much to say that *Uncle Tom's Cabin* was a fair and truthful panorama of slavery; however that may be, it opened my eyes as to who and what I was and what my country considered me, in fact, it gave me my bearing.[82]

NOTES

1. T. Parker and R. Allerton, *The Courage of His Convictions* (London: Hutchinson & Co., 1962), p. 109.

2. In this connection see the review by M. Meltzer, "Countermanipulation through Malingering," in A. Biderman and H. Zimmer, eds., *The Manipulation of Human Behavior* (New York: John Wiley & Sons, 1961), pp. 277–304.

3. In recent history, especially in Britain, low class status functioned as an important tribal stigma, the sins of the parents, or at least their milieu, being visited on the child, should the child rise improperly far above his initial station. The management of class stigma is of course a central theme in the English novel.

4. D. Riseman, "Some Observations Concerning Marginality," *Phylon*, Second Quarter, 1951, 122.

5. The case regarding mental patients is presented by T. J. Scheff in a forthcoming paper.

6. In regard to the blind, see E. Henrich and L. Kriegel, eds., *Experiments in Survival* (New York: Association for the Aid of Crippled Children, 1961), pp. 152 and 186; and H. Chevigny, *My Eyes Have a Cold Nose* (New Haven, Conn.: Yale University Press, paperbound, 1962), p. 201.

7. In the words of one blind woman, "I was asked to endorse a perfume, presumably because being sightless my sense of smell was super-discriminating." See T. Keitlen (with N. Lobsenz), *Farewell to Fear* (New York: Avon, 1962), p. 10.

8. A. G. Gowman, *The War Blind in American Social Structure* (New York: American Foundation for the Blind, 1957), p. 198.

9. For examples, see Macgregor *et al.*, *op. cit.*, throughout.

10. The notion of "normal human being" may have its source in the medical approach to humanity or in the tendency of the large-scale bureaucratic organizations, such as the nation state, to treat all members in some respects as equal. Whatever its origins, it seems to provide the basic imagery through which laymen currently conceive of themselves. Interestingly, a convention seems to have emerged in popular life-story writing where a questionable person proves his claim to normalcy by citing his acquisition of a spouse and children, and, oddly, by attesting to his spending Christmas and Thanksgiving with them.

11. A criminal's view of this nonacceptance is presented in Parker and Allerton, *op. cit.*, pp. 110–111.

12. K. B. Hathaway, *The Little Locksmith* (New York: Coward-McCann, 1943), p. 41, in Wright, *op. cit.*, p. 157.

13. *Ibid.*, pp. 46–47. For general treatments of the self-disliking sentiments, see K. Lewin, *Resolving Social Conflicts*, Part III (New York: Harper & Row, 1948); A. Kardiner and L. Ovesey, *The Mark of Oppression: A Psychosocial Study of the American Negro* (New York: W. W. Norton & Company, 1951); and E. H. Erikson, *Childhood and Society* (New York: W. W. Norton & Company, 1950).

14. F. Warfield, *Keep Listening* (New York: The Viking Press, 1957), p. 76. See also H. von Hentig, *The Criminal and His Victim* (New Haven, Conn.: Yale University Press, 1948), p. 101.

15. Keitlen, *op. cit.*, Chap. 12, pp. 117–129 and Chap. 14, pp. 137–149. See also Chevigny, *op. cit.*, pp. 85–86.

16. Henrich and Kriegel, *op. cit.*, p. 49.

17. W. Y. Baker and L. H. Smith, "Facial Disfigurement and Personality," *Journal of the American Medical Association*, CXII (1939), 303. Macgregor

et al., op. cit., p. 57 ff., provide an illustration of a man who used his big red nose for a crutch.

18. Henrich and Kriegel, *op. cit.*, p. 19.

19. *Ibid.*, p. 35.

20. Chevigny, *op. cit.*, p. 154.

21. F. Carling, *And Yet We Are Human* (London: Chatto & Windus, 1962), pp. 23–24.

22. For one review, see G. W. Allport, *The Nature of Prejudice* (New York: Anchor Books, 1958).

23. Macgregor *et al., op. cit.*, pp. 91–92.

24. From *Clinical Studies in Psychiatry*, H. S. Perry, M. L. Gawel, and M. Gibbon, eds. (New York: W. W. Norton & Company, 1956), p. 145.

25. R. Barker, "The Social Psychology of Physical Disability," *Journal of Social Issues*, IV (1948), 34, suggests that stigmatized persons "live on a social-psychological frontier," constantly facing new situations. See also Macgregor *et al., op. cit.*, p. 87, where the suggestion is made that the grossly deformed need suffer less doubt about their reception in interaction than the less visibly deformed.

26. Barker, *op. cit.*, p. 33.

27. Parker and Allerton, *op. cit.*, p. 111.

28. This special kind of self-consciousness is analyzed in S. Messinger *et al.*, "Life as Theater: Some Notes on the Dramaturgic Approach to Social Reality," *Sociometry*, XXV (1962), 98–110.

29. Parker and Allerton, *op. cit.*, p. 111.

30. Chevigny, *op. cit.*, p. 140.

31. L. A. Dexter, "A Social Theory of Mental Deficiency," *American Journal of Mental Deficiency*, LXII (1958), 923. For another study of the mental defective as a stigmatized person, see S. E. Perry, "Some Theoretical Problems of Mental Deficiency and Their Action Implications," *Psychiatry*, XVII (1954), 45–73.

32. Baker, *Out on a Limb* (New York: McGraw-Hill Book Company, n.d.), p. 22.

33. *Ibid.*, p. 73.

34. This theme is well treated in R. K. White, B. A. Wright, and T. Dembo, "Studies in Adjustment to Visible Injuries: Evaluation of Curiosity by the Injured," *Journal of Abnormal and Social Psychology*, XLIII (1948), 13–28.

35. For example, Henrich and Kriegel, *op. cit.*, p. 184.

36. See Wright, *op. cit.*, "The Problem of Sympathy," pp. 233–237.

37. S. Zawadski and P. Lazarsfeld, "The Psychological Consequences of Unemployment," *Journal of Social Psychology*, VI (1935), 239.

38. Hathaway, *op. cit.*, pp. 155–157, in S. Richardson, "The Social Psychological Consequences of Handicapping," unpublished paper presented at the 1962 American Sociological Association Convention, Washington, D.C., 7–8.

39. For a general treatment, see E. Goffman, "Alienation from Interaction," *Human Relations*, X (1957), 47–60.

40. F. Davis, "Deviance Disavowal: The Management of Strained Interaction by the Visibly Handicapped," *Social Problems*, IX (1961), 123. See also White, Wright, and Dembo, *op. cit.*, pp. 26–27.

41. H. Freeman and G. Kasenbaum, "The Illiterate in America," *Social Forces*, XXXIV (1956), 374.

42. Warfield, *op. cit.*, p. 60.

43. R. Edgerton and G. Sabagh, "From Mortification to Aggrandizement: Changing Self-Concepts in the Careers of the Mentally Retarded," *Psychiatry*, XXV (1962), 268. For further comment on sad tales, see E. Goffman, "The Moral Career of the Mental Patient," *Psychiatry*, XXII (1959), 133–134.

44. Carling, *op. cit.*, pp. 18–19.

45. E. Lemert, *Social Pathology* (New York: McGraw-Hill Book Company, 1951), p. 151.

46. A general survey is provided in H. Wechsler, "The Expatient Organization: A Survey," *Journal of Social Issues*, XVI (1960), 47–53. Titles include: Recovery, Inc., Search, Club 103, Fountain House Foundation, San Francisco Fellowship Club, Center Club. For a study of one such club, see D. Landy and S. Singer, "The Social Organization and Culture of a Club for Former Mental Patients," *Human Relations*, XIV (1961), 31–41. See also M. B. Palmer, "Social Rehabilitation for Mental Patients," *Mental Hygiene*, XLII (1958), 24–28.

47. See Baker, *op. cit.*, pp. 158–159.

48. D. R. White, "I have an ileostomy . . . I wish I didn't. But I have learned to Accept it and Live a Normal, Full Life," *American Journal of Nursing*, LXI (1961), 52: "At this time, ileostomy and colostomy clubs exist in 16 states and the District of Columbia as well as in Australia, Canada, England, and South Africa."

49. Warfield, *op. cit.*, pp. 135–136, describes a 1950 celebration of the New York hard of hearing movement, with every successive generation of leadership present, as well as representatives of every originally separate organization. A complete recapitulation of the movement's history was thus available. For comments on the international history of the movement, see K. W. Hodgson, *The Deaf and their Problems* (New York: Philosophical Library, 1954), p. 352.

50. Reported in F. Poli, *Gentlemen Convicts* (London: Rupert Hart-Davis, 1960).

51. For example, see Chevigny, *op. cit.*, Chap. 5, where the situation is presented regarding the blind.

52. Warfield, *op. cit.*, p. 78.

53. Warfield, *op. cit.*, pp. 73–74; see also Chap. 9, pp. 129–158, where a kind of confession is provided

regarding the professional life. For a description of life as a professional amputee, see H. Russell, *Victory in My Hands* (New York: Creative Age Press, 1949).

54. From the beginning such leaders may be recruited from those members of the category who are ambitious to leave the life of its members and relatively able to do so, giving rise to what Lewin (*op. cit.*, pp. 195–196) called "Leadership from the Periphery."

55. J. Stearn, *Sisters of the Night* (New York: Popular Library, 1961), p. 181.

56. N. Mailer, "The Homosexual Villain," in *Advertisements for Myself* (New York: Signet Books, 1960), pp. 200–205, provides a model confession detailing the basic cycle of bigotry, enlightening experience, and, finally recantation of prejudice through public admission. See also Angus Wilson's introduction to Carling, *op. cit.*, for a confessional record of Wilson's redefinition of cripples.

57. Ray Birdwhistell in B. Schaffner, ed., *Group Processes*, Transactions of the Second (1955) Conference. (New York: Josiah Macy, Jr. Foundation, 1956), p. 171.

58. C. H. Rolph, ed., *Women of the Streets* (London: Secker and Warburg, 1955), pp. 78–79.

59. Parker and Allerton, *op. cit.*, p. 150.

60. J. Atholl, *The Reluctant Hangman* (London: John Long, Ltd., 1956), p. 61.

61. *Berkeley Daily Gazette*, April 12, 1961.

62. The idea derives from C. G. Schwartz, "Perspectives on Deviance—Wives' Definitions of Their Husbands' Mental Illness," *Psychiatry*, XX (1957), 275–291.

63. For an example in regard to the blind, see A. Gowman, "Blindness and the Role of the Companion," *Social Problems*, IV (1956), 68–75.

64. Stearn, *op. cit.*, p. 99.

65. The range of possibilities is nicely explored in C. Brossard, "Plaint of a Gentile Intellectual," in Brossard, ed., *The Scene Before You* (New York: Holt, Rinehart & Winston, 1955), pp. 87–91.

66. Discussion of this pattern can be found in A. R. Lindesmith and A. L. Strauss, *Social Psychology*, rev. ed. (New York: Holt, Rinehart & Winston, 1956), pp. 180–183.

67. An example from the experience of a blind person may be found in R. Criddle, *Love Is Not Blind* (New York: W. W. Norton & Company, 1953), p. 21; the experience of a dwarfed person is reported in H. Viscardi, Jr., *A Man's Stature* (New York: The John Day Company, 1952), pp. 13–14.

68. Henrich and Kriegel, *op. cit.*, p. 186.

69. *Ibid.*, p. 156.

70. Orbach *et al., op. cit.*, p. 165.

71. N. Linduska, *My Polio Past* (Chicago: Pellegrini and Cudahy, 1947), p. 177.

72. Chevigny, *op. cit.*, p. 136.

73. Macgregor *et al., op. cit.*, pp. 19–20.

74. Chevigny, *op. cit.*, p. 35.

75. Keitlen, *op. cit.*, pp. 37–38. A description of the early vicissitudes of a hospitalized polio patient's identification with fellow-cripples is provided in Linduska, *op. cit.*, pp. 159–165. A fictional account of racial reidentification is provided by J. W. Johnson, *The Autobiography of an Ex-Coloured Man*, rev. ed. (New York: Hill and Wang, American Century Series, 1960), pp. 22–23.

76. A general statement may be found in two of E. C. Hughes' papers, "Social Change and Status Protest," *Phylon*, First Quarter, 1949, 58–65, and "Cycles and Turning Points," in *Men and Their Work* (New York: Free Press of Glencoe, 1958).

77. M. Yarrow, "Personality Development and Minority Group Membership," in M. Sklare, *The Jews* (New York: Free Press of Glencoe, 1960), pp. 468–470.

78. *Madeleine, An Autobiography* (New York: Pyramid Books, 1961), pp. 36–37.

79. P. Wildeblood, *Against the Law* (New York: Julian Messner, 1959), pp. 23–24.

80. Carling, *op. cit.*, p. 21.

81. C. Clausen, *I Love You Honey But the Season's Over* (New York: Holt, Rinehart & Winston, 1961), p. 217.

82. Johnson, *op. cit.*, p. 42. Johnson's novel, like others of its kind, provides a nice instance of myth-making, being a literary organization of many of the crucial moral experiences and crucial turning points retrospectively available to those in a stigmatized category.

WHITENESS AS STIGMA:
ESSENTIALIST IDENTITY WORK BY MIXED-RACE WOMEN

Debbie Storrs

I didn't like my skin color. I really didn't. I'm much too light. I don't tan. . . . All my brothers and sisters have more color to their skin. I just want pigment! I'm just tired of looking white. . . . I just wish I were darker because I'm so pale. I am very pale. (Jamie, a mixed-race young woman)

For many, the statement above is counterintuitive, perhaps even amusing or bewildering, because of the historical tendency in the United States to stigmatize people of color based on the assumption that whiteness is not only normative but desirable, beautiful, and generally superior to non-whiteness. Using Goffman's (1963) term, non-white identities are "stigmatized" by the dominant members of society. Jamie's wish for pigment challenges the stigmatization of non-whiteness and the long held conception of whiteness. Through an analysis of mixed-race women's narratives, this research reveals how women challenge normative ideas about race as well as the meaning and construction of racial identities. The women in this study identify with their non-white heritage despite stigmatized conceptions of non-whiteness and racial mixing as "spoiled" identities (Goffman 1963). Contrary to dominant racial assumptions about the superiority of whiteness, these women perceive their identities as potentially "spoiled" not by their non-whiteness, but by their whiteness—their lack of non-white racial purity and their appearance of being "too white." Given this attitude, these women manage their potentially discreditable non-white identities through identity work, including reversing the stigma associated with non-whiteness. This research contributes to the sociological literature that highlights the macro processes that construct whiteness by illustrating how whiteness is not a static identity, but, in-

stead, is in flux because individuals challenge its meanings. I capture the micro level social process of racial formation through an analysis of women's ability to rearticulate the meaning of stigma (Omi and Winant 1986). This research also adds to the symbolic interactionist literature that emphasizes face-to-face interaction, the micro processes, in the construction of self by revealing the dynamic interplay between macro and micro processes in the development of racial identity. In short, by including both micro and macro processes, this paper reveals mixed-race women's constructions of whiteness and the identity work they engage in to invoke and manage their non-white identities in the context of large racial ideologies.

METHODS

The data used in this article are drawn from a larger study that examines the racial and gendered identity constructions of mixed-race women. The sample consists of 27 women with mixed-race ancestry residing in the northwest region of the United States. More specifically, nine of the women identify their racial ancestry as Asian and Caucasian, six identify their ancestry as Native American and Caucasian, eight identify their ancestry as African American and Caucasian, one identifies her ancestry as African American and Asian, and three identify their ancestry as Mexican/Latino and Caucasian.

While this sample includes women from different racial groups, the distinctive characteristic is that they all identify as non-white. The concern of this study is to explain this identity choice while also attending to the variation among women in terms of their identity work. This variation in identity work emerges out of the unique racial histories, the macro racial forces, which are revealed in women's narratives. For example, women with Latino ancestry often recognize and discuss their mestizo background, although they differentiate this history from their own contemporary mixed-race ancestry. Mixed-race women with African American ancestry have more constraints on their racial identity than other mixed-race women largely because of the legacy of the hypo-descent policy (which holds that one drop of "black blood" is sufficient to render an individual black). One way this study differs from previous research using biracial or multiracial subjects is its comparative component, which allows for the identification of both differences and commonalities in mixed-race women's identities.

Subjects were obtained through snowball sampling methods. Initially, women were identified through personal contacts, announcements in college classrooms, and social service organizations that provide services to populations of color. The bulk of the respondents were collected by asking initial respondents if they could refer other individuals with mixed-race ancestry who might be willing to share their personal histories and experiences. Subjects participated in semi-structured interviews focusing on themes of identity, family histories, cultural knowledge, and race relations.

Because snowball sampling methods rely on interpersonal connections, subjects typically share common characteristics that help to explain their racial identities as non-white. The women in this sample share similar biographies in that their immediate social environment as children, adolescents, and adults lacks racial diversity aside from immediate non-white family members. Another unique characteristic of the sample that shapes women's identities is their involvement with race-specific organizations, classes, friends, and communities. Although women from this sample live in predominantly white communities, they actively seek out racially diverse work and social networks. Some women are involved in race-specific student associations. Others serve as board members in organizations that provide services to people of color. Many work or volunteer in a variety of occupations that provide services to people of color. Others participate in race-specific community events and most have personal friendships with persons of color.

Another important similarity among women in this sample is the historical moment in which women's identities are formed. Korgen (1998) argues that black-white biracial individuals who came of age during the Civil Rights era are more likely to identify as non-white, while those coming of age in the post-Civil Rights era are much less likely to identify as black because they came of age in a time with more identity options, such as mixed-race identity. I did not find this pattern in my research. The women in my sample, who range in age from 18 to 50, all identify as non-white, despite the growing fluidity of racial identity options. Their identities did not differ by age cohort or by specific racial ancestry. Women in this sample, baby boomers or younger, were children or young adults during the Civil Rights Movement of the 1960s. The vast majority of women came of age during the post-Civil Rights era, certainly a time of growing identity options, but also a time characterized by polarized racial politics, attacks on affirmative action, and the positive rearticulation of non-white identity within people of color (Omi 1991). Thus, while it is important to address the historical moment in terms of racial identity politics and identity options, it is equally important to examine the ways in which the meaning of racial groups changes over time. While others have examined how non-whiteness has been rearticulated, less attention has been paid to the meaning of whiteness. I highlight these unique characteristics of the sample because they help to partially explain mixed-race women's identity articulations although, as I argue in the paper, a significant explanation for their identities as non-white has to do with the meaning and stigmatization of whiteness.

IDENTITY OPTIONS

Based on early sociological studies of ethnic immigrants and subsequent generations, it was assumed that racial minorities would eventually assimilate into mainstream America and become part of the "melting pot." However, despite forced and consensual racial mixing, racial designations and identities continue to thrive. In a recent study of the role of lineage in identity formation, Waters (1991) found that while over half her subjects knew that their personal ancestries were not purely African American, all of them identified as black. In the same study, Waters reported that the majority of her respondents believed that children of a mixed white and black marriage should identify as black. Such findings reveal the continued influence of the hypo-descent policy. This historical model continues to block African American assimilation.

While the hypo-descent policy was applied specifically to African Americans, it is a gloss for a larger complex of laws that defined race as mutually exclusive categories which rested on biology and which were revealed by socially significant physical markers of difference. As Davis (1991) notes, all non-white racialized identities have historically been limited by the hypo-descent policy, physical markers of difference, and institutional placements of them within racialized categories. The constraint non-white group members face in their racial identity continues today (Waters 1990). The identities of non-whites are not voluntary. Instead, members of these groups are socially, legally, and politically constrained to identify in particular ways, preventing members from assimilating into whiteness.

Despite ideologies of hypo-descent and our society's insistence on mutually exclusive racial categories, mixed-race women have more identity options since many of them can physically pass as white. The range of identity options available to mixed-race Americans include assimilating into whiteness, articulating a multiracial identity, constructing a more fluid identity, or embracing their non-white ancestry. These identity options emerge and become possible in different historical moments.

Assimilating into whiteness, or what scholars and lay persons alike refer to as passing, has been and continues to be more of an option for those who phenotypically are more aligned with whites than others. We do not know how prevalent passing is (historically or currently), but the term refers to movement into a dominant group in order to access the privileges associated with this group membership.[1] None of the women in my sample identified as white, and, in fact, those who were assumed to be white by others found this positioning disconcerting because it contradicted their personal identities as non-white. For example, Patty, who worked in various race-

specific organizations, illustrates her rejection of passing as white:

I was the director of this organization and we had a fundraiser and this woman wanted to help assist in soliciting funds for diverse populations. And she . . . herself had identified as a lesbian so given that perspective she wanted to commend me as the executive director for targeting diverse populations. And my response was, "Well of course I do, I have a vested interest in doing so for people of color." And so she said, "Well you know it's really kind of interesting because you're so involved in it that you actually talk about this project as if you were a person of color." And I said, "Pardon me?" And she said, "Well you act like you're a person of color." And I said, "I am." And she says, "No, you're not." And I said, "Yeah I am!" And she says "No, you're white." And I said, "No, I'm not! I'm biracial—I'm Japanese, German, Irish, French." And she said, "You are?" And I was instantly pissed that how dare she say I'm white.

This story is a common one shared by many women who can pass as white but whose racial identity is aligned with their non-white ancestry. Patty's identity preference is evident in her placement of self in the panracial category of "person of color." Her subsequent revelation of her multiple racial ancestry is also typical of women. In other words, the mixed-race women in this sample do not deny their multiple racial ancestries, yet their primary identity is with their non-white ancestry. Patty's anger at the other's positioning of her as white reveals how passing into the dominant group is undesirable.

A second possibility available in the contemporary moment for individuals with mixed-race ancestry is to articulate a multiracial identity. A multiracial social movement is burgeoning in the United States, composed of loosely connected national and state-wide organizations. One of their stated goals is to gain federal recognition of a multiracial category for the U.S. Census. While the federal government has yet to add such a category, multiracial organizations have been successful in passing state legislation that provides for a multiracial listing on state government forms. On an individual level, evidence of the growing consciousness of multiraciality is found in the number of individuals who choose the "other" category in the U.S. Census. Those identifying as "other" rose 45 percent from 1980 to 1990, making it the third fastest growing racial group and the fourth largest group in absolute numbers (Fernandez 1992, p. 141).[2] While all of the women in my sample recognize and identify with their mixed-race ancestries, none identify primarily as biracial or multiracial. In addition, none of the women belong to any multiracial organization, and the majority were unfamiliar with the multiracial movement's recent unsuccessful attempt to lobby the U.S. government for a multiracial census category.

Another emerging option, particularly among the younger generation of multiracial Americans, is to embrace multiple identities. This takes many forms, including individuals who identify in different ways depending on the social context. Multiracial individuals who embrace and identify as black, white, and biracial, refusing to choose one racial label and subjectivity over another, characterize this identity articulation. Theoretically, this perspective can be found among "border intellectuals"[3] in cultural studies, postmodern theory, and literature who challenge dominant ideologies that posit rigid and impermeable racial boundaries. A variation on this trend is documented by Bernstein (1995), who describes white teens who "claim" Mexican American and other non-white racial identities and who embrace cultural artifacts, styles of dress, and music associated with non-white groups. The women in my sample, while recognizing their multiracial and biracial ancestry, identify consistently with the non-white elements of their ancestry, at least at this point in their lives, and they desire a social identity as such across social contexts. They do not seek a fluid identity as much as they attempt to construct a solid and stable non-white racial identity.

To understand why women in this sample reject these previous identity options, favoring instead to identify with their non-white ancestry, requires attention to the construction and meaning of whiteness, the application of racial stigma, and the meaning they gain from their association with non-whiteness (all of which I explore in the body of this article). In addition, we should keep in mind that individuals' racial identities are constructed from the narratives available in our culture. Not all narratives and stories are as widely circulated. In other words, "some accounts of self are more readily available to some than others" (Wetherell and Potter 1992, p. 78). Which racial accounts are more dispersed and dominant in our culture than others? The discourse of multiracial activists is slowly emerging across the nation, in some regions more so than others, but is largely absent in the predominantly white environments of the women I interviewed. The identity choices made by the white teens that Bernstein (1995) discusses are often challenged by those more firmly entrenched within communities of color, and this suggests limits to their success. The racial discourse of fluidity articulated by "border intellectuals" is not widely available to a lay audience. The inability of scholars to disseminate this particular racial discourse is not simply due to its location within academic circles, but to the dominance of other racial discourses that are widely available and discursively practiced in our culture. The dominant racial discourses I refer to are those that rest on racial essentialism and assimilation that support either a white or non-white racial identity. An assimilationist perspective assumes that those who can pass as white will do so because privileges are associated with the dominant group and because stigma has historically been applied to non-whites. This assumption does not hold for my sample, however, in large part, I argue, because of a shift in racial stigma.

RACIAL STIGMA

Historically, in the social sciences and popular culture, whiteness has represented a superior race on biological, physical, and cultural grounds. The mixed-race women in this sample reject this dominant evaluation of non-whiteness and reverse the stigma applied to racial groups. These women assign positive evaluations to their non-white ancestry, while their whiteness becomes the source of their "spoiled" ancestry. Their reversal of racial stigma is initially perplexing given the rewards in being identified as a "normal" (i.e., Caucasian). When discussing their parents' history and identities, the majority of these women describe their families pursuing the rewards of whiteness by attempting to assimilate into the white version of

America. This tendency on the part of their parents is a function of the historical moment, a time when non-whiteness was clearly associated by the dominant group with inferiority and a lack of privileges (i.e., stigmatized).

Given their parents' identification patterns, why doesn't this generation of mixed-race women continue to attempt to pass as white, to pursue the rewards of whiteness, particularly those whose physical features would make it fairly easy to do so? What possible rewards could result from identifying with their non-white ancestry, especially given the amount of energy these women must expend in their identity work? These questions can best be answered by looking at how these women construct the meaning of whiteness. These constructions, however, take place within larger contexts, groups, and interactions. In other words, while these women are active agents in the construction of their racial subjectivities, they are constrained to varying degrees by macro forces of racialization. In the next section, I briefly review the macro forces that shape and limit women's identity options, and I focus on the ways in which whiteness has become a site of negotiation.

THE SOCIAL CONSTRUCTION OF WHITENESS

One of the most significant developments in the sociological study of race relations has been the deconstruction of whiteness. Scholars of whiteness highlight how the state and other social forces have actively shaped whiteness. For example, Lopez (1996) illustrates how law constructs whiteness and non-whiteness through a variety of practices, including codifying race, defining the content of racial identities, and controlling access to resources. Omi and Winant (1986) reveal historical mechanisms that consolidated diverse European groups into a homogeneous identity of whiteness through the institutionalization of slavery, segregation, and immigration restrictions. Others focus on the more recent activities of the state in shaping and reinforcing whiteness. For example, Lipsitz (1995) discusses the racialized social policies in the post-World-War-II era that served to reinforce racial boundaries. Urban re-newal projects, federally funded highways, and FHA financing policies, according to Lipsitz, consolidated and increased the "possessive interest in whiteness" (1995, p. 369).

Despite scholarly evidence that whiteness is socially constructed and a central organizing principle in social and cultural relations, white individuals identify with particular ethnic groups, and they generally lack a racial consciousness. While in previous generations, ethnicity for white immigrants was a salient personal and social identity, today, ethnicity has become largely symbolic for most whites, although regional differences still do exist (Steinberg 1989). In other words, white ethnics identify with their ethnic ancestries, but these are generally voluntary and leisure-oriented activities (Gans 1979). For later-generation white ethnics, ethnicity is invoked at will and does not significantly shape their daily lives or their sense of self (Waters 1990). Thus, ethnic identity is largely symbolic, taking the form of consuming ethnic foods or participating in annual ethnic celebrations like St. Patrick's Day (Waters 1990). The point is that while white ethnics celebrate their ethnic heritage through symbolic cultural displays, their racial identities as white are conspicuously absent. Like males who often have no subjective consciousness as gendered beings, whites often are unconscious of their racial status as whites (Flagg 1993; McIntosh 1992; Tatum 1997; Waters 1990).

Flagg (1993) labels whites' lack of racial consciousness the "transparency phenomenon." This transparency character of whiteness is empirically illustrated in Frankenberg's research on the meaning of whiteness for Anglo feminists. For many white feminists, whiteness was "an unmarked marker, very often viewed as substantively empty and yet taken as normative" (1993, p. 65). This conception of whiteness as both normative and meaningless helps explain the historical absence of a conscious racial identity for many Euroamericans.

Recently, however, the meaning of whiteness has been reformulated into a visible and meaningful racial identity. Racial identity politics and the challenges to racial politics from persons of color have marked whiteness in ways that have not been articulated in the past. According to

Gallagher (1995), white college students find it relatively easy to transform the meaning of whiteness from privileged oppressor to socially disadvantaged group members as they embrace the ideology of an egalitarian, colorblind society. The acceptance of a colorblind and equal-opportunity society promoted by politicians and the media, and the backlash against race-based policies, encourages a white racial identity among young whites (Gallagher 1995). This reformulation of whiteness as visible and as a social disadvantage is a generational expression, structured by current racial politics. As ethnicity becomes largely symbolic among older whites (Waters 1990), and at a time of backlash against affirmative action, immigrant rights, and welfare reform, racially charged environments like the university help foster a conscious white identity among some white college students.

Gallagher's findings reveal how the meaning of whiteness is not static, but is "always constructed, always in the process of being made and unmade" (Frankenberg 1997, p. 16). Whiteness is being reformulated in various contexts, generations, and social spheres. While the mixed-race women in this sample are similar to Gallagher's white subjects in that they both challenge dominant, but subtle, constructions of whiteness, they differ significantly in the content of the construction. For Gallagher's white subjects, whiteness is under attack and whites become the subordinated and oppressed group. For the mixed-race women in this study, whiteness also becomes visible yet is stigmatized through its construction in two seemingly contradictory ways. The mixed-race women construct whiteness as normative, empty, and bland but also as oppressive, prejudicial, and discriminatory. This dual conception of whiteness helps to explain why mixed-race women do not embrace their white ancestry. These women reject assimilation into whiteness in part because whiteness is stigmatized.

WHITENESS AS NORMATIVE, MEANINGLESS, AND EMPTY

The construction of whiteness as empty is relationally linked to the construction of non-whiteness as meaningful, revealing the dichotomous nature of identity constructions. Whiteness is an empty category devoid of meaning in contrast to its opposition, racialized categories and identities that, by default, are replete with meaning. In other words, the mixed-race women's white ancestry fails, in their minds, to provide them with any substantive meaning on which to base their identities. On the other hand, their non-white ancestry becomes meaningful because it provides something they view as distinctive or "different," the key source of what it means to have a racial identity.

Jamie, whose quotation begins this article, has a "mixed" black, Jewish, and white mother and an Italian American father, yet identifies as black even though she describes herself as "very pale" and often unintentionally passes as white. When asked to explain her identity, she responds in the following way:

'Cause I guess black is different. . . . It's just different than other people. And I like to be different. I don't know; I'm short and little and so there's not much about me beside my long curly hair that's different than anybody. . . . I can actually say, "Yeah, I'm a different person."

Jamie's construction of blackness as different is based on the normative assumption of whiteness that she evaluates negatively. Through a reversal of evaluations, she stigmatizes whiteness as normative and common. Women of all racial mixtures use a similar argument to explain their identity choices. In articulating their identity in these ways, the women maintain the normative nature of whiteness but reverse the evaluation.

The women's narratives reveal the negative or stigmatized nature of the construction of whiteness as devoid of meaning and bland. This is most evident in Julia's narrative as she discusses the difference between her sisters and herself. While her two sisters share the same racial ancestry of Puerto Rican and Welsh, Julia consistently portrays herself as being more Puerto Rican than her sisters and, thus, having a more interesting personality. Her narrative is replete with contrasts between herself and her sisters on everything from behavior and food preferences (she prefers spicy food, they prefer bland food) to attitude. For Julia, Puerto Ricans constitute a racially mixed group that includes African ancestry. Given this perspective, while Julia identifies as Puerto Rican, she feels an affinity to other blacks grounded in their common racial ancestry:

There's a certain attitude that black women have that I resonate very strongly with. I don't think I exhibit it with as much zest or finesse as they do, but enough that it has made me always all my life different from my sisters. It's a sort of in your face attitude. My sister's aren't like that. I love them dearly, but they are really white bred . . . It's like their anger has been bred out of them.

Julia's use of the term "white bred" conjures up images of white bread—bland and tasteless. Similarly, she characterizes her sisters' anger as white-washed; their personalities become as bland and boring as the spiceless foods they prefer.

The discussion of whiteness is not always something that emerges directly in the women's narratives, but the conception of whiteness as an empty category, devoid of meaning and the material on which identities are based, is evident in women's discussion of their family histories. Typically, women inform me of their mixed-race ancestry by discussing their parents' racial ancestry. Women talk at length about their non-white parent's history, culture, heritage, and how this plays out in their lives without a similar discussion of their white ancestry until I explicitly ask about it. This pattern reveals the declining significance of ethnicity among fourth, fifth, and later generation whites. Due to extensive assimilation, later generation whites find little meaning in their ethnic ancestry from which to forge their identities (Waters 1990).

Only two women voluntarily discussed their white ancestry in any depth. In Julia's case, she constructs her Welsh ancestry as meaningful on the basis of aligning the Welsh with other racial minorities. Julia's conception of Welsh is in accord with her construction of Puerto Rican, since she constructs both as subordinated but powerful groups. The only other woman to investigate and discuss at any length her white ancestry is Nancy, whose father is Japanese American and mother is Polish Ukrainian. Nancy's narrative is equally structured around both of her parents' an-

cestry, unlike the other women interviewed. Nancy has been to Eastern Europe for a performing arts cultural exchange program and expresses a desire to visit her ancestral home of Ukraine. While Nancy expresses an interest in her Polish Ukrainian ancestry, she identifies as Asian American on forms and in public situations, although she often provides interested persons who ask with "a synopsis of my background: that my dad was third generation Japanese American and my mom is third generation Ukrainian American." Nancy's choice of past tense when talking about her father's ancestry (he is very much alive) is perhaps indicative of her view of her father and his family as assimilated. Throughout her narrative, she discusses her father's lack of interest in sharing his racial heritage and ancestry with her, indeed, his very inability to do so because of how assimilated his family had become over generations. The assimilation of her paternal family is evident to Nancy, since her father and paternal grandparents do not speak Japanese, and because most of her aunts and uncles have interracially married with whites. Why, then, does Nancy identify as Asian American when her Ukrainian ancestry provides her with some meaning and her Japanese ancestry has so little? Her subjectivity as non-white or Japanese emerged from a variety of factors, including the association of whiteness with oppressiveness.

WHITENESS AS OPPRESSIVE, PATRIARCHAL, AND DISCRIMINATORY

In the women's stories, the negative evaluation or stigmatization of whiteness is furthered through an association of whiteness with a history of violence and oppression. These women reject their white ancestry and culture because of their interpretation of this culture, and their ancestors, as racist, patriarchal, and discriminatory. Their narratives reveal that this negative characterization also captures, for them, the attitudes and behaviors of most whites.

Because white and non-white are oppositional categories in our American culture, non-whiteness for women is perceived and discussed using positive attributes: spiritual, caring, and nurturing. Once again, we see the traditional characterization of dichotomous categories and identities embraced, although the evaluation of each is reversed. For example, Kelley, whose father is Mexican American and whose mother is white, "loves" her father's culture more than her mother's Anglo culture because of the "spiritual side of it . . . the women in the culture are very giving, loving, and want to heal and embrace people." While not explicitly saying so, her construction of Mexican American culture as nurturing and spiritual is based on the assumption that whiteness (and specifically white femaleness) is the opposite.

The oppressive nature of whiteness is supported through personal stories of racism and prejudice that mixed-race women or their families encounter. Stories of discrimination or racism are part of the larger picture of whiteness as oppressive and whites as the oppressors. Marsha, whose mother is white and whose father is Japanese, relays a story about her mother as an example of the biases and inability of whites to understand the experiences of non-whites:

I have a younger sister who is adopted. . . . And my mother tells a story about how the social worker called her before the adoption and said, because she knew she had a half Asian daughter, and said to her, "Marlene, I want to give you a hypothetical situation. If you had two baby girls, equally healthy, equally beautiful or were equally healthy anyway, and one was Chinese and one was Caucasian, which one would you choose?" And my mother looked at me and she said, "I told her the Caucasian baby because you know I wanted your brother to have a normal family." Yeah, right. But my mother couldn't understand why that was painful.

While Marsha acknowledges that she is "half Asian," she also discursively places herself securely within the borders of non-whiteness in her story through connecting "normal" with "white." Whiteness is associated with her mother. Marsha's identification as "half Asian," as opposed to "half white," is a way of positioning herself oppositionally to her mother. Both Marsha and her mother use the construction of difference, albeit in different ways. Her mother's understanding of difference is one of deviance and abnormality. Marsha rejects this evaluation

through her implicit critique of her mother's logic in telling the story.

Her focus on her mother's and other whites' insensitivity is another mechanism by which she constructs herself in opposition to her mother and therefore whiteness. Throughout Marsha's narrative, she attempts to align herself with her Japanese American father through shared experiences with racism and their mutual assessment of whites as insensitive. For example, Marsha and her father have termed her mother's insensitivity to racial issues as "her clumsiness": "I think I've come to realize more than anything else, it was her inability to be empathetic, her clumsiness, and some bias that most, I think, white people have."

What is key in Marsha's discussion of the problems she encounters when interacting with her mother is the characterization of all whites as biased. Mixed-race women share a view of whites as biased and prejudiced by virtue of their social location in the racial hierarchy. Definitional boundaries of racial categories include assumptions and knowledge about which positions carry more privilege than other positions. Mixed-race women, particularly those who had more difficulty passing as white, are conscious of racial privilege either through their own experiences with discrimination or through the experiences of their non-white family members. The women in this study differentiate themselves from whites on the basis of oppression. In their family and personal experiences, whites are stigmatized as the oppressors. Given the dichotomous construction of racial boundaries, women portrayed non-whites in a contrasting manner by highlighting positive cultural characteristics.

The women's constructions of racial boundaries reflect their perceptions of the differing beliefs and interests among racial groups. In most cases, these perceptions are constructed from broad generalizations and, in some cases, they incorporate racial stereotypes. The positive characterization of non-white cultures and communities is common among women in this study, although they use different stereotypes to represent each group. Women with Mexican American ancestry often refer to the strength of the family and tradition in their positive characterization of Mexican culture, while women with Native American ancestry highlight spirituality and communal values with Native American culture. As an example, Joyce, whose father is Native American, relays a story about her father's assistance to an elderly, handicapped woman to illustrate this link:

My father planted gardens in her yard, and I would go with him and work in the garden, and then they would have vegetables and so would we. And he had a communal and not an individualistic sense that I think most of the American people just don't have. I think this "me" stuff has gotten out of hand. And the community aspect I think is something I got from him.

The positive characterization of non-white cultures is posited in contrast to the patriarchal and oppressive nature the women associate with whiteness. For example, Julia provides the following assessment of "Anglo culture":

Culturally, I was raised as an Anglo. . . . And all the different ways that patriarchy can make women suffer, I've suffered from. So I have no love for the white culture. I despise what it does for people. I despise the fact that it's carried over to other countries and held up as this great imperial thing that other countries should drop their culture for.

Associating patriarchy and colonialism with whiteness is again discursively dependent upon associating victimization and egalitarianism with non-white communities and groups. While this identification highlights the relationship between non-white and white, between privilege and oppression, it also reduces and reifies "white culture" and "non-white culture" to singular and unified entities.

Through such dichotomous characterizations, these women fail to recognize the critique of patriarchy, voiced by women of color, which exists within communities of "difference." The very construction of difference results in the dichotomous nature of the two characterizations, restricting more complex pictures of either community from developing.

The construction of whiteness as both empty and oppressive is not imposed upon these women. They actively construct a sense of whiteness that is diametrically opposed to their non-white ancestry through a focus on difference. Yet difference is rearticulated in positive ways which

helps create meaning used in fashioning their identities.

That such reversal of the meaning of difference occurs at all is perhaps due in large part to the need and desire of individuals to belong. The construction of difference reinforces group boundaries and meets identity needs by providing women with clear boundaries, a sense of belonging, in short, a "homeplace" (Lugones 1993). Like Bernstein's (1995) young white teens, non-whiteness provides the substance from which one can glean meaning. Mixed-race women's claims of difference do not reject or deny group difference as much as they seek a different standard of evaluation. Their claims of difference maintain the focus on racial differences in terms of physical appearance, culture, values, and personalities, but challenge the assessment of it. Difference is no longer perceived as deviant or deficient, but something that is highly prized. Thus, difference through non-white ancestry is embraced because it is psychologically fulfilling for these women, particularly when the construction of whiteness is stigmatized.

While the purpose of this article is to examine racial identity work on the part of mixed-race women, the fact that women make up the sample begs for some comment on the gendered nature of racial identity. I can only speculate on differences between mixed-race men and women's subjectivities, given that I have collected and analyzed only women's narratives, but others have suggested that there may be gender differences. The gendered division of labor that primarily relegates "kin work" to women in our society suggests that women may play a more active role as primary agents of racialization (Di Leonardo 1987). Given women's responsibility for "kin work," it comes as no surprise that women play a larger or more active role than men in the construction, maintenance, and transmission of ethnic identities (Alba 1990; Stoller 1996).

Some researchers have found gender differences in racial identities, as well. For example, Fine and Bowers (1984) argue that men are more likely to identify with higher status groups while women are more likely to identify with lower status groups. In studies of monoracial identity, scholars have consistently found that male children prefer to identify with higher status groups.

As an example, in doll studies, black boys prefer the white doll more than do black girls and are more likely to ascribe positive characteristics to it (Mahan 1976). A common explanation for male's preference to identify with higher status groups is that men are expected and encouraged to strive toward mobility while girls are not (Fine and Bowers 1984). Applied to mixed-race identity, it would be expected that mixed-race men would identify more with their white heritage, a dominant and higher status group, than their non-white heritage. Women, on the other hand, would be expected to identify less with their dominant white ancestry and more with their non-white ancestry.

The findings of this study, that mixed-race women identify with their non-white heritage, seems to conform with this pattern, but I find the status explanation insufficient. Mixed-race women identify as non-white because it provides them with meaning and because whiteness is stigmatized (framed, of course, by external categorization and racial ideologies). In other words, women identify as non-white not because they have a propensity to identify with low-status groups, but because non-whiteness is one avenue through which women can glean meaning given their stigmatization of whiteness.

Another possible explanation for the finding that race and ethnicity is less important for men is the multiple avenues available to men to attain meaning and self-construction. Racial identity is part of a larger set of interconnected subjectivities, all of which provide individuals with meaning. I suspect that for some individuals, male and female alike, racial identity is a more central component of their self-concept than other aspects like occupation, not because of some psychological tendency to identify with stigmatized groups, but because of the existing barriers to identify in other ways. Traditionally for women, central sites of identity have been those in the private sphere—as mothers, daughters, and wives—despite their participation and influence in the public realm. Men's identities have been focused in the public sphere, primarily occupational constructions of self. This is not to suggest that ethnicity or race is unimportant in men's constructions of self; only that, in terms of a hierarchy of salience, they may be less

important than other facets of one's identity. The same is true for women. Women are not simply racialized subjects. They too have multiple sites of identity that are interrelated. Race may be simply more salient for many women because they are traditionally primary agents of "kin work" and have limited opportunities for other avenues of identity.

Now let us consider how women position themselves with non-white racial boundaries. Mixed-race women's identity work provides a clear depiction of how individuals negotiate racial matters given their racially mixed ancestry and, in the case of many women, their ability to pass as white. Unlike others more firmly entrenched within racial boundaries, mixed-race women's identities as women of color are not always affirmed. Because mixed-race women's racial self-image often contradicts dominant boundary markers, they engage in more conscious actions and identity work through their everyday talk and interactions. The following section reveals the work of identity as women manage their potentially spoiled identities (because of their white racial ancestry) while embedded within a larger dominant framework and sense-making about race.

IDENTITY WORK

One of the major contributions of sociological research on race has been the emphasis on macro forces and differential power in shaping the formation of racial categories, meanings, and identities. For example, the work of Espiritu (1992), Lee (1993), and Omi and Winant (1986) has revealed the role of social movements, the state, and its institutions in forming dominant understandings of race. On the other hand, while emphasizing how social structure shapes identity, we have tended to neglect how racial identities are not simply imposed on individuals, but are achieved through interaction, presentation, and manipulation. Ponse (1978, p. 208) describes identity work as "the processes and procedures engaged in by groups designed to effect change in the meanings of particular identities." While Ponse's research focuses on the identity work of lesbians, her attention to the process of "becoming" a particular identity is helpful in understanding how individuals and groups challenge and change the meaning of racialized identities. Whiteness becomes something that mixed-race women reject because of their stigmatization of it at the same time that they negotiate for more inclusive boundaries of non-whiteness. This requires identity work. The identity work of individuals entails the use of racial narratives, symbols, and processes to inform themselves and others of their racial belonging. The identity work of mixed-race women I interviewed is especially evident given that much of the taken-for-granted symbols of racial group membership (e.g., skin color) must be challenged.

Visibility and Passing

According to Goffman (1963), since there are rewards associated with being identified as "normal," persons who can pass as such will do so in certain situations. While we can only guess at the incidence of persons of color passing as white, there is sufficient anecdotal evidence that such passing has and continues to occur. The concept of passing has focused on passing into a "normal" and thus more privileged group. If one takes a more inclusive definition of passing (i.e., passing through all racial boundaries), we could argue that, given estimates that 75 to 80 percent of blacks are products of miscegenation (Poe 1993), the vast majority of blacks are in fact passing as black. Recall that the mixed-race women in this study identified as persons of color. The concept of passing, as employed in this article, does not assume a real essence, identity, or racial self that women must reject. Instead, passing refers to a process of interaction by which women shape their identities for themselves and others in ways that contest their positioning by dominant racial standards as white.

Some mixed-race women pass into non-white boundaries with ease, while others have a much more difficult time. Goffman's (1963) differentiation between stigmatized individuals whose identities are discredited and those that are discreditable is helpful in understanding the different experiences of mixed-race women. Persons who are discreditable are those whose different-

ness from normals is not immediately visible or known. Multiracial women who can and have passed as non-white fall into this category. Like other potentially discreditable identities, mixed-race women must protect the discovery of their stigma—in this case, their whiteness. A common tactic women employ is to avoid the discovery of their stigma by highlighting cultural and physical signs of belonging. For some women, this means wearing "ethnic" looking clothes and jewelry. For others this means wearing their hair in a particular style.

Through this identity work, mixed-race women attempt to convey social information concerning their racial group membership and identity through public symbols. For example, Ellen, who identified as African American but who also cited white ancestry, claimed that others often characterized here as having "good hair," which for her symbolized their suspicion of her authenticity as a member of the black community. Ellen explains how she tried to pass physical criteria of belonging imposed upon her by others: "I would try to look black. . . . I always wanted to show my ethnicity so I would wear the braids because that was me, that was all part of me." For Ellen, wearing braids was a symbol of the blackness that resided in her—a blackness she wanted others to see and validate. Her braids were one of the physical ways in which she attempted to avoid the discovery of her whiteness.

Another strategy employed by the discreditable is selective disclosure of one's mixed-race ancestry. Ellen uses the technique and generally fails to disclose her mixed-race ancestry unless otherwise challenged. In the following example, she describes such an encounter:

This young mother came in here and she asked me, "What are you?" And I said, "I'm black, just as you are." And she said, "You look like something else; are you something else?" And I said, "Well white, just as much as you are" because she's mixed, too. She said, "I don't think you're black." And I wondered why. Is it because I speak better English. Is that what makes me so different? Or is it the clothes that I wear that makes me different? Or is it because I'm a professional? What does she mean I'm not as black or I shouldn't be black? I thought she was rude . . . maybe my hair is not as nappy but I still feel, I still feel it in my heart, it's running through my blood.

This story captures how mixed-race women must pass "racial litmus tests," methods members of groups use to help distinguish members from nonmembers, the authentic from the fake (Anzaldua 1990; Korgen 1998). At times, Ellen succeeds in passing as black, while at other times, much like the incident shared above, her identity as black is challenged. She contests this provocation by pointing out that her challenger, despite her apparently more "authentic appearance," was also racially mixed, not unlike the vast majority of African Americans.

Another group of mixed-race women, those who possess undesired traits easily identified as "normal" by "normals," would be defined as discredited. In this case, mixed-race women who have difficulty passing as non-white are discredited. Such individuals manage their spoiled identities in different ways through the use of invisible symbols of belongings and biographical constructions.

For example, Tammy, whose father is Native American and whose mother is white, began to consciously identify as Native American in her early twenties. She discovered that others often would challenge her identity as such because of the incongruency between her physical features and her identity. As a result of this discrepancy, she never felt comfortable with her physical appearance. In describing her desires to look more like her identity, she uses my physical features as a measure:

When I was growing up, I certainly knew I wasn't beautiful or cute or pretty. I always wanted to be very tall. I wanted to have long, dark hair like you have, only longer. All my life, that's what I wanted. In fact, you look much more Native American than Asian. And so I think you look more like I would like to have looked like all my life rather than who I do look like.

Tammy accomplishes two feats through this discursive act. First, Tammy revealed the internalization of narrow racial boundaries for Native American ancestry by describing her desires to physically approximate the ideal—being tall with long, dark hair. Second by positioning me

panethnically as "Asian," she effectively ignores and rejects my racially mixed heritage of Japanese and white.

Tammy's discomfort with her physical appearance is directly connected to the reception she receives from many Native Americans. Tammy complained that people make judgments and decisions about her membership based on her physical appearance. Her response is evident in the following statement:

If I could be born again. I'd like to be born more visibly Indian. I think it's one of the reasons I finally decided I wanted to be thought of as more Indian that I kept my hair black for about fifteen years. It was one attempt to try to move into what I thought would help me be more readily visible and more accepted. That was when I was in college and I dyed my hair black because that's how I wanted to identify. And that's also how I wanted others to identify me.

While Tammy managed her discredited identity through trying to approximate the ideal physical construction of Native Americans, others, including Tammy at a later age, manage their spoiled identities in other ways through the use of invisible symbols of belonging and biographical constructions, which I explore in more detail below.

Thus, depending on whether the women's non-white racial ancestry is visible, passing is more or less easy. Because these women identify whiteness in negative ways, passing entails concealing their stigmatized attribute (their white ancestry) or alternatively emphasizing the symbols associated with non-whiteness. The women interviewed in this study attempt to pass, use symbolic markers, and manipulate their histories in such a way as to better position themselves as "authentic" members of recognizable non-white groups.

These women establish non-white identities in two major ways: through the emphasis of biological markers of difference or by eliciting and using cultural symbols associated with their non-white ancestry. While some of the women use these discursive mechanisms in their identity work simultaneously, passing via cultural symbols is a more viable option for those whose stigmatized attribute of whiteness is less visible.

Structurally, both forms of identity work share a common basis in racial essentialism.

THE IDEOLOGY OF RACIAL ESSENTIALISM

Social scientists have disregarded biological notions of race while emphasizing the social construction of racial boundaries and meanings. However, the lay public has failed to make this ideological shift. This failure is evident in the narratives of mixed-race women in this study. The mixed-race respondents discursively construct their own racial subjectivities through the lens of essentialism. Essentialism is the belief in the real, invariable, fixed, essence of things (Fuss 1989). Racial essentialism is the belief that races are real, invariable, immutable, fixed, natural, and empirical (Omi and Winant 1986; Shanklin 1994). This dominant racial ideology is significant because it provides the foundations upon which the mixed-race women in this study can legitimately construct their racial identities—for themselves and often for others. Ironically, the biologically erroneous essentialist assumptions that help them to locate themselves within non-white boundaries, coupled with many women's ability to pass as white, may ultimately have the effect of widening racial borders. I return to this potential in the conclusion of the article.

Because race is assumed to be essential and biologically grounded, these women search their past and present for indicators and proof of what they believe to be their racial essence. This often entails a quest to find a self that is racially and culturally pure, although the indicators of such vary by individuals. For some, the proof and clues of one's race rest on culture—behaviors and celebrations associated with a particular racial group. Others focus their identity work on biological markers. Because discovering one's racial essence through biological markers is the more common strategy employed in their identity work, I explore this discursive strategy more closely. Skin color or shade is the definitive signifier of racial essence, although other physical markers such as hair texture, hair color, and facial features are also important. Still others privilege physical markers that are unseen—in the form of genes, blood, or bones.

PRIVILEGING THE VISIBLE: SKIN COLOR, FACIAL FEATURES, AND HAIR

Visual presentations of self help to identify, to oneself and others, one's legitimacy as a member of a social group (Stone 1962). Physical features have particularly prevalent use in the construction of racial identities and borders. The use of visible physical markers to position individuals within an American racial schema is a common feature in mixed-race women's narratives, framed as they are by larger and dominant racial ideologies. In the following discussion, Tracey, whose mother is Japanese and whose father is African American, reveals how others try to interpret her various physical features in relation to dominant ideas about racial boundaries:

People will say, "Well your hair is black, your skin is a brown color, and you've got a round face, but you also have a flat nose." The nose is what really throws people off because that's the part of me that's very African American. And I'm also kind of short and stocky.

The use of hair color and texture, skin color, and facial features to differentiate between people has a long history in racial taxonomies. Like most people, Tracey incorporates these notions in her own sense-making about race by identifying her nose and stature as African American. This was a common mechanism employed by mixed-race women as they constructed themselves as non-white. These women align themselves with their non-white heritage by identifying physical signs of difference that link them to their non-white family members.

For some of these women, physical features are not always immediately apparent, but are discovered later in life. This later discovery is also characterized by women as essentially rooted and, in their perspective, simply requiring more time to "naturally" develop. Kate, whose mother is white and whose father is believed to be black, was adopted at a very young age. On her birth certificate, she was initially identified as Caucasian, but, at the age of three, upon developing physical signs that positioned her as black, her birth certificate was changed to read "black American":

At about the age of three or three and a half, the obvious started happening. My hair started kinking up a little bit, they noticed my skin was not much darker but a little bit darker. And the records indicate that my birth mother was blond and blue eyed and so I think they had figured out that obviously she had had a relationship with somebody other than a Euroamerican.

Because Kate's birth mother did not reveal the race of the biological father, the only evidence of what is perceived as her racial essence was the developing physical markers of blackness.

The role of the state in legitimizing racial groups and identities has been amply documented in the literature (Lee 1993; Omi and Winant 1986). A key facet of this categorization and legitimization occurs by the U.S. Census. Lee's (1993) analysis of U.S. census categories reveals the federal conceptualization of races as mutually exclusive categories based on notions of racial purity. Kate's experiences with her birth certificate, the very fact that she must be racially categorized using the state's racial schema, illustrate both the state's conceptualization of race and its role in the racialization process. The state's construction and legitimization establishes mutually exclusive racial boundaries on ancestral grounds. When these are unavailable, physical features are assumed to be visible reflections of biological essences.

Skin color is the most salient physical trait employed to position people racially, but other physical traits—such as facial features, hair color and texture, and facial shape—are also commonly employed. The women's narratives reveal the historical legacy of some of the earliest racial taxonomies that employed similar criteria to construct racial boundaries and groups. The reoccurring reference to visible signs in the women's narratives reveals the widespread dissemination of essentialist racial logic.

Privileging skin color and other physical markers as the definitive signifiers of difference naturalizes race and racial categories. Women who use this strategy recount multiple incidents in which physical markers are used by both themselves and others to position them within the existing racial order. For the most part, women who use this discursive strategy do not and, according to them, cannot "pass" as white.

Privileging the Invisible: Genes, Blood, and Bones

Those who privilege unseen physical markers tend to be women with white ancestry who are light complected (i.e., the "discredited"). Women who emphasize this discursive strategy to constitute their racial identity experienced multiple problems of acceptance by communities of color because of their light skin, their ability to pass as white, and their seemingly contradictory identification as non-white.

Three of the women I interviewed did not "discover" their non-white racial heritage until they were adults. Through their narratives, they discuss what they believe to be signs of their non-white racial ancestry that were scattered throughout their life, many of which are tied to the women's beliefs about biological notions of racial essences. Julia, who is "one-fourth Norwegian, one-fourth Irish, one-fourth Welsh, and one-fourth Puerto Rican," identifies very strongly with both her Welsh and Puerto Rican ancestry. This dual identification is linked through her belief that both are "minority" cultures:

My grandmother was Welsh. The English call the Welsh the niggers of England. And they don't like them because they're dark skinned and have thick accents and could never be controlled by the English. They're very different people from the English and the Scottish and the Irish. And my grandfather was Puerto Rican and very dark skinned. I mean you could tell that he was part African American by the way he looked.

Not only are Julia's two "minority" cultures linked together by a common racial epithet, but their physical difference and commonality of darker skin color ties them together. Both Welsh and Puerto Rican are, for Julia, essentially different than the rest of her European ancestry, and this difference rests in the skin.

Despite her multiple experiences with being perceived by others as white, and even though she had only learned of her Puerto Rican ancestry at the age of 18, Julia identifies as Puerto Rican by using the most explicit form of essentialism in her theory of "race memory":

I just think that in my genes and my genetic code are also snippets and bits and pieces of the genetics of all the people who come before me in my line. And I think that those snippets and pieces carry memory with them that can be accessed and that things will trigger that. I truly believe that. And I think that's what race memory is.

Julia believes that race memory holds "snippets and bits and pieces" of genetic information ranging from walking style to food preferences to dancing abilities. For example, she believes her preference for certain kinds of Latin American music (Cubano and Puerto Rican as opposed to Mexican music) is due to race memory linked to her Puerto Rican ancestry.

While Julia's discovery and "proof" of her Puerto Ricanness is revealed through certain preferences and ways of acting, proof also materializes for her in the form of her grandfather's naturalization and immigration papers. Material proof of her ancestry is so important to Julia that she carries her grandfather's papers with her so she can "pull them out when people would question the fact that I don't call myself white."

While Julia's identity work is the most explicit form of essentialist thought encountered in this study, other women apply the same logic in more subtle ways. Women with Native American ancestry regularly use biological notions of race in their narratives, albeit less explicitly. They use blood as the metaphor for biology. Women with Native American ancestry quickly cite their percentage of Indian blood and/or discuss their enrollment status. For example, Joyce locates herself within the racial boundary of Native American during her description of her family's history by using the metaphor of blood: "So, evidently my grandfather was three-quarter Native American. And I had always identified with my father, although I didn't look like him." In this quote, it is clear that, for Joyce, biology is invisible and located in one's blood, rather than visibly present in one's skin color.

Joyce's focus on blood as the location of one's race rather than skin color was challenged during a meeting where her race and identity were contested. In the following narrative, Joyce describes her experience as a board member of a social service organization in which there was discussion about the need for Native American representation:

A member of the board said, "Well, we have someone who's part Native American." And then we had this big lecture about how I am not Native American because I'm not enrolled in a tribe and I shouldn't say that I am which I had always been very careful not to say. And it was extremely painful for me. . . . I know there are a lot of people running around wanting to be Indian. I can understand that. So I've been very careful. And yet I resent it. I can't help it if my hair is straight but is not straight black. So my red skin is in little red dots all over my arms instead of one blotch.

As this passage reveals, biologically based racial thinking is a discursive strategy employed by all three participants in this encounter. Joyce, her fellow board member, and the director call upon biological ideas to position people within and outside the group boundary of Native American, although in different ways. For the board member, this is evident in her acknowledgment of Joyce's partial Native Americanness. Assessing Joyce as part Native American rests on a belief in racial purity—the converse of which is the belief in racial mixtures, quarters, and other proportions. As for the director, she too employs biological criteria of belonging with her focus on enrollment status. The enrollment of Native Americans is based on the belief in blood quantum or degree of Indian blood. The federal government's Indian identification policy stems from the 1887 General Allotment Act in which individuals who could document one half or more Indian blood were entitled to receive land parcels (Jaimes 1992). To evoke criteria of enrollment is to evoke biological criteria based on blood.

Finally, Joyce attempts to use her visible physical features as proof of her innate Native American essence while at the same time recognizing that they fail to pass the "racial litmus test" imposed on her by others. Physical signs of Native Americanness resulted in the assessment of her "little red dots" as insignificant, requiring instead, "one blotch" of redness. Joyce's despair that her visible physical features did not coincide with her "Indian blood" reveals the multiple uses of biological markers of difference.

Through talk of blood, genes, or biology, some of these women are able to position themselves and others in non-white racialized groups despite their physical appearance. For other women, beliefs about biological essences and group belonging are manifest in physical features. Whether women use invisible or visible physical signs in their construction and discovery of racial essences, their non-white racial identities rest on their abilities to construct a coherent life story in ways that provide evidence, to themselves and others, of their inherent and lifelong racial belonging. It is the construction of a seemingly integrated and stable racial self, rooted in essentialist discourse, which I turn to next.

Construction of Continuity: Racial Histories as Coherent, Consistent, and Stable

A central theme in the women's identity work (and of essentialist racial thought) is the construction of continuity—reconstructing one's experiences and identity in such a way as to impose a coherent and continuous racial essence. These women construct a stable identity through their narratives by depicting a relatively fixed racial identity through time. For example, Joyce constructs a sense of consistency in her life as a Native American by employing a childhood memory. Evidence of her Native Americanness resides in her childhood rage toward injustice:

I remember in the fourth grade when we would read; people would call on you to read. I guess the teacher would pick the first person and they would read and then they would choose someone else. And no one wanted to choose these two little girls. They were little girls who were, one was not poor but she had moved from a Northern state and she dressed and talked differently, and kids can be really cruel. And the other one was very, very poor. And I remember I would take turns calling on them so they wouldn't be the last one to read everyday. I just remember at the time I thought it was an awful thing for a teacher to do.

Joyce's example from her own childhood is typical of women's identity work. In stories about the past, women create continuity with what they believe to be their racial essence. Joyce's personal response to this injustice is another example of how she links herself innately to Native Americans through her positive characterization

of Native Americans. Joyce's subtle description of the loving and communal nature of Native Americans is a quality that she argues she exhibited at an early age, evidenced by her response to the young girls who were excluded by others. By linking their own contemporary personalities and politics to their childhood stories of self, nonwhite parents, or ancestors, these women naturalize the invisible signs of belonging. Like skin color, these women believe values and personalities are naturally and essentially rooted.

This relationship between beliefs about racial essentialism and the racial identities they signify is the foundation of the women's narratives, and it reflects dominant ideologies of race. The women's identities are characterized by coherence and consistency through chains of experience that are viewed as leading to a particular racialized identity. Through this work, women reaffirm their racial identity, not only essentially so, but always essentially so.

The construction of racial coherence and essence requires the resolution of inconsistencies in the women's narratives. Inconsistencies include periods of time in the women's lives when affirmation (external and internal) of one's racial essence was absent, as well as periods of time in women's lives during which their perceived racial essence was unknown, ignored, or not acted upon. A significant way in which the women resolve these inconsistencies is to construct an inner racial essence and feelings of intuition. For example, Kelley, who discovered her Mexican American heritage as an adult, argues that she always knew intuitively of her Mexican ancestry:

One time I was with my father, and we were in the basement, and I remember one time finding a crucifix in the basement. I was four years old. I remember that. And it's like I'm a four-year-old kid, but I mean I remember it; it seemed intuitively right.

This passage reveals both the discovery of her heritage, symbolized materially in the form of a crucifix, a symbol of Mexicanness for her, and her intuitive understanding of what that means for her. For Kelley, finding a crucifix is symbolic of her discovery of her Mexican American ancestry, and, through this story, she develops a sense of continuity. She always knew she was Mexican American, although not consciously so.

The inconsistencies between essentialist racial beliefs and the women's discussion of time periods in their lives that were notably void of non-white identity are dismissed as aberrations in their otherwise consistent racial identities. In this essentialist framework, race is viewed as inherent and unchanging throughout the life course—although at times the consciousness of race is intuitive and not fully explored or acted upon. The women's racial biographies are constructed in ways that diminish or neglect the process of becoming or developing a racial identity; instead, they focus on discovering the racial essence that they think is innately, permanently present.

CONCLUSION

While institutional forces constrain and shape individual identities, this research reveals how misleading it is to characterize identity formation as simply a process of external categorization and constraint. The construction and deployment of identities are always embedded within relations of power, but ethnicity and race are "an acquired and used feature of human identity, available for employment . . . and subject to presentation, inhibition, manipulation, and exploitation" (Lyman and Douglas 1973, p. 351). Individuals and groups are active agents in the contestation and construction of racial categories and identities. Mixed-race women reveal this agency as they contest their racial positioning and the dominant negative evaluation of non-whiteness. Women identify as non-white and reverse the stigma, through their negative characterization of whiteness. Given this construction and many women's ability to pass as white, women's identity work takes the form of highlighting symbols associated with their non-whiteness through essentialist means.

We should be careful not to misinterpret the finding in this study that mixed-race women identify with their non-white ancestry by relying on developmental models of biracial identity. Psychological models of racial identity identify developmental stages that biracial and multiracial Americans progress through, beginning with a

stage of confusion, moving to dissonance, and finally to self-acceptance as biracial or multiracial (Jacobs 1992; Kich 1992; Kerwin 1991; Poston 1990). Because the mixed-race women in this sample do not identify as biracial or multiracial, psychological theorists of development might argue that they simply have not reached the final stage of racial identity. My data, interpreted through a symbolic interactionist perspective, indicate that because they identify as non-white for meaningful purposes, they will not progress to a biracial identity unless there are structural changes that help make a biracial category and identity as meaningful as non-white categories and identities currently are for them. If these women come to identify as biracial, this identity shift will be due to macro changes in racial ideologies and micro level processes of interaction, rather than to natural, progressive, developmental stages. In accord with symbolic interactionist theory, this study reveals the process of becoming particular identities rather than assuming a natural development toward racial identity. This is not to say that these women have not experienced developmental changes in their identities, but that there is no inherent natural order or meaning to the identities that women fashion in the sense of stages.

The identity work displayed by respondents in this study reinforces Goffman's premise that nothing is inherently stigmatized. Moreover, their identity work reveals the ways in which individuals can challenge racial stigmas through reversing what has historically been stigmatized—racial mixing and non-whiteness. At the same time, this research extends Goffman's work and other empirical examinations of stigma by taking into consideration more than face-to-face interactions and the discourse of individuals in the construction of stigma. This study illustrates how individuals must deal with macro forces that shape and limit identity options and define stigma. These women are successful in stigmatizing whiteness and, in many ways, positioning themselves within non-white borders because of larger cultural narratives concerning race relations and racial ideologies. Their creativity is evident in the way they employ dominant ideas of racial essentialism in their identity work, thereby making their racial identities more secure than the identities that Bernstein's (1995) white teens articulate. These mixed-race women can more legitimately claim, given the continued use and strength of racial essentialist thought, their non-white racial identities, despite their physical appearance.

In addition, the racial politics of the contemporary moment help facilitate the women's stigmatization of whiteness. One of the legacies of the Civil Rights Movement has been the incorporation of different perspectives and voices in college curriculums, affirmative action, and identity politics. While there is certainly a backlash against these changes, there is also the competing narrative that emphasizes past and present racial oppression and disadvantage experienced by non-whites. It is within these important contexts that the women are able to reverse the stigma of whiteness and locate themselves within non-white borders. The narratives of mixed-race women in this study illustrate that a full understanding of racial identity requires attention to both micro and macro social processes.

The theoretical implications of my findings go beyond the individual need for belonging, and they have the potential to reshape how we think about race and racial categories. The women's identity work conforms to dominant racial ideologies of essentialism, yet they also challenge racial boundaries through their self-inclusion. Discredited mixed-race women whose racial identities are inconsistent with physical characteristics associated with racial groups pose the most challenge to racial boundaries. But the respondents in this study are not the only ones who are challenging racial meanings. In some ways, the women's actions parallel the multiracial social movement that is occurring nationally. This larger movement attempts to shift racially mixed persons from a stigmatized category to one that is legitimately recognized and positively affirmed by the public. The key theme, which ties these two discursive projects together, is the search for and construction of racial meaning. While multiracial activists find their identity in the articulation of a new racial label and community, the mixed-race women in this sample find it by embracing an already constructed racial community

and subjectivity—their non-white ancestry. Both paths require identity work and a shifting of racial boundaries. For multiracial activists, the boundaries are shifted by adding another racial category, thereby moving from a system with four racial categories to one with five. For the women in this study, their identity work challenges racial boundaries by broadening them to include women like themselves. Both employ essentialism, and both discursive processes reject normative and dominant models of racial stigmatization, but in significantly different ways. Multiracial activists reject their invisibility, while individual women interviewed in this sample reverse dominant racial stigma. Neither form of identity work transpires in isolation from larger macro processes. Likewise, each form of identity work has different, yet unknown, potential in shaping dominant conceptions of race.

NOTES

1. See Daniels (1992) for an excellent historical review of passing.

2. The majority of those who selected the "other" category in the U.S. census are Latinos. Rodriguez and Guzman (1992) estimate that 40 percent of Hispanics classified themselves as "other" in both the 1980 and 1990 U.S. Census. This high proportion is likely due to the federal government's classification system that recognizes Hispanics as an ethnic, not a racial category. Another possible explanation is that many Hispanics recognize their multiple racial ancestries. In addition to the large number of Hispanics who claim the "other" category are those who are biracial or multiracial and who reject the dichotomous racial classification system of the U.S. government.

3. According to Raiskin (1994), this term is attributed to Abdul R. JanMohamed.

REFERENCES

ALBA, RICHARD. 1990. *Ethnic Identity: The Transformation of White America.* New Haven, CT: Yale University Press.

ANZALDUA, GLORIA. 1990. "En Rapport, In Opposition: Cobrando Cuentas a Las Nuestros." Pp. 142–49 in *Making Face, Making Soul,* edited by Gloria Anzaldua. San Francisco: Aunt Lute.

BERNSTEIN, NELL. 1995. "Goin' Gangsta, Choosin' Cholita." *Utne Reader,* March/April: 87–90.

DANIELS, G. REGINALD. 1992. "Passers and Pluralists: Subverting the Racial Divide." Pp. 91–107 in *Racially Mixed People in America,* edited by Maria P.P. Root. Newbury Park, CA: Sage.

DAVIS, F. JAMES. 1991. *Who Is Black? One Nation's Definition.* University Park, PA: Pennsylvania State University Press.

DI LEONARDO, MICALA. 1987. *The Varieties of Ethnic Experience: Kinship, Class, and Gender Among California Italian-Americans.* Ithaca: Cornell University Press.

ESPIRITU, YEN. 1992. *Asian American Panethnicity: Bridging Institutions and Identities.* Philadelphia: Temple University Press.

FERNANDEZ, CARLOS. 1992. "La Raza and the Melting Pot: A Comparative Look at Multiraciality." Pp. 126–43 in *Racially Mixed People in America,* edited by Maria P.P. Root. Newbury Park, CA: Sage.

FINE, MICHELLE and CHERYL BOWERS. 1984. "Racial Self-Identification: The Effects of Social History and Gender." *Journal of Applied Social Psychology* 14:136–46.

FLAGG, BARBARA. 1993. "'Was Blind, But Now I See': White Race Consciousness and the Requirement of Discriminatory Intent." *Michigan Law Review* 91:953–1017.

FRANKENBERG, RUTH. 1993. *White Women, Race Matters: The Social Construction of Whiteness.* Minnesota: University of Minnesota Press.

FRANKENBERG, RUTH. 1997. "Introduction: Local Whitenesses, Localizing Whiteness." Pp. 1–34 in *Displacing Whiteness: Essays in Social and Cultural Criticism,* edited by Ruth Frankenberg. Durham: Duke University Press.

FUSS, DIANA. 1989. *Essentially Speaking: Feminism, Nature, and Difference.* New York: Routledge.

GALLAGHER, CHARLES A. 1995. "White Reconstruction in the University." *Socialist Review* 24:165–87.

GANS, HERBERT. 1979. "Symbolic Ethnicity: The Future of Ethnic Groups and Cultures in America." *Ethnic and Racial Studies* 2:1–18.

GOFFMAN, ERVING. 1963. *Stigma: Notes on the Management of Spoiled Identity.* Englewood Cliffs, NJ: Prentice-Hall.

JACOBS, JAMES. H. 1992. "Identity Development in Biracial Children." Pp. 190–206 in *Racially Mixed People in America,* edited by Maria P.P. Root. Newbury Park: Sage.

JAIMES, ANNETTE. 1992. "Federal Indian Identification Policy: A Usurpation of Indigenous Sovereignty in North America." Pp. 123–38 in *The State of Native America,* edited by M. Annette Jaimes. Boston: South End Press.

KICH, GEORGE KITAHARA. 1992. "The Developmental Process of Asserting a Biracial Bicultural Identity." Pp. 304–17 in *Racially Mixed People in America,* edited by Maria P.P. Root Newbury Park: Sage.

KERWIN, CHRISTINE. 1991. "Racial Identity Development in Biracial Children of Black/White Racial Heritage." Ph.D. dissertation, Department of Psychology, Fordham University.

KORGEN, KATHLEEN ODELL. 1998. *From Black to Biracial: Transforming Racial Identity Among Americans.* Westport, CT: Praeger.

LEE, SHARON M. 1993. "Racial Classification in the U.S. Census: 1890–1990." *Ethnic and Racial Studies* 16:81–84.

LIPSITZ, GEORGE. 1995. "The Possessive Investment in Whiteness: Racialized Social Democracy and the 'White' Problem in American Studies." *American Quarterly* 47:369–87.

LOPEZ, IAN F. HANEY. 1996. *White By Law: The Legal Construction of Race.* New York: New York University Press.

LUGONES, MARIA. 1993. "Boomerang Perception and the Colonizing Gaze: Ginger Reflections on Horizontal Hostility." Department of Philosophy, State University of New York at Binghamton. Unpublished manuscript.

LYMAN, STANFORD M. and W. A. DOUGLAS. 1973. "Ethnicity: Strategies of Individual and Collective Impression Management." *Social Research* 40: 343–65.

MCINTOSH, PEGGY. 1992. "White Privilege and Male Privilege: A Personal Account of Coming to See Correspondence Through Work in Women's Studies." Pp. 70–81 *in Race, Class, and Gender: An Anthology,* edited by Margaret Anderson and Patricia Hill Collins. Belmont, CA: Wadsworth.

MAHAN, J. 1976. "Black and White Children's Racial Identification and Preference." *Journal of Black Psychology* 3:47–53.

OMI, MICHAEL. 1991. Shifting the Blame: Racial Ideology and Politics in the Post-Civil Rights Era. *Critical Sociology* 18:77–98.

OMI, MICHAEL and HOWARD WINANT. 1986. *Racial Formation in the U.S: From the 1960s to the 1980s.* New York: Routledge.

POE, JANITA. 1993. "Multiracial People Want a Single Name that Fits." *Chicago Tribune,* May 3:A1–A2.

PONSE, BARBARA. 1978. *Identities in the Lesbian World: The Social Construction of Self.* Westport, CT: Greenwood Press.

POSTON, W. S. CARLOS. 1990. "The Biracial Identity Development Model: A Needed Addition." *Journal of Counseling and Development* 69:152–56.

RAISKIN, JUDITH. 1994. "Inverts and Hybrids: Lesbian Rewritings of Sexual and Racial Identities." Pp. 156–71 in *The Lesbian Postmodern,* edited by Laura Doan. New York: Columbia University Press.

RODRIGUEZ, CLARA and HECTOR CORDERO GUZMAN. 1992. "Placing Race in Context." *Racial and Ethnic Studies* 15:523–41.

SHANKLIN, EUGENIA. 1994. *Anthropology and Race.* Belmont, CA: Wadsworth.

STEINBERG, STEPHEN. 1989. *The Ethnic Myth: Race, Ethnicity, and Class in America.* Boston: Beacon Press.

STOLLER, ELEANOR PALO. 1996. "Sausna, Sisu, and Sibelus: Ethnic Identity Among Finish Americans." *Sociological Quarterly* 37:145–75.

STONE, GREGORY. 1962. "Appearance and the Self." Pp. 86–118 in *Human Behavior and Social Pro-*cesses, edited by Arnold M. Rose. Boston: Houghton Mifflin.

TATUM, BEVERLY DANIEL. 1997. *"Why Are All the Black Kids Sitting Together in the Cafeteria?" And Other Conversations About Race.* New York: Basic Books.

WATERS, MARY. 1990. *Ethnic Options: Choosing Identities in America.* Berkeley, CA: University of California Press.

WATERS, MARY. 1991. "The Role of Lineage in Identity Formation Among Black Americans." *Qualitative Sociology* 14:57–76.

WETHERELL, MARGARET and JONATHAN POTTER. 1992. *Mapping the Language of Racism: Discourse and the Legitimation of Exploitation.* New York: Columbia University Press.

DEVIANCE ON RECORD: TECHNIQUES FOR LABELING CHILD ABUSERS IN OFFICIAL DOCUMENTS*

Leslie Margolin**

Some sociologists believe that wrong-doers have considerable capacity to defend and mollify attributions of deviance by offering excuses, apologies, and expressions of sorrow. For example, conceptual formulations such as Mill's (1940) "vocabularies of motive," Scott and Lyman's (1968) "accounts," Sykes and Matza's (1957) "techniques of neutralization," and Hewitt and Stokes' (1975) "disclaimers" reflect a belief in the almost limitless reparative potential of talk. In the parlance of these sociologists, deviant identities are negotiable because attributions of wrong-doing are seen to depend not only on an assessment of what the wrong-doer did but on an understanding of his or her mental state during and after the violation. As Douglas (1970:12) observes, "an individual is considered responsible for his actions if and only if . . . he has intended to commit those actions and knows the rules relevant to them. . . ."

Given these conditions, accused persons may argue that the violation in question was unanticipated, unplanned, and contrary to what they wished. Still, limited evidence exists that people win such arguments. Although account theorists (e.g., Scott and Lyman 1968:46–47) claim that "the timbers of fractured sociations" can be repaired through talk, investigators addressing the ways social control agents process putative deviants have found few instances of people talking their way out of deviant labels (cf. Margolin

*© 1992 by the Society for the Study of Social Problems. Reprinted from *Social Problems* 39:1 (February 1992), pp. 58–70 by permission of the author and the publisher.

**I am very grateful to Richard Hilbert for his many helpful insights and suggestions. Correspondence to: Margolin, Division of Counselor Education, Lindquist Center, University of Iowa, Iowa City, Iowa 52242.

1990). On the whole, social control agents tend to pigeonhole clients fairly quickly. As Waegel (1981) has shown, the organizational demand to meet deadlines, process an expected number of cases, and turn out paperwork reduces the amount of time agents can give their clients. The more bureaucrats are hurried, the greater their need to rely on shorthand methods for dealing with clients, and thus, the greater the necessity to interpret people and situations by means of stereotypes. In this regard, stereotypical or "normal" case conceptions guide responses to homicide defendants (Swigert and Farrell 1977), juvenile delinquents (Piliavin and Briar 1964), clients in a public defender's office (Sudnow 1965), skid-row residents (Bittner 1967), and shoplifters (Steffensmeier and Terry 1973).

The paperwork demand has a second effect on the putative deviant's capacity to negotiate effectively. Because oral and written communication have different potentialities for conveying information and structuring argument, agencies emphasizing the creation of records place a proportional pressure on bureaucrats to note the "recordable" features of their clients' situations. By implication, the contingencies of a case which best lend themselves to being described in written language are given the most prominence in records, and those contingencies most difficult to capture on paper (those aspects of a case best understood through face-to-face interaction) are minimized or neglected.

Studies examining the types of information bureaucrats leave out of written accounts have shown that clients' feelings are often omitted because the inner life of the individual is not only difficult to defend as objective evidence, but it is difficult to defend as evidence in writing (Kahn 1953, Lemert 1969). In face-to-face encounters, however, feelings and intentions are available through a series of gestures, tonal changes, and bodily movements which accompany the other's words (Schutz and Luckmann 1973). There is continual exchange between words and gestures. Such reciprocity cannot be duplicated in written communication, particularly when the writing is part of an official document. This means that putative deviants' capacity to argue their cases is seriously reduced when cases must be made in writing.

While documents may be a poor medium for describing internal states, bureaucrats are also reluctant to designate deviance on something as indefinite as "feelings"—theirs or the client's. The primary risk of citing the client's mental state at the time of the violation as a criterion for labeling or not labeling is that it makes agents vulnerable to accusations of subjectivity and personal bias. Since records are permanently available to supervisory scrutiny, agents feel pressure to make written assessments defendable displays of bureaucratic competence (Meehan 1986). For this reason, agents must use records to display not only "what happened" but that they performed their jobs rationally and objectively (Garfinkel 1967, Zimmerman 1969). These practical considerations oblige agents whose decision processes are recorded to place singular emphasis on the tangible aspects of the case—what the putative deviant's behavior was and what harm resulted—at the same time giving relatively little weight to clients' excuses, apologies, and expressions of sorrow.

Conceptualizing the deviant identity, then, as a mosaic assembled out of imputations of behavior and intention, this study examines how such a mosaic is pieced together in written documents. I explore how the "deviant's" point of view is documented and displayed, and how evidence is organized on paper to create the appearance that "deviance" has occurred. These dynamics are addressed through the examination of 120 case records designating child abuse.

Since the documentary reality of child abuse provides the vehicle and substantive focus of the analysis, what follows shows how child care providers are constituted as intentionally harmful to children. Like other "dividing practices" which categorize people as either healthy/sick, law abiding/criminal, or sane/insane, the separation of child abusers from normals is seen as an accomplishment of asymmetric power relations (cf. Foucault 1965, 1973, 1977). This article focuses on the power imbalance between child abuse investigators and suspects and the means by which the former impose their version of reality on the latter. Since this imposition is an accomplishment of contemporary modes of discourse (cf. Foucault 1978), I focus on investigators' vocabularies, the structure of their arguments, and the types of common sense reasoning they utilize.

METHODS

The idea for this research emerged while I was involved in a study of child abuse by babysitters. As part of that study, I had to read "official" case records documenting that child abuse had occurred. The more records I read, the more it appeared that the social workers devoted a rather large portion of their writing to describing children's injuries, as well as the violent and sexual interactions which often preceded and followed them. By contrast, the alleged perpetrator's intentions, feelings, and interpretations of what happened appeared to occupy a relatively small portion of the documents. This imbalance roused interest in view of the agency's formal regulations that social workers satisfy two criteria to establish that a caregiver committed child abuse: (1) They must establish that a caregiver performed acts which were damaging or exploitative to a child; (2) They must prove that the caregiver *intended* to damage or exploit the child—that the trauma was nonaccidental. In the article I examine how social workers managed to label child abusers in a manner consistent with these regulations without appearing to give much weight to subjective factors such as suspects' excuses and justifications.

The same consisted of 60 case records documenting physical abuse and 60 records documenting sexual abuse. They were randomly selected from all case records of child abuse by babysitters substantiated by a state agency during a two year period (N = 537). A babysitter was defined as someone who took care of a child who was not a member of the child's family, was not a boyfriend or girlfriend of the child's parent, and was not employed in a registered or licensed group care facility.

I do not treat records as ontologically valid accounts of "what happened"; rather, I treat them as a "documentary reality" (Smith 1974), indicating the ways the social workers who constructed them want to be seen by their superiors. As such,

the records provide evidence that the social workers utilized the unstated yet commonly known procedures which represent "good work." The following analysis attempts to make these procedures explicit and to show how the social workers who used them "prove" that child abuse took place by constructing good (bureaucratically sound) arguments supporting the view that a specific person intentionally damaged a child. I also explore the degree to which deviants' excuses, denials, and other accounts were incorporated into these decision processes. Finally, I look at how each type of information—descriptions of the injuries and accounts of what happened—was used as evidence that child abuse occurred and could only have been performed by the person who was labeled.

DISPLAYING VIOLENCE AND SEXUALITY

At the beginning of each record, the social worker described the physical injuries which were believed to have been inflicted on the child by the babysitter. These descriptions did not specify how the child's health or functioning were impaired but were presented as evidence that an act of transformative social import had occurred (cf. Denzin 1989). To illustrate this reporting style, one three-year-old who was spanked by his babysitter was described by the physician as having "a contusion to the buttocks and small superficial lacerations." However, the social worker who used these injuries as evidence of child abuse described them as follows:

The injuries gave the appearance of an ink blot, in that they were almost mirror images of each other, positioned in the center of each buttock. The bruising was approximately four inches long by about two and a half inches wide, and was dark red on the perimeter and had a white cast to the inside of the bruise. There was a long linear line running across the bottom of both buttocks extending almost the entire width of the child's buttock. There was lighter reddish bruising surrounding the two largest bruises on each buttock and faint bluish-red bruising extending up to the lower back. The bruising would be characterized as being red turning to a deeper reddish-purple than true bright red.

This unusually graphic style of presentation gave the bruises a special status. They were no longer simply bruises but were now defined as out of the ordinary, strange, and grotesque. By removing the bruises from everyday experience, the stage was set for redefining the babysitter who supposedly did this to the child. In this manner, a person whose social status had been taken for granted could now be seen as potentially suspicious, foreign, and malevolent (Garfinkel 1956).

A parallel line of reportage was apparent in the sexual abuse cases. To the degree that the available information permitted, reports contained no obscurity in the descriptions of sexual interactions. No detail of what happened appeared too small to be pursued, named, and included in the records as evidence (cf. Foucault 1978). This excerpt from a social worker's recorded interview with an eight-year-old girl illustrates:

S.W.: How did the bad touch happen? Can you think?
Child: I can't remember.
S.W.: Did you ever have to kiss?
Child: No.
S.W.: Anybody?
Child: Uh uh.
S.W.: Did you have to touch anybody?
Child: Yeah.
S.W.: Ah, you had to touch 'em. Where did you have to touch 'em?
Child: Down below.
S.W.: Oh, down below. Do you have a word for that body part?
Child: A thing-a-ma-jig.
S.W.: A thing-a-ma-jig. OK, let's look. . . . Is P [the suspect] a man?
Child: Yeah.
S.W.: OK, let's take a look at the man doll. Can you show me on the man doll what part you're talking about?
Child: This part.
S.W.: Oh, the part that sticks out in front. We have another word for that. Do you know the other word for that part?
Child: Dick.
S.W.: Yeah. Dick is another word for it. Another word is penis.
Child: Penis?
S.W.: Yeah.
Child: Oh.

S.W.: Can you tell me what—Did you see his body? Did you see his penis with your eyes?
Child: No.
S.W.: OK. Did he have his pants on or off?
Child: Unzipped.
S.W.: Unzipped. I see. How did his penis happen to come out of his pants?
Child: By the zipper.
S.W.: I see. Who took his penis out of his pants?
Child: He did.
S.W.: What did you have to touch his penis with?
Child: My fingers.
S.W.: I see. How did you know you had to do that?
Child: He told me to.
S.W.: What did he say?
Child: Itch it.
S.W.: Itch it. I see. Did he show you how to itch it? How did he have to itch it? One question at a time. Did he show you how to itch it?
Child: He said just go back.
S.W.: So you showed me that you're kind of scratching on it.
Child: Um hum.
S.W.: Did anything happen to his penis or his thing-a-ma-jig when you did that?
Child: No.
S.W.: OK. When he took his penis out of his pants, how did it look?
Child: Yucky.
S.W.: Yeah, I know you think it's yucky, but um, what does yucky mean? Can you tell me with some other words besides yucky?
Child: Slimy.
S.W.: Looked slimy. OK. Was it big?
Child: Yeah.
S.W.: Was it hard or soft?
Child: Soft and hard.
S.W.: OK. Explain how you mean that. . . .

I offer this dialogue not as evidence that sexual abuse did or did not occur, but rather, to display the means by which equivocal behavior is translated into the "fact" of sexual abuse. Whatever it is that "really happened" to this child, we see that her experience of it is not a concern when "documentation" is being gathered. She is an object of inquiry, not a participant (Cicourel 1968, Smith 1974). Whatever reasons compel social workers to bring her to their offices and ask these questions are their reasons not hers. And as the child learns, even features of the "event"— such as the size, hardness, and overall appearance of a penis—can assume critical importance within interviewers' frames of reference.

While social workers used these details of sexual interactions and injuries to set the stage for the attribution of deviance, I noted four cases in which the analysis of the injuries themselves played a conspicuously larger role in determining who was responsible. In these cases the injured children were too young to explain how their injuries were caused, the babysitters denied causing the injuries, and there were no witnesses. This meant that the only way the investigators were able to label the babysitters as abusive was to argue that the injuries occurred during the time the suspects were taking care of the children. The parents of the injured children testified that the children were sent to the babysitters in good health, without any marks, but returned from the babysitters with a noticeable injury. This allowed the social workers to determine responsibility through the following method: If a babysitter cannot produce any plausible alternative explanation for the child's injuries, the babysitter must be responsible for the injuries.

Since children who had allegedly been sexually abused did not have conspicuous or easily described injuries, attributing sexual abuse on the absence of any plausible alternative explanation for the injury was, of course, impossible. This would appear to severely limit social workers' capacity to document that a babysitter committed sexual abuse when the babysitter denied the charges, when the child was too young to provide coherent testimony, and when there were no other witnesses. However, this was not always the case. Like the investigators described by Garfinkel (1967:18) who were able to determine the cause of death among possible suicides with only "*this* much; *this* sight; *this* note; *this* collection of whatever is at hand," child abuse investigators showed the capacity to "make do" with whatever information was available. In one case of sexual abuse, for example, there were no witnesses, no admission from the suspect, no physical evidence, and no charge from the alleged victim; still, "evidence" was summoned to establish a babysitter's guilt. Here, the social worker cited a four-year-old girl's fears, nightmares, and other "behavior consistent with that of a child who was

sexually traumatized by a close family friend." Additionally, the babysitter in question was portrayed as a "type" capable of doing such things:

Having no physical evidence, and no consistent statement from the alleged victim, I am forced to make a conclusion based on the credibility of the child as opposed to that of the perpetrator. This conclusion is supported by similar allegations against him from an independent source. It is also supported by behavioral indications and what we know of his history.

In a second case, a social worker showed that information pointing to the suspect's homosexuality and history of sexual victimization could be used to support charges of sexual abuse when other kinds of evidence were lacking:

Although the babysitter denied having sexual contact with this child when interviewed, he did leave a note to the effect that he was attracted to males and thought that he was homosexual, and records indicate that he, himself, was sexually abused at the age of eight. Based on the interview done, the past history, and his own previous victimization, this worker feels that he did, in fact, penetrate and perpetrate himself upon the victim.

In most cases, however, portraying the suspect as a "type" was not critical to the finding of child abuse. The rationale for labeling was primarily constructed out of witnesses' testimony showing "who did what to whom."

USING WITNESSES TO DETERMINE WHO DID WHAT TO WHOM

Since the children and alleged child abusers often had different versions of what happened (40 cases), social workers needed a decision-rule to settle the question of who had the correct story. The rule used for resolving disagreements was fairly simple: The child's version was considered the true one. The children were called "credible" witnesses when describing assaults which were done to them because it was assumed they had nothing to gain by falsely accusing the babysitter. The babysitters, on the other hand, were seen as "noncredible" (when they attempted to establish their innocence) because they had everything to gain by lying. Even children as young as two and three years old were believed in preference to their adult babysitters. In fact, the main reason given for interpreting children as superior witnesses was precisely their youth, ignorance, and lack of sophistication. As one social worker observed, "It's my experience that a four-year-old would not be able to maintain such a consistent account of an incident if she was not telling the truth." Particularly in cases of sexual abuse, it was believed that the younger the witness, the more credible his or her testimony was. Social workers made the point that children who were providing details of sexual behavior would not know of such things unless they had been abused (cf. Eberle and Eberle 1986).

The children's accounts were rejected in only three instances. In one of these cases, two teenage boys claimed they witnessed a babysitter abuse a child as they peered through a window. Both the babysitter and the child said this was not true. The social worker did not feel it was necessary to explain why the babysitter would deny the allegations, but the child's denial was seen as problematic. Therefore, the social worker offered the following rationale for rejecting the child's account: "The child's refusal to say anything is not unusual because her mother was so verbally upset when she was informed of the allegations." A child's version of what happened (his denial of abuse) was rejected in a second case on the grounds that he was protecting a babysitter described as his "best friend." Finally, a 12-year-old female who repeatedly denied that anyone had touched her sexually was seen as noncredible because of her "modesty." As the social worker put it, "She did seem to have a very difficult time talking about it, and I feel she greatly minimized the incident due to her embarrassment about it."

In general, however, testimony from children was treated as the most credible source of evidence of what happened, since most social workers believe that children do not lie about the abuse done to them. By contrast, babysitters were presented as credible witnesses only when they agreed with the allegations made against them (56 cases). When they testified to the contrary, they were portrayed as biased. What does *not* happen, therefore, is the child implicating someone, the accused saying nothing happened, and the investigator siding with the accused. This

suggests an underlying idealization that precedes and supports the ones operating on the surface of most cases: *The accused is guilty.* It goes without saying that this organizational stance runs roughly opposite to the Constitutional one of "innocent until proven guilty."

Here, it might be useful to draw an analogy between the child protection workers' "investigative stance" and that of welfare investigators responsible for determining applicants' eligibility (Zimmerman 1974). In both cases, investigators adopt a thorough-going skepticism designed "to locate and display the potential discrepancy between the applicant's [or suspect's] subjective and 'interested' claims and the factual and objective (i.e., rational) account that close observance of agency procedure is deemed to produce" (Zimmerman 1974:131). However, an importance difference should be noted: During the conduct of welfare investigations, the investigated party is referred to as the "applicant," indicating that the investigation could end in a determination of either eligibility or ineligibility; by contrast, during the conduct of child abuse investigations, the investigated party is routinely identified as the "perpetrator," suggesting a previously concluded status. To illustrate, these notations documented one worker's activities during the first days of a child abuse investigation:

3/24: Home visit with police, interviewed parents, child not at home—perpetrator not in home.
3/26: Interview with detective J at Police station with CPI and child. Perpetrator arrested.

While babysitters accused of child abuse may in theory be only "suspects," at the level of practice, they are "perpetrators." This discrepancy between "theory" and "practice" is more than an example of how the formal structures of organizations are accompanied by unintended and unprogrammed structures (Bittner 1965). In this instance, child protection workers are formally enjoined to gather evidence about "perpetrators," not "suspects." Consider these guidelines from the agency's official handbook:

Information collected from the person [witness] should include precise description of size, shape, color, type, and location of injury. It may be possible to establish the credibility of the child, the responsible caretaker or the *perpetrator* as a source of this information. . . . The *perpetrator* and victim may be credible persons and need to be judged on the basis of the same factors as any other persons. (Italics added.)

The implicit message is that the goal of the child abuse investigation is not to determine an individual's guilt or innocence but to find evidence to be used in recording or "documenting" what is already taken for granted, that parties initially identified as the "perpetrator" and "victim" are in fact the "perpetrator" and "victim." Strictly speaking, then, the goal is not to determine "who did what to whom," since that information is assumed at the outset, but rather, to document that agency rules have been followed, and that the investigation was conducted in a rational, impersonal manner.

DETERMINING INTENTIONALITY

A decision-rule was also needed to determine the babysitter's intentions. While babysitters were portrayed in the allegations as malicious or exploitive, many babysitters offered a different version of their motivations. Among the babysitters accused of physical abuse, 25 acknowledged hitting the children but also claimed they intended no harm. Three said they were having a bad day, were under unusual stress, and simply "lost it." They attributed their violence to a spontaneous, noninstrumental expression of frustration. For example, one male caregiver took a two-year-old to the potty several times but the child did not go. Later he noticed that the child's diaper was wet; so he hurried him to the potty. However, just before being placed on the potty the child had a bowel movement. At that point the caregiver lost his temper and hit the child.

One woman who was labeled abusive claimed she was ill and never wanted to babysit in the first place. She only agreed to take care of a two-year-old girl because the girl's mother insisted. The mother had an unexpected schedule change at work and needed child care on an emergency basis. The abusive event occurred soon after the babysitter served lunch to the child. While the sitter rested on a couch in the living room, she

observed the girl messing with her lunch. The sitter got up and tried to settle the child. When this did not work, she took away the girl's paper plate and threw it in the garbage. At that point the girl began to cry for her mother. The babysitter returned to the living room to lie down on the couch. But the girl followed her, wailing for her mother. When the girl reached the couch, the babysitter sat up and slapped her.

Other babysitters described their violence in instrumental terms: Their goal was to discipline the children and not to hurt or injure them. They said that whatever injuries occurred were the accidental result of hitting (in one case, biting) the children harder than they meant to do. Some sitters indicated that the only reason children were injured during a disciplinary action was that the children moved just as they were being hit, exposing a sensitive part of the body to the blow. Others protested that the child's movements made it impossible to aim the blows accurately or to assess how hard they were hitting. In one case, the sitter said she was trying to hit the child across the buttocks with a stick, but the child put her hand across her buttocks to protect herself, receiving "non-intentional" bruising and swelling to the hand. A different sitter asked that the social worker consider that at the time of the violation he did not know it was against the law to beat a child with a belt. Another said he had been given permission to spank the child by the child's mother and was only following her orders. This was confirmed by the mother. After a two-and-a-half-year-old bit another child, his sitter bit him to show him "what it felt like." The sitter argued that she had done this in the past and had even told the child's mother. Thus, she believed that this was tacitly approved. Still another babysitter claimed that he struck the 11-year-old girl who was in his care in self-defense. He said that when he told her it was time for bed she began to bite and kick him. He said her injuries resulted from his efforts to calm and restrain her.

To sift out the babysitters' "official" intentions from the versions offered by the sitters themselves, several social workers explicitly invoked the following reasoning: Physical damage to the child would be considered "intentional" if the acts which produced them were intentional. Thus, a social worker wrote:

I am concluding that this injury to the child was non-accidental in that the babysitter did have a purpose in striking the child, that purpose being to discipline her in hopes of modifying her behavior.

While close examination of this logic reveals an absurdity (the injury was seen as "intentional" despite the fact that it was produced by an act aimed at an entirely different outcome, "modifying her behavior"), the practical consequence of such a formula was a simple method for determining a suspect's intentions: If a babysitter was known to intentionally hit a child, causing an injury, the social worker could conclude the babysitter intended to cause the injury. Through such a formula, the most common excuse utilized by babysitters to account for their actions, that the injury was the accidental result of a disciplinary action, was interpreted as a confession of responsibility for physical abuse.

To give another example of how this formula provided a short-cut to determining intentionality, one social worker concluded her recording as follows:

Physical abuse is founded in that the caretaker did hit the child on the face because she was throwing a temper tantrum and left a bruise approximately one inch long under the right eye. This constitutes a non-accidental injury. The bruise is still visible after five days.

In cases involving allegations of physical abuse, the problem of figuring out what the babysitter was really contemplating at the time of the violation never came up as a separate issue because the alleged perpetrator's motivation to injure the child was seen as the operational equivalent of two prior questions, "Does the child have an injury resulting from a blow?" and "Did the babysitter intentionally strike the child?" When each of these questions was answered affirmatively, intent to harm the child was inferred. Thus, it was possible for a social worker to observe, "It was this writer's opinion that the babysitter was surprised at the injury she left on the child by spanking the child," and later conclude, "the injury occurred as a result of a non-accidental incident."

One record included comments from witnesses which stated that a babysitter pushed a five-year-old boy after the child socked a cat. All agreed that the injury was not a direct consequence of the push but resulted when the child lost balance and fell over. Despite the social worker's explicit recognition that the child's injury was neither planned nor anticipated (she wrote that "the injury will probably not be repeated due to the sitter's awareness of the seriousness of disciplining a child by reacting rather than thinking"), the report of physical abuse was, nonetheless, founded "due to the fact that the injury occurred in the course of a disciplinary action."

In another record, a male babysitter admitted to spanking a child, causing red marks on his buttocks. Although the child's father said he "did not believe the sitter meant to spank as hard as he did," and the police officer who was present concluded that "based on the information obtained in this investigation, I could find no intent on the sitter's part to assault this child," the social worker found the determination of physical abuse nonproblematic. Since the child received the injury in the course of a spanking, child abuse occurred.

There were only two cases of sexual abuse in which the alleged abuser acknowledged touching the child in a manner consistent with the allegations, but at the same time denied sexual intent. In one of these cases, the alleged abuser said he only touched a 10-year-old boy's genitals in the process of giving him a bath. In the other case, the alleged abuser claimed he only touched the girl's body as part of an anatomy lesson, to show her where her rib and pelvic bones were located. Both of these accounts were dismissed as preposterous. The social workers expressed the opinion that sexual intent was the only possible reason anyone would enact the types of behavior attributed to the accused in the allegations. In short, an equation was drawn between specific behaviors attributed to the accused and their states of mind. If it was established that the babysitter behaved toward the child in ways commonly understood as sexual (e.g., fondling), establishing intent, as a separate dimension of the investigation, was seen as redundant. Thus, social workers were able to conclude their investigations of sexual abuse, as one investigator did, by utilizing the following formula: "The child, a credible witness, indicated that her babysitter did fondle her genitals. Therefore, this is a founded case of intent to commit sexual abuse."

To summarize, in cases of both physical and sexual abuse, the intent to commit these acts was seen as a necessary component of the specific behaviors used to accomplish them. Hitting which resulted in an injury was always treated as if it was a direct indicator of the motivation to injure. Similarly, behavior commonly known as "sexual" was always treated as if it was identical with the suspect's intent to sexually exploit. The fact that social workers sometimes described the suspects' surprise and horror at the physical damage their violence caused the child did not make the attribution of "intent to harm" more problematic because suspects' accounts were not organizationally defined as indicators of intent. Consistent with Mills (1940), motives for child abuse are not features of the perpetrator's psyche, but rather, of the bureaucracy and profession. That 50 of the babysitters labeled as abusive denied performing the actions imputed to them, and another 14 were not interviewed at all (either because they could not be located or refused to speak to the social worker) demonstrated that it was possible to "officially" determine babysitters' intentions without confirmatory statements from the babysitters themselves.

DISCUSSION

Sociologists have often questioned official records on the grounds of their accuracy, reliability, and representativeness. However, the methods through which and by which deviance is routinely displayed in records have rarely been investigated (cf. Cicourel and Kitsuse 1963, Kitsuse and Cicourel 1963). This study has treated as problematic the standardized arguments and evidence which social workers use in official documents to prove that child abuse has taken place. In this regard, child abuse is seen as an accomplishment of a bureaucratic system in which members agree to treat specific phenomena as if they were "child abuse."

The proof of abuse was problematic since more than half of the suspects either denied the accusations or were not interviewed. Social workers "made do" without supportive testimony from suspects by routinely defining them as "noncredible" witnesses. Also, social workers managed to conform to agency regulations requiring proof that suspects intended to harm or exploit children by agreeing to treat specific observables as if they represented the intent to harm or exploit.

Thus, the designation of child abuse was simplified. Testimony from the person most likely to disagree with this label, the accused, did not have to be considered. This is not to say that testimony from the accused might overcome the processes of institutional sense-making. It is to suggest, rather, that defining the accused as noncredible makes the designation of child abuse more "cut and dried," defendable, and recordable, since abuse that might otherwise be denied, excused, or justified, either in whole or in part, can then be fully attributed to suspects.

While it can be argued that simplifying the means by which suspects are labeled is desirable for a society concerned about keeping dangerous people away from children, the negative consequences should be acknowledged. As already shown, individuals who assign child abuse labels have more power than suspects, making it impossible for parties at risk of being labeled to "negotiate" on an equal footing with labelers. Indeed, any disjuncture between suspects' and investigators' versions of "what really happened" do not have to be resolved prior to the attribution of child abuse (cf. Pollner 1987:77–81). Since investigators have the capacity to impose their versions of reality on suspects, the only "resolution" needed from the investigators' perspective entails finding ways to make their decisions defendable in writing.

As might be expected, the personal, social, and legal stigma resulting from designating this label is enormous. Once the impression has been formed that a person is a child abuser, the expectation exists that he or she will continue to be abusive. Moreover, there is little a person can do to remove this label. It exists as part of a permanent record that can be recalled whenever a person's care capacities or moral standing are questioned (cf. Rosenhan 1973). If, as Smith (1974:259) argues, the creation of written records "mediates relations among persons in ways analogous to how Marx conceived commodities mediating relations among individuals," then for the relations (and identities) constituted by records, there is no intersubjective world in which members share the passage of time, and, in the words of Schutz, "grow old together" (cited in Smith 1974:259). There is no interpersonal negotiation or becoming, but only "fact" as sedimented in the records themselves.

While most who write about child abuse are enmeshed in that system, either as practitioners or idealogues and so are strained to defend its existence, in recent years critics have shown concern about the growing numbers of people labeled as child abusers (Besharov 1986, Eberle and Eberle 1986, Elshtain 1985, Johnson 1985, Pride 1986, Wexler 1985). Most trace this "over-attribution" of child abuse to professional and lay people's "emotionally charged desire to 'do something' about child abuse, fanned by repeated and often sensational media coverage" (Besharov 1986:19). However, Conrad and Schneider (1980:270) provide a more general explanation: "bureaucratic 'industries' with large budgets and many employees . . . depend for their existence on the acceptance of a particular deviance designation. They become 'vested interests' in every sense of the term." To take their analysis one step farther, "bureaucratic industries" have a vested interest not only in a label, but in a labeling process—specifically, in finding ways of reducing complexity and making labeling accomplishable.

Piven and Cloward's (1971) analysis of the regulating functions of welfare programs suggests why these bureaucracies have expanded in recent years. If income support programs expand and contract to control turmoil resulting from instability in labor markets, it is possible that social agencies geared to controlling child care grow in response to instability in the child care system. This hypothesis warrants attention if for no other reason than that mothers' dramatic increases in labor force participation over the last three decades, and the commensurate increase in young children's time in nonparental care, have closely paralleled the emergence of child abuse as a major social issue. However, this single causal mode of explanation would be more compelling if it were not that history reveals other periods in which institutional momentum developed around "saving children" under a variety of different conditions (Best 1990, Finestone 1976, Platt 1969). This suggests that any explanation of why such social movements wax and wane, taking their particular form at each point in history, needs to account for many interacting factors, including the prevailing moralities and family institutions as well as opportunities for effectively marketing these problems to a wide audience (cf. Best 1990).

To conclude, this study has shown some of the ways in which the construction of documents labels deviance. The main findings include bureaucrats' determination to translate sex and violence into endlessly accumulated verbal detail, to "make do" with whatever information is available, to fashion proofs of child abuse based on the new "common sense" that children's testimony is more credible than adults', and to develop simple, accomplishable ways of imputing intentionality that are unaffected by suspects' accounts.

REFERENCES

BESHAROV, DOUGLAS J. 1986. "Unfounded allegations—A new child abuse problem." *The Public Interest* 83:18–33.

BEST, JOEL. 1990. *Threatened Children: Rhetoric and Concern about Child-Victims.* Chicago: The University of Chicago Press.

BITTNER, EGON. 1965. "The concept of organization." *Social Research* 32:239–255.

———. 1967. "The police on skid row: A study of peace keeping." *American Sociological Review* 32:699–715.

CICOUREL, AARON V. 1968. *The Social Organization of Juvenile Justice.* New York: John Wiley and Sons.

CICOUREL, AARON V., and JOHN I. KITSUSE. 1963. *The Educational Decision-Makers.* New York: Bobbs-Merrill.

CONRAD, PETER, and JOSEPH W. SCHNEIDER. 1980. *Deviance and Medicalization.* St. Louis: C.V. Mosby.

DENZIN, NORMAN K. 1989. *Interpretive Interactionism.* Newbury Park, Calif.: Sage.

Douglas, Jack D. 1970. "Deviance and respectability: The social construction of moral meanings." In Jack D. Douglas (ed.), *Deviance and Respectability* (pp. 3–30). New York: Basic Books.

Eberle, Paul, and Shirley Eberle. 1986. *The Politics of Child Abuse.* Secaucus, N.J.: Lyle Stuart.

Elshtain, Jean Bethke. 1985. "Invasion of the child savers: How we succumb to hype and hysteria." *The Progressive* 49:23–26.

Finestone, Harold. 1976. *Victims of Change: Juvenile Delinquents in American Society.* Westport, Conn.: Greenwood Press.

Foucault, Michel. 1965. *Madness and Civilization.* New York: Random House.

———. 1973. *The Birth of the Clinic.* New York: Pantheon.

———. 1977. *Discipline and Punish.* New York: Pantheon.

———. 1978. *The History of Sexuality.* Vol. 1. New York: Pantheon.

Garfinkel, Harold. 1956. "Conditions of successful degradation ceremonies." *American Journal of Sociology* 61:420–424.

———. 1967. *Studies in Ethnomethodology.* Englewood Cliffs, N.J.: Prentice-Hall.

Hewitt, John P., and Randall Stokes. 1975. "Disclaimers." *American Sociological Review* 40:1–11.

Johnson, John M. 1985. "Symbolic salvation: The changing meanings of the child maltreatment movement." *Studies in Symbolic Interaction* 6: 289–305.

Kahn, Alfred J. 1953. *A Court for Children.* New York: Columbia University Press.

Kitsuse, John I., and Aaron V. Cicourel. 1963. "A note on the use of official statistics." *Social Problems* 11:131–139.

Lemert, Edwin M. 1969. "Records in juvenile court." In Stanton Wheeler (ed.), *On Record: Files and Dossiers in American Life* (pp. 355–389). New York: Russell Sage Foundation.

Margolin, Leslie. 1990. "When vocabularies of motive fail: The example of fatal child abuse." *Qualitative Sociology* 13:373–385.

Meehan, Albert J. 1986. "Record-keeping practices in the policing of juveniles." *Urban Life* 15:70–102.

Mills, C. Wright. 1940. "Situated actions and vocabularies of motive." *American Sociological Review* 5:904–913.

Piliavin, Irving, and Scott Briar. 1964. "Police encounters with juveniles." *American Sociological Review* 70:206–214.

Piven, Frances Fox, and Richard A. Cloward. 1971. *Regulating the Poor: The Functions of Public Welfare.* New York: Pantheon Books.

Platt, Anthony M. 1969. *The Child Savers: The Invention of Delinquency.* Chicago: The University of Chicago Press.

Pollner, Melvin. 1987. *Mundane Reason: Reality in Everyday and Sociological Discourse.* Cambridge: Cambridge University Press.

Pride, Mary. 1986. *The Child Abuse Industry.* Westchester, Ill.: Crossway.

Rosenhan, D.L. 1973. "On being sane in insane places." *Science* 179:250–258.

Schutz, Alfred, and Thomas Luckmann. 1973. *The Structures of the Life-World.* Translated by R. M. Zaner and H. T. Engelhardt, Jr. Evanston, Ill.: Northwestern University Press.

Scott, Marvin B., and Stanford M. Lyman. 1968. "Accounts." *American Sociological Review* 22:664–670.

Smith, Dorothy E. 1974. "The social construction of documentary reality." *Sociological Inquiry* 44: 257–268.

Steffenmeier, Darrell J., and Robert M. Terry. 1973. "Deviance and respectability: An observational study of reactions to shoplifting." *Social Forces* 51:417–426.

Sudnow, David. 1965. "Normal crimes: Sociological features of the penal code in a public defender office." *Social Problems* 12:255–276.

Swigert, Victoria, and Ronald Farrell. 1977. "Normal homicides and the law." *American Sociological Review* 42:16–32.

Sykes, Gresham M., and David Matza. 1957. "Techniques of neutralization: A theory of delinquency." *American Sociological Review* 22:664–670.

Waegel, William B. 1981. "Case routinization in investigative police work." *Social Problems* 28: 263–275.

Wexler, Richard. 1985. "Invasions of the child savers: No one is safe in the war against abuse." *The Progressive* 49:19–22.

Zimmerman, Don H. 1969. "Record-keeping and the intake process in a public welfare agency." In Stanton Wheeler (ed.), *On Record: Files and Dossiers in American Life* (pp. 319–354). New York: Russell Sage Foundation.

———. 1974. "Fact as a practical accomplishment." In Roy Turner (ed.), *Ethnomethodology* (pp. 128–143). Middlesex, Eng.: Penguin Books.

ON BEHALF OF LABELING THEORY*

Erich Goode**

By the early 1960s labeling theory had become the major approach in the sociology of deviant behavior. But by the early 1970s the antilabeling stance became almost as fashionable as labeling had been a decade earlier. The interim witnessed many dozens of critiques. Most—although not all—share three fundamental flaws. First, they tend to be polemical rather than constructive. Instead of urging labeling theorists to sharpen their conceptual tools with the proffered criticisms, their authors seem intent on *extirpating* labeling theory. A second problem with these critiques is that they rarely render a faithful likeness of the original. The perspective has typically been caricatured, made to affirm principles that no labeling theorist has ever written or believed. Third, and most important: Our critics seem incapable of recognizing the crucial difference between what specific labeling theorists have (supposedly) written in specific works and the potential power of the perspective, where future deviance theorists could go with the perspective's root concepts and insights were they to be systematically rethought and developed.

I would like to re-examine a number of key concepts and assertions made both by critics of labeling theory and by authors seen as labeling theorists. I intend to offer a commentary on the validity of these criticisms, a stock-taking of what has and has not been said by the "reactive"

perspective, and some thoughts on where a labeling perspective should take us—even if it has not yet done so.

A convincing case could be made for the assertion that labeling theory does not exist in the first place. A field has been fabricated by observers and critics out of the raw material of a few arresting passages, phrases and concepts. Examined carefully, the ideas of the supposed school's adherents sound increasingly less alike, at times revealing more discord than the harmony marking a genuine tradition of thought.

It has been said that the concept of "secondary deviation" is central to labeling theory (Schur, 1971:10). However, the author of this concept, Edwin Lemert, rejects what may be the key idea in any "reactive" perspective in the study of deviance: that the relationship between action and reaction is problematic. Lemert, in counterpoint, invokes "objective aspects of deviance" and "values universal in nature" (1972:22). Consequently, it is difficult to comprehend just what might be meant when it is asserted that Edwin Lemert is a labeling theorist.

Kai Erikson penned what is the single most often quoted article in the labeling tradition, "Notes on the Sociology of Deviance" (1962). But the monograph in which this essay forms the first chapter (Erikson, 1966) rests squarely within the functionalist tradition, as the leading functionalist (Merton, 1971:829) has noted. It may be that there are points of agreement between functionalism and labeling theory (just as there are, say, between functionalism and Marxism), but a theorist whose most important work is primarily functionalist in its orientation cannot be said to be primarily a labeling theorist.

John Kitsuse is the author of "Societal Reaction to Deviant Behavior" (1962), probably the second most frequently quoted paper within the supposed labeling perspective. It is widely regarded as a classic example of labeling theoriz-

*© 1975 by The Society for the Study of Social Problems. Reprinted from *Social Problems*, 22 (June, 1975), pp. 570–583 by permission of the author and the publisher.

**This paper is part of a larger investigation supported by a fellowship from the John Simon Guggenheim Memorial Foundation; I am grateful for its generous support. In addition, the Research Foundation of the State University of New York permitted me a summer unencumbered by teaching responsibilities by awarding me a Faculty Research Fellowship. I would also like to thank Gerald Suttles, Forrest Dill, Robert Stevenson, and Terry J. Rosenberg for critical comments on an earlier draft of this paper; they have been most helpful.

ing. But Kitsuse is also the coauthor of another paper that points to a number of gaps, rigidities, and fallacies in current labeling theorists' thinking (Rains and Kitsuse, 1973). Since these criticisms contradict the image of labeling theory that has common currency, it would be difficult to pin the labeling theorist label on John Kitsuse.

Howard Becker's work is more frequently cited than that of any other labeling theorist. Yet Becker has written a number of illuminating comments on the "straw theory" nearly everyone takes to be labeling theory (1973). Labeling theory, Becker writes, is, first of all, not a *theory* in the strict sense of the word as it is generally understood. Second, it wasn't meant to "explain" deviant behavior; it is not the literal "cause" of the cats evaluated in the first place. Third: Public stigmatization is neither a necessary nor a sufficient condition for an individual's commitment to a career in deviance. Becker agrees with Cohen (1965) in stating that this is an empirical question; no theory can simply assume it. Last, not only should labeling theory not be called a theory, it probably shouldn't be called "labeling" anything. Since the literal application of a negative label to specific individuals committing specific acts is neither the most essential nor even the most fundamental process within the scope of this perspective, perhaps the term "labeling" should be dropped altogether. Becker, along with Rubington and Weinberg (1973), suggests the "interactionist" perspective.

If the four most often invoked figures in labeling theory—Lemert, Erikson, Kitsuse, and Becker—cannot be called labeling theorists (that is, do not accept tenets ascribed as central to labeling theory), who is one? We search in vain for a set of theories, or any systematic, unified body of work to which we can point and say, this is labeling theory, its authors are labeling theorists. There is no real school of labeling theory—outside of the label, the public characterization. We do have a few paragraphs, some insights, a few lines of reasoning aimed at several targets. We have the makings of a perspective, a number of powerful sensitizing concepts that have been inappropriately specified and stereotyped into what appears to be a monolithic edifice.

LABELING: WHAT SOMETHING IS

Early attempts to study deviant behavior made the assumption that acts social scientists attached names to inherently belonged in naturally occurring categories. Forms of deviance were thought to constitute clinical entities, predefined for the scientist. Attempts to devise theories of deviant behavior had to be based on phenomena having objective, formal, universal features applicable regardless of time and place, perceived by an external observer (the scientist), but not necessarily by the subject scrutinized by the scientist. Just what this scientific quest meant took on a distinctive and even peculiar flavor. After all, the literal-minded would say, "subjectivity" is the opposite of "objectivity." Ergo, "subjectivity" has no place in the science of sociology.

Labelists rejected the validity of the necessity for studying "objective" categories of human behavior. "All categories of mankind are phenomenological constructs employed by the members of mankind" (Lofland, 1969:123). Even before we know just what forms of behavior are thought of as deviant, we have to understand how features of those forms of behavior are assembled and categorized, how some specific act comes to be seen as an instance of a larger category of behavior. No class of objects, people, or acts "belongs" together under the same name inherently and automatically. A number of women strolling the beaches of Ipanema, a suburb of Rio de Janeiro, took to wearing topless bathing suits. In the spring of 1973 the Director of Censorship and Entertainment of the Rio police department ordered topless female bathers to be arrested for "practicing an obscene act." Any woman who bared her breasts, this official declared, committed "violent aggression against society." No doubt the reader does not share this conception of "aggression" or "violence." Is it proper to call same-gender genital contact "homosexuality" when it takes place in one setting devoid of the opposite sex (in prison, for example), in a society that strongly encourages it—say, among the Siwans of Africa (Ford and Beach, 1951: 131–132)—in another subculture of male hustlers who adopt no homosexual self-image, follow a rigid code as to what is permitted with others whom they call homosexuals, have intercourse with their girlfriends, and eventually discontinue the practice (Reiss, 1961)? Sociologically, these acts are "the same behavior" only in the most superficial respect; they might in fact, be called behavioral analogues. While it is true, as Gibbs points out, arguing for some measure of "objectivism" in studying deviance, that "less than absolute perceptual uniformity within a social unit does not negate the notion of types of acts" (1972:47), the variations in definitions as to what specific acts fall into what general (deviant) categories are sufficiently great as to treat this as problematic rather than automatic.

This "subjectivistic" view troubles many sociologists. In commenting on the current stress on interpretations of deviant behavior rather than on the behavior itself, Hirschi argues for a return to viewing categories of behavior in terms of objective criteria: "The person may not have committed a 'deviant' act, but he did (in many cases) do *something* . . . And it is just possible that . . . if he were left alone he would *do it again*" (Hirschi, 1973:169). "Extreme relativism," agrees Edwin Lemert, "leaves the unfortunate impression that almost any meaning can be assigned to human attributes and actions."

Practically all societies in varying degrees and ways disapprove of incest, adultery, promiscuity, cruelty to children, laziness, disrespect for parents and elders, murder, rape, theft, lying and cheating. Perhaps the point to make is that certain kinds of actions are likely to be judged deleterious in any context . . . It is not so much that they violate rules as it is that they destroy, downgrade, or jeopardize values universal in nature (Lemert, 1972:22).

One problem with these assertions is that none of the forms of behavior mentioned comprises a universally agreed-upon category. Just what is regarded as incest isn't the same everywhere; different societies regard different sets of potential sex partners as incestuous. In some civilizations only members of one's immediate family, plus aunts, uncles and grandparents qualify. In others, "the interpretation of incest is so broad as to include as potential sex partners half the available population" (Ford and Beach, 1951:113).

The very inclusion of an act within a certain category implies a certain attitude toward it. "Murder," "incest," and "robbery"—terms you and I use to characterize acts we deem to fit— may (or may not) be universally condemned, but if they are, it is because each of these words is already predefined and "loaded with moral disapproval" (Nisbet, 1970:282). In many past societies of the world the "murder" (from our point of view, not theirs) of a commoner by a nobleman did not arouse much moral outrage or even disapproval. Under the reign of King Shaka of the Zulu the king "murdered" citizens at will. His behavior was not only not condemned, but it was applauded, even by his soon-to-be victims, as a sign of the monarch's potency (Walter, 1969).

Thus, when an "objectivist" says of an actor engaged in a given and supposedly deviant form of behavior, "he did do *something*," we can only be left with a feeling of emptiness. *Just what is it, specifically, that he did?* Can we automatically and mechanically equate acts that are externally similar regardless of what they mean to the participants involved?

Everything is not relative, of course; the college sophomore's banalization of a basically powerful idea seems to make a travesty of it. (In fact, a diluted "objectivism," if properly understood, can be seen as a kind of relativism, because looking at categories as having universal properties is only one of many viable, available perspectives that could be adopted by an observer—in this case, someone usually called a "social scientist.") There is a definite utility to looking at social behavior in an "objectivistic" fashion. The point is that while adopting subjective categories and realities will yield crucial consequences and pay-offs, adopting objective categories and realities constructed by social scientists but not seen by participants also has important consequences and pay-offs.

Societies differ significantly in what is considered a normal consumption of alcohol. Heavy drinking in one will be considered average in another. This subjective definition helps us to understand certain things concerning drinking. (For instance, the social organization of the control and condemnation of "excessive" drinking.) But it doesn't help very much in understanding other significant facts. Alcohol does have certain effects on the body. The "objectivistic" view will help discover what these effects will be, while the subjectivistic views constructed by members of the society in which drinking takes place probably will not.

We may simply want to know how frequently and with what consequences intercourse occurs, let's say, between cross-cousins, regardless of how it is seen by the members of the society in which it takes place or by the cousins themselves, regardless of whether it is defined as "incest" in the first place. We may wish to find out how it comes to pass that some men or women do not see themselves, and are not seen by their peers, as engaging in "homosexual" behavior when, to our eyes, they seem to be doing so in the formal, "objective" sense. (As Gerald Suttles pointed out to me, the fact that participants do not share the distinctions sociologists make is itself a problem to be explained. Likewise, I would add, the participants may want to know how sociologists managed to concoct the categories through which *they* see the world.) It is a perfectly legitimate enterprise, this "objectivistic" line of inquiry, but limited. It becomes invalid when investigators: (1) believe it to be the whole story; (2) lose sight of the fact that their categorizations may have nothing to do with those held by participants; (3) wish to understand behavior as it is lived and experienced; or (4) fail to recognize the relevance of subjective distinctions in the sphere they study. In short, we have to know *when whose perspective is relevant.*

EMPATHY

Hirschi (1973) is troubled by the use of empathy in the social sciences. He feels that understanding the world through the eyes of the deviant leads the researcher into an empirical blunder: It blinds the sociologist to the less attractive features of deviance.

Being empathetic means that we have to come as close to the behavior under study as we possibly can, given the limitations of our biography, morality, and ideology. Empathy means that the sociologist has mentally, emotionally, and experientially to enter the world of the people he or she wishes to understand. Advocates do not claim that this is the only acceptable means of studying deviance. It does mean that the practitioner of deviant behavior often sees the world in a fairly distinct fashion. It is therefore a crucial and theoretically fruitful dimension of deviance.

This approach has also been called "appreciative" sociology (Matza, 1969:15–40). Perhaps this term is a bit misleading. Deviants may despise what they do or themselves for doing it—witness the child molester (McCaghy, 1967), the stripper (Skipper and McCaghy, 1970), the alcoholic. To assume that prostitutes necessarily enjoy their work would be to fall victim to the "happy hooker" syndrome (Goode and Troiden, 1974:108). In short, deviants may not "appreciate" their own behavior at all. If we were to assume that they do would be anything but empathetic. Their "appreciation" of their deviant behavior is an empirical question.

Empathy does not mean being conned or duped by our subject, by the practitioner of the deviant behavior we study. It does not, above all, indicate a simple-minded gullibility. In fact, it means the reverse: To be conned is to be the victim of an external social facade the deviant presents to the outside world. To empathize is to see the world from a first-hand perspective, to acquire an insider's view, and hence, to recognize the nature of the con job being presented to and believed by those not practiced or adept in the art of empathy. The subject—the deviant—is acutely aware of the fronts he or she presents to the world. Empathy involves knowing just how these fronts operate, not believing in their validity.

An example of this principle may be found in the review of Harold Garfinkel's book, *Studies in Ethnomethodology* (1967), written by the positivistically inclined sociologist James S. Coleman (1968). Garfinkel describes the case of "Agnes," who was born a biological boy, but passed as a woman for several years after taking female hormones during adolescence, and eventually underwent a sex-change operation. Garfinkel's approach attempts to be empathetic. Since Agnes defined herself as a woman, and successfully "accomplished" womanhood—that is, performed convincingly, and was so regarded by the outside world—the sociologist, too, could regard her, even before her operation, as an accomplished woman.

Coleman takes strong exception to this view. He argues that in adopting the empathetic stance, the researcher becomes "trapped in the confidence game." The "fatal flaw" in identifying with one's subjects, Coleman feels, is that the observer becomes incapable of standing outside the social world described to see it "objectively," as it really is, rather than as our subjects *think* it is.

There are two fallacies concerning Coleman's reasoning. First, Agnes really did know that she was born with the anatomical equipment of a male. She did know that she had been taking hormones to induce female secondary sex characteristics in herself. And she was aware of her lies to the physicians examining her. She knew only too well the fronts, the tricks, the ruses she fabricated to hide her secret from others. So Agnes was fully aware of the leap from being a technically biological male to becoming an hormonally and surgically induced female. If Garfinkel and his colleagues had really seen the world as Agnes did, they would have been aware of all this. Their error was not in adopting empathy as an assumption and a reasearch strategy, as Coleman claims, but in *not being empathetic enough*. They had believed in Agnes's front *to* the world, not in her version *of* the world.

And the second flaw in Coleman's "objectivistic" posture toward Agnes is in assuming the unidimensionality of gender, that formal, objective properties determine the essential reality of a phenomenon. It is quite irrelevant exactly how Agnes induced female characteristics in herself. *She truly believed herself to be a woman.* She saw her male sex organs as an excrescence, a pathological growth, much like cancer. Her efforts, she felt, corrected a mistake of nature. Her operation was a vindication of her true sexuality (Garfinkel, 1967:116–185). (Agnes and Coleman agree on the major point: that gender is *essentialistic*, that one has a "true," ultimate, definitive sexuality. They differ only on the criteria. Both versions can be regarded as one out of many ways of looking at gender.) To believe that Agnes "really" was, after all, and above all, a "boy"—as Coleman insists on referring to her throughout his review—is to fail to notice something truly remarkable taking place before one's very eyes. It is to fail as an empiricist.

Empathy does not mean *surrender*, either; it does not mean that the deviant "is always right." Ideological systems describing, explaining and justifying one's own behavior tend to be detailed and subtle. (Although those describing other people's are often shallow and simplified.) Outsiders who are not plugged into what people think and say about what they do, who they are, and what they believe, gloss over the filigree-like fertility of their subjects' worldview. Deviants do not present an "I am always right" impression to one another, nor to themselves. (Perhaps the paranoid is an exception.) But they do to outsiders. Frequent, heavy users of hard drugs—alcoholics, speed freaks, heroin addicts—do not present the effects of the drug they use in a uniformly positive light, not to insiders, not to themselves, and not to empathetic researchers who make a genuine effort to understand their world. The closer one comes to that world the more brutally honest they are about what their drug of choice is doing to their mind and body.

NUTS, SLUTS, AND PREVERTS

A sizable proportion of sociological writings on deviance within the labeling tradition has investigated what has come to be called the *nuts, sluts, and deviated preverts* variety of behavior (Liazos, 1972). The study of deviance concentrates on condemned and stigmatized behavior and people; what is studied is specifically only that which is included within these circumscribed boundaries. This means that deviance sociologists have to ignore a great deal of behavior and people that do not fit in with the formal definition, but are similar in interesting ways. This past fascination with dramatic and "immoral" behavior has led to ignoring "the unethical, illegal and destructive actions of powerful individuals, groups and institutions in our society" (Liazos, 1972:111). The "value engaged labelists" express their "class bias" by focusing on the behavior of the powerless and ignoring that of the powerful. In so doing, they avoid examining the workings of the power elite in the drama of deviant behavior, thereby supporting the status quo (Thio, 1973).

This is a valid characterization and criticism of labeling theory as it has been practiced specifically and historically. But critics of this stripe make the assumption that the blunder is inherent to the labeling perspective. In fact, this restriction on what behavior a "reactive" viewpoint can and cannot examine and what levels of society it delves into is entirely self-imposed. I will argue that it is not a logical or a necessary implication of labeling theory. The "interactionist" perspective toward deviance does not automatically restrict our attention to "nuts, sluts, and preverts," to the deviance of the powerless; it can direct our attention to the very phenomena these critics wish to examine. Far from being a kind of ringside seat on a parade of freaks, weirdos, and colorful characters, our perspective should insist on raising the question why certain kinds of acts tend to be condemned while others are not. Inevitably this leads to an examination of the distribution of power in the society under study.

As sociologists further back than Sutherland have pointed out, the thief in the white collar steals far more from the public pocket than the conventional street criminal. If we were to ask a cross-section of the public why crimes such as armed robbery and burglary should receive stiff penalties, the typical reply would be that they represent a great "threat to society." The same public is indifferent toward, fails to condemn—and yet, is being bilked by—the white collar criminal. Why? A recent estimate of bank losses indicated that bank robbers stole approximately 27 million dollars in 1973, while in the same year approximately 150 million was stolen by the bank's own trusted employees. Yet armed robbery was considered significantly more "serious" a crime to a sample of respondents than embezzlement (Rossi, et al., 1974). The public loses incalculably more again from corporate crimes and yet condemns them even less. Which, then, is more deviant?

Consider drug use, possession, and sale. Selling heroin was the third most "serious" crime evaluated by the respondents in the study just cited—ranking below only the planned killing of a policeman and the planned killing of a person

for a fee. It was deemed more serious than all forms of forcible rape and the planned killing of a spouse. Even *using* heroin was more strongly condemned than killing someone in a bar-room brawl. Selling marijuana ranked as more serious than the forcible rape of one's former spouse and "killing spouse's lover after catching them together" (Rossi, et al., 1974).

The possession, use, and sale of illegal, recreational drugs is clearly a form of deviant behavior. However, a mechanical and simple-minded interpretation of labeling deviant behavior would be to confine our efforts exclusively to those drug-related forms of behavior that are condemned by the public. A sophisticated interpretation of the labeling perspective would study drug use with the intention of understanding why externally similar forms of behavior are accorded markedly different degrees of condemnation. Certain legal drug sellers—the alcohol, tobacco, and the pharmaceutical industries—are responsible for far more drug-related deaths, overdoses, medical damage, and human misery than purveyors of illegal drugs. Yet we never cast drug manufacturing executives into the role of deviants. Any meaningful examination of drug use is forced to grapple with this paradox (Goode, 1972).

An adequate understanding of labeling theory demands that damaging but respectable (i.e., non-deviant) behavior be studied. These disjunctions between public condemnation and "objective" social damage should intrigue us. If we define deviance by public condemnation, we have to find out both the "why" of it—why some behavior attracts a label of immorality—was well as the "why not": why other forms of behavior are not considered immoral. We can never fully understand what is deviant until we get a good look at what isn't. By looking at both, we realize that it is not "social cost" nor any "objective threat to society" that accounts for behavior labeled as deviant or crystallized into formal law. We couldn't deal with this issue if we concentrated exclusively on deviant (or criminal) behavior itself.

The forms of behavior that Marxists and radicals consider—those they criticize labeling theorists for ignoring—oppression, exploitation, racism, sexism, imperialism, certainly do far more damage to human life than most (or any) acts of obvious deviance. And yet behavior that falls under their umbrella is not generally regarded as deviant. Many of us might feel that they *should* be condemned by the public. Some no doubt feel that a theory, like labeling theory, should not be taken seriously if we *can't* call such actions deviant. But the fact that they are not deviant in the public mind should excite our curiosity. Deviance is not centrally about oppression, although it overlaps with it in important ways. Oppression is certainly a basic feature in some forms of deviant behavior, just as the quality of deviance is entirely lacking in much oppressive behavior.

This divergence leads to the issue of how definitions of deviance favorable to those in power manage to win out over definitions that would threaten established ideological and material interests. As Marx and Engels pointed out over a century and a quarter ago in *The German Ideology*, the ruling class tends to dominate a society's intellectual and ideological life, its notions of true and false, of good and bad. Consequently it often happens that the relatively powerless in a given society, the economically deprived, are more likely to have their behavior defined as deviant and are less capable of resisting an imputation of deviance than the affluent and powerful. Thus, the study of deviance often parallels the study of powerlessness. Why this essentially Marxist idea should enrage Marxists is puzzling.

WHAT IS DEVIANCE?
WHO IS THE DEVIANT?

Pushed to its logical extreme, the idea of relativity is self-defeating. If what is considered deviant is relative generally to time and place, it is relative even more specifically to each individual instance of time and place. Judgments of the reactions to behavior vary not only across societies and contexts in general, but across specific situations as well. It follows that what is deviance is completely *sui generis* and literally emergent out of actually occurring instances of behavior and reactions to behavior. This is Pollner's "Model II" version of deviance: "the deviant character of the act . . . depends upon, or more emphatically, is constituted by the subsequent response of the community. . . . There is no deviance apart from the response. . . . If the labeling is constitutive of deviance, then the fact that no one reacts to an act as deviant means that it is not deviant" (Pollner, 1974:29, 33).

It becomes impossible, adopting this view, to predict a priori whether a given act will be judged as deviance until we know whether it already has been so judged. Behavior that has escaped the scrutiny and condemnation by alters is not deviant at all. If act A is identical in all respects to act B, differing only in that A has been observed and condemned while B has not, then A is an instance of deviance and B is not. Becker tried to bridge this chasm by introducing the distinction between *deviance* and *rule-breaking* behavior (1963:14), thereby creating a form of behavior that formally breaks the rules but is not perceived as deviance—"secret deviance" (1963:20). But by employing the dimension of literal condemnation "secret deviance" is not deviant at all; it could not exist within Becker's scheme. Of all aspects of his model, perhaps this conceptual difficulty attracted more criticism than any other. It pleased no one, including Becker himself.

Becker's later formulation attempted to resolve this problem. It is not necessary to call behavior deviant if and only if it has already been condemned. Certain acts can be considered deviant "because these acts are likely to be defined as deviant when discovered" (Becker, 1973:181). Referring to his earlier conceptualization of "secret" deviance, Becker comments: "If we begin by saying that an act is deviant when it is so defined, what can it mean to call an act an instance of secret deviance? Since no one has defined it as deviant it cannot, by definition, be deviant; but 'secret' indicates that *we* know it is deviant, even if no one else does" (1973:187). This difficulty forces us to refer to certain acts as *potentially* deviant. Acts have differing degrees of probability attached to them of being condemned. If we knew the situations in which they occurred and the characteristics of the various actors involved, we would have a clearer idea of just what these probabilities are. This probabilistic conception of deviance permits us to transcend the dilemma that plagued earlier theorists. Behavior is deviant, then, "if it falls within a class of behavior for which there is probability of negative sanctions subsequent to its detection" (Black and Reiss, 1970:63).

Taken literally, the "everything is relative" vulgarization implies that almost any behavior is deviant—to some people. And that no form of behavior is deviant—that is, to absolutely everyone. This is of course literally true, but not very helpful. The idea of "potential" deviance forces us to recognize that not all groups in a society are equally powerful nor are they equal in the numeric sense. Examining different definitions of evidence as if they all got equal time, as if they operated in a kind of ethical free enterprise system, belies the hierarchical nature of deviance. Most important is the issue of which moral codes are dominant, which forms of behavior stand a high likelihood of condemnation. Different acts command varying probabilities of exciting moral outrage among segments of the community; these probabilities can be determined, even if only approximately. A completely situational view of deviance can be intellectually paralyzing. The probabilistic view rescues us from the solipsistic logical extreme of absolute situational relativity and the empirical obtuseness of behavioral universality.

Does the probabilistic view imply that the deviant shares the majority view of what and who should be condemned? Critics of the labeling theory holding a leftish, conflict viewpoint (Mankoff, 1971; Chambliss, 1974) find "significant traces of consensual thinking" in labelists. "The societal reaction paradigm implies that labelers really share the same *Weltanschauung* as rule-breakers" (Mankoff, 1971: 212). This would make labeling theory a variety of a "value consensus" perspective. This position represents a basic misunderstanding.

Several analytically and empirically distinct dimensions are confused in this criticism. It is crucial to separate them. They are:

1. *sharing* the conformist's normative values—that is, believing that rule-breaking (for the deviant, what one is doing) is morally wrong;

2. *knowing* what the majority definition of deviance and conformity actually are;
3. *caring*, in the moral sense, that one will be condemned by the majority's definition of right and wrong;
4. caring about the *consequences* that flow from committing wrong-doing among conformists;
5. taking the negative reactions of conformists to one's own deviance *into account.*

The labelist assumes that rule-breakers and deviants are typically aware of the general society's definitions of right and wrong; most know that what they are doing would be regarded as deviance by a substantial proportion of their fellow members of society. And they are usually motivated to avoid punishment and condemnation, taking care to keep their behavior from public view. The labelist, in other words, *assumes* dimension (2), and takes dimensions (4) and (5) to be an empirical question, although usually true. Dimensions (1) and (3) are usually not true (although they may be). Believing that they are typically the case would make one a "value consensus" theorist. Such assumptions are most decidedly not part of the perspective of anyone known as a labeling theorist. It is necessary, then, to make a distinction between *knowing* and *caring*, and between knowing and caring about how others *feel* and *what they can do to you*, what sanctions they have at their command. Confusing these dimensions mangles one's interpretation of the interactionist perspective.

If we can determine what deviance is a priori (without turning into a value consensus theorist), does the same hold for identifying the deviant? The word "deviant" is, of course, both an adjective and a noun. Used as an adjective, as in "deviant behavior," it has the same meanings as, but is simply grammatically different from, "deviance." "Deviant" takes on a radically different meaning if it is used as a noun. We all know that *doing* deviance is not the same thing as *being a deviant.* And that one possible avenue to becoming "a" deviant is through the application of a stigmatizing label—Tannenbaum's "dramatization of evil" (1938:19). In this sense to be a deviant is to have one's entire character publicly discredited, tainted, and morally damned. A deviant is one who is widely thought to be routinely immoral by others, who is seen to "belong" to a collectively stigmatized group or category, whose behavior has become so scandalous to others that he or she is thought to be the sort of person who is expected to do immoral, evil, disgraceful, diabolical, irritating things. By this definition, one may be a deviant only if one has, in fact, already been collectively condemned by others.

However, this process of public labeling is atypical. Most of the people who would be considered "deviants" were their behavior to become known to the general public do not conform to this definition. Most people who claim affiliation with a stigmatized group or category never themselves literally become publicly stigmatized as deviants. Consider homosexuals. "Most homosexuals live out their lives . . . without their sexual activities ever having been made a public issue. . . . Members of the gay community define themselves as essentially *being homosexual* and tend to organize their lives around the fact of possessing the *symbolic* (as opposed to publicly applied) stigma." Their special claim to being deviant "results *not* from . . . *acts of labeling*, typically at least, but through a more informal and amorphous process of *being labeled*, or having an identity infused with the cognizance of its public opprobrium" (Warren and Johnson, 1972:76, 77). In short, one can be *a* deviant through the process of *self-labeling*: accepting an identity that one is aware is saturated with public scorn. One may not accept the validity of these public characterizations. One may not even care about them. But one is rarely ignorant of them. This awareness necessitates adjustments, accommodations, and coping mechanisms. In short, one can be committed to a deviant career—and be a deviant—without having been literally so labeled by the public.

Some students of behavior are distressed by the fact that the concepts "deviance" and "deviant" are not precisely parallel. By the definitions I proposed here, it is possible to know in advance (roughly, at any rate) what acts stand a high likelihood of being judged as deviant by specific relevant audiences. This is not acceptable for defining individuals as "deviants," however. Acts can be regarded as potentially deviant; people cannot. When we refer to behavior, contingencies *constitute* the character of the act. When we refer to people, contingencies *qualify* their character. When we think of or refer to behavior, ancillary features may or may not render it an instance of a larger, deviant, form of behavior (to a specific audience, of course). "Killing" by itself is not necessarily regarded as deviance; the extenuating circumstances and the contextual features of the act determine whether it is a deviant form of killing, i.e., murder. The many contingencies and auxiliary aspects, its context, the motives regarded as acceptable, are sufficiently qualifying *as to classify it altogether*. These can, however, be spelled out. To cite another instance, one ethnomethodologists are especially fond of, to throw a baby out of a 10-story window is usually taken to be an instance of "insanity." But if the man who does it is a fireman, the building is in flames, and there is a safety net below, it is seen as an instance of "heroism," not madness. The extenuating features of the behavior do not merely qualify it—they constitute it. So that we can refer to murder or incest or homosexuality as deviance in general (given specific audiences) because the referent has *already* been stripped of all qualifying features.

It is quite otherwise with the attachment of a deviant label to specific individuals. People can be many more things than a drunk, an adulterer, an embezzler. Conventional audiences are often willing to admit that, yes, he did a horrible thing—but he's not a horrible *man*. The power of ancillary and contingent features of the individuals in question to determine their deviant status is sufficiently great as to demand that we reserve judgment concerning whether or not a given perpetrator of a clearly deviant act is, in fact, *a* deviant until we know his or her relevant qualifying features, and what they mean to relevant audiences. The escalation from deviant acts to deviant character type is sufficiently problematic that the only way of dealing with the problem is to reserve judgment until learning whether a given individual *has already* been regarded as a deviant by relevant audiences—including himself or herself. Specific people live biographical and historical lives; abstract acts are frozen in time. In addition, the passage of time washes many sins away. The compilation of additional features that are conventional or praiseworthy does not render the deviant acts of the past respectable, but they may render the individual respectable.

CONCLUSION

Labeling theory isn't a theory at all. Perhaps it isn't even as grandiose an edifice as a general perspective. It is merely one way of looking not at deviance in general, but at some specific *features* of deviance. Aspects of labeling theory are relevant for some issues in examining deviant behavior and irrelevant for many others. Some of the basic and fundamental issues raised by labeling theorists—what something is, what category it "belongs" to, what is deviant, who is a deviant—are always relevant, even when examining deviance in a fairly conventional fashion. But accepting the importance of these issues does not mean, as Hirschi (1973:169–170) seems to have concluded, that this makes deviance "impossible to study." It does mean that the first step in the study of deviance has to be a consideration of these crucial issues. The exquisitely reciprocal relationship between action and reaction makes a simple study of "pure" behavior extremely misleading. Included within the scope of what behavior *is* has to be what it *means*—to the various relevant audiences. Hirschi is incorrect in saying that this makes the study of deviance impossible. But what it does mean is that the issues he takes to be "straightforward empirical questions" quite simply aren't.

Beyond this, a number of critics have pointed out labeling theory's limited scope. The question of etiology, for example (Gibbs, 1966) may very well be beyond the scope of labeling theory; it was never intended to be an explanation of causality. Of course, it would help those studying etiology to specify just what they are trying to find the cause of. But no one would hold that labeling creates a given form of behavior de novo. There may be forms of behavior on which labeling has some etiological impact, but generally, this avenue is unlikely to prove fruitful.

Far from a theory of deviance, the major ideas in labeling theory are at the level of what Herbert Blumer (1969:147–151) calls *sensitizing concepts*. The simple fact of the limitations of the scope of labeling theory is rarely recognized; if it is, it is taken as a devastating defect. Commentators discuss the labeling issue as if different theories are in stiff competition, or locked in mortal combat. "Theoretical" discussions degenerate into polemics making a point is equated with blasting an opponent's arguments into oblivion. Perhaps if there is anything like a universal rule, I suppose it would be this: The bombardier always attracts more attention than the bricklayer.

REFERENCES

BECKER, HOWARD S. 1963. *Outsiders: Studies in the Sociology of Deviance.* New York: Free Press.

——— 1973. "Labeling theory reconsidered." In *Outsiders,* 2nd edition.

BLACK, DONALD J., and ALBERT J. REISS, JR. 1970. "Police control of juveniles." *American Sociological Review* 35 (February): 63–77.

BLUMER, HERBERT. 1969. *Symbolic Interactionism: Perspective and Method.* Englewood Cliffs, N.J.: Prentice Hall.

CHAMBLISS, WILLIAM J. 1974. "Functional and Conflict Theories of Crime." New York: MSS Modular Publications.

COHEN, ALBERT K. 1965. "The sociology of the deviant act: anomie theory and beyond." *American Sociological Review* 30 (February): 5–14.

COLEMAN, JAMES S. 1968. "Review of Harold Garfinkel's studies in ethnomethodology." *American Sociological Review* 30 (February): 126–130.

ERIKSON, KAI T. 1962. "Notes on the sociology of deviance." *Social Problems* 9 (Spring): 307–314.

——— 1966. *Wayward Puritans: A Study in the Sociology of Deviance.* New York: John Wiley.

FORD, CLELLAN S., and FRANK A. BEACH. 1951. *Patterns of Sexual Behavior.* New York: Harper and Row.

GARFINKEL, HAROLD. 1967. *Studies in Ethnomethodology.* Englewood Cliffs, N.J.: Prentice Hall.

GIBBS, JACK P. 1966. "Conceptions of deviant behavior: the old and the new." *Pacific Sociological Review 9* (Spring): 9–14.

——— 1972. "Issues in defining deviance." In Robert A. Scott and Jack D. Douglas (eds.), *Theoretical Perspectives on Deviance.* New York: Basic Books.

GOODE, ERICH. 1972. *Drugs in American Society.* New York: Alfred Knopf.

GOODE, ERICH, and RICHARD R. TROIDEN (eds.) 1974. *Sexual Deviance and Sexual Deviants.* New York: William Morrow.

HIRSCHI, TRAVIS. 1973. "Procedural rules and the study of deviance." *Social Problems* 21 (Fall): 159–173.

KITSUSE, JOHN I. 1962. "Societal reaction to deviant behavior: problems of theory and method." *Social Problems 9* (Winter): 247–256.

LEMERT, EDWIN M. 1972. *Human Deviance, Social Problems, and Social Control.* Englewood Cliffs, N.J.: Prentice Hall.

LIAZOS, ALEXANDER. 1972. "The poverty of the sociology of deviance: nuts, sluts, and preverts." *Social Problems 20* (Summer): 103–120.

LOFLAND, JOHN. 1969. *Deviance and Identity.* Englewood Cliffs, N.J.: Prentice Hall.

MANKOFF, MILTON. 1971. "Societal reaction and career deviance: a critical analysis." *The Sociological Quarterly 12* (Spring): 204–218.

MATZA, DAVID. 1969. *Becoming Deviant.* Englewood Cliffs, N.J.: Prentice Hall.

McCaghy, Charles. 1967. "Child molesters: a study of their careers as deviants." In Marshall B. Clinard and Richard Quinney, *Criminal Behavior Systems: A Typology.* New York: Holt, Rinehart and Winston.

MERTON, ROBERT K. 1971. "Social problems and sociological theory." In Robert K. Merton and Robert Nisbet (eds.), *Contemporary Social Problems.* New York: Harcourt Brace Jovanovich.

NISBET, ROBERT. 1970. *The Social Bond.* New York: Alfred Knopf.

POLLNER, MELVIN. 1974. "Sociological and commonsense models of the labeling process." In Roy Turner (ed.), *Ethnomethodology: Selected Readings.* Baltimore: Penguin Books.

RAINS, PRUDENCE, and JOHN I. KITSUSE. 1973. "Comments on the Labeling Approach to Deviance." Unpublished manuscript.

REISS, ALBERT J. 1961. "The social integration of queers and peers." *Social Problems 9* (Fall): 102–120.

ROSSI, PETER H., et al. 1974. "The seriousness of crimes: normative structure and individual differences." *American Sociological Review* 39 (April): 224–237.

RUBINGTON, EARL, and MARTIN S. WEINBERG (eds.). 1973. *Deviance: The Interactionist Perspective.* New York: Macmillan, 2nd edition.

SCHUR, EDWIN M. 1971. *Labeling Deviant Behavior.* New York: Harper and Row.

SKIPPER, JAMES K., JR., and CHARLES McCAGHY. 1970. "Stripteasers: the anatomy and career contingencies of a deviant occupation." *Social Problems* 17 (Winter): 391–405.

TANNENBAUM, FRANK. 1938. *Crime and the Community.* New York: Columbia University Press.

THIO, ALEX. 1973. "Class bias in the sociology of deviance." *The American Sociologist* 8 (February): 1–12.

WALTER, EUGENE VICTOR. 1969. *Terror and Resistance.* New York: Oxford University Press.

WARREN, CAROL A.B., and JOHN M. JOHNSON. 1972. "A critique of labeling theory from the phenomenological perspective." In Robert A. Scott and Jack D. Douglas (eds.), *Theoretical Perspectives on Deviance.* New York: Basic Books.

Conflict Theory

Conflict theories of deviant behavior are of several types, but all of them focus on the central element of power in defining deviance and its social control. Conflict theorists (unlike functionalists) do not believe that societal consensus maintains social order. On the contrary, they assert that most societies are made up of groups with conflicting values, and those with the most power will define certain behaviors of weaker groups as deviant or criminal. Generally, there are cultural, political, economic, and Marxist versions of conflict theory.

Steven Spitzer's article, "Toward a Marxian Theory of Deviance," lays out the basic tenets of Marxian analysis and applies them to the study of deviance. Marx's writings did not attend much to matters of deviance and crime. Spitzer's analysis draws out the implications of Marxian theory for both the creation and control of deviance and explains how in a class society deviance and crime are more likely to be found in the "lowest sediment" of the relative surplus population. Elements of this population may threaten the established order of production, and must be controlled if existing economic relations are to be preserved. He predicts that as this class is more clearly defined, it becomes more problematic in terms of control, and that more of the state's resources are necessary to effect this end.

Along similar lines, Robert Bohm offers an explication and defense of what has come to be known as "Radical Criminology." This theoretical perspective contains numerous related theories that generally challenge those posited by mainstream criminology. Bohm contrasts radical versus conflict criminologies and finds fundamental differences between them. He then goes on to examine each of the schools of thought within radical criminology, paying particular attention to the issue of how social control is managed by the state and the varying interpretations of how this control comes about.

Alexander Liazos' piece, "The Poverty of the Sociology of Deviance," provides an important challenge that the field of deviance become more inclusive of forms of deviance in society. Liazos posits in the early 1970s that at that time the study of deviance largely neglected deviant behaviors of the political and economic elite, and that despite their claims, sociologists had ignored the role of power in defining deviance. Drawing on the work of C. Wright Mills, he argues that while the field had progressed since that time, it was still biased in terms of the subjects it chose for study. One neglected area, introduced by Liazos, is what he terms "covert institutional violence," which is built into the social structure itself. Liazos also claims that the effort by some sociologists to show that deviants are not so much different than conformists is defeated by the fact that certain categories of behavior but not others are focused on. His forceful argument against the exclusive emphasis on "nuts, sluts, and preverts" (intentionally misspelled in the original) has helped to broaden and diversify the study of deviance over the past two decades.

TOWARD A MARXIAN THEORY OF DEVIANCE*

Steven Spitzer

THE PRODUCTION OF DEVIANCE IN CAPITALIST SOCIETY

The concept of deviance production offers a starting point for the analysis of both deviance and control. But for such a construct to serve as a critical tool it must be grounded in a historical and structural investigation of society. For Marx, the crucial unit of analysis is the mode of production that dominates a given historical period. If we are to have a Marxian theory of deviance, therefore, deviance production must be understood in relationship to specific forms of socioeconomic organization. In our society, productive activity is organized capitalistically and it is ultimately defined by "the process that transforms on the one hand, the social means of subsistence and of production into capital, on the other hand the immediate producers into wage labourers" (Marx, 1967:714).

There are two features of the capitalist mode of production important for purposes of this discussion. First, as a mode of production it forms the foundation of infrastructure of our society. This means that the starting point of our analysis must be an understanding of the economic organization of capitalist societies and the impact of that organization on all aspects of social life. But the capitalist mode of production is an important

starting point in another sense. It contains contradictions which reflect the internal tendencies of capitalism. These contradictions are important because they explain the changing character of the capitalist system and the nature of its impact on social, political, and intellectual activity. The formulation of a Marxist perspective on deviance requires the interpretation of the process through which the contradictions of capitalism are expressed. In particular, the theory must illustrate the relationship between specific contradictions, the problems of capitalist development, and the production of a deviant class.

The superstructure of society emerges from and reflects the ongoing development of economic forces (the infrastructure). In class societies this superstructure preserves the hegemony of the ruling class through a system of class controls. These controls, which are institutionalized in the family, church, private associations, media, schools, and the state, provide a mechanism for coping with the contradictions and achieving the aims of capitalist development.

Among the most important functions served by the superstructure in capitalist societies is the regulation and management of problem populations. Because deviance processing is only one of the methods available for social control, these groups supply raw material for deviance production, but are by no means synonymous with deviant populations. Problem populations tend to share a number of social characteristics, but most important among these is the fact that their behavior, personal qualities, and/or position

*Reprinted from "Toward a Marxian Theory of Deviance," by Steven Spitzer, *Social Problems*, 22 (June, 1975), pp. 641–651. © 1975 by The Society for the Study of Social Problems. Reprinted by permission of the publisher and the author.

threaten the *social relations of production* in capitalist societies. In other words, populations become generally eligible for management as deviant when they disturb, hinder, or call into question any of the following:

1. capitalist modes of appropriating the product of human labor (e.g., when the poor "steal" from the rich);
2. the social conditions under which capitalist production takes place (e.g., those who refuse or are unable to perform wage labor);
3. patterns of distribution and consumption in capitalist society (e.g., those who use drugs for escape and transcendence rather than sociability and adjustment);
4. the process of socialization for productive and non-productive roles (e.g., youth who refuse to be schooled or those who deny the validity of "family life");[1]
5. the ideology which supports the functioning of capitalist society (e.g., proponents of alternative forms of social organization).

Although problem populations are defined in terms of the threat and costs that they present to the social relations of production in capitalist societies, these populations are far from isomorphic with a revolutionary class. It is certainly true that some members of the problem population may under specific circumstances possess revolutionary potential. But this potential can only be realized if the problematic group is located in a position of functional indispensability within the capitalist system. Historically, capitalist societies have been quite successful in transforming those who are problematic and indispensable (the proto-revolutionary class) into groups who are either problematic and dispensable (candidates for deviance processing) or indispensable but not problematic (supporters of the capitalist order). On the other hand, simply because a group is manageable does not mean that it ceases to be a problem for the capitalist class. Even though dispensable problem populations cannot overturn the capitalist system, they can represent a significant impediment to its maintenance and growth. It is in this sense that they become eligible for management as deviants.

Problem populations are created in two ways—either directly through the expression of fundamental contradictions in the capitalist mode of production or indirectly through disturbances in the system of class rule. An example of the first process is found in Marx's analysis of the "relative surplus-population."

Writing on the "General Law of Capitalist Accumulation" Marx explains how increased social redundance is inherent in the development of the capitalist mode of production.

With the extension of the scale of production, and the mass of the labourers set in motion, with the greater breadth and fullness of all sources of wealth, there is also an extension of the scale on which greater attraction of labourers by capital is accompanied by their greater repulsion. . . . The labouring population therefore produces, along with the accumulation of capital produced by it, the means by which itself is made relatively superfluous, . . . and it does this to an always increasing extent (Marx, 1967:631).

In its most limited sense the production of a relative surplus-population involves the creation of a class which is economically redundant. But insofar as the conditions of economic existence determine social existence, this process helps explain the emergence of groups who become both threatening and vulnerable at the same time. The marginal status of these populations reduces their stake in the maintenance of the system while their powerlessness and dispensability renders them increasingly susceptible to the mechanisms of official control.

The paradox surrounding the production of the relative surplus-population is that this population is both useful and menacing to the accumulation of capital. Marx describes how the relative surplus-population "forms a disposable industrial army, that belongs to capital quite as absolutely as if the latter had bred it at its own cost," and how this army, "creates, for the changing needs of the self-expansion of capital, a mass of human material always ready for exploitation" (Marx, 1967:632).

On the other hand, it is apparent that an excessive increase in what Marx called the "lowest sediment" of the relative surplus-population might seriously impair the growth of capital. The social expenses and threat to social harmony created by a large and economically stagnant surplus-population could jeopardize the preconditions for accumulation by undermining the ideology of equality so essential to the legitimation of production relations in bourgeois democracies, diverting revenues away from capital investment toward control and support operations, and providing a basis for political organization of the dispossessed.[2] To the extent that the relative surplus-population confronts the capitalist class as a threat to the social relations of production, it reflects an important contradiction in modern capitalist societies: A surplus-population is a necessary product of and condition for the accumulation of wealth on a capitalist basis, but it also creates a form of social expense which must be neutralized or controlled if production relations and conditions for increased accumulation are to remain unimpaired.

Problem populations are also generated through contradictions which develop in the system of class rule. The institutions which make up the superstructure of capitalist society originate and are maintained to guarantee the interests of the capitalist class. Yet these institutions necessarily reproduce, rather than resolve, the contradictions of the capitalist order. In a dialectical fashion, arrangements which arise in order to buttress capitalism are transformed into their opposite—structures for the cultivation of internal threats. An instructive example of this process is found in the emergence and transformation of educational institutions in the United States.

The introduction of mass education in the United States can be traced to the developing needs of corporate capitalism (cf. Karier, 1973; Cohen and Lazerson, 1972; Bowles and Gintis, 1972; Spring, 1972). Compulsory education provided a means of training, testing and sorting, and assimilating wage-laborers, as well as withholding certain populations from the labor market. The system was also intended to preserve the values of bourgeois society and operate as an "inexpensive form of police" (Spring, 1973:31). However, as Gintis (1973) and Bowles (1973) have suggested, the internal contradictions of schooling can lead to effects opposite of those intended. For the poor, early schooling can make

explicit the oppressiveness and alienating character of capitalist institutions, while higher education can instill critical abilities which lead students to "bite the hand that feeds them." In both cases educational institutions create troublesome populations (i.e., dropouts and student radicals) and contribute to the very problems they were designed to solve. . . .

Two more or less discrete groupings are established through the operations of official control. These groups are a product of different operating assumptions and administrative orientations toward the deviant population. On the one hand, there is *social junk*, which, from the point of view of the dominant class, is a costly yet relatively harmless burden to society. The discreditability of social junk resides in the failure, inability, or refusal of this group to participate in the roles supportive of capitalist society. Social junk is most likely to come to official attention when informal resources have been exhausted or when the magnitude of the problem becomes significant enough to create a basis for "public concern." Since the threat presented by social junk is passive, growing out of its inability to compete and its withdrawal from the prevailing social order, controls are usually designed to regulate and contain rather than eliminate and suppress the problem. Clear-cut examples of social junk in modern capitalist societies might include the officially administered aged, handicapped, mentally ill, and mentally retarded.

In contrast to social junk, there is a category that can be roughly described as *social dynamite*. The essential quality of deviance managed as social dynamite is its potential actively to call into question established relationships, especially relations of production and domination. Generally, therefore, social dynamite tends to be more youthful, alienated, and politically volatile than social junk. The control of social dynamite is usually premised on an assumption that the problem is acute in nature, requiring a rapid and focused expenditure of control resources. This is in contrast to the handling of social junk, frequently based on a belief that the problem is chronic and best controlled through broad reactive rather than intensive and selective measures. Correspondingly, social dynamite is normally processed through the legal system with its capacity for active intervention, while social junk is frequently (but not always)[3] administered by the agencies and agents of the therapeutic and welfare state.

Many varieties of deviant populations are alternatively or simultaneously dealt with as either social junk and/or social dynamite. The welfare poor, homosexuals, alcoholics, and "problem children" are among the categories reflecting the equivocal nature of the control process and its dependence on the political, economic, and ideological priorities of deviance production. The changing nature of these priorities and their implications for the future may be best understood by examining some of the tendencies of modern capitalist systems.

MONOPOLY CAPITAL AND DEVIANCE PRODUCTION

Marx viewed capitalism as a system constantly transforming itself. He explained these changes in terms of certain tendencies and contradictions immanent within the capitalist mode of production. One of the most important processes identified by Marx was the tendency for the organic composition of capital to rise. Simply stated, capitalism requires increased productivity to survive, and increased productivity is only made possible by raising the ratio of machines (dead labor) to men (living labor). This tendency is self reinforcing since, "the further machine production advances, the higher becomes the organic composition of capital needed for an entrepreneur to secure the average profit" (Mandel, 1968:163). This phenomenon helps us explain the course of capitalist development over the last century and the rise of monopoly capital (Baran and Sweezy, 1966).

For the purposes of this analysis there are at least two important consequences of this process. First, the growth of constant capital (machines and raw material) in the production process leads to an expansion in the overall size of the relative surplus-population. The reasons for this are obvious. The increasingly technological character of production removes more and more laborers from productive activity for longer periods of time. Thus, modern capitalist societies have been required progressively to reduce the number of productive years in a worker's life, defining both young and old as economically superfluous. Especially affected are the unskilled, who become more and more expendable as capital expands.

In addition to affecting the general size of the relative surplus-population, the rise of the organic composition of capital leads to an increase in the relative stagnancy of that population. In Marx's original analysis he distinguished between forms of superfluous population that were floating and stagnant. The floating population consists of workers who are "sometimes repelled, sometimes attracted again in greater masses, the number of those employed increasing on the whole, although in a constantly decreasing proportion to the scale of production" (1967:641). From the point of view of capitalist accumulation, the floating population offers the greatest economic flexibility and the fewest problems of social control because they are most effectively tied to capital by the "natural laws of production." Unfortunately (for the capitalist at least), these groups come to comprise a smaller and smaller proportion of the relative surplus-population. The increasing specialization of productive activity raises the cost of reproducing labor and heightens the demand of highly skilled and "internally controlled" forms of wage labor (Gorz, 1970). The process through which unskilled workers are alternatively absorbed and expelled from the labor force is thereby impaired, and the relative surplus-population comes to be made up of increasing numbers of persons who are more or less permanently redundant. The boundaries between the "useful" and the "useless" are more clearly delineated, while standards for social disqualification are more liberally defined.

With the growth of monopoly capital, therefore, the relative surplus-population begins to take on the character of a population which is more and more absolute. At the same time, the market becomes a less reliable means of disciplining these populations, and the "invisible hand" is more frequently replaced by the "visible fist." The implications for deviance production are twofold: (1) problem populations become gradually more problematic—both in terms of their size and their insensitivity to economic controls, and (2) the resources of the state need to be applied in greater proportion to protect capitalist relations of production and ensure the accumulation of capital.

NOTES

1. To the extent that a group (e.g., homosexuals) blatantly and systematically challenges the validity of the bourgeois family, it is likely to become part of the problem population. The family is essential to capitalist society as a unit for consumption, socialization, and the reproduction of the socially necessary labor force (cf. Frankford and Snitow, 1972; Secombe, 1973; Zaretsky, 1973).

2. O'Connor (1973) discusses this problem in terms of the crisis faced by the capitalist state in maintaining conditions for profitable accumulation and social harmony.

3. It has been estimated, for instance, that one third of all arrests in America are for the offense of public drunkenness. Most of these apparently involve "sick" and destitute "skid row alcoholics" (Morris and Hawkins, 1969).

REFERENCES

BARAN, PAUL, and PAUL M. SWEEZY. 1966. *Monopoly Capital.* New York: Monthly Review Press.

BOWLES, SAMUEL. 1973. "Contradictions in United States higher education." Pp. 165–199 in James H. Weaver (ed.), *Modern Political Economy: Radical Versus Orthodox Approaches.* Boston: Allyn & Bacon.

BOWLES, SAMUEL, and HERBERT GINTIS. 1972. "I.Q. in the U.S. class structure." *Social Policy* 3 (November/December):65–96.

COHEN, DAVID K., and MARVIN LAZERSON. 1972. "Education and the corporate order." *Socialist Revolution* (March/April): 48–72.

FRANKFORD, EVENLY, and ANN SNITOW. 1972. "The trap of domesticity: Notes on the family." *Socialist Revolution* (July/August): 83–94.

GINTIS, HERBERT. 1973. "Alienation and power." Pp. 431–465 in James H. Weaver (ed.), *Modern Political Economy: Radical Versus Orthodox Approaches.* Boston: Allyn & Bacon.

GORZ, ANDRE. 1970. "Capitalist relations of production and the socially necessary labor force." Pp. 155–171 in Arthur Lothstein (ed.), *All We Are Saying. . . .* New York: G. P. Putnam.

KARIER, CLARENCE J. 1973. "Business values and the educational state." Pp. 6–29 in Clarence J. Karier, Paul Violas, and Joel Spring (eds.), *Roots of Crisis: American Education in the Twentieth Century.* Chicago: Rand McNally.

MANDEL, ERNEST. 1968. *Marxist Economic Theory,* Vol. 1. New York: Monthly Review Press.

MARX, KARL. 1964. *Class Struggles in France, 1848–1850.* New York: International Publishers.

———. 1967. *Capital,* Vol. 1. New York: International Publishers.

MORRIS, NORVAL, and GORDON HAWKINS. 1969. *The Honest Politician's Guide to Crime Control.* Chicago: University of Chicago Press.

O'CONNOR, JAMES. 1973. *The Fiscal Crisis of the State.* New York: St. Martin's Press.

SECOMBE, WALLY. 1973. "The housewife and her labour under capitalism." *New Left Review* (January–February): 3–24.

SPRING, JOEL. 1972. *Education and the Rise of the Corporate State.* Boston: Beacon Press.

———. 1973. "Education as a form of social control." Pp. 30–39 in Clarence J. Karier, Paul Violas, and Joel Spring (eds.), *Roots of Crisis: American Education in the Twentieth Century.* Chicago: Rand McNally.

ZARETSKY, ELI. 1973. "Capitalism, the family and personal life: parts 1 & 2." *Socialist Revolution* (January–April/May–June): 69–126, 19–70.

Radical Criminology
An Explication*

Robert M. Bohm

A growing controversy has developed over "radical" criminology,[1] a theoretical perspective and practical exigency that challenges the hegemony of traditional "classical" and "positive" criminologies as well as insurgent criminologies based on "labeling" and "conflict" theories.[2] However, much of the polemic related to radical criminology is directed at a "straw man." A review of the literature reveals that radical criminology has been variously termed "The New Criminology" (Taylor et al., 1974; Phillipson, 1973; Chambliss and Mankoff, 1976; Meier, 1976; Hackler, 1977; Bonomo and Wenger, 1978; Inciardi, 1979; Toby, 1979; Pelfrey, 1980), "Marxist" criminology (Young, 1976; Greenberg, 1976; Quinney, 1977; Beirne, 1979; Klockars, 1976; Akers, 1979), "materialist" criminology (Werkentin et al., 1974; Taylor et al., 1976; Inciardi, 1979), "dialectical" criminology (Quinney, 1979), "radical" criminology (Wright, 1973; Gibbons and Garabedian, 1974; Young, 1975; Platt, 1975; Taylor et al., 1975; Turk, 1975; Gordon, 1976; Scull, 1977; Toby, 1979; Pelfrey, 1980), "socialist" criminology (Young, 1975), and "critical" criminology (Wright, 1973; Sykes, 1974; Davis, 1975; Taylor et al., 1975; Schumann, 1976; Michalowski and Bohlander, 1976; Keller, 1976; Inciardi, 1979; Wollan, 1979; Pelfrey, 1980).[3] Thus, while radical criminologists obviously share many philosophical, theoretical, and practical assumptions, the preceding list of terms suggests that both they and their critics hold to and appreciate these assumptions with differing degrees of sensitivity, sophistication, and subtlety. Moreover, there are important philosophical, theoretical, practical, and, as indicated above, nominal differences between radical criminologists that are oftentimes ignored by critics and enthusiasts alike. Consequently, the purpose of this study is to begin to explicate some of the shared assumptions of radical criminologists, and some of their differences as well.

RADICAL CRIMINOLOGY VERSUS CONFLICT CRIMINOLOGY[4]

While both "radical" and "conflict" criminologists are critical of traditional classical and positive criminologies, and are conversant with Marxism, there are fundamental differences between them. In particular, radical criminologists are more specific than conflict criminologists in their identification of the explanatory variables that presumably account for crime. As Beirne (1979: 375–377) explains:

The conflict theorists were rarely precise in delineating quite in what "power" and "conflict" consisted, how power manifested itself, how conflict was resolved, and why it was resolved at all; but they nevertheless agreed that power and conflict were at the root of social organization. . . . Conflict theory was generally so vague in its basic assumptions, and so wide-ranging in its scope, that it might easily incorporate (or co-opt) a variety of different perspectives, including Marxism, within the compass of its structure.

Similarly, Taylor et al. (1975: 23) explain that conflict criminology "is highly various in form and in content, but very rarely does it aspire to a coherent or systematic account of the workings of the total society." Likewise Platt (1975: 98–99) argues that while conflict criminologists:

are often critical of the established order, the lack of a historical and dialectical perspective inevitably sets the stage for nihilism or a wishy-washy relativism . . . [conflict criminologists] catalogue various inadequacies and injustices in the present system, but stop short of condemning capitalism or fall back to apologetic relativism. . . . The cynicism implicit in [conflict] ideology is closely tied to elitism and paternalism. [Conflict criminologists] do not envision ordinary working people as the motive force in history, but rather see en-

*From Robert M. Bohm, *Criminology*, vol. 19, No. 4, pp. 565–589, copyright © 1982 by American Society of Criminology. Reprinted by permission of Sage Publications, Inc.

lightened experts fighting a losing battle against an "ignorant public" and corrupt government.

Finally, as Keller (1976: 283) maintains:

a crucial difference between the two schools of criminology is the degree to which they focus on the political and economic structures of society as explanatory variables in the study of crime. While the conflict school specifies stratification as a criminogenic factor, the critical [i.e., radical] school specifies the political economy of capitalism as the criminogenic factor. Only the critical [i.e., radical] school specifies the political and economic structures that promote conflict and therefore produce crime.

Ironically, the major weakness of conflict criminology noted by radical criminologists (i.e., its lack of specificity) is considered by conflict criminologists as a major strength (i.e., its abstractness). Contrary to what they assume radical criminologists believe, conflict criminologists argue that power in society is not the exclusive possession of a "capitalist ruling class," but rather that different groups in society possess and exercise varying degrees of power. As Vold and Bernard (1979: 322) explain:

The value of non-Marxist conflict theory is that it holds that, in any society—whether Marxist or capitalist or fascist—there will be conflicting values and interests among the various segments of society, and that the resolution of those conflicts will depend on the power of the conflicting groups.

In addition, and again presumably in contrast to the beliefs of radical criminologists, conflict criminologists maintain that conflict is not historically or socially limited to a particular type of society (e.g., capitalism) but is a fundamental element of all societies.

One problem with these arguments made by conflict criminologists about the views held by radical criminologists regarding the conflict position is that the conflict criminologists apparently misunderstand the radical argument. First, radical criminologists do not deny that conflict is a fundamental element of all societies. Second, radical criminologists recognize the existence of a plethora of conflicting interest groups that wield varying degrees of power in society. However, for radical criminologists the existence of more or less powerful and oftentimes conflicting interest

groups does not preclude the existence of "classes" (especially under capitalism)—instead, they are considered two different phenomena. The primary difference between "interest groups" and "classes" is that usually an individual may voluntarily align himself with any number of interest groups, while his class position in society is dictated by his relation to the means of production, whether or not he owns property, and the type of property he owns (Mills, 1975: 84; Plamenatz, 1963: 293).

Additionally, radical criminologists generally stress that the ownership and control of productive private property is the basis of power in society, while conflict criminologists seem to emphasize that power is the basis of private property. For conflict criminologists, however, the basis of this power in society is rarely specified. When it is specified, it is usually attributed to the characteristics of an elite (Beirne, 1979; Platt, 1975). In short, both radical criminologists and conflict criminologists assume that conflict is a pervasive and fundamental element of society—whether capitalist, precapitalist, or postcapitalist. However, radical criminologists assume, apparently in contrast to conflict criminologists, that the particular nature of conflict in society is fundamentally related to the historical and social distribution of productive private property in that society.

The final difference between radical and conflict criminology to be discussed here involves a difference in the policy implications of the two criminologies. According to Keller (1976: 350): "While conflict criminology can be described as basically reformist, critical (i.e., radical) criminology can be described as revolutionary." In this regard, consider the following statement of a conflict criminologist:

Conflict theory could result in specific recommendations for social reform, in order to establish a fairer and more just society. This would not necessarily entail the overthrow of the existing social order, any more than did the recommendations derived from the theories of human ecology or of anomie. The question of how conflicts between segments of society can be fairly and equitably resolved is not limited to one type of society, and will not be resolved by the overthrow of a particular social order [Vold and Bernard, 1979: 322].

As conflict criminologists argue, and radical criminologists generally concur, all detrimental forms of conflict will not be resolved by the overthrow of a particular social order. However, according to radical criminologists, those detrimental conflicts peculiar to capitalism, as well as those detrimental conflicts that transcend capitalism but still reinforce capitalist productive relationships (e.g., sexism and racism), cannot be resolved without the overthrow of capitalism.

A NOTE ON THE METONYM "THE NEW CRIMINOLOGY"

Although the radical criminology that gained popularity in the last decade is certainly different from traditional classical and positive criminologies, it is not new. Actually, the term "The New Criminology" is a misnomer for three reasons. First, and on a very superficial level, when a new theory in criminology is promulgated, it is sometimes hailed as "The New Criminology." Compare, for example, Max G. Schlapp and Edward H. Smith's *The New Criminology* (1928) which introduced their glandular conception of crime causation (Lopez-Rey, 1970: 130). Obviously, Schlapp and Smith's *The New Criminology* differs fundamentally from "The New Criminology" associated with radical criminology.

Second, reference to "The New Criminology" sometimes confuses two distinct and oftentimes contradictory positions. For example, at the 1978 annual conference of the Academy of Criminal Justice Sciences, a panel on "new criminology" consisted of proponents of "conflict-critical-radical-Marxian criminology" and "psychobiological criminology" (Pelfrey, 1980:54).[5]

Finally and most importantly, since the roots of radical criminology can be traced at least from Bonger (1916), the perspective is far from new. In short, it is perhaps more accurate to refer to the emergence of radical criminology as a renaissance rather than a "New Criminology."

PHILOSOPHICAL, THEORETICAL, AND PRACTICAL SIMILARITIES IN RADICAL CRIMINOLOGY

In general, radical criminologists focus their attention to the social arrangements in society, especially on political and economic structures and the institutions of capitalism. They argue that capitalism, characterized by its competitive ethos, is an exploitative and alienating social order in which inequality is institutionalized by an elite ruling class whose vested interests depend on the perpetuation of a capitalist society (Taylor et al., 1974, 1975; Gordon, 1973; Wright, 1973; Spitzer, 1975; Keller, 1976; Pearce, 1976; Quinney, 1977).

It is important not to misunderstand that for radical criminologists, the pernicious effects of capitalism (wars, depressions, unemployment, inflation, recession, crime, and so forth)[6] are not directly caused by income or property inequality or poverty per se. Rather, it is the competitive and exploitative inter- and intraclass relations of capitalism that engender income or property inequality, poverty, and many of the other problems noted above that are recurrent under capitalism. According to radical criminologists, crime in capitalist societies is often a rational response to coerced social arrangements or a "by-product" of the political economy (Gordon, 1973: 163, 200; Quinney, 1977: 93; Pearce, 1976).

For radical criminologists, it is the class struggle both between and among those who own and control the means of production and distribution and those who do not that is at the source of *all* crime in capitalist societies (Quinney, 1977: 91; 1979: 446; Chambliss, 1976: 7). The class struggle between the "ruling class" and the "working class" (and, it might be added, the "nonworking class"), as well as the struggle within each class, generates competitive individualism in each class and manifests itself in the pursuit, criminal or otherwise, of property wealth and economic self-aggrandizement (Wright, 1973: 9; Center for Research on Criminal Justice, 1977: 14; Taylor et al., 1975: 3).

This is not to imply that radical criminologists proffer no explanation for violent crime. On the contrary, according to Quinney (1977: 53–54), violent crime (e.g., murder, assault, and rape), which is usually intraclass in nature, results from the brutalization of life under the conditions of capitalism. In short, as Taylor et al. (1975: 23) explain: "It is not that man behaves as an animal because of his 'nature': It is that he is not fundamentally allowed by virtue of the social arrangements of production to do otherwise."

Nor does this necessarily mean that noncapitalist societies will be crime-free, but rather that noncapitalist societies should have different types of crime and much lower rates of crime (as traditionally defined) "because the less intense class struggle should reduce the forces leading to and the functions of crime" (Chambliss, 1976: 9).

It is important to emphasize that radical criminologists define the concept of "crime" differently than is the custom of traditional criminologists. Because they assume that criminal law is all too often manipulated to benefit particular interests to the detriment of all others, radical criminologists argue that the legal definition of crime is both too narrow and too broad in scope. Radical criminologists maintain that "crime" should be defined as a violation of human rights. As Platt (1975: 103) explains:

A radical perspective defines crime as a violation of politically defined human rights: the truly egalitarian rights to decent food and shelter, to human dignity and self-determination, rather than the so-called right to compete for an unequal share of wealth and power.

A radical definition of crime includes "imperialism, racism, capitalism, sexism and other systems of exploitation which contribute to human misery and deprive people of their human potentiality" (Platt, 1975: 103; also see Schwendinger and Schwendinger, 1975 for a similar definition). While many of the behaviors currently proscribed by criminal law would be included in this radical definition, it is nonetheless the case that other behaviors now considered to be crimes would be excluded (e.g., victimless crimes or crimes of consumption), and that some behaviors not now considered to be crimes would be added (e.g., racism, sexism, imperialism).

The objection may be legitimately raised that this radical definition of crime based on the violation of human rights is itself too broad and vague. In confronting a similar dilemma, Edmund Cahn (1966), the noted legal philosopher, once wrote that although it is often difficult to determine what is just, most men can easily identify what is unjust. Perhaps in a like manner, it may be equally difficult to determine what a "human right" is, but it is generally assumed by radical criminologists that most people know when a "human right" has been violated.

In any event, a major priority of radical criminologists is the reconceptualization of the definition of crime in terms of violations of "human rights" (Platt, 1975: 103; Schwendinger and Schwendinger, 1975: 132). Related to this priority is the ethical obligation to demonstrate that the criminal law upon which the definition of crime is based is:

used by the state and the ruling class to secure the survival of the capitalist system, and, as capitalist society is further threatened by its own contradictions, criminal law will be increasingly used in the attempt to maintain domestic order [Quinney, 1974: 16; also see Young, 1975: 89].

Another ethical obligation of radical criminologists is to expose the criminal justice system as a "state-initiated" and "state-supported" effort to rationalize social control and eventually to replace the criminal justice system with "popular" or "socialist justice" (Quinney, 1977: 10 and 22–23; Pearce, 1976: 50; Wright, 1973: 388).

Consequently, contrary to the beliefs of many liberal criminologists, radical criminologists argue that reform of capitalist institutions, especially those of the criminal justice system, cannot legitimately be expected to eradicate the initial causes of crime for two reasons:

First, capitalism depends quite substantially on the preservation of the conditions of competition and inequality. Those conditions . . . will tend to lead almost inevitably to relatively pervasive criminal behavior; without those conditions, the capitalist system would scarcely work at all. Second, as many have argued, the general presence of racism in this country, though capitalists may not in fact have created it, tends to support and maintain the power of the capitalists as a class by providing cheap labor and dividing the working class [Gordon, 1976: 206].

For nearly all radical criminologists, the solution to the problem of crime is a socialist society (Quinney, 1974: 198; 1977: 162; Wright, 1973: 337; Young, 1976: 20; Pearce, 1976) in which, unlike capitalism, human diversity will presumably be appreciated (Taylor et al., 1974: 282; Young, 1975: 90). This in turn will require the development of a political consciousness among all people who are exploited and alienated by the capitalist system (Quinney, 1977: 104–105; Pearce, 1976: 45). Finally, and perhaps most importantly for radical criminologists, only through "praxis" (human action) will this new socialist society be achieved (Taylor et al., 1975: 11; Platt, 1975: 105).

Marxist Criminology

In some ways, Marxist criminology is an inappropriate metonym for radical criminology. Marx actually wrote very little about crime and criminal justice (Quinney, 1975: 192; Chambliss, 1976: 2). However, on one occasion he and Engels did explain that "crime, i.e., the struggle of the isolated individual against the prevailing conditions, is not the result of pure arbitrariness. . . . On the contrary, it depends on the same conditions as that rule" (1970: 107). In other ways, Marxist criminology is perhaps the most appropriate metonym for radical criminology. In this regard, Quinney (1975: 192) explains:

I am suggesting a critical philosophy for understanding the legal order. That philosophy is based on a critical development of a Marxist thought for our age. Only a Marxist critique allows us to break out of the ideology and conditions of the age.

Moreover, Pearce (1976: 104) maintains that not only does a Marxist analysis provide a better explanation of "reality" (i.e., the "reality" of crime and crime control under capitalism), but it also explains the functions of the inaccurate portrayal. Similarly, Chambliss (1976: 2) writes that "Marxism . . . provides a useful starting point . . . because of the very general nature of Marx's sociological theory and the logical extension of it to crime and criminal law." Finally, as Taylor et al. (1975: 45) argue:

The analysis of particular forms of crime, or particular types of criminal, outside of their context in history and society has been shown, in our view, to be a meaningless activity. . . . We have ourselves been forced, logically, to turn for such an analysis (and such a criminology) to Marx.

Thus, "Marxism" provides radical criminologists with a theoretical framework that interrelates the capitalist mode of production, the state,

law, crime control, and crime—as well as other relevant factors. The importance of this integrated understanding is conveyed by Taylor et al. (1974: 278), who write:

The conditions of our time are forcing a reappraisal of (the) compartmentalization of issues and problems. It is not just that the traditional focus of applied criminology on the socially deprived working-class adolescent is being thrown into doubt by the criminalization of vast numbers of middle-class youth. . . . Neither is it only that the crisis of our institutions has deepened to the point where the "master institutions" of the state, and of the political economy, are unable to disguise their own inability to adhere to their own rules and regulations. . . . It is largely that the total interconnectedness of these problems and others is being revealed. A criminology which is to be adequate to an understanding of these developments . . . will need to deal with the society as a totality.

In short, an understanding of any one factor (e.g., capitalism, the state, law, crime control, or crime), in this view, necessitates an understanding of each of the other factors in relation of one to another.

Unfortunately for radical criminologists, there is sufficient ambiguity in Marx's and Engels's writing to allow for at least three different interpretations of how various factors are interrelated. The three interpretations to be discussed in later sections of this article include: (1) the "ruling class determinist" or "instrumentalist"; (2) the "economic determinist" or "structuralist"; and (3) the "dialectical" or "critical."[7]

PHILOSOPHICAL AND THEORETICAL DIFFERENCES IN RADICAL CRIMINOLOGY

Materialist Criminology

Marx and Engels's materialistic conception of history ("historical-materialism") was an explicit repudiation of the German idealism prevalent at the time. For Marx and Engels, the idealistic assumption—that by changing one's beliefs about "reality," one can change "reality"—was not only false, but a particularly insidious form of class domination under capitalism. Marx and Engels (1970: 123) argued: "The philosophers have only 'interpreted' the world in various ways; the point is to 'change' it." Only in a communist (i.e., a classless) society, Marx and Engels believed, would man finally be free from class domination. Moreover, they suggested that a materialistic conception of history and society would provide the evidence (e.g., human misery and contradictions in society) of the forthcoming liberation of all people from conditions of oppression (domination). In sum, for Marx and Engels (1970: 61), "liberation is an historical and not a mental act, and it is brought about by historical conditions, the development of industry, commerce, agriculture, the conditions of intercourse."

It is this interpretation of historical-materialism that typically informs the work of materialist criminologists. For example, Bonger (1916) relates the cause of crime to the absence of a "social disposition" in man, and he argues that it is the mode of production[8] that is able to develop the social predisposition innate in man or to prevent this disposition from being developed. In certain cases (e.g., capitalism), he adds, the mode of production may even destroy the social disposition entirely. Taylor et al. (1975: 47), in expounding the need for a materialist sociology of law, suggest that such a sociology must reveal, among other things, "the primacy not of legal thought, but of material conditions, as the determinants of normative change in general, and criminal and legal norms in particular." Similarly, Quinney (1975: 191) asserts that Marxism "is the one form of analysis that is historically specific and locates the problems of the age in the economic-class relations." Elsewhere (1977: v), Quinney adds that in order to understand criminal justice:

We must investigate the larger issues of the historical development of capitalism, the material basis of crime (including both crime control and criminality), the class structure of advanced capitalism, the role of the capitalist state, and the political economy of criminal justice. Eventually our task is to document the development of control policies in the history of the United States in relation to the economic and political development of the nation.

Chambliss (1976: 2–3), likewise, remarks that:

The Marxian analysis begins with the observation that the needs, characteristics, ideologies, and institutions of a particular society are a reflection of that society's historical condition—especially the material conditions (the mode of production) at that particular historical moment.

Finally, Young (1976: 14) maintains that "central to our concern is the explanation of law and criminality in terms of the dominant mode of production and the class nature of society."

However, as previously mentioned, there is sufficient ambiguity in Marx's and Engels's conception of historical-materialism to suggest at least three interpretations of how various factors (e.g., capitalism, the state, law, and other "superstructures") are interrelated. In this section, the "ruling class determinist" ("instrumentalist") and "economic determinist" ("structuralist") versions of how the state is manipulated are described.[9]

According to the ruling class determinist or instrumentalist interpretation:

The functioning of the state is . . . understood in terms of the instrumental exercise of power by people in strategic positions, either directly through the manipulation of state policies or indirectly through the exercise of pressure on the state [Gold et al., 1975: 34].

Furthermore, in this view the capitalist ruling class is typically perceived as a homogeneous group largely devoid of internal conflicts (Beirne, 1979: 379). Consequently, the materialist criminologist who assumes a ruling class determinist or instrumentalist view of the state generally focuses his research "on studying the nature of the class which rules, the mechanisms which tie this class to the state, and the concrete relationships between state policies and class interests" (Gold et al., 1975: 32; also Beirne, 1979: 379).[10]

In the economic determinist or structuralist interpretation, on the other hand, the functions of the state are presumed to be determined by the structures of society (e.g., "the market" or "the law") rather than by the people who occupy positions of state power or by individual capitalists (Gold et al., 1975). According to the economic determinist or structuralist interpretation, it is the long-run stability of capitalism rather than the short-run interests of individual capitalists that determines state policy (Gold et al., 1975; Beirne, 1979).

A major problem structuralists have with instrumentalists is the instrumentalist's belief in the existence of a homogeneous ruling class whose individual members manifest an unambiguous classwide interest and influence on the state. Structuralists argue that the capitalist ruling class is comprised of specific capitalists and capitalist class factions that represent parochial and individualized interests. Instrumentalists, on the other hand, while admitting a tendency "toward voluntarism to explain state activities," argue that "structuralists have almost entirely eliminated conscious action from their analysis" (Gold et al., 1975: 39).

Dialectical Criminology

Several radical criminologists, presumably following Marx,[11] advocate a "dialectical" criminology. For example, Scull (1977: 11), in his examination of the contemporary effort to "decarcerate" various deviant populations, writes that his study:

will seek to demonstrate the superiority of explanations which focus directly on the complex dialectical interplay between transformations in the social control apparatus (and thus in the shapes and forms of deviance) and changes in the wider social system.

The most outspoken advocate of a dialectical criminology, however, is Quinney. In *Class, State and Crime*, Quinney (1977: 32) explains:

The "dialectical method" allows us to comprehend the world as a complex of processes, in which all things go through a continuous process of coming into being and passing away. All things are studied in the context of their historical development. . . . In dialectical analysis we critically understand our past, informing our analysis with the possibilities for our future.

Elsewhere, and contrary to those radical criminologists who exclusively endorse a materialist criminology, Quinney (1979: 445–446) maintains that:

History is made both subjectively and objectively, as the result of class struggle *and* as the development of the economic modes of production. . . . Thus, all social life, including everything associated with crime, must be understood in terms of the objective economic conditions of production and the subjective struggle between classes that is related to these conditions.

Finally, Young (1976: 14), in defense of a dialectical criminology, concludes that it is necessary "to move beyond this oscillation between vulgar materialism and idealism which is so characteristic of bourgeois thought."

There are at least two implications of this criticism of an exclusively materialist (and oftentimes positivistic) criminology—especially, as noted in the last section, with regard to materialist interpretations of the state. First, for dialectical criminologists, the tendency of materialist criminologists to treat the capitalist state as either an "instrument" in the hands of the ruling class or a determinant of the "structures" of society is rejected, because both views represent undialectical analyses. Instead, in a dialectical analysis, the capitalist state is viewed as both "a structure constrained by the logic of the society within which it functions and as an organization manipulated behind the scenes by the ruling class and its representatives" (Gold et al., 1975: 46). Moreover, in the dialectical view, "the extent to which actual state policies can be explained through structural or instrumental processes is historically contingent" (Gold et al., 1975: 46).

The second implication of the criticism made by dialectical theorists of materialist interpretations of the state is that for dialectical theorists, "'modern states' have major emancipatory forces and are not 'merely' repressive vehicles" (Frankel, 1979: 222). As Frankel (1979: 231) queries:

Are we to only see the bourgeois state in negative terms and ignore the protests of reactionary religious, political and economic forces who are desperately trying to limit state intervention against discriminatory social practices based on puritan bigotry, racist and sexist notions of superiority, plus dozens of other nonuniversalistic notions of human beings?

In other words, the capitalist state, in a dialectical view, is not simply the instrument for the defense and reproduction of capitalism's "exchange value" commodities, but is also the producer of "use value" goods and services (e.g., some of the goods and services provided by hospitals, schools, and welfare agencies) which are not in themselves directly reproducing dominant capitalist social relations (Frankel, 1979: 223–225). Consequently, for Frankel (1979: 237) and other dialectical theorists:

Because the state is involved in everything from wage fixing to sexual, racial, urban and ecological policies, any political organization which claims to be revolutionary must abandon the notion that certain struggles are primary and others secondary.

This latter observation of Frankel's is directly related to those of the radical criminologists (e.g., Taylor et al., 1975: 20 and Quinney, 1977: 156) who envision, as did Marx, the eventual "withering away of the state."[12]

PRAXIS AND METHODOLOGY ISSUES

Radical Criminology

Radical criminology is perhaps the most utilized and encompassing metonym for this general criminological position. It is, for example, a more general term than either Marxist criminology or socialist criminology (to be explicated in the next section). That is, a Marxist is always radical (i.e., revolutionary), while a socialist may or may not be. "Communitarians" and "social democrats" are examples of nonradical (i.e., nonrevolutionary) socialists.

The distinguishing characteristic of radical criminology is its emphasis on "praxis" (human action) as a means of both bringing about changes in society and ascertaining the "adequacy" (i.e., "truth") of radical criminological theories upon which the changes in society are based.

In regard to bringing about changes in society, Becker and Horowitz (1972: 52–53) maintain that to be radical "rests on a desire to change society in a way that will increase equality and maximize freedom," and on an effort to make "a distinctive contribution to the struggle for change." Although Becker and Horowitz's argument is about radical sociology, it applies equally well to radical criminology. Specifically, a radical criminology, in this view, provides the knowledge for: (1) "unmasking forms of domination"; (2) "clarification of what has been confused"; and (3) "critique of organizational constraints" (Becker and Horowitz, 1972:

54–56).[13] In this view, the elements of radical criminology differ little from the elements of critical criminology (to be discussed in the last section). However, what may ultimately separate radical criminology from critical criminology is the implication that the struggle or praxis to change society in a way that will increase equality and maximize freedom (i.e., the transformation from capitalism to communism) will be revolutionary.[14]

The reason that radical criminologists advocate a revolution in order to effect the transformation of capitalism is that only through revolution, they believe, can the mode of production be changed. As Harrington (1976: 137) explains:

The essential objection to the capitalist is not that he steals surplus labor from the worker, and the crucial demand is not to share his luxuries with the populace on a democratic basis. . . . What concerns Marx is that this process of accumulation is carried out in an antisocial fashion that causes depressions, wars and countless other miseries. The point then, is not simply to make the distribution of wealth fairer, but to change the mode of production of wealth so that it is no longer accomplished by means of periodic crises and the brutalization of the producers.

As previously noted, for radical criminologists it is the inter- and intraclass relations of capitalism that generate crime under capitalism:

The causes of crime are rooted in the capitalist system, particularly in its economic policies which guarantee high unemployment and job instability, and in its political policies which reproduce competitive and exploitative social relations [Center for Research on Criminal Justice, 1977: 197].

Furthermore, although "logically, violence, the shedding of blood, is no essential part of revolution as Marx and Engels conceived of it," Plamenatz (1963: 310) indicates that Marx and Engels "thought there would be violence when the proletariat took over power, in most countries if not in all." According to Lenin (1970: 25):

The supersession of the bourgeois state by the proletarian state is impossible without a violent revolution. . . . The necessity of systematically imbuing the masses with "this" and precisely this view of violent revolution lies at the root of "all" the teachings of Marx and Engels.

However, with regard to this presumed necessity for revolution, the radical criminologist may be well advised not to forget Kant's warning:

Perhaps a fall of personal despotism or of avaricious or tyrannical oppression may be accomplished by revolution, but never a true reform in ways of thinking. Rather, new prejudices will serve as well as old ones to harness the great unthinking masses [Kant, 1959: 86].

Regarding the necessity of ascertaining the "adequacy" (i.e., "truth") of radical criminological theories in praxis, Taylor et al. (1975: 24) write:

Radical theory and practice can become a full-blown form of political practice (where currently it appears largely as a political assertion) if it can find ways of changing the social world whilst investigating it.

For Taylor et al. (1975: 24), then, the radical criminologist "must engage in theory and research as praxis." Platt (1975: 105), likewise, asserts that "a radical commitment to practice consists of 'practical critical activity' and participating in ongoing political struggles." Similarly, Quinney (1975: 190) writes that "more than negative thinking is required in a philosophy that will move us to a radical reconstruction of our lives—indeed, to revolution itself." For Quinney (1975: 188), "the liberating force of radical criticism is the movement from revelation to the development of a new consciousness and an active life in which we transcend the established existence."

Socialist Criminology

Besides many of the same considerations already discussed, socialist criminologists, like Marx and other radical criminologists, typically acknowledge the necessity for a transition period between capitalism and communism. As Marx explains:

Between capitalist and communist society lies the period of the revolutionary transformation of the one into the other. There corresponds to this also a political transition period in which the state can be nothing but "the revolutionary dictatorship of the proletariat" [in Lenin, 1970: 102].

For Marx, "the revolutionary dictatorship of the proletariat" is a metaphor for socialism and the "antithesis" of capitalism. Similarly, Quinney (1977: 151) maintains that:

The transition to socialism is the ultimate trend of history operating within capitalist society. The transformation of capitalism to socialism thus depends on the prior development of capitalism. Socialism is nothing less than the dialectical abolition of capitalism. . . . At the root of the transition from capitalism to socialism is the fact that "socialism is in practice nothing but what capitalism is potentially." However, since the potential cannot be satisfied under capitalism, socialism becomes necessary.

For the socialist and radical criminologist, then, "only with the collapse of capitalist society and the creation of a new society, based on socialist principles, will there be a solution to the crime problem" (Quinney, 1975: 199). Likewise, the Center for Research on Criminal Justice (1977: 197) maintains that "ultimately, building a humane and decent society in the United States will depend on our ability to build a socialist movement that can put an end to all forms of exploitation."

Nevertheless, there are radical criminologists who remain unconvinced of the merits of revolution in general and socialism in particular. As Schumann (1976: 293) warns: "It is necessary to be sensitive to conflicts which cannot simply be derived from class dichotomy" (e.g., "the deep rooted discrimination of women, which is existent in many types of societies"). "If class theory does not grasp all relevant social conflicts in capitalist societies," adds Schumann (1976: 293):

revolution may not suspend the causes of all social conflicts either. If little attention is paid to this possibility there may be a danger to apologetically legitimize criminalization in post-capitalist societies.

Another potential hazard in the transformation to socialism is described by Kennedy (1976: 55), who writes that "just as the new state makes legal much of what once was criminal, so it also makes criminal much of what once was legal, as both civil and criminal laws are transformed." The problem here, for the revolutionaries, is that one form of exploitation may simply be replaced by another form.

Critical Criminology

Like "The New Criminology," the term critical criminology is really a misnomer. Although critical criminologists are typically critical of dissonant criminological positions, few are critical of their own position. Some of the problems unaddressed by so-called critical criminologists include: (1) how an individual becomes "conscious" of both his own and another's "class interests"; (2) how an individual realizes his (class) interests once he has become "conscious" of them (i.e., the relationship between theory and praxis); (3) whether the changes which occur in human behavior are always "rational," that is, in keeping with new interests which are created; (4) how long it takes for new conditions to produce new people; and (5) why socialism is not the inevitable panacea for the iniquities of capitalism in general and crime in particular. Since these problems have been discussed elsewhere (Bohm, 1980), the first four will not be discussed again here. However, since the last problem—why socialism is not the inevitable panacea for the iniquities of capitalism in general and crime in particular—is directly relevant to our previous examination of socialist criminology, a few remarks seem in order.

As noted in the last section, Quinney (1977: 151), like Marx, maintains:

The transition to socialism is the ultimate trend of history operating within capitalist society. . . . At the root of the transition from capitalism to socialism is the fact that "socialism is in practice nothing but what capitalism is potentially." However, since the potential cannot be satisfied under capitalism, socialism becomes necessary.

Thus, the initial problem is not whether socialism is a panacea for crime, but whether, as Quinney suggests, socialism is the "ultimate trend of history operating within capitalist society." Upon reflection, and contrary to the hopes of many critical criminologists, the answer must be a resounding no! As history has well documented, there have been several antitheses of capitalism (e.g., social democracy, bourgeois socialism or state capitalism, nazism or fascism, Bolshevism, Stalinism, Maoism, and so forth). Moreover, none of these antitheses of capitalism

is Marx's conception of socialism. Thus, as Becker and Horowitz (1972: 53) warn: "To demand allegiance to any social system as the mark of a radical perspective is to ignore the 100-year history of inequality within what has passed for socialism." Therefore, those critical criminologists who currently advocate socialism (in whatever form) as the inevitable successor to capitalism and as a solution to crime apparently have lost their own "critical edge." They have failed to be critical about their own historical situation. As Schroyer (1975: 35) maintains:

Whereas the notion of the socialist alternative of industrial development was at one time a revolutionary conception, it is today a vague concept that can no longer express the concrete ideal of a liberated society. We need to reflect on the meaning of emancipation in the context of the 1970's and reconceptualize the conditions of liberation from a higher level of industrial domination. And we must anticipate the social forms that will enable us to realize freedom.[15]

Extending Schroyer's observation into the 1980s and directing it to critical criminologists, we must acknowledge the failure of the most visible historical alternatives to capitalism and rethink our historical position.

SUMMARY

As noted in the preceding discussion, those theorists conveniently termed radical criminologists generally assume that the particular configuration of crime in capitalist societies is the product of the competitive and exploitative inter- and intra-class relations inherent in a capitalist political-economy. Crime, in this view, is behavior that contributes to human misery and deprives people of their human potentiality. Furthermore, it is generally believed that criminal law, on which the definition of crime is based, and the various components of the criminal justice system are state-initiated and state-supported forms of social control manipulated by a ruling class, through the state, to secure the survival of the capitalist system. There are, however, differences among radical criminologists as to the nature of capitalist manipulation. On the one hand, some radical criminologists assume that the state, criminal law, and the criminal justice system are instruments manipulated by individual members of the capitalist ruling class, through their agents, on behalf of their parochial interests. On the other hand, other radical criminologists assume that the policies of the state, criminal law, and the operation of the criminal justice system are determined by impersonal structures of capitalism such as the "market." Radical criminologists also differ on whether the policies of the state, criminal law, and the components of the criminal justice system are inherently repressive, or whether they have emancipatory potential as well. Some radical criminologists assume that the emancipatory potential of the state, criminal law, and criminal justice system is increased under noncapitalist modes of production.

Additionally, radical criminologists generally assume that the source of domination in society is mystified. For some, the capitalist ruling class has intentionally obscured their domination over society. For others, the source of domination in society is obscured by the ideology of free enterprise inherent in a capitalist mode of production. In any event, since the source of domination in society is obscured, radical criminologists generally contend that the adequacy (i.e., "truth") of criminological theories must be ascertained in praxis.

Finally, for most radical criminologists, the solution to crime in capitalist societies is the abolition of the capitalist mode of production. For some, however, a socialist society is the inevitable antithesis of a capitalist society and a panacea for crime, while for others, it is neither. Moreover, for those radical criminologists who advocate socialism as the inevitable antithesis of capitalism and a panacea for crime, there is differing opinion as to whether the transformation of capitalism to socialism must be effected by violent revolution or whether nonviolent revolution will suffice.

As indicated above, the theoretical perspective conveniently termed radical criminology comprises a rich complexity of largely unexplored assumptions and propositions that would seem to preclude the dismissal of the entire perspective as simply "old sentimentality" (Toby, 1979), "old baloney," (Toby, 1980), "structurally irresponsi-

ble," or "theoretically at a dead end" (Klockars, 1976). Unfortunately, much of the polemic surrounding radical criminology is probably a reflex response to its association with Marxism. This response, however, is neither scholarly nor critical and, in the end, it is unproductive in regard to the attempt to expand and enliven criminological theory.

NOTES

1. For convenience, the term "radical" criminology will be used in this article to designate the "general" position.

2. "Labeling theory" has also been termed "skeptical deviance theory" (Taylor et al., 1975) and "misfit sociology" (Pearson, 1975). For examples of criticisms of traditional "classical" and "positive" criminologies, as well as "labeling" theories, see Taylor et al., 1974; Quinney, 1974; Davis, 1975; and Vold and Bernard, 1979. Some differences between "conflict" criminology and "radical" criminology will be discussed in the body of the article.

3. As can be seen from the duplication of theorists under different categories, it is not uncommon to find theorists either confusing two or more positions or shifting between two or more positions. With regard to the latter, compare, for example, the positions of Quinney, 1977 and 1979 (although not listed, see Quinney, 1974, for yet another position); Taylor et al., 1974 and 1975; and Chambliss and Seidman, 1971 and Chambliss and Mankoff, 1976. The point to be emphasized is that these positions are not necessarily mutually exclusive. Additionally, the reader should be aware that this article was originally completed and submitted in October of 1980 in response to the infamous February, 1979 edition of *Criminology* devoted to radical criminology. Since that time, and contrary to the predictions of some of the contributors to the 1979 edition, radical criminology has experienced increased interest and has generated a growing literature. For example, at the 1981 annual meetings of the Southern Sociological Society, a panel session devoted to new developments in criminological theory produced four of five papers from a radical criminological perspective. Moreover, several significant contributions have been added to the literature. Among these are: Balkan et al., 1980; Inciardi, 1980; and Greenberg, 1981. This is in addition to the journals that are devoted to radical criminology which include: *Crime and Social Justice, Contemporary Crises,* as well as the January, 1981 edition of *Crime and Delinquency.* Thus, in the time that has

elapsed since the author's pen was laid to rest on this article, much has been written about and on radical criminology, and consequently, some of the ideas that the author originally considered "novel" in the essay seem less novel in light of what has followed. Nevertheless, it is hoped that some of the ideas expressed will still be new for some readers. Finally, the aforementioned terms used by different authors to describe radical criminology are employed as subtopic headings in the body of the article to distinguish different, although sometimes overlapping, positions within the general perspective of radical criminology.

4. Examples of "conflict" criminology include Vold, 1958; Turk, 1969; Chambliss and Seidman, 1971; Vold and Bernard, 1979.

5. For an example of "psycho-biological criminology" see Jeffery, 1977.

6. Admittedly, these factors are not limited to capitalist societies. They have existed in precapitalist and noncapitalist societies. However, they take on a special configuration in capitalist societies that differentiates them from the same factors in noncapitalist societies.

7. The first two interpretations—the "ruling-class determinist" or "instrumentalist" and the "economic determinist" or "structuralist"—are variants of "materialist" criminology and will be discussed together in the section entitled "Materialist Criminology." The third interpretation—the "dialectical" or "critical"—will be discussed in a separate section entitled "Dialectical Criminology."

8. According to Marx and Engels (1970: 42), the "mode of production" denotes the way men produce their means of subsistence. However, they also warn that the "mode of production" is not simply the way men reproduce their physical existence, but rather a definite form of activity of these individuals, a definite form of expressing their life, a definite "mode of life" on their part. As individuals express their life, so they are. What they are, therefore, coincides with their production, both with "what" they produce and with "how" they produce. The nature of individuals thus depends on the material conditions determining their production [Marx and Engels, 1970: 42].

Although they discuss other "modes of production" (e.g., slavery, feudalism, socialism), of central concern to them was the "capitalist mode of production."

9. The law or crime control could have just as easily been used instead of the state to exemplify the "instrumentalist" and "structuralist" interpretations. Furthermore, it is these two interpretations that reflect the "positivistic" tendencies in Marx and Engels's writings that have been noted by several writers (e.g., Ollman, 1976: 54; Bernstein, 1976: 189; Bender, 1975: 82).

10. For examples of this type of research, see Domhoff, 1967, 1979; Lundberg, 1968; and Milliband, 1969.

11. According to Harrington (1976: 42), it was not Marx, but Engels, who invented the "omniscient theory of society and nature, called 'dialectical materialism' which is not to be found, even as a momentary indiscretion, in the writings of Marx."

12. Again, it should be noted that these same criticisms made by dialectical theorists about materialist interpretations of the state could be expanded to cover typical materialist interpretations of the law and crime control.

13. Interestingly, Becker and Horowitz (1972: 55) add that "the poor and downtrodden are never 'radical'—what they do is 'natural,' in keeping with their 'interests.' The radical violates the canon of self-interest or group interest."

14. It is this criteria that differentiates radical criminology from other liberal or ameliorative criminologies.

15. See Gouldner (1976) for a similar view.

REFERENCES

AKERS, R. L. (1979). "Theory and ideology in Marxist criminology." *Criminology* 16 (February): 527–544.

BALKAN, S., R. J. BERGER, and J. SCHMIDT. (1980). *Crime and Deviance in America.* Belmont, CA: Wadsworth.

BECKER, H. S., and I. L. HOROWITZ. (1972). "Radical politics and sociological research: observations on methodology and ideology." *Amer. J. of Sociology* 78 (July): 48–66.

BEIRNE, P. (1979). "Empiricism and the critique of Marxism on law and crime." *Social Problems* 26 (April): 373–385.

BENDER, F. L. [ed.] (1975). *The Betrayal of Marx.* New York: Harper & Row.

BERNSTEIN, R. J. (1976). *The Restructuring of Social and Political Theory.* Philadelphia: Univ. of Pennsylvania Press.

BOHM, R. M. (1980). "Reflexivity and critical criminology." Presented at the annual meetings of the American Society of Criminology, San Francisco.

BONGER, W. A. (1916). *Criminology and Economic Conditions.* Boston: Little, Brown.

BONOMO, T. A. and M. G. WENGER. (1978). "A critique of radical criminology on surplus population: an examination of Quinney's thesis." Presented at the annual meetings of the American Society of Criminology, Dallas.

CAHN, L. [ed.] (1966). *Confronting Injustice.* Boston: Little, Brown.

Center for Research on Criminal Justice (1977). *The Iron Fist and the Velvet Glove.* Berkeley, CA: Center for Research on Criminal Justice.

CHAMBLISS, W. J. (1976). "Functional and conflict theories of crime: the heritage of Emile Durkheim and Karl Marx," pp. 1–28 in W. J. Chambliss and M. Mankoff (eds.) *Whose Law What Order?* New York: John Wiley.

———. and M. MANKOFF [eds.] (1976). *Whose Law What Order?* New York: John Wiley.

———. and R. B. SEIDMAN (1971). *Law, Order and Power.* Reading, MA: Addison-Wesley.

DAVIS, N. J. (1975). *Sociological Constructions of Deviance: Perspectives and Issues in the Field.* Dubuque, IA: William C. Brown.

DOMHOFF, G. W. (1979). *The Powers That Be: Processes of Ruling Class Domination in America.* New York: Vintage.

———. (1967). *Who Rules America?* Englewood Cliffs, NJ: Prentice Hall.

FRANKEL, B. (1979). "On the state of the state: Marxist theories of the state after Leninism." *Theory and Society* 7: 199–242.

GIBBONS, D. C. and P. GARABEDIAN (1974). "Conservative, liberal and radical criminology: some trends and observations," pp. 51–65 in C. E. Reasons (ed.) *The Criminologist: Crime and the Criminal.* Pacific Palisades, CA: Goodyear.

GOLD, D. A., C. Y. H. LO, and E. O. WRIGHT (1975). "Recent developments in Marxist theories of the capitalist state." *Monthly Rev.* (October/November): 29–43, 36–51.

GORDON, D. M. (1976). "Class and the economics of crime," pp. 193–214 in W. J. Chambliss and M. Mankoff (eds.) *Whose Law What Order?* New York: John Wiley.

———. (1973). "Capitalism, class, and crime in America." *Crime and Delinquency* (April): 163–186.

GOULDNER, A. W. (1976). *The Dialectic of Ideology and Technology: The Origins, Grammar, and Future of Ideology.* New York: Seabury.

GREENBERG, D. F. [ed.] (1981). *Crime and Capitalism.* Palo Alto, CA: Mayfield.

———. (1976). "On one-dimensional Marxist criminology." *Theory and Society* 3: 610–621.

HACKLER, J. (1977). "The new criminology: ideology or explanation." *Canadian J. of Criminology and Corrections* 19: 192–195.

HARRINGTON, M. (1976). *The Twilight of Capitalism.* New York: Simon & Schuster.

INCIARDI, J. A. [ed.] (1980). *Radical Criminology: The Coming Crises.* Beverly Hills, CA: Sage.

———. (1979). "From the editor's desk." *Criminology* 16 (February): 443–444.

JEFFERY, C. R. (1977). *Crime Prevention Through Environmental Design.* Beverly Hills, CA: Sage.

KANT, I. (1959). *Foundations of the Metaphysics of Morals and What is Enlightenment?* Indianapolis: Liberal Arts Press.

KELLER, R. L. (1976). "A sociological analysis of the conflict and critical criminologies." Ph.D. dissertation, University of Montana.

KENNEDY, M. C. (1976). "Beyond incrimination," pp. 34–65 in W. J. Chambliss and M. Mankoff (eds.) *Whose Law What Order?* New York: John Wiley.

KLOCKARS, C. B. (1976). "The contemporary crises of Marxist criminology." *Criminology* 16 (February): 477–515.

LENIN, V. I. (1970). *The State and Revolution.* Peking: Foreign Languages Press.

LOPEZ-REY, M. (1970). *Crime: An Analytical Appraisal.* New York: Praeger.

LUNDBERG, F. (1968). *The Rich and the Super-Rich.* New York: Lyle Stuart.

MARX, K. and F. ENGELS. (1974). *The Communist Manifesto.* New York: Washington Square Press.

———. (1970). *The German Ideology.* New York: International Publishers.

MEIER, R. F. (1976). "The new criminology: continuity in criminological theory." *J. of Criminal Law and Criminology* 67 (December): 461–469.

MICHALOWSKI, R. J. and E. W. BOHLANDER (1976). "Repression and criminal justice in capitalist America." *Soc. Inquiry* 46 (2): 95–106.

MILLIBAND, R. (1969). *The State in Capitalist Society.* New York: Basic Books.

MILLS, C. W. (1975). *The Marxists.* New York: Dell.

OLLMAN, B. (1976). *Alienation* (2nd Ed.) Cambridge, MA: Cambridge Univ. Press.

PEARCE, F. (1976). *Crimes of the Powerful.* London: Pluto.

PEARSON, G. (1975). "Misfit sociology and the politics of socialization," pp. 147–166 in I. Taylor et al. (eds.) *Critical Criminology.* Boston: Routledge & Kegan Paul.

PELFREY, W. V. (1980). *The Evolution of Criminology.* Cincinnati: Anderson.

PHILLIPSON, M. (1973). "Critical theorizing and the new criminology." *British J. of Criminology* 13 (October): 398–400.

PLAMENATZ, J. (1963). *Man and Society,* Vol. 2. New York: McGraw-Hill.

PLATT, T. (1975). "Prospects for a radical criminology in the USA," pp. 95–112 in I. Taylor et al. (eds.) *Critical Criminology.* Boston: Routledge & Kegan Paul.

QUINNEY, R. (1979). "The production of criminology." *Criminology* 16 (February): 445–457.

———. (1977). *Class, State and Crime.* New York: McKay.

———. (1975). "Crime control in capitalist society: a critical philosophy of legal order," pp. 181–202 in I. Taylor, et al. *Critical Criminology.* Boston: Routledge & Kegan Paul.

———. (1974). *Critique of Legal Order: Crime Control in Capitalist Society.* Boston: Little, Brown.

REASONS, C. E. (1974). "Law and the making of criminals," pp. 99–105 in C. E. Reasons (ed.) *The Criminologist: Crime and the Criminal.* Pacific Palisades, CA: Goodyear.

SCHROYER, T. (1975). *The Critique of Domination.* Boston: Beacon.

SCHUMANN, K. F. (1976). "Theoretical presuppositions for criminology as a critical enterprise." *Int. J. of Criminology and Penology* 4 (August): 285–294.

SCHWENDINGER, H. and J. SCHWENDINGER (1975). "Defenders of order or guardians of human rights?" pp. 113–146 in I. Taylor et al. (eds.) *Critical Criminology.* Boston: Routledge & Kegan Paul.

SCULL, A. T. (1977). *Decarceration.* Englewood Cliffs, NJ: Prentice Hall.

SPITZER, S. (1975). "Toward a Marxian theory of deviance." *Social Problems* 22 (June): 638–651.

SYKES, G. M. (1974). "The rise of critical criminology." *J. of Criminal Law and Criminology* 65 (June): 206–213.

TAYLOR, I., P. WALTON, and J. YOUNG (1975). *Critical Criminology.* Boston: Routledge & Kegan Paul.

———. (1975). "Critical criminology in Britain: review and prospects," pp. 6–62 in I. Taylor et al.

(eds.) *Critical Criminology.* Boston: Routledge & Kegan Paul.

———. (1974). *The New Criminology: For a Social Theory of Deviance.* New York: Harper & Row.

TOBY, J. (1980). "The new criminology is the old baloney," pp. 124–132 in J. A. Inciardi (ed.) *Radical Criminology: The Coming Crises.* Beverly Hills, CA: Sage.

———. (1979). "The new criminology is the old sentimentality." *Criminology* 16 (February): 516–526.

TURK, A. (1975). "Radical criminology." *Crime and Social Justice* 4: 42.

———. (1969). *Criminality and Legal Order.* Chicago: Rand McNally.

VOLD, G. B. (1958). *Theoretical Criminology.* New York: Oxford.

———. and T. J. BERNARD. (1979). *Theoretical Criminology* (2nd Ed.). New York: Oxford.

WERKENTIN, F., M. HOFFERBERT, and M. BAUERMAN (1974). "Criminology as policy science or: how old is the new criminology?" *Crime and Social Justice* 2 (Fall–Winter): 24–41.

WOLLAN, L. A. (1979). "After labeling and conflict." *Criminology* 16 (February): 545–560.

WRIGHT, E. O. (1973). *The Politics of Punishment.* New York: Harper Colophon.

YOUNG, J. (1976). "Foreword," pp. 11–21 in F. Pearce, *Crimes of the Powerful.* London: Pluto.

———. (1975). "Working-class criminology," pp. 63–94 in I. Taylor et al. (eds.) *Critical Criminology.* Boston: Routledge & Kegan Paul.

THE POVERTY OF THE SOCIOLOGY OF DEVIANCE
NUTS, SLUTS, AND PREVERTS*

Alexander Liazos**

C. Wright Mills left a rich legacy to sociology. One of his earliest, and best, contributions was "The Professional Ideology of Social Pathologists" (1943). In it, Mills argues that the small-town, middle-class background of writers of social problems textbooks blinded them to basic problems of social structure and power, and led them to emphasize melioristic, patchwork types of solutions to America's "problems," ranging from rape in rural districts to public housing, and emphasized the orderly the structure of small-town America; anything else was pathology and disorganization. Moreover, these "problems," "ranging from rape in rural districts to public housing," were not explored systematically and theoretically; they were not placed in some larger political, historical, and social context. They were merely listed and decried.[1]

Since Mills wrote his paper, however, the field of social problems, social disorganization, and social pathology has undergone considerable changes. Beginning in the late 1940s and the 1950s, and culminating in the 1960s, the field of "deviance" has largely replaced the social problems orientation. This new field is characterized by a number of features which distinguish it from the older approach.[2]

First, there is some theoretical framework, even though it is often absent in edited collections (the Rubington and Weinberg (1968) edited book is an outstanding exception). Second, the small-town morality is largely gone. Writers claim they will examine the phenomena at hand—prostitution, juvenile delinquency, mental illness, crime, and others—objectively, not considering them as necessarily harmful and immoral. Third, the statements and theories of the field are based on much more extensive, detailed, and theoretically oriented research than were those of the 1920s and 1930s. Fourth, writers attempt to fit their theories to some central theories, concerns, and problems found in the general field of sociology; they try to transcend mere moralizing.

The "deviant" has been humanized; the moralistic tone is no longer ever-present (although it still lurks underneath the explicit disavowals); and theoretical perspectives have been developed. Nevertheless, all is not well with the field of "deviance." Close examination reveals that writers of this field still do not try to relate the phenomena of "deviance" to larger social, historical, political, and economic contexts. The emphasis is still on the "deviant" and the "problems" *he* presents to himself and others, not on the society within which he emerges and operates.

I examined 16 textbooks in the field of "deviance," eight of them readers, to determine the state of the field. (They are preceded by an asterisk in the references.) Theoretically, eight take the labelling-interactionist approach; three more tend to lean to that approach; four others argue for other orientations (anomie, structural-functional, etc.) or, among the readers, have an "eclectic" approach; and one (McCaghy, *et al.*, 1968) is a collection of biographical and other statements by "deviants" themselves, and thus

*© 1972 by the Society for the Study of Social Problems. Reprinted from *Social Problems,* 20 (Summer, 1972), pp. 103–120 by permission of the author and the publisher.

**The subtitle of this paper came from two sources. (a) A Yale undergraduate once told me that the deviance course was known among Yale students as "nuts and sluts." (b) A former colleague of mine at Quinnipiac College, John Bancroft, often told me that the deviance course was "all about those preverts." When I came to write this paper, I discovered that these descriptions were correct, and concise summaries of my argument. I thank both of them. I also want to thank Gordon Fellman for a very careful reading of the first draft of the manuscript, and for discussing with me the general and specific issues I raise here.

may not be said to have a theoretical approach (although, as we shall see, the selection of the types of statements and "deviants" still implies an orientation and viewpoint). A careful examination of these textbooks revealed a number of ideological biases. These biases became apparent as much from what these books leave unsaid and unexamined, as from what they do say. The field of the sociology of deviance, as exemplified in these books, contains three important theoretical and political biases.

1. All writers, especially those of the labelling school, either state explicitly or imply that one of their main concerns is to *humanize* and *normalize* the "deviant," to show that he is essentially no different from us. But by the very emphasis on the "deviant" and his identity problems and sub-culture, the opposite effect may have been achieved. The persisting use of the label "deviant" to refer to the people we are considering is an indication of the feeling that these people are indeed different.

2. By the overwhelming emphasis on the "dramatic" nature of the usual types of "deviance"—prostitution, homosexuality, juvenile delinquency, and others—we have neglected to examine other, more serious and harmful forms of "deviance." I refer to *covert institutional violence* (defined and discussed below) which leads to such things as poverty and exploitation, the war in Vietnam, unjust tax laws, racism and sexism, and so on, which cause psychic and material suffering for many Americans, black and white, men and women.

3. Despite explicit statements by these authors of the importance of *power* in the designation of what is "deviant," in their substantive analyses they show a profound unconcern with power and its implications. The really powerful, the upper classes, and the power elite, those Gouldner (1968) calls the "top dogs," are left essentially unexamined by these sociologists of deviance.

I.

Always implicit, and frequently explicit, is the aim of the labelling school to humanize and normalize the "deviant." Two statements by Becker and Matza are representative of this sentiment.

In the course of our work and for who knows what private reasons, we fall into deep sympathy with the people we are studying, so that while the rest of society

views them as unfit in one or another respect for the deference ordinarily accorded a fellow citizen, we believe that they are at least as good as anyone else, more sinned against than sinning (Becker, 1967: 100–101).

The growth of the sociological view of deviant phenomena involved, as major phases, the replacement of a correctional stance by an appreciation of the deviant subject, the tacit purging of a conception of pathology by a new stress on human diversity, and the erosion of a simple distinction between deviant and conventional phenomena, resulting from intimate familiarity of the world as it is, which yielded a more sophisticated view stressing complexity (Matza, 1969: 10).

For a number of reasons, however, the opposite effect may have been achieved; and "deviants" still seem different. I began to suspect this reverse effect from the many essays and papers I read while teaching the "deviance" course. The clearest example is the repeated use of the word "tolerate." Students would write that we must not persecute homosexuals, prostitutes, mental patients, and others, that we must be "tolerant" of them. But one tolerates only those one considers less than equal, morally inferior, and weak; those equal to oneself, one accepts and respects; one does not merely allow them to exist, one does not "tolerate" them.

The repeated assertion that "deviants" are "at least as good as anyone else" may raise doubts that this is in fact the case, or that we believe it. A young woman who grew up in the South in the 1940s and 1950s told Quinn (1954:146): " 'You know, I think from the fact that I was told so often that I must treat colored people with consideration, I got the feeling that I could mistreat them if I wanted to.' " Thus with "deviants" if in fact they are as good as we are, we would not need to remind everyone of this fact; we would take it for granted and proceed from there. But our assertions that "deviants" are not different may raise the very doubts we want to dispel. Moreover, why would we create a separate field of sociology for "deviants" if there were not something different about them? May it be that even we do not believe our statements and protestations?

The continued use of the word "deviant" (and its variants), despite its invidious distinctions and connotations, also belies our explicit statements on the equality of the people under consideration. To be sure, some of the authors express uneasiness over the term. For example, we are told,

In our use of this term for the purpose of sociological investigation, we emphasize that we do not attach any value judgement, explicitly or implicitly, either to the word "deviance" or to those describing their behavior or beliefs in this book (McCaghy, *et al.*, 1968:v).

Lofland (1969:2, 9–10) expresses even stronger reservations about the use of the term, and sees clearly the sociological, ethical, and political problems raised by its continued use. Yet, the title of his book is *Deviance and Identity*.

Szasz (1970: xxv–xxvi) has urged that we abandon use of the term:

Words have lives of their own. However much sociologists insist that the term "deviant" does not diminish the worth of the person or group so categorized, the implication of inferiority adheres to the word. Indeed, sociologists are not wholly exempt from blame: they describe addicts and homosexuals as deviants, but never Olympic champions or Nobel Prize winners. In fact, the term is rarely applied to people with admired characteristics, such as great wealth, superior skills, or fame—whereas it is often applied to those with despised characteristics, such as poverty, lack of marketable skills, or infamy.

The term "social deviants" . . . does not make sufficiently explicit—as the terms "scapegoat" or "victim" do—that majorities usually categorize persons or groups as "deviant" in order to set them apart as inferior beings and to justify their social control, oppression, persecution, or even complete destruction.

Terms like victimization, persecution, and oppression are more accurate descriptions of what is really happening. But even Gouldner (1968), in a masterful critique of the labelling school, while describing social conflict, calls civil-rights and anti-war protesters "political deviants." He points out clearly that these protesters are resisting openly, not slyly, conditions they abhor. Gouldner is discussing political struggles; oppression and resistance to oppression; conflicts over values, morals, interests, and power; and victimization. Naming such protesters "deviants," even if *political* deviants, is an indication of the deep penetration within our minds of certain prejudices and orientations.

Given the use of the term, the definition and examples of "deviant" reveal underlying sentiments and views. Therefore, it is important that we redefine drastically the entire field, especially since it is a flourishing one: "Because younger sociologists have found deviance such a fertile and exciting field for their own work, and because students share these feelings, deviance promises to become an even more important area of sociological research and theory in the coming years" (Douglas, 1970a:3).

The lists and discussions of "deviant" acts and persons reveal the writers' biases and sentiments. These are acts which, "like robbery, burglary or rape [are] of a simple and dramatic predatory nature . . ." (The President's Commission on Law Enforcement and the Administration of Justice, in Dinitz, *et al.*, 1969:105). All 16 texts, without exception, concentrate on actions and persons of a "dramatic predatory nature," on "preverts." This is true of both the labelling and other schools. The following are examples from the latter:

Ten different types of deviant behavior are considered: juvenile delinquency, adult crime, prison sub-cultures, homosexuality, prostitution, suicide, homicide, alcoholism, drug addiction and mental illness (Rushing, 1969: preface).

Traditionally, in American sociology the study of deviance has focused on criminals, juvenile delinquents, prostitutes, suicides, the mentally ill, drug users and drug addicts, homosexuals, and political and religious radicals (Lefton, *et al.*, 1968:v).

Deviant behavior is essentially violation of certain types of group norms; a deviant act is behavior which is proscribed in a certain way. [It must be] in a disapproved direction, and of sufficient degree to exceed the tolerance limit of the community. . . . [such as] delinquency and crime, prostitution, homosexual behavior, drug addiction, alcoholism, mental disorders, suicide, marital and family maladjustment, discrimination against minority groups, and, to a lesser degree, role problems of old age (Clinard, 1968:28).

Finally, we are told that these are some examples of deviance every society must deal with: ". . . . mental illness, violence, theft, and sexual misconduct, as well as . . . other similarly difficult behavior" (Dinitz, *et al.*, 1969:3).

The list stays unchanged with the authors of the labelling school.

... in Part I, "The Deviant Act," I draw rather heavily on certain studies of homicide, embezzlement, "naive" check forgery, suicide and a few other acts ... in discussing the assumption of deviant identity (Part II) and the assumption of normal identity (Part III), there is heavy reference to certain studies of paranoia, "mental illness" more generally, and Alcoholics Anonymous and Synanon (Lofland, 1969:34).

Homicide, suicide, alcoholism, mental illness, prostitution, and homosexuality are among the forms of behavior typically called deviant, and they are among the kinds of behavior that will be analyzed (Lofland, 1969:1). Included among my respondents were political radicals of the far left and the far right, homosexuals, militant blacks, convicts and mental hospital patients, mystics, narcotic addicts, LSD and marijuana users, illicit drug dealers, delinquent boys, racially mixed couples, hippies, health-food users, and bohemian artists and village eccentrics (Simmons, 1969:10).

Simmons (1969:27, 29, 31) also informs us that in his study of stereotypes of "deviants" held by the public, these are the types he gave to people: homosexuals, beatniks, adulterers, marijuana smokers, political radicals, alcoholics, prostitutes, lesbians, ex-mental patients, atheists, ex-convicts, intellectuals, and gamblers. In Lemert (1967) we find that except for the three introductory (theoretical) chapters, the substantive chapters cover the following topics: alcohol drinking, four; check forgers, three; stuttering, two; and mental illness, two. Matza (1969) offers the following list of "deviants" and their actions that "must be appreciated if one adheres to a naturalistic perspective:" paupers, robbers, motorcycle gangs, prostitutes, drug addicts, promiscuous homosexuals, thieving Gypsies, and "free love" Bohemians (1969:16). Finally, Douglas' collection (1970a) covers these forms of "deviance": abortion, nudism, topless barmaids, prostitutes, homosexuals, violence (motorcycle and juvenile gangs), shoplifting, and drugs.

The omissions from these lists are staggering. The covert, institutional forms of "deviance" (part II, below) are nowhere to be found. Reading these authors, one would not know that the most destructive use of violence in the last decade has been the war in Vietnam, in which the United States has heaped unprecedented suffering on the people and their land; more bombs have been dropped in Vietnam than in the entire World War II. Moreover, the robbery of the corporate world—through tax breaks, fixed prices, low wages, pollution of the environment, shoddy goods, etc.—is passed over in our fascination with "dramatic and predatory" actions. Therefore, we are told that "while they certainly are of no greater social importance to us than such subjects as banking and accounting [or military violence], subjects such as marijuana use and motorcycle gangs are of far greater interest to most of us. While it is only a coincidence that our scientific interests correspond with the emotional interest in deviants, it is a happy coincidence and, I believe, one that should be encouraged" (Douglas, 1970a:5). And Matza (1969:17), in commenting on the "appreciative sentiments" of the "naturalistic spirit," elaborates on the same theme: "We do not for a moment wish that we could rid ourselves of deviant phenomena. We are intrigued by them. They are an intrinsic, ineradicable, and vital part of human society."

An effort is made to transcend this limited view and substantive concern with dramatic and predatory forms of "deviance." Becker (1964:3) claims that the new (labelling) deviance no longer studies only "delinquents and drug addicts, though these classical kinds of deviance are still kept under observation." It increases its knowledge "of the processes of deviance by studying physicians, people with physical handicaps, the mentally deficient, and others whose doings were formerly not included in the area." The powerful "deviants" are still left untouched, however. This is still true with another aspect of the new deviance. Becker (1964:4) claims that in the labelling perspective "we focus attention on the other people involved in the process. We pay attention to the role of the non-deviant as well as that of the deviant." But we see that it is the ordinary non-deviants and the low-level agents of social control who receive attention, not the powerful ones (Gouldner, 1968).

In fact, the emphasis is more on the *subculture* and *identity* of the "deviants" themselves rather than on their oppressors and persecutors. To be sure, in varying degrees all authors discuss the agents of social control, but the fascination and emphasis are on the "deviant" himself. Studies of prisons and prisoners, for example, focus on prison subcultures and prisoner rehabilitation; there is little or no consideration of the social, political, economic, and power conditions which consign people to prisons. Only now are we beginning to realize that most prisoners are *political prisoners*—that their "criminal" actions (whether against individuals, such as robbery, or conscious political acts against the state) result largely from current social and political conditions, and are not the work of "disturbed" and "psychopathic" personalities. This realization came about largely because of the writings of political prisoners themselves: Malcolm X (1965), Eldridge Cleaver (1968), and George Jackson (1970), among others.[3]

In all these books, notably those of the labelling school, the concern is with the "deviant's" subculture and identity: his problems, motives, fellow victims, etc. The collection of memoirs and apologies of "deviants" in their own words (McCaghy, *et al.,* 1968) covers the lives and identities of 'prevert' deviants:" prostitutes, nudists, abortionists, criminals, drug users, homosexuals, the mentally ill, alcoholics, and suicides. For good measure, some "militant deviants" are thrown in: Black Muslims, the SDS, and a conscientious objector. But one wonders about other types of "deviants:" how do those who perpetrate the covert institutional violence in our society view themselves? Do they have identity problems? How do they justify their actions? How did the robber barons of the late 19th century steal, fix laws, and buy politicians six days of the week and go to church on Sunday? By what process can people speak of body counts and kill ratios with cool objectivity? On these and similar questions, this book (and all others)[4] provides no answers; indeed, the editors seem unaware that such questions should or could be raised.

Becker (1964), Rubington and Weinberg (1968), Matza (1969), and Bell (1971) also focus on the identity and subculture of "prevert deviants." Matza, in discussing the assumption of "deviant identity," uses as examples, and elaborates upon, thieves and marijuana users. In all these books, there are occasional references to and questions about the larger social and political structure, but these are not explored in any depth; and the emphasis remains on the behavior, identity, and rehabilitation of the "deviant" himself. This bias continues in the latest book which, following the fashions of the times, has chapters on hippies and militant protesters (Bell, 1971).

Even the best of these books, Simmons's *Deviants* (1969), is not free of the overwhelming concentration of the "deviant" and his identity. It is the most sympathetic and balanced presentation of the lives of "deviants": their joys, sorrows, and problems with the straight world and fellow victims. Simmons demystifies the processes of becoming "deviant" and overcoming "deviance." He shows, as well as anyone does, that these victims *are* just like us; and the differences they possess and the suffering they endure are imposed upon them. Ultimately, however, Simmons too falls prey to the three biases shown in the work of others: (a) the "deviants" he considers are only of the "prevert" type; (b) he focuses mostly on the victim and his identity, not on the persecutors; and (c) the persecutors he does discuss are of the middle-level variety, the agents of more powerful others and institutions.

Because of these biases, there is an implicit, but very clear, acceptance by these authors of the current definitions of "deviance." It comes about because they concentrate their attention on those who have been *successfully labelled as "deviant,"* and not on those who break laws, fix laws, violate ethical and moral standards, harm individuals and groups, etc., but who either are able to hide their actions, or, when known, can deflect criticism, labelling, and punishment. The following are typical statements which reveal this bias.

". . . no act committed by members of occupational groups [such as white-collar crimes], however unethical, should be considered as crime unless it is punishable by the state in some way" (Clinard, 1968:269). Thus, if some people can manipulate laws so that their unethical and destructive acts are not "crimes," we should cater to their power and agree that they are not criminals.

Furthermore, the essence of the labelling school encourages this bias, despite Becker's (1963:14) assertion that ". . . insofar as a scientist uses "deviant" to refer to any rule-breaking behavior and takes as his subjects of study only those who have been *labelled* deviant, he will be hampered by the disparities between the two categories." But as the following statements from Becker and others show, this is in fact what the labelling school does do.

Deviance is "created by society . . . *social groups create deviance by making the rules whose infraction constitutes deviance,* and by applying those rules to particular people and labelling them as outsiders" (Becker, 1963:8–9). Clearly, according to this view, in cases where no group has labelled another, no matter what the other group or individuals have done, there is nothing for the sociologist to study and dissect.

Rules are not made automatically. Even though a practice may be harmful in an objective sense to the group in which it occurs, the harm needs to be discovered and pointed out. People must be made to feel that something ought to be done about it (Becker, 1963:162).

What is important for the social analyst is not what people are by his lights or by his standards, but what it is that people construe one another and themselves to be for what reasons and with what consequences (Lofland, 1969:35).

. . . deviance is in the eyes of the beholder. For deviance to become a social fact, somebody must perceive an act, person, situation, or event as a departure from social norms, must categorize that perception, must report the perception to others, must get them to accept this definition of the situation, and must obtain a response that conforms to this definition. Unless all these requirements are met, deviance as a social fact does not come into being (Rubington and Weinberg, 1968:v).

The implication of these statements is that the sociologist accepts current, successful definitions of what is "deviant" as the only ones worthy of his attention. To be sure, he may argue that those labelled "deviant" are not really different from the rest of us, or that there is no act intrinsically "deviant," etc. By concentrating on cases of successful labelling, however, he will not penetrate beneath the surface to look for other forms of "deviance"—undetected stealing, violence, and destruction. When people are not powerful enough to make the "deviant" label stick on others, we overlook these cases. But is it not as much a *social fact,* even though few of us pay much attention to it, that the corporate economy kills and maims more, is more violent, than any violence committed by the poor (the usual subjects of studies of violence)? By what reasoning and necessity is the "violence" of the poor in the ghettoes more worthy of our attention than the military bootcamps which numb recruits from the horrors of killing the "enemy" ("Oriental human beings," as we learned during the Calley trial)? But because these acts are not labelled "deviant," because they are covert, institutional, and normal, their "deviant" qualities are overlooked and they do not become part of the province of the sociology of deviance. Despite their best liberal intentions, these sociologists seem to perpetuate the very notions they think they debunk, and others of which they are unaware.

II.

As a result of the fascination with "nuts, sluts, and preverts," and their identities and subcultures, little attention has been paid to the unethical, illegal, and destructive actions of powerful individuals, groups, and institutions in our society. Because these actions are carried out quietly in the normal course of events, the sociology of deviance does not consider them as part of its subject matter. This bias is rooted in the very conception and definition of the field. It is obvious when one examines the treatment, or, just as often, lack of it, of the issues of violence, crime, and white-collar crime.

Discussions of violence treat only one type: the "dramatic and predatory" violence committed by individuals (usually the poor and minorities) against persons and property. For example, we read, "crimes involving violence, such as criminal homicide, assault, and forcible rape, are concentrated in the slums" (Clinard, 1968:123). Wolfgang, an expert on violence, has developed a whole theory on the "subculture of violence" found among the lower classes (e.g., in Rushing, 1969:233–40). And Douglas (1970a:part 4, on violence) includes readings on street gangs and the Hell's Angels. Thompson (1966), in his book on the Hell's Angels, devotes many pages to an exploration of the Angels' social background. In addition, throughout the book, and especially in his concluding chapter, he places the Angels' violence in the perspective of a violent, raping, and destructive society, which refuses to confront the reality of the Angels by distorting, exaggerating, and romanticizing their actions. But Douglas reprints none of these pages; rather, he offers us the chapter where, during a July 4 weekend, the Angels were restricted by the police within a lakeside area, had a drunken weekend, and became a tourist sideshow and circus.

In short, violence is presented as the exclusive property of the poor in the slums, the minorities, street gangs, and motorcycle beasts. But if we take the concept *violence* seriously, we see that much of our political and economic system thrives on it. In violence, a person is *violated*—there is harm done to his person, his psyche, his body, his dignity, his ability to govern himself (Garver, in Rose, 1969:6). Seen in this way, a person can be violated in many ways; physical force is only one of them. As the readings in Rose (1969) show, a person can be violated by a system that denies him a decent job, or consigns him to a slum, or causes him brain damage by near-starvation during childhood, or manipulates him through the mass media, and so on endlessly.

Moreover, we must see that *covert institutional violence* is much more destructive than overt individual violence. We must recognize that people's lives are violated by the very normal and everyday workings of institutions. We do not see such events and situations as violent because they are not dramatic and predatory; they do not make for fascinating reading on the lives of preverts; but they kill, maim, and destroy many more lives than do violent individuals.

Here are some examples. Carmichael and Hamilton (1967:4), in distinguishing between *individual* and *institutional* racism, offer examples of each:

When white terrorists bomb a black church and kill five black children, that is an act of individual racism, widely deplored by most segments of the society. But when in that same city—Birmingham, Alabama—five

hundred black babies die each year because of lack of proper food, shelter, and medical facilities, and thousands more are destroyed and maimed physically, emotionally and intellectually because of conditions of poverty and discrimination in the black community, that is a function of institutional racism.

Surely this is violence; it is caused by the normal, quiet workings of institutions run by respectable members of the community. Many whites also suffer from the institutional workings of a profit-oriented society and economy; poor health, dead-end jobs, slum housing, hunger in rural areas, and so on, are daily realities in their lives. This is surely much worse violence than any committed by the Hell's Angels or street gangs. Only these groups get stigmatized and analyzed by sociologists of deviance, however, while those good people who live in luxurious homes (fixing tax laws for their benefit) off profits derived from an exploitative economic system—they are the pillars of their community.

Violence is committed daily by the government, very often by lack of action. The same system that enriches businessmen farmers with billions of dollars through farm subsidies cannot be bothered to appropriate a few millions to deal with lead poisoning in the slums. Young children.

. . . get it by eating the sweet-tasting chips of peeling tenement walls, painted a generation ago with leaded paint.

According to the Department of Health, Education, and Welfare, 400,000 children are poisoned each year, about 30,000 in New York City alone. About 3,200 suffer permanent brain damage, 800 go blind or become so mentally retarded that they require hospitalization for the rest of their lives, and approximately 200 die.

The tragedy is that lead poisoning is totally man-made and totally preventable. It is caused by slum housing. And there are now blood tests that can detect the disease, and medicines to cure it. Only a lack of purpose sentences 200 black children to die each year (Newfield, 1971).[5]

Newfield goes on to report that on May 20, 1971, a Senate-House conference eliminated $5 million from an appropriations budget. In fact, 200 children had been sentenced to death and thousands more to maiming and suffering.

Similar actions of violence are committed daily by the government and corporations; but in these days of misplaced emphasis, ignorance, and manipulation we do not see the destruction inherent in these actions. Instead, we get fascinated, angry, and misled by the violence of the poor and the powerless. We see the violence committed during political rebellions in the ghettos (called "riots" in order to dismiss them), but all along we ignored the daily violence committed against the ghetto residents by the institutions of the society: schools, hospitals, corporations, the government. Check any of these books on deviance, and see how much of this type of violence is even mentioned, much less explored and described.

It may be argued that some of this violence is (implicitly) recognized in discussions of "white-collar" crime. This is not the case, however. Of the 16 books under consideration, only three pay some attention to white-collar crime (Cohen, 1966; Clinard, 1968; Dinitz, *et al.*, 1969); and of these, only the last covers the issue at some length. Even in these few discussions, however, the focus remains on the *individuals* who commit the actions (on their greediness, lack of morality, etc.), not on the economic and political institutions within which they operate. The selection in Dinitz, *et al.* (1969:99–109), from the President's Commission on Law Enforcement and the Administration of Justice, at least three times (pp. 101, 103, 108) argues that white-collar crime is "pervasive," causes "financial burdens" ("probably far greater than those produced by traditional common law theft offenses"), and is generally harmful. At least in these pages, however, there is no investigation of the social, political, and economic conditions which make the pervasiveness, and lenient treatment, of white-collar crime possible.

The bias against examining the structural conditions behind white-collar crime is further revealed in Clinard's suggestions on how to deal with it (in his chapter on "The Prevention of Deviant Behavior"). The only recommendation in three pages of discussion (704–7) is to teach everyone more "respect" for the law. This is a purely moralistic device; it pays no attention to the structural aspects of the problem, to the fact that even deeper than white-collar crime is ingrained a whole network of laws, especially tax laws, administrative policies, and institutions which systematically favor a small minority. More generally, discussions on the prevention of "deviance" and crime do not deal with institutional violence, and what we need to do to stop it.[6]

But there is an obvious explanation for this oversight. The people committing serious white-collar crimes and executing the policies of violent institutions are respectable and responsible individuals, not "deviants" this is the view of the President's Commission on Law Enforcement and the Administration of Justice.

Significantly, the Antitrust Division does not feel that lengthy prison sentences are ordinarily called for [for white-collar crimes]. It "rarely recommends jail sentences greater than 6 months—recommendations of 30-day imprisonment are most frequent." (Dinitz, *et al.*, 1969:105.)

Persons who have standing and roots in a community, and are prepared for and engaged in legitimate occupations, can be expected to be particularly susceptible to the threat of criminal prosecution. Criminal proceedings and the imposition of sanctions have a much sharper impact upon those who have not been hardened by previous contact with the criminal justice system (in Dinitz, *et al.*, 1969:104).

At the same time, we are told elsewhere by the Commission that white-collar crime is pervasive and widespread; "criminal proceedings and the imposition of sanctions" do not appear to deter it much.

The executives convicted in the Electrical Equipment case were respectable citizens. "Several were deacons or vestrymen of their churches." The rest also held prestigious positions: president of the Chamber of Commerce, bank director, little-league organizer, and so on (Dinitz, *et al.* 1969:107). Moreover, "generally . . . in cases of white-collar crime, neither the corporations as entities nor their responsible officers are invested with deviant characters. . ." (Cohen, 1966:30). Once more, there is quiet acquiescence to this state of affairs. There is no attempt to find out why those who steal millions and whose actions violate lives are not "invested with deviant characters." There is no consideration given to the possibility that, as responsible intellectuals, it is our duty to explore and expose the structural causes for corporate and other serious crimes, which make for much more suffering than does armed robbery. We seem satisfied merely to observe what is, and leave the causes unexamined.

In conclusion, let us look at another form of institutional "deviance." The partial publication of the Pentagon papers (June 1971) made public the conscious lying and manipulation by the government to quiet opposition to the Vietnam war. But lying pervades both government and economy. Deceptions and outright lies abound in advertising (see Henry, 1963). During the 1968 campaign, Presidential candidate Nixon blessed us with an ingenious form of deception. McGinniss (1969:149–50) is recording a discussion that took place before Nixon was to appear on live TV (to show spontaneity) the day before the election and answer, unrehearsed, questions phoned in by the viewing audience.

"I understand Paul Keyes has been sitting up for two days writing questions," Roger Ailes said.
"Well, not quite," Jack Rourke said. He seemed a little embarrassed.
"What is going to happen?"
"Oh . . ."
"It's sort of semiforgery, isn't it?" Ailes said. "Keyes has a bunch of questions Nixon wants to answer. He's written them in advance to make sure they're properly worded. When someone calls in with something similar, they'll use Keyes' question and attribute it to the person who called. Isn't that it?"
"More or less," Jack Rourke said.

In short, despite the supposedly central position of *social structure* in the sociological enterprise, there is general neglect of it in the field of "deviance." Larger questions, especially if they deal with political and economic issues, are either passed over briefly or overlooked completely. The focus on the actions of "nuts, sluts, and preverts" and the related slight of the criminal and destructive actions of the powerful, are instances of this avoidance.

III.

Most of the authors under discussion mention the importance of *power* in labelling people "deviant." They state that those who label (the victimizers) are more powerful than those they label (the victims). Writers of the labelling school make this point explicitly. According to Becker (1963:17), "who can . . . force others to accept their rules and what are the causes of their success? This is, of course, a question of political and economic power." Simmons (1969:131) comments that historically, "those in power have used their positions largely to perpetuate and enhance their own advantages through coercing and manipulating the rest of the populace." And Lofland (1969:19) makes the same observation in his opening pages:

It is in the situation of a very powerful party opposing a very weak one that the powerful party sponsors the *idea* that the weak party is breaking the rules of society. The very concepts of "society" and its "rules" are appropriated by powerful parties and made synonymous with their interests (and, of course, believed in by the naive, e.g., the undergraduate penchant for the phrases "society says . . . ," "society expects . . . ," "society does . . .").

But this insight is not developed. In none of the 16 books is there an extensive discussion of how power operates in the designation of deviance. Instead of a study of power, of its concrete uses in modern, corporate America, we are offered rather fascinating explorations into the identities and subcultures of "deviants," and misplaced emphasis on the middle-level agents of social control. Only Szasz (1961, 1963, and notably 1970) has shown consistently the role of power in one area of "deviance," "mental illness." Through historical and contemporary studies, he has shown that those labelled "mentally ill" (crazy, insane, mad, lunatic) and institutionalized have always been the powerless: women, the poor, peasants, the aged, and others. Moreover, he has exposed repeatedly the means used by powerful individuals and institutions in employing the "mental illness" label to discredit, persecute, and eliminate opponents. In short, he has shown the political element in the "mental illness" game.

In addition, except for Szasz, none of the authors seems to realize that the stigma of prostitution, abortion, and other "deviant" acts unique to women comes about in large part from the powerlessness of women and their status in society.

Moreover, to my knowledge, no one has bothered to ask why there have always been women prostitutes for men to satisfy their sexual desires, but very few men prostitutes for women to patronize. The very word *prostitute* we associate with women only, not men. Both men and women have been involved in this "immoral" act, but the stigma has been carried by the women alone.

All 16 books, some more extensively than others, discuss the ideology, modes of operation, and views of *agents of social control,* the people who designate what is to be "deviant" and those who handle the people so designated. As Gouldner (1968) has shown, however, these are the lower and middle level officials, not those who make basic policy and decisions. This bias becomes obvious when we look at the specific agents discussed.

For example, Simmons (1969:18) tells us that some of "those in charge at every level" are the following: "university administrators, patrolmen, schoolmasters, and similar public employees. . . ." Do university administrators and teachers run the schools alone? Are they teaching and enforcing their own unique values? Do teachers alone create the horrible schools in the slums? Are the uniformity, punctuality, and conformity teachers inculcate their own psychological hangups, or do they represent the interests of an industrial-technological-corporate order? In another sphere, do the police enforce their own laws?

Becker (1963:14) has shown consistent interest in agents of social control. However, a close examination reveals limitations. He discusses "moral crusaders" like those who passed the laws against marijuana. The moral crusader, "the prototype of the rule creator," finds that "the existing rules do not satisfy him because there is some evil which profoundly disturbs him." But the only type of rule creator Becker discusses is the moral crusader, no other. The political manipulators who pass laws to defend their interests and persecute dissenters are not studied. The "unconventional sentimentality," the debunking motif Becker (1964:4–5) sees in the "new deviance" is directed toward the police, the prison officials, the mental hospital personnel, the "average" person and his prejudices. The basic social, political, and economic structure, and those commanding it who guide the labelling and persecution, are left untouched. We have become so accustomed to debunking these low-level agents that we do not even know how to begin to direct our attention to the ruling institutions and groups (for an attempt at such an analysis, see Liazos, 1970).

In a later paper, Becker (1967) poses an apparently insoluble dilemma. He argues that, in studying agents of social control, we are always forced to study subordinates. We can never really get to the top, to those who "really" run the show, for if we study X's superior Y, we find Z above him, and so on endlessly. Everyone has somebody over him, so there is no one at the top. But this is a clever point without substance. In this hierarchy some have more power than others and some are at the top; they may disclaim their position, of course, but it is our job to show otherwise. Some people in this society do have more power than others: parents over children, men over women; some have considerable power over others: top administrators of institutions, for one; and some have a great deal of power, those Domhoff (1967) and others have shown to be the ruling class. It should be our task to explore and describe this hierarchy, its bases of strength, its uses of the "deviant" label to discredit its opponents in order to silence them, and to find ways to eliminate this hierarchy.

Discussions of the police reveal the same misplaced emphasis on lower and middle level agents of social control. In three of the books (Matza, 1969:182–95; Rubington and Weinberg, 1968: ch. 7; Dinitz, *et al.,* 1969:40–47), we are presented with the biases and prejudices of policemen; their modes of operation in confronting delinquents and others; the pressures on them from various quarters; etc. In short, the focus is on the role and psychology of the policeman.

All these issues about the policeman's situation need to be discussed, of course; but there is an even more important issue which these authors avoid. We must ask, who passes the laws the police enforce? Whose agents are they? Why do the police exist? Three excellent papers (Cook, 1968; A. Silver, in Bordua, 1967; T. Hayden, in Rose, 1969) offer some answers to these questions. They show, through a historical description of the origins of police forces, that they have always been used to defend the status quo, the interests of the ruling powers. When the police force was created in England in the early 1800s, it was meant to defend the propertied classes from the "dangerous classes" and the "mob."[7] With the rise of capitalism and industrialism, there was much unrest from the suffering underclass; the professional police were meant to act as a buffer zone for the capitalist elite. Similarly, in America during the early part of this century, especially in the 1930s, police were used repeatedly to attack striking workers and break their strikes. During the Chicago "police riot" of 1968, the police were not merely acting out their aggressions and frustrations; as Hayden shows, they acted with the consent, direction, and blessing of Mayor Daley and the Democratic party (which party represents the "liberal" wing of the American upper class).

It must be stressed that the police, like all agents of social control, are doing someone else's work. Sometimes they enforce laws and prejudices of "society," the much maligned middle class (on sex, marijuana, etc.); but at other times it is not "society" which gives them their directives, but specific interested groups, even though, often, "society" is manipulated to express its approval of such actions. Above all, we must remember that *"in a fundamentally unjust society, even the most impartial, professional, efficient enforcement of the laws by the police cannot result in justice"* (Cook, 1968:2). More generally, in an unjust and exploitative society, no matter how "humane" agents of social control are, their actions necessarily result in repression.

Broad generalization is another device used by some of these authors to avoid concrete examination of the uses of power in the creation and labelling of "deviance." Clairborne (1971) has called such generalization *"schlock."* The following are some of the tactics he thinks are commonly used in writing popular *schlock* sociology (some sociologists of deviance use similar tactics, as we shall see).

The Plausible Passive: "New scientific discoveries are being made every day. . . . These new ideas are being put to work more quickly . . ." [Toffler, in *Future Shock,* is] thereby rather neatly obscuring the fact that scientists and engineers (mostly paid by industry) are making the discoveries and industrialists (often with the aid of public funds) are putting them to work. An alternative to the Plausible Passive is the Elusive Impersonal: "Buildings in New York literally disappear overnight." What Toffler is trying to avoid saying is that contractors and real estate speculators *destroy* buildings overnight (Clairborne, 1971:118).

Rampant Reification, by which "conceptual abstractions are transformed into causal realities," also abounds. Toffler:

speaks of the "roaring current of change" as "an elemental force" and of "that great, growling engine of change—technology." Which of course completely begs the question of what fuels the engine and whose hand is on the throttle. One does not cross-examine an elemental force, let alone suggest that it may have been engendered by monopoly profits (especially in defense and aerospace) or accelerated by government incentives (e.g., open or concealed subsidies, low capital gains tax, accelerated depreciation—which Nixon is now seeking to reinstitute) (Clairborne, 1971:118).

There are parallels in the sociology of deviance. Clinard (1968:ch. 4) argues that urbanization and the slum are breeding grounds for "deviant behavior." But these conditions are reified, not examined concretely. He says about urbanization and social change:

Rapid social and cultural change, disregard for the importance of stability of generations, and untempered loyalties also generally characterize urban life. New ideas are generally welcome, inventions and mechanical gadgets are encouraged, and new styles in such arts as painting, literature, and music are often approved (1968:90).

But the slum, urbanization, and change are not reified entities working out their independent wills. For example, competition, capitalism, and the profit motive—all encouraged by a government controlled by the upper classes—have had something to do with the rise of slums. There is a general process of urbanization, but at given points in history it is fed by, and gives profits to, specific groups. The following are a few historical examples: the land enclosure policies and practices of the English ruling classes in the 17th and 18th centuries; the building of cheap housing in the 19th century by the owners of factory towns; and the profits its derived from "urban renewal" (which has destroyed neighborhoods, created even more crowded slums, etc.) by the building of highways, luxury apartments, and stores.

Another favorite theme of *schlock* sociology is that "All Men Are Guilty." That means nothing can be done to change things. There is a variation of this theme in the sociology of deviance when we are told that (a) all of us are deviant in some way, (b) all of us label some others deviant, and (c) "society" labels. Such statements preclude asking concrete questions: does the "deviance" of each of us have equal consequences for others? Does the labelling of each of us stick, and with what results?

For example, Simmons (1969:124) says:

... I strongly suspect that officials now further alienate more culprits than they recruit back into conventional society, and I think they imprison at least as many people in deviance as they rehabilitate. We must remember that, with a sprinkling of exceptions, officials come from, are hired by, and belong to the dominant majority.

Who is that dominant majority? Are they always the numerical majority? Do they control the labelling and correctional process all by themselves? These questions are not raised.

Another case of *schlock* is found in Matza's discussion (lack of it, really) of "Leviathan" (1969, especially ch. 7). It is mentioned as a potent force in the labelling and handling of "deviance." But, vainly, one keeps looking for some exploration into the workings of "Leviathan." It remains a reified, aloof creature. What is it? Who controls it? How does it label? Why? Matza seems content to try to mesmerize us by mentioning it constantly (Leviathan is capitalized throughout); but we are never shown how it operates. It hovers in the background, it punishes, and its presence somehow cowers us into submission. But it remains a reified force whose presence is accepted without close examination.

The preceding examples typify much of what is wrong with the sociology of deviance: the lack of specific analysis of the role of power in the labelling process; the generalizations which, even when true, explain little; the fascination with "deviants" the reluctance to study the "deviance" of the powerful.

IV.

I want to start my concluding comments with two disclaimers.

a. I have tried to provide some balance and perspective in the field of "deviance," and in doing so I have argued against the exclusive emphasis on *nuts, sluts,* and *preverts* and their identities and subcultures. I do not mean, however, that the usually considered forms of "deviance" are unworthy of our attention. Suicide, prostitution, madness, juvenile delinquency, and others *are* with us; we cannot ignore them. People do suffer when labelled and treated as "deviant" (in *this* sense, "deviants" *are* different from conformists). Rather, I want to draw attention to phenomena which also belong to the field of "deviance."[8]

b. It is because the sociology of deviance, especially the labelling approach, contains important, exciting, and revealing insights, because it tries to humanize the "deviant," and because it is popular, that it is easy to overlook some of the basic ideological biases still pervading the field. For this reason, I have tried to explore and detail some of these biases. At the same time, however, I do not mean to dismiss the contributions of the field as totally negative and useless. In fact, in my teaching I have been using two of the books discussed here, Simmons (1969) and Rubington and Weinberg (1968).

The argument can be summarized briefly. (1) We should not study only, or predominantly, the popular and dramatic forms of "deviance." Indeed, we should banish the concept of "deviance" and speak of oppression, conflict, persecution, and suffering. By focusing on the dramatic forms, as we do now, we perpetuate most people's beliefs and impressions that such "deviance" is the basic cause of many of our troubles, that these people (criminals, drug addicts, political dissenters, and others) are the real "troublemakers" and, necessarily, we neglect conditions of inequality, powerlessness, institutional violence, and so on, which lie at the bases of our tortured society. (2) Even when we do study the popular forms of "deviance," we do not avoid blaming the victim for his fate; the continued use of the term "deviant" is one clue to this blame. Nor have we succeeded in normalizing him; the focus on the "deviant" himself, on his identity and subculture, has tended to confirm the popular prejudice that he is different.

NOTES

1. Bend and Vogenfanger (1964) examined social problems textbooks of the early 1960s; they found there was little theory or emphasis on social structure in them.

2. What I say below applies to the "labelling-interactionist" school of deviance of Becker, Lemert, Erikson, Matza, and others: to a large degree, however, most of my comments also apply to the other schools.

3. The first draft of this paper was completed in July, 1971. The killing of George Jackson at San Quentin on August 21, 1971, which many people see as a political murder, and the Attica prisoner rebellion of early September, 1971, only strengthen the argument about political prisoners. Two things became clear: (a) Not only a few "radicals," but many prisoners (if not a majority) see their fate as the outcome of political forces and decisions, and themselves as political prisoners (see Fraser, 1971). Robert Chrisman's argument (in Fraser, 1971) points to such a conclusion clearly: "To maintain that all black offenders are, by their actions, politically correct, is dangerous romanticism. Black antisocial behavior must be seen in and of its own terms and corrected for enhancement of the black community." But there is a political aspect, for black prisoners' condition "derives from the political inequity of black people in America. A black prisoner's crime may or may not have been a political action against the state, but the state's action against him is always political." I would stress that the same is true of most white prisoners, for they come mostly from the exploited poorer classes and groups. (b) The state authorities, the political rulers, by their deeds if not their words, see such prisoners as political men and threats. The death of George Jackson, and the brutal crushing of the Attica rebellion, attest to the authorities' realization, and fear, that here were no mere riots with prisoners letting off steam, but authentic political actions, involving groups and individuals conscious of their social position and exploitation.

4. With the exception of E. C. Hughes, in Becker (1964).

5. As Gittlin and Hollander (1970) show, the children of poor whites also suffer from lead poisoning.

6. Investigation of the causes and prevention of institutional violence would probably be biting the hand that feeds the sociologist, for we read that the government and foundations (whose money comes from corporate profits) have supported research on "deviant behavior," especially its prevention. "This has meant particularly that the application of sociological theory to research has increased markedly in such areas as delinquency, crime, mental disorder, alcoholism, drug addiction, and discrimination" (Clinard, 1968:742). That's where the action is, not on white-collar crime, nor on the covert institutional violence of the government and economy.

7. See Rudé (1966) on the role of mobs of poor workers and peasants in 18th and 19th century England and France.

8. The question of "what deviance is to the deviant" (Gordon Fellman, private communication), not what the labelling, anomie, and other schools, or the present radical viewpoint say about such a person, is not dealt with here. I avoid this issue not because I think it unimportant, rather because I want to concentrate on the political, moral, and social issues raised by the biases of those presently writing about the "deviant."

REFERENCES

BECKER, HOWARD S. *1963. *Outsiders.* New York: Free Press.

———. *1964. (ed.) *The Other Side.* New York: Free Press.

———.1967. "Whose side are we on?" *Social Problems* 14: 239–247 (reprinted in Douglas, 1970a, 99–111; references to this reprint).

BELL, ROBERT R. *1971. *Social Deviance: A Substantive Analysis.* Homewood, Illinois: Dorsey.

BEND, EMIL and MARTIN VOGENFANGER. 1964. "A new look at Mills' critique," in *Mass Society in Crisis.* Bernard Rosenberg, Israel Gerver, F. William Howton (eds.). New York: Macmillan, 1964, 111–122.

BORDUA, DAVID (ed.) 1967. *The Police.* New York: Wiley. Carmichael, Stokeley and Charles V. Hamilton.

———. 1967. *Black Power.* New York: Random House.

CLAIRBORNE, ROBERT. 1971. "Future schlock." *The Nation,* Jan. 25, 117–120.

CLEAVER, ELDRIDGE. 1968. *Soul On Ice.* New York: McGraw-Hill.

CLINARD, MARSHALL B. *1968. *Sociology of Deviant Behavior.* (3rd ed.) New York: Holt, Rinehart, and Winston.

COHEN, ALBERT K. *1966. *Deviance and Control.* Englewood Cliffs, N.J.: Prentice Hall.

COOK, ROBERT M. 1968. "The police." *The Bulletin of the American Independent Movement* (New Haven, Conn.), 3:6, 1–6.

DINITZ, SIMON, RUSSELL R. DYNES, and ALFRED C. CLARKE (eds.) *1969. *Deviance.* New York: Oxford University Press.

DOMHOFF, WILLIAM G. 1967. *Who Rules America?* Englewood Cliffs, N.J.: Prentice Hall.

DOUGLAS, JACK D. *1970a. (ed.) *Observations of Deviance.* New York: Random House.

———. *1970b. (ed.) *Deviance and Respectability: The Social Construction of Moral Meanings.* New York: Basic Books.

FRASER, C. GERALD. 1971. "Black prisoners finding new view of themselves as political prisoners." *New York Times,* Sept. 16.

GITTLIN, TODD and NANCI HOLLANDER. 1970. *Uptown: Poor Whites in Chicago.* New York: Harper and Row.

GOULDNER, ALVIN W. 1968. "The sociologist as partisan: Sociology and the welfare state." *American Sociologist* 3:2, 103–116.

HENRY, JULES. 1963. *Culture Against Man.* New York: Random House.

JACKSON, GEORGE. 1970. *Soledad Brother.* New York: Bantam Books.

LEFTON, MARK, J. K. SKIPPER, and C. H. McCAGHY (eds.) *1968. *Approaches to Deviance.* New York: Appleton-Century-Crofts.

LEMERT, EDWIN M. *1967. *Human Deviance, Social Problems, and Social Control.* Englewood Cliffs, N.J.: Prentice Hall.

LIAZOS, ALEXANDER. 1970. Processing for Unfitness: socialization of "emotionally disturbed" lower-class boys into the mass society. Ph.D. dissertation, Brandeis University.

LOFLAND, JOHN. *1969. *Deviance and Identity.* Englewood Cliffs, N.J.: Prentice Hall.

MALCOLM X. 1965. *The Autobiography of Malcolm X.* New York: Grove.

MATZA, DAVID. *1969. *Becoming Deviant.* Englewood Cliffs, N.J.: Prentice Hall.

McCAGHY, CHARLES H., J. K. SKIPPER, and M. LEFTON (eds.) *1968. *In Their Own Behalf: Voices from the Margin.* New York: Appleton-Century-Crofts.

McGINNISS, JOE. 1969. *The Selling of the President, 1968.* New York: Trident.

MILLS, C. WRIGHT. 1943. "The professional ideology of social pathologists." *American Journal of Sociology* 49: 165–180.

NEWFIELD, JACK. 1971. "Let them eat lead." *New York Times,* June 16, p. 45.

QUINN, OLIVE W. 1954. "The transmission of racial attitudes among white southerners." *Social Forces* 33:1, 41–47 (reprinted in E. Schuler, *et al.,* eds., *Readings in Sociology,* 2nd ed., New York: Crowell, 1960, 140–150).

ROSE, THOMAS (ed.) 1969. *Violence in America.* New York: Random House.

RUBINGTON, EARL and M. S. WEINBERG (eds.) *1968. *Deviance: The Interactionist Perspective.* New York: Macmillan.

RUDE, GEORGE. 1966. *The Crowd in History.* New York: Wiley.

RUSHING, WILLIAM A. (ed.) *1969. *Deviant Behavior and Social Processes.* Chicago: Rand McNally.

SIMMONS, J. L. *1969. *Deviants.* Berkeley, Cal.: Glendessary.

SZASZ, THOMAS S. 1961. *The Myth of Mental Illness.* New York: Harper and Row.

———. 1963. *Law, Liberty, and Psychiatry.* New York: Macmillan.

———. 1970. *The Manufacture of Madness.* New York: Harper and Row.

THOMPSON, HUNTER S. 1966. *Hell's Angels.* New York: Ballantine.

Learning

Another useful perspective for understanding deviance is that of learning theory. In general, such theories examine the processes by which deviant behavior and values are learned through group interaction. Learning theorists focus on group behavior and affiliation and how individuals internalize norms associated with such groups.

Gresham Sykes and David Matza's classic article, "Techniques of Neutralization," describes the rationalizations that juveniles offer for their deviant and criminal behavior. Such rationalizations are learned through group interaction and allow for one to engage in deviant behavior by suspending conventional norms that generally control behavior. Elaborating upon Sutherland's work (discussed below), they argue that techniques of neutralization make up a significant component of the definitions favorable to law violation and must be learned and accepted before one is able to engage in deviance. These techniques allow one to drift in and out of law-abiding behavior and are learned in group interaction. Sykes and Matza classify five major types of neutralization techniques, and later theorists have added others. The five techniques they describe are: the denial of responsibility, the denial of injury, the denial of victim, the condemnation of condemners, and the appeal to higher loyalties. All of these learned techniques allow the enactment of deviance and are part of a larger system of attitudes and beliefs that are important for understanding delinquency and other acts of lawbreaking.

In "Becoming a Marihuana User," Howard Becker argues that this form of drug use can best be understood not by theories that focus on traits which predispose one to engage in the behavior, but rather by the sequence of learning that leads to "the use of marihuana for pleasure." Using personal accounts of users, Becker shows that persons "learn" the technique for using marihuana to produce this effect, as well as learning to perceive certain effects through experimentation, which usually occurs in a social context. Finally, learning to enjoy the effects of the drug allows for possible continued use. Conceptions of the drug change during this learning process, which helps the user develop motivations or dispositions to use marihuana that could not have been present before actually experiencing its effects.

One of the more famous learning theories is Edwin Sutherland's theory of "differential association." Sutherland attempted to create a theory that would account for all criminal behavior, including what he termed "white-collar crime." He maintained that crime was learned, just as anything else is learned by members of society. That is, the knowledge necessary to commit deviant acts, along with the motives, values, and skills, are acquired through personal interactions that take place in groups. Deviant groups are those where there is "an excess of definitions favorable to law violation over those favorable to conformity." The theory has been criticized on the grounds that it is too vague and untestable. Some crimes such as check forgery and embezzlement do not fit the differential association model. Despite these limitations, many forms of deviant and criminal behavior fit Sutherland's model, and it has had a major impact on the field of deviance theory.

One of the variations on Sutherland's theory of differential association is found in Daniel Glaser's formulation of "differential identification." According to Glaser, it is not always necessary to have direct group interaction to acquire the values and knowledge to commit acts of deviance and crime. A person may simply identify with a real or imaginary group or persons from whose perspective deviance is acceptable. Here the emphasis is on the choice of models, rather than the direct interaction with deviant subgroups.

TECHNIQUES OF NEUTRALIZATION
A THEORY OF DELINQUENCY*

Gresham M. Sykes and David Matza

As Morris Cohen once said, one of the most fascinating problems about human behavior is why men violate the laws in which they believe. This is the problem that confronts us when we attempt to explain why delinquency occurs despite a greater or lesser commitment to the usages of conformity. A basic clue is offered by the fact that social rules or norms calling for valued behavior seldom if ever take the form of categorical imperatives. Rather, values or norms appear as *qualified* guides for action, limited in their applicability in terms of time, place, persons, and social circumstances. The moral injunction against killing, for example, does not apply to the enemy during combat in time of war, although a captured enemy comes once again under the prohibition. Similarly, the taking and distributing of scarce goods in a time of acute social need is felt by many to be right, although under other circumstances private property is held inviolable. The normative system of a society, then, is marked by what Williams has termed *flexibility*;

it does not consist of a body of rules held to be binding under all conditions.[1]

This flexibility is, in fact, an integral part of the criminal law in that measures for "defenses to crimes" are provided in pleas such as non-age, necessity, insanity, drunkenness, compulsion, self-defense, and so on. The individual can avoid moral culpability for his criminal action—and thus avoid the negative sanctions of society—if he can prove that criminal intent was lacking. *It is our argument that much delinquency is based on what is essentially an unrecognized extension of defenses to crimes, in the form of justifications for deviance that are seen as valid by the delinquent but not by the legal system or society at large.*

These justifications are commonly described as rationalizations. They are viewed as following deviant behavior and as protecting the individual from self-blame and the blame of others after the act. But there is also reason to believe that they precede deviant behavior and make deviant behavior possible. It is this possibility that Sutherland mentioned only in passing and that other writers have failed to exploit from the viewpoint

*"Techniques of Neutralization: Theory of Delinquency" by Gresham M. Sykes and David Matza. *American Sociological Review,* 22 (Dec., 1957).

of sociological theory. Disapproval flowing from internalized norms and conforming others in the social environment is neutralized, turned back, or deflected in advance. Social controls that serve to check or inhibit deviant motivational patterns are rendered inoperative, and the individual is freed to engage in delinquency without serious damage to his self-image. In this sense, the delinquent both has his cake and eats it too, for he remains committed to the dominant normative system and yet so qualifies its imperatives that violations are "acceptable" if not "right." Thus the delinquent represents not a radical opposition to law-abiding society but something more like an apologetic failure, often more sinned against than sinning in his own eyes. We call these justifications of deviant behavior techniques of neutralization; and we believe these techniques make up a crucial component of Sutherland's "definitions favorable to the violation of law." It is by learning these techniques that the juvenile becomes delinquent, rather than by learning moral imperatives, values, or attitudes standing in direct contradiction to those of the dominant society. In analyzing these techniques, we have found it convenient to divide them into five major types.

THE DENIAL OF RESPONSIBILITY

Insofar as the delinquent can define himself as lacking responsibility for his deviant actions, the disapproval of self or others is sharply reduced in effectiveness as a restraining influence. As Justice Holmes has said, even a dog distinguishes between being stumbled over and being kicked, and modern society is no less careful to draw a line between injuries that are unintentional, i.e., where responsibility is lacking, and those that are intentional. As a technique of neutralization, however, the denial of responsibility extends much further than the claim that deviant acts are an "accident" or some similar negation of personal accountability. It may also be asserted that delinquent acts are due to forces outside of the individual and beyond his control such as unloving parents, bad companions, or a slum neighborhood. In effect, the delinquent approaches a "billiard ball" conception of himself in which he sees himself as helplessly propelled into new situa-

tions. From a psychodynamic viewpoint, this orientation toward one's own actions may represent a profound alienation from self, but it is important to stress the fact that interpretations of responsibility are cultural constructs and not merely idiosyncratic beliefs. The similarity between this mode of justifying illegal behavior assumed by the delinquent and the implications of a "sociological" frame of reference or a "humane" jurisprudence is readily apparent.[2] It is not the validity of this orientation that concerns us here, but its function of deflecting blame attached to violations of social norms and its relative independence of a particular personality structure.[3] By learning to view himself as more acted upon than acting, the delinquent prepares the way for deviance from the dominant normative system without the necessity of a frontal assault on the norms themselves.

THE DENIAL OF INJURY

A second major technique of neutralization centers on the injury or harm involved in the delinquent act. The criminal law has long made a distinction between crimes which are *mala in se* and *mala prohibita*—that is, between acts that are wrong in themselves and acts that are illegal but not immoral—and the delinquent can make the same kind of distinction in evaluating the wrongfulness of his behavior. For the delinquent, however, wrongfulness may turn on the question of whether or not anyone has clearly been hurt by his deviance, and this matter is open to a variety of interpretations. Vandalism, for example, may be defined by the delinquent simply as "mischief"—after all, it may be claimed, the persons whose property has been destroyed can well afford it. Similarly, auto theft may be viewed as "borrowing," and gang fighting may be seen as a private quarrel, an agreed-upon duel between two willing parties, and thus of no concern to the community at large. We are not suggesting that this technique of neutralization, labeled the denial of injury, involves an explicit dialectic. Rather, we are arguing that the delinquent frequently, and in a hazy fashion, feels that his behavior does not really cause any great harm despite the fact that it runs counter to law. Just as the link between the individual and his acts may be broken by the denial of responsibility, so may the link between acts and their consequences be broken by the denial of injury. Since society sometimes agrees with the delinquent, e.g., in matters such as truancy, "pranks," and so on, it merely reaffirms the idea that the delinquent's neutralization of social controls by means of qualifying the norms is an extension of common practice rather than a gesture of complete opposition.

THE DENIAL OF THE VICTIM

Even if the delinquent accepts the responsibility for his deviant actions and is willing to admit that his deviant actions involve an injury or hurt, the moral indignation of self and others may be neutralized by an insistence that the injury is not wrong in light of the circumstances. The injury, it may be claimed, is not really an injury; rather, it is a form of rightful retaliation or punishment. By a subtle alchemy the delinquent moves himself into the position of an avenger and the victim is transformed into a wrong-doer. Assaults on homosexuals or suspected homosexuals, attacks on members of minority groups who are said to have gotten "out of place," vandalism as revenge on an unfair teacher or school official, thefts from a "crooked" store owner—all may be hurts inflicted on a transgressor, in the eyes of the delinquent. As Orwell has pointed out, the type of criminal admired by the general public has probably changed over the course of years and Raffles no longer serves as a hero;[4] but Robin Hood, and his latter-day derivatives such as the tough detective seeking justice outside the law, still capture the popular imagination, and the delinquent may view his acts as part of a similar role.

To deny the existence of the victim, then, by transforming him into a person deserving injury is an extreme form of a phenomenon we have mentioned before, namely, the delinquent's recognition of appropriate and inappropriate targets for his delinquent acts. In addition, however, the existence of the victim may be denied for the delinquent, in a somewhat different sense, by the circumstances of the delinquent act itself. Insofar as the victim is physically absent, unknown, or a vague abstraction (as is often the case in delinquent acts committed against property), the awareness of the victim's existence is weakened. Internalized norms and anticipations of the reactions of others must somehow be activated if they are to serve as guides for behavior; and it is possible that a diminished awareness of the victim plays an important part of determining whether or not this process is set in motion.

THE CONDEMNATION OF THE CONDEMNERS

A fourth technique of neutralization would appear to involve a condemnation of the condemners or, as McCorkle and Korn have phrased it, a rejection of the rejectors.[5] The delinquent shifts the focus of attention from his own deviant acts to the motives and behavior of those who disapprove of his violations. His condemners, he may claim, are hypocrites, deviants in disguise, or impelled by personal spite. This orientation toward the conforming world may be of particular importance when it hardens into a bitter cynicism directed against those assigned the task of enforcing or expressing the norms of the dominant society. Police, it may be said, are corrupt, stupid, and brutal. Teachers always show favoritism and parents always "take it out" on their children. By a slight extension, the rewards of conformity—such as material success—become a matter of pull or luck, thus decreasing still further the stature of those who stand on the side of the law-abiding. The validity of this jaundiced viewpoint is not so important as its function in turning back or deflecting the negative sanctions attached to violations of the norms. The delinquent, in effect, has changed the subject of the conversation in the dialogue between his own deviant impulses and the reactions of others; and by attacking others, the wrongfulness of his own behavior is more easily repressed or lost to view.

THE APPEAL TO HIGHER LOYALTIES

Fifth, and last, internal and external social controls may be neutralized by sacrificing the demands of the larger society for the demands of the smaller social groups to which the delinquent belongs, such as the sibling pair, the gang, or the friendship clique. It is important to note that the delinquent does not necessarily repudiate the imperatives of the dominant normative system, despite his failure to follow them. Rather, the delinquent may see himself as caught up in a dilemma that must be resolved, unfortunately, at the cost of violating the law. One aspect of this situation has been studied by Stouffer and Toby in their research on the conflict between particularistic and universalistic demands, between the claims of friendship and general social obligations, and their results suggest that "it is possible to classify people according to a predisposition to select one or the other horn of a dilemma in role conflict."[6] For our purposes, however, the most important point is that deviation from certain norms may occur not because the norms are rejected but because others' norms, held to be more pressing or involving a higher loyalty, are accorded precedence. Indeed, it is the fact that both sets of norms are believed in that gives meaning to our concepts of dilemma and role conflict.

The conflict between the claims of friendship and the claims of law, or a similar dilemma, has of course long been recognized by the social scientist (and the novelist) as a common human problem. If the juvenile delinquent frequently resolves his dilemma by insisting that he must "always help a buddy" or "never squeal on a friend," even when it throws him into serious difficulties with the dominant social order, his choice remains familiar to the supposedly law-abiding. The delinquent is unusual, perhaps, in the extent to which he is able to see the fact that he acts in behalf of the smaller social groups to which he belongs as a justification for violations of society's norms, but it is a matter of degree rather than of kind.

"I didn't mean it." "I didn't really hurt anybody." "They had it coming to them." "Everybody's picking on me." "I didn't do it for myself." These slogans or their variants, we hypothesize, prepare the juvenile for delinquent acts. These "definitions of the situation" represent tangential or glancing blows at the dominant normative system rather than the creation of an opposing ideology; and they are extensions of patterns of thought prevalent in society rather than something created *de novo*.

Techniques of neutralization may not be powerful enough to fully shield the individual from the force of his own internalized values and the reactions of conforming others, for as we have pointed out, juvenile delinquents often appear to suffer from feelings of guilt and shame when called into account for their deviant behavior. And some delinquents may be so isolated from the world of conformity that techniques of neutralization need not be called into play. Nonetheless, we would argue that techniques of neutralization are critical in lessening the effectiveness of social controls and that they lie behind a large share of delinquent behavior. Empirical research in this area is scattered and fragmentary at the present time, but the work of Redl,[7] Cressey,[8] and others has supplied a body of significant data that has done much to clarify the theoretical issues and enlarge the fund of supporting evidence. Two lines of investigation seem to be critical at this stage. First, there is need for more knowledge concerning the differential distribution of techniques of neutralization, as operative patterns of thought, by age, sex, social class, ethnic group, etc. On a priori grounds it might be assumed that these justifications for deviance will be more readily seized by segments of society for whom a discrepancy between common social ideals and social practice is most apparent. It is also possible, however, that the habit of "bending" the dominant normative system—if not "breaking" it—cuts across our cruder social categories and is to be traced primarily to patterns of social interaction within the familial circle. Second, there is need for a greater understanding of the internal structure of techniques of neutralization, as a system of beliefs and attitudes, and its relationship to various types of delinquent behavior. Certain techniques of neutralization would appear to be better adapted to particular deviant acts than to others, as we have suggested, for example, in the case of offenses against property and the denial of the victim. But the issue remains far from clear and stands in need of more information.

In any case, techniques of neutralization appear to offer a promising line of research in enlarging and systematizing the theoretical grasp of juvenile delinquency. As more information is

uncovered concerning techniques of neutralization, their origins, and their consequences, both
juvenile delinquency in particular and deviation
from normative systems in general may be illu-
minated.

NOTES

1. Cf. Robin Williams, Jr., *American Society,* New
York: Knopf, 1951, p. 28.

2. A number of observers have wryly noted that
many delinquents seem to show a surprising awareness
of sociological and psychological explanations for
their behavior and are quick to point out the casual role
of their poor environment.

3. It is possible, of course, that certain personality
structures can accept some techniques of neutralization

more readily than others, but this question remains
largely unexplored.

4. George Orwell, *Dickens, Dali, and Others,* New
York: Reynal, 1946.

5. Lloyd W. McCorkle and Richard Korn, "Resocialization Within Walls," *The Annals of the American
Academy of Political and Social Science,* 293 (May,
1954), pp. 88–98.

6. See Samuel A. Stouffer and Jackson Toby, "Role
Conflict and Personality," in *Toward a General Theory of Action,* edited by Talcott Parsons and Edward
A. Shils, Cambridge, Mass.: Harvard University Press,
1951, p. 494.

7. See Fritz Redl and David Wineman, *Children
Who Hate,* Glencoe, Ill.: The Free Press, 1956.

8. See D. R. Cressey, *Other People's Money,* Glencoe, Ill.: The Free Press, 1953.

BECOMING A MARIHUANA USER*

Howard S. Becker

An unknown, but probably quite large, number
of people in the United States use marihuana.
They do this in spite of the fact that it is both illegal and disapproved.

The phenomenon of marihuana use has received much attention, particularly from psychiatrists and law enforcement officials. The research
that has been done, as is often the case with research on behavior that is viewed as deviant, is
mainly concerned with the question: why do they
do it? Attempts to account for the use of marihuana lean heavily on the premise that the presence of any particular kind of behavior in an individual can best be explained as the result of some
trait which predisposes or motivates him to engage in that behavior. In the case of marihuana
use, this trait is usually identified as psychologi-

*"Becoming a Marihuana User" by Howard S. Becker.
American Journal of Sociology, 59 (Nov., 1953), pp. 235–242.
Reprinted by permission of the author and the University of
Chicago Press.

cal, as a need for fantasy and escape from psychological problems the individual cannot face.[1]

I do not think such theories can adequately account for marihuana use. In fact, marihuana use
is an interesting case for theories of deviance, because it illustrates the way deviant motives actually develop in the course of experience with the
deviant activity. To put a complex argument in a
few words: Instead of the deviant motives leading to the deviant behavior, it is the other way
around; the deviant behavior in time produces the
deviant motivation. Vague impulses and desires—in this case, probably most frequently a
curiosity about the kind of experience the drug
will produce—are transformed into definite patterns of action through the social interpretation of
a physical experience which is in itself ambiguous. Marihuana use is a function of the individual's conception of marihuana and of the uses to
which it can be put, and this conception develops
as the individual's experience with the drug increases.[2]

The research reported [here] deals with the career of the marihuana user, [specifically, with] the development of the individual's immediate physical experience with marihuana . . . What we are trying to understand here is the sequence of changes in attitude and experience which lead to the use of marihuana for pleasure. This way of phrasing the problem requires a little explanation. Marihuana does not produce addiction, at least in the sense that alcohol and the opiate drugs do. The user experiences no withdrawal sickness and exhibits no ineradicable craving for the drug.[3] The most frequent pattern of use might be termed "recreational." The drug is used occasionally for the pleasure the user finds in it, a relatively casual kind of behavior in comparison with that connected with the use of addicting drugs. The report of the New York City Mayor's Committee on Marihuana emphasizes this point:

A person may be a confirmed smoker for a prolonged period, and give up the drug voluntarily without experiencing any craving for it or exhibiting withdrawal symptoms. He may, at some time later on, go back to its use. Others may remain infrequent users of the cigarette, taking one or two a week, or only when the "social setting" calls for participation. From time to time we had one of our investigators associate with a marihuana user. The investigator would bring up the subject of smoking. This would invariably lead to the suggestion that they obtain some marihuana cigarettes. They would seek a "tea-pad," and if it was closed the smoker and our investigator would calmly resume their previous activity, such as the discussion of life in general or the playing of pool. There were apparently no signs indicative of frustration in the smoker at not being able to gratify the desire for the drug. We consider this point highly significant since it is so contrary to the experience of users of other narcotics. A similar situation occurring in one addicted to the use of morphine, cocaine or heroin would result in a compulsive attitude on the part of the addict to obtain the drug. If unable to secure it, there would be obvious physical and mental manifestations of frustration. This may be considered presumptive evidence that there is no true addiction in the medical sense associated with the use of marihuana.[4]

In using the phrase "use for pleasure," I mean to emphasize the noncompulsive and casual character of the behavior. (I also mean to eliminate from consideration here those few cases in which marihuana is used for its prestige value only, as a symbol that one is a certain kind of person, with no pleasure at all being derived from its use.)

The research I am about to report was not so designed that it could constitute a crucial test of the theories that relate marihuana use to some psychological trait of the user. However, it does show that psychological explanations are not in themselves sufficient to account for marihuana use and that they are, perhaps, not even necessary. Researchers attempting to prove such psychological theories have run into two great difficulties, never satisfactorily resolved, which the theory presented here avoids. In the first place, theories based on the existence of some predisposing psychological trait have difficulty in accounting for that group of users, who turn up in sizable numbers in every study,[5] who do not exhibit the trait or traits which are considered to cause the behavior. Second, psychological theories have difficulty in accounting for the great variability over time of a given individual's behavior with reference to the drug. The same person will at one time be unable to use the drug for pleasure, at a later stage be able and willing to do so, and still later again be unable to use it in this way. These changes, difficult to explain from a theory based on the user's needs for "escape" are readily understandable as consequences of changes in his conception of the drug. Similarly, if we think of the marihuana user as someone who has learned to view marihuana as something that can give him pleasure, we have no difficulty in understanding the existence of psychologically "normal" users.

In doing the study, I used the method of analytic induction. I tried to arrive at a general statement of the sequence of changes in individual attitude and experience which always occurred when the individual became willing and able to use marihuana for pleasure, and never occurred or had not been permanently maintained when the person was unwilling to use marihuana for pleasure. The method requires that *every* case collected in the research substantiate the hypothesis. If one case is encountered which does not substantiate it, the researcher is required to change the hypothesis to fit the case which has proven his original idea wrong.[6]

To develop and test my hypothesis about the genesis of marihuana use for pleasure, I conducted fifty interviews with marihuana users. I had been a professional dance musician for some years when I conducted this study and my first interviews were with people I had met in the music business. I asked them to put me in contact with other users who would be willing to discuss their experiences with me. Colleagues working on a study of users of opiate drugs made a few interviews available to me which contained, in addition to material on opiate drugs, sufficient material on the use of marihuana to furnish a test of my hypothesis.[7] Although in the end half of the fifty interviews were conducted with musicians, the other half covered a wide range of people, including laborers, machinists, and people in the professions. The sample is, of course, in no sense "random"; it would not be possible to draw a random sample, since no one knows the nature of the universe from which it would have to be drawn.

In interviewing users, I focused on the history of the person's experience with marihuana, seeking major changes in his attitude toward it and in his actual use of it, and the reasons for these changes. Where it was possible and appropriate, I used the jargon of the user himself.

The theory starts with the person who has arrived at the point of willingness to try marihuana. . . . He knows others use marihuana to "get high," but he does not know what this means in any concrete way. He is curious about the experience, ignorant of what it may turn out to be, and afraid it may be more than he has bargained for. The steps outlined below, if he undergoes them all and maintains the attitudes developed in them, leave him willing and able to use the drug for pleasure when the opportunity presents itself.

LEARNING THE TECHNIQUE

The novice does not ordinarily get high the first time he smokes marihuana, and several attempts are usually necessary to induce this state. One explanation of this may be that the drug is not smoked "properly," that is, in a way that insures sufficient dosage to produce real symptoms of intoxication. Most users agree that it cannot be smoked like tobacco if one is to get high:

Take in a lot of air, you know, and . . . I don't know how to describe it, you don't smoke it like a cigarette, you draw in a lot of air and get it deep down in your system and then keep it there. Keep it there as long as you can.

Without the use of some such technique[8] the drug will produce no effects, and the user will be unable to get high:

The trouble with people like that [who are not able to get high] is that they're just not smoking it right, that's all there is to it. Either they're not holding it down long enough, or they're getting too much air and not enough smoke, or the other way around or something like that. A lot of people just don't smoke it right, so naturally nothing's gonna happen.

If nothing happens, it is manifestly impossible for the user to develop a conception of the drug as an object which can be used for pleasure, and use will therefore not continue. The first step in the sequence of events that must occur if the person is to become a user is that he must learn to use the proper smoking technique so that his use of the drug will produce effects in terms of which his conception of it can change.

Such a change is, as might be expected, a result of the individual's participation in groups in which marihuana is used. In them the individual learns the proper way to smoke the drug. This may occur through direct teaching:

I was smoking like I did an ordinary cigarette. He said, "No, don't do it like that." He said, "Suck it, you know, draw in and hold it in your lungs till you . . . for a period of time."

I said, "Is there any limit of time to hold it?"

He said, "No, just till you feel that you want to let it out, let it out." So I did that three or four times.

Many new users are ashamed to admit ignorance and, pretending to know already, must learn through the more indirect means of observation and imitation:

I came on like I had turned on many times before, you know. I didn't want to seem like a punk to this cat. See, like I didn't know the first thing about it—how to smoke it, or what was going to happen, or what. I just watched him like a hawk—I didn't take my eyes off him for a second, because I wanted to do everything just as he did it. I watched how he held it, how he smoked it, and everything. Then when he gave it to me I just came on cool, as though I knew exactly what the score was. I held it like he did and took a poke just the way he did.

No one I interviewed continued marihuana use for pleasure without learning a technique that supplied sufficient dosage for the effects of the drug to appear. Only when this was learned was it possible for a conception of the drug as an object which could be used for pleasure to emerge. Without such a conception marihuana use was considered meaningless and did not continue.

LEARNING TO PERCEIVE THE EFFECTS

Even after he learns the proper smoking technique, the new user may not get high and thus not form a conception of the drug as something which can be used for pleasure. A remark made by a user suggested the reason for this difficulty in getting high and pointed to the next necessary step on the road to being a user:

As a matter of fact, I've seen a guy who was high out of his mind and didn't know it.

[How can that be, man?]

Well, it's pretty strange, I'll grant you that, but I've seen it. This guy got on with me, claiming that he'd never got high, one of those guys, and he got completely stoned. And he kept insisting that he wasn't high. So I had to prove to him that he was.

What does this mean? It suggests that being high consists of two elements: the presence of symptoms caused by marihuana use and the recognition of these symptoms and their connection by the user with his use of the drug. It is not enough, that is, that the effects be present; alone, they do not automatically provide the experience of being high. The user must be able to point them out to himself and consciously connect them with having smoked marihuana before he can have this experience. Otherwise, no matter what actual effects are produced, he considers that the drug has had no effect on him: "I figured it either had no effect on me or other people were exaggerating its effect on them, you know. I thought it was probably psychological, see."

Such persons believe the whole thing is an illusion and that the wish to be high leads the user to deceive himself into believing that something is happening when, in fact, nothing is. They do not continue marihuana use, feeling that "it does nothing" for them.

Typically, however, the novice has faith (developed from his observation of users who do get high) that the drug actually will produce some new experience and continues to experiment with it until it does. His failure to get high worries him, and he is likely to ask more experienced users or provoke comments from them about it. In such conversations he is made aware of specific details of his experience which he may not have noticed or may have noticed but failed to identify as symptoms of being high:

I didn't get high the first time. . . . I don't think I held it in long enough. I probably let it out, you know, you're a little afraid. The second time I wasn't sure, and he [smoking companion] told me, like I asked him for some of the symptoms or something, how would I know, you know. . . . So he told me to sit on a stool. I sat on—I think I sat on a bar stool—and he said, "Let your feet hang," and then when I got down my feet were real cold, you know.

And I started feeling it, you know. That was the first time. And then about a week after that, sometime pretty close to it, I really got on. That was the first time I got on a big laughing kick, you know. Then I really knew I was on.

One symptom of being high is an intense hunger. In the next case the novice becomes aware of this and gets high for the first time:

They were just laughing the hell out of me because like I was eating so much. I just scoffed [ate] so much food, and they were just laughing at me, you know. Sometimes I'd be looking at them, you know, wondering why they're laughing, you know, not knowing what I was doing. [Well, did they tell you why they were laughing eventually?] Yeah, yeah, I come back, "Hey, man, what's happening?" Like, you know, like I'd ask, "What's happening?" and all of a sudden I feel weird, you know. "Man, you're on, you know. You're on pot [high on marihuana]." I said, "No, am I?" Like I don't know what's happening.

The learning may occur in more indirect ways:

I heard little remarks that were made by other people. Somebody said, "My legs are rubbery," and I can't remember all the remarks that were made because I was very attentively listening for all these cues for what I was supposed to feel like.

The novice, then, eager to have this feeling, picks up from other users some concrete referents of the term "high" and applies these notions to his own experience. The new concepts make it possible for him to locate these symptoms among his own sensations and to point out to himself a "something different" in his experience that he connects with drug use. It is only when he can do this that he is high. In the next case, the contrast between two successive experiences of a user makes clear the crucial importance of the awareness of the symptoms in being high and re-emphasizes the important role of interaction with other users in acquiring the concepts that make this awareness possible:

[Did you get high the first time you turned on?] Yeah, sure. Although, come to think of it, I guess I really didn't. I mean, like that first time it was more or less of a mild drunk. I was happy, I guess, you know what I mean. But I didn't really know I was high, you know what I mean. It was only after the second time I got high that I realized I was high the first time. Then I knew that something different was happening.

[How did you know that?] How did I know? If what happened to me that night would of happened to you, you would've known, believe me. We played the first tune for almost two hours—one tune! Imagine, man! We got on the stand and played this one tune, we started at nine o'clock. When we got finished I looked at my watch, it's a quarter to eleven. Almost two hours on one tune. And it didn't seem like anything.

I mean, you know, it does that to you. It's like you have much more time or something. Anyway, when I saw that, man, it was too much. I knew I must really be high or something if anything like that could happen. See, and then they explained to me that that's what it did to you, you had a different sense of time and everything. So I realized that that's what it was. I knew then. Like the first time, I probably felt that way, you know, but I didn't know what's happening.

It is only when the novice becomes able to get high in this sense that he will continue to use marihuana for pleasure. In every case in which use continued, the user had acquired the necessary concepts with which to express to himself the fact that he was experiencing new sensations caused by the drug. That is, for use to continue, it is necessary not only to use the drug so as to produce effects but also to learn to perceive these effects when they occur. In this way marihuana acquires meaning for the user as an object which can be used for pleasure.

With increasing experience the user develops a greater appreciation of the drug's effects; he continues to learn to get high. He examines succeeding experiences closely, looking for new effects, making sure the old ones are still there. Out of this there grows a stable set of categories for experiencing the drug's effects whose presence enables the user to get high with ease.

Users, as they acquire this set of categories, become connoisseurs. Like experts in fine wines, they can specify where a particular plant was grown and what time of year it was harvested. Although it is usually not possible to know whether these attributions are correct, it is true that they distinguish between batches of marihuana, not only according to strength, but also with respect to the different kinds of symptoms produced.

The ability to perceive the drug's effects must be maintained if use is to continue; if it is lost, marihuana use ceases. Two kinds of evidence support this statement. First, people who become heavy users of alcohol, barbiturates, or opiates do not continue to smoke marihuana, largely because they lose the ability to distinguish between its effects and those of the other drugs.[9] They no longer know whether the marihuana gets them high. Second, in those few cases in which an individual uses marihuana in such quantities that he is always high, he is apt to feel the drug has no effect on him, since the essential element of a noticeable difference between feeling high and feeling normal is missing. In such a situation, use is likely to be given up completely, but temporarily, in order that the user may once again be able to perceive the difference.

LEARNING TO ENJOY THE EFFECTS

One more step is necessary if the user who has now learned to get high is to continue use. He must learn to enjoy the effects he has just learned to experience. Marihuana-produced sensations are not automatically or necessarily pleasurable. The taste for such experience is a socially acquired one, not different in kind from acquired tastes for oysters or dry martinis. The user feels dizzy, thirsty; his scalp tingles; he misjudges time and distances. Are these things pleasurable? He isn't sure. If he is to continue marihuana use, he must decide that they are. Otherwise, getting high, while a real enough experience, will be an unpleasant one he would rather avoid.

The effects of the drug, when first perceived, may be physically unpleasant or at least ambiguous:

It started taking effect, and I didn't know what was happening, you know, what it was, and I was very sick. I walked around the room, walking around the room trying to get off, you know; it just scared me at first, you know. I wasn't used to that kind of feeling.

In addition, the novice's naïve interpretation of what is happening to him may further confuse and frighten him, particularly if he decides, as many do, that he is going insane:

I felt I was insane, you know. Everything people done to me just wigged me. I couldn't hold a conversation, and my mind would be wandering, and I was always thinking, oh, I don't know, weird things, like hearing music different. . . . I get the feeling that I can't talk to anyone. I'll goof completely.

Given these typically frightening and unpleasant first experiences, the beginner will not continue use unless he learns to redefine the sensations as pleasurable:

It was offered to me, and I tried it. I'll tell you one thing. I never did enjoy it at all. I mean it was just nothing that I could enjoy. [Well, did you get high when you turned on?] Oh, yeah, I got definite feelings from it. But I didn't enjoy them. I mean I got plenty of reactions, but they were mostly reactions of fear. [You were frightened?] Yes. I didn't enjoy it. I couldn't seem to relax with it, you know. If you can't relax with a thing, you can't enjoy it, I don't think.

In other cases the first experiences were also definitely unpleasant, but the person did become a marihuana user. This occurred, however, only after a later experience enabled him to redefine the sensations as pleasurable:

[This man's first experience was extremely unpleasant, involving distortion of spatial relationships and sounds, violent thirst, and panic produced by these symptoms.] After the first time I didn't turn on for about, I'd say, ten months to a year. . . . It wasn't a moral thing; it was because I'd gotten so frightened, bein' so high. An' I didn't want to go through that again, I mean, my reaction was, "Well, if this is what they call bein' high, I don't dig [like] it." . . . So I didn't turn on for a year almost, accounta that. . . .

Well, my friends started, an' consequently I started again. But I didn't have any more, I didn't have that same initial reaction, after I started turning on again.

[In interaction with his friends he became able to find pleasure in the effects of the drug and eventually became a regular user.]

In no case will use continue without a redefinition of the effects as enjoyable.

This redefinition occurs, typically, in interaction with more experienced users who, in a number of ways, teach the novice to find pleasure in this experience which is at first so frightening.[10] They may reassure him as to the temporary character of the unpleasant sensations and minimize their seriousness, at the same time calling attention to the more enjoyable aspects. An experienced user describes how he handles newcomers to marihuana use:

Well, they get pretty high sometimes. The average person isn't ready for that, and it is a little frightening to them sometimes. I mean, they've been high on lush [alcohol], and they get higher that way than they've ever been before, and they don't know what's happening to them. Because they think they're going to keep going up, up, up till they lose their minds or begin doing weird things or something. You have to like reassure them, explain to them that they're not really flipping or anything, that they're gonna be all right. You have to just talk them out of being afraid. Keep talking to them, reassuring, telling them it's all right. And come on with your own story, you know: "The same thing happened to me. You'll get to like that after awhile." Keep coming on like that; pretty soon you talk them out of being scared. And besides they see you doing it and nothing horrible is happening to you, so that gives them more confidence.

The more experienced user may also teach the novice to regulate the amount he smokes more carefully, so as to avoid any severely uncomfortable symptoms while retaining the pleasant ones.

Finally, he teaches the new user that he can "get to like it after awhile." He teaches him to regard those ambiguous experiences formerly defined as unpleasant as enjoyable. The older user in the following incident is a person whose tastes have shifted in this way, and his remarks have the effect of helping others to make a similar redefinition:

A new user had her first experience of the effects of marihuana and became frightened and hysterical. She "felt like she was half in and half out of the room" and experienced a number of alarming physical symptoms. One of the more experienced users present said, "She's dragged because she's high like that. I'd give anything to get that high myself. I haven't been that high in years."

In short, what was once frightening and distasteful becomes, after a taste for it is built up, pleasant, desired, and sought after. Enjoyment is introduced by the favorable definition of the experience that one acquires from others. Without this, use will not continue, for marihuana will not be for the user an object he can use for pleasure.

In addition to being a necessary step in becoming a user, this represents an important condition for continued use. It is quite common for experienced users suddenly to have an unpleasant or frightening experience, which they cannot define as pleasurable, either because they have used a larger amount of marihuana than usual or because the marihuana they have used turns out to be of a higher quality than they expected. The user has sensations which go beyond any conception he has of what being high is and is in much the same situation as the novice, uncomfortable and frightened. He may blame it on an overdose and simply be more careful in the future. But he may make this the occasion for a rethinking of his attitude toward the drug and decide that it no longer can give him pleasure. When this occurs and is not followed by a redefinition of the drug as capable of producing pleasure, use will cease.

The likelihood of such a redefinition occurring depends on the degree of the individual's participation with other users. Where this participation is intensive, the individual is quickly talked out of his feeling against marihuana use. In the next case, on the other hand, the experi-ence was very disturbing, and the aftermath of the incident cut the person's participation with other users to almost zero. Use stopped for three years and began again only when a combination of circumstances, important among which was a resumption of ties with users, made possible a redefinition of the nature of the drug:

It was too much, like I only made about four pokes, and I couldn't even get it out of my mouth, I was so high, and I got real flipped. In the basement, you know, I just couldn't stay in there anymore. My heart was pounding real hard, you know, and I was going out of my mind; I thought I was losing my mind completely. So I cut out of this basement, and this other guy, he's out of his mind, told me, "Don't, don't leave me, man. Stay here." And I couldn't.

I walked outside, and it was five below zero, and I thought I was dying, and I had my coat open; I was sweating, I was perspiring. My whole insides were all . . . , and I walked about two blocks away, and I fainted behind a bush. I don't know how long I laid there. I woke up, and I was feeling the worst, I can't describe it at all, so I made it to a bowling alley, man, and I was trying to act normal, I was trying to shoot pool, you know, trying to act real normal, and I couldn't lay and I couldn't stand up and I couldn't sit down, and I went up and laid down where some guys that spot pins lay down, and that didn't help me, and I went down to a doctor's office. I was going to go in there and tell the doctor to put me out of my misery . . . because my heart was pounding so hard, you know. . . . So then all weekend I started flipping, seeing things there and going through hell, you know, all kinds of abnormal things. . . . I just quit for a long time then.

[He went to a doctor who defined the symptoms for him as those of a nervous breakdown caused by "nerves" and "worries." Although he was no longer using marihuana, he had some recurrences of the symptoms which led him to suspect that "it was all his nerves."] So I just stopped worrying, you know; so it was about thirty-six months later I started making it again. I'd just take a few pokes, you know. [He first resumed use in the company of the same user-friend with whom he had been involved in the original incident.]

A person, then, cannot begin to use marihuana for pleasure, or continue its use for pleasure, unless he learns to define its effects as enjoyable, unless it becomes and remains an object he conceives of as capable of producing pleasure.

In summary, an individual will be able to use marihuana for pleasure only when he goes through a process of learning to conceive of it as an object which can be used in this way. No one becomes a user without (1) learning to smoke the drug in a way which will produce real effects; (2) learning to recognize the effects and connect them with drug use (learning, in other words, to get high); and (3) learning to enjoy the sensations he perceives. In the course of this process he develops a disposition or motivation to use marihuana which was not and could not have been present when he began use, for it involves and depends on conceptions of the drug which could only grow out of the kind of actual experience detailed above. On completion of this process he is willing and able to use marihuana for pleasure.

He has learned, in short, to answer "Yes" to the question: "Is it fun?" The direction his further use of the drug takes depends on his being able to continue to answer "Yes" to this question and, in addition, on his being able to answer "Yes" to other questions which arise as he becomes aware of the implications of the fact that society disapproves of the practice: "Is it expedient?" "Is it moral?" Once he has acquired the ability to get enjoyment by using the drug, use will continue to be possible for him. Considerations of morality and expediency, occasioned by the reactions of society, may interfere and inhibit use, but use continues to be a possibility in terms of his conception of the drug. The act becomes impossible only when the ability to enjoy the experience of being high is lost, through a change in the user's conception of the drug occasioned by certain kinds of experience with it.

NOTES

1. See, as examples of this approach, the following: Eli Marcovitz and Henry J. Meyers, "The Marihuana Addict in the Army," *War Medicine,* VI (December, 1944), 382–391; Herbert S. Gaskill, "Marihuana, an Intoxicant," *American Journal of Psychiatry,* CII (September, 1945), 202–204; Sol Charen and Luis Perelman, "Personality Studies of Marihuana Addicts," *American Journal of Psychiatry,* CII (March, 1946), 674–682.

2. This theoretical point of view stems from George Herbert Mead's discussion of objects in *Mind, Self, and Society* (Chicago: University of Chicago Press, 1934), pp. 277–280.

3. Cf. Rogers Adams, "Marihuana," *Bulletin of the New York Academy of Medicine,* XVIII (November, 1942), 705–730.

4. The New York City Mayor's Committee on Marihuana, *The Marihuana Problem in the City of New York* (Lancaster, Pennsylvania: Jacques Cattell Press, 1944), pp. 12–13.

5. Cf. Lawrence Kolb, "Marihuana," *Federal Probation,* II (July, 1938), 22–25; and Walter Bromberg, "Marihuana: A Psychiatric Study," *Journal of the American Medical Association,* CXIII (July 1, 1939), 11.

6. The method is described in Alfred R. Lindesmith, *Opiate Addiction* (Bloomington, Indiana: Principia Press, 1947), chap. 1. There has been considerable discussion of this method in the literature. See, particularly, Ralph H. Turner, "The Quest for Universals in Sociological Research," *American Sociological Review,* 18 (December, 1953), 604–611, and the literature cited there.

7. I wish to thank Solomon Kobrin and Harold Finestone for making these interviews available to me.

8. A pharmacologist notes that this ritual is in fact an extremely efficient way of getting the drug into the blood stream. See R. P. Walton, *Marihuana: America's New Drug Problem* (Philadelphia: J. B. Lippincott, 1938), p. 48.

9. "Smokers have repeatedly stated that the consumption of whiskey while smoking negates the potency of the drug. They find it very difficult to get 'high' while drinking whiskey and because of that smokers will not drink while using the 'weed.'" (New York City Mayor's Committee on Marihuana, *The Marihuana Problem in the City of New York, op. cit.,* p. 13.)

10. Charen and Perelman, *op. cit.,* p. 679.

DIFFERENTIAL ASSOCIATION*

Edwin H. Sutherland

The scientific explanation of a phenomenon may be stated either in terms of the factors which are operating at the moment of the occurrence of a phenomenon or in terms of the processes operating in the earlier history of that phenomenon. In the first case the explanation is mechanistic, in the second historical or genetic; both are desirable. The physical and biological scientists favor the first of these methods and it would probably be superior as an explanation of criminal behavior. Efforts at explanations of the mechanistic type have been notably unsuccessful, perhaps largely because they have been concentrated on the attempt to isolate personal and social pathologies. Work from this point of view has, at least, resulted in the conclusion that the immediate factors in criminal behavior lie in the person-situation complex. Person and situation are not factors exclusive of each other, for the situation which is important is the situation as defined by the person who is involved. The tendencies and inhibitions at the moment of the criminal behavior are, to be sure, largely a product of the earlier history of the person, but the expression of these tendencies and inhibitions is a reaction to the immediate situation as defined by the person. The situation operates in many ways, of which perhaps the least important is the provision of an opportunity for a criminal act. A thief may steal from a fruit stand when the owner is not in sight but refrain when the owner is in sight; a bank burglar may attack a bank which is poorly protected but refrain from attacking a bank protected by watchmen and burglar alarms. A corporation which manufactures automobiles seldom or never violates the Pure Food and Drug Law but a meat-packing corporation violates this law with great frequency.

The second type of explanation of criminal behavior is made in terms of the life experience of a person. This is an historical or genetic explanation of criminal behavior. This, to be sure, assumes a situation to be defined by the person in terms of the inclinations and abilities which the person has acquired up to that date. The following paragraphs state such a genetic theory of criminal behavior on the assumption that a criminal act occurs when a situation appropriate for it, as defined by a person, is present.

GENETIC EXPLANATION OF CRIMINAL BEHAVIOR

The following statement refers to the process by which a particular person comes to engage in criminal behavior.

1. *Criminal behavior is learned.* Negatively, this means that criminal behavior is not inherited, as such; also, the person who is not already trained in crime does not invent criminal behavior, just as a person does not make mechanical inventions unless he has had training in mechanics.

2. *Criminal behavior is learned in interaction with other persons in a process of communication.* This communication is verbal in many respects but includes also "the communication of gestures."

3. *The principal part of the learning of criminal behavior occurs within intimate personal groups.* Negatively, this means that the impersonal agencies of communication, such as picture shows and newspapers, play a relatively unimportant part in the genesis of criminal behavior.

4. *When criminal behavior is learned, the learning includes (a) techniques of committing the crime, which are sometimes very complicated, sometimes very simple; (b) the specific direction of motives, drives, rationalizations, and attitudes.*

5. *The specific direction of motives and drives is learned from definitions of the legal codes as favorable or unfavorable.* In some societies an individual is surrounded by persons who invariably define the legal codes as rules to be observed, while in others he is surrounded by persons whose definitions are favorable to the violation of the legal

*Selections from *Principles of Criminology* by Edwin H. Sutherland. (Philadelphia: J. B. Lippincott Co.), 1947, pp. 5–9.

codes. In our American society these definitions are almost always mixed and consequently we have culture conflict in relation to the legal codes.

6. *A person becomes delinquent because of an excess of definitions favorable to violation of law over definitions unfavorable to violation of law.* This is the principle of differential association. It refers to both criminal and anti-criminal associations and has to do with counteracting forces. When persons become criminal, they do so because of contacts with criminal patterns and also because of isolation from anti-criminal patterns. Any person inevitably assimilates the surrounding culture unless other patterns are in conflict; a Southerner does not pronounce "r" because other Southerners do not pronounce "r." Negatively, this proposition of differential association means that associations which are neutral so far as crime is concerned have little or no effect on the genesis of criminal behavior. Much of the experience of a person is neutral in this sense, e.g., learning to brush one's teeth. This behavior has no negative or positive effect on criminal behavior except as it may be related to associations which are concerned with the legal codes. This neutral behavior is important especially as an occupier of the time of a child so that he is not in contact with criminal behavior during the time he is so engaged in the neutral behavior.

7. *Differential associations may vary in frequency, duration, priority, and intensity.* This means that associations with criminal behavior and also associations with anti-criminal behavior vary in those respects. "Frequency" and "duration" as modalities of associations are obvious and need no explanation. "Priority" is assumed to be important in the sense that lawful behavior developed in early childhood may persist throughout life, and also that delinquent behavior developed in early childhood may persist throughout life. This tendency, however, has not been adequately demonstrated, and priority seems to be important principally through its selective influence. "Intensity" is not precisely defined but it has to do with such things as the prestige of the source of a criminal or anti-criminal pattern and with emotional reactions related to the associations. In a precise description of the criminal behavior of a person these modalities would be stated in quantitative form and a mathematical ratio be reached. A formula in this sense has not been developed and the development of such a formula would be extremely difficult.

8. *The process of learning criminal behavior by association with criminal and anti-criminal patterns involves all of the mechanisms that are involved in any other learning.* Negatively, this means that the learning of criminal behavior is not restricted to the process of imitation. A person who is seduced, for instance, learns criminal behavior by association but this process would not ordinarily be described as imitation.

9. *While criminal behavior is an expression of general needs and values, it is not explained by those general needs and values since non-criminal behavior is an expression of the same needs and values.* Thieves generally steal in order to secure money, but likewise honest laborers work in order to secure money. The attempts by many scholars to explain criminal behavior by general drives and values, such as the happiness principle, striving for social status, the money motive, or frustration, have been and must continue to be futile since they explain lawful behavior as completely as they explain criminal behavior. They are similar to respiration, which is necessary for any behavior but which does not differentiate criminal from non-criminal behavior.

It is not necessary, at this level of explanation, to explain why a person has the associations which he has; this certainly involves a complex of many things. In an area where the delinquency rate is high a boy who is sociable, gregarious, active, and athletic is very likely to come in contact with the other boys in the neighborhood, learn delinquent behavior from them, and become a gangster; in the same neighborhood the psychopathic boy who is isolated, introvert, and inert may remain at home, not become acquainted with the other boys in the neighborhood, and not become delinquent. In another situation, the sociable, athletic, aggressive boy may become a member of a scout troop and not become involved in delinquent behavior. The person's associations are determined in a general context of social organization. A child is ordinarily reared in a family; the place of residence of the family is determined largely by family income; and the delinquency rate is in many respects related to the rental value of the houses. Many other factors enter into this social organization, including many of the small personal group relationships.

The preceding explanation of criminal behavior was stated from the point of view of the person who engages in criminal behavior. It is possible, also, to state theories of criminal behavior from the point of view of the community, nation, or other group. The problem, when thus stated, is generally concerned with crime rates and involves a comparison of the crime rates of various groups or the crime rates of a particular group at different times. One of the best explanations of crime rates from this point of view is that a high crime rate is due to social disorganization. The term "social disorganization" is not entirely satisfactory and it seems preferable to substitute for it the term "differential social organization." The postulate on which this theory is based, regardless of the name, is that

crime is rooted in the social organization and is an expression of that social organization. A group may be organized for criminal behavior or organized against criminal behavior. Most communities are organized both for criminal and anti-criminal behavior and in that sense the crime rate is an expression of the differential group organization. Differential group organization as an explanation of a crime rate must be consistent with the explanation of the criminal behavior of the person, since the crime rate is a summary statement of the number of persons in the group who commit crimes and the frequency with which they commit crimes.

DIFFERENTIAL IDENTIFICATION*

Daniel Glaser

We described identification somewhat unconventionally as "the choice of another, from whose perspective we view our own behavior." What we have called "differential identification" reconceptualizes Sutherland's theory in role-taking imagery, drawing heavily on Mead as well as on later refinements of role theory."[1] Most persons in our society are believed to identify themselves with both criminal and non-criminal persons in the course of their lives. Criminal identification may occur, for example, during direct experience in delinquent membership groups, through positive reference to criminal roles portrayed in mass media, or as a negative reaction to forces opposed to crime. The family probably is the principal non-criminal reference group, even for criminals. It is supplemented by many other groups of anti-criminal "generalized others."

The theory of differential identification, in essence, is that *a person pursues criminal behav-*

ior to the extent that he identifies himself with real or imaginary persons from whose perspective his criminal behavior seems acceptable. Such a theory focuses attention on the interaction in which choice of models occurs, including the individual's interaction with himself in rationalizing his conduct. This focus makes differential identification theory integrative, in that it provides a criterion of the relevance, for each individual case of criminality, of economic conditions, prior frustrations, learned moral creeds, group participation, or other features of an individual's life. These features are relevant to the extent that they can be shown to affect the choice of the other from whose perspective the individual views his own behavior. The explanation of criminal behavior on the basis of its imperfect correlation with any single variable of life-situations, if presented without specifying the intervening identification, evokes only a disconnected image of the relationship between the life-situation and the criminal behavior.

Sutherland supported the differential association theory by evidence that a major portion of criminality is learned through participation in criminal groups. Differential identification is a

*"Criminality Theories and Behavioral Images" by Daniel Glaser. *The American Journal of Sociology,* 61 (March, 1956), pp. 440–441. Reprinted by permission of the author and the University of Chicago Press.

less disconnected explanation for such learning, and it also does not seem vulnerable to most of the objections to differential association. Because opposing and divisive roles frequently develop within groups, because our identification may be with remote reference groups or with imaginary or highly generalized others, and because identifications may shift rapidly with dialectical processes of role change and rationalization during social interaction, differential association, as ordinarily conceived, is insufficient to account for all differential identification.

In practice, the use of differential identification to explain lone crimes where the source of learning is not readily apparent (such as extremes of brutality or other abnormality in sex crimes) gives rise to speculation as to the "others" involved in the identification. The use of this theory to explain a gang member's participation in a professional crime against property presents fewer difficulties. In so far as the former types of offense are explained by psychiatrists without invoking instincts or other mystical forces, they usually are interpreted, on a necessarily speculative basis, in terms of the self-conception which the offender develops in supporting his behavior and the sources of that self-conception. Such differential identification, in the case of most unusual and compulsive crimes, offers a less disconnected explanation than explanations derived from the alternative theories.[2]

The one objection to the theory of differential association which cannot be met by differential identification is that it does not account for "accidental" crimes. Differential identification treats crime as a form of voluntary (i.e., anticipatory) behavior, rather than as an accident. Indeed, both legal and popular conceptions of "crime" exclude acts which are purely accidental, except for some legislation on felonious negligence, to which our discussion of criminality must be considered inapplicable. Even for the latter offenses, however, it is noteworthy that the consequences of accidentally committing a crime may be such as to foster identification with criminal-role models (whether one is apprehended for the accidental crime or not).

During any period, *prior identifications* and *present circumstances* dictate the selection of the persons with whom we identify ourselves. Prior identifications which have been pleasing tend to persist, but at any time the immediate circumstances affect the relative ease (or salience) of alternative identifications. That is why membership groups so frequently are the reference groups, although they need not be. That, too, is why those inclined to crime usually refrain from it in situations where they play satisfying conventional roles in which crime would threaten their acceptance. From the latter situations their identification with non-criminal others may eventually make them anticriminal. This is the essence of rehabilitation.[3]

There is evidence that, with the spread of urban secularism, social situations are becoming more and more deliberately rather than traditionally organized. Concurrently, roles are increasingly adjusted on the basis of the apparent authority or social pressure in each situation.[4] Our culture is said to give a common level of aspiration but different capacities of attainment according to socioeconomic class. At the same time, it is suggested, economic sources of status are becoming stronger while non-economic sources are becoming weaker. Therefore, when conventional occupational avenues of upward mobility are denied, people are more and more willing to seek the economic gains anticipated in crime, even at the risk of losing such non-economic sources of status as acceptance by non-criminal groups.[5] All these alleged features of urbanism suggest a considerable applicability of differential identification to "situational" and "incidental" crimes; focus on differential identification with alternative reference groups may reveal "situational imperatives" in individual life-histories.

Differential identification may be considered tautological, in that it may seem merely to make "crime" synonymous with "criminal identification." It is more than a tautology, however, if it directs one to observations beyond those necessary merely for the classification of behavior as criminal or non-criminal. It is a fruitful empirical theory leading one to proceed from the legalistic classification to the analysis of behavior as identification and role-playing.[6]

NOTES

1. Cf. D. Glaser, "A Reconsideration of Some Parole Prediction Factors," *American Sociological*

Review, XIX (June, 1954), 335–41; G. H. Mead, *Mind, Self, and Society* (Chicago: University of Chicago Press, 1934); N. N. Foote, "Identification as the Basis for a Theory of Motivation," *American Sociological Review,* XVI (February, 1951), 14–22; C. W. Mills, "Situated Actions and Vocabularies of Motive," *American Sociological Review,* V (December, 1940), 904–913; T. Shibutani, "Reference Groups as Perspectives," *American Journal of Sociology,* LX (May, 1955), 562–69.

2. For an outstanding illustration of what becomes differential identification rather than the usual conception of differential association, applied to compulsive crimes, see Donald R. Cressey, "Differential Association and Compulsive Crimes," *Journal of Criminal Law, Criminology, and Police Science,* XLV (May–June, 1954), 29–40.

3. Cf. Donald R. Cressey, "Contradictory Theories in Correctional Group Therapy Programs," *Federal Probation,* XVIII (June, 1954), 20–26.

4. This evidence has come most dramatically from recent studies of race relations. Cf. Joseph D. Lohman and Dietrich C. Reitzes, "Note on Race Relations in Mass Society," *American Journal of Sociology,* LVIII (November, 1952), 240–46; Dietrich C. Reitzes, "The Role of Organizational Structures," *Journal of Social Issues,* IX, No. 1 (1953), 37–44; William C. Bradbury, "Evaluation of Research in Race Relations," *Inventory of Research in Racial and Cultural Relations,* V (winter-spring, 1953), 99–133.

5. Cf. Merton, *Social Theory and Social Structure* (Glencoe, Ill.: Free Press, 1949), chap. iv. It may be noteworthy here that classification of Illinois parolees by status ratings of the jobs to which they were going was more predictive than classification by the status of their father's occupation or by whether their job was of higher, lower, or equal status than their father's occupation. Regardless of their class background, the parolee's infractions seemed primarily to be a function of their failure to approach middle-class status (cf. Daniel Glaser, "A Reformulation and Testing of Parole Prediction Factors" [unpublished Ph.D. dissertation, University of Chicago, 1954], pp. 253–59).

6. A number of examples of useful tautologies in social science are presented in Arnold Rose, *Theory and Method in the Social Sciences* (Minneapolis: University of Minnesota Press, 1954), pp. 328–38. Insofar as a proposition is of heuristic use, however, one may question whether it is appropriately designated a "tautology."

Feminism

During the last decade, feminist scholarship has expanded throughout many disciplines, including the areas of criminology and deviance theory. Feminism generally refers to the idea that women experience subordination on the basis of their sex. Feminist scholars are interested in understanding the origins and ramifications of this inequality. While there are different strains of feminist theory found in the literature, researchers usually relate their work to male-dominated institutions in order to discover patterns of sexual bias. As far as deviance theory is concerned, women have been largely ignored, both in past theorizing and research. When they were included, their importance and roles were essentially trivialized. This situation is changing as scholars turn their attention to issues of female deviance and crime, victimization, and the treatment of women by formal institutions of social control.

In "Girls' Crime and Woman's Place," Meda Chesney-Lind, a leading feminist scholar in the field of deviance and crime, argues that existing theories of deviance and delinquency are inadequate for explaining female delinquency and official reactions to girls' deviance. By reviewing the available evidence on female offending, she cites the need for a feminist model of female delinquency. The juvenile justice system is found

to be a major force in women's oppression, as it has historically served to reinforce obedience to the demands of patriarchal authority. Chesney-Lind calls for increased research into female delinquency and the reactions of social control institutions to such behavior in order to develop theories that are sensitive to the context of patriarchy.

Ryan Bishop and Lillian S. Robinson discuss the nature of international commercial sex in Thailand in their piece, "In the Night Market." Taken from a book on the topic, the authors conducted extensive fieldwork to examine the structural and personal dimensions of the profitable and popular sex tourist industry. They characterize the experiences of customers and workers in terms of "international sexual alienation" which is part of a larger system of "totalizing alienation" under which both industrialized sexuality and industrialized leisure exist. They conclude that understanding sexual alienation as a system helps explain the purchase of sex as a commodity, including both the appeal and popularity of such activity.

In the article, "On the Backs of Working Prostitutes," Annette Jolin uses feminist theory to examine major issues related to prostitution policy. Her analysis explores why prostitution remains as controversial as it was 4000 years ago, why feminists are involved in the controversy, and what effects this controversy has on working prostitutes. Looking at the historical record, Jolin argues that answers can be found in the institutionalized sexual double standard of Western patriarchal societies and economic arrangements involving promiscuity, chastity, and inequality. She concludes that prostitution theories do not adequately address the actual problems experienced by prostitutes and calls for a new feminist synthesis that addresses both rights to choose and rights to protections.

"Appearance and Delinquency" by Jill Leslie Rosenbaum and Meda Chesney-Lind, is another example of the new feminist scholarship in the field of deviance. Focusing on official reactions to female deviants, this novel study finds that culturally derived standards of attractiveness are used in determining the treatment women receive in the criminal justice system. Using data from the California Youth Authority, Rosenbaum and Chesney-Lind find that a variety of physical descriptions regarding appearance and attractive-

ness was mentioned in official files. This was more likely to be the case for those charged with immorality. The study provides an interesting glimpse of the world view of those who process female offenders and presents evidence that officials may look upon attractive girls who engage in sexual "immorality" more harshly.

In the article "Identity, Strategy, and Feminist Politics," Patricia Gagne examines the impact of feminist activism on the decision to grant clemency to women incarcerated for killing or assaulting abusive intimate partners or stepfathers. Identifying the tactics and strategies employed by the feminist battered women's movement, she finds that incarcerated battered women used their careers and personal relationships to form consciousness-raising groups in prison that established a social movement community that gained access to authorities and the public. Gagne discusses how feminists created an opportunity structure resulting in clemency and what strategies and tactics other social movements need to consider in hostile cultural and political environments.

GIRLS' CRIME AND WOMAN'S PLACE
TOWARD A FEMINIST MODEL OF FEMALE DELINQUENCY*

Meda Chesney-Lind

I ran away so many times. I tried anything, man, and they wouldn't believe me. . . . As far as they are concerned they think I'm the problem. You know, runaway, bad label. (Statement of a 16-year-old girl who, after having been physically and sexually assaulted, started running away from home and was arrested as a "runaway" in Hawaii.)

You know, one of these days I'm going to have to kill myself before you guys are gonna listen to me. I can't stay at home. (Statement of a 16-year-old Tucson run-

away with a long history of physical abuse [Davidson, 1982, p. 26].)

Who is the typical female delinquent? What causes her to get into trouble? What happens to her if she is caught? These are questions that few members of the general public could answer quickly. By contrast, almost every citizen can talk about "delinquency," by which they generally mean male delinquency, and can even generate some fairly specific complaints about, for example, the failure of the juvenile justice system to deal with such problems as "the alarming increase in the rate of serious juvenile crime" and

*From Meda Chesney-Lind, *Crime and Delinquency,* vol. 35, No. 1, pp. 5–29, copyright © 1989 by Sage Publications, Inc. Reprinted by permission of Sage Publications, Inc.

the fact that the juvenile courts are too lenient on juveniles found guilty of these offenses (Opinion Research Corporation, 1982).

This situation should come as no surprise since even the academic study of delinquent behavior has, for all intents and purposes, been the study of male delinquency. "The delinquent is a rogue male" declared Albert Cohen (1955, p. 140) in his influential book on gang delinquency. More than a decade later, Travis Hirschi, in his equally important book entitled *The Causes of Delinquency,* relegated women to a footnote that suggested, somewhat apologetically, that "in the analysis that follows, the 'non-Negro' becomes 'white,' and the girls disappear."

This pattern of neglect is not all that unusual. All areas of social inquiry have been notoriously gender blind. What is perhaps less well understood is that theories developed to describe the misbehavior of working- or lower-class male youth fail to capture the full nature of delinquency in America; and, more to the point, are woefully inadequate when it comes to explaining female misbehavior and official reactions to girls' deviance.

To be specific, delinquent behavior involves a range of activities far broader than those committed by the stereotypical street gang. Moreover, many more young people than the small visible group of "troublemakers" that exist on every intermediate and high school campus commit some sort of juvenile offense and many of these youth have brushes with the law. One study revealed, for example, that 33% of all the boys and 14% of the girls born in 1958 had at least one contact with the police before reaching their eighteenth birthday (Tracy Wolfgang, and Figlio, 1985, p. 5). Studies that solicit from youth themselves the volume of their delinquent behavior consistently confirm that large numbers of adolescents engage in at least some form of misbehavior that could result in their arrest. As a consequence, it is largely trivial misconduct, rather than the commission of serious crime, that shapes the actual nature of juvenile delinquency. One national study of youth aged 15–21, for example, noted that only 5% reported involvement in a serious assault, and only 6% reported having participated

in a gang fight. In contrast, 81% admitted to having used alcohol, 44% admitted to having used marijuana, 37% admitted to having been publicly drunk, 42% admitted to having skipped classes (truancy), 44% admitted having had sexual intercourse, and 15% admitted to having stolen from the family (McGarrell and Flanagan, 1985, p. 363). Clearly, not all of these activities are as serious as the others. It is important to remember that young people can be arrested for all of these behaviors.

Indeed, one of the most important points to understand about the nature of delinquency, and particularly female delinquency, is that youth can be taken into custody for both criminal acts and a wide variety of what are often called "status offenses." These offenses, in contrast to criminal violations, permit the arrest of youth for a wide range of behaviors that are violations of parental authority: "running away from home," "being a person in need of supervision," "minor in need of supervision," being "incorrigible," "beyond control," truant, in need of "care and protection," and so on. Juvenile delinquents, then, are youths arrested for either criminal or noncriminal status offenses; and, as this discussion will establish, the role played by uniquely juvenile offenses is by no means insignificant, particularly when considering the character of female delinquency.

Examining the types of offenses for which youth are actually arrested, it is clear that again most are arrested for the less serious criminal acts and status offenses. Of the one and a half million youth arrested in 1983, for example, only 4.5% of these arrests were for such serious violent offenses as murder, rape, robbery, or aggravated assault (McGarrell and Flanagan, 1985, p. 479). In contrast, 21% were arrested for a single offense (larceny theft) much of which, particularly for girls, is shoplifting (Shelden and Horvath, 1986).

Table 1 presents the five most frequent offenses for which male and female youth are arrested and from this it can be seen that while trivial offenses dominate both male and female delinquency, trivial offenses, particularly status offenses, are more significant in the case of girls' arrests; for example, the five offenses listed in Table 1 account for nearly three-quarters of

TABLE 1 Rank Order of Adolescent Male and Female Arrests for Specific Offenses, 1977 and 1986

	Male					Female				
	1977	% of Total Arrests	1986	% of Total Arrests		1977	% of Total Arrests	1986	% of Total Arrests	
	(1) Larceny-Theft	18.4	(1) Larceny-Theft	20.4		(1) Larceny-Theft	27.0	(1) Larceny-Theft	25.7	
	(2) Other Offenses	14.5	(2) Other Offenses	16.5		(2) Runaway	22.9	(2) Runaway	20.5	
	(3) Burglary	13.0	(3) Burglary	9.1		(3) Other Offenses	14.2	(3) Other Offenses	14.8	
	(4) Drug Abuse Violations	6.5	(4) Drug Abuse Violations	7.0		(4) Liquor Laws	5.5	(4) Liquor Laws	8.4	
	(5) Vandalism	6.4	(5) Vandalism	6.3		(5) Curfew & Loitering Violations	4.0	(5) Curfew & Loitering Violations	4.7	

	1977	1986	% N Change		1977	1986	% N Change
Arrests for Serious Violent Offenses[a]	4.2%	4.7%	+2.3	Arrest for Serious Violent Offenses	1.8%	2.0%	+1.7
Arrests of All Violent Offenses[b]	7.6%	9.6%	+10.3	Arrests of All Violent Offenses	5.1%	7.1%	+26.0
Arrests for Status Offenses[c]	8.8%	8.3%	−17.8	Arrests for Status Offenses	26.9%	25.2%	14.7

SOURCE: Compiled from Federal Bureau of Investigation (1987, p. 169).
a. Arrest for murder and nonnegligent manslaughter, robbery, forcible rape, and aggravated assault.
b. Also includes arrests for other assaults.
c. Arrest for curfew and loitering law violation and runaway.

female offenses and only slightly more than half of male offenses.

More to the point, it is clear that, though routinely neglected in most delinquency research, status offenses play a significant role in girls' official delinquency. Status offenses accounted for about 25.2% of all girls' arrests in 1986 (as compared to 26.9% in 1977) and only about 8.3% of boys' arrests (compared to 8.8% in 1977). These figures are somewhat surprising since dramatic declines in arrests of youth for these offenses might have been expected as a result of the passage of the Juvenile Justice and Delinquency Prevention Act in 1974, which, among other things, encouraged jurisdictions to divert and deinstitutionalize youth charged with noncriminal offenses. While the figures in Table 1 do show a decline in these arrests, virtually all of this decline occurred in the 1970s. Between 1982 and 1986 girls' curfew arrests increased by 5.1% and runaway arrests increased by a striking 24.5%. And the upward trend continues; arrests of girls for running away increased by 3% between 1985 and 1986 and arrests of girls for curfew violations increased by 12.4% (Federal Bureau of Investigation, 1987, p. 171).

Looking at girls who find their way into juvenile court populations, it is apparent that status offenses continue to play an important role in the character of girls' official delinquency. In total, 34% of the girls, but only 12% of the boys, were referred to court in 1983 for these offenses (Snyder and Finnegan, 1987, pp. 6–20). Stating these figures differently, they mean that while males constituted about 81% of all delinquency referrals, females constituted 46% of all status offenders in courts (Snyder and Finnegan, 1987, p. 20). Similar figures were reported for 1977 by Black and Smith (1981). Fifteen years earlier, about half of the girls and about 20% of the boys were referred to court for these offenses (Children's Bureau, 1965). These data do seem to signal a drop in female status offense referrals, though not as dramatic a decline as might have been expected.

For many years statistics showing large numbers of girls arrested and referred for status offenses were taken to be representative of the different types of male and female delinquency.

However, self-report studies of male and female delinquency do not reflect the dramatic differences in misbehavior found in official statistics. Specifically, it appears that girls charged with these noncriminal status offenses have been and continue to be significantly overrepresented in court populations.

Teilmann and Landry (1981) compared girls' contribution to arrests for runaway and incorrigibility with girls' self-reports of these two activities, and found a 10.4% overrepresentation of females among those arrested for runaway and a 30.9% overrepresentation in arrests for incorrigibility. From these data they concluded that girls are "arrested for status offenses at a higher rate than boys, when contrasted to their self-reported delinquency rates" (Teilmann and Landry, 1981, pp. 74–75). These findings were confirmed in another recent self-report study. Figueira-McDonough (1985, p. 277) analyzed the delinquent conduct of 2,000 youths and found "no evidence of greater involvement of females in status offenses." Similarly, Canter (1982) found in the National Youth Survey that there was no evidence of greater female involvement, compared to males, in any category of delinquent behavior. Indeed, in this sample, males were significantly more likely than females to report status offenses.

Utilizing Canter's national data on the extensiveness of girls self-reported delinquency and comparing these figures to official arrests of girls (see Table 2) reveals that girls are underrepresented in every arrest category with the exception of status offenses and larceny theft. These figures strongly suggest that official practices tend to exaggerate the role played by status offenses in girls' delinquency.

Delinquency theory, because it has virtually ignored female delinquency, failed to pursue anomalies such as these found in the few early studies examining gender differences in delinquent behavior. Indeed, most delinquency theories have ignored status offenses. As a consequence, there is considerable question as to whether existing theories that were admittedly developed to explain male delinquency can adequately explain female delinquency. Clearly, these theories were much influenced by the

TABLE 2 Comparison of Sex Differences in Self-Reported and Official Delinquency for Selected Offenses

	Self-Report[a] M/F Ratios (1976)	1976	Official Statistics[b] M/F Arrest Ratio 1986
Theft	3.5:1 (Felony Theft)		
	3.4:1 (Minor Theft)	2.5:1	2.7:1
Drug Violation	1:1	5.1:1	6.0:1
	(Hard Drug Use)		(Drug Abuse Violations)
Vandalism	5.1:1	12.3:1	10.0:1
Disorderly Conduct	2.8:1	4.5:1	4.4:1
Serious Assault	3.5:1	5.6:1	5.5:1
	(Felony Assault)		(Aggravated Assault)
Minor Assault	3.4:1	3.8:1	3.4:1
Status Offenses	1.6:1	1.3:1	1.1:1
			(Runaway, Curfew)

a. Extracted from Rachelle Canter (1982, p. 383).
b. Compiled from Federal Bureau of Investigation (1987, p. 173).

notion that class and protest masculinity were at the core of delinquency. Will the "add women and stir approach" be sufficient? Are these really theories of delinquent behavior as some (Simons, Miller, and Aigner, 1980) have argued?

This article will suggest that they are not. The extensive focus on male delinquency and the inattention to the role played by patriarchal arrangements in the generation of adolescent delinquency and conformity has rendered the major delinquency theories fundamentally inadequate to the task of explaining female behavior. There is, in short, an urgent need to rethink current models in light of girls' situation in patriarchal society.

To understand why such work must occur, it is first necessary to explore briefly the dimensions of the androcentric bias found in the dominant and influential delinquency theories. Then the need for a feminist model of female delinquency will be explored by reviewing the available evidence on girls' offending. This discussion will also establish that the proposed overhaul of delinquency theory is not, as some might think, solely an academic exercise. Specifically, it is incorrect to assume that because girls are charged with less serious offenses, they actually have few problems and are treated gently when they are drawn into the juvenile justice system. Indeed, the extensive focus on disadvan-

taged males in public settings has meant that girls' victimization and the relationship between that experience and girls' crime has been systematically ignored. Also missed has been the central role played by the juvenile justice system in the sexualization of girls' delinquency and the criminalization of girls' survival strategies. Finally, it will be suggested that the official actions of the juvenile justice system should be understood as major forces in girls' oppression as they have historically served to reinforce the obedience of all young women to demands of patriarchal authority no matter how abusive and arbitrary.

THE ROMANCE OF THE GANG OR THE *WEST SIDE STORY* SYNDROME

From the start, the field of delinquency research focused on visible lower-class male delinquency, often justifying the neglect of girls in the most cavalier of terms. Take, for example, the extremely important and influential work of Clifford R. Shaw and Henry D. McKay who, beginning in 1929, utilized an ecological approach to the study of juvenile delinquency. Their impressive work, particularly *Juvenile Delinquency in Urban Areas* (1942) and intensive biographical case studies such as Shaw's *Brothers in Crime* (1938) and *The Jack-Roller* (1930), set the stage for much of the subcultural research on gang

essentialism

delinquency. In their ecological work, however, Shaw and McKay analyzed only the official arrest data on male delinquents in Chicago and repeatedly referred to these rates as "delinquency rates" (though they occasionally made parenthetical reference to data on female delinquency) (see Shaw and McKay, 1942, p. 356). Similarly, their biographical work traced only male experiences with the law; in *Brothers in Crime,* for example, the delinquent and criminal careers of five brothers were followed for fifteen years. In none of these works was any justification given for the equation of male delinquency with delinquency.

Early fieldwork on delinquent gangs in Chicago set the stage for another style of delinquency research. Yet here too researchers were interested only in talking to and following the boys. Thrasher studied over a thousand juvenile gangs in Chicago during roughly the same period as Shaw and McKay's more quantitative work was being done. He spent approximately one page out of 600 on the five of six female gangs he encountered in his field observation of juvenile gangs. Thrasher (1927, p. 228) did mention, in passing, two factors he felt accounted for the lower number of girl gangs: "First, the social patterns for the behavior of girls, powerfully backed by the great weight of tradition and custom, are contrary to the gang and its activities; and secondly, girls, even in urban disorganized areas, are much more closely supervised and guarded than boys and usually well incorporated into the family groups or some other social structure."

Another major theoretical approach to delinquency focuses on the subculture of lower-class communities as a generating milieu for delinquent behavior. Here again, noted delinquency researchers concentrated either exclusively or nearly exclusively on male lower-class culture. For example, Cohen's work on the subculture of delinquent gangs, which was written nearly twenty years after Thrasher's, deliberately considers only boys' delinquency. His justification for the exclusion of the girls is quite illuminating:

My skin has nothing of the quality of down or silk, there is nothing limpid or flute-like about my voice, I am a total loss with needle and thread, my posture and carriage are wholly lacking in grace. These imperfections cause me no distress—if anything, they are grati-

fying—because I conceive myself to be a man and want people to recognize me as a full-fledged, unequivocal representative of my sex. My wife, on the other hand, is not greatly embarrassed by her inability to tinker with or talk about the internal organs of a car, by her modest attainments in arithmetic or by her inability to lift heavy objects. Indeed, I am reliably informed that many women—I do not suggest that my wife is among them—often affect ignorance, frailty and emotional instability because to do otherwise would be out of keeping with a reputation for indubitable femininity. In short, people do not simply want to excel; they want to excel as a man or as a woman [Cohen, 1955, p. 138].

From this Cohen (1955, p. 140) concludes that the delinquent response "however it may be condemned by others on moral grounds, has at least one virtue: it incontestably confirms, in the eyes of all concerned, his essential masculinity." Much the same line of argument appears in Miller's influential paper on the "focal concerns" of lower-class life with its emphasis on importance of trouble, toughness, excitement, and so on. These, the author concludes, predispose poor youth (particularly male youth) to criminal misconduct. However, Cohen's comments are notable in their candor and probably capture both the allure that male delinquency has had for at least some male theorists as well as the fact that sexism has rendered the female delinquent as irrelevant to their work.

Emphasis on blocked opportunities (sometimes the "strain" theories) emerged out of the work of Robert K. Merton (1938) who stressed the need to consider how some social structures exert a definite pressure upon certain persons in the society to engage in nonconformist rather than conformist conduct. His work influenced research largely through the efforts of Cloward and Ohlin who discussed access to "legitimate" and "illegitimate" opportunities for male youth. No mention of female delinquency can be found in their *Delinquency and Opportunity* except that women are blamed for male delinquency. Here, the familiar notion is that boys, "engulfed by a feminine world and uncertain of their own identification . . . tend to 'protest' against femininity" (Cloward and Ohlin, 1960, p. 49). Early efforts by Ruth Morris to test this hypothesis utilizing different definitions of success based on the gender of respondents met with mixed success. Attempting to assess boys' perceptions about access to economic power status while for girls the variable concerned itself with the ability or inability of girls to maintain effective relationships, Morris was unable to find a clear relationship between "female" goals and delinquency (Morris, 1964).

The work of Edwin Sutherland emphasized the fact that criminal behavior was learned in intimate personal groups. His work, particularly the notion of differential association, which also influenced Cloward and Ohlin's work, was similarly male oriented as much of his work was affected by case studies he conducted of male criminals. Indeed, in describing his notion of how differential association works, he utilized male examples (e.g., "In an area where the delinquency rate is high a boy who is sociable, gregarious, active, and athletic is very likely to come in contact with the other boys, in the neighborhood, learn delinquent behavior from them, and become a gangster" [Sutherland, 1978, p. 131]). Finally, the work of Travis Hirschi on the social bonds that control delinquency ("social control theory") was, as was stated earlier, derived out of research on male delinquents (though he, at least, studied delinquent behavior as reported by youth themselves rather than studying only those who were arrested).

Such a persistent focus on social class and such an absence of interest in gender in delinquency is ironic for two reasons. As even the work of Hirschi demonstrated, and as later studies would validate, a clear relationship between social class position and delinquency is problematic, while it is clear that gender has a dramatic and consistent effect on delinquency causation (Hagan, Gillis, and Simpson, 1985). The second irony, and one that consistently eludes even contemporary delinquency theorists, is the fact that while the academics had little interest in female delinquents, the same could not be said for the juvenile justice system. Indeed, work on the early history of the separate system for youth, reveals that concerns about girls' immoral conduct were really at the center of what some have called the "childsaving movement" (Platt, 1969) that set up the juvenile justice system.

"THE BEST PLACE TO CONQUER GIRLS"

The movement to establish separate institutions for youthful offenders was part of the larger Progressive movement, which among other things was keenly concerned about prostitution and other "social evils" (white slavery and the like) (Schlossman and Wallach, 1978; Rafter, 1985, p. 54). Childsaving was also a celebration of women's domesticity, though ironically women were influential in the movement (Platt, 1969; Rafter, 1985). In a sense, privileged women found, in the moral purity crusades and the establishment of family courts, a safe outlet for their energies. As the legitimate guardians of the moral sphere, women were seen as uniquely suited to patrol the normative boundaries of the social order. Embracing rather than challenging these stereotypes, women carved out for themselves a role in the policing of women and girls (Feinman, 1980; Freedman, 1981; Messerschmidt, 1987). Ultimately, many of the early childsavers' activities revolved around the monitoring of young girls', particularly immigrant girls', behavior to prevent their straying from the path.

This state of affairs was the direct consequence of a disturbing coalition between some feminists and the more conservative social purity movement. Concerned about female victimization and distrustful of male (and to some degree female) sexuality, notable women leaders, including Susan B. Anthony, found common cause with the social purists around such issues as opposing the regulation of prostitution and raising the age of consent (see Messerschmidt, 1987). The consequences of such a partnership are an important lesson for contemporary feminist movements that are, to some extent, faced with the same possible coalitions.

Girls were the clear losers in this reform effort. Studies of early family court activity reveal that virtually all the girls who appeared in these courts were charged for immorality or waywardness (Chesney-Lind, 1971; Schlossman and Wallach, 1978; Shelden, 1981). More to the point, the sanctions for such misbehavior were extremely severe. For example, in Chicago (where the first family court was founded), one-half of the girl delinquents, but only one-fifth of the boy delinquents, were sent to reformatories between 1899–1909. In Milwaukee, twice as many girls as boys were committed to training schools (Schlossman and Wallach, 1978, p. 72); and in Memphis females were twice as likely as males to be committed to training schools (Shelden, 1981, p. 70).

In Honolulu, during the period 1929–1930, over half of the girls referred to court were charged with "immorality," which meant evidence of sexual intercourse. In addition, another 30% were charged with "waywardness." Evidence of immorality was vigorously pursued by both arresting officers and social workers through lengthy questioning of the girl and, if possible, males with whom she was suspected of having sex. Other evidence of "exposure" was provided by gynecological examinations that were routinely ordered in virtually all girls' cases. Doctors, who understood the purpose of such examinations, would routinely note the condition of the hymen: "admits intercourse hymen rupture," "no laceration," "hymen ruptured" are typical of the notations on the forms. Girls during this period were also twice as likely as males to be detained where they spent five times as long on the average as their male counterparts. They were also nearly three times more likely to be sentenced to the training school (Chesney-Lind, 1971). Indeed, girls were half of those committed to training schools in Honolulu well into the 1950s (Chesney-Lind, 1973).

Not surprisingly, large numbers of girl's reformatories and training schools were established during this period as well as places of "rescue and reform." For example, Schlossman and Wallach note that 23 facilities for girls were opened during the 1910–1920 decade (in contrast to the 1850–1910 period where the average was 5 reformatories per decade [Schlossman and Wallach, 1985, p. 70]), and these institutions did much to set the tone of official response to female delinquency. Obsessed with precocious female sexuality, the institutions set about to isolate the females from all contact with males while housing them in bucolic settings. The intention was to hold the girls until marriageable age and to occupy them in domestic pursuits during their sometimes lengthy incarceration.

The links between these attitudes and those of juvenile courts some decades later are, of course, arguable; but an examination of the record of the court does not inspire confidence. A few examples of the persistence of what might be called a double standard of juvenile justice will suffice here.

A study conducted in the early 1970s in a Connecticut training school revealed large numbers of girls incarcerated "for their own protection." Explaining this pattern, one judge explained, "Why most of the girls I commit are for status offenses. I figure if a girl is about to get pregnant, we'll keep her until she's sixteen and then ADC (Aid to Dependent Children) will pick her up" (Rogers, 1972). For more evidence of official concern with adolescent sexual misconduct, consider Linda Hancock's (1981) content analysis of police referrals in Australia. She noted that 40% of the referrals of girls to court made specific mention of sexual and moral conduct compared to only 5% of the referrals of boys. These sorts of results suggest that all youthful female misbehavior has traditionally been subject to surveillance for evidence of sexual misconduct.

Gelsthorpe's (1986) field research on an English police station also revealed how everyday police decision making resulted in disregard of complaints about male problem behavior in contrast to active concern about the "problem behavior" of girls. Notable, here, was the concern about the girl's sexual behavior. In one case, she describes police persistence in pursuing a "moral danger" order for a 14-year-old picked up in a truancy run. Over the objections of both the girl's parents and the Social Services Department and in the face of a written confirmation from a surgeon that the girl was still premenstrual, the officers pursued the application because, in one officers words, "I know her sort . . . free and easy. I'm still suspicious that she might be pregnant. Anyway, if the doctor can't provide evidence we'll do her for being beyond the care and control of her parents, no one can dispute that. Running away is proof" (Gelsthorpe, 1986, p. 136). This sexualization of female deviance is highly significant and explains why criminal activities by girls (particularly in past years) were overlooked so long as they did not appear to signal defiance of parental control (see Smith, 1978).

In their historic obsession about precocious female sexuality, juvenile justice workers rarely reflected on the broader nature of female misbehavior or on the sources of this misbehavior. It was enough for them that girls' parents reported them out of control. Indeed, court personnel tended to "sexualize" virtually all female defiance that lent itself to that construction and ignore other misbehavior (Chesney-Lind, 1973, 1977; Smith, 1978). For their part, academic students of delinquency were so entranced with the notion of the delinquent as a romantic rogue male challenging a rigid and unequal class structure, that they spent little time on middle-class delinquency, trivial offenders, or status offenders. Yet it is clear that the vast bulk of delinquent behavior is of this type.

Some have argued that such an imbalance in theoretical work is appropriate as minor misconduct, while troublesome, is not a threat to the safety and well-being of the community. This argument might be persuasive if two additional points could be established. One, that some small number of youth "specialize" in serious criminal behavior while the rest commit only minor acts, and, two, that the juvenile court rapidly releases those youth that come into its purview for these minor offenses, thus reserving resources for the most serious youthful offenders.

The evidence is mixed on both of these points. Determined efforts to locate the "serious juvenile offender" have failed to locate a group of offenders who specialize only in serious violent offenses. For example, in a recent analysis of a national self-report data set, Elliott and his associates noted "there is little evidence for specialization in serious violent offending; to the contrary, serious violent offending appears to be embedded in a more general involvement in a wide range of serious and non-serious offenses" (Elliott, Huizinga, and Morse, 1987). Indeed, they went so far as to speculate that arrest histories that tend to highlight particular types of offenders reflect variations in police policy, practices, and processes of uncovering crime as well as underlying offending patterns.

More to the point, police and court personnel are, in turns out, far more interested in youth they charge with trivial or status offenses than anyone imagined. Efforts to deinstitutionalize "status offenders," for example, ran afoul of juvenile justice personnel who had little interest in releasing youth guilty of noncriminal offenses (Chesney-Lind, 1988). As has been established, much of this is a product of the system's history that encouraged court officers to involve themselves in the noncriminal behavior of youth in order to "save" them from a variety of social ills.

Indeed, parallels can be found between the earlier Progressive period and current national efforts to challenge the deinstitutionalization components of the Juvenile Justice and Delinquency Prevention Act of 1974. These come complete with their celebration of family values and concerns about youthful independence. One of the arguments against the act has been that it allegedly gave children the "freedom to run away" (Office of Juvenile Justice and Delinquency Prevention, 1985) and that it has hampered "reunions" of "missing" children with their parents (Office of Juvenile Justice, 1986). Suspicions about teen sexuality are reflected in excessive concern about the control of teen prostitution and child pornography.

Opponents have also attempted to justify continued intervention into the lives of status offenders by suggesting that without such intervention, the youth would "escalate" to criminal behavior. Yet there is little evidence that status offenders escalate to criminal offenses, and the evidence is particularly weak when considering female delinquents (particularly white female delinquents) (Datesman and Aickin, 1984). Finally, if escalation is occurring, it is likely the product of the justice system's insistence on enforcing status offense laws, thereby forcing youth in crisis to live lives of escaped criminals.

The most influential delinquency theories, however, have largely ducked the issue of status and trivial offenses and, as a consequence, neglected the role played by the agencies of official control (police, probation officers, juvenile court judges, detention home workers, and training school personnel) in the shaping of the "delinquency problem." When confronting the less than distinct picture that emerges from the actual distribution of delinquent behavior, however, the conclusion that agents of social control have considerable discretion in labeling or choosing not to label particular behavior as "delinquent" is inescapable. This symbiotic relationship between delinquent behavior and the official response to that behavior is particularly critical when the question of female delinquency is considered.

TOWARD A FEMINIST THEORY OF DELINQUENCY

To sketch out completely a feminist theory of delinquency is a task beyond the scope of this article. It may be sufficient, at this point, simply to identify a few of the most obvious problems with attempts to adapt male-oriented theory to explain female conformity and deviance. Most significant of these is the fact that all existing theories were developed with no concern about gender stratification.

Note that this is not simply an observation about the power of gender roles (though this power is undeniable). It is increasingly clear that gender stratification in patriarchal society is as powerful a system as is class. A feminist approach to delinquency means construction of explanations of female behavior that are sensitive to its patriarchal context. Feminist analysis of delinquency would also examine ways in which agencies of social control—the police, the courts, and the prisons—act in ways to reinforce woman's place in male society (Harris, 1977; Chesney-Lind, 1986). Efforts to construct a feminist model of delinquency must first and foremost be sensitive to the situations of girls. Failure to consider the existing empirical evidence on girls' lives and behavior can quickly lead to stereotypical thinking and theoretical dead ends.

An example of this sort of flawed theory building was the early fascination with the notion that the women's movement was causing an increase in women's crime; a notion that is now more or less discredited (Steffensmeier, 1980; Gora, 1982). A more recent example of the same sort of thinking can be found in recent work on the "power-control" model of delinquency

(Hagan, Simpson, and Gillis, 1987). Here, the authors speculate that girls commit less delinquency in part because their behavior is more closely controlled by the patriarchal family. The authors' promising beginning quickly gets bogged down in a very limited definition of patriarchal control (focusing on parental supervision and variations in power within the family). Ultimately, the authors' narrow formulation of patriarchal control results in their arguing that mother's work force participation (particularly in high status occupations) leads to increases in daughters' delinquency since these girls find themselves in more "egalitarian families."

This is essentially a not-too-subtle variation on the earlier "liberation" hypothesis. Now, mother's liberation causes daughter's crime. Aside from the methodological problems with the study (e.g., the authors argue that female-headed households are equivalent to upper-status "egalitarian" families where both parents work, and they measure delinquency using a six-item scale that contains no status offense items), there is a more fundamental problem with the hypothesis. There is no evidence to suggest that as women's labor force participation has increased, girls' delinquency has increased. Indeed, during the last decade when both women's labor force participation accelerated and the number of female-headed households soared, aggregate female delinquency measured both by self-report and official statistics either declined or remained stable (Ageton, 1983; Chilton and Datesman, 1987; Federal Bureau of Investigation, 1987).

By contrast, a feminist model of delinquency would focus more extensively on the few pieces of information about girls' actual lives and the role played by girls' problems, including those caused by racism and poverty, in their delinquency behavior. Fortunately, a considerable literature is now developing on girls' lives and much of it bears directly on girls' crime.

CRIMINALIZING GIRLS' SURVIVAL

It has long been understood that a major reason for girls' presence in juvenile courts was the fact that their parents insisted on their arrest. In the early years, conflicts with parents were by far the most significant referral source; in Honolulu 44% of the girls who appeared in court in 1929 through 1930 were referred by parents.

Recent national data, while slightly less explicit, also show that girls are more likely to be referred to court by "sources other than law enforcement agencies" (which would include parents). In 1983, nearly a quarter (23%) of all girls but only 16% of boys charged with delinquent offenses were referred to court by non-law enforcement agencies. The pattern among youth referred for status offenses (for which girls are overrepresented) was even more pronounced. Well over half (56%) of the girls charged with these offenses and 45% of the boys were referred by sources other than law enforcement (Snyder and Finnegan, 1987, p. 21; see also Pope and Feyerherm, 1982).

The fact that parents are often committed to two standards of adolescent behavior is one explanation for such a disparity—and one that should not be discounted as a major source of tension even in modern families. Despite expectations to the contrary, gender-specific socialization patterns have not changed very much and this is especially true for parents' relationships with their daughters (Katz, 1979). It appears that even parents who oppose sexism in general feel "uncomfortable tampering with existing traditions" and "do not want to risk their children becoming misfits" (Katz, 1979, p. 24). Clearly, parental attempts to adhere to and enforce these traditional notions will continue to be a source of conflict between girls and their elders. Another important explanation for girls' problems with their parents, which has received attention only in more recent years, is the problem of physical and sexual abuse. Looking specifically at the problem of childhood sexual abuse, it is increasingly clear that this form of abuse is a particular problem for girls.

Girls are, for example, much more likely to be the victims of child sexual abuse than are boys. Finkelhor and Baron estimate from a review of community studies that roughly 70% of the victims of sexual abuse are female (Finkelhor and Baron, 1986, p. 45). Girls' sexual abuse also tends to start earlier than boys (Finkelhor and Baron, 1986, p. 48); they are more likely than

boys to be assaulted by a family member (often a stepfather) (DeJong, Hervada, and Emmett, 1983; Russell, 1986), and, as a consequence, their abuse tends to last longer than male sexual abuse (DeJong, Hervada, and Emmett, 1983). All of these factors are associated with more severe trauma—causing dramatic short- and long-term effects in victims (Adams-Tucker, 1982). The effects noted by researchers in this area move from the more well known "fear, anxiety, depression, anger and hostility, and inappropriate sexual behavior" (Browne and Finkelhor, 1986, p. 69) to behaviors of greater familiarity to criminologists, including running away from home, difficulties in school, truancy, and early marriage (Browne and Finkelhor, 1986).

Herman's study of incest survivors in therapy found that they were more likely to have run away from home than a matched sample of women whose fathers were "seductive" (33% compared to 5%). Another study of women patients found that 50% of the victims of child sexual abuse, but only 20% of the nonvictim group, had left home before the age of 18 (Meiselman, 1978).

Not surprisingly, then, studies of girls on the streets or in court populations are showing high rates of both physical and sexual abuse. Silbert and Pines (1981, p. 409) found, for example, that 60% of the street prostitutes they interviewed had been sexually abused as juveniles. Girls at an Arkansas diagnostic unit and school who had been adjudicated for either status or delinquent offenses reported similarly high levels of sexual abuse as well as high levels of physical abuse; 53% indicated they had been sexually abused, 25% recalled scars, 38% recalled bleeding from abuse, and 51% recalled bruises (Mouzakitas, 1981).

A sample survey of girls in the juvenile justice system in Wisconsin (Phelps et al., 1982) revealed that 79% had been subjected to physical abuse that resulted in some form of injury, and 32% had been sexually abused by parents or other persons who were closely connected to their families. Moreover, 50% had been sexually assaulted ("raped" or forced to participate in sexual acts) (Phelps et al., 1982, p. 66). Even higher figures were reported by McCormack and her associates (McCormack, Janus, and Burgess, 1986) in their study of youth in a runaway shelter in Toronto. They found that 73% of the females and 38% of the males had been sexually abused. Finally, a study of youth charged with running away, truancy, or listed as missing persons in Arizona found that 55% were incest victims (Reich and Gutierres, 1979).

Many young women, then, are running away from profound sexual victimization at home, and once on the streets they are forced further into crime in order to survive. Interviews with girls who have run away from home show, very clearly, that they do not have a lot of attachment to their delinquent activities. In fact, they are angry about being labeled as delinquent, yet all engaged in illegal acts (Koroki and Chesney-Lind, 1985). The Wisconsin study found that 54% of the girls who ran away found it necessary to steal money, food, and clothing in order to survive. A few exchanged sexual contact for money, food, and/or shelter (Phelps et al., 1982, p. 67). In their study of runaway youth, McCormack, Janus, and Burgess (1986, pp. 392–393) found that sexually abused female runaways were significantly more likely than their nonabused counterparts to engage in delinquent or criminal activities such as substance abuse, petty theft, and prostitution. No such pattern was found among male runaways.

Research (Chesney-Lind and Rodriguez, 1983) on the backgrounds of adult women in prison underscores the important links between women's childhood victimizations and their later criminal careers. The interviews revealed that virtually all of this sample were the victims of physical and/or sexual abuse as youngsters; over 60% had been sexually abused and about half had been raped as young women. This situation prompted these women to run away from home (three-quarters had been arrested for status offenses) where once on the streets they began engaging in prostitution and other forms of petty property crime. They also begin what becomes a lifetime problem with drugs. As adults, the women continue in these activities since they possess truncated educational backgrounds and virtually no marketable occupational skills (see also Miller, 1986).

Confirmation of the consequences of childhood sexual and physical abuse on adult female criminal behavior has also recently come from a large quantitative study of 908 individuals with substantiated and validated histories of these victimizations. Widom (1988) found that abused or neglected females were twice as likely as a matched group of controls to have an adult record (16% compared to 7.5). The difference was also found among men, but it was not as dramatic (42% compared to 33%). Men with abuse backgrounds were also more likely to contribute to the "cycle of violence" with more arrest for violent offenses as adult offenders than the control group. In contrast, when women with abuse backgrounds did become involved with the criminal justice system, their arrests tended to involve property and order offenses (such as disorderly conduct, curfew, and loitering violations) (Widom, 1988, p. 17).

Given this information, a brief example of how a feminist perspective on the causes of female delinquency might look seems appropriate. First, like young men, girls are frequently the recipients of violence and sexual abuse. But unlike boys, girls' victimization and their response to that victimization is specifically shaped by their status as young women. Perhaps because of the gender and sexual scripts found in patriarchal families, girls are much more likely than boys to be victim of family related sexual abuse. Men, particularly men with traditional attitudes toward women, are likely to define their daughters or stepdaughters as their sexual property (Finkelhor, 1982). In a society that idealizes inequality in male/female relationships and venerates youth in women, girls are easily defined as sexually attractive by older men (Bell, 1984). In addition, girls' vulnerability to both physical and sexual abuse is heightened by norms that require that they stay at home where their victimizers have access to them.

Moreover, their victimizers (usually males) have the ability to invoke official agencies of social control in their efforts to keep young women at home and vulnerable. That is to say, abusers have traditionally been able to utilize the uncritical commitment of the juvenile justice system toward parental authority to force girls to obey them. Girls' complaints about abuse were, until recently, routinely ignored. For this reason, statutes that were originally placed in law to "protect" young people have, in the case of girls' delinquency, criminalized their survival strategies. As they run away from abusive homes, parents have been able to employ agencies to enforce their return. If they persisted in their refusal to stay in that home, however intolerable, they were incarcerated.

Young women, a large number of whom are on the run from homes characterized by sexual abuse and parental neglect, are forced by the very statutes designed to protect them into the lives of escaped convicts. Unable to enroll in school or take a job to support themselves because they fear detection, young female runaways are forced into the streets. Here they engage in panhandling, petty theft, and occasional prostitution in order to survive. Young women in conflict with their parents (often for very legitimate reasons) may actually be forced by present laws into petty criminal activity, prostitution, and drug use.

In addition, the fact that young girls (but not necessarily young boys) are defined as sexually desirable and, in fact, more desirable then their older sisters due to the double standard of aging means that their lives on the streets (and their survival strategies) take on unique shape—one again shaped by patriarchal values. It is no accident that girls on the run from abusive homes, or on the streets because of profound poverty, get involved in criminal activities that exploit their sexual object status. American society has defined as desirable youthful, physically perfect women. This means that girls on the streets, who have little else of value to trade, are encouraged to utilize this "resource" (Campagna and Poffenberger, 1988). It also means that the criminal subculture views them from this perspective (Miller, 1986).

FEMALE DELINQUENCY, PATRIARCHAL AUTHORITY, AND FAMILY COURTS

The early insights into male delinquency were largely gleaned by intensive field observation of delinquent boys. Very little of this sort of work has been done in the case of girls' delinquency, though it is vital to an understanding of girls' definitions of their own situations, choices, and behavior (for exceptions to this see Campbell, 1984; Peacock, 1981; Miller, 1986; Rosenberg and Zimmerman, 1977). Time must be spent listening to girls. Fuller research on the settings, such as families and schools, that girls find themselves in and the impact of variations in those settings should also be undertaken (see Figueira-McDonough, 1986). A more complete understanding of how poverty and racism shape girls' lives is also vital (see Messerschmidt, 1986; Campbell, 1984). Finally, current qualitative research on the reaction of official agencies to girls' delinquency must be conducted. This latter task, admittedly more difficult, is particularly critical to the development of delinquency theory that is as sensitive to gender as it is to race and class.

It is clear that throughout most of the court's history, virtually all female delinquency has been placed within the larger context of girls' sexual behavior. One explanation for this pattern is that familial control over girls' sexual capital has historically been central to the maintenance of patriarchy (Lerner, 1986). The fact that young women have relatively more of this capital has been one reason for the excessive concern that both families and official agencies of social control have expressed about youthful female defiance (otherwise much of the behavior of criminal justice personnel makes virtually no sense). Only if one considers the role of women's control over their sexuality at the point in their lives that their value to patriarchal society is so pronounced, does the historic pattern of jailing of huge numbers of girls guilty of minor misconduct make sense.

This framework also explains the enormous resistance that the movement to curb the juvenile justice system's authority over status offenders encountered. Supporters of the change were not really prepared for the political significance of giving youth the freedom to run. Horror stories told by the opponents of deinstitutionalization about victimized youth, youthful prostitution, and youthful involvement in pornography (Office of Juvenile Justice and Delinquency Prevention, 1985) all neglect the unpleasant reality that most of these behaviors were often in direct response to earlier victimization, frequently by parents, that officials had, for years, routinely ignored. What may be at stake in efforts to roll back deinstitutionalization efforts is not so much "protection" of youth as it is curbing the right of young women to defy patriarchy.

In sum, research in both the dynamics of girls' delinquency and official reactions to that behavior is essential to the development of theories of delinquency that are sensitive to its patriarchal as well as class and racial context.

REFERENCES

ADAMS-TUCKER, CHRISTINE. 1982. "Proximate Effects of Sexual Abuse in Childhood." *American Journal of Psychiatry* 193:1252–1256.

AGETON, SUZANNE S. 1983. "The Dynamics of Female Delinquency, 1976–1980." *Criminology* 21:555–584.

BELL, INGE POWELL. 1984. "The Double Standard: Age." In *Women: A Feminist Perspective*, edited by Jo Freeman. Palo Alto, CA: Mayfield.

BLACK, T. EDWIN and CHARLES P. SMITH. 1981. *A Preliminary National Assessment of the Number and Characteristics of Juveniles Processed in the Juvenile Justice System.* Washington, DC: Government Printing Office.

BROWNE, ANGELA and DAVID FINKELHOR. 1986. "Impact of Child Sexual Abuse: A Review of Research." *Psychological Bulletin* 99:66–77.

CAMPAGNA, DANIEL S. and DONALD L. POFFENBERGER. 1988. *The Sexual Trafficking in Children.* Dover, DE: Auburn House.

CAMPBELL, ANN. 1984. *The Girls in the Gang.* Oxford: Basil Blackwell.

CANTER, RACHELLE J. 1982. "Sex Differences in Self-Report Delinquency." *Criminology* 20:373–393.

CHESNEY-LIND, MEDA. 1971. *Female Juvenile Delinquency in Hawaii.* Master's thesis, University of Hawaii.

———— 1973. "Judicial Enforcement of the Female Sex Role." *Issues in Criminology* 3:51–71.

———— 1978. "Young Women in the Arms of the Law." In *Women, Crime and the Criminal Justice System,* edited by Lee H. Bowker. Boston: Lexington.

———— 1986. "Women and Crime: The Female Offender." *Signs* 12:78–96.

———— 1988. "Girls and Deinstitutionalization: Is Juvenile Justice Still Sexist?" *Journal of Criminal Justice Abstracts* 20:144–165.

———— and Noelie Rodriguez. 1983. "Women Under Lock and Key." *Prison Journal* 63:47–65.

Children's Bureau, Department of Health, Education and Welfare. 1965. *1964 Statistics on Public Institutions for Delinquent Children.* Washington, DC: Government Printing Office.

CHILTON, ROLAND and SUSAN K. DATESMAN. 1987. "Gender, Race and Crime: An Analysis of Urban Arrest Trends, 1960–1980." *Gender and Society* 1:152–171.

CLOWARD, RICHARD A. and LLOYD E. OHLIN. 1960. *Delinquency and Opportunity.* New York: Free Press.

COHEN, ALBERT K. 1955. *Delinquent Boys: The Culture of the Gang.* New York: Free Press.

DATESMAN, SUSAN and MIKEL AICKIN. 1984. "Offense Specialization and Escalation Among Status Offenders." *Journal of Criminal Law and Criminology* 75:1246–1275.

DAVIDSON, SUE, ed. 1982. *Justice for Young Women.* Tucson, AZ: New Directions for Young Women.

DEJONG, ALLAN R., ARTURO R. HERVADA, and GARY A. EMMETT. 1983. "Epidemiologic Variations in Childhood Sexual Abuse." *Child Abuse and Neglect* 7:155–162.

ELLIOTT, DELBERT, DAVID HUIZINGA, and BARBARA MORSE. 1987. "A Career Analysis of Serious Violent Offenders." In *Violent Juvenile Crime: What Can We Do About It?* edited by Ira Schwartz. Minneapolis, MN: Hubert Humphrey Institute.

Federal Bureau of Investigation. 1987. *Crime in the United States 1986.* Washington, DC: Government Printing Office.

FEINMAN, CLARICE. 1980. *Women in the Criminal Justice System.* New York: Praeger.

FIGUEIRA-McDONOUGH, JOSEFINA. 1985. "Are Girls Different? Gender Discrepancies Between Delinquent Behavior and Control."*Child Welfare* 64:273–289.

———— 1986. "School Context, Gender, and Delinquency." *Journal of Youth and Adolescence* 15:79–98.

FINKELHOR, DAVID. 1982. "Sexual Abuse: A Sociological Perspective." *Child Abuse and Neglect* 6:95–102.

———— and LARRY BARON. 1986. "Risk Factors for Child Sexual Abuse." *Journal of Interpersonal Violence* 1:43–71.

FREEDMAN, ESTELLE. 1981. *Their Sisters' Keepers.* Ann Arbor: University of Michigan Press.

GELSTHORPE, LORAINE. 1986. "Towards a Skeptical Look at Sexism." *International Journal of the Sociology of Law* 14:125–152.

GORA, JOANN. 1982. *The New Female Criminal: Empirical Reality or Social Myth.* New York: Praeger.

HAGAN, JOHN, A. R. GILLIS, and JOHN SIMPSON. 1985. "The Class Structure of Gender and Delinquency:

Toward a Power-Control Theory of Common Delinquent Behavior." *American Journal of Sociology* 90:1151–1178.

HAGAN, JOHN, JOHN SIMPSON, and A. R. GILLIS. 1987. "Class in the Household: A Power-Control Theory of Gender and Delinquency." *American Journal of Sociology* 92:788–816.

HANCOCK, LINDA. 1981. "The Myth that Females are Treated More Leniently than Males in the Juvenile Justice System." *Australian and New Zealand Journal of Criminology* 16:4–14.

HARRIS, ANTHONY. 1977. "Sex and Theories of Deviance." *American Sociological Review* 42:3–16.

HERMAN, JULIA L. 1981. *Father-Daughter Incest.* Cambridge, MA: Harvard University Press.

KATZ, PHYLLIS A. 1979. "The Development of Female Identity." In *Becoming Female: Perspectives on Development,* edited by CLAIRE B. KOPP. New York: Plenum.

KOROKI, JAN and MEDA CHESNEY-LIND. 1985. *Everything Just Going Down the Drain.* Hawaii: Youth Development and Research Center.

LERNER, GERDA. 1986. *The Creation of Patriarchy.* New York: Oxford.

McCORMACK, ARLENE, MARK-DAVID JANUS, and ANN WOLBERT BURGESS. 1986. "Runaway Youths and Sexual Victimization: Gender Differences in an Adolescent Runaway Population." *Child Abuse and Neglect* 10:387–395.

McGARRELL, EDMUND F. and TIMOTHY J. FLANAGAN, eds. 1985. *Sourcebook of Criminal Justice Statistics—1984.* Washington, DC: Government Printing Office.

MEISELMAN, KAREN. 1978. *Incest.* San Francisco: Jossey-Bass.

MERTON, ROBERT K. 1938. "Social Structure and Anomie." *American Sociological Review* 3(October):672–682.

MESSERSCHMIDT, JAMES. 1986. *Capitalism, Patriarchy, and Crime: Toward a Socialist Feminist Criminology.* Totowa, NJ: Rowman & Littlefield.

——— 1987. "Feminism, Criminology, and the Rise of the Female Sex Delinquent, 1880–1930." *Contemporary Crises* 11:243–263.

MILLER, ELEANOR. 1986. *Street Woman.* Philadelphia: Temple University Press.

MILLER, WALTER B. 1958. "Lower Class Culture as the Generating Milieu of Gang Delinquency." *Journal of Social Issues* 14:5–19.

MORRIS, RUTH. 1964. "Female Delinquency and Relational Problems." *Social Forces* 43:82–89.

MOUZAKITAS, C. M. 1981. "An Inquiry into the Problem of Child Abuse and Juvenile Delinquency." In *Exploring the Relationship Between Child Abuse and Delinquency,* edited by R. J. Hunner and Y. E. Walkers. Montclair, NJ: Allanheld, Osmun.

National Female Advocacy Project. 1981. *Young Women and the Justice System: Basic Facts and Issues.* Tucson, AZ: New Directions for Young Women.

Office of Juvenile Justice and Delinquency Prevention. 1985. *Runaway Children and the Juvenile Justice and Delinquency Prevention Act: What is the Impact?* Washington, DC: Government Printing Office.

——— 1986. *America's Missing and Exploited Children. Report and Recommendations of the U.S. Attorney General's Advisory Board on Missing Children.* Washington, DC: Government Printing Office.

Opinion Research Corporation. 1982. "Public Attitudes Toward Youth Crime: National Public Opinion Poll." Mimeographed. Minnesota: Hubert Humphrey Institute of Public Affairs, University of Minnesota.

PEACOCK, CAROL. 1981. *Hand Me Down Dreams.* New York: Schocken.

PHELPS, R. J. et al. 1982. *Wisconsin Female Juvenile Offender Study Project Summary Report.* Wisconsin: Youth Policy and Law Center, Wisconsin Council on Juvenile Justice.

PLATT, ANTHONY M. 1969. *The Childsavers.* Chicago: University of Chicago Press.

POPE, CARL and WILLIAM H. FEYERHERM. 1982. "Gender Bias in Juvenile Court Dispositions." *Social Service Review* 6:1–17.

RAFTER, NICOLE HAHN. 1985. *Partial Justice.* Boston: Northeastern University Press.

REICH, J. W. and S. E. GUTIERRES. 1979. "Escape/Aggression Incidence in Sexually Abused Juvenile Delinquents." *Criminal Justice and Behavior* 6:239–243.

ROGERS, KRISTINE. 1972. "'For Her Own Protection . . . ': Conditions of Incarceration for Female Juvenile Offenders in the State of Connecticut." *Law and Society Review* (Winter):223–246.

ROSENBERG, DEBBY and CAROL ZIMMERMAN. 1977. *Are My Dreams Too Much To Ask For?* Tucson, AZ: New Directions for Young Women.

RUSSELL, DIANA E. 1986. *The Secret Trauma: Incest in the Lives of Girls and Women.* New York: Basic Books.

SCHLOSSMAN, STEVEN and STEPHANIE WALLACH. 1978. "The Crime of Precocious Sexuality: Female Juvenile Delinquency in the Progressive Era." *Harvard Educational Review* 48:65–94.

SHAW, CLIFFORD R. 1930. *The Jack-Roller.* Chicago: University of Chicago Press.

—— 1938. *Brothers in Crime*. Chicago: University of Chicago Press.

—— and HENRY D. MCKAY. 1942. *Juvenile Delinquency in Urban Areas*. Chicago: University of Chicago Press.

SHELDEN, RANDALL. 1981. "Sex Discrimination in the Juvenile Justice System: Memphis, Tennessee, 1900–1917." In *Comparing Female and Male Offenders*, edited by Marguerite Q. Warren. Beverly Hills, CA: Sage.

—— and JOHN HORVATH. 1986. "Processing Offenders in a Juvenile Court: A Comparison of Males and Females." Paper presented at the annual meeting of the Western Society of Criminology, Newport Beach, CA, February 27-March 2.

SILBERT, MIMI and AYALA M. PINES. 1981. "Sexual Child Abuse as an Antecedent to Prostitution." *Child Abuse and Neglect* 5:407–411.

SIMONS, RONALD L., MARTIN G. MILLER, and STEPHEN M. AIGNER. 1980. "Contemporary Theories of Deviance and Female Delinquency: An Empirical Test." *Journal of Research in Crime and Delinquency* 17:42–57.

SMITH, LESLEY SHACKLADY. 1978. "Sexist Assumptions and Female Delinquency." In *Women, Sexuality and Social Control*, edited by Carol Smart and BARRY SMART. London: Routledge & Kegan Paul.

SNYDER, HOWARD N. and TERRENCE A. FINNEGAN. 1987. *Delinquency in the United States*. Washington, DC: Department of Justice.

STEFFENSMEIER, DARRELL J. 1980. "Sex Differences in Patterns of Adult Crime, 1965–1977." *Social Forces* 58:1080–1109.

SUTHERLAND, EDWIN. 1978. "Differential Association." In *Children of Ishmael: Critical Perspectives on Juvenile Justice*, edited by Barry Krisberg and James Austin. Palo Alto, CA: Mayfield.

TEILMANN, KATHERINE S. and PIERRE H. LANDRY, Jr. 1981. "Gender Bias in Juvenile Justice." *Journal of Research in Crime and Delinquency* 18:47–80.

THRASHER, FREDERIC M. 1927. *The Gang*. Chicago: University of Chicago Press.

TRACY, PAUL E., MARVIN E. WOLFGANG, and ROBERT M. FIGLIO. 1985. *Delinquency in Two Birth Cohorts: Executive Summary*. Washington, DC: Department of Justice.

WIDOM, CATHY SPATZ. 1988. "Child Abuse, Neglect, and Violent Criminal Behavior." Unpublished manuscript.

IN THE NIGHT MARKET
TOURISM, SEX, AND COMMERCE IN CONTEMPORARY THAILAND

Ryan Bishop and Lillian S. Robinson

If you want the best blow job in the world, say so . . . [The manager]'ll tell you which girls specialize in the field. If you want anal, say so. If you want to watch two or three girls making love to each other and then join in, say so. Be specific and graphic: they've heard it all before, and will direct you toward the right girl(s). . . . [In the room, after the bath and body massage,] you'll dry off, move to the bed, and do whatever it was you paid to do. It's all very leisurely, you've got two hours to play. On occasion . . . a girl might possess some extremely powerful Thai stick, and will ask you to join her in a smoke. It's up to you, but if you don't, you can be sure she'll have had a better time than you (and have blotted you completely out in the process). Whatever, almost without exception in my experience, these girls are very, very good at what they do.

That said, it would be well to remember that what these girls "do" . . . is not what they "are." Often, they are quite funny and bright. Even if not, if you never cease to remember that they are, before anything else, human beings with human feelings, chances are good you'll truly enjoy yourself, and you will have made her life, for a moment, at least, not as completely horrible as it might have been.[1]

This epigraph comes from a provocative site of postmodern expression, the Internet's World Sex Guide—specifically, from a 1994 text entitled "Sex in Thailand: The Basics," written as a *vade mecum* for the neophyte sex customer by an anonymous author who describes himself as a longtime traveler to Southeast Asia. In this selection, he is explaining the practices—you might even call them the etiquette—of Bangkok's recreational massage parlors.

The epigraph also brings together a number of the themes addressed in this essay: the nature of international commercial sex in Thailand; the enormous material and affective disparity—the sheer inequality—between the participants; and the focus on the mentality and motives of the subject "you," the Western male, proud possessor of foreign exchange that may seem like chump change to "you" but represents a fortune to a Thai peasant girl—and possessor, as well, of a sexuality alienated enough to make "you" travel halfway around the world to purchase its satisfaction.

To begin the discussion proper—and, in some places, highly improper—we have to step back several long paces from this close-up of the massage-parlor transaction. What is the largest industry in the world? You may be excused if you say "sex." But however widespread commercial sex may be, neither the monetary amounts nor the number of people working in administration, transportation, and so on—*in addition* to those toiling at the point of production and those who supervise, manage, and profit—makes it at all comparable to, say, the petroleum industry. Answering "sex," is a bit like the conventional reference to prostitution as "the world's oldest profession," a remark suggesting that commercial sex is so long established a practice that it constitutes the first-known instance of exchange for value received. Indeed, reference to the purportedly ancient origins of prostitution supports the idea that it is ingrained in human behavior, if not a natural activity. By contrast, it is our position that large-scale international commercial sex is neither natural nor inevitable, and it is oddly comforting to believe that in arguing against it,

we are struggling against neither nature nor human nature but "merely" global capitalism and the simultaneously violent and alienated sexual cultures it (so to speak) engenders.

Again we ask: what *is* the world's largest industry—comparable in scale, finances, and numbers of workers at all levels in a great many occupations to the oil business? The answer is tourism, travel, which is both the most lucrative and the most labor-intensive industry in the world today. Tourism owes its ascendancy to a variety of material factors: the conversion of the military aircraft industry to civilian production in the aftermath of World War II and the subsequent development of the jumbo jet; the granting of longer annual vacations to First World workers, especially in western Europe where, depending on the country, four and even five or six weeks of paid leave are the norm; and, for nations in the postcolonial world, powerful modernization imperatives, that is, the need to become a participant, however unequally, in the global marketplace.[2] Tourism began to expand in the early 1960s, promoted by the United Nations, national governments, and tourism-specific conferences and organizations as a route to world peace and mutual understanding.[3] In regard to international development planning, tourism was long understood as a solution to the problems of modernization, one that created wealth yet avoided the environmental and human costs of heavy, "smokestack" industry like those experienced in the West during the Industrial Revolution.

It is in this context that we describe the particulars of sex tourism in Thailand. In the late 1960s, the Thai economy became increasingly dependent on the presence of U.S. and other foreign military personnel. The large American air bases and the investment and labor required to build, staff, and serve them were supplemented by the consequences of the contracts that Thailand, along with a half dozen other localities, signed with the U.S. Department of Defense in 1967, to provide R and R to thousands of servicemen a week rotated directly in from the Vietnam war zone. R and R stands for Rest and Recreation, although many of the U.S. soldiers called it "I and I," for Intercourse and Intoxication, because that's what they used it for. The food, lodging, transportation, entertainment, and other comforts provided for the troops meant profits for a wide range of businesses. But the principal attraction of Thailand was the I and I.

Because Thailand's enormous sex industry was already in place—for the indigenous prostitution trade in Thailand remains much larger than its international aspect in terms of numbers of sex providers and customers, though much smaller in terms of profits generated—a new sexual institution was developed. In addition to brothels, massage parlors, sexual exhibitions, and pick-up bars, there emerged the girlie or go-go bar, resembling in some ways the "singles" dance bars that sprang up in late-1960s America. Indeed, the Thai girlie bars had the same strobe lights, loud rock music, alcohol, dancing, and sexual quests. The difference was that whereas a U.S. bar typically had one or two provocatively clad go-go dancers suspended high above the customers' heads, sometimes in cages, with both the dance floor and the negotiations for sexual encounters open to customers of both sexes, the Bangkok bars provided dozens, even hundreds, of dancers, performing with their crotches at eye level and presented not primarily as entertainers but as potential sexual partners for male customers. There were virtually no female customers. That's the scene as it was and as it remains. Entering one of those bars in the 1990s feels like stepping back into a singles bar in the 1970s, with the flashing disco lights and Creedence Clearwater Revival playing at maximum volume,[4] and, still no female bar customers with their troubling subjectivity, their ability to say "no thanks" to an offer of a drink or a one-night stand, their power to answer the question, "What's your sign?" with the words, "Keep Off."

Why have those bars remained and flourished, crowded every night of the year with very young Thai dancer-prostitutes from the north and northeast of the kingdom, the regions that traditionally supply many of Thailand's beauty queens—so many dancers that their shifts on-stage, where they are best displayed to the most customers at once, are limited to a couple of cuts on the tape, before others take their places? Why are the bars crowded with mostly middle-aged white men

from North America, western Europe, and Australia (all called *farang* by the Thais) looking for the special sort of good time these girls can provide? Meanwhile, elsewhere in Bangkok, very large numbers of Japanese and Arab men pack different bars and other sex-tourism locales.

What happened is that in 1971, a World Bank delegation to Thailand headed by the bank's president, Robert S. McNamara, met with officials at the highest levels of the Thai political and economic structure. Although the war in Indochina still raged, they were already rightly concerned about what would happen to the Thai economy once the foreign troops left the region. McNamara, who, by no means incidentally, had been the U.S. secretary of defense in 1967 when the R and R contracts were signed, arranged to send some of the World Bank's development experts to Thailand to make recommendations. These experts' report—issued in 1975, the year the last Americans left Vietnam—recommended that Thailand base its postwar economy on the development of mass tourism.[5] A World Bank recommendation means, of course, that loans and credits will be available for the course outlined in the recommendation, but not for other economic objectives.

Mass tourism means chiefly package tours—airfare, hotel, ground transportation, and perhaps meals and guides, included in a single fee. But even at bargain rates, Thailand is a long and therefore never very cheap flight from most parts of the world where people get paid vacations. It was thus too expensive to appeal to many family travelers or honeymooners, and so the focus had to be on men traveling alone. And what delights did Thailand have to offer them? The sexual pleasure that had been established for the GIs on R and R. Japanese tours, in fact, usually include the sexual entertainment in the comprehensive fee. By contrast, Americans and Europeans, although attracted by brochures pitching the greater sexual availability and subservience of Thai women and the cultural differences that purportedly make them so available, prefer the illusion of a free choice on both sides—even of a relationship. So the tour includes their airfare and perhaps their literal accommodations, while they seek out their own sexual accommodations from the variety available in every bar.

On a macroeconomic level, the result is that the tourism business brings in more than $4 billion a year to the Thai economy. Indeed, as of the mid-1980s, tourism had surpassed rice exports as Thailand's major source of foreign exchange.[6] More than 70 percent of the tourists to Thailand are men traveling on their own, but in certain resort towns that are known as prostitution centers, that figure rises to well over 90 percent. Millions of tourists a year, many more millions of individual sexual transactions, billions of dollars, most of it going to the transnational corporations that own airlines and hotel chains. No one knows or can even estimate accurately how many of these dollars are directly generated by the sex industry, which is, after all, an illegal business, but that industry is certainly responsible for filling the jumbo jets.

The phenomenon involves millions of individual encounters in the bars and other commercial sex venues. These human and economic interactions may have been arranged by international planning and lending mechanisms, but on a personal level, what brings Thai women (as well as children of both sexes) and foreign men to this site of cross-cultural sexual communication?

For the sex workers, the answer lies in their own and their families' overwhelming poverty. The north and northeast regions of Thailand are distinguished from the central area, where Bangkok is located, by ethnic as well as class differences. These were always poor areas, dependent on subsistence farming, and in the past three decades, it has become nearly impossible to subsist on subsistence farming there. We speculate that national policies regarding water usage and irrigation, agricultural credits, and even landholding have deliberately impoverished these regions in order to create an army of unskilled workers to staff the favored areas of the economy.[7] The result has been an exodus from the villages of the north and northeast to Bangkok and to the new beach-resort towns. For young people without specific job skills, work is available in domestic service, construction, hotel and restaurant work, and production in the sweatshops manufacturing clothing, athletic shoes, and toys. (The Mighty Morphin Power Rangers that were the most popular U.S. Christmas toy a few

years ago were manufactured by Thai women workers whose daily salary could not purchase even one Morphin.) Most of the young workers do become domestics, hotel cleaners, kitchen workers, and factory operatives and so can relieve their families of the burden of their support and become minimally self-sufficient.

For them to do more than this, however—to contribute to the support of their families, a duty in traditional Thai culture—the sex industry is their only source of a great number of better-paid unskilled jobs. Some families indenture their daughters to brothels in return for a loan at an interest rate as high as 100 percent that the girls must work off. But recruitment, especially for the international dimension of the sex industry, does not entail such debt bondage but is instead a forced labor-market choice for many young girls. The result is that many villages are made up of families—parents, grandparents, siblings, and perhaps the young sex worker's own children—each supported by the labor of one prostitute in Bangkok. The money she sends home is sufficient to feed the family, even build a new house, keep younger siblings in school, dig a well for drinking water, and perhaps buy seed and fertilizer or even a water buffalo for the farm but not to enable another economic situation to replace the continuing dependence on sex work.[8] This could not be permitted, because from the planners' point of view, the tourism, and especially the sex industry's need for a gender- and age-specific labor force, will continue indefinitely.

In our own interviews with Thai bar girls, and those of other researchers, the economic motivations for and effects of their occupation were invariably central. Common to all the girls was their fear, fear of the short-run violence that can be inflicted with impunity on a body that has already been defined as being at once profitable, enjoyable, and essentially worthless. Although this fear also included that of long-range disease and early death, it was the terror of each encounter with a stranger and what he might do that resonated most clearly.

The following is an excerpt from an interview with a "freelance" prostitute we call Nong. The narrator is Ryan Bishop:

Leaning over a beer and shouting over the general din, I asked her, "Would you prefer to do another kind of work?"

"Of course. Who wouldn't?"

"Some *farangs* say that many, if not most, of the women love the bars: the men, the drinking, the dancing, the money, the attention. They say all this gets in the women's systems. Then, if they try to do another type of work or simply get out of this job and go home, they can't do it."

Shaking her head, Nong responds, "No, I don't think so." She blows a plume of smoke into the air. "Most are here because they have no education and no real choice."

"Are you ever afraid to go with a man?"

Her eyes widen. "Sure! All the time. Every time. You never know what a man is going to do," she says, clutching her throat.

"One guy tried to strangle me, and I hit him with the ashtray. Now I always look for the ashtray when I go with a man I don't know."

"Is that often now?"

"No. I have a pretty steady group of men who are nice to me, which is why I go with them. But some months, the rent is due and my son's school needs to be paid—no money in the bank—so I go here [German Beer Garden] or the T-Room [an after-hours bar, the Thermae]. I don't know if you've ever, you know, been starving or scrambling for food for your child. You do some crazy things. That's when I have to smile sweetly at guys who are really shit, you know. Each time, too, there's that fear along your back, near your spine—fear of losing that guy's attention and money, fear of not getting enough money, fear that he might hurt me. If I have some money, I can tell the guys I don't like to fuck off. If I don't, then it's smiling at this shithead who's grabbing me all over my body." She moves her hands in illustration.

[After discussing other prostitutes' hopes for the future, I asked her,] "What do *you* dream of?"

"A bookshop, you know. One that sells coffee, too. Maybe some music playing lightly in the background— quiet and cool. People could rent the books, too. They wouldn't even have to buy them."[9]

What motivates the customers, and how do they talk about their experiences? In addition to literary sources, our book *Night Market* relies on the interviews conducted by Bishop, and the sex diaries that customers put on the Internet when they return home. It all adds up to a picture that we call *international sexual alienation.*

This is Bishop's report of the statement of an informant to whom we gave the synechdochic name Peter:

An American in his early forties, Peter had made many trips to Thailand as a sex tourist before inheriting a sum of money that allowed him to become an expat with the luxury of being gainfully unemployed. We asked him how to have a good time in Bangkok, how best to take advantage of what . . . [the red-light districts] had to offer the sex tourist. These were issues Peter had spent much time thinking about and empirically experiencing. . . . Over his third beer, Peter launched into advice-giving mode. "First, check into a hotel near Nana and dump your load. I mean your bags AND your load. Call room service and ask them to send up some tart. Tell 'em you're horny and you've got a purply [a 500 baht note, then worth $20] for her if she's good. No muss, no fuss.

"OK. It's midafternoon. You've checked in and shot your pre-wad. Now go dive into a buffet in a nearby hotel and fuel up. One of the upscale ones that have *farang* food and no Thai customers. The Landmark's good and right across from *soi* 7, where you KNOW you'll be heading to next.

"Walk over to the GBG [German Beer Garden] when you're done eating. Hell, you can even eat there if you're horny enough and want to scope out the freelancers before it gets too late. Now, here you've got a couple of choices. You want to take the edge off here, mind you, not to get fucking married. They've got a decent supply of purply freelancers wandering in and out of here ALL the time. They'll take one look at you and they know. THEY KNOW!!!

"OK. Pick one. Any one! We're talking short-time here, buddy. Who knows, maybe you get lucky and want to keep her on, but check her out first. There's plenty more where she comes from, so don't sweat it. Take her back to the Crowne if your own place is too far away, or wherever, and do the deed. Take the edge off, bro, so you're not drooling later and do something foolish like spend too much or get shackled to a scuz. These girls aren't stupid either. Last thing they want is some horny buffalo crawling all over them.

"Dump her. Take a bath. Have a nap. Read the paper, watch the Bloody Boring Corporation on TV. Get a massage, a manicure, pedicure, haircut and BJ [blow-job] somewhere. Suttisan's a good area for this. Just ask them if they 'sa-moke.' In Thai-English, 'Sa-moke di may?' [Smoke is ok, huh?] another purple, big deal. You're being treated like royalty from top to bottom at twenty bucks a throw.

"Now you're moving into big Mango mode. You're getting' down and dirty and you're lovin' it! Admit it! You can't do this at home! OK, now you're ready for the main course. You got a few options here, depending on what you want and how much you want to drop.

"The Japs got the best girls now, in Thaniya Plaza. Much better than what we've got. But if you want you can hang around outside and lap up their leavings. Sloppy seconds from Japs are basically virgins anyway, except for the S&Mers. Patpong: OK, some fine looking babes still there, but supermercenary. A few BJ shops but you've had that already. Getting expensive down there now and the girls have an attitude. Me, I'd stay away from it myself. Cowboy: Fine but too tame. Some nice girls you can actually talk to, but if you're in town for a day or two, talk *is not what you're after.*

"Go to Nana. Yeah. Nana. Definitely. This is where it's at now—up and coming. Some good shows, some decent bars, middle-of-the-road—reasonable prices and a few places to do short-timers right there so you don't have to break your stride. I've been VERY lucky there. Highly recommended. Take your time, though. Pick a winner and watch a show. Get a stiffy, give her your best smile, flash a few baht, buy her a couple of drinks and you're in.

"But listen up. You might not even score there. Might not find what you're after. If not, then there is always hope. THERE IS STILL HOPE IN THE WORLD AS LONG AS THE T-ROOM IS OPEN, which it will be for fucking ever. I'm talking about the Chicken Farm . . . HQ . . . the T-Room . . . the meeting place . . . the best little whorehouse in the world.

"And it swings into action when the other bars CLOSE!

"Go there. Sit down if you can. Order a set of Mekong. A couple of mamasans are always wandering around looking for buffaloes like you to buy them *khanam* [treats]. Tell them what you want. Big tits, little tits; Khmer dancer; *tua lek* [small body]; *tua yai* [big body]; BJ; twosome, threesome; WHATEVER! You've found your kingdom, revel in it. We only live once. Why do you think God made the Thermae?"[10]

What is most impressive in what we call "Peter's performance piece," is the way, from the shooting of that memorable "pre-wad" onward, that the subject "you" constantly ejaculates yet is constantly holding back, saving up for the big score that is always still ahead. That and the way the price of each sexual experience becomes a category of judgment: the girls in the Patpong red-light district may be pretty, but they have an "attitude" (inferentially bad); that is, they are "supermercenary," whereas the cheaper ones at Nana Entertainment Plaza are "nicer." And "you" want to avoid the twin pitfalls lying in wait for the unwary foreigner: If you don't "take the edge off" (with your second lay of the day, mind you), you might do something foolish "like spend too much or get shackled to a scuz."

Early familiarity with Peter's recurrent assimilation of ejaculation and spending—reminiscent of Victorian sexual discourse in which the latter was the most common colloquial term for the former—alerted us to the prevalence of the same motif in the Internet sex diaries. The standard "prostitution by country" entry in the World Sex Guide gives information about the legal situation, age of consent, typical prices for various acts, what acts or gestures sex workers in the particular country refuse to engage in, and where to find street prostitutes and more specialized workers.

For Thailand, however, the listings go on and on, including etiquette guides like the one cited in the epigraph, other guides that provide names and addresses of recommended establishments, and diaries in which the traveler, on his return, gives a detailed description of his stay. Typically, these narratives relate the price of everything. (Oscar Wilde, of course, would add "and the value of nothing.") They begin with the fare charged for ground transportation from the airport and proceed through accommodations and intercity travel to sex, so that every suck and stroke has its dollar value and every sexual experience is rated as a waste of money, a great bargain, or a splurge that paid off big time.

From here, the material connections become even more revealing. One correspondent, not a native speaker of English, complains about a "dumb" masseuse who didn't know she was supposed to massage muscles, not bones. When the couple get into bed, she's also a dud in the blowjob department, because *he* can't get an erection. He observes that "I thought about helping her with thinking at something REALLY nice, but then I thought, 'what for do I pay?'"[11] *She* is supposed to do all the work, after all, so why should he participate in his own arousal, which is to say, be part of his own sexuality, even to the extent of conjuring up an erotic fantasy?

This mentality leads to narratives in which, as in one posting, the loss of a credit card and the wait for its replacement become a suspense-enhancing motif or, in another, romance is destroyed and "heartbreak" ensues when a prostitute gets "greedy"—that is, when she tells the *farang* she has been seeing "steadily" for several days that, according to her roommate, 1,000 baht, not 500, should be the price for an all-night session. He whines to the reader that he is really disappointed because he thought "goodwill" had been established and that "she was different."[12] It is only fitting that another long diary posting is headed, in lieu of a title, "The following is a true account of my trip to Thailand; Note: $1 = 25 Baht."[13]

The ultimate experience, therefore, is getting something for nothing, as in this passage:

One thing I'll never forget . . . is my last night. I had specifically sought out one of the "Miss Thailands" spotted the previous evening and spent my last entertainment money on her. Afterwards, I returned to the bar of my previous night's carnal delights and ran into my "Sweetie" from . . . last night. Well, she just about insisted about 1:00 A.M. that we return to my hotel. When I explained about no $$$, she replied, 'No problem, you fl-end, you no pay!' I am sure it's not a first, but getting a freebie from a beautiful Patpong bar girl ranks way up there on my list! It also filled the time until my 5:00 A.M. taxi to the airport.[14]

In her book *Patpong Sisters,* Cleo Odzer explains how she was won over to the position that far from being in need of "saving," the bar girls she studied are actually freer than other Thai women. Odzer does express sympathy for the economic plight of her prostitute-subjects, yet her account, like those on the World Sex Guide, is larded with references to exactly how much she is spending for what. More to the point, although she is supposedly willing to pay her subjects for their time and is sometimes generous with those she befriends (taking them on research trips to their home villages and on vacations to Ko Samet or Pattaya), she becomes easily exasperated at the way their families and boyfriends avail themselves of her ability to pay for things. Moreover, the prostitutes themselves often seem to her to be out for whatever they can get. (Why, they act like whores!)

And when Odzer becomes involved with Jek, a Patpong tout or pimp, the issue of repaying her 500 baht ($20) loan to him acquires the same dramatic significance as the Internet account of the girl who spoiled a beautiful relationship by unexpectedly raising her price. Odzer has no compunction about sharing her *bed* with Jek, losing herself "in a blend of East and West," but both before and after they have sex for the first time, she muses, "Did I trust him in the apartment with my computer and other electronic gadgets? Not really."[15]

Although she spares us no detail of the emotional "price" she pays as this relationship runs its course, it is only after Odzer has reclaimed her sense of *farang* entitlement that she takes on the full sex-tourist mentality. Thus, in her memories of her romantic night with a trekking guide, she relates the "flirty looks" they exchanged the next day as he poled the raft around "perilous turns and protruding rocks," recalling that "he'd promised to take me on a *free tour* of Chiang Mai on his motorbike that night."[16] The aphrodisiac delights of getting something for nothing must never be underestimated! And all this time, Odzer is the one complaining that the denizens of the red-light district just don't know how to sustain an authentic, noncommercial human relationship!

The first night the two of us (Bishop and Robinson) went to Soi Cowboy together, one of our *farang* companions gestured around the bar and exclaimed, "Look at these guys: they're so obviously the losers of the Western world!" A bar girl expressed the same view: "When they're in their country, they can't get a girlfriend. They're very lonely. Work, work, work and come back here."[17] By contrast, what has always struck us is the ordinariness of the men crowding the bars: it requires no stretch of the imagination to transport mentally almost any of them to a restaurant table in his own country, facing a noncommercial companion of his own age and nation. These men are "losers" only because they prefer a game with even fewer rules and with guaranteed certainty as to the result. That is, they prefer the sexual event as a transaction, even if some of them are also capable of mystifying its commercial aspects.

The bar girl also is right, though, when she connects their situation to "work, work, work." In a sense, sex tourism is as much a part of the men's working lives as is the routine itself of their jobs. Thanh-Dam Truong points out the "interplay between leisure policy and leisure industry" and the way "the economic value of leisure or 'free time' as unoccupied time . . . [has been] incorporated into the logic of production and consumption."[18] Industrialized sexuality as a form of industrialized leisure can thus be understood as intrinsic to the system in which work is defined and carried out—a system, in other words, of *totalizing alienation.* That sex tourism was built on an infrastructure established for military R and R and extended through corporate recreational contracts only underscores the totality of the work-leisure institutional continuum.

Seeing the system as one of international sexual alienation offers a perspective on the kind of sexuality that the sex industry features and recognizes it as part of the global economic system of exchange, domination, and exploitation. Thus, ignoring Marx's definition of alienation as appropriated labor, Brock and Thistlethwaite focus on the sorts of alienation engendered by the system, arguing that capitalism

tends to make the person unstable as a social, discursive, somatic, and psychic entity. . . . [T]he lack of congruity between life and work, what Marx called alienation, is characteristic of . . . [capitalist] societies. This alienation is an important mechanism of power that supports prostitution, because the body must be regarded as a commodity in order for the sex industry to obtain workers.[19]

They point out that one of the most important ways in which capitalism enables the sex industry to function "is the reduction of the human body to property."[20] This also helps explain commentator Kathleen Barry's moral imperative: *"When the human being is reduced to a body, objectified to sexually service another, whether or not there is consent, violation of the human being has occurred."*[21] Seeing it as sexual alienation means placing this violation in the context of all the other violations inherent in a system in which work is performed by "labor power"—a dehumanized but not disembodied quality of human beings who are sometimes identified as "hands."

This conclusion suggests that we must try to understand sexual alienation as a system, just as we understand capitalism itself as a system, in which we in the First World are implicated, as

well as those who labor or profit in other sectors. And like capitalism, the system of sexual alienation has an international dimension—postcolonial but far from postimperial. Accordingly, to try to change the Thai sex industry, we must deepen our understanding not only of exotic phenomena like beautiful teenagers performing suggestive dances in distant bars but also of far more familiar and boring experiences, like how our economic system can condition our most intimate responses, including our sexuality, so that all of us are part of a sexual as well as an economic system. The conditions under which we all may be trying to work out and take responsibility for a nonalienated sexuality necessarily include the cultural climate that gives some of our compatriots the means and the desire to purchase sex as a commodity in a drastically unequal market. For international sexual alienation, as we say in concluding the introduction to *Night Market,* makes the sexual transactions in the bars and massage parlors a phenomenon at once exotic and close to home, both apart from us and a part of us.[22]

NOTES

This essay was written for presentation as a lecture by Lillian S. Robinson, relying on research reflected in a collaborative study by Ryan Bishop and Lillian S. Robinson, *Night Market: Sexual Cultures and the Thai Economic Miracle* (New York: Routledge, 1998). The lecture was delivered by Robinson at Georgetown University, Ohio University, and East Carolina University in the spring of 1998. The thoughtful comments and questions from all three audiences helped clarify and focus the argument for this version.

1. "Sex in Thailand: The Basics," World Sex Guide, Prostitution by Country: Thailand, Internet Posting 23 August 1994. This document is discussed in chap. 5 of *Night Market,* "Imagining Sexual Others."

2. See Harry G. Matthews, *International Tourism: A Political and Social Analysis* (Cambridge, MA: Schenkman, 1977); Linda Richter, *The Politics of Tourism in Asia* (Honolulu: University of Hawaii Press, 1989); Tranh-Dam Truong, *Sex, Money and Morality: Prostitution and Tourism in South-East Asia* (London: Zed Books, 1990); Michael Hitchcock, Victor T. King, and Michael J. G. Parnwell, eds., *Tourism in South-East Asia* (London: Routledge, 1993).

3. See, for example, Luther Hodges, foreword to *The Future of Tourism in the Pacific and the Far East,*

by Harry G. Clements (Washington, DC: U.S. Department of Commerce, 1961); *Recommendations on International Travel and Tourism* (Rome: United Nations, 1963); *The Hague Declaration on Tourism* (The Hague: Inter-Parliamentary Conference on Tourism, 1989).

4. Lillian S. Robinson, "In the Penile Colony: Touring Thailand's Sex Industry," *The Nation,* November 1, 1993, 492–97, which is included in chap. 1 of Bishop and Robinson, *Night Market,* describes the go-go bars.

5. Truong, *Sex, Money and Morality,* 162–63.

6. Richter, *The Politics of Tourism in Asia,* 84–89; Pasuk Phongpaichit and Chris Baker, *Thailand: Economy and Politics* (Kuala Lumpur: Oxford University Press, 1995).

7. Chap. 4 of Bishop and Robinson, *Night Market,* "A Very Political Economy," lays the groundwork for this position, esp. 98–99; see, as well, Catherine Hill, "Planning for Prostitution: An Analysis of Thailand's Sex Industry," in *Women's Lives and Public Policy: The International Experience,* ed. Meredeth Turshan and Briavel Holcomb (Westport, CT: Greenwood Press, 1993), 133–44.

8. Pasuk Phongpaichit, *From Peasant Girls to Bangkok Masseuses* (Geneva: International Labour Organisation, 1982).

9. Bishop and Robinson, *Night Market,* 189–91.

10. Ibid., 153–55.

11. World Sex Guide, posting dated July 1995, emphasis in original.

12. Paranoia.com/faq/prostitution, March 27, 1995.

13. World Sex Guide, posting dated September 19, 1996.

14. Ibid., posting dated April 1996.

15. Cleo Odzer, *Patpong Sisters: An American Woman's View of the Bangkok Sex World* (New York: Blue Moon-Arcade, 1994), 110.

16. Ibid., 305, emphasis added.

17. Dave Walker and Richard S. Ehrlich, eds., *"Hello My Big Big Honey!" Love Letters to Bangkok Bar Girls and Their Revealing Interviews* (Bangkok: Dragon Dance, 1992), 153.

18. Truong, *Sex, Money and Morality,* 98.

19. Gail Nakashima Brock and Susan Brooks Thistlethwaite, *Casting Stones: Prostitution and Liberation in Asia and the United States* (Minneapolis: Fortress Press, 1996), 108.

20. Ibid., 110.

21. Kathleen Barry, *The Prostitution of Sexuality* (New York: New York University Press, 1995), 23, emphasis in original.

22. Bishop and Robinson, *Night Market,* 15.

ON THE BACKS OF WORKING PROSTITUTES
FEMINIST THEORY AND PROSTITUTION POLICY*

Annette Jolin

Why is prostitution as controversial today as it was 4000 years ago? Why are feminists embroiled in the prostitution controversy? And what is it about prostitution that defies resolution? I argue that the answers to these questions can be found in a fundamental contradiction in Western culture, a contradiction that arises from the institutionalization of a sexual double standard in patriarchal societies, wherein prostitution owes its

existence to an interplay of social and economic arrangements that involve promiscuity, chastity, and inequality.

Throughout its long history, prostitution has neither enjoyed uncontested acceptance nor endured total condemnation. In times of acceptance, as in times of condemnation, prostitution was always controversial. That conflict has always involved one or more of the elements in the promiscuity-chastity-inequality model of prostitution. Whatever form this conflict takes, however, it is always the women[1] who work as prostitutes who suffer. This is perhaps easier to

*From Annette Jolin, *Crime and Delinquency,* vol. 40, no. 2, pp 69–83, copyright © 1994 by Sage Publications Inc. Reprinted by permission of author and Sage Publications, Inc.

understand in times when men, rather than women, dominate the prostitution debate, but even today when the prostitution controversy largely involves a debate *between* women and ending male dominance—about ending inequality, it is still the prostitute who suffers. The schism between women is deep. This divisiveness among women, as we shall see, exists for good reason, but it is also the case that today, after more than a century of feminism, the United States is one of the few industrial societies where prostitutes are defined as criminals.

THE PROMISCUITY-CHASTITY-INEQUALITY MODEL OF PROSTITUTION

Prostitution is an activity, which in broad terms can be identified as the exchange of sex for money: Women typically provide the sex and men the money (Lerner 1986, p. 131).

The controversial character of prostitution, and the often bitter social conflicts arising from disagreements about it, are the result of a profound cultural contradiction, which originates in the desire of men to ensure promiscuity for themselves and chastity for women. Men want sex with different women and they want women who have sex with only one man, a theoretical impossibility to which men have found a practical, albeit controversial, solution, one that requires "setting aside" a few women to meet the needs of men without substantially reducing the availability of chaste women or threatening the chastity of wives.

Historically, the process of "setting aside" a group of women and keeping them there succeeded because men had the power to overcome the resistance of women to being set aside. Voluntary entrance of women into prostitution seems highly unlikely, given a social order that linked female worth and economic survival to marriage, and marriageability to chastity.

In summary, prostitution in patriarchal society resulted from the following arrangements:

1. Male sexuality was defined to include promiscuity.
2. Female sexuality was defined to dictate chastity.
3. Men had the power to enforce both.

I refer to these arrangements as the promiscuity-chastity-inequality model of prostitution etiology. The term *inequality* is used to reflect men's social and economic dominance over women. The term *equality* refers to the social and economic equality of women with men.[2]

As the model suggests, prostitution owes its existence to a sexual double standard, the implementation of which is predicated on the economic and social dominance of men over women. It is not surprising that prostitution, which incorporates male sexual duplicity and inequality between the sexes, has inspired moral crusaders and social reformers to speak out against it. Until the mid-19th century, those who spoke out against prostitution were almost exclusively men. Only since then have women become involved in the public debate.

HISTORICAL CONTROVERSIES

The following discussion of prostitution controversies makes use of only a few of the examples that have been documented over the course of nearly 4000 years. History is replete with challenges to prostitution, followed by decades, even centuries, of relatively quiet tolerance. Yet neither support nor challenges have ever succeeded in freeing prostitution from controversy. For example, it rarely enjoyed greater social acceptance than it did among ancient Greeks, where all forms of prostitution flourished, and where upper-class prostitutes frequently attained prominence as highly cultured companions of powerful Greek citizens (for detailed discussions of prostitution in history, see Roberts 1992; Bullough and Bullough 1987; Henriques 1962). But despite public admiration and the association with powerful men, even these prostitutes were refused the status of wife and with it, the ultimate affirmation of legitimacy for women in Greek society, thus ensuring that the bad woman-good woman, today more popularly known as the whore-Madonna, dichotomy remains intact.

Once Christianity was firmly established, tolerance for prostitution took on a functionalist character. Religious leaders such as Augustine and St. Thomas Aquinas urged tolerance on the grounds that prostitution, an admittedly troublesome social phenomenon, nonetheless served a basic need, which if left unmet would lead to greater harm than prostitution itself. St. Thomas Aquinas, for example, compared the function of prostitution to that of a sewer in a palace: "If the sewer were removed, the palace would be filled with pollution; similarly if prostitution was removed the world would be filled with sodomy and other crimes" (Bullough and Bullough 1987, p. 120). Although Aquinas presented an argument in support of tolerance for prostitution, he clearly viewed it as an evil, albeit the lesser of two evils. This line of reasoning is as old as prostitution itself and, through the years, has taken a variety of forms (Davis 1937; Schreiber 1986; Sieverts and Schneider 1977; Middendorf 1959; Simmel 1971; Kahmann and Lanzerath 1981; Otis 1985; Roberts 1992).

But tolerance, not infrequently, was replaced by movements to abolish prostitution. For instance, when Lutheran thinking came to prevail in 16th-century Europe, all pretense of tolerance disappeared. Martin Luther advocated the abolition of prostitution on moral grounds. He pointed to the moral reprehensiveness of promiscuity (Otis 1985, p. 41) and depicted prostitutes as emissaries of the devil who were sent to destroy faith (Bullough and Bullough 1978, p. 142). Lutheran sexual morality decreed chastity for all, promiscuity for none.

The history of prostitution provides many more examples of forms of tolerance as well as forms of condemnation. Taken together, historical accounts reveal an interesting pattern. In times of tolerance, prostitution engenders discomfort in society largely because it poses a threat to female chastity and marriage. For example, the Greeks freely tolerated prostitution but went to great lengths to protect the chastity of their wives and daughters. They physically segregated chaste women from other women, and reserved their praise and ascription of legitimacy for mothers and chaste wives. As Roberts (1992) puts it: "The 'respectable' wives and wives-to-be of free Athenian citizens spend almost their entire lives under conditions that can only be described as house-arrest" (p. 14). At other times in history, when the strict segregation of chaste women from prostitutes was not possible, those

who urged tolerance pointed out that far from a threat to married life, prostitution actually should be considered a safeguard to marriage. Prostitution, it was reasoned, allowed men to meet their sexual needs in a monetary exchange which, according to Davis (1937) and Simmel (1971, p. 121), poses no threat to marriage: "Money serves most matter-of-factly and completely for venal pleasure which rejects any continuation of the relationship beyond sensual satisfaction: money is completely detached from the person and puts an end to any further ramifications." Sex with prostitutes, unlike that with nonprostitutes, is therefore devoid of emotional entanglements and is consequently much less of a threat to marriage than sex that entails actual or potential emotional attachment. Hence prostitution, given male promiscuity, serves to enhance the stability of marriage.

In times of condemnation, on the other hand, prostitution embodied moral degeneracy, and the moral outrage against promiscuity became the focus in all efforts to get rid of it. Most of these were based on Christian moral objections to sexual promiscuity, as there were for Luther, for example. Other attempts to get rid of prostitution cited links between sexual promiscuity and threats to public health such as the plague and most recently AIDS. But on closer examination, these public health arguments are revealed as religiously informed, moral condemnations of promiscuity.

It is not until the middle of the 19th century that we find concerns about prostitution linked to either inequality—setting women aside, or chastity—as the norm for female sexuality.

PROSTITUTION AND 19TH-CENTURY FEMINISM

The 19th-century feminist movement in the United States gave women an opportunity to voice their opinions about prostitution. Then, as now, their voices were not in harmony. Some activist women called for the eradication of prostitution by citing the moral degeneracy of male promiscuity, whereas others urged that society give prostitution legitimacy as an expression of female sexuality outside of marriage. Representatives of the former view included eminent feminists Elizabeth Cady Stanton and Susan B. Anthony. In 1871, they successfully fought government proposals to legalize prostitution. Legitimizing prostitution, they argued along with social purity reformers, was nothing less than capitulating "to the morality of Sodom and Gomorrah" (Pleck 1987, pp. 89–90). Social purity reformers viewed male sexuality in general, and promiscuity in particular, as the source of a variety of social ills, among them prostitution. Prostitutes were cast as being among the "innocents," like many wives and children, victims of licentious men (Pleck 1987; Jenness 1993).

Other feminists regarded Stanton and Anthony's victory as a disaster. They felt that suppressing prostitution was a threat to free love and to a woman's ability to exercise sexual and economic choice. Victoria Woodhull opposed Stanton and Anthony's stance on prostitution, both because she favored free sexual expression for women, and because in her view, marriage was potentially worse for women than prostitution.

The marriage law [which] is the most damnable Social Evil Bill—the most consummate outrage on woman—that was ever conceived. Those who are called prostitutes . . . are free women sexually, when compared to the poor wife. They are at liberty, at least to refuse; but she knows no such escape. (Woodhull as cited in Rosen 1982, p. 56).

Free love advocates clearly questioned the traditional view of chastity—the one man-one *pure* woman rule—in the prostitution debate. If the lives of chaste wives are no better, and in some ways conceivably worse than those of promiscuous women, what is the value of chastity? And free love advocates were not alone in questioning marriage as the "naturally" superior social arrangement for women. Engels ([1884] 1942), for example, wrote that bourgeois marriage

turns often enough into crassest prostitution—sometimes of both partners, but far more commonly of the woman, who only differs from the ordinary courtesan in that she does not let out her body on piece-work as a wage-worker, but sells it once and for all into slavery. (p. 63)

This is one of the first times that the institution of marriage was portrayed as potentially less acceptable than prostitution. And with it, chastity, as it is originally defined in the promiscuity-chastity-inequality model, becomes the focus of the attack on prostitution.

All 19th-century feminists agreed, however, that inequality was bad for women, that the social and economic forces that permitted setting women aside for prostitution (i.e., inequality) were indeed a problem. What divided them were different conceptions about the role of prostitution in women's struggle for equality. Social purity feminists like Stanton and Anthony saw prostitution as the embodiment of female *inequality*, and free love feminists like Woodhull saw prostitution as the embodiment of female *equality*. For Stanton and Anthony, the prostitute represented the victim of male sexuality and dominance; for Woodhull she represented an empowered woman who had cast aside the shackles of chastity and marriage. In its fundamental form, this describes the polar positions in the ideological divide among contemporary feminists as well (Tong 1984). And not even today, more than a century later, according to Barbara Meil-Hobson (1987), "neither those who cast the prostitute as victim or those who viewed her as empowered could create an ideological consensus" (p. 223).

THE PROSTITUTION CONTROVERSY AMONG CONTEMPORARY FEMINISTS

Prostitution rarely, if ever, becomes a topic of great social concern in and of itself. Prostitution debates tend to emerge in the context of larger social reform movements, occasioned by the need to correct widespread injustices or other social ills. These reform movements, with their own philosophics and language, shape the framework of the prostitution debate. Luther, for example, discussed prostitution as part of religious reform aimed at eradicating the moral and spiritual decay of medieval Catholicism. He discussed it in the context of morally corrupt sexuality and religious degeneracy. The mid-19th-century feminist debates reflected both the broad civil rights agenda and the large-scale social purity reform efforts underway at that time.

The 20th-century prostitution debate has its origins in the civil rights and feminist movements of the 1960s (Meil-Hobson 1987; Daly and Chesney-Lind 1988). In its fundamental form, the modern framework for discussing prostitution echoes that of the preceding century (Tong 1984; Jenness 1993). Thus contemporary feminist perspectives, philosophies, and language cast prostitution as a civil rights issue involving either the right to free sexual expression or the right to be protected from male sexual exploitation (the male sexual brute in 19th-century language).

While prostitution has almost exclusively become a feminist concern, it is also a debate that today is primarily argued in terms of inequality. Chastity and promiscuity, as originally defined in the prostitution model, have lost much of their relevance as sources of controversy among feminists. Sexual liberation, the availability of divorce, and increased female labor force participation have weakened the cultural significance of both. Women no longer are openly forced into marriage as the sole conveyor of social and economic well-being and, as a consequence, the question of female chastity has lost part of its importance and relevance. Choosing to be sexually promiscuous is no longer the sole prerogative of men. A woman may opt to be promiscuous, albeit within narrower limits than a man, without jeopardizing her value as a woman or her social and economic standing.[3]

Contemporary feminists are in full agreement that the social and economic forces that allow men to set aside women, that is, inequality, are bad for all women and must be changed, but how to bring about these changes continues to be a deeply divisive issue for contemporary feminists[4] (Davis 1993; Meil-Hobson 1987; Tong 1984; Schur 1984; Jenness 1993; Bell 1987; Pheterson 1989; Roberts 1992; Hydra 1988; Alexander 1987). Modern feminists have been unable to resolve questions of this sort: Is it sexual or economic inequality that keeps women from attaining equality? Should protecting women from male sexual subjugation entail restricting women's ability to make choices? Are women victims or entrepreneurs?

The inequality-equality element in the prostitution model has evolved as a highly complex and controversial concept in the prostitution debate among feminists. In fundamental terms, although there are variants of each, feminists divide into two broad groups regarding the role of prostitution in women's fight for equality:

1. Women who stress emancipation from male sexual oppression (prostitute as victim) as the primary equity issue in the prostitution debate—the sexual equality first (SEF) group; and
2. Women who stress freedom of choice (prostitute as worker) as the primary equity issue in the prostitution debate—the free choice first (FCF) group.

Women for whom sexual equality is of primary importance argue that prostitution represents institutionalized sexual inequality and, as such, constitutes prima facie evidence of women's social and economic inequality. Therefore, to bring about equality for women, all instances of institutionalized sexual inequality must be sought out and eradicated. This, they contend, will eliminate the sexual double standard as well as the forced sexual subjugation of women to men.

Those feminists who stress freedom of choice as the primary element in the struggle to overcome women's inequality assert that all steps toward equality must be accompanied by women's freedom to choose even when it involves prostitution. They further maintain that, given the social changes of the last century and a half, choice is eminently relevant in the inequality-equality debate, whether it involves attempts to gain social and economic or sexual equality. Insofar as women today are no longer bound by earlier definitions of promiscuity and marriage no longer represents their only path to social standing and economic security, freedom of choice becomes the central issue in debates about women's equality. Choice in sexual matters is as much as equality issue for women as is choice in the economic, social, or political arenas.

The Sexual Equality First (SEF) Approach

This argument asserts that equality for women depends directly on their ability to eliminate male sexual oppression. Although proponents of this view do not deny the importance of choice in the fight for equality, they contend that until women are equal members of society, free choice is essentially illusionary. To attain equality, and with it, genuine freedom of choice, choices that involve male sexual dominance undermine the pursuit of equality and must therefore be restricted.

Two prominent representatives of this approach are radical feminist theorists Catherine MacKinnon (1987) and Andrea Dworkin (1989). They talk about the power-sex nexus in patriarchal societies, where male power is inextricably linked with female sexual subjugation. Women's equality, their argument asserts, sexual and otherwise, cannot be achieved so long as prostitution, which is predicated on the sexual subordination of women to men, continues to exist.

This argument stresses the interplay between male sexual dominance and gender inequality in the etiology of prostitution—the institutionalized expression of a male sexual double standard predicated on female economic and social inequality. Prostitution, in other words, which institutionalizes women's dependence on men, is intrinsically exploitative, as is evident in its most extreme form—in female sexual slavery (Barry 1981; Cole 1987).

Some European feminists have expressed similar ideas in slightly different words. They describe prostitution as the clearest expression of the relationship between dominant sexuality, male power, and control. "Prostitution," they argue, "is little more than rape in installments" (Hoigard and Finstad 1987; cited in Tübinger Projektgruppe 1989, pp. 100–101). Thus the pursuit of female equality, perhaps even female survival, necessitates getting rid of prostitution.

The Free Choice First (FCF) Approach

For freedom of choice proponents, the freedom to choose must accompany the pursuit of equality in all of its phases. Choice is at all times linked to full and equal personhood. Restricting choice for a woman, for any reason, reduces her status as a full and equal human being.

For feminists of this persuasion, the fight for women's equality depends on the rejection of *all* attempts *by men or women* to forcibly impose their will on women. Taking away a woman's choice by forcibly imposing one's will on her re-

quires that the person whose will prevails has greater power than the person whose choice is preempted. As long as men have the ability to impose their will by overcoming women's resistance, the power balance between men and women is weighted in favor of men. Making choices for others nearly always implies having control over them. This is particularly true when making choices for others that are deemed "for their own good." Making such choices for others assumes inequality. Thus the freedom to choose is an inalienable precondition for equality. For someone to deny a woman choice reflects the very inequalities that women seek to eliminate. Thus "saving a woman from herself" by restricting her choice denies her equality, and with it, her status as a full human being. Thus, *if freely chosen*, prostitution is an expression of women's status as equal, not a symptom of women's subjugation.

From Theory to Practice: Sexual Equality First vs. Free Choice First Arguments

So long as one remains at the level of theory, choosing between these two approaches is less a matter of succumbing to the inescapable logic of one or the other argument than it is a matter of personal preference. Both are persuasive and both are flawed. Feminists from both sides of the prostitution divide have delivered ample documentation of the flaws in each other's arguments. As an observer, one can either believe that true equality for women will not exist so long as women sell their bodies to men or one can believe that true equality will not exist so long as women are prevented from exercising choice, including the choice to sell their bodies to men. The chances of resolving this issue, either logically or empirically, are no greater than the chances of resolving the nature-nurture argument.

Theoretical considerations notwithstanding, prostitution theories, perhaps more than many other theories, today as in the past, have real consequences for the women who work as prostitutes. Throughout history, prostitutes, not theorists, *lived* the results of the prevailing sexual zeitgeist, no matter how injurious and inhumane these consequences were. That this should have been so is perhaps no surprise if one considers that most theorists were men. Even if they were sympathetic to the prostitute's lot, they were still likely entrenched in the prevailing patriarchal social order. That this should continue to be the case after nearly a century and a half of feminism is not as surprising as it is regrettable.

Prostitution Policy and the Sexual Equality First Perspective

For SEF feminists, the existence of prostitution presents a priori proof of women's inequality. To achieve true equality therefore requires that prostitution must cease to exist. Appropriately translated into 20th-century prostitution policy, this means criminalizing prostitution.[5] But endorsing criminalization puts SEF feminists in the untenable position of supporting fundamentally contradictory approaches: As feminists in general, they work to liberate women from sexual restrictions, but as feminists in the prostitution debate, they work to impose restrictions on women's sexuality. In other words, SEF feminists advocate women's sexual freedom unless it occurs in exchange for money. This makes it hard to dismiss critics such as Walkowitz (1982) and Coles and Coles (1978), who suggest that these feminists fail to recognize the difference of their middle-class interests from those of the women involved in prostitution, for whom sex is an economic issue first and an equality issue second, if at all. In other words, giving priority to issues of sexuality over issues of economic survival is a luxury in which many women cannot indulge. When the availability of choosing prostitution as an income-producing activity is eliminated, the economic impact will be felt by some women more so than others. It will further curtail economic options for lower-class women because most prostitutes come from that class (Alexander 1987). And as critics suggest, SEF feminists will not be the ones to suffer economic setbacks from the abolition of prostitution. In response to such criticism, proponents of the SEF perspective, except for a very small minority, are tentative in their support of criminalization and have instead aligned themselves most closely, but not without reservation with what Tong (1984, p. 58) calls laissez-faire decriminalization. This form of decriminalization involves repealing all laws and regulations that impinge on prostitution (City Club of Portland 1984, p. 54). But SEF feminists are uneasy and, at most, are willing to endorse decriminalization as a short-term strategy (Schur 1984, p. 172). In the long run, they insist, the continued existence of prostitution is irreconcilable with women's equality. Such ambivalent attitudes "may explain why no campaign around prostitution has materialized within the American feminist movement" (Meil-Hobson 1987, p. 220).

Prostitution Policy and the Free Choice First Perspective

For FCF proponents, choice is inalienably linked to full and equal personhood. Restricting a woman's choice or right to engage in prostitution denies her equality and with it, her status as a full and equal human being. Prostitution, as an act of sexual self-determination, becomes an expression of women's status as an equal, not a symptom of woman's subjugation. This view is most vigorously supported by feminist sex workers and feminist prostitutes' rights groups, which include Call Off Your Old Tired Ethics (COYOTE) in San Francisco, Hooking is Real Employment (HIRE) in Atlanta, the Canadian Organization for the Rights of Prostitutes (CORP), Projekt Hydra in Germany, and the International Committee for Prostitutes' Rights (ICPR), which was organized during the Second World Whores' Congress in 1986 in Brussels.

For many of the FCF or prostitute rights proponents, prostitution is seen first and foremost as an economic issue. This perspective was colorfully expressed by Margo St. James (1989): "A blow job is better than no job" (p. 21). For these feminists, women's inequality rests as much, if not more, in economic and social inequality as it does in sexual inequality. Mariana Valverde (1987), a feminist freedom of choice proponent, accuses MacKinnon and Dworkin of doing a "disservice to the women's movement by claiming sexuality as the site of women's oppression"

(p. 30). Valverde sees this as a dangerous reduction of the many complex social and economic factors involved in women's inequality. What is needed instead, according to Gail Pheterson (1989), is "the recognition of prostitutes' rights as an emancipation and labor issue rather than as an issue of criminality, immorality or disease" (p. 26).

But critics of this perspective point out that so long as female inequality exists, choice may be a dangerous illusion. Members of the prostitute collective, Women Hurt in Systems of Prostitution Engaged in Revolt (WHISPER), put it this way:

We will no longer whisper furtively about the ways that we have been used and hurt by men, while they brag about, celebrate and profit from our abuse. We also reject the self-appointed "experts" or spokepersons who pimp prostitution as a pleasurable, lucrative, economic alternative that women freely choose, while they decline this "choice" for themselves. (cited by Hobson 1987, p. 221)

Despite their profound disagreements, both groups of feminists proclaim decriminalization as their prostitution policy of choice. While SEF proponents, as we noted above, are ambivalent in their endorsement of decriminalization, FCF advocates give it their unqualified, enthusiastic support. Yet neither ambivalence nor unqualified support have had much of an impact on prostitution policy in the United States. Prostitution, to this day, remains a criminal act in all but a few jurisdictions.

Although prostitution policies are not limited to criminalization and decriminalization, the feminist debate has virtually ignored the other primary approach to prostitution policy: legalization. Neither SEF nor FCF feminists appear to regard legalization as a policy worth considering. This stance seems to be largely based on a general distrust, by both groups, that a male-dominated state system could develop "women centered systems of state licensing" (Tong 1984, p. 58). Instead, most feminists foresee that legalization strategies would lead to the expansion of state control in women's lives. For example, mandatory medical examinations for prostitutes would mean "increased male control of women's

bodies," and as such would do little more than further "highlight the gender and class bias in prostitution policy" (Meil-Hobson 1987, p. 217). Insofar as most legalization policies enable the state to determine where, when, and how prostitution can be pursued, legalization allows the state—a predominantly male institution—to regulate female sexual conduct, and, as such, represents yet another form of male sexual domination for women. Legalization, therefore, presents an obstacle to both sexual equality and free choice.

THE WORKING PROSTITUTE AS CRIMINAL

Criminalizing prostitution has been dismissed by feminists of both perspectives on the grounds that it intensifies female inequality and furthers discrimination against women. In addition to all other inequities, this policy means that prostitutes bear the additional physical, psychological, and economic burdens of being identified as criminals (Tong 1984; Schur 1984; City Club of Portland 1984; Millett 1970; Jenness 1993). An attempt, during the mid-1970s, to reduce the gender inequities in criminal prostitution policies led to the widespread enactment of gender neutral prostitution laws in the United States, but 20 years later arrest patterns still show the vast overrepresentation of women among arrestees. In Portland, Oregon in 1984, 79% of the prostitution arrests involved women (City Club Report, p. 43). St. James (1987, p. 82) reports similar findings, noting that only one third of the men arrested for prostitution were clients, the rest were male prostitutes, which has not brought about much lightening of the burden for women prostitutes.

Prostitution theories, it has become clear, do not address that actual problems experienced by prostitutes, and neither do the strategies that flow from these theories. The fact that, despite feminists' advocacy of decriminalization, prostitution in 1993 continues to be a crime underscores this point. And, for the street prostitute, criminalization translates into a very real, very long, and very painful list of daily victimizations and indignities, to which she can add the further burden of becoming the victim of feminist prostitution ideology. This is a cruel irony, when one considers that much of the motivation, especially among SEF feminists, stems from the wish to protect women from victimization.

The fact that criminalization has prevailed as prostitution policy in the United States could mean that SEF feminists did little more than pay lip service in their endorsement of decriminalization, which undermined the efforts of FCF feminists and, as a consequence, preserved the status quo. It could also mean that longstanding cultural values that are not central to the contemporary feminist debate, such as concerns about the moral reprehensibility of promiscuity, present greater obstacles to change than feminists anticipated.

However, as the central argument in this discussion of prostitution and prostitution-associated controversies maintains, the cultural origins of prostitution have exposed in the past, and will continue to expose, prostitution to a variety of legitimate challenges. Until such time as a woman's sexual conduct is of her choice (equality), and neither detracts from (promiscuity) nor enhances (chastity) her worth, prostitution will continue to exist and it will continue to be fraught with controversy.

But because in the meantime real women live real lives as prostitutes, and some prostitution policies are less harmful to women than others, it is incumbent upon feminists to create a synthesis in the dialectic of the rights to choose and the rights to protections. Both depictions, of the prostitute as a woman empowered and of the prostitute as a woman enslaved, capture but a fraction of the women who work as prostitutes. After 150 years of feminism—of women working with women—we as feminists must work with all women.

NOTES

1. For purposes of this article, prostitution will be defined as an activity wherein women provide the sex and men provide the money—commonly known as female prostitution. The scope of this article is purposely limited to the discussion of female prostitution. Male prostitution, which has its own long-standing history (Roberts 1992) and shares many of the economic, social class, and stigmatization issues with female prosti-

tution, is therefore not reflected in any of the subsequent discussion.

2. Lerner (1986, p. 236) notes that a distinction must be made between equality and emancipation. The former refers to obtaining equality with men and the latter refers to gaining freedom from restrictions. Equality as it is used here leads to emancipation, and inequality to lack thereof. In patriarchal societies, social and economic inequality or dominance is associated with sexual emancipation, whereas the lack of social and economic dominance is associated with sexual restrictions (chastity) or forced sexual activities (prostitution). Thus, in the context of the present discussion, the terms equality and inequality are causally related to emancipation.

3. These changes notwithstanding, comments in discussions about AIDS among the population at large suggest that fears about the sinfulness of promiscuity are far from forgotten.

4. According to Daly and Chesney-Lind (1988, p. 502), some of the divisiveness is related to difficulties with the definition of feminism itself. Feminists confront a variety of difficulties when they try to define feminism. Delmar (1986), for example, offers what she thinks might be a baseline definition, with which she hopes most women might be able to agree. Feminism, she suggests, accepts that women experience discrimination because of their sex, and that due to this discrimination, they have needs that are negated and unsatisfied, and that the satisfaction of these needs requires a radical change. Beyond that, Delmar says, "things immediately become more complicated" (p. 8). And indeed, the contemporary prostitution debate takes place in Delmar's "beyond."

5. There are private nonprofit groups, such as the Portland, Oregon-based Council for Prostitution Alternatives, that provide broad-based support for women who wish to leave prostitution. Despite these efforts, the dominant social response to prostitution remains treating prostitutes as criminals.

REFERENCES

ALEXANDER, PRISCILLA. 1987. "Prostitution: A Difficult Issue for Feminists." Pp. 184–214 in *Sex Work Writing by Women in the Sex Industry*, edited by F. Delacoste and P. Alexander. Pittsburgh, PA: Cleis Press.

BARRY, KATHLEEN. 1981. *Female Sexual Slavery*. New York: Avon.

BELL, LAURIE. 1987. *Good Girls/Bad Girls*. Seattle: Seal Press.

BULLOUGH, VERN and BONNIE BULLOUGH. 1978. *Prostitution: An Illustrated Social History*. New York: Crown.

———. 1987. *Women and Prostitution: A Social History.* Buffalo, NY: Prometheus.

City Club of Portland. 1984. "Report on Adult Prostitution in Portland." Special Issue. *Bulletin* 65(August 31).

COLE, SUSAN G. 1987. "Sexual Politics: Contradictions and Explosions." Pp. 33–36 in *Good Girls/Bad Girls,* edited by L. Bell. Seattle: Seal Press.

COLES, ROBERT and JANE HALLOWELL COLES. 1978. *Women of Crisis.* New York: Dell.

DALY, KATHLEEN and MEDA CHESNEY-LIND. 1988. "Feminism and Criminology." *Justice Quarterly* 5:497–98.

DAVIS, KINGSLEY. 1937. "The Sociology of Prostitution." *American Sociological Review* 2:746–55.

DAVIS, NANETTE J. 1993. *Prostitution: An International Handbook on Trends, Problems, and Policies.* Westport, CT: Greenwood.

DELMAR, ROSALIND. 1986. "What Is Feminism?" Pp. 8–33 in *What is Feminism?* edited by J. Mitchell and A. Oakley. New York: Pantheon.

DWORKIN, ANDREA. 1989. *Pornography.* New York: Dutton.

ENGELS, FRIEDERICH. [1884] 1942. *The Origin of the Family, Private Property, and the State.* New York: International.

HENRIQUES, FERNANDO. 1962. *Prostitution and Society.* New York: Grove Press.

HOIGARD, CECILIE and LIV FINSTAD. 1987. *Seitenstrassen. Geld, Macht und Liebe oder der Mythos von der Prostitution.* Hamburg: Reinbeck.

Hydra, Prostituiertenprojekt. 1988. *Beruf Hure.* Hamburg: Verlag am Galgenberg.

JENNESS, VALERIE. 1993. *Making It Work: The Prostitutes' Rights Movement in Perspective.* New York: de Gruyter.

KAHMANN, JURGEN and HUBERT LANZERATH. 1981. *Weibliche Prostitution in Hamburg.* Heidelberg: Kriminalistik.

LERNER, GERDA. 1986. *The Creation of Patriarchy.* New York: Oxford University Press.

MACKINNON, CATHERINE A. 1987. *Feminism Unmodified: Discourses on Life and Law.* Cambridge, MA: Harvard University Press.

MEIL-HOBSON, BARBARA. 1987. *Uneasy Virtue.* New York: Basic Books

MIDDENDORF, D. 1959. "Die Sittlichkeitsdelikte in historischer und internationaler Sicht." In *Bekampfung der Sittlichkeitsdelikte.* Wiesbaden: Bundeskriminalamt.

MILLETT, KATE. 1970. *Sexual Politics.* Garden City, NY: Doubleday.

OTIS, LEAH. 1985. *Prostitution in Medieval Society.* Chicago: University of Chicago Press.

PHETERSON, GAIL. 1989. *A Vindication of the Rights of Whores.* Seattle: Seal Press.

PLECK, ELIZABETH. 1987. *Domestic Tyranny.* New York: Oxford University Press.

ROBERTS, NICKIE. 1992. *Whores in History: Prostitution in Western Society.* London: HarperCollins.

ROSEN, RUTH. 1982. *The Lost Sisterhood: Prostitution in America, 1900–1918.* Baltimore: Johns Hopkins University Press.

ST. JAMES, MARGO. 1987. "The Reclamation of Whores." Pp. 81–87 in *Good Girls/Bad Girls,* edited by L. Bell. Seattle: Seal Press.

SCHREIBER, MANFRED. 1986. "Prostitution und Kriminalpolitik." Unpublished lecture, University of Munich.

SCHUR, EDWIN M. 1984. *Labeling Women Deviant: Gender, Stigma, and Social Control.* Philadelphia: Temple University Press.

SIEVERTS, RUDOLPH and HANS SCHNEIDER. 1977. *Handwörterbuch der Kriminologie.* Berlin: de Gruyter.

SIMMEL, GEORG. 1971. "Prostitution." Pp. 121–25 in *On Individuality and Social Forms,* edited by D. E. Levine. Chicago: University of Chicago Press.

TONG, ROSEMARY. 1984. *Women, Sex, and the Law.* Totowa, NJ: Rowman and Allanheld.

Tubinger Projektgruppe Fraunhandel. 1989. *Frauenhandel in Deutschland.* Bonn: J.H.W. Dietz.

VALVERDE, MARIANA. 1987. "Too Much Heat, Not Enough Light." Pp. 27–33 in *Good Girls/Bad Girls,* edited by L. Bell. Seattle: Seal Press.

WALKOWITZ, JUDITH. 1982. "Male Vice and Feminist Virtue: Feminism and the Politics of Prostitution in Nineteenth Century Britain." *History Workshop* 13:79–83.

APPEARANCE AND DELINQUENCY
A RESEARCH NOTE*

Jill Leslie Rosenbaum and Meda Chesney-Lind

Women are judged by culturally derived standards of attractiveness. These culturally created standards affect women in all walks of life, including it appears, the way they are treated by the criminal justice system. Research has shown that perception of physical appearance can have a significant impact on an individual's success in a variety of endeavors. These endeavors include dating opportunities (Crause and Mehrabian 1977; Stretch and Figley 1980; Walster, Aronson, Abrahams, and Rottman 1966), the initiation of relationships (Murstein and Christy 1976; Price and Vandenberg 1979; White 1980), teachers' evaluations of students (Clifford and Walster 1973; Dion 1973), and corporate success (Heilman and Stopeck 1985; Heilman and Sarawatari 1979).

The role of appearance in judgments of criminal responsibility and the punishment of such behavior have also been the focus of a variety of psychological studies (Efran 1974; Sigall and Ostrove 1975; Stewart 1980). These studies consistently indicate that physical attractiveness influences judgments of wrongdoing. Dion (1973) found that adult judgments of children's transgressions were affected by the attractiveness of the child. Transgressions, both mild and severe, were perceived to be less undesirable when committed by an attractive child than an unattractive child. Furthermore, subjects were less likely to attribute chronic antisocial behavior to attractive than to unattractive children.

The work of Sigall and Ostrove (1975) suggests that the sentences given to offenders are often conditioned by the appearance of the offender. Attractive female offenders, whose offense was not appearance-related (burglary),

received greater leniency than unattractive offenders. However, when the offense was attractiveness-related (swindle), attractive offenders received harsher sentences than their unattractive counterparts. These findings are consistent with those of Efran (1974), whose work has shown that attractive defendants are much less likely to be found guilty than unattractive defendants. This becomes especially pronounced when males are judging the culpability of females. Sigall and Ostrove (1975) and Efran (1974) also indicate that when a female offender is seen as using her attractiveness to assist in the commission of a crime, attractive defendants were more likely to be found guilty.

Studies of appearance also demonstrate that society has higher expectations for attractive individuals; some of these expectations pertain exclusively to women. For instance, attractive women are assumed to be more feminine and have a more socially desirable personality, and as a result, they are assumed to have greater overall happiness in their personal, social, and professional lives (Dion, Berscheid, and Walster 1973). It is also assumed that they are less likely to remain single, more likely to marry earlier, be better spouses, and be better sexual partners as well.

Although the lives of attractive women are assumed to be far superior to those of less attractive women, some believe that attractive women have less integrity, and thus managerial opportunities for them may be hindered. In fact, Heilman and Sarawatari (1979) concluded that women with more masculine characteristics are believed to have greater ability than women with feminine characteristics. Thus, although attractive women are thought to be more feminine, they are also thought to be less well-suited for nontraditional female roles.

Finally, Emerson (1969) noted that judges and other juvenile court personnel often expressed considerable interest in the appearance of girls appearing before the court he observed. He noted a judge's interest in whether runaway girls were "clean" after having been away from home for more than a day or two; the assumption was that if they were clean and/or heavily made up, they might be engaging in prostitution (Emerson 1969, p. 112). Emerson observed that appearance was taken as an indication of sexual morality or immorality. Numerous notations on the sexual and moral activities of girls, but not of boys, were also noted by Hancock (1981) in her study of police records in Victoria, Australia.

Attractiveness can be somewhat of a double-edged sword. The situation becomes all the more complex for girls and women who find their way into the criminal justice system for offenses either directly or indirectly related to their sexuality and sexual deportment (Schlossman and Wallach 1978; Rafter 1990). This pattern has been especially marked in the case of young women coming into the juvenile justice system.

Since the establishment of the first juvenile court, there has been ongoing interest by judges and other court workers in the sexual activity of girls. In the early days of the court (1899–1920), there was a clear bias against girls deemed sexually active and a harsh official response to their misbehavior. Virtually all of the girls who appeared before the first juvenile courts were charged with immorality or waywardness (Chesney-Lind 1971; Schlossman and Wallach 1978; Shelden 1981; Rafter 1990), and the response of the courts to this noncriminal behavior frequently was incarceration. For example, between 1899–1909 in Chicago (where the first family court was founded), one-half of the female delinquents, but only one-fifth of the male delinquents, were sent to reformatories. In Milwaukee, twice as many girls as boys were committed to training schools (Schlossman and Wallach 1978, p. 72), and in Memphis, females were twice as likely as males to be committed to training schools (Shelden 1981, p. 70).

In Honolulu during 1929–1930, over half of the girls referred to court were charged with immorality, which meant evidence (or inferences drawn) of sexual intercourse. In addition, another 30% were charged with waywardness. Evidence of immorality was vigorously pursued both by arresting officers and social workers through lengthy questioning of the girl and, if possible, males with whom she was suspected of having sex. Other evidence of exposure was provided by gynecological examinations, which were routinely ordered. Doctors, who understood the purpose of such examinations, would routinely note the condition of the hymen: "admits intercourse-hymen ruptured," "no laceration," and "hymen ruptured" were typical of their notations. Girls during this period were also twice as likely as boys to be detained, and they remained in detention five times as long on the average as their male counterparts. They were also nearly three times more likely to be sentenced to training schools (Chesney-Lind 1971) where well into the 1950s, they continued to be half of those committed in Honolulu (Chesney-Lind 1973).

Not surprisingly, a large number of reformatories and training schools for girls were established during this period as places of "rescue and reform." For example, Schlossman and Wallach (1978, p. 70) note that 23 facilities were opened between 1919 and 1920. By contrast, an average of 5 reformatories per decade were opened between 1850 and 1910. The opening of these institutions did much to set the tone of the official response to female delinquency. Obsessed with precocious female sexuality, the institutions set about to isolate females from all contact with males. They were housed in bucolic settings, where they were held until they were of marriageable age and were kept occupied with domestic pursuits during their sometimes lengthy incarceration.

The links between these attitudes and those of juvenile courts some decades later are, of course, arguable, but a clear holdover from this early obsession with girls' moral behavior is the overrepresentation of girls in court populations charged with status offenses (Chesney-Lind and Shelden 1992). Related to this pattern is the large number of girls who found their way into training schools for these offenses.

National statistics reflect the official enthusiasm for the incarceration of girls during the early part of this century; their share of the population of juvenile correctional facilities increased from

1880 (when girls were 19% of the population) to 1923 (when girls were 28%). By 1950, girls had climbed to 34% of the total and in 1960 they were still 27% of those in correctional facilities. By 1980, this pattern appeared to be reversed and girls were again 19% of those in correctional facilities (Calahan 1986, p. 130) and in 1989, girls accounted for 11.9% of those held in public detention centers and training schools (Allen-Hagen 1991, p. 4).

The decline in incarceration of juvenile females in public facilities run by the juvenile justice system is directly linked to an intense debate on the issue of the institutionalization of young people, especially youth charged with noncriminal status offenses (e.g., running away from home, being incorrigible, truant, or in danger of leading a lewd and lascivious lifestyle). In particular, the Juvenile Justice and Delinquency Prevention Act (JJDPA) of 1974 stressed the need to divert and deinstitutionalize youth charged with status offenses and provided states with a number of incentives to achieve this goal.

These figures, then, represent some very good news to those concerned with the court's sexual policing of girls. Prior to the passage of the JJDPA of 1974, nearly three quarters (71%) of the girls and 23% of the boys in the nation's training schools were incarcerated for status offenses (Schwartz, Stekette, and Schneider 1990). Between 1974 and 1979, the number of girls admitted to public detention facilities and training schools dropped by 40%. Since then, however, the deinstitutionalization trend has slowed in some areas of the country, particularly at the detention level. Between 1979 and 1989, for example, the number of girls held in these same public facilities actually increased by 10% (Jamieson and Flanagan 1987; Flanagan and McGarrell 1986; Allen-Hagen 1991). These figures have also been accompanied by sharp increases in the last decade (1981–1990) of arrests of girls for running away (up 19%) and curfew violation (up 36.6%). Again, these figures represent a shift away from the decline in arrests of youth for status offenses that was seen in the late 1970s.

Critical to any understanding of the dynamics of gender bias in the juvenile justice system, then, is an appreciation of the gendered nature of delinquency, and particularly status offenses. It should be understood that status offenses have also served as "buffer charges" for the court's historic, but now implicit interest in monitoring girls' sexual activities and their obedience to parental authority (Gold 1971, p. 571). In essence, modern status offense charges mask the court's historic interest in girls' propriety and obedience to parental authority (Chesney-Lind and Shelden 1991).

Because of the recent but eroding success of the JJDPA of 1974, it is perhaps essential to review the dynamics of sexism within the juvenile justice system immediately prior to the passage of this act. The study reported here, although relatively modest, documents one aspect of the sexism that girls encountered as they entered institutions in the 1960s: the interest of criminal justice professionals in the physical appearance of girls.

DATA AND METHODS

This analysis is based on the records of 159 women who, as juveniles, were committed to the California Youth Authority (CYA) during the 1960s. Records were requested on all 240 of the girls who were sentenced to the CYA between 1961 and 1965 from San Francisco and the Sacramento Valley. There were 59 cases unavailable because the juvenile records had been purged and another 22 cases could not be located. For the 159 cases where data was available, the records included the complete CYA files containing all comments/reports regarding the ward and the case by CYA intake workers, counselors, teachers, living unit personnel, chaplains, social workers, and psychologists (for more information regarding data collection, see Warren and Rosenbaum 1986).

The racial composition of these 159 cases was 51% Caucasian, 30% African American, 9% Latino, and the remaining 10% were Asian or Native American. Two-thirds of the girls had been committed to the CYA for status offenses and, more specifically, 49% were charged with running away from home, 28% for being "beyond control," 12% for "being in danger of a lewd and lascivious lifestyle," 7% for truancy, and 4% curfew. To say that these girls were committed for status offenses actually under-states the role of status offenses in their delinquency records; this group of girls committed 698 offenses prior to their commitment to the CYA. The average number of arrests was six, and over 90% of these were status offenses. There were no racial differences observed in the distribution of these offenses.

Each file was examined by two independent coders who coded data on the type of offenses committed prior to CYA commitment, the gender of the social worker who did the evaluation of the ward, whether mention was made of the ward's appearance, and if so, the description given of the girl's appearance.[1] Reliability among the coders was over 96%. Because all of the girls in the sample were part of an experimental program and were randomly assigned to treatment programs, the length of their incarceration was not coded.

FINDINGS

Female case workers did intake evaluations on 29% (46) of the 159 cases, whereas males were responsible for 71% (113) of them. When female CYA personnel conducted the intake evaluation, there was no mention of physical appearance in any of the 46 cases for which they were responsible. This was not the case when males performed the evaluation; appearance was mentioned in 63% (75) of the cases.

A variety of physical descriptions were recorded for the 75 wards whose appearance was mentioned in the files. These show male staff concern with the physical maturity of the girls, as well as some evidence of racial stereotyping; indeed, of those where evaluative judgments about appearance were made, 60% were made about minority group females. Moreover, those viewing these young women of color adhered to "representations of race" (hooks 1992) that negate any beauty that does not conform to White standards of appearance, while celebrating those images that mimic White appearance. Take, for example, the following comments:

S is a tall pretty Mexican girl whose appearance belies her Mexican heritage.

The ward is a very attractive, light complexioned Negro girl.

She is an attractive, fair skinned girl whose light brown hair is dyed a yellowish-blond color.

The ward is a fairly attractive dark-skinned girl. She shows some rather mild Negroid features, but these are not very pronounced and would not be noticeable unless attention were called to them.

From the descriptions of the girls' appearance, four general categories emerged: attractive, unattractive, plain/wholesome, and "well-built."[2] Of the wards whose appearance was mentioned, 26% (19) were described as attractive (e.g., "the ward is an attractive, physically mature 13-year-old"), whereas 38% (27) were described as unattractive (e.g., "Her appearance is rather uninteresting and unattractive"); 19% as plain or wholesome; and 17% (14) were described as well-built (see Figure 1).

Differences emerged when the relationship between the type of offense and the mention of appearance in the intake evaluations was examined. About 50% (56) of the girls who had been evaluated by a male had at least one immorality charge against them. When females who had been charged with immorality offenses (being in danger of leading a lewd and lascivious life and prostitution) were compared with those who had

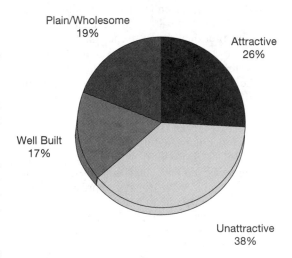

FIGURE 1 Type of Description Given

no such charge, differences in the mention of appearance became especially pronounced. For instance, for those charged with one or more counts of immorality, a physical description was present in 93% (55) of the cases. However, when no immorality charges were present, a physical description was included in only 37% (20) of the cases (see Table 1). Looking at the data from another perspective, in cases where no description of the girl's appearance was present, 89% (34) had no charges of immorality. As indicated in Table 1, a significant relationship ($X^2 = 37.5$) was found between having at least one immorality charge and having mention made of the girl's appearance in her file.

Differences also existed with respect to the type of offenses present and the description given. All of the girls who were described as attractive and all of the girls who were described as well-built had been charged with at least one immorality offense. However, only 26% of the girls described as plain/wholesome and 34% of those described as unattractive had similar charges against them. Although these numbers are small, the magnitude of the difference is clearly significant.

MORE RECENT DATA

To assess whether or not appearance remains an issue today, more recent data from the CYA and also Hawaii were examined. In the process of collecting data from the CYA files of all girls who were wards of the CYA in 1990, close attention was paid to any mention of the girl's appearance. Similar attention was paid in a separate examination of the case files of all boys and girls who were confined in the Hawaii Youth Correctional Facility in 1989.

TABLE 1 Appearance by Presence of Immorality Charges

	Appearance Described	No Description Included	
Immorality charges	93(55)	7(4)	100(59)
No immorality charges	37(20)	63(34)	100(54)

XX^2 = 37.4, 1 *df*, significance = .000.

Although there were 214 girls who were wards of the CYA in 1990, comments regarding appearance were found in only eight files. All, except one who was described as slovenly and unattractive, were simply described as attractive. Five of the eight had arrests for violent crime, the other three had long records for property and drug offenses. Although the vast majority of the girls' arrests during the 1960s were for status offenses, only 4% of their 1990 counterparts' arrests were for status offenses.

In Hawaii, however, comments such as the following were still found in girls' files in 1990:

[Minor is] highly sexual and very seductive . . . she is thought to be sexually active.

[Minor's] neck was loaded with hickies.

Other comments found in girls' files in Hawaii concerned when and where they had been arrested for curfew violations. One file, for example, noted that these arrests "did occur in the early morning hours" or that "[minor] was arrested by the police on four occasions, two while on Hotel Street and twice while in Waikiki. [Minor] associates with a suspected pimp and prostitute and it is suspected that she is engaging in prostitution" (Saiki 1990, pp. 49–50). This same research effort noted that no such comments appeared in boys' files and that a third of the girls held in training schools were being held solely for "probation violation," which is a mechanism for continuing to incarcerate status offenders (Saiki 1990, p. 23). The Hawaii study found that roughly half of the girls incarcerated during spring 1990 were "bootstrapped" status offenders (Costello and Worthington 1991) and even for those girls who had committed criminal offenses, their offenses were far less serious than the boys and "the bulk of their juvenile offenses consisted of status offenses" (Saiki 1990, p. 48).

DISCUSSION

The emphasis on physical appearance found in this small study, and the link between this interest in girls' appearance and their noncriminal delinquent behavior is more important than it might first seem. In essence, these observations provide a window into the worldview of the keepers of young women during the years prior to the passage of the JJDPA of 1974; sadly, they may also reflect a bias that remains in the states that have been resistant to the deinstitutionalization efforts signaled by the passage of that act. Like earlier studies, which found a large number of girls in institutions subjected to physical examinations to determine if they were virgins (see Chesney-Lind and Shelden 1992), interest in the physical appearance of girls, and particularly their physical maturity, indicates substantial interest in the sexual behavior of girls and illuminates another important dimension of the sexual policing of girls (Cain 1989).

Particularly troubling are the comments which indicate a presumed association between "beauty," specifically male Caucasian standards of beauty, and sexual behavior. Certainly the fact that these girls were incarcerated for noncriminal offenses indicates the seriousness with which the criminal justice system viewed their transgressions. In short, these data provide some support for the notion, suggested by Sigall and Ostrove (1975), as well as that by Efran (1974), that judges, social workers, and other criminal justice professionals (particularly if they are male) may look upon attractive girls who engage in sexual "immorality" more harshly. They may also overlook some of the same behaviors in less attractive girls.

Such a fascination with appearance is also at odds with the literature on street prostitutes. These studies indicate that the pace and pressure of this life does not produce "attractive" young women, but instead tends to take a physical toll on the girls engaged in the behavior (Weisberg 1985, p. 116). Indeed, some descriptions of prostitutes describe them as unattractive, overweight, with poor complexions and bad teeth (Winick and Kinsie 1972, p. 35).

The remarks found in the files, which were made by male intake workers, suggest a fascination with the appearance of the girls who were charged with immorality. Clearly there was considerable concern with their physical maturity and physical attraction. The comments regarding the girls' appearance suggest that status offenses may have functioned as buffer charges for suspected sexual behavior. Although it appears that at least in California, where girls are no longer incarcerated for noncriminal offenses, this no longer seems to be a problem, national data suggest that in some states, like Hawaii, the detention and incarceration of girls for noncriminal status offenses persists; thus the concerns raised by this article may, sadly, not be of simply historic interest.

NOTES

1. Nowhere on any of the CYA forms was there any particular place for a physical description of the ward. Comments were found throughout the narratives by the CYA personnel who became involved with the case. As far as we can tell, the issue of appearance was never discussed with regard to policy. It seemed to be merely an issue for the intake personnel.

2. These categories are broad and somewhat evasive; however, they were the factors that emerged during this analysis. It is important to remember that attractiveness is in the eye of the beholder and we, as researchers, are merely reporting the subjective assessments that we found.

REFERENCES

ALLEN-HAGEN, BARBARA. 1991. *Children in Custody 1989.* Washington, DC: Bureau of Justice Statistics.

CAIN, MAUREEN. 1989. *Growing Up Good: Policing the Behavior of Girls in Europe.* London: Sage.

CALAHAN, M. W. 1986. *Historical Corrections Statistics in the United States 1950–1984.* Washington, DC: U.S. Department of Justice.

CHESNEY-LIND, MEDA. 1971. *Female Juvenile Delinquency in Hawaii.* Master's thesis, University of Hawaii at Manoa.

———. 1973. Judicial enforcement of the female sex role. *Issues in Criminology* 8:51–70.

CHESNEY-LIND, MEDA and RANDALL SHELDEN. 1992. *Girls, Delinquency, and the Juvenile Justice System.* Pacific Grove, CA: Brooks/Cole.

CLIFFORD, MARK and ELAINE WALSTER. 1973. "The Effect of Physical Attractiveness on Teacher Expectations." *Sociology of Education* 46:248–58.

COSTELLO, J. C. and N. L. WORTHINGTON. 1991. Incarcerating status offenders: Attempts to circumvent the Juvenile Justice and Delinquency Prevention Act. *Harvard Civil Rights-Civil Liberties Law Review* 16:41–81.

CRAUSE, BRYANT B. and ALBERT MEHRABIAN. 1977. "Affiliation of Opposite-Sexed Strangers." *Journal of Research in Personality* 11:38–47.

DION, KAREN. 1973. "Physical Attractiveness and Evaluation of Children's Transgressions." *Journal of Personality and Social Psychology* 24:207–18.

DION, KAREN, ELLEN BERSCHEID, and ELAINE WALSTER. 1973. "What Is Beautiful Is Good." *Journal of Personality and Social Psychology* 24:285–90.

EFRAN, MICHAEL. 1974. "The Effect of Physical Appearance on the Judgement of Guilt, Interpersonal Attraction, and Severity of Recommended Punishment." *Journal of Experimental Research in Personality* 8:45–54.

EMERSON, ROBERT. 1969. *Judging Delinquents.* Chicago: Aldine.

FLANAGAN, TIMOTHY J. and EDMUND F. McGARRELL, eds. 1986. *Sourcebook of Criminal Justice Statistics—1985.* Washington, DC: U.S. Department of Justice.

GOLD, STEVEN. 1971. "Equal Protection for Girls in Need of Supervision in New York State." *New York Law Forum* 17:570–91.

HANCOCK, L. 1981. "The Myth That Females Are Treated More Leniently Than Males in the Juvenile Justice System." *Australian and New Zealand Journal of Sociology* 16:4–14.

HEILMAN, MADELINE and LOIS SARAWATARI. 1979. "When Beauty Is Beastly: The Effects of Appearance and Sex on Evaluations of Job Applicants for Managerial and Nonmanagerial Jobs." *Organizational Behavior and Human Performance* 23: 360–72.

HEILMAN, MADELINE and MELANIE STOPECK. 1985. "Attractiveness and Corporate Success: Different Causal Attributions for Males and Females." *Journal of Applied Psychology* 70:379–88.

HOOKS, BELL. 1992. *Black Looks.* Boston: South End Press.

JAMIESON, KATHERINE M. and TIMOTHY FLANAGAN, eds. 1987. *Sourcebook of Criminal Justice Statistics—1986.* Washington, DC: U.S. Department of Justice, Bureau of Justice Statistics.

MURSTEIN, B. and P. CHRISTY. 1976. "Physical Attractiveness and Marriage Adjustment in Middle Aged Couples." *Journal of Personality and Social Psychology* 34:537–42.

PRICE, RICHARD and STEVEN VANDENBERG. 1979. "Matching for Physical Attractiveness in Married Couples." *Personality and Social Psychology Bulletin* 5:398–99.

RAFTER, NICOLE. 1990. *Partial Justice: Women, Prisons and Social Control.* New Brunswick, NJ: Transaction Books.

SAIKI, SCOTT. 1990. "Girls, Double Standards and Status Offenses in Hawaii's Juvenile Court." Unpublished paper. William Richardson School of Law, University of Hawaii.

SCHLOSSMAN, STEVE and STEPHANIE WALLACH. 1978. "The Crime of Precocious Sexuality: Female Delinquency in the Progressive Era." *Harvard Educational Review* 48:65–94.

SCHWARTZ, IRA M., M. STEKETTE, and V. SCHNEIDER. 1990. "Federal Juvenile Justice Policy and the Incarceration of Girls." *Crime & Delinquency* 36:503–20.

SHELDEN, RANDALL. 1981. "Sex Discrimination in the Juvenile Justice System: Memphis, Tennessee, 1900–1971." In *Comparing Male and Female Offenders,* edited by M. Q. Warren. Beverly Hills, CA: Sage.

SIGALL, HAROLD and NANCY OSTROVE. 1975. "Beautiful But Dangerous: Effects of Offender Attractiveness and Nature of Crime on Juridic Judgement." *Journal of Personality and Social Psychology* 31:410–14.

STEWART, JOHN. 1980. "Defendant's Attraction as a Factor in the Outcome of Criminal Trials: An Observational Study." *Journal of Applied Social Psychology* 10:348–61.

STRETCH, RICHARD and CHARLES FIGLEY. 1980. "Beauty and the Beast: Predictions of Interpersonal Attraction in a Dating Experiment." *Psychology, a Quarterly Journal of Human Behavior* 17:34–43.

WALSTER, ELAINE, E. ARONSON, D. ABRAHAMS, and L. ROTTMAN. 1966. "Importance of Physical Attractiveness in Dating Behavior." *Journal of Personality and Social Psychology* 4:508–16.

WARREN, MARGUERITE Q. and JILL ROSENBAUM. 1986. "Criminal Careers of Female Offenders." *Criminal Justice and Behavior* 13:393–418.

WEISBERG, D. KELLY. 1985. *Children of the Night: A Study of Adolescent Prostitution.* Lexington, MA: Lexington Books.

WHITE, GREGORY. 1980. "Physical Attractiveness and Courtship Progress." *Journal of Personality and Social Psychology* 39:660–68.

WINICK, CHARLES and PAUL M. KINSIE. 1972. *The Lively Commerce.* New York: Signet.

Identity, Strategy, and Feminist Politics
Clemency for Battered Women Who Kill*

Patricia Gagné**

The feminist battered women's movement has been widely credited with creating public awareness of wife abuse as a social problem, establishing safe places for victims of intimate violence, working to eliminate gender bias in the law, and creating equal protection for battered women (Davis 1988; Dobash and Dobash 1992; Schechter 1982; Tierney 1982). Most studies of the battered women's movement of the 1970s and 1980s were grounded in resource mobilization theory (see McCarthy and Zald 1973, 1977). While the early developments in resource mobilization focused on availability of resources and the ability of activists to organize them, a subsequent strand focused on the social and political context as an opportunity for action (Jenkins 1983). Most analyses of the battered women's movement have taken the first approach, focusing on shelters as social movement organizations (but see Schechter 1982). As a result of the focus on shelters, as opposed to an examination of activists agitating for change in other arenas, analysts have argued that the movement has been, or is in danger of being, coopted (Ferraro 1983; Johnson 1981; Schechter 1982).[1]

Resource mobilization theory is grounded in theories of liberal democracy, which narrowly define politics as separate from civic society, personal life, and social movements (Acklesberg 1988; Ferree 1992). With its narrow and rigidly defined conceptualization of social movements, resource mobilization theory is problematic in the examination of women's movements, primarily because it is based upon a white, middle class, masculine (or liberal democratic) tradition of personal and civic life and participation in politics (Ferree 1992). That is, it assumes that activists are people outside of institutionalized positions of authority. It overlooks the liberal feminist goal of placing women in key political positions and other careers where they will work to create social change, excludes the radical feminist concept that the personal is political, and obviates an examination of acts of "everyday resistance" (Collins 1990).

Feminists have challenged the tenet that institutionalized politics are separable from personal life or activism (Acklesberg 1988; Alonso 1992; Cassell 1977; Elshtain 1981; Evans 1979; Kauffman 1989; Morgen and Bookman 1988; Mouffe 1992). Similarly, post-modern, critical, feminist, and new social movement theorists have argued that a merging of political and non-political spheres of life has taken place in post-industrial societies (Acklesberg 1988; Alonso 1992; Bernstein 1985; Elshtain 1981; Foucault 1979; Habermas 1985; Melucci 1980; Morgen and Bookman 1988; Mouffe 1992; Offe 1985; Taylor and Whittier 1992; Touraine 1985). Therefore, an examination of the feminist battered women's movement that is based upon liberal democratic assumptions will overlook the activism that has taken place in non-traditional arenas (such as the work place), institutional politics, or personal relationships and will obscure examinations of activists' efforts to create a political and cultural context conducive to movement success.

Drawing on a case study of the 1990 decision by then Ohio Governor Richard Celeste to grant

*©1996 by the Society for the Study of Social Problems. Reprinted from *Social Problems*, 43:1 (February 1996), pp. 77–93 by permission of the author and publisher.

**My thanks to Angela Browne, Ann Goetting, J. Craig Jenkins, Mark Richard, Joseph Scott, Verta Taylor, Richard Tewksbury, and three anonymous reviewers for their comments on this work. This research was funded by a grant from the Elizabeth Gee Fund for Research on Women from the Center for Women's Studies and a Research Intense Summer Fellowship from the Department of Sociology, both at The Ohio State University, and by a Project Completion Grant from the College of Arts and Sciences at the University of Louisville. Correspondence: Department of Sociology, University of Louisville, Louisville, KY 40292.

clemency to 26 women who were incarcerated for killing or assaulting abusive intimate partners or stepfathers, this paper examines the strategies and tactics used by feminists in the battered women's movement to lay the groundwork for and establish a clemency review process. I have chosen to focus on the Ohio movement for the following reasons: It was the first multiple clemency decision of its type; it was directly influenced by feminists in the women's and battered women's movements; to date, it has resulted in the largest number of women being released from prison at one time; and finally, it appears to have set a precedent that was followed by similar decisions by three other governors, and by feminist organizing efforts in 17 other states. By examining this event in light of social movement and political theories that challenge the assumptions of liberal democratic theories, my goals are to: (1) document an historical event that might otherwise be lost; (2) challenge the notion that the battered women's movement was coopted in the 1980s; (3) identify movement tactics that worked in an environment relatively conducive to change; (4) hypothesize about strategies and tactics that might work in a less hospitable era; and (5) to conceptually expand our understanding of what constitutes activism.

METHODS

The data for this article come from 45 intensive, semi-structured, tape recorded interviews with members of the Ohio battered women's movement and key informants in state government.[2] I used a snowball sampling method, beginning with First Lady Dagmar Celeste, who was involved in the women's and battered women's movements from the 1960s and who was influential in promoting women's prison reform and the clemency review. In addition to Dagmar Celeste, my sample included members of her staff, many of the founders of the battered women's movement, the governor, cabinet members, aides to the governor and cabinet, employees of the Ohio Department of Rehabilitation and Correction, members of a statewide network of direct service providers, former members of three support groups for incarcerated battered women, defense

attorneys, judges, feminist and pro-feminist Ohio legislators, and 12 of the 26 women who were granted clemency.[3] I transcribed all of the interviews verbatim.

All of the never-incarcerated activists and authorities in my sample were middle-class professionals, and all but three, two women and one man, were white. Of the clemency recipients I interviewed, seven were African American and five were white.[4] Seven of them worked in blue or pink collar jobs, two received Aid to Families with Dependent Children, and three collected Supplemental Security Income. Although many never-incarcerated activists discussed efforts to diversify the movement, my sample suggests that in Ohio they were predominately white and middle class, working to expand the movement to include an ethnically and socioeconomically diverse population.

I analyzed the data using principles of analytic induction and grounded theory (Charmaz 1983; Strauss and Corbin 1990) and triangulated interview data with archival materials.[5] I have also drawn upon an extensive collection of newspaper and magazine articles from Ohio and the national press and video recorded television talk shows and news magazines on which the women who received clemency appeared.

HISTORICAL OVERVIEW OF THE MOVEMENT

The Ohio battered women's movement emerged out of the larger women's movement, with early activism concentrated in Columbus and Cleveland. The roots of the later clemency movement were based predominately in Cleveland, with community ties later expanding throughout the state. In Cleveland the movement began in 1974 with women from a wide array of feminist organizations uniting through an organization they called Women Together to confront the issue of woman abuse.[6] Similar to national trends (Schechter 1982), the Ohio movement incorporated diverse tactics. While working to change the legal system, these feminists established organizations that would provide temporary refuge from violence, run exclusively by and for women. In 1975 Women Together founded a hotline, and in

December 1976 it opened the first shelter for battered women in the State of Ohio in the home of then Lieutenant Governor Richard Celeste. When it was founded, the shelter was committed to social change, with services based on feminist principles of self-help and empowerment.

Despite efforts to provide them with alternatives, women frequently and repeatedly returned to violent and abusive partners. By the late 1970s, feminists at Women Together, like those doing similar work throughout the United States, began to understand that battered women experience a range of post-traumatic psychological responses to abuse, similar to those of victims of other types of violence or trauma (see Browne 1993). Subsequently, the psychological response to battered women became reified as "battered woman syndrome," a subcategory of post-traumatic stress disorder (Walker 1984). Interestingly, in the course of trying to create social change, the focus perceptibly shifted to trying to explain why battered women fail to leave abusive partners. In trying to address this question, a debate ensued among feminists and mental health workers as to the potential merits and problems of categorizing as a mental disorder what many feminists labeled a *normal* response to fear and an *appropriately* angry response to abuse (see Browne 1987; 1993; Schneider 1986). Although many woman left abusive relationships or successfully ended violence through other means, some responded to ongoing or accelerated abuse by killing or trying to kill their partners. In many states, when they went to trial such women found they were restricted from introducing testimony about the abuse they had endured or their resulting states of mind. In trying to address these women's needs, some activists and scholars advocated the use of expert testimony to explain battered woman syndrome to juries. This strategy would introduce evidence of past abuse and challenge the gender biases of self-defense law by explaining the woman's state of mind at the time of the offense (see Gillespie 1989). Feminist legal scholars raised potential problems in the use of battered woman syndrome. They argued that it could be used against women who did not neatly fit pre-established criteria and had the potential to become another example of the ten-

dency to label women's normal angry responses as mental illness (Browne 1993; Schneider 1986; see also Chesler 1989 and Schur 1984). While the desirability of working to admit expert testimony was debated, individual state courts and legislatures varied in their willingness to recognize battered woman syndrome, permit evidence of past abuse, or allow expert testimony. As the legal debate about battered women's responses to violence was beginning to unfold, the Ohio movement became directly involved in it when a former shelter resident shot and killed her abusive common law husband. In 1978 Women Together, in conjunction with the woman's lawyer, decided to challenge existing law by trying to introduce battered woman syndrome expert testimony at trial.

At the time, battered woman syndrome had little scientific merit or legal recognition, and the decision turned out to be a costly one in Ohio. The trial court refused to allow the testimony, and in 1981 that decision was upheld by the Ohio Supreme Court (*State v. Thomas* 1981, '66 Ohio St. 2d 51).[7] Despite this major setback, activists remained committed to challenging the law and improving their own and society's understanding of the trauma experienced by battered women. The case became symbolic of the Ohio movement's dual focus on gender inequities in the law and women's response to abuse.

By the early 1980s, most Woman Together founders left the shelter to establish professional careers, which they viewed as a means of advancing the feminist agenda. Many had become frustrated with the limitations and defeats they experienced as outsider challengers. The strategy they adopted was to infiltrate and appropriate the institutions they sought to change. For example, one founder, who had worked for ERA America in addition to her other feminist activism, explained her decision to run for elected office by saying:

I was in every state when [the ERA] was defeated. . . . That's when I decided to run for the legislature. I said, "I can do this better than these turkeys. This is not a problem."

Founders became legislators, judges, victim advocates, expert witnesses, government administrators, doctors, counselors, and professors. In 1982, many became activists within the administrative branch of state government when Celeste was elected to his first term as governor.

As movement founders left the shelter, a new cohort of feminists and mental health professional took over Women Together, and the shelter vacillated between the models advocated by each group (see Davis 1988), ultimately devising an approach that incorporated elements of both. In 1989 a network of feminist shelters—the Ohio Domestic Violence Network (ODVN)—was formed to re-establish the movement's emphasis on social change. That year ODVN worked to pass House Bill 484, an attempt to overrule the *Thomas* decision. While ODVN lobbied from outside the House and Senate, movement founders worked within the legislature and administration, laying the groundwork for clemency. In March 1990, the Ohio Supreme Court reversed itself in the case of *State v. Koss* (1990 49 Ohio St. 3d 213).[8] In August HB 484 was signed into law.

While HB 484 was being debated, the Celeste Administration began to work to implement the clemencies. For several years, Dagmar Celeste had been visiting women on death row at the Ohio Reformatory for Women (ORW), where she became involved in prison reform and numerous aspects of inmates' lives. Sometime during the mid-1980s, she first raised with the governor the issue of a large scale clemency for battered women. His staff reviewed the issue and reported back that there was no precedent for such an action. The matter was subsequently dropped until 1989 when the first lady and her staff began to press the issue. That year the governor ordered research to determine the number of women incarcerated for crimes related to battering and to document the existence of battered woman syndrome among Ohio's female inmate population.[9] In December 1989 he ordered that a clemency application and review process be established.[10] One-hundred-fifteen women applied, and in December 1990 26 were granted clemency.[11]

In light of these events the question remains: How was such a controversial decision made at a time many analysts have labeled postfeminist (Bolotin 1982; Friedan 1985; Stacey 1987; Steinem 1983) and when the national and state political contexts were increasingly conservative? Further, for social movement scholars and activists, the more important question is: Given the conservative backlash against women and the increasingly punitive incarceration models, which of the Ohio movement's tactics have the greatest likelihood of resulting in success in politically hostile settings? To address these questions, I examine the context of the Ohio clemency decisions, the way the issues were presented to authorities, the strategy and tactics used by activists in this movement, and the role of politically established persons in carrying out the movement's mandate.

CREATING OPPORTUNITY

Resource mobilization theorists contend that the context in which a social movement occurs is an important component in its emergence and success (Jenkins 1987; McAdam 1982; Morris 1984; Piven and Cloward 1977; Tilly 1988). Because of the assumption that movements react to opportunities provided, there has been little examination of their efforts to alter the political structure or climate. Nonetheless, this is what the Ohio battered women's movement did.

The Context

In 1982 Richard Celeste was elected governor by a decisive majority. His success was due, in part, to the recession and high unemployment that had hit the state, particularly in the "rust belt," and to a strong anti-Republican sentiment. Voters were liberal on economic, but not social, issues. To fight against further erosion of jobs and the decline of schools, voters elected Democrats to office across the board. In 1986 Celeste ran for re-election against James Rhodes, a candidate who had already served four terms as governor (in two, two-term periods). At that time, Ohio's economy was on the rebound, and again voters elected Celeste to office by a decisive margin. In neither term was Celeste elected on social issues, nor did he campaign on them strongly. While he had the legal authority to grant clemency to whomever he chose, he lacked a political mandate on left wing or feminist social issues. Although he had received the backing of activists advocating for social change, his staff understood the political risks of being too socially progressive, and they worked to protect him from such demands.

When he took office in 1983, the governor provided Dagmar Celeste with a staff and office space in the State House and depended on her to get involved with many of the issues affecting Ohio citizens. She called upon feminist colleagues and friends, many of whom had helped found the women's and battered women's movements, to help her create a "First Lady's Agenda." Some of those women served in the "First Lady's Unit," but more were selected by the governor to serve in cabinet and sub-cabinet level positions as directors of government agencies and in a variety of other positions. During the second term, these women organized the Women's Interagency Task Force, a network of feminists representing governmental departments and agencies. The Task Force met on a regular basis to discuss social policy as it related to women, review what agencies were doing about women's issues, provide an annual review of the governor's budget from a feminist perspective, and coordinate efforts on behalf of women throughout the state. The result was more efficient mobilization of a feminist community, which increased its influence throughout the state. With backing from the Task Force, as the term progressed, the First Lady's Unit increased pressure on members of the governor's staff who thought certain issues "too controversial" for the governor to address.

Feminists created support for clemency by raising public, judicial, and legislative awareness of gender biases in self-defense law and by pressing for change. In 1989 ODVN and feminists in the legislature pressed the passage of HB 484, despite well-organized opposition from conservative legislators and prosecutors. At the same time, feminist therapists, expert witnesses, and advocates worked to educate judges and Supreme Court justices about battered woman syndrome and its role in domestic homicides. By passing HB 484 and doing the background work that led to the *Koss* decision, they helped to create a context in which clemency reviews could be justified, particularly for women who, according to the law in 1990, had not received fair trials. Feminists developed the context of opportunity the governor needed, but more work had to be done to put the review process in place.

EMERGENT FRAMES AND THE RHETORIC OF WIFE ABUSE

Collective action frames are dynamic efforts by movements to "package" an issue by creating a sense of injustice and attributing blame for it to a particular social group or agent (Snow and Benford 1992). In an informal sense, the movement creates a theory about the source and solutions to the problem and presents it to the public and/or authorities. On a larger scale, master frames are more abstract theories that guide the discourse of movements within the social movement sector (Snow and Benford 1992). Like theories to a paradigm, the collective action frames of individual movements are likely to adhere to the discourse of the larger master frame.

The master frame of the movements of the 1960s and early 1970s focused on structural and cultural inequality, with goals such as equal rights, justice, and freedom from oppression. When the battered women's movement first emerged in the mid-1970s, the cycle of protest that had begun in the 1950s was reaching the end of its heyday (Jenkins 1987). When the battered women's movement became well established in the late 1970s the cycle of protest was in decline (Jenkins 1987) and the anti-feminist, pro-family backlash was gaining momentum (Crawford 1980; Faludi 1991). At the same time, mental health professionals began to reframe battered women's issues in non-oppositional terms and to encroach on the movement (Johnson 1981; Schechter 1982). By the end of the 1970s, the majority of shelters were non-feminist in orientation (Ferraro 1983; Johnson 1981). At the same time, the master frame of that cycle of protest had begun to shift toward personal development, and many radical feminists began to turn toward a cultural or eco-feminist analysis. Whereas radicals were social constructionist in orientation and sought to eliminate the sex-class system, cultural and eco-feminists based their discourse on essentialist premises, with a focus on elevating women's inherent virtues and putting greater emphasis on women's spiritual growth (Echols 1989). In Ohio, the battered women's movement shifted from a focus on gender equality to one of difference, incorporating elements of a debate that has been going on for more than a century.

Alternative Visions and Overlapping Discourse

To bring about social change, a movement must create an alternative vision of the world (Dobash and Dobash 1992). But, to enhance their chances of mobilizing potential participants and achieving their goals, activists must develop a collective action frame that agrees, in whole or in part, with something the public already believes. Alternatively, the movement must convert the public to its collective action frame, a strategy that is likely to require greater resources and more time (Klandermans 1992). In movements where there are no pragmatic repercussions for holding out, ideological purity has fewer consequences. However, where individuals' lives are endangered or when people are in prison, time is of the essence. In Ohio, activists incorporated cultural and eco-feminism's emphasis on gender differences and spiritual growth with their goal of social and structural change. As the movement's collective action frame shifted, the First Lady's Unit's goals were presented in the language of recovery and peaceful families—a frame they believed to be culturally resonant with mainstream society (McAdam 1994)—but the goals of personal empowerment, the elimination of gender biases in the law, and the eradication of violence against women remained. For example, among feminists working in the legislature and through the courts, recognition of women's psychological response to ongoing, severe abuse was framed in terms specific to women. Feminist lobbyists and legislators pointed to the fact that women rarely kill, unless they are under extreme duress. Relying on assumptions that women are less violent and less able to protect themselves, and arguing that police had refused to help many of the women who had been convicted of killing their partners, feminists argued that legal recognition of women's response to battering was warranted.[12]

Resources and opportunities are central to social change, particularly when movement goals are dependent on the development of collective consciousness and identity (Buechler 1990). Prison support and educational groups were an important part of the movement for clemency, but it took the work of non-inmate feminists to get them established at the Ohio Reformatory for Women (ORW). To mobilize the resources needed to establish such groups for battered women, feminists frequently framed demands in terms such as "peaceful families," "recovery," and "spiritual growth." In 1989 Dagmar Celeste became involved in efforts at ORW to build a chapel so that church services and recovery groups could be expanded. In a series of memoranda[13] among her, the governor, their aides, and officials at the prison and in the Department of Rehabilitation and Correction, the governor and first lady referred to the need to provide every inmate with an opportunity for "spiritual growth" and the chance to "recover from addiction." ORW added "support" and "educational" groups for battered women, as well as numerous additional recovery groups. These groups provided a "womanspace, a space free from male intrusion where women could . . . nurture each other and themselves" (Jagger 1983:270). As a manifestation of radical feminism, these groups provided a place where women could practice the skills and strengths they were forbidden to use in abusive relationships and patriarchal society and develop alternative ways of perceiving reality and reacting to their circumstances (Jagger 1983). In short, they functioned very much like consciousness raising groups of the 1960s and 1970s, with strikingly similar results. As women participated in groups for battered women, they began to understand the social forces that had shaped their lives. Most entered their groups believing they deserved to be punished for their crimes, but as consciousness of the patriarchal context of their lives was raised, a politicized collective identity emerged among them and they began to work for clemency. As incarcerated women came to believe they deserved to be released, it was incumbent on non-inmate feminists to help them get their cases reviewed. To do that, feminists worked as "ideological outsiders" within the government and its agencies.

FEMINIST STRATEGY AND THE TACTICS OF PERSONAL POLITICS

Similar to Collins's (1986) analysis of black female intellectuals' creative use of their own marginality within academic institutions, feminists in the Ohio battered women's movement were ideological outsiders within the institutions they sought to change. There they adopted and modified a strategy of "self-limiting radicalism," challenging the tenets of liberal democracy but accepting the legitimate existence of the state and capitalist economy (Cohen 1985). Activists using this strategy struggle to redraw public and private boundaries by creating democratic public spaces and transforming formerly private domains into social arenas for the renegotiation of identity and other movement demands (Cohen 1985). Similar to the women's movement (Buechler 1990), one of the most important legacies of the Ohio battered women's movement was the creation of a community of informally linked activists, capable of rapid and intense mobilization around specific issues, particularly when it required acting outside of social movement organizations. As movement founders moved into careers, they adopted a strategy I call "insider self-limiting radicalism," by remaining ideologically outside the systems they sought to change. Within state government, they were a minority who worked to advance feminist goals.

Framing Demands for Prison Reform

Had the first lady and members of the network advocated the formation of feminist consciousness raising groups for incarcerated women, it is likely the governor's staff and prison authorities would have resisted their efforts. However, by focusing on "recovery" services they were able to establish groups that became a key factor in creating a social movement community within the women's prison.

Consciousness Raising and the Politicization of Identity

The central task of the Ohio battered women's movement in achieving clemency was to create a collective identity among women inmates (see Melucci 1989). All the women I met who had attended educational or support groups for battered women talked about realizing they were not alone in their experiences. They explained how other women in their groups helped them understand how they had been dominated and controlled and how society had failed to help them. For example, when I asked what she had learned in her group, one clemency recipient said:

By listening to other women [I could see] the control, the isolation, where they want to cut you off from the world, that type of thing. . . . I could relate to how she felt about that, because I went through that, you know? How they want to control your whole life and they don't want you to have any friends and . . . your whole world's just you and the abuser.

In time women began to see themselves as survivors, rather than perpetual victims, and to understand how they came to be controlled, abused, and ultimately trapped in violent relationships.

Talking about their experiences was central in helping the women "reclaim" their definition of self, a step central to the politicization of identity (see D'Emilio 1983; Herman and Miall 1990). Based on my interviews with clemency recipients, activists, and authorities, I found that the importance of reclaiming identity is threefold. First, privately discussing the violent relationship with women who have claimed the identity "survivor" helps the "victim" reinterpret her experiences within the social context and begin to redefine herself.[14] As the victim redefines herself as a survivor, she realizes her strengths and how society has socialized her to be weak, failed to protect her, and blamed her for her own victimization. Second, as the public witnesses the reclaiming and public identification with a previously stigmatized status, old stereotypes and definitions are challenged and the identity is publicly renegotiated and redefined. Third, by publicly discussing and redefining the issues, their private nature is challenged and transformed from a personal to a social problem, deserving of social recompense.

From prison the women carried on a campaign to educate authorities and the public about battered woman syndrome. They told about their experiences with violent and abusive spouses and parents and the injustices they had endured in the criminal justice system. For most these efforts involved letter writing campaigns and meeting with public officials who were frequently brought to the prison by the first lady or feminist legislators. They met with legislators to talk about their experiences, their reactions to abuse, battered woman syndrome, and the need for laws recognizing it. They shared their experiences in closed meetings with the governor's staff and in groups organized to garner media attention, such as a meeting Dagmar Celeste's staff arranged with Miss America. They told their stories on television news magazines and to anyone else who would listen. Their goals were to educate government officials and the public about wife abuse and build public sympathy for their cases. One legislator explained how meeting with the women helped him understand what battered women endure and why it was necessary to change the law and remedy past inequities. He said:

I wanted to really talk to a real person who's been through this. . . . One woman told me how the windows were nailed shut. When the guy left . . . he took the phone with him and warned her that if she left the house . . . or contacted the authorities, that her children were going to be in serious harm's way. . . . And this had gone on for a decade. So one day, he came home and that was it. . . . He was going to abuse her physically, sexually, too. . . . She shot him dead with a shotgun. And she was in her . . . ninth year of incarceration.

The women's stories matched real lives with the theories and put faces on the statistics. With what they learned in prison, the governor's aides and supporters of HB 484 were able to win the votes of those who opposed the legislation.

As women began to realize there were alternatives to abuse and that their actions could make a difference, they began to resist abuses of power in other domains and demand justice. In prison, those who had witnessed or experienced harassment, sexual assault, or unfair treatment by prison employees began to report it and, when possible, testified in court. For example, one woman told me she and a roommate had witnessed the sexual assault of a third woman by a corrections officer. The three made a pact that they would take "no more abuse." After reporting what had happened, they testified against the officer, who was ultimately convicted. Intolerance of abuse continued when the women returned home. There they began to confront their daughters' abusive partners and teach the young women how to protect themselves. Five of the women had decided to avoid relationships with men altogether. One of them explained:

I have not interacted with men, I mean I have friends, but I have not entertained a relationship. . . . I am not ready. . . . I am gonna stay by myself 'cause I cannot tolerate this no more.

Only three of the women I talked with had had problems with men since being released. One, whose entire family was abusive, tolerated the violence because, as she explained, "I know he loves me." A second left a man she had met who had become abusive. The third was very assertive in communicating that she would not tolerate abuse. When her partner pushed her, she had him arrested and pressed charges. When I talked to her, the two were in couples' counseling and recovery groups and were trying to "work things out." Still, she was adamant that although she loved him, she knew she "deserved better than that." These forms of everyday resistance were made possible because women acknowledged that they had been abused and, in the process, learned to protect themselves and help others.

While inmates' actions were central in the transformation of identity, their voices alone were not enough to result in clemency. That goal required activism outside the prison. To accomplish that, the systems by which women had been dominated had to be appropriated and used to their own benefit.

Appropriating and Career Activism

One outcome of many of the social movements of the 1960s and 1970s was the creation of job opportunities for activists (McAdam 1988; McCarthy and Zald 1973). However, as the "cycle of protest" (Tarrow 1991) wound down for many movements of the period, activists found themselves in an increasingly tight activist job market (McAdam 1988). Nonetheless, the presence of the growing women's movement gave women expanding career outlets for their activism (McAdam 1988). A major distinction between the experiences of men in the new left and feminists is that the former eschew participation in "the establishment," while many feminists have looked upon career success as one potential means of addressing the economic and power inequities between women and men. For example, a 1960s student radical would look upon the offer of a position as judge as an effort at cooptation, while feminists have sought such positions as avenues to reinterpret or change the law.

Feminist activism on the job entails working to advance the goals of the women's movement as part of one's career. Within the Ohio battered women's movement, efforts to institutionalize change ranged from municipal court systems to the Supreme Court, the state legislature, and the Celeste Administration. At the municipal level, feminist judges, attorneys, shelter directors, and other direct service providers worked together to coordinate the police and judicial response to battering. Throughout the state the Governor's Task Force on Family Violence endeavored to understand and coordinate services for battered women and other victims of family violence. Feminist doctors worked to train their colleagues about family violence. Feminists in the Ohio Public Defender's Office were active in supporting legislation and working to educate their colleagues about battered woman syndrome. After *State v. Koss*, the Supreme Court created a task force to educate judges about domestic violence and battered woman syndrome and called upon movement founders who had established themselves in government careers to work with them. Feminist researchers and correctional staff, working to document the presence of battered woman syndrome among Ohio's female inmate population, stood their ground as the integrity of their work was challenged by their supervisors, and they ensured that the cases of all women who were eligible for review made it to the governor's office. Feminists within the First Lady's Unit and in the cabinet worked to educate the governor and his staff about wife abuse.

The battered women's movement has not taken over the Ohio legislature, judiciary, prison system, the executive branch of government, or any of the many state agencies feminists work in or run. But feminists used their jobs to achieve their goals. Their unwillingness to leave their convictions at the workplace door brought the movement into the very institutions that would grant legitimacy to the changes they sought to make. It may not be true of all movements, but because identity is central to feminist movements, it is inevitable that as activists gain entrée to new arenas, the distinction between the movement and social institutions will become blurred. Similarly, as women resist oppression in their personal lives, the distinction between the personal and the political will be obscured.

Intimacy and Activism

At the end of my interviews, I asked participants if there was a clear separation in their minds between their activism, their jobs, and their personal lives. All of the women, and all but three of the men,[15] said no. One of the women explained the connections among these facets of her life:

I think they're all of a piece. . . . I can't imagine compartmentalizing life. . . . You're acting from a core of whoever you are.

When I asked them to give examples of how their activism was carried on in their personal lives, many women described their efforts to negotiate egalitarian intimate relationships. Many referred to their marriages as partnerships that they and their spouses had worked to establish. Others referred to the music they would or would not listen to and the movies they refused to see. Those with children talked about their efforts to rear them to be socially conscious, nonsexist, and non-violent. My data are replete with examples of how women pursued feminist goals in their intimate relationships and home lives. Such acts of resistance, collectively, have advanced efforts to renegotiate women's identities and lives.

Political Partnerships and Everyday Resistance

Among politicians, there is a precarious separation that has historically been expected to exist between personal and public life. It is almost as if the public expects office holders to be sequestered from their families. Conversations about political issues should, ideally, not take place among family members or between spouses. If they do, either no influence should be exerted or any opinion expressed by the non-office holder should be ignored. Basing their opinions on liberal, non-feminist assumptions about the division that *should* exist between public and private domains, the public resents the privileged access family members have to office holders and demands that the division between public and private be at least symbolically maintained.

As women have continued to become more educated and have their own careers, the likelihood has increased that male politicians will marry women with political opinions, agendas, and goals of their own. The election of feminists to public office is one way the women's movement has worked to achieve its goals. But elected officials are constrained in ways their spouses and family members are not. Partnership politics increases the likelihood that social movements will gain entrée to arenas of official decision making. Therefore, the election of pro-feminist men who share power with their wives is a potential source of entrée to arenas of power and authority for women's movements.

In Ohio, Governor Celeste lent institutional support to his partnership with the first lady by providing her with a staff and offices in the State House. He empowered her to work toward feminist goals by actively seeking her input, instructing his staff to work with her, and including her in high-level meetings. The governor valued her contributions. Nonetheless, while she kept a low profile, working behind the scenes until the last year of their second term in office, Dagmar Celeste's influence did not come without resentment and resistance from the public, the governor's staff, and other public servants. Governor Celeste explained:

The staff of the governor serves the governor and thinks that anything else that intrudes is just that, an intrusion, and an unwarranted intrusion. That's family, that's first lady, whatever it might be. . . . Here we are doing the business of the state, why do we need to worry about something that the first lady's interested in? And so I think it's fair to say that there was never a wonderfully smooth relationship between the first lady's staff and the governor's office staff.

Despite resistance, the governor insisted that the first lady's concerns be addressed through official channels. Their relationship is an example of Cohen's (1985) concept of self-limiting radicalism. By challenging the separation between their public and private lives, they created "democratic public spaces" accessible to marginalized groups, including incarcerated women and feminists. Dagmar Celeste's unofficial position gave her a degree of freedom not available to the governor. Nonetheless, because she was not elected to office, her efforts were met with resentment and resistance. Dagmar Celeste used the metaphor of a strategic game to explain their relationship and efforts to create social change. She said:

I've often viewed the role of the first lady as the queen in a chess game. . . . The whole God damn game . . . is built on protecting the king. . . . And what's interesting in chess . . . is that the queen has a lot more mobility than anybody else. . . . She can move up . . . he can't move at all! . . . Chess is not a feminist game, [she laughs] because there's no point in having a queen, except to protect the king. . . . I would make coalitions with people who didn't serve his interests, if they served a feminist interest. And eventually he would come to see that they served his interest, because if he wanted to be what he said he wanted to be as a progressive feminist politician, eventually, it came to serve his interests.

By challenging the expected boundaries between their personal and political lives, the governor and first lady forged a partnership that allowed her to create alliances that played a central role in providing access to and for marginalized groups. As the spouse of an elected official, committed to feminist principles and goals, she provided an arena through which the women's and battered women's movements could achieve their goals. Without the political partnership that existed between the governor and first lady, the networks she facilitated among feminists throughout the state, and her willingness to violate liberal personal and political boundaries, the leadership within state government that was required to bring about the clemency review process would have been missing. While elected officials are important gatekeepers to many social movement goals, spouses have an enormous potential to push that gate open or leave it closed.

CONCLUSION

Social movements are frequently thought of as outside challenges to systems of authority, a conceptualization that is incomplete when analyzing women's and other new social movements. The assumption underlying the Ohio battered women's movement's strategy was that any separation of the personal from the political was unthinkable. This tenet was the foundation of the creation of wife abuse as a social problem, the empowerment of battered women within and out of prison, and the appropriation of three branches of the government, numerous state agencies, and the correctional system. Feminist identity entails a willingness to challenge established social arrangements, gender relations, and definitions of women, and to apply a feminist analysis to the social settings in which women find themselves and those they wish to enter. As the Ohio battered women's movement's founders left the shelter, they sought careers where they could work more effectively to achieve feminist goals. As they spread throughout the state and infiltrated all branches of government, they held to their feminist analysis of wife abuse and maintained contact with each other. In their personal lives, they sought social change and created partnerships with spouses who sought their input and were amenable to their influence. Through this strategy of infiltrating all three branches of government and violating public/private separations in their intimate relationships, feminists empowered at least one marginalized group to have great input in the democratic decision-making process. They did this by creating democratic public spaces in arenas previously considered beyond the realm of democracy. The most influential of these spaces were the political partnership between the governor and first lady and the consciousness raising groups at the Ohio Reformatory for Women.

Previous examinations of the battered women's movement have focused primarily on shelters as social movement organizations and have concluded that the feminist principles of the movement have been coopted by mental health professionals. In Ohio I found a well organized network of feminist shelters that worked toward social change on the local and state levels, despite an anti-feminist/pro-family cultural backlash, an increasingly conservative political environment, and efforts by mental health professionals to redefine the issues. While they staffed the "front lines," the majority of activism that made the clemencies possible occurred in arenas traditionally considered outside the domain of social movements.

Because they did not respect the boundaries between public and private, feminists successfully forced a recognition of the social factors that frequently entrap women in violent relationships. As ideological outsiders within the systems they wanted to change, they created a climate more favorable to clemency by framing issues in terms authorities were likely to understand and accept. This rhetorical compromise helped feminists establish a social movement community within the prison. In Ohio, feminists achieved their goals by carrying their activism into their careers and personal lives and by recognizing that political change occurs at the level of individual identity, as it did when women inmates began to advocate for their own clemencies. Feminists could only achieve these goals by resisting individual explanations of wife abuse, focusing on the need for personal transformation and social change, and remaining ideologically outside the systems they wanted to appropriate and change.

In periods that are inhospitable to movement goals, activists must identify strategies and tactics that are most likely to result in the achievement of movement goals. Based on the success of the Ohio battered women's movement, I have identified six tactics that may assist other movements during inhospitable or hostile cycles. First, movements can elect public officials sympathetic to their views and infiltrate positions of authority in order to swing the political pendulum in their favor. Along these lines, they must recognize the increasingly important role of political spouses in providing or denying access to political decision makers and other authorities. Second, movements can work toward social change in every aspect of their personal and public lives, bearing in mind that identity transformation among non-activists is a powerful potential source of movement growth. Third, movements can work to create democratic spaces in previously private or non-democratic arenas. Fourth, unless they are able to build a powerful coalition, strong enough to challenge authorities and sway public opinion, movements can engage in rhetorical compromise by framing their demands in terms more likely to resonate with authorities and the public. Fifth, movements can work to create coalitions with activists from across the ideological spectrum, finding a role for all groups and coordinating their activities. Sixth, movements can work from within and outside the system, exerting influence on every pressure point and providing access to, and on behalf of, already marginalized groups. If social scientists are to understand the dynamics of social change, we must continue to examine social movements. However, as I have demonstrated in this paper, an examination of outsider challengers or activism that takes place through social movement organizations or in "public" places gives us only a partial understanding of how change occurs, how demands become institutionalized, and how new challengers arise and infiltrate the systems they wish to change. Further research is needed to examine to what extent these tactics have been used by other activists, in both left and right wing movements.

NOTES

1. Within the majority of articles arguing that the movement has been coopted, the term is generally poorly defined. However, cooptation, as it is discussed in the context of the battered women's movement, generally refers to a shift away from feminist principles of pragmatic assistance, self-help, consciousness raising, empowerment, and non-hierarchical organization to a mental health or social welfare model that relies heavily on counseling, rigid rules, and bureaucratic organization, and that assumes that the problem is rooted in individual pathology or within a dysfunctional family system (see Davis 1988).

2. Although it may appear that part of my research was ethnographic in nature, I was not involved in activism or decision making during any stage of the organizing or clemency review process. My involvement in this project began when then former First Lady Dagmar Celeste suggested to my advisor that someone needed to research the clemency decisions.

3. One of the women died shortly after being released and another has returned to prison. Of the remainder, five did not respond to telephone calls and letters, and four refused to be interviewed, saying they wanted to put the past behind them and get on with their lives. I was unable to locate three.

4. The racial and ethnic make-up of the women who received clemency are as follows: 11 whites, 14 African Americans, and 1 Hispanic.

5. Archival data included all relevant files in the Celeste Administration records, newsletters from early women's movement organizations and the first shelter in Ohio, correspondence and meeting minutes from numerous social movement organizations and government agencies, drafts of legislation, speeches, Supreme Court decisions, court records, notes from prison support groups, and progress reports and historical summaries from government agencies and movement organizations. Archival data were used to verify dates, events, and exact wording of official documents, the interaction of key players, and to fill in the gaps surrounding forgotten or overlooked events.

6. The feminist organizations that emerged in the 1970s were loosely coordinated by an "organization of organizations" (Morris 1984) called WomanSpace. This organization provided resources that expedited the shelter's opening.

7. The grounds cited by the Court were that the syndrome was irrelevant and immaterial to the issue of whether the defendant acted in self-defense, that it was within the understanding of the jury and insufficiently developed as a matter of commonly accepted scientific knowledge, and that its prejudicial impact outweighed its probative value (*State v. Thomas* 1981 66 Ohio St. 2d).

8. In this decision, Justice Alice Robie Resnick wrote that "The battered woman syndrome has gained substantial scientific acceptance to warrant admissibility into evidence" (*State v. Koss* 1990, 49 Ohio St. 3d 213). In the decision, she cited numerous feminists' books and articles that documented and debated the syndrome, the American Psychological Association's recognition of it (which had been advocated by feminist therapists and psychologists), and the Ohio Legislature's introduction of a bill that would recognize battered woman syndrome in law as evidence that the syndrome deserved recognition by the court. Several activists expressed the opinion that the court reversed itself because legislation appeared imminent.

9. Two studies were conducted by the Research Department of the Ohio Department of Rehabilitation

and Correction. The first found that 203 women were incarcerated for crimes related to domestic violence, with 97 cases identified in which battered woman syndrome was verified or claimed by the inmate (Black 1990). The second involved interviews with 20 women who exhibited traits of battered woman syndrome (Sussman 1990). That study was used to help the parole board and others involved in researching the clemencies understand what battered woman syndrome was. It was later used at a seminar sponsored by the governor and organized by the first lady to teach defense attorneys, judges, and other legal practitioners about the syndrome and has been read by incarcerated battered women seeking to understand their experiences.

10. In the clemency review process, the inadmissibility of battered woman syndrome expert testimony at the time women went to trial or were convicted was the rationale for the clemencies. The governor and his aides did not use the formal psychological definition of battered woman syndrome in their review of women's cases. Rather, they looked for five things: (1) evidence of long term, systematic abuse; (2) evidence of having come to terms with their experiences; (3) behavior while in prison; (4) prior criminal record; and (5) the length of time they had already served, with all women, including those granted clemency, needing to have served at least two years.

11. An obstacle faced by 34 of the women, whom the governor sent back for further review by the parole board, was their failure or inability to fully document their cases.

12. Schneider (1986) has cogently argued that battered woman syndrome relies on stereotypes of femininity and that women who do not fit the criteria of the perfect victim are likely to be harmed by a focus on battered woman syndrome.

13. December 28, 1989 through February 26, 1990. Governor Celeste Files, Series 4124, Box 4, Ohio Historical Society.

14. In groups open only to inmates, women varied in their degree of reclaiming identity, with each helping the others at various stages of the consciousness raising process. In addition to these private group sessions, a seminar was developed by an organization of inmates serving life sentences. At that seminar, formerly incarcerated battered women who killed abusers shared their life experiences with clemency applicants. The overwhelming response from inmates who attended was that the seminar was empowering and that more opportunities like it should be made available to women in prison. (This response is based on program evaluation forms filled out by all inmates who attended the seminar.)

15. Two of those men were authorities, expected to maintain a separation between their personal and official lives. The third was an activist who had worked to establish boundaries between his job, activism, and home life so that he could devote more time to his family.

REFERENCES

ACKLESBERG, MARTHA A. 1988. "Communities, resistance, and women's activism: Some implications for a democratic polity." In *Women and the Politics of Empowerment*, eds. Ann Bookman and Sandra Morgen, 297–313. Philadelphia: Temple University Press.

ALONSO, ANA MARÍA 1992. "Gender, power, and historical memory: Discourses of Serrano resistance." In *Feminists Theorize the Political*, eds. Judith Butler and Joan W. Scott, 404–425. New York: Routledge.

BERNSTEIN, RICHARD J. 1985. "Introduction." In *Habermas and Modernity*, ed. Richard J. Bernstein, 1–32. Cambridge: The MIT Press.

BLACK, MAUREEN 1990. "Battered Spousal/Woman Syndrome Project: Report." Columbus: Ohio Department of Rehabilitation and Correction.

BOLOTIN, S. 1982. "Views from the post-feminist generation." *New York Times Magazine*, October: 29–31, 103–116.

BROWNE, ANGELA 1987. *When Battered Women Kill*. New York: The Free Press.

1993. "Violence against women by male partners: Prevalence, outcomes, and policy implications." *American Psychologist* 48:1077–1087.

BUECHLER, STEVEN M. 1990. *Women's Movements in the United States*. New Brunswick: Rutgers University Press.

CASSELL, JOAN 1977. *A Group Called Women: Sisterhood and Symbolism in the Feminist Movement*. Prospect Heights, Ill.: Waveland Press.

CHARMAZ, KATHY 1983. "The Grounded theory method: An explication and interpretation." In *Contemporary Field Research: A Collection of Readings*, ed. Robert M. Emerson, 109–126. Prospect Heights, Ill.: Waveland Press.

CHESLER, PHYLLIS 1989. *Women and Madness*. New York: Harcourt Brace Jovanovich.

COHEN, JEAN L. 1985. "Strategy or identity: New theoretical paradigms and contemporary social movements." *Social Research* 52:663–716.

COLLINS, PATRICIA HILL 1986. "Learning from the outsider within: The sociological significance of black feminist thought." *Social Problems* 33: 514–532.

1990. *Black Feminist Thought: Knowledge, Consciousness, and the Politics of Empowerment.* London: HarperCollins Academic.

CRAWFORD, ALAN 1980. *Thunder on the Right: The "New Right" and the Politics of Resentment.* New York: Pantheon Books.

D'EMILIO, JOHN 1983. *Sexual Politics, Sexual Communities: The Making of a Homosexual Minority in the United States, 1940–1970.* Chicago: University of Chicago Press.

DOBASH, R. EMERSON, and RUSSELL P. DOBASH 1992. *Women, Violence and Social Change.* New York: Routledge.

ECHOLS, ALICE 1989. *Daring to Be Bad: Radical Feminism in America 1967–1975.* Minneapolis: University of Minnesota Press.

ELSHTAIN, JEAN BETHKE 1981. *Public Man, Private Woman: Women in Social and Political Thought.* Princeton: Princeton University Press.

EVANS, SARA 1979. *Personal Politics.* New York: Vintage Books.

FALUDI, SUSAN 1991. *Backlash: The Undeclared War Against American Women.* New York: Crown Publishers, Inc.

FERRARO, KATHLEEN J. 1983. "Negotiating trouble in a battered women's shelter," *Urban Life* 12:287–306.

FERREE, MYRA MARX 1992. "The political context of rationality: Rational choice theory and resource mobilization." In *Frontiers in Social Movement Theory*, eds. Aldon D. Morris and Carol McClurg Mueller, 29–52. New Haven, Conn.: Yale University Press.

FERREE, MYRA MARX, and BETH B. HESS 1985. *Controversy and Coalition: The New Feminist Movement.* Boston: Twayne Publishers.

FOUCAULT, MICHEL 1979. *Discipline and Punish: The Birth of the Prison.* New York: Random House.

FRIEDAN, BETTY 1985. "How to get the women's movement moving again." *New York Time Magazine*, November 3:26–28, 66–67, 84–86, 89–90, 106–108.

GILLESPIE, CYNTHIA K. 1989. *Justifiable Homicide: Battered Women, Self-Defense, and the Law.* Columbus: Ohio State University Press.

HABERMAS, JÜRGEN 1985. "Neoconservative culture criticism in the United States and West Germany: An intellectual movement in two political cultures." In *Habermas and Modernity*, ed. Richard J. Bernstein, 78–94. Cambridge: The MIT Press.

HERMAN, NANCY J., and CHARLENE E. MIALL 1990. "The positive consequences of stigma: Two case studies in mental and physical disability." *Qualitative Sociology* 13:251–269.

JAGGER, ALLISON 1983. *Feminist Politics and Human Nature.* Sussex, England: Harvester Press.

JENKINS, J. CRAIG 1983. "Resource mobilization theory and the study of social movements." *Annual Review of Sociology* 9:527–553.

1987. "Interpreting the story 1960s: Three theories in search of a political age." *Research in Political Sociology* 3:269–303.

JOHNSON, JOHN M. 1981. "Program enterprise and official cooptation in the battered women's shelter movement. *American Behavioral Scientist* 24: 827–842.

KAUFFMAN, L.A. 1989. "The anti-politics of identity." *Socialist Review* 20:67–80.

KLANDERMANS, BERT 1992. "The social construction of protest and multiorganizational fields." In *Frontiers in Social Movement Theory*, eds. Aldon D. Morris and Carol McClurg Mueller, 77–103. New Haven, Conn.: Yale University Press.

McADAM, DOUG 1982. *Political Process and the Development of Black Insurgency, 1930–1970.* Chicago: University of Chicago Press.

1988. *Freedom Summer.* New York: Oxford University Press.

1994. "Culture and social movements." In *New Social Movements: From Ideology to Identity*, eds. Enrique Laraña, Hank Johnston, and Joseph Gusfield, 36–57. Philadelphia: Temple University Press.

McCARTHY, JOHN D., and MAYER N. ZALD 1973. *The Trend of Social Movements in America: Professionalization and Resource Mobilization.* Morristown, N.J.: General Learning Corporation.

1977. "Resource mobilization and social movements: A partial theory." *American Journal of Sociology* 82:1212–1240.

MELUCCI, ALBERTO 1980. "The new social movements: A theoretical approach." *Social Science Information* 19:199–226.

1989. *Nomads of the Present: Social Movements and Individual Needs in Contemporary Society.* Philadelphia: Temple University Press.

MORGEN, SANDRA, and ANN BOOKMAN 1988. "Rethinking women and politics: An introductory essay." In *Women and the Politics of Empowerment*, eds. Ann Bookman and Sandra Morgen, 3–29. Philadelphia: Temple University Press.

MORRIS, ALDON D. 1984. *The Origins of the Civil Rights Movement: Black Communities Organizing for Change.* New York: The Free Press.

MOUFFE, CHANTAL 1992. "Feminism, citizenship, and radical democratic politics." In *Feminists Theorize the Political*, eds. Judith Butler and Joan W. Scott, 369–384. New York: Routledge.

OFFE, CLAUS 1985. "New social movements; Challenging the boundaries of institutional politics." *Social Research* 52:817–868.

PIVEN, FRANCES FOX, and RICHARD A. CLOWARD 1977. *Poor People's Movements: Why They Succeed, How They Fail*. New York: Random House.

SCHECHTER, SUSAN 1982. *Women and Violence: The Visions and Struggles of the Battered Women's Movement*. Boston: South End Press.

SCHNEIDER, ELIZABETH M. 1986. "Describing and changing: Women's self-defense work and the problem of expert testimony on battering." *Women's Rights Law Reporter* 9:195–222.

SCHUR, EDWIN M. 1984. *Labeling Women Deviant: Gender, Stigma, and Social Control*. Philadelphia: Temple University Press.

SNOW, DAVID A., and ROBERT D. BENFORD 1992. "Master frames and cycles of protest." In *Frontiers in Social Movement Theory*, eds. Aldon D. Morris and Carol McClurg Mueller, 133–155. New Haven, Conn.: Yale University Press.

STACEY, J. 1987. "Sexism by a subtler name? Postindustrial conditions and postfeminist consciousness in the Silicon Valley." *Socialist Review* 17:7–28.

STEINEM, GLORIA 1983. "Why younger women are more conservative." In *Outrageous Acts and Everyday Rebellions*, ed. Gloria Steinem, 211–218. New York: Holt, Rinehart and Winston.

STRAUSS, ANSELM, and JULIET CORBIN 1990. *Basics of Qualitative Research: Grounded Theory Procedures and Techniques*. Newbury Park, Calif.: Sage.

SUSSMAN, VICKI 1990. "Battered women who commit violent offenses: A study of battered women incarcerated at the Ohio Reformatory for Women." Columbus, Ohio: Bureau of Planning and Research, Ohio Department of Rehabilitation and Correction.

TARROW, SIDNEY 1991. *Struggle, Politics, and Reform: Collective Action, Social Movements, and Cycles of Protest*. Ithaca, N.Y.: Center for International Studies, Cornell University.

TAYLOR, VERTA, and NANCY WHITTIER 1992. "Collective identity in social movement communities: Lesbian feminist mobilization." In *Frontiers in Social Movement Theory*, eds. Aldon D. Morris and Carol McClurg Mueller, 104–129. New Haven, Conn.: Yale University Press.

TIERNEY, KATHLEEN J. 1982. "The battered women movement and the creation of the wife beating problem." *Social Problems* 29:207–220.

TILLY, CHARLES 1988. "Social movements, old and new." *Research in Social Movements, Conflict and Change* 10:1–18. Greenwich, Conn.: JAI Press.

TOURAINE, ALAIN 1985. "An introduction to the study of social movements." *Social Research* 52:749–787.

WALKER, LENORE 1984. *The Battered Woman Syndrome*. New York: Springer Publishing Co.

PART III

DEVIANT BEHAVIORS

Alcohol and Drug Use

In Joseph Gusfield's classic work, "Moral Passage," an account is given as to how deviant behavior regarding drinking was defined in the United States. Using an interactionist approach, Gusfield examines how symbolic processes helped shape the movement to limit and control the personal consumption of alcohol. His analysis shows how deviant categories have distinct social histories, and how the reactions of specific groups provided the grounds for a "moral passage" of the act of drinking from one status (conventional) to another (deviant).

Howard Becker's piece, "Marihuana Use and Social Control," examines factors that both encourage and limit the use of marihuana as a recreational drug. Becker's analysis focuses on issues such as supply, secrecy, and morality in explaining the use of marihuana, and how social controls that limit its use are broken down, allowing individuals to become marihuana users.

In "Deviance as a Situated Phenomenon," James Orcutt uses questionnaires administered to a sample of students to examine their interpretations of marihuana and alcohol use in eight different social situations. He finds that the interpretations of the use of marihuana and alcohol as "deviant" vary depending on the situation in which they occur, but notes that the nature of the act itself also influences reactions. His study supports the idea that deviance is neither a totally relativistic concept nor a concrete thing, but rather lies somewhere in between.

In "Gender, Power, and Alternative Living Arrangements in the Inner-City Crack Culture," Lisa Maher, Eloise Dunlap, Bruce Johnson, and Ansley Hamid use extensive field notes and personal interviews to study the lives of impoverished crack-abusing women. They find that the most common alternative living arrangement was for women to live in the household of a male with a dependable income for whom they typically provided sex, drugs, domestic service, or companionship. Some women lived in "freakhouses" where they entertained sexual customers and shared drugs. Maher and her colleagues find that these alternative living arrangements reflect the relative powerlessness as well as the high levels of sexual exploitation and degradation of women in the inner-city crack culture.

MORAL PASSAGE
THE SYMBOLIC PROCESS IN PUBLIC
DESIGNATIONS OF DEVIANCE*

Joseph R. Gusfield

Recent perspectives on deviant behavior have focused attention away from the actor and his acts and placed it on the analysis of public reactions in labelling deviants as "outsiders."[1] This perspective forms the background for the present paper. In it I will analyze the implications which defining behavior as deviant has for the public designators. Several forms of deviance will be distinguished, each of which has a different kind of significance for the designators. The symbolic import of each type, I argue, leads to different public responses toward the deviant and helps account for the historical changes often found in treatment of such delinquents as alcoholics, drug addicts, and other "criminals," changes which involve a passage from one moral status to another.

INSTRUMENTAL AND SYMBOLIC FUNCTIONS OF LAW[2]

Agents of government are the only persons in modern societies who can legitimately claim to represent the total society. In support of their acts, limited and specific group interests are denied while a public and societal interest is claimed.[3] Acts of government "commit the group to action or to perform coordinated acts for general welfare."[4] This representational character of governmental officials and their acts makes it possible for them not only to influence the allocation of resources but also to define the public norms of morality and to designate which acts violate them. In a pluralistic society these defining and designating acts can become matters of political issue because they support or reject one or another of the competing and conflicting cultural groups in the society.

Let us begin with a distinction between *instrumental* and *symbolic* functions of legal and governmental acts. We readily perceive that acts of officials, legislative enactments, and court decisions often affect behavior in an instrumental manner through a direct influence on the actions of people. The Wagner Labor Relations Act and the Taft-Hartley Act have had considerable impact on the conditions of collective bargaining in the United States. Tariff legislation directly affects the prices of import commodities. The instrumental function of such laws lies in their enforcement; unenforced they have little effect.

Symbolic aspects of law and government do not depend on enforcement for their effect. They are symbolic in a sense close to that used in literary analysis. The symbolic act "invites consideration rather than overt reaction."[5] There is a dimension of meaning in symbolic behavior which is not given in its immediate and manifest significance but in what the action connotes for the audience that views it. The symbol "has acquired a meaning which is added to its immediate intrinsic significance."[6] The use of the wine and wafer in the Mass or the importance of the national flag cannot be appreciated without knowing their symbolic meaning for the users. In analyzing law as symbolic we are oriented less to behavioral consequences as a means to a fixed end; more to meaning as an act, a decision, a gesture important in itself.

An action of a governmental agent takes on symbolic import as it affects the designation of public norms. A courtroom decision or a legislative act is a gesture which often glorifies the values of one group and demeans those of another. In their representational character, governmental actions can be seen as ceremonial and ritual performances, designating the content of public

*© 1967 by the Society for the Study of Social Problems. Reprinted from *Social Problems,* 15: (Fall, 1967), pp. 175–188 by permission of the author and the publisher.

morality. They are the statement of what is acceptable in the public interest. Law can thus be seen as symbolizing the public affirmation of social ideals and norms as well as a means of direct social control. This symbolic dimension is given in the statement, promulgation, or announcement of law unrelated to its function in influencing behavior through enforcement.

It has long been evident to students of government and law that these two functions, instrumental and symbolic, may often be separated in more than an analytical sense. Many laws are honored as much in the breach as in performance.[7] Robin Williams has labelled such institutionalized yet illegal and deviant behavior the "patterned evasion of norms." Such evasion occurs when law proscribes behavior which nevertheless occurs in a recurrent socially organized manner and is seldom punished.[8] The kinds of crimes we are concerned with here quite clearly fall into this category. Gambling, prostitution, abortion, and public drunkenness are all common modes of behavior although laws exist designating them as prohibited. It is possible to see such systematic evasion as functioning to minimize conflicts between cultures by utilizing law to proclaim one set of norms as public morality and to use another set of norms in actually controlling that behavior.

While patterned evasion may perform such harmonizing functions, the passage of legislation, the acts of officials, and decisions of judges nevertheless have a significance as gestures of public affirmation. First, the act of public affirmation of a norm often persuades listeners that behavior and norm are consistent. The existence of law quiets and comforts those whose interests and sentiments are embodied in it.[9] Second, public affirmation of a moral norm directs the major institutions of the society to its support. Despite patterned practices of abortion in the United States, obtaining abortions does require access to a subterranean social structure and is much more difficult than obtaining an appendectomy. There are instrumental functions to law even where there is patterned evasion.

A third impact of public affirmation is the one that most interests us here. The fact of affirmation through acts of law and government expresses the public worth of one set of norms, of

one sub-culture vis-à-vis those of others. It demonstrates which cultures have legitimacy and public domination, and which do not. Accordingly it enhances the social status of groups carrying the affirmed culture and degrades groups carrying that which is condemned as deviant. We have argued elsewhere that the significance of Prohibition in the United States lay less in its enforcement than in the fact that it occurred.[10] Analysis of the enforcement of Prohibition law indicates that it was often limited by the unwillingness of Dry forces to utilize all their political strength for fear of stirring intensive opposition. Great satisfaction was gained from the passage and maintenance of the legislation itself.[11]

Irrespective of its instrumental effects, public designation of morality is itself an issue generative of deep conflict. The designating gestures are dramatistic events, "since it invites one to consider the matter of motives in a perspective that, being developed in the analysis of drama, treats language and thought primarily as modes of action."[12] For this reason the designation of a way of behavior as violating public norms confers status and honor on those groups whose cultures are followed as the standard of conventionality, and derogates those whose cultures are considered deviant. My analysis of the American Temperance movement has shown how the issue of drinking and abstinence became a politically significant focus for the conflicts between Protestant and Catholic, rural and urban, native and immigrant, middle class and lower class in American society. The political conflict lay in the efforts of an abstinent Protestant middle class to control the public affirmation of morality in drinking. Victory or defeat were consequently symbolic of the status and power of the cultures opposing each other.[13] Legal affirmation or rejection is thus important in what it symbolizes as well or instead of what it controls. Even if the law was broken, it was clear whose law it was.

DEVIANT NONCONFORMITY AND DESIGNATOR REACTION

In Durkheim's analysis of the indignant and hostile response to norm-violation, all proscribed actions are threats to the existence of the norm.[14]

Once we separate the instrumental from the symbolic functions of legal and governmental designation of deviants, however, we can question this assumption. We can look at norm-violation from the standpoint of its effects on the symbolic rather than the instrumental character of the norm. Our analysis of patterned evasion of norms has suggested that a law weak in its instrumental functions may nevertheless perform significant symbolic functions. Unlike human limbs, norms do not necessarily atrophy through disuse. Standards of charity, mercy, and justice may be dishonored every day yet remain important statements of what is publicly approved as virtue. The sexual behavior of the human male and the human female need not be a copy of the socially sanctioned rules. Those rules remain as important affirmations of an acceptable code, even though they are regularly breached. Their roles as ideals are not threatened by daily behavior. In analyzing the violation of norms we will look at the implications of different forms of deviance on the symbolic character of the norm itself. *The point here is that the designators of deviant behavior react differently to different norm-sustaining implications of an act.* We can classify deviant behavior from this standpoint.

The Repentant Deviant

The reckless motorist often admits the legitimacy of traffic laws, even though he has broken them. The chronic alcoholic may well agree that both he and his society would be better if he could stay sober. In both cases the norm they have violated is itself unquestioned. Their deviation is a moral lapse, a fall from a grace to which they aspire. The homosexual who seeks a psychiatrist to rid himself of his habit has defined his actions similarly to those who have designated him as a deviant. There is a consensus between the designator and the deviant; his repentance confirms the norm.

Repentance and redemption seem to go hand-in-hand in court and church. Sykes and Matza have described techniques of neutralization which juvenile delinquents often use with enforcement agencies.

The juvenile delinquent would appear to be at least partially committed to the dominant social order in that he frequently exhibits guilt or shame when he violates its proscriptions, accords approval to certain conforming figures and distinguishes between appropriate and inappropriate targets for his deviance.[15]

A show of repentance is also used, say Sykes and Matza, to soften the indignation of law enforcement agents. A recent study of police behavior lends support to this. Juveniles apprehended by the police received more lenient treatment, including dismissal, if they appeared contrite and remorseful about their violations than if they did not. This difference in the posture of the deviant accounted for much of the differential treatment favoring middle-class "youngsters" as against lower-class "delinquents."[16]

The Sick Deviant

Acts which represent an attack upon a norm are neutralized by repentance. The open admission of repentance confirms the sinner's belief in the sin. His threat to the norm is removed and his violation has left the norm intact. Acts which we can perceive as those of sick and diseased people are irrelevant to the norm; they neither attack nor defend it. The use of morphine by hospital patients in severe pain is not designated as deviant behavior. Sentiments of public hostility and the apparatus of enforcement agencies are not mobilized toward the morphine-user. His use is not perceived as a violation of the norm against drug use, but as an uncontrolled act, not likely to be recurrent.[17]

While designations of action resulting from sickness do not threaten the norm, significant consequences flow from such definitions. Talcott Parsons has pointed out that the designation of a person as ill changes the obligations which others have toward the person and his obligations toward them.[18] Parsons's description sensitizes us to the way in which the sick person is a different social object than the healthy one. He has now become an object of welfare, a person to be helped rather than punished. Hostile sentiments toward sick people are not legitimate. The sick person is not responsible for his acts. He is excused from the consequences which attend the healthy who act the same way.[19]

Deviance designations, as we shall show below, are not fixed. They may shift from one form to another over time. Defining a behavior pattern as one caused by illness makes a hostile response toward the actor illegitimate and inappropriate. "Illness" is a social designation, by no means given in the nature of medical fact. Even lefthandedness is still seen as morally deviant in many countries. Hence the effort to define a practice as a consequence of illness is itself a matter of conflict and a political issue.

The Enemy Deviant

Writing about a Boston slum in the 1930s, William F. Whyte remarks:

The policeman is subject to sharply conflicting pressures. On one side are the "good people" of Eastern City, who have written their moral judgments into law and demand through their newspapers that the law be enforced. On the other side are the people of Cornerville, who have different standards and have built up an organization whose perpetuation depends upon the freedom to violate the law.[20]

Whyte's is one of several studies that have pointed out the discrepancies between middle-class moralities embodied in law and lower-class moralities which differ sharply from them.[21] In Cornerville, gambling was seen as a "respectable" crime, just as antitrust behavior may be in other levels of the social structure. In American society, conflicts between social classes are often also cultural conflicts reflecting moral differences. Coincidence of ethnic and religious distinctions with class differences accentuates such conflicts between group values.

In these cases, the validity of the public designation is itself at issue. The publicly defined deviant is neither repentant nor sick, but is instead an upholder of an opposite norm. He accepts his behavior as proper and derogates the public norm as illegitimate. He refuses to internalize the public norm into his self-definition. This is especially likely to occur in instances of "business crimes." The buyer sees his action as legitimate economic behavior and resists a definition of it as

immoral and thus prohibitable. The issue of "off-track" betting illustrates one area in which clashes of culture have been salient.

The designation of culturally legitimate behavior as deviant depends upon the superior power and organization of the designators. The concept of convention in this area, as Thrasymachus defined Justice for Socrates, is the will of the stronger. If the deviant is the politically weaker group, then the designation is open to the changes and contingencies of political fortunes. It becomes an issue of political conflict, ranging group against group and culture against culture, in the effort to determine whose morals are to be designated as deserving of public affirmation.

It is when the deviant is also an enemy and his deviance is an aspect of group culture that the conventional norm is most explicitly and energetically attacked. When those once designated as deviant have achieved enough political power they may shift from disobedience to an effort to change the designation itself. This has certainly happened in the civil rights movement. Behavior viewed as deviant in the segregationist society has in many instances been moved into the realm of the problematic, now subject to political processes of conflict and compromise.

When the deviant and the designator perceive each other as enemies, and the designator's power is superior to that of the deviant, we have domination without a corresponding legitimacy. Anything which increases the power of the deviant to organize and attack the norm is thus a threat to the social dominance symbolized in the affirmation of the norm. Under such conditions the need of the designators to strengthen and enforce the norms is great. The struggle over the symbol of social power and status is focused on the question of the maintenance or change of the legal norm. The threat to the middle class in the increased political power of Cornerville is not that the Cornerville resident will gamble more; he already does gamble with great frequency. The threat is that the law will come to accept the morality of gambling and treat it as a legitimate business. If this happens, Boston is no longer a city dominated by middle-class Yankees but becomes one dominated by lower-class immigrants, as many think has actually happened in Boston. The maintenance of a norm which defines gambling as deviant behavior thus symbolizes the maintenance of Yankee social and political superiority. Its disappearance as a public commitment would symbolize the loss of that superiority.

The Cynical Deviant

The professional criminal commits acts whose designation as deviant is supported by wide social consensus. The burglar, the hired murderer, the arsonist, the kidnapper all prey on victims. While they may use repentance or illness as strategies to manage the impressions of enforcers, their basic orientation is self-seeking, to get around the rules. It is for this reason that their behavior is not a great threat to the norms although it calls for social management and repression. It does not threaten the legitimacy of the normative order.

DRINKING AS A CHANGING FORM OF DEVIANCE

Analysis of efforts to define drinking as deviant in the United States will illustrate the process by which designations shift. The legal embodiment of attitudes toward drinking shows how cultural conflicts find their expression in the symbolic functions of law. In the 160 years since 1800, we see all our suggested types of non-conforming behavior and all the forms of reaction among the conventional segments of the society.

The movement to limit and control personal consumption of alcohol began in the early nineteenth century, although some scattered attempts were made earlier.[22] Colonial legislation was aimed mainly at controlling the inn through licensing systems. While drunkenness occurred, and drinking was frequent, the rigid nature of the colonial society, in both North and South, kept drinking from becoming an important social issue.[23]

The Repentant Drinker

The definition of the drinker as an object of social shame begins in the early nineteenth century and reaches full development in the late 1820s and early 1830s. A wave of growth in Temperance organizations in this period was sparked by the conversion of drinking men to abstinence under the stimulus of evangelical revivalism.[24] Through drinking men joining together to take the pledge, a norm of abstinence and sobriety emerged as a definition of conventional respectability. They sought to control themselves and their neighbors.

The norm of abstinence and sobriety replaced the accepted patterns of heavy drinking countenanced in the late eighteenth and early nineteenth century. By the 1870s rural and small-town America had defined middle-class morals to include the Dry attitude. This definition had little need for legal embodiment. It could be enunciated in attacks on the drunkard which assumed that he shared the normative pattern of those who exhorted him to be better and to do better. He was a repentant deviant, someone to be brought back into the fold by moral persuasion and the techniques of religious revivalism.[25] His error was the sin of lapse from a shared standard of virtue. "The Holy Spirit will not visit, much less will He dwell within he who is under the polluting, debasing effects of intoxicating drink. The state of heart and mind which this occasions to him is loathsome and an abomination."[26]

Moral persuasion thus rests on the conviction of a consensus between the deviant and the designators. As long as the object of attack and conversion is isolated in individual terms, rather than perceived as a group, there is no sense of his deviant act as part of a shared culture. What is shared is the norm of conventionality; the appeal to the drinker and the chronic alcoholic is to repent. When the Woman's Anti-Whiskey Crusade of 1873–1874 broke out in Ohio, church women placed their attention on the taverns. In many Ohio towns these respectable ladies set up vigils in front of the tavern and attempted to prevent men from entering just by the fear that they would be observed.[27] In keeping with the evangelical motif in the Temperance movement, the Washingtonians, founded in 1848, appealed to drinkers and chronic alcoholics with the emotional trappings and oratory of religious meetings, even though devoid of pastors.[28]

Moral persuasion, rather than legislation, has been one persistent theme in the designation of the drinker as deviant and the alcoholic as depraved. Even in the depictions of the miseries and poverty of the chronic alcoholic, there is a decided moral condemnation which has been the hallmark of the American Temperance movement. Moral persuasion was ineffective as a device to wipe out drinking and drunkenness. Heavy drinking persisted through the nineteenth century and the organized attempts to convert the drunkard experienced much backsliding.[29] Nevertheless, defections from the standard did not threaten the standard. The public definition of respectability matched the ideal of the sober and abstaining people who dominated those parts of the society where moral suasion was effective. In the late nineteenth century those areas in the which temperance sentiment was strongest were also those in which legislation was most easily enforceable.[30]

The Enemy Drinker

The demand for laws to limit alcoholic consumption appears to arise from situations in which the drinkers possess power as a definitive social and political group and, in their customary habits and beliefs, deny the validity of abstinence norms. The persistence of areas in which Temperance norms were least controlling led to the emergence of attempts to embody control in legal measures. The drinker as enemy seems to be the greatest stimulus to efforts to designate his act as publicly defined deviance.

In its early phase the American Temperance movement was committed chiefly to moral persuasion. Efforts to achieve legislation governing the sale and use of alcohol do not appear until the 1840s. This legislative movement had a close relationship to the immigration of Irish Catholics and German Lutherans into the United States in this period. These non-evangelical and/or non-Protestant people made up a large proportion of the urban poor in the 1840s and 1850s. They brought with them a far more accepting evaluation of drinking than had yet existed in the United States. The tavern and the beer parlor had a distinct place in the leisure of the Germans and the Irish. The prominence of this place was intensified by the stark character of the developing American slum.[31] These immigrant cultures did not contain a strong tradition of Temperance norms which might have made an effective appeal to a sense of sin. To be sure, excessive drunkenness was scorned, but neither abstinence nor constant sobriety were supported by the cultural codes.

Between these two groups—the native American, middle-class evangelical Protestant and the immigrant European Catholic or Lutheran occupying the urban lower class—there was little room for repentance. By the 1850s the issue of drinking reflected a general clash over cultural values. The Temperance movement found allies in its political efforts among the nativist movements.[32] The force and power of the anti-alcohol movements, however, were limited greatly by the political composition of the urban electorate, with its high proportion of immigrants. Thus the movement to develop legislation emerged in reaction to the appearance of cultural groups least responsive to the norms of abstinence and sobriety. The very effort to turn such informal norms into legal standards polarized the opposing forces and accentuated the symbolic import of the movement. Now that the issue had been joined, defeat or victory was a clear-cut statement of public dominance.

It is a paradox that the most successful move to eradicate alcohol emerged in a period when America was shifting from a heavy-drinking society, in which whiskey was the leading form of alcohol, to a moderate one, in which beer was replacing whiskey. Prohibition came as the culmination of the movement to reform the immigrant cultures and at the height of the immigrant influx into the United States.

Following the Civil War, moral persuasion and legislative goals were both parts of the movement against alcohol. By the 1880s an appeal was made to the urban, immigrant lower classes to repent and to imitate the habits of the American middle class as a route to economic and social mobility. Norms of abstinence were presented to the non-abstainer both as virtue and as expedience.[33] This effort failed. The new, and larger, immigration of 1890–1915 increased still further the threat of the urban lower class to the native American.

The symbolic effect of Prohibition legislation must be kept analytically separate from its instrumental, enforcement side. While the urban middle class did provide much of the organizational leadership to the Temperance and Prohibition movements, the political strength of the movement in its legislative drives was in the rural areas of the United States. Here, where the problems of drinking were most under control, where the norm was relatively intact, the appeal to a struggle against foreign invasion was the most potent. In these areas, passage of legislation was likely to make small difference in behavior. The continuing polarization of political forces into those of cultural opposition and cultural acceptance during the Prohibition campaigns (1906–1919), and during the drive the Repeal (1926–1933), greatly intensified the symbolic significance of victory and defeat.[34] Even if the Prohibition measures were limited in their enforceability in the metropolis there was no doubt about whose law was public and what way of life was being labelled as opprobrious.

After Repeal, as Dry power in American politics subsided, the designation of the drinker as deviant also receded. Public affirmation of the temperance norm had changed and with it the definition of the deviant had changed. Abstinence was itself less acceptable. In the 1950s the Temperance movement, faced with this change in public norms, even introduced a series of placards with the slogan, "It's Smart *Not* to Drink."

Despite this normative change in the public designation of drinking deviance, there has not been much change in American drinking patterns. Following the Prohibition period the consumption of alcohol has not returned to its pre-1915 high. Beer has continued to occupy a more important place as a source of alcohol consumption. "Hard drinkers" are not as common in America today as they were in the nineteenth century. While there has been some increase in moderate drinking, the percentage of adults who are abstainers has remained approximately the same (one-third) for the past 30 years. Similarly, Dry sentiment has remained stable, as measured by local opinion results.[35] In short, the argument over deviance designation has been largely one of normative dominance, not of instrumental social control. The process of deviance designation in drinking needs to be understood in terms of symbols of cultural dominance rather than in the activities of social control.

The Sick Drinker

For most of the nineteenth century, the chronic alcoholic as well as the less compulsive drinker was viewed as a sinner. It was not until after Repeal (1933) that chronic alcoholism became defined as illness in the United States. Earlier actions taken toward promotion of the welfare of drinkers and alcoholics through Temperance measures rested on the moral supremacy of abstinence and the demand for repentance. The user of alcohol could be an object of sympathy, but his social salvation depended on a willingness to embrace the norm of his exhorters. The designation of alcoholism as sickness has a different bearing on the question of normative superiority. It renders the behavior of the deviant indifferent to the status of norms enforcing abstinence.

This realization appears to have made supporters of Temperance and Prohibition hostile to efforts to redefine the deviant character of alcoholism. They deeply opposed the reports of the Committee of Fifty in the late nineteenth century.[36] These volumes of reports by scholars and prominent men took a less moralistic and a more sociological and functional view of the saloon and drinking than did the Temperance movement.

The soundness of these fears is shown by what did happen to the Temperance movement with the rise of the view that alcoholism is illness. It led to new agencies concerned with drinking problems. These excluded Temperance people from the circle of those who now define what is deviant in drinking habits. The National Commission on Alcoholism was formed in 1941 and the Yale School of Alcoholic Studies formed in 1940. They were manned by medical personnel, social workers, and social scientists, people now alien to the spirit of the abstainer. Problems of drinking were removed from the church and placed in the hands of the universities and the medical clinics. The tendency to handle drinkers through protective and welfare agencies rather than through police or clergy has become more frequent.

"The bare statement that 'alcoholism is a disease' is most misleading since ... it conceals what is essential—that a step in public policy is being recommended, not a scientific discovery announced."[37] John Seeley's remark is an apt one. Replacement of the norm of sin and repentance by that of illness and therapy removes the onus of guilt and immorality from the act of drinking and the state of chronic alcoholism. It replaces the image of the sinner with that of a patient, a person to be helped rather than to be exhorted. No wonder that the Temperance movement has found the work of the Yale School, and often even the work of Alcoholics Anonymous, a threat to its own movement. It has been most limited in its cooperation with these organizations and has attempted to set up other organizations which might provide the face of Science in league with the tone of the movement.[38]

The redefinition of the alcoholic as sick thus brought into power both ideas and organizations antithetical to the Temperance movement. The norm protected by law and government was no longer the one held by the people who had supported Temperance and Prohibition. The hostility of Temperance people is readily understandable; their relative political unimportance is crucial to their present inability to make that hostility effective.

MOVEMENTS OF MORAL PASSAGE

In this paper we have called attention to the fact that deviance designations have histories; the public definition of behavior as deviant is itself changeable. It is open to reversals of political power, twists of public opinion, and the development of social movements and moral crusades. What is attacked as criminal today may be seen as sick next year and fought over as possibly legitimate by the next generation.

Movements to redefine behavior may eventuate in a moral passage, a transition of the behavior from one moral status to another. In analyzing movements toward the redefinition of alcohol use, we have dealt with moral crusades which were restrictive and others which were permissive toward drinking and toward "drunkards." (We might have also used the word "alcoholics,"

suggesting a less disapproving and more medical perspective.) In both cases, however, the movements sought to change the public designation. While we are familiar with the restrictive or enforcing movements, the permissive or legitimizing movement must also be seen as a prevalent way in which deviants throw off the onus of their actions and avoid the sanctions associated with immoral activities.

Even where the deviants are a small and politically powerless group they may nevertheless attempt to protect themselves by influence over the process of designation. The effort to define themselves as ill is one plausible means to this end. Drug addiction as well as drunkenness is partially undergoing a change toward such redefinition.[39] This occurs in league with powerful groups in society, such as social workers, medical professionals, or university professors. The moral passage achieved here reduces the sanctions imposed by criminal law and the public acceptance of the deviant designation.

The "lifting" of a deviant activity to the level of a political, public issue is thus a sign that its moral status is at stake, that legitimacy is a possibility. Today the moral acceptance of drinking, marijuana and LSD use, homosexuality, abortion, and other "vices" is being publicly discussed, and movements championing them have emerged. Such movements draw into them far more than the deviants themselves. Because they become symbols of general cultural attitudes they call out partisans for both repression and permission. The present debate over drug addiction laws in the United States, for example, is carried out between defenders and opposers of the norm rather than between users and non-users of the drugs involved.

As the movement for redefinition of the addict as sick has grown, the movement to strengthen the definition of addiction as criminal has responded with increased legal severity. To classify drug users as sick and the victims or clients as suffering from "disease" would mean a change in the agencies responsible for reaction from police enforcement to medical authorities. Further, it might diminish the moral disapproval with which drug use, and the reputed euphoric effects connected with it, are viewed by supporters of present legislation. Commenting on the clinic plan to permit medical dispensing of narcotics to licensed addicts, U.S. Commissioner of Narcotics Anslinger wrote:

This plan would elevate a most despicable trade to the avowed status of an honorable business, nay, to the status of practice of a time-honored profession; and drug addicts would multiply unrestrained, to the irrevocable impairment of the moral fiber and physical welfare of the American people.[40]

In this paper we have seen that redefining moral crusades tends to generate strong countermovements. The deviant as a cultural opponent is a more potent threat to the norm than is the repentant, or even the sick deviant. The threat to the legitimacy of the norm is a spur to the need for symbolic restatement in legal terms. In these instances of "crimes without victims" the legal norm is *not* the enunciator of a consensus within the community. On the contrary, it is when consensus is least attainable that the pressure to establish legal norms appears to be greatest.

NOTES

1. Howard S. Becker, *Outsiders: Studies in the Sociology of Deviance,* Glencoe: The Free Press, 1963, Chap. 1. A similar view is presented in John Kitsuse, "Societal Reaction to Deviant Behavior," *Social Problems,* 9 (Winter, 1962), pp. 247–256; Kai Erikson, "Sociology of Deviance," in E. McDonagh and J. Simpson, editors, *Social Problems,* New York: Holt, Rinehart and Winston, Inc., 1965, pp. 457–464, p. 458.

2. The material of this section is more fully discussed in my book *Symbolic Crusade: Status Politics and the American Temperance Movement,* Urbana: University of Illinois Press, 1963, esp. Chap. 7.

3. See the analysis of power as infused with collective goals in Parsons's criticism of C. Wright Mills, *The Power Elite:* Talcott Parsons, "The Distribution of Power in American Society," *World Politics,* 10 (October, 1957), p. 123, 144.

4. Francis X. Sutton, "Representation and the Nature of Political Systems," *Comparative Studies in Society and History,* 2 (October, 1959), pp. 1–10. In this paper Sutton shows that in some primitive societies, political officials function chiefly as representatives to other tribes rather than as law enforcers or policy makers.

5. Phillip Wheelwright, *The Burning Fountain,* Bloomington: Indiana University Press, 1964, p. 23.

6. Talcott Parsons, *The Social System,* Glencoe: The Free Press, 1954, p. 286.

7. Murray Edelman has shown this in his analysis of the discrepancy between legislative action and administrative agency operation. Murray Edelman, *The Symbolic Uses of Politics,* Urbana: University of Illinois Press, 1964.

8. Robin Williams, *American Society,* New York: A. A. Knopf, 1960, pp. 372–396. Hyman Rodman's analysis of "lower-class value stretch" suggests yet another ambiguity in the concept of norm. He found that in Trinidad among lower-class respondents that *both* marriage and non-legal marital union are normatively accepted, although marriage is preferred. Hyman Rodman, "Illegitimacy in the Caribbean Social Structure," *American Sociological Review,* 31 (October, 1966), pp. 673–683.

9. Edelman, *op. cit.,* Chap. 2. The author refers to this as a process of political quiescence. While Edelman's symbolic analysis is close to mine, his emphasis is on the reassurance function of symbols in relation to presumed instrumental affects. My analysis stresses the conflict over symbols as a process of importance apart from instrumental effects.

10. Gusfield, *op. cit.,* pp. 117–126.

11. Joseph Gusfield, "Prohibition: The Impact of Political Utopianism," in John Braeman, editor, *The 1920's Revisited,* Columbus: Ohio State University Press, forthcoming; Andrew Sinclair, *The Era of Excess,* New York: Harper Colophon Books, 1964, Chap. 10, pp. 13–14.

12. Kenneth Burke, *A Grammar of Motives,* New York: Prentice Hall, 1945, p. 393. Burke's writings have been the strongest influence on the mode of analysis presented here. Two other writers, whose works have been influential, themselves influenced by Burke, are Erving Goffman and Hugh D. Duncan.

13. Gusfield, *Symbolic Crusade, op. cit.,* Chap. 5.

14. Émile Durkheim, *The Division of Labor in Society,* trans. George Simpson, Glencoe: The Free Press, 1947, especially at pp. 96–103. For a similar view see Lewis Coser, "Some Functions of Deviant Behavior and Normative Flexibility," *American Journal of Sociology,* 68 (September, 1962), pp. 172–182.

15. Gresham Sykes and David Matza, "Techniques of Neutralization: A Theory of Delinquency," *American Sociological Review,* 22 (December, 1957), pp. 664–670, at p. 666.

16. Irving Piliavin and Scott Briar, "Police Encounters with Juveniles," *American Journal of Sociology,* 70 (September, 1964), pp. 206–214.

17. This of course does not mean that the patient using morphine may not become an addict.

18. Talcott Parsons and Renée Fox, "Illness, Therapy and the Modern Urban Family," *Journal of Social Issues,* 8 (1952), pp. 31–44.

19. A somewhat similar distinction as that presented here can be found in Vilhelm Aubert and Sheldon Messinger, "The Criminal and the Sick," in V. Aubert, *The Hidden Society,* New York: The Bedminster Press, 1965, pp. 25–54.

20. William F. Whyte, *Street-Corner Society,* Chicago: University of Chicago Press, 2nd edition, 1955, p. 138.

21. See William Westley's analysis of the differences between the morality shared by the lower class and the police in contrast to that of the courts over such matters as gambling, prostitution, and sexual perversion. The courts take a sterner view of gamblers and prostitutes than do the police, who take a sterner view of the sexual offender. William Westley, "Violence and the Police," *American Journal of Sociology,* 59 (July, 1953), pp. 34–42.

22. The best single account of Temperance activities before the Civil War is that of John Krout, *The Origins of Prohibition,* New York: A. A. Knopf, 1925.

23. *Ibid.,* Chapters 1 and 2; also see Alice Earle, *Home Life in Colonial Days,* New York: Macmillan and Co., 1937, pp. 148–149; 156–165.

24. Gusfield, *Symbolic Crusade, op. cit.,* pp. 44–51.

25. *Ibid.,* pp. 69–86.

26. *Temperance Manual* (no publisher listed, 1836), p. 46.

27. See the typical account by Mother Stewart, one of the leaders in the 1873–74 Woman's War on Whiskey, in Eliza D. Steward, *Memories of the Crusade,* Columbus, Ohio: W. G. Hibbard, 2nd edition, 1889, pp. 139–143; also see *Standard Encyclopedia of the Alcohol Problem,* 6 (Westerville, Ohio: American Issue Publishing Co., 1930), pp. 2902–2905.

28. Krout, *op. cit.,* Chap. 9.

29. See the table of consumption of alcoholic beverages, 1850–1957, in Mark Keller and Vera Efron, "Selected Statistics on Alcoholic Beverage," reprinted in Raymond McCarthy, editor, *Drinking and Intoxication,* Glencoe: The Free Press, 1959, p. 180.

30. Joseph Rowntree and Arthur Sherwell, *State Prohibition and Local Option,* London: Hodden and Stoughton, 1900, using both systematic observation and analysis of Federal tax payments, concluded (p. 253) that ". . . local veto in America has only been found operative outside the larger towns and cities."

31. See the accounts of drinking habits among Irish and German immigrants in Oscar Handlin, *Boston's Immigrants,* Cambridge, Massachusetts: Harvard University Press, 1941, pp. 191–192, 201–209; Marcus Hansen, *The Immigrant in American History,* Cambridge, Massachusetts: Harvard University Press, 1940.

32. Ray Billington, *The Protestant Crusade, 1800–1860,* New York: Macmillan, 1938, Chap. 15; Gusfield, *Symbolic Crusade, op. cit.,* pp. 55–57.

33. William F. Whyte, *op. cit.,* p. 99. Whyte has shown this as a major attitude of social work and the settlement house toward slum-dwellers he studied in the 1930s. "The community was expected to adapt itself to the standards of the settlement house." The rationale for adaptation lay in its effects in promoting social mobility.

34. Although a well-organized Temperance movement existed among Catholics, it was weakened by the Protestant drive for Prohibition: See Joan Bland, *Hibernian Crusade,* Washington, D.C.: Catholic University Press, 1951.

35. See my analysis of American drinking in the post-Repeal era. Gusfield, "Prohibition: The Impact of Political Utopianism," *op. cit.*

36. The Committee of Fifty, a group of prominent educators, scientists, and clergymen sponsored and directed several studies of drinking and the saloon. Their position as men unaffiliated to temperance organizations was intended to introduce unbiased investigation, often critical of Temperance doctrine. For two of the leading volumes see John Shaw Billing's, *The Physiological Aspects of the Liquor Problem,* Boston and New York: Houghton, Mifflin and Co., 1903; Raymond Calkins, *Substitutes for the Saloon,* Boston and New York: Houghton, Mifflin and Co., 1903.

37. John Seeley, "Alcoholism Is a Disease: Implications for Social Policy," in D. Pittman and C. Snyder, editors, *Society, Culture and Drinking Patterns,* New York: John Wiley and Sons, 1962, pp. 586–593, at p. 593. For a description of the variety of definitions of alcoholism and drunkenness, as deviant and nondeviant, see the papers by Edwin Lemert, "Alcohol, Values and Social Control" and by Archer Tongue, "What the State Does About Alcohol and Alcoholism," both in the same volume.

38. The WCTU during the 1950s persistently avoided support to Alcoholics Anonymous. The Yale School of Alcohol Studies was attacked and derogated in Temperance literature. A counter-organization, with several prominent pro-Dry scientists, developed, held seminars, and issued statements in opposition to Yale School publications.

39. Many of the writings of sociologists interested in drug addiction have contained explicit demands for

such redefinitions. See Becker, *op. cit.;* Alfred Lindesmith, *The Addict and the Law,* Bloomington: Indiana University Press, 1965, and David Ausubel, *Drug Addiction,* New York: Random House, 1958. The recent movement to redefine marijuana and LSD as legitimate is partially supported by such writings but is more saliently a movement of enemy deviants. The activities of Timothy Leary, Allen Ginsberg, and the "hipsters" is the most vocal expression of this movement.

40. Harry Anslinger and William Tompkins, *The Traffic in Narcotics,* New York: Funk and Wagnalls Co., Inc., 1953, p. 186.

Marihuana Use and Social Control*

Howard S. Becker**

When deviant behavior occurs in a society—behavior which flouts its basic values and norms—one element in its coming into being is a breakdown in social controls, those mechanisms which ordinarily operate to maintain valued forms of behavior. In complex societies, the process is somewhat more complicated since breakdowns in social control are often the consequences of the person becoming a participant in a subculture whose controls operate at cross-purposes to those of the larger society. Important factors in the genesis of deviant behavior, then, may be sought in those processes by which people are emancipated from the larger set of controls and become responsive to those of the subculture.

Social controls affect individual behavior, in the first instance, through the use of power, the application of sanctions. Valued behavior is rewarded and negatively valued behavior is punished. Control would be difficult to maintain if such enforcement were always needed, so that

more subtle mechanisms performing the same function arise. Among these is the control of behavior achieved by affecting the conceptions persons have of the to-be-controlled activity, and of the possibility or feasibility of engaging in it. These conceptions arise in social situations in which they are communicated by persons regarded as reputable and validated in experience. Such situations may be so ordered that individuals come to conceive of the activity as distasteful, inexpedient, or immoral, and therefore do not engage in it.

Such a perspective invites us to analyze the genesis of deviant behavior in terms of events which render sanctions ineffective and experiences which shift conceptions so that the behavior becomes a conceivable possibility to the person. This paper is devoted to an analysis of this process in the instance of marihuana use. Its basic question is: what is the sequence of events and experiences by which a person comes to be able to carry on the use of marihuana, in spite of the elaborate social controls functioning to prevent such behavior?

A number of potent forces operate to control the use of marihuana in this country. The act is illegal and punishable by severe penalties. Its illgality makes access to the drug difficult, placing immediate obstacles before anyone who wishes to use it. Actual use can be dangerous, for arrest and imprisonment are always possible conse-

*© 1955 by the Society for the Study of Social Problems. Reprinted from *Social Problems,* 54 (July, 1955), pp. 35–44 by permission of the author and the publisher.

**The research on which this paper is based was done while I was a member of the staff of the Chicago Narcotics Survey, a project done by the Chicago Area Project, Inc., under a grant from the National Mental Health Institute. I wish to thank Eliot Freidson, Erving Goffman, Anselm Strauss, and R. Richard Wohl for reading and commenting on an earlier version.

quences. In addition, those who are discovered in their use of the drug by family, friends, or employers may be subject to various kinds of informal but highly effective sanctions and social punishments; ostracism, withdrawal of affection, etc. Finally, a set of traditional views has grown up, defining the practice as a violation of basic moral imperatives, as an act leading to loss of self-control, paralysis of the will, and eventual slavery to the drug. Such views are commonplace and are an effective force preventing marihuana use.

The development of marihuana-using activity in an individual may be divided into three stages, each representing a distinct shift in the person's relations to these social controls of the larger society and those of the subculture in which marihuana use is found. The first stage is represented by the *beginner,* the person smoking marihuana for the first time; the second, by the *occasional user,* whose use is sporadic and dependent on chance factors; and the third, by the *regular user,* for whom use becomes a systematic daily routine.

The analysis will be pursued in terms of the processes by which the various kinds of social controls become progressively less effective as the user moves from level to level of use or, alternatively, the ways in which they prevent such movement by remaining effective. The major kinds of controls to be considered are: (a) control through limiting of supply and access to the drug; (b) control through the necessity of keeping non-users from discovering that one is a user; (c) control through definition of the act as immoral. The rendering ineffective of these controls, at the levels and in the combinations to be described, may be taken as an essential condition for continued and increased marihuana use.

One explanatory note is in order. It is obvious that people do not do things simply because they are not prevented from doing them. More positive motivations are necessarily present. This paper does not deal with the genesis of these positive motivations involved in the continuation and increase of marihuana use (except in passing), focusing rather on the barriers to use, and taking the motivation more or less for granted. I have described one important element in this motivation elsewhere. This is the knowledge that one can gain pleasure by smoking marihuana, achieved in a process of learning to smoke the drug so that definite symptoms occur, learning to recognize these effects and connect them with the use of the drug, and learning to find these effects enjoyable. This learning takes place in interaction with more experienced users who present the novice with the necessary symbols and concepts with which to organize this otherwise vague and ambiguous experience. By and large, however, the motivation to continue use will, in this discussion, be taken for granted and emphasis placed on the breakdown of deterrents to this.

The analysis is based on fifty intensive interviews with marihuana users from a variety of social backgrounds and present positions in society.[1] The interviews focused on the history of the person's experience with the drug, seeking major changes in his attitude toward it and in his actual use of it and the reasons for these changes. Generalizations stating necessary conditions for the maintenance of use at each level were developed in initial interviews, and tested against and revised in the light of each succeeding one. The stated conclusions hold true for all the cases collected and may tentatively be considered as true of all marihuana users in this society, at least until further evidence forces their revision.[2]

SUPPLY

Marihuana use is limited, in the first instance, by laws making possession or sale of drugs punishable by severe penalties. This confines its distribution to illicit sources which are not available to the ordinary person. In order for a person to begin marihuana use, he must begin participation in some group through which these sources of supply become available to him, ordinarily a group organized around values and activities opposing those of the larger conventional society.

In those unconventional circles in which marihuana is already used, it is apparently just a matter of time until a situation arises in which the newcomer is given a chance to smoke it:

I was with these guys that I knew from school, and one had some, so they went to get high and they just figured that I did too, they never asked me, so I didn't want to be no wallflower or nothin', so I didn't say nothin' and went out in the back of this place with them. They were doing up a couple of cigarettes.

In other groups marihuana is not immediately available, but participation in the group provides connections to others in which it is:

But the thing was, we didn't know where to get any. None of us knew where to get it or how to find out where to get it. Well, there was this one chick there . . . she had some spade girl friends and she had turned on before with them. Maybe once or twice. But she knew a little more about it than any of the rest of us. So she got hold of some, through these spade friends, and one night she brought down a couple of sticks.

In either case, such participation provides the conditions under which marihuana becomes available for first use. It also provides the conditions for the next level of occasional use, in which the individual smokes marihuana sporadically and irregularly. When an individual has arrived through earlier experiences at a point where he is able to use marihuana for pleasure, use tends at first to be a function of availability. The person uses the drug when he is with others who have a supply; when this is not the case his use ceases. It tends therefore to fluctuate in terms of the conditions of availability created by his participation with other users; a musician at this stage of use said:

That's mostly when I get high, is when I play jobs. And I haven't played hardly at all lately . . . See, I'm married twelve years now, and I really haven't done much since then. I had to get a day job, you know, and I haven't been able to play much. I haven't had many gigs, so I really haven't turned on much, you see.

Like I say, the only time I really get on is if I'm working with some cats who do, then I will too. Like I say, I haven't been high for maybe six months. I haven't turned on in all that time. Then, since I come on this job, that's three weeks, I've been high every Friday and Saturday. That's the way it goes with me.

(This man was observed over a period of weeks to be completely dependent on other members of the orchestra in which he worked and on musicians who dropped into the tavern in which he was playing for any marihuana he used.)

If an occasional user begins to move on toward a more regularized and systematic mode of use, he can do it only by finding some more sta-

ble source of supply than more-or-less chance encounters with other users, and this means establishing connections with persons who make a business of dealing in narcotics. Although purchases in large quantities are necessary for regular use, they are not ordinarily made with that intent; but, once made, they do render such use possible, as it was not before. Such purchases tend to be made as the user becomes more responsive to the controls of the drug-using group:

I was running around with this whole crowd of people who turned on then. And they were always turning me on, you know, until it got embarrassing. I was really embarrassed that I never had any, that I couldn't reciprocate. . . . So I asked around where I could get some and picked up for the first time.

Also, purchasing from a dealer is more economical, since there are no middlemen and the purchaser of larger quantities receives, as in the ordinary business world, a lower price.

However, in order to make these purchases, the user must have a "connection"—know someone who makes a business of selling drugs. These dealers operate illicitly, and in order to do business with them one must know where to find them and be identified to them in such a way that they will not hesitate to make a sale. This is quite difficult for persons who are very casually involved in drug-using groups. But as a person becomes more identified with these groups, and is considered more trustworthy, the necessary knowledge and introductions to dealers become available to him. In becoming defined as a member, one is also defined as a person who can safely be trusted to buy drugs without endangering anyone else.

Even when the opportunity is made available to them, many do not make use of it. The danger of arrest latent in such an act prevents them from attempting it:

If it were freely distributed, I think that I would probably keep it on hand all the time. But . . . (You mean if it wasn't against the law?) Yeah. (Well, so does that mean that you don't want to get involved . . .) Well, I don't want to get too involved, you know. I don't want to get too close to the people who traffic in, rather heavily in it. I've never had any difficulty much in getting any stuff. I just . . . someone usually has some and you can get it when you want it. Why, just why, I've never happened to run into those more or less direct contacts, the pushers, I suppose you'd explain it on the basis of the fact that I never felt the need for scrounging or looking up one.

Such fears operate only so long as the attempt is not made, for once it has been successfully accomplished the individual is able to use the experience to revise his estimate of the danger involved; the notion of danger no longer prevents purchase. Instead, the act is approached with a realistic caution which recognizes without overemphasizing the possibility of arrest. The purchaser feels safe so long as he observes elementary, common-sense precautions. Although many of the interviewees had made such purchases, only a few reported any difficulty of a legal kind and these attributed it to the failure to take such precautions.

For those who do establish such connections, regular use is often interrupted by the arrest or disappearance of the man from whom they purchase their supply. In such circumstances, regular use can continue only if the user is able to find a new source of supply. This young man had to give up use for a while when:

Well, like Tom went to jail, they put him in jail. Then Cramer, how did it happen . . . Oh yeah, like I owed him some money and I didn't see him for quite a while and when I did try to see him he had moved and I couldn't find out from anyone where the cat went. So that was that connection . . . (So you just didn't know where to get it?) No. (So you stopped?) Yeah.

This instability of sources of supply is an important control over regular use, and reflects indirectly the use of legal sanctions by the community in the arrest of those trafficking in drugs. The enforcement of the law controls use by making access more difficult because of this instability of sources, rather than through its acting as a direct deterrent to users. Each level of use, from beginning to routine, thus has its typical mode of supply, which must be present for such use to occur. In this sense, the social mechanisms which operate to limit availability of the drug limit its use. However, participation in groups in which marihuana is used creates the conditions under which these controls

which limit access to it no longer operate. Such participation also involves increased sensitivity to the controls of the drug-using group, so that there are forces pressing toward use of the new sources of supply. Changes in the mode of supply in turn create the conditions for movement to a new level of use. Consequently, it may be said that changes in group participation and membership lead to changes in level of use by affecting the individual's access to marihuana under present conditions in which the drug is available only through illicit outlets.

SECRECY

Marihuana use is limited also to the extent that individuals actually find it inexpedient or believe that they will find it so. This inexpediency, real or presumed, arises from the fact or belief that if non-users discover that one uses the drug, sanctions of some important kind will be applied. The user's conception of these sanctions is vague, because few of them seem ever to have had such an experience or to have known anyone who did. Although he does not know what specifically to expect in the way of punishments, the outlines are clear: He fears repudiation by people whose respect and acceptance he requires both practically and emotionally. That is, he expects that his relationships with non-users will be disturbed and disrupted if they should find out, and limits and controls his behavior accordingly.

This kind of control breaks down in the course of the user's participation with other users and in the development of his experience with the drug, as he comes to realize that, though it might be true that sanctions would be applied if non-users found out, they need never find out. At each level of use, there is a growth in this realization which makes the new level possible.

For the beginner, these considerations are very important and must be overcome if use is to be undertaken at all. These fears are challenged by the sight of others—more experienced users—who apparently feel there is little or no danger and appear to engage in the activity with impunity. If one does "try it once," he may still his fears by observations of this kind. Participation with other users thus furnishes the beginner with the rationalizations with which first to attempt the act.

Further participation in the marihuana use of these groups allows the novice to draw the further conclusion that the act can be safe no matter how often indulged in, as long as one is careful and makes sure that non-users are not present or likely to intrude. This kind of perspective is a necessary prerequisite for occasional use, in which the drug is used when other users invite one to join them. While it permits this level of use, such a perspective does not allow regular use to occur for the worlds of user and non-user, while separate to a degree allowing the occasional use pattern to persist, are not completely segregated. The points where these worlds meet appear dangerous to the occasional user who must, therefore, confine his use to those occasions on which such meeting does not seem likely.

Regular use, on the other hand, implies a systematic and routine use of the drug which does not take into account such possibilities and plan periods of "getting high" around them. It is a mode of use which depends on another kind of attitude toward the possibility of non-users finding out, the attitude that marihuana use can be carried on under the noses of non-users, or, alternatively, on the living of a pattern of social participation which reduces contacts with non-users almost to the zero point. Without this adjustment in attitude, participation, or both, the user is forced to remain at the level of occasional use. These adjustments take place in terms of two categories or risks involved: First, that non-users will discover marihuana in one's possession and second, that one will be unable to hide the effects of the drug when he is "high" while with non-users.

The difficulties of the would-be regular user, in terms of possession, are illustrated in the remarks of a young man who unsuccessfully attempted regular use while living with his parents:

I never did like to have it around the house, you know. (Why?) Well, I thought maybe my mother might find it or something like that. (What do you think she'd say?) Oh, well, you know, like . . . well, they never do mention it, you know, anything about dope addicts or anything like that but it would be a really bad thing in my case, I know, because of the big family I come from. And my sisters and brothers, they'd put me

down the worst. (And you don't want that to happen?) No, I'm afraid not.

In such cases, envisioning the consequences of such a secret being discovered prevents the person from maintaining the supply essential to regular use. Use remains erratic; since it must depend on encounters with other users and cannot occur whenever the user desires.

Unless he discovers some method of overcoming this difficulty, the person can progress to regular use only when the relationship deterring use is broken. People do not ordinarily leave their homes and families in order to smoke marihuana regularly. But if they do, for whatever reason, regular use, heretofore proscribed, becomes a possibility. Confirmed regular users often take into very serious account the effect on their drug use of forming new social relationships with non-users:

I wouldn't marry someone who would be belligerent if I do (smoke marihuana), you know. I mean, I wouldn't marry a woman who would be so untrusting as to think I would do something . . . I mean, you know, like hurt myself or try to hurt someone.

If such attachments are formed, use tends to revert to the occasional level:

(This man had used marihuana quite intensively but his wife objected to it.) Of course, largely the reason I cut off was my wife. There were a few times when I'd feel like . . . didn't actually crave for it but would just like to have had some. (He was unable to continue using the drug except irregularly, on those occasions when he was away from his wife's presence and control.)

If the person moves almost totally into the user group, the problem ceases in many respects to exist, and it is possible for regular use to occur except when some new connection with the more conventional world is made.

If a person uses marihuana regularly and routinely it is almost inevitable—since even in urban society such roles cannot be kept completely separate—that he one day find himself "high" while in the company of non-users from whom he wishes to keep his marihuana use secret. Given the variety of symptoms the drug may produce, it is natural for the user to fear that he might reveal through his behavior that he is "high," that he might be unable to control the symptoms and thus give away his own secret. Such phenomena as difficulty in focusing one's attention and in carrying on normal conversation create a fear that everyone will know exactly why one is behaving in this way, that the behavior will be interpreted automatically as a sign of drug use.

Those who progress to regular use manage to avoid this dilemma. It may happen, as noted above, that they come to participate almost completely in the subcultural group in which the practice is carried on, so that they simply have a minimal amount of contact with non-users about whose opinions they care. Since this isolation from conventional society is seldom complete, the user must learn another method of avoiding the dilemma, one which is the most important method for those whose participation is never so completely segregated. This consists in learning to control the drug's effects while in the company of non-users, so that they can be fooled and the secret successfully kept even though one continues participation with them. If one cannot learn this, there exists some group of situations in which he dare not get "high" and regular use is not possible:

Say, I'll tell you something that just kills me, man, I mean it's really terrible. Have you ever got high and then had to face your family? I really dread that. Like having to talk to my father or mother, or brothers, man, it's just too much. I just can't make it. I just feel like they're sitting there digging (watching) me, and they know I'm high. It's a horrible feeling. I hate it.

Most users have these feelings and move on to regular use, if they do, only if an experience of the following order occurs, changing their conception of the possibilities of detection:

(Were you making it much then, at first?) No, not too much. Like I said, I was a little afraid of it. But it was finally about 1948 that I really began to make it strong. (What were you afraid of?) Well, I was afraid that I would get high and not be able to op (operate), you dig, I mean, I was afraid to let go and see what would happen. Especially on jobs. I couldn't trust myself when I was high. I was afraid I'd get too high, and pass out completely, or do stupid things. I didn't want to get too wigged.
(How did you ever get over that?) Well, it's just one of those things, man. One night I turned on and I just suddenly felt real great, relaxed, you know, I was really swinging with it. From then on I've just been

able to smoke as much as I want without getting into any trouble with it. I can always control it.

The typical experience is one in which the user finds himself in a position where he must do something while he is "high" that he is quite sure he cannot do in that condition. To his surprise, he finds that he can do it and can hide from others the fact that he is under the drug's influence. One or more occurrences of this kind allow the user to conclude that his caution has been excessive and based on a false premise. If he desires to use the drug regularly he is no longer deterred by this fear, for he can use such an experience to justify the belief that non-users need never know:

(The suggestion was made that many users find it difficult to perform their work tasks effectively while high. The interviewee, a machinist, replied with the story of how he got over this barrier.)
It doesn't bother me that way. I had an experience once that proved that to me. I was out on a pretty rough party the night before. I got pretty high. On pot (marihuana) and lushing, too. I got so high that I was still out of my mind when I went to work the next day. And I had a very important job to work on. It had to be practically perfect—precision stuff. The boss had been priming me for it for days, explaining how to do it and everything.
(He went to work high and, as far as he could remember, must have done the job, although there was no clear memory of it since he was still quite high.)
About a quarter to four, I finally came down and I thought, "Jesus! What am I doing?" So I just cut out and went home. I didn't sleep all night hardly, worrying about whether I had f..ked up on that job or not. I got down the next morning, the boss puts the old "mikes" on the thing, and I had done the f..kin' job perfectly. So after that I just didn't worry any more. I've gone down to work really out of my mind on some mornings. I don't have any trouble at all.

This problem is not equally important for all users, for there are those whose social participation is such that it cannot arise; all their associates know they use marihuana and none of them care, while their conventional contacts are few and unimportant. In addition, some persons achieve idiosyncratic solutions which allow them to act "high" and have it ignored:

They (the boys in his neighborhood) can never tell if I'm high. I usually am, but they don't know it. See, I

sort of groovy!

always had the reputation, all through high school, of being kind of goofy, so no matter what I do, nobody pays much attention. So I can get away with being high practically anyplace.

In short, persons limit their use of marihuana in proportion to the degree of their fear, realistic or otherwise, that non-users who are important to them will discover that they use drugs and react in some punishing way. This kind of control breaks down as the user discovers that his fears are excessive and unrealistic, as he comes to conceive of the practice as one which can be kept secret with relative ease. Each level of use can occur only when the person has revised his conception of the dangers involved in such a way as to allow it.

MORALITY

This section discusses the role of conventional notions of morality as a means through which marihuana use is controlled. The basic moral imperatives which operate here are those which require the individual to be responsible for his own welfare, and to be able to control his behavior rationally. The stereotype of the dope fiend portrays a person who violates these imperatives. A recent description of the marihuana user illustrates the principal features of this stereotype:

In the earliest stages of intoxication the will power is destroyed and inhibitions and restraints are released; the moral barricades are broken down and often debauchery and sexuality result. Where mental instability is inherent, the behavior is generally violent. An egotist will enjoy delusions of grandeur, the timid individual will suffer anxiety, and the aggressive one often will resort to acts of violence and crime. Dormant tendencies are released and while the subject may know what is happening, he has become powerless to prevent it. Constant use produces an incapacity for work and a disorientation of purpose.

One must add to this, of course, the notion that the user becomes a slave to the drug, that he voluntarily surrenders himself to a habit from which there is no escape. The person who takes such a stereotype seriously is presented with a serious obstacle to drug use. Use will ordinarily be begun, maintained and increased only when

some other way of viewing the practice is accepted by the individual.

The beginner has at some time shared these views. In the course of his participation in some unconventional segment of society, however, he is likely to acquire a more "emancipated" view of the moral standards implicit in this characterization of the drug user, at least to the point that he will not reject activities out of hand simply because they are conventionally condemned. The observation of others using the drug may further tempt him to apply his rejection of conventional standards to the specific instance of marihuana use. Such participation, then, tends to provide the conditions under which these controls can be circumvented at least sufficiently for first use to be attempted.

In the course of further experience in these groups, the novice acquires a whole series of rationalizations and justifications with which he may answer objections to occasional use if he decides to engage in it. If he should raise himself the objections of conventional morality he finds ready answers available in the folklore of marihuana using groups.

One of the most common rationalizations is that conventional persons indulge in much more harmful practices and that a comparatively minor vice like marihuana smoking cannot really be wrong when such things as the use of alcohol are so commonly accepted:

(You don't dig (like) alcohol then?) No, I don't dig it at all. (Why not?) I don't know. I just don't. Well, see, here's the thing. Before I was at the age where kids start drinking I was already getting on (using marihuana) and I saw the advantages of getting on, you know, I mean there was no sickness and it was much cheaper. That was one of the first things I learned, man. Why do you want to drink? Drinking is dumb, you know. It's so much cheaper to get on and you don't get sick, and it's not sloppy and takes less time. And it just grew to be the thing, you know. So I got on before I drank, you know. . . .

(What do you mean that's one of the first things you learned?) Well, I mean, as I say, I was just first starting to play jobs as a musician when I got on and I was also in a position to drink on the jobs, you know. And these guys just told me it was silly to drink. They didn't drink either.

Additional rationalizations enable the user to suggest to himself that the drug's effects, rather than being harmful, are in fact beneficial:

I have had some that made me feel like . . . very invigorated and also it gives a very strong appetite. It makes you very hungry. That's probably good for some people who are underweight.

Finally, the user, at this point, is not using the drug all the time. His use is scheduled, there being times when he considers it appropriate and times when he does not. The fact of this schedule allows him to assure himself that he controls the drug, rather than the drug controlling him, and becomes a symbol of the harmlessness of the practice. He does not consider himself a slave to the drug, because he can and does abide by this schedule, regardless of the amount of use the particular schedule may allow. The fact that there are times when he does not, on principle, use the drug, can be used as proof to himself of his freedom with respect to it.

I like to get on and mostly do get on when I'm relaxing, doing something I enjoy like listening to a real good classical record or maybe like a movie or something like that or listening to a radio program. Something I enjoy doing, not participating in, like . . . I play golf during the summer, you know, and a couple of guys I play with got on, turned on while they were playing golf and I couldn't see that because, I don't know, when you're participating in something you want your mind to be on that and nothing else, and if you're . . . because I think, I know it makes you relax and . . . I don't think you can make it as well.

Occasional use can occur in an individual who accepts these views, for he has reorganized his moral notions in such a way as to permit it, primarily by acquiring the conceptions that conventional moral notions about drugs do not apply to this drug and that, in any case, his use of it has not become excessive.

If use progresses to the point of becoming regular and systematic, these questions may again be raised for the user, for he begins now to look, to himself as well as others, like the uncontrolled "dope fiend" of popular mythology. He must convince himself again, if use is to continue at this level that he has not crossed this line. The

problem, and one possible resolution, are presented in this statement by a regular user:

I know it isn't habit forming but I was a little worried about how easy it would be to put down, so I tried it. I was smoking it all the time, then I just put it down for a whole week to see what would happen. Nothing happened. So I knew it was cool (all right). Ever since then I've used it as much as I want to. Of course, I wouldn't dig being a slave to it or anything like that, but I don't think that that would happen unless I was neurotic or something, and I don't think I am, not to that extent.

The earlier rationalization with regard to the beneficial effects of the drug remain unchanged and may even undergo a considerable elaboration. But the question raised in the last quotation proves more troublesome. In view of his increased and regularized consumption of the drug, the user is not sure that he is really able to control, that he has not possibly become the slave of a vicious habit. Tests are made—use is given up and the consequences awaited—and when nothing untoward occurs, the user is able to draw the conclusion that there is nothing to fear.

The problem is, however, more difficult for some of the more sophisticated users who derive their moral directives not so much from conventional thinking as from popular psychiatric "theory." Their use troubles them, not in conventional terms, but because of what it may indicate about their mental health. Accepting current thinking about the causes of drug use, they reason that no one would use drugs in any large amounts unless "something" were "wrong" with him, unless there were some neurotic maladjustment which made drugs necessary. The fact of marihuana smoking becomes a symbol of psychic weakness and, ultimately, moral weakness. This prejudices the person against further regular use and causes a return to occasional use unless some new rationale is discovered.

Well, I wonder if the best thing is not to get on anything at all. That's what they tell you. Although I've heard psychiatrists say, "Smoke all the pot (marihuana) you want, but leave the horse (heroin) alone."

(Well, that sounds reasonable.) Yeah, but how many people can do it? There aren't very many . . . I think that seventy-five percent or maybe even a bigger percent of the people that turn on have a behavior pattern that would lead them to get on more and more pot to get more and more away from things. I think I have it myself. But I think I'm aware of it so I think I can fight it.

The notion that to be aware of the problem is to solve it constitutes such a rationale in the above instance. Where such justifications cannot be discovered, use continues on an occasional basis, the user explaining his reasons in terms of his conception of psychiatric theory:

Well, I believe that people who indulge in narcotics and alcohol and drinks, any stimulants of that type, on that level, are probably looking for an escape from a more serious condition than the more or less occasional user. I don't feel that I'm escaping from anything. I think that, however, I realize that I have a lot of adjustment to accomplish yet . . . So I can't say that I have any serious neurotic condition or inefficiency that I'm trying to handle. But in the case of some acquaintances I've made, people who are chronic alcoholics or junkies (opiate addicts) or pretty habitual smokers, I have found accompanying that condition some maladjustment in their personality, too.

Certain morally toned conceptions about the nature of drug use and drug users thus influence the marihuana user. If he is unable to explain away or ignore these conceptions, use will not occur at all, and the degree of use appears to be related to the degree to which these conceptions no longer are influential, having been replaced by rationalizations and justifications current among users.

DISCUSSION

The extent of an individual's use of marihuana is at least partly dependent on the degree to which conventional social controls fail to prevent his engaging in the activity. Apart from other possible necessary conditions, it may be said that marihuana use can occur at the various levels described only when the necessary events and shifts in conception of the activity have removed the individual from the influence of these controls and substituted for them the controls of the subcultural group.

This kind of analysis seems to put some experiential flesh on the bare bones of the contention that the assumption of roles in a deviant subculture accounts for deviant behavior. There is, of course, a close relationship between the two. But a good deal of theoretical and practical difficulty is avoided by introducing an intervening process of change in social participation and individual conception made possible, but not inevitable by subcultural membership, and which becomes itself the explanatory factor. In this way, the element of truth in the simpler statement is conserved while the difficulties posed by those who participate in such groups without engaging in the deviant behavior are obviated. For such membership only provides the possibility, not the necessity, of having those experiences which will produce the behavior. The analysis may be made finer by then considering those contingencies which tend to determine whether or not the member of such a group actually has the necessary experiences.

Such a view necessarily implies the general hypothesis, of some interest to students of culture and personality, that the holding of a social position, in and of itself, cannot be considered to explain an individual's behavior. Rather, the analysis of behavior must take account of social roles in a more subtle fashion, by asking what possibilities of action and what experiences which might shape the individual's appreciation and tendency to make use of those possibilities are provided by a given role. Such a viewpoint continues to insist on the analytic importance of the role concept, which calls our attention to the patterning of an individual's experience by the position which he holds in an organized social group, but adds to this an emphasis on the experience itself as it shapes conduct and the process by which this shaping occurs.

NOTES

1. Most of the interviews were done by me. I wish to thank Solomon Korbin and Harold Finestone for allowing me to make use of interviews done by them.

2. This is an application of the method of analytic induction described in.

REFERENCES

H. J. Anslinger and William F. Tompkins. *The Traffic in Narcotics,* New York: Funk and Wagnalls Company, 1953, pp. 21–2.

Howard S. Becker. "Becoming a Marihuana User," *American Journal of Sociology,* LIX (November, 1953), 235–42.

Alfred R. Lindesmith. *Opiate Addiction,* Bloomington: Principia Press, 1947.

DEVIANCE AS A SITUATED PHENOMENON
VARIATIONS IN THE SOCIAL INTERPRETATION OF MARIJUANA AND ALCOHOL USE*

James D. Orcutt**

INTRODUCTION

A relativistic orientation has become preeminent in recent theoretical work in the field of deviance (Douglas, 1971; Rubington and Weinberg, 1973; Davis, 1972; Matza, 1969; Schur, 1971). In contrast to earlier structural or normative theories of deviant behavior, relativistic theories do not treat deviance as an objectively given quality of certain acts or actors. Rather, deviance is viewed as analytically identifiable only *in relation to* interpretational and interactional processes through which acts and actors are *socially defined* as deviant. Erikson (1966:11), for example, states: "Deviance is not a property *inherent in* certain forms of behavior; it is a property *conferred upon* these forms by the audiences which directly or indirectly witness them" (emphasis in original). Assignment of this symbolic property to a certain act may depend as much or more on various characteristics of the actors, audiences, and situations involved than on the nature of the act itself. Thus, an actor's behavior is but one of a number of contingencies which must be considered in relativistic analyses of social definitions of deviance.

Unfortunately, this relativistic orientation has served more as a focal point for critique, debate, and speculation than as a heuristic stimulus for empirical research (see Gibbs, 1966; 1972; Schur, 1971: 7–36; Davis, 1972). In particular, few studies have dealt with the relativistic argument that social interpretations of "deviant behavior" are situationally problematic. Audience interpretations of a given act as deviant or nondeviant are taken to be highly dependent upon the social circumstances within which that act is embedded. The same act interpreted as deviant under one set of circumstances might be seen as quite acceptable under other circumstances. As an illustration of this argument, Douglas (1971:139) cites the following example adapted from Blum (1970):

> . . . a woman observed on the streets of a city to be wailing might well be thought to be "mentally ill." Yet once we know that she has just been in an automobile accident in which a loved one has been killed, her behavior can be seen to be "normal grief" and not "mental illness." Only the situational context makes this clear to us.

Deviance theorists in the "ethnomethodological" tradition, such as Douglas, Blum, and McHugh (1970) have been especially insistent on treating deviance as a "situated" phenomenon. However, a concern with situational variations in interpretational processes is also evident in more conventional theories of societal reaction and labeling (Kitsuse, 1962; Rubington and Weinberg, 1973: 1–10). Yet with the exception of several studies on police work (Piliavin and Briar, 1964; Bittner, 1967a; 1967b; Black and Reiss, 1970; Black, 1970), deviance research has overlooked this problem.

Previous theoretical discussions of situated interpretations of deviance have been rather abstract and have not provided systematic guidelines for research. This study will attempt to specify several situational factors which influence the interpretational process. The influences of these factors will be examined empirically, using survey data which compare interpretive reactions to marijuana use and alcohol use in various situations.

*© 1978 by the Society for the Study of Social Problems. Reprinted from *Social Problems,* 22 (February 1975), pp. 346–356 by permission of the author and publisher.

**Presented at the 1974 Annual Meeting of the Southern Sociological Society, Atlanta. The author wishes to thank Donald A. Biggs for facilitating this research and to acknowledge the support of a grant from the Office for Student Affairs, University of Minn.

SITUATIONAL VARIATIONS
IN THE INTERPRETATIONAL PROCESS

One of the earliest and clearest statements of the relativistic orientation is Kitsuse's (1962) analysis of societal reactions to deviance. Deviance, for Kitsuse, must be defined and analyzed from the point of view of those who interpret and react to behavior as deviant. Accordingly, he conceptualizes "deviance" as a three-stage process "by which the members of a group, community, or society (1) interpret behavior as deviant, (2) define persons who so behave as a certain kind of deviant, and (3) accord them the treatment considered appropriate to such deviants" (Kitsuse, 1962:248). These stages represent empirically related, but analytically distinct sources of variation in social definitions of deviance. The initiating stage in Kitsuse's formulation—interpretations of behavior as deviant—is of primary interest here.[1] Although Kitsuse (1962:255) indicates that the "interpretational process may be activated by a wide range of situational behavior," he does not present a detailed analysis of these situational variations.

In a recent paper, Orcutt (1973) attempts to extend Kitsuse's work by relating it to laboratory studies of deviation in small groups. On the basis of a reanalysis of two small group studies, he identifies three situational conditions which appear to influence naïve group members' interpretations of "deviation" performed by experimental confederates during group discussions. Group members' attitudinal hostility toward a confederate tends to increase to the extent that the confederate's behavior is perceived (1) to interfere with central situational goals, (2) to be stable, i.e., unresponsive to social influence and situational change, and (3) to be motivated by pervasive personal dispositions of the confederate rather than by immediate social events in the situation. These three conditions refer to joint perceptual relationships between the confederate's actions and the situational context from which interpretations of deviant behavior are derived. Cumulative combinations of these perceptual conditions are used by group members as grounds for assigning "deviance" as a situated meaning to the confederate's actions. Consistent with Kitsuse's formulation, Orcutt argues that such interpretations subsequently provide members with evidence for defining the confederate as deviant *in character* and with justification for reacting to him accordingly.

Orcutt's (1973) analysis of situational contingencies in the interpretational process is limited by its reliance on indirect inference from previously published research. A more adequate analysis of these conditional factors would require that the situational context be systematically varied while holding the actor's behavior constant. The present study attempts such an analysis. Respondents in the investigation reported here were asked to interpret the acceptability or unacceptability of marijuana use or alcohol use in various hypothetical situations. Situational circumstances were systematically varied according to three conditions suggested by Orcutt's reanalysis of small group studies.

The first of these conditions relates to *situational goals* and varies according to whether drug use occurs in a *task* situation or in a *socioemotional* situation. The use of either marijuana or alcohol should generally be perceived as consistent with the goals of a socioemotional situation, such as a party, but as a potential source of interference with goal-attainment in a task situation. Therefore, the acts of marijuana use or alcohol use will tend to be interpreted as deviant when situated in a task setting.

The situational *stability* of marijuana or alcohol use is also varied. In some of the items presented to respondents, drug-using behavior was described as *intra*-situational, i.e., a single, situationally circumscribed occurrence. Other items described marijuana or alcohol use as *inter*-situational, i.e., the act of drug use was presented as a stable pattern of repeated occurrences across several situations. Attribution theorists (Heider, 1958; Kelley, 1967) argue that the certainty with which inferences or interpretations can be made regarding an act will be an increasing function of the consistency of the act's occurrence across situations. When drug use is perceived as a stable *inter*-situational pattern, it will be more likely to be interpreted as deviant. Some support for this hypothesis is supplied by Johnston's (1973:74) recent study of attitudes toward drug use.

The third and final situational variation considered in this study relates to *motivations* attributed to the marijuana or alcohol user. A central issue for attribution theories in social psychology (Heider, 1958; Kelley, 1967), as well as for relativistic theories of deviance (McHugh, 1970), is whether situational circumstances or personal motives of the actor are perceived to be responsible for the occurrence of an act. Situational causes are frequently viewed as legitimate "excuses" for a deviant act (Scott and Lyman, 1963). An attempt is made to tap this aspect of situational interpretations in the present study by varying drug-using situations according to a distinction between *social* and *personal* motivations for use. Social motivations were depicted in situations which reflect mutual social participation in marijuana or alcohol use. Personal motivations were implied where drug use is presented as an individualistic attempt to cope with the situation. Interpretations of deviance should be more likely under the latter condition.

In addition to its focus on these three situational variations, the present study also attempts to take into consideration recent criticism advanced by Lemert (1972) of relativistic theories of deviance. Lemert cautions against the tendency of some theorists to overemphasize subjective social definitions and to ignore the objective nature of the deviant act itself. He argues that "(t)he extreme relativism in some statements of labeling theory leaves the unfortunate impression that almost any meaning can be assigned to human attributes and actions" (1972:22). Deviance research should attend both to objective factors and to subjective factors and "it has to be heeded continually that deviance outcomes flow from interaction between the two sets of factors . . ." (1972:21).

In order to deal empirically with Lemert's arguments, the research reported here incorporates comparisons between two objectively different acts, marijuana use and alcohol use. Half of the respondents in this study were presented with situational variations in marijuana use, while the other half were asked to interpret alcohol use in the same situations. These two acts are similar enough to permit standardization of situational variations, but sufficiently different to permit comparative assessment of unique effects of an act upon respondents' interpretations. For example, is marijuana use *generally* interpreted as more deviant than alcohol use, irrespective of situational contexts? Also, does the nature of these acts "interact," in Lemert's words, with certain situational features to produce unique interpretations of deviance? This analysis will focus on these substantive questions as well as on the relativistic problem of situated deviance.

METHODOLOGY

Items describing situational variations in recreational drug use were included on questionnaires administered to a purposive sample of University of Minnesota undergraduates during the Winter Quarter of 1972. The questionnaires were distributed and completed during regular meetings of eight large classes in four undergraduate divisions.[2] Two forms of the questionnaire—a Marijuana Form and an Alcohol Form—were distributed alternately to students in adjoining seats. Approximately half of the items on the two forms were identical. The other half of the items dealt specifically with one drug or the other. The Marijuana Form was completed by 460 undergraduates and the Alcohol Form was completed by 465. These two sub-samples did not differ significantly in sociodemographic characteristics or in levels of recreational drug use.

Respondents' interpretations of situational variations were measured by a series of eight items, listed in Table 1. These items were randomly mixed with four filler items. Respondents who completed the Marijuana Form were asked to rate situated descriptions of marijuana use, while respondents who completed the Alcohol Form were asked to rate alcohol use. Ratings were recorded in a five-point Likert response format ranging from "quite acceptable" to "quite unacceptable" with "indifferent" as the midpoint.[3] The eight critical items presented all possible factorial combinations of the three situational variations, i.e., situational goal (Socioemotional/Task), stability of use (Intra-situational/Inter-situational) and user motivation (Social motivation/Personal motivation). Therefore, including the marijuana-alcohol comparison across

TABLE 1 Percentages Accepting of or Indifferent to Marijuana Use and Alcohol Use by Situational Item Variations

Situational Items	Conditional Variations*			Accepting or Indifferent		Significance of Difference (by Chi-Square)
	Situational Goal	Stability of Use	User Motivation	Mari.	Alco.	
1—A college student smokes marijuana (drinks alcohol) at a small party with his friends who are also using marijuana (alcohol).	Socio-emotional	Intra-situation	Social motivation	82.8%	97.0%	p < .001
2—A college student working as a salesman smokes marijuana (drinks alcohol) with one of his clients who has offered it to him.	TASK	Intra-situation	Social motivation	39.0%	81.0%	p < .001
3—A college student smokes marijuana (drinks alcohol) two or three times a week when he gets together with friends in the evening.	Socio-emotional	INTER-SITUATION	Social motivation	70.9%	79.0%	p < .01
4—During a boring party, a college student withdraws to a quiet corner to get high on marijuana (alcohol) to help him feel better.	Socio-emotional	Intra-situation	PERSONAL MOTIVATION	41.7%	34.9%	p < .05
5—A college student uses marijuana (alcohol) to ease his anxieties about meeting others before going to any kind of a party.	Socio-emotional	INTER-SITUATION	PERSONAL MOTIVATION	39.6%	48.5%	p < .01
6—A college student working in an office regularly smokes marijuana (drinks alcohol) with his co-workers during their lunch break.	TASK	INTER-SITUATION	Social motivation	29.6%	31.5%	N.S.
7—On a particularly trying day at his part-time job, a college student smokes marijuana (drinks alcohol) during his lunch break to help him face the rest of his work.	TASK	Intra-situation	PERSONAL MOTIVATION	26.5%	20.9%	N.S.
8—Every day before going to his job, a college student smokes marijuana (drinks alcohol) to help him cope with his work situation.	TASK	INTER-SITUATION	PERSONAL MOTIVATION	9.3%	4.9%	p < .025

*Conditions expected to increase "deviant" interpretations shown in capital letters.

independent sub-samples, these items were designed as a 2 x 2 x 2 x 2 factorial, with repeated measures on three factors.

RESULTS

Table 1 lists the situational items and the conditional variations that each presented. This table also presents the percentages of respondents who either rated an item as quite acceptable, acceptable, or indifferent. These categories seem reasonable as an operationalization of *non-deviant* interpretations of situated instances of recreational drug use. Percentages are given separately for interpretations of marijuana use (N = 460) and alcohol use (N = 465). Finally, the significance level of differences between drug percentages is given for each item.

Cumulative Effects of Situational Variations

The items in Table 1 have been ranked in four groups. The item presenting no "deviant" situational conditions is listed first (Item 1), the three items with one "deviant" condition next (Items 2–4), followed by items presenting two "deviant" conditions (Items 5–7) and the item with three "deviant" conditions (Item 8). A general indication of the cumulative influence of the situational conditions can be gained by reading percentages down this table within drugs.

With two interesting exceptions, decreasing acceptance of marijuana and alcohol use can be observed as a greater number of "deviant" conditions becomes implicated in the situational context. Interpretations of alcohol use show an especially dramatic cumulative change. Although 97 percent of the alcohol sub-sample accept drinking in the completely "non-deviant" situation (Item 1), only five percent accept alcohol use in the completely "deviant" situation (Item 8). Therefore, *depending on the situational context,* interpretations of alcohol use undergo a virtually complete reversal from nondeviant to deviant. Situational variations have a similar, but less pronounced cumulative effect on interpretations of marijuana use. Percentages of acceptance range from 83 percent to nine percent. These general cumulative trends clearly indicate that social interpretations of these acts are systematically responsive to variations in situational contexts.

One exception to the general cumulative trend involves marijuana use in a task situation which is "non-deviant" in other respects (Item 2). Marijuana use in this situation is slightly less acceptable than is use in a situation where *both* stability and motivation are "deviant" (Item 5). This finding suggests that the respondents place special weight on situational goals when interpreting marijuana use as deviant. In fact, the four situations involving task goals are also the four situations where marijuana use is most likely to be interpreted as deviant.

The other exception to the general cumulative trend occurs when alcohol use is presented in the context of a personal motivation to "withdraw" from a boring party (Item 4). Curiously, alcohol use is rated as less acceptable in this particular situation than in another situation involving both intersituational use *and* personal motivation (Item 5, "easing anxieties about meeting others before going to any party"). This theoretically troublesome result is undoubtedly due to the specific reference to "withdrawal" in the former item. Such a use of alcohol implies extreme detachment from the social situation, while "easing anxieties about meeting others" still implies an element of social motivation. Ironically, this subtle and unintended difference between the "personal motivations" described in these items highlights a particular sensitivity to motivational considerations in social interpretations of alcohol use. The implications of this sensitivity can be seen more clearly in comparisons across drugs.

Comparisons Between Marijuana Use and Alcohol Use

The data indicate that the act of marijuana use is not uniformly interpreted as more deviant than is the act of alcohol use, at least among college students. As shown in Table 1, alcohol use is significantly more acceptable than marijuana use in only four of eight situational contexts. Greater acceptance of alcohol use is limited mainly to relatively "non-deviant" contexts, where only one or no "deviant" situational conditions are involved.

Alcohol use is much more acceptable than marijuana use in the task situation where other conditions are "non-deviant" (Item 2, salesman "drinks" vs. "smokes" with a client). This finding reflects the functional importance and "normality" of alcohol use in situations involving business transactions, a situated activity which has yet to be institutionalized for marijuana. Consistent with Lemert's argument, this is an instance where the objective nature of the act "interacts" with the situational context to produce a unique interpretation of deviance.

Differences between interpretations of marijuana use and alcohol use tend to diminish or reverse as soon as personal motivation is perceived to enter into the situated activity. In three out of four items involving personal motivations, the acceptability of marijuana use is greater than that of alcohol use. Table 1 clearly shows the precipitous decline in acceptance of alcohol that results when personal motivations become a factor in situational interpretations. These patterns relate to the earlier comment regarding the interpretive significance of the motivational circumstances of alcohol use. Compared to alcohol use, interpretations of marijuana use appear to be less contingent on situational variations in motivations attributed to the user.

DISCUSSION

The situational variations examined in this analysis do produce substantial and predictable chances in respondents' interpretations of marijuana and alcohol use. Each of the three situational conditions has at least some effect on respondents' interpretations and the cumulative effects of these variations are dramatic. This is particularly so in the case of alcohol use, where interpretations vary from almost unanimous acceptance to unanimous nonacceptance. In short, what is nondeviant in some situations is deviant in others. These data generally lend empirical substance to relativistic discussions of deviance as a situated phenomenon.

However, Lemert's caution against "radical" relativism also finds justification in these data. Several findings indicate that the nature of the act itself has important influences on respondents' interpretations. In contrast to marijuana use, alcohol use tends to receive substantial disapproval only after personal motivations are situationally attributed to the act. Once alcohol use is perceived to be associated with personal motivations, interpretive differences between this act and the act of marijuana use diminish considerably. On the other hand, marijuana use is clearly viewed as deviant in a typical task situation where alcohol use is overwhelmingly accepted by the respondents. An understanding of these results requires analysis of differences between the acts themselves.

Respondents may view marijuana use and alcohol use differently in terms of *typical* motivations for these acts. Respondents seem tacitly to assume that alcohol use is socially motivated, unless notified otherwise by situational circumstances. It is likely that a similar tacit assumption is not made with regard to marijuana use. Given the typical nature of marijuana use among American college students, the act itself might imply some degree of personal motivation in any situation. These observations are consistent with research and theory which documents the general motivational and functional importance of alcohol as a "social mixer" and the more personalized, experiential motivations associated with marijuana use (Orcutt, 1972; Cahalan *et al.,* 1969; Goode, 1972).

These remarks suggest that respondents may use *either the situational context of the act or the act itself* as sources of evidence for motivational attributions. Even when marijuana is used in a situation that does not present explicit evidence of personal motivation, the act *per se* will still serve as an alternative source which carries this information. In the case of alcohol use, however, the situation must explicitly imply personal motivations, since the act *per se* does not.

This explanation helps to account for the responsiveness of interpretations of alcohol use to situational perceptions of personal motivation. The situation, and not the act, is the primary source of motivational evidence. Insight is also gained into the markedly discrepant interpretations of marijuana use and alcohol use in the "salesman-client" task situation. If alcohol use is assumed to be socially motivated, it can be accepted as an activity which facilitates interpersonal interaction and the attainment of task goals. On the other hand, if marijuana use is assumed to be personally motivated, it will tend to be viewed as a potential impediment to the attainment of task goals. Task activities require focused involvement in and attention to the *interpersonal* situation. The act of marijuana use instead implies a motivation to focus inward on *interpersonal* experience. In the task situation, then, marijuana use will be perceived as motivationally inconsistent with task requirements and interpreted as deviant.

CONCLUSION

The results of this study indicate the usefulness of relativistic conceptions of situated deviance. Situational circumstances appear to account for a considerable degree of the perceptual variance in respondents' interpretations of marijuana and alcohol use as deviant acts. At the same time, the findings caution against a radical relativism which would deny interpretive significance to the nature of the act itself.

Unfortunately, this study fails to come to grips with the interactional implications of relativistic theorizing, a weakness it shares with most of the research literature on deviance (Orcutt, 1973). The relationship between subjective interpretations of deviant acts and overt reactions to such acts by social audiences remains conceptually and empirically problematic. The kinds of situational conditions hypothetically varied in this survey investigation could conceivably be manipulated in experimental and quasi-experimental designs which focus on behavioral reactions to situated deviance.

Relativistic theories have raised new and important problems for the field of deviance. But it is time attention was shifted from the endless round of critique and debate of these ideas to the more crucial task of empirical evaluation.

NOTES

1. Behavioral evidence is not a necessary condition for imputations of deviance to an actor (Katz, 1972). In most empirical instances, however, definitions of an actor as deviant and reactions to the actor's deviance are based on interpretations of behavior as deviant.

2. Probability sampling procedures were precluded by time and budgetary limitations, but an attempt was made to obtain a broad, if not precisely representative, cross-section of the undergraduate population. Classes were selected for the sample according to two main criteria: (1) enrollment exceeding 100 students and (2) required for departmental majors in four diverse undergraduate colleges. Questionnaires were distributed to approximately equal numbers of students from classes in the Colleges of Liberal Arts (N = 304), Business Administration (N = 301), and Agriculture, Forestry and Home Economics (N = 322). A smaller number of students were in classes in the Institute of Technology (N = 85). Of the 1,012 questionnaires distributed, 92.3 percent were usable. Unusable questionnaires were mainly those filled out by graduate students and those that were incomplete. When compared with undergraduate enrollment parameters, the sample tends to overrepresent males (68.3 percent versus 58.4 percent) and to underrepresent freshmen (14.4 percent versus 23.1 percent).

3. The items were presented to respondents as follows:

What is appropriate in one situation may not be appropriate in another. Below are 12 descriptions of situations in which marijuana [alcohol] might be used. Rate the acceptability of marijuana [alcohol] use in each situation as you see it. Enter your ratings on the back page according to the following codes:

1 = I feel that marijuana [alcohol] use would be QUITE ACCEPTABLE under these circumstances.

2 = I feel that marijuana [alcohol] use would be SOMEWHAT ACCEPTABLE under these circumstances.

3 = I would feel INDIFFERENT regarding marijuana [alcohol] use under these circumstances.

4 = I feel that marijuana [alcohol] use would be SOMEWHAT UNACCEPTABLE under these circumstances.

5 = I feel that marijuana [alcohol] use would be QUITE UNACCEPTABLE under these circumstances.

REFERENCES

BITTNER, E. 1967a. "The police on skid-row: A study of peace keeping." *American Sociological Review* 32(October): 699–715.

1967b. "Police discretion in emergency apprehension of mentally ill persons." *Social Problems* 14(Winter): 278–292.

BLACK, D. J. 1970. "Production of crime rates." *American Sociological Review* 35(August): 733–748.

BLACK, D. J. and A. J. REISS, JR. 1970. "Police control of juveniles." *American Sociological Review* 35 (February): 63–77.

BLUM, A. F. 1970. "The sociology of mental illness," pp. 31–60 in Jack D. Douglas (ed.), *Deviance and Respectability: The Social Construction of Moral Meanings.* New York: Basic Books.

CAHALAN, DON, IRA H. CISIN, and HELEN M. CROSSLEY. 1969. *American Drinking Practices.* New Brunswick: Rutgers Center of Alcohol Studies.

DAVIS, N. J. 1972. "Labeling theory in deviance research: A critique and reconsideration." *Sociological Quarterly* 13(Autumn): 447–474.

DOUGLAS, JACK D. 1971. *Deviance and Respectability.* New York: Basic Books.

DOUGLAS, JACK D. 1971. *American Social Order: Social Rules in a Pluralistic Society.* New York: The Free Press.

GIBBS, J. 1972. "Issues in defining deviant behavior," pp. 39–68 in Robert A. Scott and Jack D. Douglas (eds.), *Theoretical Perspectives on Deviance.* New York: Basic Books.

1966. "Conceptions of deviant behavior: The old and the new." *Pacific Sociological Review* 9(Spring): 9–14.

GOODE, ERICH. 1972. *Drugs in American Society.* New York: Knopf.

HEIDER, FRITZ. 1958. *The Psychology of Interpersonal Relations.* New York: Wiley.

JOHNSTON, LLOYD. 1973. *Drugs and American Youth.* Ann Arbor: Institute for Social Research.

KATZ, J. 1972. "Deviance, charisma, and rule-defined behavior." *Social Problems* 20(Fall): 186–202.

KELLEY, H. H. 1967. "Attribution theory in social psychology," pp. 192–240 in David Levine (ed.), *Nebraska Symposium on Motivation, 1967.* Lincoln: University of Nebraska Press.

KITSUSE, J. I. 1962. "Societal reaction to deviant behavior: Problems of theory and method." *Social Problems* 9(Winter): 247–256.

LEMERT, EDWIN M. 1972. *Human Deviance, Social Problems, and Social Control* (2nd ed.). Englewood Cliffs, NJ: Prentice Hall.

MATZA, DAVID. 1969. *Becoming Deviant.* Englewood Cliffs, NJ: Prentice Hall.

McHUGH, P. 1970. "A common-sense conception of deviance." Pp. 61–88 in Jack D. Douglas (ed.), *Deviance and Respectability: The Social Construction of Moral Meanings.* New York: Basic Books.

ORCUTT, J. D. 1973. "Societal reaction and the response to deviation in small groups." *Social Forces* 52(December): 259–267.

1972. "Toward a sociological theory of drug effects: A comparison of marijuana and alcohol." *Sociology and Social Research* 56(January): 242–253.

PILIAVIN, I. and S. BRIAR. 1964. "Police encounters with juveniles." *American Journal of Sociology* 69(September): 206–214.

RUBINGTON, EARL and MARTIN S. WEINBERG. 1973. *Deviance: The Interactionist Perspective* (2nd ed.). New York: Macmillan.

SCHUR, EDWIN M. 1971. *Labeling Deviant Behavior: Its Sociological Implications.* New York: Harper and Row.

SCOTT, M. B. and S. M. LYMAN. 1963. "Accounts." *American Sociological Review* 33(February): 46–62.

Gender, Power, and Alternative Living Arrangements in the Inner-City Crack Culture*

Lisa Maher
Eloise Dunlap
Bruce D. Johnson
Ansley Hamid**

The advent of crack cocaine has had a profound effect on the economic and social life of many low-income inner-city communities (Johnson, Williams, Dei, and Sanabria 1990). The crack economy has also extracted a much higher price from its participants than previous drug eras, taking an excessive toll on users' lives (Hamid 1990). Within this context, shelter has become a crucial and sought-after commodity. This article will document processes by which impoverished crack-abusing women resolve their human needs for shelter and personal safety and describe the strategies they pursue in constructing little-known alternative living arrangements for themselves. The core question addressed is this: Among inner-city women without legal income (for instance, who have no legal employment or welfare payments), who are excluded from assistance by their family and kin networks, and who expend most of their monetary and labor resources to procure and use crack, how and where do they find shelter with some semblance of personal security?

Recent scholarship on homelessness (Barak 1991; Hopper and Hamburg 1984; Jencks and Peterson 1991; Ropers 1988; Rossi 1989; Venderstaay 1992) has documented many forces associated with the increased numbers of homeless persons in America but has neglected two themes. Although the homeless literature occasionally mentions the importance of crack abuse (Jencks and Peterson 1991), few studies have sought to specify the mechanisms by which crack abusers become homeless. Moreover, homeless women living without children are rarely mentioned or studied; such women appear to constitute less than 10% of persons living in shelters or other institutions where homeless persons are found. The relative absence of homeless crack-using females in the homeless literature may be largely due to their success in obtaining alternative living arrangements, which keep them out of shelters and institutional settings.

The literature on crack use and sex-for-crack (Boyle and Anglin 1993; Carlson and Siegel 1991; Edlin et al. 1992; Goldstein, Ouellet, and Fendrich 1992; Inciardi, Lockwood, and Pottieger 1993; Inciardi, Pottieger, Forney, Chitwood, and McBride 1990; Ratner 1993a; Weatherby et al. 1992) reveals many factors that contribute to women becoming crack abusers and having no conventional place to live. First and foremost has been the influence of social and economic forces in limiting options for low-income women. Since 1965, inner-city minority neighborhoods have been marked by persistent poverty, structural unemployment, and urban dispossession. In many neighborhoods, the drug economy has become a way of life and a means of survival for a significant segment of the local population (Bourgois 1989, 1995; Dunlap and

*From *The Journal of Research in Crime and Delinquency,* 33(2), pp. 181–205. Copyright © 1996 by Sage Publications, Inc. Reprinted by permission of Sage Publications, Inc.

**This study was supported by the National Institute on Drug Abuse (NIDA) (1R01 DA 05126-07) and NIDA Minority Research Supplemental Award (1 R03 DA 06413-01), as well as the Harry Frank Guggenheim Foundation. The opinions expressed in this article do not represent the official position of the U.S. government, the National Institute on Drug Abuse, National Development and Research Institutes, Inc. (NDRI), John Jay College of Criminal Justice, or the National Drug and Alcohol Research Centre. The authors express their appreciation to Richard Curtis, Ali Manwar, Doris Randolf, and Charles Small for their many contributions to this research.

Johnson 1992; Hamid 1992a; Johnson et al. 1990; Kasarda 1992; Moore 1991; Sullivan 1989). Few of the women studied here had held employment in legal jobs during the preceding decade, and at the time of interview most failed to comply with welfare regulations; thus they were not in receipt of any legitimate income.

These crack-abusing women typically grew up in family and kin systems severely affected by these structural forces. Little prepared these women for licit jobs or conventional marriages. Few women had even one parent who held steady employment, and welfare support was often intermittent and never enough. Mothers or other caregivers (typically a grandmother or aunt) supplemented income by informal sector activity (e.g., serving alcohol at afterhours clubs, working for a numbers runner, etc.—see Dunlap 1992; Maher, Dunlap, and Johnson, forthcoming). For many women, both community and family level involvement facilitated access to informal sector labor markets. Within some families, alcohol, heroin, marijuana, and cocaine use and abuse, as well as the illicit sale of such substances, had been a primary economic activity across several generations (Dunlap and Johnson 1994; Dunlap, Johnson, and Maher, forthcoming).

The majority of women respondents here (see following) initiated illicit drug use prior to 1985–1986, when crack use became widespread in New York City. Many were former heroin and cocaine powder users with a history of intravenous drug use. A significant minority also used alcohol and marijuana on a near-daily basis (Golub and Johnson 1994; Johnson et al. 1985). However, despite the fact that most were not drug neophytes, these women's lives were severely disrupted by crack use. The demands of crack use and the crack lifestyle forced many of them to develop new and innovative ways of meeting their instrumental needs. In particular, the advent of crack had a dramatic effect on the nature, frequency, and dollar value of sexual acts in street-level sex markets (Maher 1996; Maher and Curtis 1992). Although the exchange of sex-for-drugs is not a new phenomenon, recent accounts have highlighted its significance and frequency in inner-city drug use settings (e.g., Carlson and Siegel 1991; Edlin et al. 1992;

Fullilove and Fullilove 1989; Goldstein et al. 1992; Inciardi et al. 1993, p. 96; Inciardi et al. 1991; Ratner 1993a; Weatherby et al. 1992).

The cumulative effect of these influences was a large number of crack-abusing women who had no legal income, expended all their illegal income on crack, had no relatives or friends who allowed them in their households, and were excluded by male crack sellers who dominated them sexually or as employers. One of the most pressing problems confronted by the crack-using women encountered in this research—in addition to their constant mission (the search for crack and the illegal activities this typically entailed)—was the search for shelter and respite from the street. Although they vacillated between homelessness and periods of temporary residence with family, kin, friends and associates, most of the women in this study could be classified as homeless and certainly almost all had experienced homelessness at some point. Day after day, month after month, these women had no conventional place to go to sleep, eliminate, bathe, eat, rest, relax, and restore themselves. Using ethnographic data based on observations and interviews with active women crack users, this article documents the existence of a set of gendered "solutions" to the problems of homelessness and residential instability encountered by women crack users.

METHODOLOGY

This article combines data from two ethnographic projects conducted in New York City over the period 1989–1992. These projects spanned seven low-income neighborhoods and included data from a broad sample of women crack users of different ages and race-ethnic backgrounds who exhibited considerable diversity in terms of their drug use careers.

One study, the Natural History of Crack Distribution/Abuse, is an ethnographic study of the structure, functioning, and economics of cocaine and crack distribution in low-income, minority communities in New York City. The data set generated for this project constituted one of the richest in the field, containing several thousand pages of transcribed recorded material and drawing on the insights of a variety of informants and a multidisciplinary team of ethnographic researchers. (Further details of this study and the methods used are outlined in Dunlap and Johnson 1994; Dunlap et al. 1990; Williams, Dunlap, Johnson, and Hamid 1992). As of 1992, 23 African American women, 9 Latinas, and 1 White woman had been studied. Although these women were active sellers and distributors of crack (and often other drugs), the vast majority were rarely able to afford housing and were usually without a regular conventional place to live.

The second study (Maher 1995) consisted of a multisite ethnographic study focusing on the economic lives of women crack users in three Brooklyn neighborhoods. In the course of this 3-year project, field observations and interviews were conducted with more than 200 women crack users. Although the majority of subjects were African American women (36%) and Latinas (44%), a significant minority (20%) were European American women. A majority were polydrug users and nearly all were homeless or involved in lifestyles that exhibited a high degree of residential instability. These women were both perpetrators and victims of violence, and all were engaged in lawbreaking activity—principally street-level sexwork—at the time of the study (for further details of this study and the sampling procedures see Maher 1995; Maher and Curtis 1994).

These two ethnographic research endeavors were conducted in the same city over the same time period, although in different neighborhoods and with slightly different focal study groups. In both studies, women ethnographers (Dunlap and Maher) conducted extensive fieldwork (recording hundreds of pages of field notes) and completed extensive in-depth tape-recorded interviews (generating thousands of transcript pages) with their selected subjects. In most cases, specific female subjects were contacted and observed on different days and times during the year—ensuring that the reliability of their living arrangements was routinely documented over time. In both studies, the ethnographers intentionally visited the women at their current living arrangements, thereby observing and validating the actual conditions in which subjects lived.

A major theme emerged in both studies: The majority of these women did not have a conventional place (a home or apartment where someone [rarely the subject] paid the rent and maintained the household) to sleep, rest, eat, eliminate, bathe, and store possessions. Instead, these woman crack users, regardless of whether primarily active in sexwork or drug distribution and sales, demonstrated considerable effort and skill in finding places to stay for relatively limited time periods. These alternate living arrangements reflected their persistence and extensive experience in continuously locating a place day-by-day and week-by-week to restore themselves. This rich descriptive repository of field notes, field diaries, and transcribed tape-recorded interviews documented both similarities and variations in local social and economic conditions as well as how the larger context of drug use, income generation, and gender relations affected these women. (It should be noted that many male crack users exhibited similar difficulties in finding places to live and often resorted to nonconventional living arrangements, but the focus of this article is upon female crack users and the gendered nature of their arrangements.)

As the following sections demonstrate, for many of the women in this study, homelessness served both to cement and intensify their involvement in and commitment to the street-level drug economy. However, the nature, form, and physical location of accommodations utilized by these women exhibited wide variation, as did the relationships to which such coresidencies gave rise. Although in this context the considerable evidence of exchange and support patterns gives lie to the stereotype of the predatory thirsty crackhead, it needs to be borne in mind that such relationships are also responses to the exigencies of life on the margins. The variability of these alternative living arrangements and the social relations they reflected and spawned are discussed below.

Starting Out: A Little Help From Your Friends

The more I looked into homelessness, the more it appeared to be misstated as merely a problem of being without shelter: homelessness is more properly viewed as the most aggravated state of a more prevalent problem, **extreme poverty** (Rossi 1989, p. 8).

For many poor people, homelessness is the end result of a gradual and piecemeal shift from a tenuous existence that encompasses economic and social marginality, substandard housing, and family breakdown. Among the socially and economically isolated, and the precariously housed to begin with, the experiences of most of the women in this study appear to fit this model of homelessness as "the last stage in the downward spiral of poverty and abandonment" (Vanderstaay 1992, p. 60). Even though drug use clearly accelerates this process, a majority of women maintained precarious accommodations prior to problematic drug use. For some women, involvement in drug sales led to arrest or eviction, serving to expedite official homelessness, as reported by Carol, a 41-year-old African American woman.

I had my own apartment, myself and my daughter. I started selling crack. From my house. [For who?] Some Jamaican. [Yeah, how did you get hooked up with that?] Through my boyfriend. They wanted to sell from my apartment. They were supposed to pay me something like $150 a week rent, and then something off the profits. They used to, you know, fuck up the money, like not give me the money. Eventually I went through a whole lot of different dealers. Eventually I stopped payin' my rent because I wanted to get a transfer out of there to get away from everything 'cause soon as one group of crack dealers would get out, another group would come along. [So how long did that go on for?] About four years. Then I lost my apartment, and I sat out in the street.

Whereas the majority of women in this study had not sold drugs from their apartments, the experiences of those who had done so suggest that such arrangements only rarely represent a form of female entrepreneurship and are typically short-lived (but see the case study of Rachel for an exception—Dunlap and Johnson 1996; Dunlap, Johnson, Manwar 1994; Dunlap et al. 1990).

Initially, whether they were evicted, pushed out, or left of their own accord, many of the women in this study avoided formal acknowledgment of their homeless status by becoming "couch people"—alternating between households among extended kin networks (see Dunlap and Johnson 1992) or roaming from friend to (so-called) friend in search of short-term accommodations. As is evident in the following quotation from Jonelle, a 32-year-old African American woman, such offers are usually limited to a shower or brief rest or perhaps an overnight stay, usually in exchange for drugs.

[So where do you stay mostly now?] Walk the street. [You don't have one particular place where you go?] Oh, we got a girlfriend named Jeanette that lives on J———, you know. She let us go up there and wash up or sometimes I might fall asleep up there, but I'm not—I don't consider myself stayin' with her though. [Does she charge you anything to go there?] Not really. . . . With her, she's just lookin' to get high. You come with some "get high" which most likely we'll do, and you turn her on and you know it's cool.

Occasionally, women were able to negotiate short-term living arrangements with other women drug users. More often than not, however, such hospitality was contingent on the approval of coresident males. As Sugar, a 36-year-old Latina, reported:

I found me a new room. [Yeah, how did that happen?] So you know, uh, Angel, she lives right here on I——— and T——— okay, she's one of my co-workers. And her old man said, "Hey let her stay here," you know. And I appreciate that. [You have to pay them?] She never said nothing like that, but of course I've got to give them something. Yeah, you know. [Throw them something anyway.] Of course, definitely. But I mean they didn't make any kind of formal arrangement? [They just kind of expect you to, when you have, to, you know?] Um-huh.

Contingent on the strength and nature of the relationship, a few women were able to negotiate longer term arrangements when various forms of payment were provided, as did Shorty, a 22-year-old Latina.

I was living with a friend of mine and her husband, and then this guy came along and started living there too, and they were into getting high and stuff; and at that time, I was getting high too. [On what?] On crack. You know, and I was having a very hard time there, and I didn't have no financial help, as far as my husband working, he wasn't working, I wasn't on welfare or nothing like that. So, finally these guys weren't satisfied with the money we were giving them. They wanted me to support their habit, buy food and pay rent money. You know? [How much were you giving them?] I was giving them $75 a week for both of us, which wasn't bad. I could deal with that, but then they wanted, you know, crack. I had to buy them crack too, plus feed her, her husband, and this guy that started living there.

However, such arrangements rarely last when the household is immersed in drug use. ~~Even long-standing relationships between women are rapidly depleted by one or both party's use of drugs,~~ as happened between Dee Dee, a 29-year-old African American woman, and her "home-girl," Rita.

She lives in the projects on Marcy. She used to live right around the corner from me. She's one of the first people that we lived with when we came in this neighborhood. But then they abandoned her building. [Is she somebody that you could stay at her house?] Yeah, but everybody, you know, to get in the door it's like you got to have something for them. And I don't really feel like they're such a friend, you know. I told her when I first came there, I said, "Look I got a bag of dope. I'll give you some, all right." I'm like, "Just give me a wash cloth and a towel. That's all I want to do. I want to take a shower and clean up and then I'll talk to you," you know. So of course I was taking my time. I wanted to relax and really get clean, you know. So when I come out it's like a big thing now. It's like, "Well you just walk in my house, and just walk into my shower," and all this is 'cause all the time I'm in the bathroom she's thinking I'm gettin' high. She think I don't have no more dope. So I played it off like I didn't. I said, "You know what the bag was so small, I did the whole thing." And honey she must have caught on fire, right; and when I seen her attitude, and I felt like—and I really had the bag of dope. I just wanted to see how she was gonna act. And she acted just like I thought. "And you ain't got nothin' for me, you're not welcome here." So when I seen it was like that I said, "Yeah well I'll just go, and I won't come again."

These accounts illustrate that although the need for reciprocity was clearly understood, the terms were often vague, suggesting that among this population, conflict over the precise nature of reciprocal obligations would be frequent and perhaps inevitable. For the most part, however, the women crack users in this study were rarely in a position to extend shelter to each other. Most of them were homeless, a majority were estranged from both their families of orientation and procreation and all could be characterized as possessing severely limited economic and social resources. For a majority of women, this meant that they had three choices—either resort to the city shelter system, go it alone on the streets, or rely on men.

Engaging the System: Welfare Hotels and Shelter Accommodation

Without exception, the women in this study identified ~~Single Room Occupancy (SRO) or welfare hotels, as criminogenic, dangerous, and conducive to drug use.~~ Although Jenny, a 25-year-old European American, had experimented with drug use in the context of her relationship with a violent and abusive husband, it was not until after they split up that she began to use heroin, cocaine powder, and crack. Evicted from her apartment in Queens because she could no longer afford to pay the rent, Jenny and her two children were made homeless and wandered the streets before eventually being relocated to an SRO hotel in mid-town Manhattan. Her story clearly illustrates the way in which ~~social and economic factors converge with situational factors, such as the availability of drugs and~~ the proximity of experienced (usually male) users/sellers to render homeless women even more vulnerable.

After I split up with him [husband] I couldn't pay the rent, and he wouldn't give me no money unless I let him stay with me. So I had to take him to court. But in the meantime, I still couldn't pay my rent. So I went down to Welfare, and Welfare wouldn't pay that amount. So they got me in the welfare hotel in the Holland. . . . So I had to go to the Holland Hotel on 42nd Street between Eighth and Ninth Avenues. And it was like pimps, crack, dope, you know, drug hotel—pimp hotel. And I was, like, I never knew anything about this stuff you know 'cause I came from Queens, in a quiet area. . . . He [drug seller and pimp] conned me into staying with him, and I did, you know. I was vulnerable, hungry, you know. I lost my welfare, and they were kicking me out of the hotel; and he had a room in the same hotel; the Holland, which he paid the security guards to have it. It wasn't like welfare benefits. He just paid to keep that room and I was staying there because I had no other place to stay, and then he turned me out to the streets. I was sniffing dope, coke, and smoking a lot of crack. [Yeah, and he turned you onto all those drugs.] Yeah and that's how I became like really hooked because I had a habit and I didn't know [it].

Boy, a 29-year-old African American woman, was one of the few women who from time to time made use of this system. Her views of the shelter system were reinforced by many other women, most of whom refused to even contemplate shelter accommodation.

I was scared the firs' time I ever went to a shelter. [When was this?] It was about eighteen months ago. An' I was scared. They took me to a single shelter, I only stayed two days an' I wen' to 116 Street. Is called [Women's Shelter], the wors'es shelter ya can ever go to 'cos deres dikes and everythin' there. An' dat taught me a lot. Thassa woman shelter. I wouldn' put ma dog in it. But I havta stay. There's two accommodations dere, dykes and crack. There's nine a y'all inna room. If you look at one person—"You looked at ma woman, I'm gon' kick your ass." Y'know dykes are the worsest things there ever is. I don' like it, but I havta deal wid it, so you can' really—in nis place you don' get ta lay down. You gotta get up eight a'clock inna morning. An' you don' get ta go back upstairs till, like, six a'clock in afternoon. [What do most of the women do during the day?] I sit ou'side. I sit right ou'side. But I don' 'cumulate wid none o' dem nere because once you start ta be frens wid dem, dey're wrapped up in nat system. [So do some women do crack?] Crack it up inside the place, they be crackin' it up ou'side the place. Shootin' up. Sellin'. I mean I was like marked. Is like an animal house.

Although the women in this study were critical of the conditions of shelter life in general, they reserved greatest hostility for those that worked in the system. In particular, women received little comfort or indeed protection from the security guards employed to police behavior and maintain order in the shelter system (see Rossi 1989, p. 199; Waterston 1993). Guards were widely perceived as being involved in drug use, and, in particular, female guards were frequently cited as being implicated in lesbian relationships with shelter residents.

Is bad when dere own guards do it. How can da guards protect you when they do the same thing? You got guards dat go together. You got guards dat smoke. How can you protect me if you're smokin' an' you a dyke? So you're 'cumulated wid da rest a them. If you

have a fight with a dyke, okay, the guard's gonna be onna dyke's side, not yours, so you fucked.

The violence and criminality endemic to shelter life also promote the use of instrumental aggression (Campbell 1993) by women in an effort to ward off potential aggressors. As Boy explained in response to a question about how she protected herself:

Myself. Okay, when I went there Tuesday I laid ma law straight, I hadda argument, but dey know me from before, alrigh'. I jus' let you know. Okay, iss a certain way you can look at a person, y'know. An' nas wa' I did, y'know. An' by me bein' there before, people know, don' mess wid me, I'm not one a dem suckers. See if you go in nere wimpy, they're gonna kick your ass. But if ya go in nere lay ya law down, an' don' fuck wid no one. Thas all—you don' fuck wid dem, dey won' fuck wid you.

Although women appeared more likely to reside in shelters during pregnancy, shelters specifically for pregnant women were similarly perceived by Boy.

Dey placed me inta [S-Shelter] I don' wanna be dere, y'understan'. I don' like ta be wid a groupa people. Now dey got me inna room, dere's thirteen beds in this room. [Thirteen pregnant women?] Yeah. An' iss like eleven o'clock, I'm ready ta doze off, y'know. Dere playin' cards an' playin' music, an' lights on. Iss like you never can sleep when ya wanna sleep. Ya can't watch TV when ya wanna watch TV. Y' gotta sign fa soap, ya gotta sign fa toilet tissue. Iss jus' like bein' inna detention home. [Do the women fight with each other?] Dey argue like cats 'n' dogs okay, ya got it inside an' ya got it outside. Right around the corner on the side of the building is a crack area. On number one crack dealers. [What do they sell, mix?] Yeah. Crack, dope, heroin, um wass dat stuff, dat orange stuff? [Methadone?] Methadone. Anythin' you want they got, okay? It makes it bad on us. Because at night you hear, "You took ma money bitch" an' "ba, ba, ba."

These accounts suggest that for many women, current system responses to female homelessness were perceived in a negative light. At best, hotels and shelters "constitute a subculture that makes any attempt toward sobriety extremely difficult" (Zimmer and Schretzman 1991, p. 174). At worst, they provided an environment that served to amplify drug and alcohol use, fostered involvement in illegal activities, and encouraged the neglect or abuse of children. Most of the women interviewed in this research preferred to take their chances elsewhere. Thus the recent proliferation of alternative living arrangements can also be seen, in part, as a response to the city's failure to meet these women's needs.

Going to the Curb: Squatting and Sleeping on the Street

For most women, city accommodations failed to provide a viable alternative even when the only other option was to sleep on the street or in an abandoned building (see also Boyle and Anglin 1993). Queen Bee, a 25-year-old African American user/seller, was squatting in an abandoned apartment building. She held the keys to two apartments on the fourth floor of this building. Cable wire attached to a city outlet brought electricity into both apartments. Water was acquired from the fire hydrant outside. As the following field note excerpt suggests, the conditions of life were both unsafe and unsanitary.

The first apartment can only be explained as a garbage can. It is extremely disorganized and reeks of garbage and decay. The floors are littered with old clothing and rags and each room is adorned with broken pieces of discarded furniture and piles of refuse. Queen Bee took me into this apartment to retrieve a lamp, consisting of a bulb screwed into a broken base, before quickly proceeding to the other apartment. This apartment is also filthy and smells terrible but is in slightly better condition than its neighbor. There is a long hallway and several rooms open off it but it is too dark to see into these rooms. The only source of light emanates from the lamp Queen Bee is holding. We enter a room off to the right of the hallway containing an old beat up dresser with a mirror, two chairs in decayed condition, a stool, various boxes, a tray table with a hot plate on it, and assorted other junk. The dresser is covered with empty vials, about eight empty lighters, and a lot of debris. Queen Bee uses a sweep of her arm to clear the contents of the dresser top and create a space for the lamp.

This abandoned building was an active drug dealing spot. Several other individuals besides Queen Bee dealt drugs from this spot. Booby traps were set for police and strangers. The steps on the third landing had been rigged. Everyone lived above this landing and anyone that did not know his or her way around this particular step would fall through to the first floor.

Similarly, Princess, a 32-year-old African American woman also chose to create her own living arrangements. Unlike Queen Bee, however, Princess did not have access to an abandoned building and her accommodations were strictly curbside. As she related:

[Where did you go when you moved out?] Well I started staying here, there. Mainly I break night a lot so, mainly in the streets. Not that I have to be in the streets. Just that I don' choose to take these drug vices into my family's home.

Princess rationalized her choice by saying that she preferred to stay on the street rather than in someone's house because, in her opinion, either way people were out to rip you off. As she saw it, in some ways sleeping rough may even reduce the risk of victimization insofar as she believed that there was less chance of others thinking that you had anything to steal.

I'll stay here [in the lot], y'know I paid anywhere I went, but besides gettin' robbed, y'know 'cos when you stay in somebody's house all they do is rip you off. I've gotten by better in the streets, y'know. That's right. You sleep, fall asleep in the streets nobody think you got nothin'. So they're not gonna search you for anything. You know you wake up with any dime—you go to somebody's house and you have nothing, not even a wake up.

Sleeping on the street, or sleeping rough, typically entailed the construction of a makeshift shelter, usually in the form of a cardboard box shanty or lean-to against a wall or fence. Ironically, these structures were referred to in one study neighborhood as "condos." For most women, however, the high likelihood both of victimization and of police harassment meant that condos were not a viable option unless they were in partnership with a male. Following the eviction of Dream from her apartment, three African American couples who had been staying there were forced to relocate to a vacant lot where they set up a large communal condo. Below, Dee Dee, a 29-year-old African American woman described this arrangement.

In the backa da lot, dere a couch back dere. Wen I'm finally pooped, I can' take it no more, I step back dere and fall asleep. An' iss gota Johnny pump das open. [But it's not too good when it rains.] No, but we done made it like a canopy or whatever wid de pallets on each side o' da couch. [How many people are staying over there?] Iss really six of us there, but we be in there at different times. An' if there's not enough room for the nex' one we lay a pallet out. We got enough blankets and stuff. We put a blanket on the pallet an' lay out there. [But anyone can go in there?] They can yeah, there's nothin' stoppin' 'em, but dey don'. Iss not as popular as dat lot dere. Guess a lot o' people know about it but never think to go in there. Jus' an empty lot, a parkin' lot. An' iss got trees ona sides dat block us out, iss cool for now.

Although most males who were part of street-level drug-using networks were neither inclined nor particularly well placed to provide for women's needs, some relationships endured. Latisha, a 32-year-old African American woman and her mate, Tre, resided in an abandoned truck situated on an empty lot hidden from the roadside by undergrowth and adjoining a large warehouse. Even though it was located a 30-min walk away from the drug market area, Latisha and Tre made this journey at least once a day. Latisha and Tre managed to successfully hide the fact that they lived in this truck from other drug users (and for a time, from the ethnographer) by claiming that they lived in an apartment in an adjacent neighborhood. Following the ethnographer's visit to the site, Latisha discussed their accommodation.

It's very hot in the summer. You have to keep the doors open when you're sleepin' and God forbid if you try to put a cover on you, and mosquitoes, my God. [What about rats?] Well, you see the bag hangin' up over the ceiling. Thas where we put the food. If we didn't eat it all we have to hang it up in the ceiling because the rats would smell it and come in. You gotta remember you're on the outside and those are big rats. [What about other people in the neighborhood?] They know that we're around and we don't bother them or steal or nothing. . . . I keep myself pretty much clean, I mean I can't take a bath every day, but we have access to hot water. The guy across the street give us hot water. [So you take a bath over there?] No, we fill up buckets, we got a big barrel, you fill the barrel, get in and wash. Outside. Last winter was three feet of snow and I still went outside.

Although involved in a physically abusive relationship, Latisha saw herself as fortunate in that she at least had a "roof over her head." Moreover, sleeping rough was not an option for women who depended on street-level sexwork because of the undesirable message it sends out to customers.

I refuse to just sleep right over here [in the drug market area]. I don't want people to see me lyin' out here on the sidewalk. Dates come through these areas too and they see a girl laying out here and then they see her back on the street. You know, it's gonna be hard for you, they figure out you ain't shit.

Within the street-level drug economy, sexwork, as a primary means of economic sustenance necessitated a basic level of attention to looks, physical hygiene, and, ironically, moral propriety (see Maher 1995).

Older Males

By far the most common alternative living arrangement for the women in this study was as part of the household of an older male for a period of time. Most of the women in this sample patronized older men to secure and satisfy their needs for shelter. However, as Hamid (1992b) has argued, these relationships cannot be considered in isolation from the economic position of young minority women generally.

While the real income and other benefits of elderly men or senior citizens have improved appreciably in the past two decades . . . young women have seen their income decline steeply over the same period of time. (p. 344)

By middle-class standards, these older men do not control significant resources, but in the inner-city context, the resources of a steady income and maintenance of an apartment enabled them to obtain a sense of mastery or control over women. These older males usually had some form of dependable or steady income, such as a low-wage job, pension, social security, or retirement benefits. They owned or had a long-established lease on a house or apartment and were well positioned to provide women crack smokers (and sometimes their children, as well) with shelter and a place to wash and rest up, and sometimes food.

Although individual arrangements exhibited considerable variation, these accommodations always came at a price. Women typically paid in either sex or drugs or less often, cash, and sometimes all three. In addition to sexual availability and drugs, these older men received the companionship of younger women and, in some instances, were able to exert considerable control over them. Some also extracted further benefits in the form of unpaid domestic labor, such as cleaning, cooking, and laundry.

Cash for Shelter.

Although few of the women were able to negotiate these relationships with older males on strictly economic terms by paying in either cash or crack, Connie, a 24-year-old gay Latina, maintained that she was able to keep the transaction at a purely financial level.

[Where do you stay now?] At my [male] friend's house on W——. [The friend smokes crack too?] Yes. [You have to—] Pay him. Pay him cash, right, in order for me to sleep and take a bath. [What, he doesn't ask for sex or anything like that?] No, He's an old, old man. Well, I tell him I don't like mens. I tell him, and I don't like mens. [You like women?] Exactly. [You pay him by the night or by the week?] Oh, I give him ten, fifteen dollars a day.

Crack for Shelter.

Similarly, Jo-Beth, a 23-year-old and Candy, a 41-year-old [both European American] were part of a group of women who stayed at the apartment of an elderly Latino on a regular basis and claimed they always paid in crack.

I'm in this old man's house. He's a crack-head. A lot of the girls go there. You give him crack. [Do you find that there's a lot of old guys that smoke?] I don't know. I don't hang out with old guys. I pay my way. (Jo-Beth)

I bought a nickel crack for this old man right here so I can come in here. It cost me a nickel or two to get here. And he's still not happy. If you go out ten times a day, if it be ten times, you got to bring him a bottle [of crack]. It took me so long to make that damn money and the bastard, me so sick. At least I had that nickel to get in here, you know. (Candy)

Sex for Shelter.

More often than not, however, sex was part of the deal. Shorty, a 22-year-old Latina recalled a typical former relationship.

Well, he's the type of guy that used to help all the girls from the Avenue. And they would go up there and take a shower and sleep, you know. He was like very perverted, and to get a place to sleep, you had to do something with him, you know? "For a couple of weeks, I'll help you out," so we started staying there, but he had a drinking problem and was perverted. [Did he use crack also?] No, he used to drink. Just drink. And when my husband wasn't there, he would try to get fresh with me, 'cause you know, he's a pervert. So that didn't go over too tough, either.

Whole networks of women crack users informed one another of possible sites of shelter with older males, as Jackie, a 29-year-old Afro-Caribbean woman, explained.

Mo used to live right upstairs in a bad apartment. And he invite the same Joclyn up to, you know—fuck around . . . . After a while it was like everybody get—ya know, the word pass around, and people see how people live here, a lot of girls used to live there, and guys use to be lookin' for girls, too. . . . Everybody tell you all about him and ya know, everybody start livin' there . . . gettin' high, gettin' high, gettin' high.

Frequently, the older males who offered their space to be entertained by these women were retired and many were alcoholics. However, some older men were initiated or "turned on" to smoking crack through their associations with these younger women. In many places, a typical scene involved a group of old men who were playing cards and drinking beer while women smoked crack. Later, the old men might take their pick of the females and some would also smoke crack. In addition to older retired males, middle-aged working men may also offer various forms of hospitality to women crack users. For example, George, an electrical engineer, worked everyday—often with a charge from "Scottie" for the road. According to women, George treated them to a less exploitative time: they showered, cooked, listened to music, and beamed up together.

Companionship/Affection for Shelter.
In several instances, these older men were dates or former dates who claimed affections for individual women. For example, Tameka, a 41-year-old African American woman, met her common law husband as a date in a local bar and remained in this union throughout the study period.

He told me he said, "Look I'm not worth the fuck all I want is companionship," he said, "Look I'll give you $50 you go home with me." So I said, "Cool, no problem." We never did anything together or anything like that other than lay in the bed and sleep, and that was it. . . . whoever he bought with him they would take his money. Because I knew that it was somebody that I wanted to see again who would be there for me. . . . So I knew if I rolled [stole from] him he wouldn't have wanted me. So I didn't roll him and thank God I didn't, and the man's been there ever since.

Similarly, Peggy, a 34-year-old European American woman, lived with an older Italian man who worked as a numbers runner. Although not a drug user, Peggy's boyfriend gave her money to purchase drugs in an effort to keep her from prostitution. The relationship, however, was not without its problems.

The man that I live with, I met on the stroll up here. We would see each other once a week, then he would come twice a week, then he would come three, four times a week, take me to lunch, take me to dinner, take me to the house . . . And then, I never moved out. . . . Well, it's my home. I'm living there eight months already. I mean, he knew what he was getting. But, I cook, I clean the house, I wait on him hand and foot. He never was married, so I'm like his baby. I was never home when he got home from work and that's all he asks, that I'm home. He don't care if there's no food, if the house is burning; as long as I'm there when he gets home. He says, "I'm going to chain you," and he did one day. I swear to God! He put shackles on my feet. I freaked out.

Domestic Duties for Shelter.
Chef, a 27-year-old African American woman, lived with Clyde (70 years old), who had his own apartment for many years. Clyde did not use crack nor allow Chef to bring others into his apartment. She was required to keep the apartment and his clothes clean, cook the food, and to complete a number of other well-defined domestic duties in return for staying there. Sex was not involved.

Similarly, Linda, a 31-year-old European American woman, negotiated a deal with an older man whereby she was given food, shelter, and a few dollars in return for her services as a sitter for his elderly invalid mother, an arrangement she later described as "too good to be true."

I've been babysittin' the old lady. I'm still over there but, you know, he's got a lot of problems—he drinks. Yeah, her son. [How much do they pay you for watchin' over her?] You know whatever. I don't have a set thing, you know. I'm just happy with the roof over my head. [How old is this guy?] Fifty-five. [You don't have to take care of him?] No, only when he gets drunk, real, real drunk. He just wants me to cuddle up next to him. I don't do anything, but I get mad 'cause he wakes me up. You know, he drinks all night until two, three, four o'clock in the morning, and he has the radio blastin', and then he comes and wakes me up. He goes on and on.

However, despite variations in the nature of the commodity exchanged, living arrangements with older males typically took the form of short-term instrumental associations. Over a 2-month period during fieldwork observations, Linda had had four such associations.

Remember I told you I was living on J——? You know that guy died? [Since then where have you been staying?] Well I was staying with this other guy on the Southside, on B——, you know. How do I know him? Well I used to go out with him. You know I give him a blow job to stay there, you know. But then he threw me out, 'cause he says, "I don't want no more injections in the house." He don't get high. He drinks, you know, when he got the money. [Since then where have you been staying?] I found this other guy, right. But he got on a program, and he was doing good, you know. So then I left there. So now I'm staying with this other guy, this old man, he don't get high or nothing. [How'd you hook up with him?] I used to date him. But now, he just lets me stay up there. He's a little bit off. So I told [him], "Hey easy with the sex" (laughing).

Most women, by virtue of their crack use and depleted economic and social resources, were forced to rely on short-lived associations with older males during which they exchanged drugs, sex, cash, or services (or some combination thereof) for shelter. Although most of these men used alcohol and some also used crack, these males were peripheral to street-level drug-using or selling networks. They were simply older neighborhood males, who, by virtue of their apartments and somewhat better economic status, were able to offer these younger women shelter—in exchange they received a number of benefits, including sexual favors, drugs, money, and domestic labor. But there was a fine line between these households and their commodified forms as "freakhouses" and other commercial settings for crack consumption.

Freakhouses and Other Commercial Settings

In many impoverished inner-city neighborhoods, crack has become the "de facto currency of the realm"—a liquid asset with cash value that can be exchanged for shelter, sex, food, and other durables (Inciardi et al. 1991). The rise of the freakhouse, which specialized in sex-for-crack exchanges between chronic crack-using women and men who were less heavy consumers (or were nonusing males), exemplified crack's capacity for the commodification of human relationships. In New York City, freakhouses generally took the following form.

The elderly man receives sexual services and gifts of crack from a core group of five or six crack-abusing women. In exchange they gain a sanctuary in highly transient lifestyles where they can wash, prepare meals, or feel at home. They promptly attract several other crack-abusing women, and the combined "harem" lures male users and working men of all ages. The latter come to "freak" (use any and all of the women sexually—a favorite pastime is "flipping," with the male going from one to as many women that are present in continuous succession), and some use crack (but many do not). The visitors pay the old man or one of his appointees cash or crack for any activity: going out to buy crack, beer, or cigarettes; use of private space (by the half hour); or access to the women (Hamid 1992b, p. 344).

Joe, a 31-year-old Afro-Caribbean male, inherited a beautiful frame house when his mother died. A regular crack user, Joe was not employed at the time of the study and used the house to accommodate a core of six female crack users and a shifting number of crack-using transients. Although he was unable to pay the monthly mortgage, his female house guests kept Joe in drugs. The presence of women willing to provide sexual services in exchange for crack quickly turned Joe's place into a freakhouse. However, freakhouses are sustained by male sexual desires that extend beyond the inner-city crack culture. The freakhouse created and maintained a setting for sexual commodities neither readily accessible nor cheaply available in the commercial marketplace of street-level sexwork.

The social and economic organization of such households ranges from anarchic to authoritarian (see also Ouellet, Wiebel, Jiminez, and Johnson 1993). Isolated from other sources of social and economic support, many women initially entertained freakhouse accommodation and the accompanying sexual demands as a response to scarcity and deprivation. However, whereas the freakhouse was by definition a commercial setting for sexual transactions and crack/drug use, often the relationships among individual residents suggest that it functioned along the lines of a household unit, however unstable and exploitative. According to both owners and other residents, many freakhouses exhibited social obligations of affection and limited trust developed among household members. Residents exchanged food, money, goods, services—and drugs—and sometimes considered each other as family. Members looked out for each other and provided protection against serious violence. For the most part, then, freakhouses provided a more congenial setting than other commercial locations.

In contrast to the freakhouse, this research also identified a number of commercial settings variously described as crack houses or shooting galleries, which often catered to both intravenous drug users and crack smokers (but rarely present were nonusing males interested only in sex). These settings tended to operate along the lines of the traditional heroin shooting gallery (e.g., see Murphy and Waldorf 1991) insofar as they created a relatively secure environment where street-level drug users gathered primarily to consume drugs. Although some establishments provided rooms for rent on a half-hourly basis for sexual transactions, payment was typically extracted in exchange for entry and a range of drug-related services including equipment hire and the purchase of drugs. Within such establishments, the margin of profit, or house take, depended on how long people stayed and how much they consumed—encouraging excessive use and a high incidence of theft and violence (Inciardi et al. 1993; Ouellet et al. 1993; Ratner 1993b).

Women known to the owners were permitted to spend the night in these establishments in return for either drugs or cash. Commercial sexual transactions were generally not permitted in these settings, although a minority facilitated sex-for-drugs exchanges and some provided private rooms for rental on a half-hourly basis. Unlike freakhouses, however, these commercial settings were drug focused, rather than sex focused. Women made important distinctions between the two types of settings—freakhouses and crack house/shooting gallery operations—on the basis of perceived safety. Personal and material safety emerged as primary considerations in the search for shelter, and these women were extremely reluctant to stay in locations identified as commercial consumption settings.

Pappy's I don't trust. I have walked passed it and I don't trust it because if dey see somebody with you and it looks like somebody das got a lot of money dey rob them. Dey set them up. Pappy's, dey [potential dates] look at his place and say, "Oh, all these guys out here, no I don' want to go," and dey would drive off. (Keisha)

Uh, well you know it's so busy over there at Pap's house. And man, I swear to God, I can't hold nothin'. I can't have nothin' there. They took my wick [tampon] from out my underwear while I was sleepin'. (Sugar)

[You ever stay at Kizzy's place?] No I don't like it there, she robs you when you're there. She robs your stuff while you're there and then say she doesn't know what happened to it. [Have you been robbed there?] Yeah. I bought a sweat suit for $75 and when I woke up the top of my sweatsuit was gone. She said she didn't know what happened to it. (Rachel)

Within the inner-city crack culture studied here, settings for drug use and sexual transactions can be located along a continuum of alternative living arrangements that attest to crack's capacity for commodification. Whereas the more commercially oriented settings are more strictly drug focused and the less commercial tend to exploit the potent combination of sex and crack, strictly commercial settings are further differentiated by the absence of exchanges rooted in domestic labor, companionship, and affection. The reality for many crack-using women was a choice between a rock and a hard place—between submitting to the exploitation and potential sexual degradation offered within the relative safety of the freakhouse or retaining sexual autonomy at the increased risk of physical and material victimization in other commercial settings. For many women, the relative insulation from the exigencies of street life provided by being a sexual partner/drug conduit to elderly males or freakhouse owners (and their clientele) appeared to render such arrangements the least undesirable option.

DISCUSSION

Recent research has drawn attention to the existence of new opportunities for female participation in street-level drug markets and the influence of structural changes on the gender composition of street networks (e.g., Baskin, Sommers, and Fagan 1993; Mieczkowski 1994). As Fagan has suggested:

Some women have constructed careers in illegal work that have insulated them from the exploitation and destructive behaviors that characterize heavy cocaine and crack use. . . . Signs of the changing status of women in drug markets are evident in the relatively high incomes some achieve, and the relatively insignificant role of prostitution in generating income (Fagan 1994, p. 210).

However, the findings of this research suggest that many crack-using women are seriously impoverished and unable to maintain stable living arrangements. This was true both of women who engaged in street-level drug distribution and sales activities (Bourgois and Dunlap 1993; Dunlap et al. 1995) and those who relied primarily on the street-level sex economy (Maher 1995; Maher and Curtis 1992). The women in this study clearly lacked the necessary resources for maintaining physical security and economic independence and for assuring sexual autonomy. Many expended their incomes exclusively on crack consumption with little or nothing left over to pay rent or meet other basic needs.

The failure of the city system to meet these women's needs meant that for most, shelters and welfare hotels were regarded as the least desirable accommodation option. The alternatives, however, were loaded with risk and uncertainty and skewed by the gendered distribution of power within the inner-city crack culture. In particular, the costs of sleeping rough and in commercial establishments were high and included risks of theft and violent victimization. On the other hand, older males provided an elastic source of accommodation. Many of them lived alone and welcomed crack-using women as companions or house guests. Within the context of this particular form of alternative living arrangement, women remained vulnerable to exploitation by virtue of their relative powerlessness vis-à-vis older men with apartments and economic resources. It is ironic then, that these households—some of which spawned new depths of sexual degradation and new forms of indentured labor—were seen by women to minimize the risk of victimization. However, when viewed in the context of other options for accommodation, such arrangements reflected women's search for what they clearly regarded as the least vulnerable situations.

CONCLUSION

Rather than seek to isolate the sexual and economic practices of women crack users, this article has sought to identify and describe some of the changing contexts in which these practices are situated. Bolstered by wide-spread sex-segmentation in the street-level drug economy, the relative powerlessness and economic marginality of women crack users undergirded an array of alternative living arrangements that fueled female participation in both prostitution and sex-for-drug exchanges. Although important distinctions clearly existed between the sex trade on the streets and sexual activities in the context of crack use behind closed doors, these women's

accounts suggest that women crack users continue to experience significant levels of exploitation and degradation (see also Bourgois and Dunlap 1993). Within this context, the advent of crack cocaine has served to reproduce, rather than rupture, existing gender divisions.

This study indicates that however freed from the confines of family life, the lives of these women remained firmly anchored within the confines of a gender regime that served to disadvantage them both as social actors and economic agents. Although women crack users have ostensibly been liberated from the confines of oppressive pimping structures that characterized previous eras of street-level sexwork (Maher and Curtis 1992), reliance on males for drugs, shelter, and other commodities prompted new forms of female dependence (see also Goldstein et al. 1992, p. 360; Inciardi et al. 1993, p. 85). Moreover, the data presented here indicate that drug dealers, lookouts, and participants in the street-level drug economy were not the only males to whom women crack users relinquished their meager incomes and their bodies.

The proliferation of alternative living arrangements devised by female crack users in the inner city has clearly prompted shifts in gender relations. Women crack users, in developing creative responses to homelessness, have redefined the boundaries of household forms and the nature of domestic economies. Within these contexts, gender relations have been reconstituted. However, underlying imbalances of power continue to structure the positioning of women in the street-level drug economy and the cultural meanings that attach to female drug use and homelessness. Even though the crack culture serves to amplify existing gender inequalities, it does not create them (Maher 1995). The privileged access of males, and older males in particular, to social, cultural, and economic resources, works to ensure that they remain the principal beneficiaries of these reconstituted gender relations.

REFERENCES

Barak, G. 1991. *Gimme Shelter: A Social History of Homelessness in Contemporary America.* New York: Praeger.

BASKIN, D., I. SOMMERS, and J. A. FAGAN. 1993. "The Political Economy of Violent Female Street Crime." *Fordham Urban Law Journal* 20:401–7.

BOURGOIS, P. 1989. "In Search of Horatio Alger: Culture and Ideology in the Crack Economy." *Contemporary Drug Problems* 16:619–49.

BOURGOIS, P. 1995. *In Search of Respect: Selling Crack in El Barrio.* New York: Cambridge University Press.

BOURGOIS, P. and E. DUNLAP. 1993. "Exorcising Sex-for-Crack: An Ethnographic Perspective From Harlem." Pp. 97–132 in *Crack Pipe as Pimp: An Ethnographic Investigation of Sex-for-Crack Exchanges,* edited by M. S. Ratner. New York: Lexington Books.

BOYLE, K. and M. D. ANGLIN. 1993. "To the Curb: Sex Bartering and Drug Use Among Homeless Crack Users in Los Angeles." Pp. 159–86 in *Crack Pipe as Pimp: An Ethnographic Investigation of Sex-for-Crack Exchanges,* edited by M. S. Ratner. New York: Lexington Books.

CAMPBELL, A. 1993. *Out of Control: Men, Women and Aggression.* London: Pandora.

CARLSON R. G. and H. A. SIEGEL. 1991. "The Crack Life: An Ethnographic Overview of Crack Use and Sexual Behavior Among African-Americans in a Midwest Metropolitan City." *Journal of Psychoactive Drugs* 23:11–20.

DUNLAP, E. 1992. "Impact of Drugs on Family Life and Kin Networks in the Inner-City African-American Single-Parent Household." Pp. 181–207 in *Drugs, Crime and Social Isolation: Barriers to Urban Opportunity,* edited by A. Harrell and G. Peterson. Washington, D.C., Urban Institute Press.

DUNLAP, E. and B. D. JOHNSON, 1992. "The Setting for the Crack Era: Macro Forces, Micro Consequences 1960–1992." *Journal of Psychoactive Drugs* 24:307–21.

———. 1994. "Gaining Access and Conducting Ethnographic Research Among Drug Dealers." Presented at the meeting of the Society for Applied Anthropology, Cancun, Mexico, April.

———. 1996. "Family/Resources in the Development of a Female Crack Seller Career: Case Study of a Hidden Population." *Journal of Drug Issues* 26:177–200.

DUNLAP, E., B. D. JOHNSON, and L. Maher. Forthcoming. "Female Crack Dealers in New York City: Who They Are and What They Do." *Women and Criminal Justice.*

DUNLAP, E., B. D. JOHNSON, and A. Manwar. 1994. "A Successful Female Crack Dealer: Case Study of a Deviant Career." *Deviant Behavior* 15:1–25.

DUNLAP, E., B. D. JOHNSON, H. SANABRIA, E. HOLLIDAY, V. LIPSEY, M. BARNETT, W. HOPKINS, I. SOBEL, D. RANDOLPH, and K. CHIN. 1990. "Studying Crack Users and Their Criminal Careers: Scientific and Artistic Aspects of Locating Hard-to-Reach Subjects and Interviewing Them About Sensitive Topics." *Contemporary Drug Problems* 17:121–44.

EDLIN, B. R., K. L. IRWIN, D. D. LUDWIG, H. V. MCCOY, Y. SERRANO, C. WORD, B. P. BOWSER, S. FARUQUE, C. B. MCCOY, R. F. SCHILLING, and S. D. HOLMBERG. 1992. "High-Risk Sex Behavior Among Young Street-Recruited Crack Cocaine Smokers in Three American Cities: An Interim Report." *Journal of Psychoactive Drugs* 24:363–71.

FAGAN, J. A. 1994. "Women and Drugs Revisited: Female Participation in the Cocaine Economy." *Journal of Drug Issues* 24:179–225.

FULLILOVE, M. T. and R. E. FULLILOVE. 1989. "Intersecting Epidemics: Black Teen Crack Use and Sexually Transmitted Diseases." *Journal of the American Medical Association* 44:146–53.

GOLDSTEIN, P. J., L. J. OUELLET, and M. FENDRICH. 1992. "From Bag Brides to Skeezers: A Historical Perspective on Sex-for-Drugs Behavior." *Journal of Psychoactive Drugs* 24:349–61.

GOLUB, A. and B. D. JOHNSON. 1994. "The Shifting Importance of Alcohol and Marijuana as Gateway Substances Among Serious Drug Abusers. *Journal of Alcohol Studies* 55:607–14.

HAMID, A. 1990. "The Political Economy of Crack-Related Violence." *Contemporary Drug Problems* 17:31–78.

———. 1992a. "The Developmental Cycle of a Drug Epidemic: The Cocaine Smoking Epidemic of 1981–1991." *Journal of Psychoactive Drugs* 24:337–48.

———. 1992b. "Drugs and Patterns of Opportunity in the Inner-City: The Case of Middle Aged, Middle Income Cocaine Smokers." Pp. 209–39 in *Drugs, Crime, and Social Isolation: Barriers to Urban Opportunity,* edited by Adele Harrell and George Peterson. Washington, DC: Urban Institute Press.

HOPPER, K. and J. HAMBURG. 1984. *The Making of America's Homeless: From Skid Row to New Poor, 1945–1984.* New York: Community Service Society.

INCIARDI, J. A., D. LOCKWOOD, and A. E. POTTIEGER. 1993. *Women and Crack Cocaine.* New York: Macmillan.

INCIARDI, J. A., A. E. POTTIEGER, M. A. FORNEY, D. D. CHITWOOD, and D. C. MCBRIDE. 1991. "Prostitution, IV Drug Use, and Sex-for-Crack Exchanges Among Serious Delinquents: Risks for HIV Infection." *Criminology* 29:221–35.

JENCKS, C., and P. E. PETERSON. 1991. *The Urban Underclass.* Washington, DC: Brookings Institution.

JOHNSON, B. D., P. J. GOLDSTEIN, E. PREBLE, J. SCHMEIDLER, D. S. LIPTON, B. SPUNT, and T. MILLER. 1985. *Taking Care of Business: The Economics of Crime by Heroin Abusers.* Lexington, MA: Lexington Books.

JOHNSON, B. D., T. WILLIAMS, K. DEI, and H. SANABRIA. 1990. "Drug Abuse and the Inner City: Impact on Hard Drug Users and the Community." Pp. 9–67 in *Drugs and Crime,* Vol. 13, *Crime and Justice Series,* edited by Michael Tonry and James Q. Wilson. Chicago: University of Chicago Press.

KASARDA, J. D. 1992. "The Severely Distressed in Economically Transforming Cities." Pp. 45–98 in *Drugs, Crime, and Social Isolation: Barriers to Urban Opportunity,* edited by Adele Harrell and George Peterson. Washington, DC: Urban Institute Press.

MAHER, L. 1995. "Dope Girls: Gender, Race and Class in the Drug Economy." Ph.D. Dissertation, Rutgers University, Newark, New Jersey.

———. 1996. "Hidden in the Light: Occupational Norms Among Crack-using Street-level Sex Workers." *Journal of Drug Issues,* 26:145–175.

MAHER, L. and R. CURTIS. 1992. "Women on the Edge of Crime: Crack Cocaine and the Changing Contexts of Street-level Sex Work in New York City." *Crime, Law and Social Change* 18:221–58.

———. 1994. "In Search of the Female Urban Gansta: Change, Culture and Crack Cocaine." Pp. 147–66 in *The Criminal Justice System and Women,* edited by B. Raffel Price and N. J. Sokoloff. 2nd ed. New York: McGraw-Hill.

MAHER, L., E. DUNLAP, and B. D. JOHNSON. "Black Women's Pathways to Involvement in Illicit Drug Distribution and Sales: An Ethnographic Analysis." In review.

MIECZKOWSKI, T. 1994. "The Experiences of Women Who Sell Crack: Some Descriptive Data From the Detroit Crack Ethnography Project." *Journal of Drug Issues* 24:227–48.

MOORE, J. W. 1991. *Going Down to the Barrio: Homeboys and Homegirls in Change.* Philadelphia: Temple University Press.

MURPHY, S. and D. WALDORF. 1991. "Kickin' Down to the Street Doc: Shooting Galleries in the San Francisco Bay Area." *Contemporary Drug Problems* 18:9–29.

OUELLET, L. J., W. W. WIEBEL, A. D. JIMINEZ, and W. A. JOHNSON. 1993. "Crack Cocaine and the Transformation of Prostitution in Three Chicago Neighborhoods." Pp. 69–96 in *Crack Pipe as Pimp: An Ethnographic Investigation of Sex-for-Crack Exchanges,* edited by M. S. Ratner. New York: Lexington Books.

RATNER, M. S., ed. 1993a. *Crack Pipe as Pimp: An Ethnographic Investigation of Sex-for-Crack Exchanges.* New York: Lexington Books.

———. 1993b. "Sex, Drugs and Public Policy: Studying and Understanding the Sex-for-Crack Phenomenon." Pp. 1–36 in *Crack Pipe as Pimp: An Ethnographic Investigation of Sex-for-Crack Exchanges,* edited by M. S. Ratner. New York: Lexington Books.

ROPERS, R. H. 1988. *The Invisible Homeless: A New Urban Ecology.* New York: Insight Books.

ROSSI, P. H. 1989. *Down and Out in America: The Origins of Homelessness.* Chicago: University of Chicago Press.

SULLIVAN, M. L.. 1989. *Getting Paid: Youth Crime and Work in the Inner City.* Ithaca, NY: Cornell University Press.

VANDERSTAAY, S. 1992. *Street Lives: An Oral History of Homeless Americans.* Philadelphia: New Society.

WATERSTON, A. 1993. *Street Addicts in the Political Economy.* Philadelphia: Temple University Press.

WEATHERBY, N. L., J. M. SCHULTZ, D. D. CHITWOOD, H. V. McCOY, C. B. McCOY, D. D. LUDWIG, and B. R. EDLIN. 1992. "Crack Cocaine Use and Sexual Activity in Miami, Florida." *Journal of Psychoactive Drugs* 24:373–80.

WILLIAMS, T., E. DUNLAP, B. D. JOHNSON, and A. HAMID. 1992. "Personal Safety in Dangerous Places." *Journal of Contemporary Ethnography* 21:343–74.

ZIMMER, R. and M. SCHRETZMAN. 1991. "Issues for Homeless Women and Their Children." Pp. 173–77 in *Alcohol and Drugs Are Women's Issues,* Vol. 1, *A Review of the Issues,* edited by P. Roth. Metuchen, NJ: Women's Action Alliance and Scarecrow Press.

Sexual Deviance

In the selection "The Madam as Teacher," Barbara Sherman Heyl examines the social organization of the house training of prostitutes. Hers is a study on one aspect of the entry into prostitution as an occupation that focuses attention on female trainer-trainee relationships. Sherman Heyl describes the process of "turning out," or the teaching of basic rules and skills necessary for the successful running of a house of prostitution. During such professional socialization, identity changes take place that are tied to the social organization of the brothel. In describing this socialization process, the study notes essential differences between house prostitution and streetwalking and callgirl operations.

Laud Humphreys' study of what he termed the "Tearoom Trade" is a classic as well as a controversial study of homosexual relations that take place in public restrooms. The study has been harshly criticized for the unethical research techniques employed (the study was conducted before the existence of "human subjects" review boards) regarding the treatment of subjects who were observed undercover and misled during later interviews. Humphreys' defense of such tactics was not accepted by large portions of the scientific community. Yet, the findings of his study stand as an important contribution to the understanding of homosexuality as a social phe-

nomenon. The selection from his book of the same title focuses on the social organization of the sexual encounters themselves. What is perhaps more important in terms of the overall understanding of such relations is that when interviewed later, it was found that most of the individuals involved in tearoom encounters were married men with heterosexual self-identities who had no interest or identification with the homosexual subculture other than engaging in the sexual acts described in this chapter.

Rape constitutes an act of violence as well as the sexual abuse of women. How rape is considered by rapists themselves is the topic of Diana Scully and Joseph Marolla's research entitled, "Convicted Rapists' Vocabulary of Motive." Using personal interviews with rapists, the authors attempt to understand the ways in which perpetrators of such acts employ techniques that allow them to excuse and justify their violent sexual acts against women. Contrasting the "admitters" and "deniers," the authors find that the former are more prone to excuse rape while the latter tend to justify it. Sexist images and stereotypes are used by both groups in providing a "vocabulary of motive" for rape.

In their article "Topless Dancers," William Thompson and Jackie Harred provide a look at how stigma is managed in a deviant occupation.

In order to engage in nude dancing, women must arrange their social identities to deflect embarrassment and negative societal reactions. Using a symbolic interactionist framework for analysis, Thompson and Harred interviewed over forty topless dancers and found that they socially and symbolically redefined their work to reduce or neutralize negative reactions toward themselves and their work. The authors also draw upon techniques of neutralization to explain how dancers rationalized their behavior and avoided feeling the effects of stigma.

Joanna Gregson Higginson examines the excuses and justifications used by teenage mothers to account for their involvement with older boyfriends in her piece, "Defining, Excusing, and Justifying Deviance." Using data gathered through a participant-observation study, she found that teens who used justifications claimed that their consent made the relationships "non-deviant," while other teens who used excuses perceived themselves as victims of their older boyfriends and believed that statutory rape laws needed to be regularly enforced.

THE MADAM AS TEACHER
THE TRAINING OF HOUSE PROSTITUTES*

Barbara Sherman Heyl

Although the day of the elaborate and conspicuous high-class house of prostitution is gone, houses still operate throughout the United States in a variety of altered forms. The business may be run out of trailers and motels along major highways, luxury apartments in the center of a metropolis or rundown houses in smaller, industrialized cities. (Recent discussions of various aspects of house prostitution include: Gagnon and Simon, 1973:226–7; Hall, 1973:115–95; Heyl, 1974; Jackson, 1969:185–92; Sheehy, 1974:185–204; Stewart, 1972; and Vogliotti, 1975:25–80.) Madams sometimes find themselves teaching young women how to become professional prostitutes. This paper focuses on one madam who trains novices to work at the house level. I compare the training to Bryan's (1965) account of the apprenticeship of call girls and relate the madam's role to the social organization of house prostitution.

Bryan's study of thirty-three Los Angeles call girls is one of the earliest interactionist treatments of prostitution. His data focus on the process of entry into the occupation of the call girl and permit an analysis of the structure and content of a woman's apprenticeship. He concluded that the apprenticeship of call girls is mainly directed toward developing a clientele, rather than sexual skills (1965:288, 296–7). But while Bryan notes that pimps seldom train women directly, approximately half of his field evidence in fact derives from pimp-call girl apprenticeships. Thus, in Bryan's study (as well as in subsequent work on entry into prostitution as an occupation) there was a missing set of data on the more typical female trainer-trainee relationship and on the content and the process of training at other levels of the business in nonmetropolitan settings. This paper attempts to fill this gap.

I. ANN'S TURN-OUT ESTABLISHMENT

A professional prostitute, whether she works as a streetwalker, house prostitute, or call girl, can usually pick out one person in her past who "turned her out," that is, who taught her the basic techniques and rules of the prostitute's occupation.[1] For women who begin working at the house level, that person may be a pimp, another "working girl," or a madam. Most madams and managers of prostitution establishments, however, prefer not to take on novice prostitutes, and they may even have a specific policy against hiring turn-outs (see Erwin (1960:204–5) and Lewis (1942:222)). The turn-out's inexperience may cost the madam clients and money; to train the novice, on the other hand, costs her time and energy. Most madams and managers simply do not want the additional burden.

It was precisely the madam's typical disdain for turn-outs that led to the emergence of the house discussed in this paper—a house specifically devoted to training new prostitutes. The madam of this operation, whom we shall call Ann, is forty-one years old and has been in the prostitution world twenty-three years, working primarily at the house level. Ann knew that pimps who manage women at this level have difficulty placing novices in houses. After operating several houses staffed by professional prostitutes, she decided to run a school for turn-outs partly as a strategy for acquiring a continually changing staff of young women for her house. Pimps are the active recruiters of new prostitutes, and Ann found that, upon demonstrating that she could transform the pimps' new, square women into trained prostitutes easily placed in professional houses, pimps would help keep her business staffed.[2] Ann's house is a small operation in a middle-sized industrial city (population 300,000), with a limited clientele of primarily working-class men retained as customers for ten to fifteen years and offered low rates to maintain their patronage.

Although Ann insists that every turn-out is different, her group of novices is remarkably homogeneous in some ways. Ann has turned out approximately twenty women a year over the six years while she has operated the training school. Except for one Chicano, one black, and one American Indian, the women were all white. They ranged in age from eighteen to twenty-seven. Until three years ago, all the women she hired had pimps. Since then, more women are independent (so-called "outlaws"), although many

come to Ann sponsored by a pimp. That is, in return for being placed with Ann, a turn-out gives the pimp a percentage of her earnings for a specific length of time. At present eighty percent of the turn-outs come to Ann without a long-term commitment to a pimp. The turn-outs stay at Ann's on the average of two to three months. This is the same average length of time Bryan (1965:290) finds for the apprenticeship in his call-girl study. Ann seldom has more than two or three women in training at any one time. Most turn-outs live at the house, often just a large apartment near the older business section of the city.

II. THE CONTENT OF THE TRAINING

The data for the following analysis are of three kinds. First, tape recordings from actual training sessions with fourteen novices helped specify the structure and content of the training provided. Second, lengthy interviews with three of the novices and multiple interviews with Ann were conducted to obtain data on the training during the novice's first few days at the house before the first group training sessions were conducted and recorded by Ann. And third, visits to the house on ten occasions and observations of Ann's interaction with the novices during teaching periods extended the data on training techniques used and the relationship between madam and novice. In addition, weekly contact with Ann over a four-year period allowed repeated review of current problems and strategies in training turn-outs.

Ann's training of the novice begins soon after the woman arrives at the house. The woman first chooses an alias. Ann then asks her whether she has ever "Frenched a guy all the way," that is, whether she has brought a man to orgasm during the act of fellatio. Few of the women say they have. By admitting her lack of competence in a specialized area, the novice has permitted Ann to assume the role of teacher. Ann then launches into instruction on performing fellatio. Such instruction is important to her business. Approximately eighty percent of her customers are what Ann calls "French tricks." Many men visit prostitutes to receive sexual services, including fellatio, their wives or lovers seldom perform. This may be particularly true of the lower- and working-class clientele of the houses and hotels of prostitution (Gagnon and Simon, 1973:230). Yet the request for fellatio may come from clients at all social levels; consequently, it is a sexual skill today's prostitute must possess and one she may not have prior to entry into the business (Bryan, 1965:293; Winick and Kinsie, 1971:180, 207; Gray, 1973:413).

Although Ann devotes much more time to teaching the physical and psychological techniques of performing fellatio than she does to any other sexual skill, she also provides strategies for coitus and giving a "half and half"—fellatio followed by coitus. The sexual strategies taught are frequently a mixture of ways for stimulating the client sexually and techniques of self-protection during the sexual acts. For example, during coitus, the woman is to move her hips "like a go-go dancer's" while keeping her feet on the bed and tightening her inner thigh muscles to protect herself from the customer's thrust and full penetration. Ann allows turn-outs to perform coitus on their backs only, and the woman is taught to keep one of her arms across her chest as a measure of self-defense in this vulnerable position.

After Ann has described the rudimentary techniques for the three basic sexual acts—fellatio, coitus, and "half and half"—she begins to explain the rules of the house operation. The first set of rules concerns what acts the client may receive for specific sums of money. Time limits are imposed on the clients, roughly at the rate of $1 per minute; the minimum rate in this house is $15 for any of the three basic positions. Ann describes in detail what will occur when the first client arrives: he will be admitted by either Ann or the maid; the women are to stand and smile at him, but not speak at him (considered "dirty hustling"); he will choose one of the women and go to the bedroom with her. Ann accompanies the turn-out and the client to the bedroom and begins teaching the woman how to check the man for any cuts or open sores on the genitals and for any signs of old or active venereal disease. Ann usually rechecks each client herself during the turn-out's first two weeks of work. For the first few days Ann remains in the room while the turn-out and client negotiate the sexual

contract. In ensuing days Ann spends time helping the woman develop verbal skills to "hustle" the customer for more expensive sexual activities.

The following analysis of the instruction Ann provides is based on tape recordings made by Ann during actual training sessions in 1971 and 1975. These sessions took place after the turn-outs had worked several days but usually during their first two weeks of work. The tapes contain ten hours of group discussion with fourteen different novices. The teaching tapes were analyzed according to topics covered in the discussions, using the method outlined in Barker (1963) for making such divisions in the flow of conversation and using Bryan's analysis of the call girl's apprenticeship as a guide in grouping the topics. Bryan divides the content of the training of call girls into two broad dimensions, one philosophical and one interpersonal (1965:291–4). The first emphasizes a subcultural value system and sets down guidelines for how the novice *should* treat her clients and her colleagues in the business. The second dimension follows from the first but emphasizes actual behavioral techniques and skills.

The content analysis of the taped training sessions produced three major topics of discussion and revealed the relative amount of time Ann devoted to each. The first two most frequently discussed topics can be categorized under Bryan's dimension of interpersonal skills; they were devoted to teaching situational strategies for managing clients. The third topic resembles Bryan's value dimension (1965:291–2).

The first topic stressed physical skills and strategies. Included in this category were instruction on how to perform certain sexual acts and specification of their prices, discussion of particular clients, and instruction in techniques for dealing with certain categories of clients, such as "older men" or "kinky" tricks. This topic of physical skills also included discussion of, and Ann's demonstration of, positions designed to provide the woman maximum comfort and protection from the man during different sexual acts. Defense tactics, such as ways to get out of a sexual position and out of the bedroom quickly, were practiced by the novices. Much time was devoted to analyzing past encounters with particular clients. Bryan finds similar discussions of individual tricks among novice call girls and their trainers (1965:293). In the case of Ann's turn-outs these discussions were often initiated by a novice's complaint or question about a certain client and his requests or behavior in the bedroom. The novice always received tips and advice from Ann and the other women present on how to manage that type of bedroom encounter. Such sharing of tactics allows the turn-out to learn what Gagnon and Simon call "patterns of client management" (1973:231).

Ann typically used these discussions of bedroom difficulties to further the training in specific sexual skills she had begun during the turn-out's first few days at work. It is possible that the addition of such follow-up sexual training to that provided during the turn-out's first days at the house results in a more extensive teaching of actual sexual skills than that obtained either by call girls or streetwalkers. Bryan finds that in the call-girl training—except for fellatio—"There seems to be little instruction concerning sexual techniques as such, even though the previous sexual experience of the trainee may have been quite limited" (1965:293). Gray (1973:413) notes that her sample of streetwalker turn-outs were rarely taught specific work strategies:

They learned these things by trial and error on the job. Nor were they schooled in specific sexual techniques: Usually they were taught by customers who made the specific requests.

House prostitution may require more extensive sexual instruction than other forms of the business. The dissatisfied customer of a house may mean loss of business and therefore loss of income to the madam and the prostitutes who work there. The sexually inept streetwalker or call girl does not hurt business for anyone but herself; she may actually increase business for those women in the area should dissatisfied clients choose to avoid her. But the house depends on a stable clientele of satisfied customers.

The second most frequently discussed topic could be labeled: client management/verbal skills. Ann's primary concern was teaching what she calls "hustling." "Hustling" is similar to what

Bryan terms a "sales pitch" for call girls (1965:292), but in the house setting it takes place in the bedroom while the client is deciding how much to spend and what sexual acts he wishes performed. "Hustling" is designed to encourage the client to spend more than the minimum rate.[3] The prominence on the teaching tapes of instruction in this verbal skill shows its importance in Ann's training of novices.

On one of the tapes Ann uses her own turning-out experience to explain to two novices (both with pimps) why she always teaches hustling skills as an integral part of working in a house.

Ann as a Turn-out[4]

Ann: Of course, I can remember a time when I didn't know that I was supposed to hustle. So that's why I understand that it's difficult to *learn* to hustle. When I turned out it was $2 a throw. They came in. They gave me their $2. They got a hell of a fuck. And that was it. Then one Saturday night I turned *forty-four* tricks! And Penny [the madam] used to put the number of tricks at the top of the page and the amount of money at the bottom of the page— she used these big ledger books. Lloyd [Ann's pimp] came in at six o'clock and he looked at that book and he just *knew* I had made all kinds of money. Would you believe I had turned forty-two $2 tricks and two $3 tricks—because two of 'em got generous and gave me an extra buck! [Laughs] I got my ass whipped. And I was so tired—I thought I was going to die—I was 15 years old. And I got my ass whipped for it. [Ann imitates an angry Lloyd:] "Don't you know you're supposed to ask for more money?!" No, I didn't. Nobody told me that. All they told me was it was $2. So that is learning it the *hard* way. I'm trying to help you learn it the *easy* way, if there is an easy way to do it.

In the same session Ann asks one of the turn-outs (Linda, age eighteen) to practice her hustling rap.

Learning the Hustling Rap

Ann: I'm going to be a trick. You've checked me. I want you to carry it from there. [Ann begins role-playing: she plays the client; Linda, the hustler.]

Linda: [mechanically] What kind of party would you like to have?

Ann: That had all the enthusiasm of a wet noodle. I really wouldn't *want* any party with that because you evidently don't want to give me one.

Linda: What kind of party would you *like* to have?

Ann: I usually take a half and half.

Linda: Uh, the money?

Ann: What money?

Linda: The money you're supposed to have! [loudly] 'Cause you ain't gettin' it for free!

Ann: [Upset] Linda, if you *ever,* ever say that in my joint . . . Because that's fine for street hustling. In street hustling, you're going to *have* to hard-hustle those guys or they're not going to come up with anything. Because they are going to *try* and get it for free. But when they walk in here, they *know* they're not going to get it for free to begin with. So try another tack—just a little more friendly, not quite so hard-nosed. [Returning to role-playing:] I just take a half and half.

Linda: How about fifteen [dollars]?

Ann: You're leading into the money too fast, honey. Try: "What are you going to spend?" or "How much money are you going to spend?" or something like that.

Linda: How much would you like to spend?

Ann: No! Not "like." 'Cause they don't *like* to spend anything.

Linda: How much *would* you like to spend?

Ann: Make it a very definite, positive statement: "How much are you going to spend?"

Ann considers teaching hustling skills her most difficult and important task. In spite of her lengthy discussion on the tapes of the rules and techniques for dealing with her customer sexually, Ann states that it may take only a few minutes to "show a girl how to turn a trick." A substantially longer period is required, however, to teach her to hustle. To be adept at hustling, the woman must be mentally alert and sensitive to the client's response to what she is saying and doing and be able to act on those perceptions of his reactions. The hustler must maintain a steady patter of verbal coaxing, during which her tone of voice may be more important than her actual words.

In Ann's framework, then, hustling is a form of verbal sexual aggression. Referring to the problems in teaching novices to hustle, Ann notes that "taking the aggressive part is something women are not used to doing; particularly young women." No doubt, hustling is difficult to teach partly because the woman must learn to discuss sexual acts, whereas in her previous experience, sexual behavior and preferences had been negotiated nonverbally (see Gagnon and Simon, 1973:228). Ann feels that to be effective, each woman's "hustling rap" must be her own—one that comes naturally and will strike the clients as sincere. All of that takes practice. But Ann is aware that the difficulty in learning to hustle stems more from the fact that it involves inappropriate sex-role behavior. Bryan concludes that it is precisely this aspect of soliciting men on the telephone that causes the greatest distress to the novice call girl (1965:293). Thus, the call girl's income is affected by how much business she can bring in by her calls, that is, by how well she can learn to be socially aggressive on the telephone. The income of the house prostitute, in turn, depends heavily on her hustling skills in the bedroom. Ann's task, then, is to train the novice, who has recently come from a culture where young women are not expected to be sexually aggressive, to assume that role with a persuasive naturalness.

Following the first two major topics—client management through physical and verbal skills—the teaching of "racket" (prostitution world) values was the third ranking topic of training and discussion on the teaching tapes. Bryan notes that the major value taught to call girls is "that of maximizing gains and minimizing effort, even if this requires transgressions of either a legal or moral nature" (1965:291). In her training, however, Ann avoids communicating the notion that the novices may exploit the customers in any way they can. For example, stealing or cheating clients is grounds for dismissal from the house. Ann cannot afford the reputation among her tricks that they risk being robbed when they visit her. Moreover, being honest with clients is extolled as a virtue. Thus, Ann urges the novices to tell the trick if she is nervous or unsure, to let him know she is new to the business. This is in direct contradiction to the advice pimps usually give their new women to hide their inexperience from the trick. Ann asserts that honesty in this case means that the client will be more tolerant of mistakes in sexual technique, be less likely to interpret hesitancy as coldness, and be generally more helpful and sympathetic. Putting her "basic principle" in the form of a simple directive, Ann declares: "Please the trick, but at the same time get as much money for pleasing him as you possibly can." Ann does not consider hustling to be client exploitation. It is simply the attempt to sell the customer the product with the highest profit margin. That is, she would defend hustling in terms familiar to the businessman or sales manager.

That Ann teaches hustling as a value is revealed in the following discussion between Ann and Sandy—a former hustler and longtime friend of Ann. Sandy, who married a former trick and still lives in town, has come over to the house to help instruct several novices in the hustling business.

Whores, Prostitutes, and Hustlers

Ann: [To the turn-outs:] Don't get uptight that you're hesitating or you're fumbling, within the first week or even the first five years. Because it takes that long to become a good hustler. I mean you can be a whore in one night. There's nothing to that. The first time you take money you're a whore.

Sandy: This girl in Midtown [a small, midwestern city] informed me—I had been working there awhile—that I was a "whore" and she was a "prostitute." And I said: "Now what the hell does that mean?" Well the difference was that a prostitute could pick her customer and a whore had to take anybody. I said: "Well honey, I want to tell you something. I'm neither one." She said: "Well, you *work*." I said: "I know, but I'm a *hustler*. I make *money* for what I do."

Ann: And this is what I turn out—or try to turn out—hustlers. Not prostitutes. Not whores. But hustlers.

For Ann and Sandy the hustler deserves high status in the prostitution business because she has mastered a specific set of skills that, even with many repeat clients, earn her premiums above the going rate for sexual acts.

In the ideological training of call girls Bryan finds that "values such as fairness with other working girls, or fidelity to a pimp, may occasionally be taught" (1965:291–2); the teaching tapes revealed Ann's affirmation of both these virtues. When a pimp brings a woman to Ann, she supports his control over that woman. For ex-

ample, if during her stay at the house, the novices break any of the basic rules—by using drugs, holding back money (from either Ann or the pimp), lying or seeing another man—Ann will report the infractions to the woman's pimp. Ann notes: "If I don't do that and the pimp finds out, he knows I'm not training her right, and he won't bring his future ladies to me for training." Ann knows she is dependent on the pimps to help supply her with turn-outs. Bryan, likewise, finds a willingness among call girls' trainers to defer to the pimps' wishes during the apprenticeship period (1965:290).

Teaching fairness to other prostitutes is particularly relevant to the madam who daily faces the problem of maintaining peace among competing women at work under one roof. If two streetwalkers or two call girls find that they cannot get along, they need not work near one another. But if a woman leaves a house because of personal conflicts, the madam loses a source of income. To minimize potential negative feelings among novices, Ann stresses mutual support, prohibits "criticizing another girl," and denigrates the "prima donna"—the prostitute who flaunts her financial success before the other women.

In still another strategy to encourage fair treatment of one's colleagues in the establishment, Ann emphasizes a set of rules prohibiting "dirty hustling"—behavior engaged in by one prostitute that would undercut the business of other women in the house. Tabooed under the label of "dirty hustling" are the following: appearing in the line-up partially unclothed; performing certain disapproved sexual positions, such as anal intercourse; and allowing approved sexual extras without charging additional fees. The norms governing acceptable behavior vary from house to house and region to region, and Ann warns the turn-outs to ask about such rules when they begin work in a new establishment. The woman who breaks the work norms in a house, either knowingly or unknowingly, will draw the anger of the other women and can be fired by a madam eager to restore peace and order in the house.

Other topics considered on the tapes—in addition to physical skills, "hustling" and work values—were instruction on personal hygiene and grooming, role-playing of conversational skills with tricks on topics not related to sex or hustling ("living room talk"), house rules not related to hustling (such as punctuality, no perfume, no drugs), and guidelines for what to do during an arrest. There were specific suggestions on how to handle personal criticism, questions, and insults from clients. In addition, the discussions on the tapes provided the novices with many general strategies for becoming "professionals" at their work, for example, the importance of personal style, enthusiasm ("the customer is always right"), and a sense of humor. In some ways these guidelines resemble a beginning course in salesmanship. But they also provide clues, particularly in combination with the topics on handling client insults and the emphasis on hustling, on how the house prostitute learns to manage a stable and limited clientele and cope psychologically with the repetition of the clients and the sheer tedium of the physical work (Hughes, 1971:342–5).

III. TRAINING HOUSE PROSTITUTES—A PROCESS OF PROFESSIONAL SOCIALIZATION

Observing how Ann trains turn-outs is a study in techniques to facilitate identity change (see also Davis, 1971 and Heyl, 1975, chapter 2). Ann uses a variety of persuasive strategies to help give the turn-outs a new occupational identity as a "professional." One strategy is to rely heavily on the new values taught the novice to isolate her from her previous lifestyle and acquaintances. Bryan finds that "the value structure serves, in general, to create in-group solidarity and to alienate the girl, 'square' society" (1965:292). Whereas alienation from conventional society may be an indirect effect of values taught to call girls, in Ann's training of house prostitutes the expectation that the novice will immerse herself in the prostitution world ("racket life") is made dramatically explicit.

In the following transcription from one of the teaching tapes, the participants are Ann (age thirty-six at the time the tape was made), Bonnie (an experienced turn-out, age twenty-five) and Kristy (a new turn-out, age eighteen). Kristy has recently linked up with a pimp for the first time and volunteers to Ann and Bonnie her difficulty

in adjusting to the racket rule of minimal contact with the square world—a rule her pimp is enforcing by not allowing Kristy to meet and talk with her old friends. Ann (A) and Bonnie (B) have listened to Kristy's (K) complaints and are making suggestions. (The notation "B-K" indicates that Bonnie is addressing Kristy.)

B-K: What you gotta do is sit down and talk to him and weed out your friends and find the ones he thinks are suitable companions for you—in your new type of life.
K-B: None of them.
A-K: What about *his* friends?
K-A: I haven't met many of his friends. I don't like any of 'em so far.
A-K: You are making the same mistake that makes me so goddamned irritated with square broads! You're taking a man and trying to train *him,* instead of letting the man train you.
K-A: What?! I'm not trying to train him, I'm just. . . .
A-K: All right, you're trying to force him to accept your friends.
K-A: I don't care whether he accepts them or not. I just can't go around not talking to anybody.
A-K: "Anybody" is your old man! He is your world. And the people he says you can talk to are the people that are your world. But what you're trying to do is force your square world on a racket guy. It's like oil and water. There's just no way a square and a racket person can get together. That's why when you turn out you've got to change your mind completely from square to racket. And you're still trying to hang with squares. You can't do it.

Strauss's (1969) concept of "coaching" illuminates a more subtle technique Ann employs as she helps the novice along, step by step, from "square" to "racket" values and lifestyle. She observes carefully how the novice progresses, elicits responses from her about what she is experiencing, and then interprets those responses for her. In the following excerpt from one of the teaching tapes, Ann prepares two novices for feelings of depression over their newly made decisions to become prostitutes.

Turn-out Blues

Ann: And while I'm on the subject—depression. You know they've got a word for it when you have a baby—it's called "postpartum blues." Now, I call it "turn-out blues." Every girl that ever turns out has 'em. And, depending on the girl, it comes about the third or fourth day. You'll go into a depression for no apparent reason. You'll wake up one morning and say: "Why in the hell am I doing this? Why am I here? I wanna go home!" And I can't do a thing to help you. The only thing I can do is to leave you alone and hope that you'll fight the battle yourself. But knowing that it will come and knowing that everybody else goes through it too does help. Just pray it's a busy night! So if you get blue and you get down, remember: "turn-out blues"— everybody gets it. Here's when you'll decide whether you're going to stay or you're gonna quit.

Ann's description of "turn-out blues" is a good example of Strauss's account (1969:111–2) of how coaches will use prophecy to increase their persuasive power over their novices. In the case of "turn-out blues," the novice, if she becomes depressed about her decision to enter prostitution, will recall Ann's prediction that this would happen and that it happens to all turn-outs. This recollection may or may not end the woman's misgivings about her decision, but it will surely enhance the turn-out's impression of Ann's competence. Ann's use of her past experience to make such predictions is a form of positive leverage; it increases the probability that what she says will be respected and followed in the future.

In Bryan's study the call girls reported that their training was more a matter of observation than direct instruction from their trainer (1965:294). Ann, on the other hand, relies on a variety of teaching techniques, including lecturing and discussion involving other turn-outs who are further along in the training process and can reinforce Ann's views. Ann even brings in guest speakers, such as Sandy, the former hustler, who participates in the discussion with the novices in the role of the experienced resource person. "Learning the Hustling Rap," above, offers an example of role-playing—another teaching technique Ann frequently employs to help the turn-outs develop verbal skills. Ann may have to rely on more varied teaching approaches than the call-girl trainer because: (1) Ann herself is not working, thus her novices have fewer opportunities to watch their trainer interact with clients than do the call-girl novices; and (2) Ann's liveli-

hood depends more directly on the success of her teaching efforts than does that of the call-girl trainer. Ann feels that if a woman under her direction does not "turn out well," not only will the woman earn less money while she is at her house (affecting Ann's own income), but Ann could also lose clients and future turn-outs from her teaching "failure."[5]

The dissolution of the training relationship marks the end of the course. Bryan claims that the sharp break between trainer and trainee shows that the training process itself is largely unrelated to the acquisition of a skill. But one would scarcely have expected the trainee to report "that the final disruption of the apprenticeship was the result of the completion of adequate training" (1965:296). Such establishments do not offer diplomas and terminal degrees. The present study, too, indicates that abrupt breaks in the training relationship are quite common. But what is significant is that the break is precipitated by personal conflicts exacerbated by both the narrowing of the skill-gap between trainer and trainee and the consequent increase in the novice's confidence that she can make it on her own. Thus, skill acquisition counts in such an equation, not in a formal sense ("completion of adequate training"), but rather in so far as it works to break down the earlier bonds of dependence between trainer and trainee.

IV. THE FUNCTION OF TRAINING AT THE HOUSE LEVEL OF PROSTITUTION

Bryan concludes that the training is necessitated by the novice's need for a list of clients in order to work at the call-girl level and not because the actual training is required to prepare her for such work. But turn-outs at the house level of prostitution do not acquire a clientele. The clients are customers of the house. In fact, the madam usually makes sure that only she has the names or phone numbers of her tricks in order to keep control over her business. If Ann's turn-outs (unlike call girls) do not acquire a clientele in the course of their training, why is the training period necessary?

Although Ann feels strongly that training is required to become a successful hustler at the house level, the function served by the training can be seen more as a spin-off of the structure of the occupation at that level: Madams of establishments will often hire only trained prostitutes. Novices who pose as experienced hustlers are fairly easily detected by those proficient in the business working in the same house; to be found out all she need do is violate any of the expected norms of behavior: wear perfume, repeatedly fail to hustle any "over-money" or engage in dirty hustling. The exposure to racket values, which the training provides, may be more critical to the house prostitute than to the call girl. She must live and work in close contact with others in the business. Participants in house prostitution are more integrated into the prostitution world than are call girls, who can be and frequently are "independent"—working without close ties to pimps or other prostitutes. Becoming skilled in hustling is also less important for the call girl, as her minimum fee is usually high, making hustling for small increments less necessary. The house prostitute who does not know how to ask for more money, however, lowers the madam's income as well—another reason why madams prefer professional prostitutes.

The training of house prostitutes, then, reflects two problems in the social organization of house prostitution: (1) Most madams will not hire untrained prostitutes; and (2) the close interaction of prostitutes operating within the confines of a house requires a common set of work standards and practices. These two factors differentiate house prostitution from call-girl and streetwalking operations and facilitate this madam's task of turning novices into professional prostitutes. The teaching madam employs a variety of coaching techniques to train turn-outs in sexual and hustling skills and to expose them to a set of occupational rules and values. Hers is an effort to prepare women with conventional backgrounds for work in the social environment of a house of prostitution where those skills and values are expected and necessary.

NOTES

1. This situation-specific induction into prostitution may be contrasted with the "smooth and almost imperceptible" transition to the status of poolroom "hustler" noted by Polsky (1969:80–1).

2. In the wider context of the national prostitution scene, Ann's situation reflects the "minor league" status of her geographical location. In fact, she trains women from other communities who move on to more lucrative opportunities in the big city. See the stimulating applications of the concept of "minor league" to the study of occupations in Faulkner (1974).

3. The term "hustling" has been used to describe a wide range of small-time criminal activities. Even within the world of prostitution, "hustling" can refer to different occupational styles; see Ross's description of the "hustler" who "is distinguished from ordinary prostitutes in frequently engaging in accessory crimes of exploitation," such as extortion or robbery (1959:16). The use of the term here is thus highly specific, reflecting its meaning in Ann's world.

4. The indented sections (for example, "Ann as a Turn-out" and "Learning the Hustling Rap") are transcriptions from the teaching tapes. Redundant expressions have been omitted, and the author's comments on the speech tone or delivery are bracketed. Words italicized indicate emphasis by the speaker.

5. These data bear only on the skills and values to which Ann *exposes* the turn-outs; confirmation of the effects of such exposure awaits further analysis and is a study in its own right. See Bryan's (1965) study of the impact of the occupational perspective taught by call-girl trainers on the individual attitudes of call girls. See Davis (1971:315) for a description of what constitutes successful "in-service training" for streetwalkers.

REFERENCES

BARKER, ROGER G. (ED.). 1963. *The Stream of Behavior: Explorations of Its Structure and Content*. New York: Appleton-Century-Crofts.

BRYAN, JAMES H. 1965. "Apprenticeships in prostitution." *Social Problems* 12 (Winter):287–97. 1966. "Occupational ideologies and individual attitudes of call girls." *Social Problems* 13 (Spring):441–50.

DAVIS, NANETTE J. 1971. "The prostitute: Developing a deviant identity." Pp. 297–332 in James M. Henslin (ed.). *Studies in the Sociology of Sex*. New York: Appleton-Century-Crofts.

ERWIN, CAROL. 1960. *The Orderly Disorderly House*. Garden City, N.Y.: Doubleday.

FAULKNER, ROBERT R. 1974. "Coming of age in organizations: A comparative study of career contingencies and adult socialization." *Sociology of Work and Occupations* 1 (May):131–73.

GAGNON, JOHN H. and WILLIAM SIMON. 1973. *Sexual Conduct: The Social Sources of Human Sexuality*. Chicago: Aldine.

GRAY, DIANA. 1973. "Turning-out: A study of teenage prostitution." *Urban Life and Culture* 1 (January):401–25.

HALL, SUSAN. 1973. *Ladies of the Night.* New York: Trident Press.

HEYL, BARBARA S. 1974. "The madam as entrepreneur." *Sociological Symposium* 11 (Spring):61–82.

———. 1975. "The house prostitute: A case study." Unpublished Ph.D. dissertation, Department of Sociology, University of Illinois-Urbana.

HUGHES, EVERETT C. 1971. "Work and self." Pp. 338–47 in *The Sociological Eye: Selected Papers.* Chicago: Aldine-Atherton.

JACKSON, BRUCE. 1969. *A Thief's Primer.* Toronto, Ontario: Macmillan.

LEWIS, GLADYS ADELINA (ED.) 1942. *Call House Madam: The Story of the Career of Beverly Davis.* San Francisco: Martin Tudordale.

POLSKY, NED. 1969. *Hustlers, Beats and Others.* Garden City, N.Y.: Doubleday.

ROSS, H. LAURENCE. 1959. "The 'hustler' in Chicago." *Journal of Student Research* 1:13–19.

SHEEHY, GAIL. 1974. *Hustling: Prostitution in Our Wide-Open Society.* New York: Dell.

STEWART, GEORGE I. 1972. "On first being a john." *Urban Life and Culture* 1 (October):255–74.

STRAUSS, ANSELM L. 1969. *Mirrors and Masks: The Search for Identity.* San Francisco: Sociology Press.

VOGLIOTTI, GABRIEL R. 1975. *The Girls of Nevada.* Secaucus, N.J.: Citadel Press.

WINICK, CHARLES and PAUL M. KINSIE. 1971. *The Lively Commerce: Prostitution in the United States.* Chicago: Quadrangle Books.

TEAROOM TRADE[*]

Laud Humphreys

While the agreements resulting in "one-night-stands" occur in many settings—the bath, the street, the public toilet—and may vary greatly in the elaborateness or simplicity of the interaction preceding culmination in the sexual act, their essential feature is the expectation that sex can be had without obligation or commitment.[1]

At shortly after five o'clock on a weekday evening, four men enter a public restroom in the city park. One wears a well-tailored business suit; another wears tennis shoes, shorts, and teeshirt; the third man is still clad in the khaki uniform of his filling station; the last, a salesman, has loosened his tie and left his sports coat in the car. What has caused these men to leave the company of other homeward-bound commuters on the freeway? What common interest brings these men, with their divergent backgrounds, to this public facility?

They have come here not for the obvious reason, but in a search for "instant sex." Many men—married and unmarried, those with heterosexual identities and those whose self-image is a homosexual one—seek such impersonal sex, shunning involvement, desiring kicks without commitment. Whatever reasons—social, physiological, or psychological—might be postulated for this search, the phenomenon of impersonal sex persists as a widespread but rarely studied form of human interaction.

There are several settings for this type of deviant activity—the balconies of movie theaters, automobiles, behind bushes—but few offer the advantages for these men that public restrooms provide. "Tearooms," as these facilities are called in the language of the homosexual subculture,[2] have several characteristics that make them attractive as locales for sexual encounters without involvement.

*Reprinted with permission from Humphreys, Laud. *Tearoom Trade: Impersonal Sex in Public Places.* Enlarged Edition (New York: Aldine de Gruyter). Copyright © 1970, 1975 R. A. Laud Humphreys.

According to its most precise meaning in the argot, the only "true" tearoom is one that gains a reputation as a place where homosexual encounters occur. Presumably, any restroom could qualify for this distinction, but comparatively few are singled out for this function at any one time. For instance, I have researched a metropolitan area with more than ninety public toilets in its parks, only twenty of which are in regular use as locales for sexual games. Restrooms thus designated join the company of automobiles and bathhouses as places for deviant sexual activity second only to private bedrooms in popularity.[3] During certain seasons of the year—roughly, that period from April through October that midwestern homosexuals call "the hunting season"—tearooms may surpass any other locale of homoerotic enterprise in volume of activity.

Public restrooms are chosen by those who want homoerotic activity without commitment for a number of reasons. *They are accessible, easily recognized by the initiate, and provide little public visibility.* Tearooms thus offer the advantages of both public and private settings. They are available and recognizable enough to attract a large volume of potential sexual partners, providing an opportunity for rapid action with a variety of men. When added to the relative privacy of these settings, such features enhance the impersonality of the sheltered interaction.

AVAILABILITY

In the first place, tearooms are readily accessible to the male population. They may be located in any sort of public gathering place: department stores, bus stations, libraries, hotels, YMCAs, or courthouses. In keeping with the drive-in craze of American society, however, the more popular facilities are those readily accessible to the roadways. The restrooms of public parks and beaches—and, more recently, the rest stops set at programmed intervals along superhighways—are now attracting the clientele that, in a more pedestrian age, frequented great buildings of the inner cities. . . . [M]y research is focused on the activity that takes place in the restrooms of public parks, not only because (with some seasonal variation) they provide the most action but also be-

cause of other factors that make them suitable for sociological study.

It is a function of some societies to make these facilities for elimination available to the public. Perhaps the public toilet is one of the marks of "civilization," at least as perceived by European and post-European culture. I recall a letter from a sailor stationed in North Africa during World War II in which he called the people "uncivilized" because they had no public restrooms and used streets and gutters for the purpose of elimination.

For the cultural historian, American park restrooms merit study as physical traces of modern civilization. The older ones are often appended to pavilions or concealed beneath the paving of graceful colonnades. One marble-lined room in which I have done research occupies half of a Greek temple-like structure, a building of beautiful lines and proportions. A second type, built before the Great Depression, are the toilet facilities located in park administration buildings, maintenance shops, or garages. For the most part, these lack the artistic qualities of the first type. Partly because they are not as accessible from the roads and partly because they are too easily approached by supervisory personnel and other interfering "straights," these restrooms enjoy homosexual popularity only during the months when other outlets are closed.

With the depression of the 1930s a new variety of public toilet appeared on the park scene. Ten of the twelve tearooms in which I made systematic observations . . . were of this category. Although the floor plans and building materials used vary from city to city, the majority of restrooms I have seen were constructed during this period. These have been built by the Work Projects Administration and, in any one community, seem to have been stamped from the same die. In the city where most of my research took place, they are constructed of a native white stone with men's and women's facilities back-to-back under one red roof. They have heavy wooden doors, usually screened from public view by a latticework partition attached to the building's exterior. In most of these doors, there is an inset of opaque French panes.

Each of the toilet facilities in the building has two windows of the same opaque glass, situated at either side of the room. The outside of these apertures is always covered with heavy screen. Against the blank wall opposite the door there are (from left to right) three urinals and two stalls, although smaller restrooms may provide only two urinals and one stall. Some of the facilities still have wash basins intact, situated in the corner to the left as one enters the door, but few of these are in working order. There is an occasional wastebasket. Paper towels are seldom provided, and there are no other furnishings in the rooms (see Figure 1).

Few park restrooms date back to the 1940s, when the nation was concerned with building those other major outlets for homosexual activity, the military posts. Apparently, most public construction in the 1950s was connected with the rush to provide more athletic facilities—swimming pools, golf courses, skating rinks, and the like.

The past decade has witnessed the construction of new, functional, cement-block facilities. Most of these structures are located along the expressways, but a number are appearing in the parks and playgrounds of our cities. These relief stations may be viewed as an expression of the current interest in urban planning: some replace buildings no longer fit for use; others are located on the newly created urban playgrounds; and the bulk accompany the nation's answer to problems of mass transportation. However one may interpret the new construction as a reflection of the course of American history, it should be a boon to the tearoom customers. Most of the newly built restrooms are isolated structures with ready access to the roads and thus meet the prime requisites of tearoom activity.

According to some older respondents, the real turning point for the tearoom trade arrived with the WPA. One man, who has been active in the homosexual subculture for more than forty years, puts it this way:

I suppose there has been such activity since the invention of plumbing. I first started out in one of those pavilion places. But the real fun began during the depression. There were all those new buildings, easy to reach, and the automobile was really getting popular about then. . . . Suddenly, it just seemed like half the men in town met in the tearooms.

Not all of the new buildings were easy to reach, but those that were soon found popularity for homosexual activity. Tearoom ecology, like that of society at large, is highly affected by the

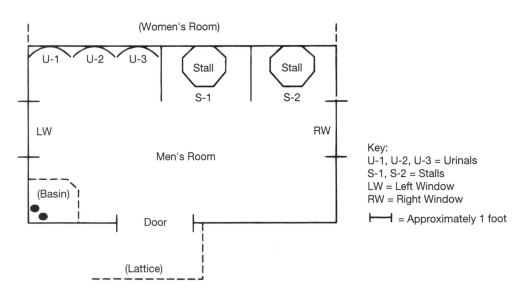

FIGURE 1 Diagram of Typical Public Park Restroom

location of transportation routes. Whether by accident or design, most large city parks are located close to major thoroughfares and freeways. Because the activity in tearooms reaches its peak at the close of the workday, restrooms will draw more customers if located near principal commuting routes of the metropolitan area. The two facilities that I found to attract the greatest numbers for homosexual relations were adjacent to four-lane traffic arteries. All others in which any noteworthy amount of activity was observed were located within five minutes' driving time of the expressways that circle and cross the city.

LOCATING THE ACTION

There is a great deal of difference in the volumes of homosexual activity that these accommodations shelter. In some, one might wait for months before observing a deviant act (unless solitary masturbation is considered deviant). In others, the volume approaches orgiastic dimensions. One summer afternoon, for instance, I witnessed twenty acts of fellatio in the course of an hour while waiting out a thunderstorm in a tearoom. For one who wishes to participate in (or study) such activity, the primary consideration is one of finding where the action is.

Occasionally, tips about the more active places may be gained from unexpected sources. Early in my research, I was approached by a man (whom I later surmised to be a park patrolman in plain clothes) while waiting at the window of a tearoom for some patrons to arrive. After finishing his business at the urinal and exchanging some remarks about the weather (it had been raining), the man came abruptly to the point: "Look, fellow, if you're looking for sex, this isn't the place. We're clamping down on this park because of trouble with the niggers. Try the john at the northeast corner of [Reagan] Park. You'll find plenty of action there." He was right. Some of my best observations were made at the spot he recommended. In most cases, however, I could only enter, wait, and watch—a method that was costly in both time and gasoline. After surveying a couple of dozen such rooms in this way, however, I became able to identify the more popular tearooms by observing certain physical evidence,

the most obvious of which is the location of the facility. During the warm seasons, those restrooms that are isolated from other park facilities, such as administration buildings, shops, tennis courts, playgrounds, and picnic areas, are the more popular for deviant activity. The most active tearooms studied were all isolated from recreational areas, cut off by drives or lakes from baseball diamonds and picnic tables.

I have chosen the term "purlieu" (with its ancient meaning of land severed from a royal forest by perambulation) to describe the immediate environs best suited to the tearoom trade. Drives and walks that separate a public toilet from the rest of the park are almost certain guides to deviant sex. The ideal setting for homosexual activity is a tearoom situated on an island of grass, with roads close by on every side. The getaway car is just a few steps away; children are not apt to wander over from the playground; no one can surprise the participants by walking in from the woods or from over a hill; it is not likely that straight people will stop there at all. According to my observations, the women's side of these buildings is seldom used.

Active tearooms are also identifiable by the number of automobiles parked nearby. If two or more cars remain in front of a relatively isolated restroom for more than ten minutes, one may be reasonably certain that homosexual activity is in progress inside. This sign that the sexual market is in operation is an important one to the participants, who seldom enter a park restroom unless the presence of other unoccupied cars indicates that potential partners are inside. A lone arriver will usually wait in his auto until at least one other has parked nearby. That this signal is obscured when a golf course, zoo, or other facility that draws automobiles is located in close proximity may help explain the popularity of the isolated restroom.

Another means of recognizing the active tearoom requires closer inspection. Here, I refer to the condition of the windows and doors. Men who play the tearoom game must be able to know when someone is approaching. A door that squeaks or sticks is of great assistance; however, the condition of the windows is even more important. If they are of opaque glass, are nailed shut, or have no broken panes, the researcher may presume that the facility is seldom used for homosexual encounters.

In a western city, I have observed an exception to this rule. One of the popular meeting places there was a restroom located beneath the pavement of a colonnade. There were vents but no windows. The only access to this tearoom, however, was by means of a circular, metal stairway, and clanging footfalls could be heard well before the intruder was far enough down to see into the room. Normally, popular tearooms have at least one pane broken from each window, unless the windows have been opened. Fragments of glass that remain between the window frame and an outside screen are indicative of destruction that was initiated from within the restroom rather than by outside vandals. As [one] account of a teen-age attack . . . indicates, occasional damage to the buildings comes from outside. But one of the first acts of participants after the spring opening or renovation of a facility is to break out a few carefully selected panes so that insiders can see who is approaching.

Graffiti were expected to provide some indication of restroom usage for deviant activity. On the basis of quantity alone, however, inscriptions vary most directly with the time since the latest repainting or cleansing of the walls or with the type of wall covering used. There also seems to be a relationship between the quantity of such markings and the neighborhood in which the facility is situated. Restrooms in lower class and commercial neighborhoods or close to schools tend to invite more of such writings than those in middle class or residential areas.

The *type* of graffiti found does correlate with use of the room for homosexual purposes. In the more active tearooms, I have often noticed inscriptions such as: "show hard—get sucked," "will suck cocks—10/12/66—all morning," or "I have eight inches—who wants it?" One respondent says that the presence of recent markings such as these reassures him that he has come to the right place for action. Active homosexual locales are conspicuously lacking in initials, sketches of nude females, poetry, and certain of the classic four-letter words. Writings on the walls of the true tearooms are straightforward, functional messages, lacking the fantasy content of the graffiti in most men's rooms. Moreover, this research suggests that involvement in homosexual encounters may preclude the leisure time necessary for some of the more creative types of graffiti production.

VOLUME AND VARIETY

The availability of facilities they can recognize attracts a great number of men who wish, for whatever reason, to engage in impersonal homoerotic activity. Simple observation is enough to guide these participants, the researcher, and, perhaps, the police to active tearooms. It is much more difficult to make an accurate appraisal of the proportion of the male population who engage in such activity over a representative length of time. Even with good sampling procedures, a large staff of assistants would be needed to make the observations necessary for an adequate census of this mobile population.[4] All that may be said with some degree of certainty is that the percentage of the male population who participate in tearoom sex in the United States is somewhat less than the 16 percent of the adult white male population Kinsey found to have "at least as much of the homosexual as the heterosexual in their histories."[5]

Participants assure me that it is not uncommon in tearooms for one man to fellate as many as ten others in a day. I have personally watched a fellator take on three men in succession in a half hour of observation. One respondent, who has cooperated with the researcher in a number of taped interviews, claims to average three men each day during the busy seasons.

I have seen some wait in turn for this type of service. Leaving one such scene on a warm September Saturday, I remarked to a man who left close behind me: "Kind of crowded in there, isn't it?" "Hell, yes," he answered. "It's getting so you have to take a number and wait in line in these places!"

There are many who frequent the same facility repeatedly. Men will come to be known as regular, even daily, participants, stopping off at the same tearoom on the way to or from work. One physician in his late fifties was so punctual in his appearance at a particular restroom that I began to look forward to our daily chats. This robust, affable respondent said he had stopped at this tearoom every evening of the week (except Wednesday, his day off) for years "for a blow-job." Another respondent, a salesman whose schedule is flexible, may "make the scene" more than once a day—usually at his favorite men's room. At the time of our formal interview, this man claimed to have had four orgasms in the past twenty-four hours.

According to participants I have interviewed, those who are looking for impersonal sex in tea-rooms are relatively certain of finding the sort of partner they want . . .

You go into the tearoom. You can pick up some really nice things in there. Again, it is a matter of sex real quick; and, if you like this kind, fine—you've got it. You get one and he is done; and, before long, you've got another one.

. . . when they want it:

Well, I go there; and you can always find someone to suck your cock, morning, noon, or night. I know lots of guys who stop by there on their way to work—and all during the day.

It is this sort of volume and variety that keeps the tearooms viable as market places of the one-night-stand variety.

Of the bar crowd in gay (homosexual) society, only a small percentage would be found in park restrooms. But this more overt, gay bar clientele constitutes a minor part of those in any American city who follow a predominantly homosexual pattern. The so-called closet queens and other types of covert deviants make up the vast major-ity of those who engage in homosexual acts— and these are the persons most attracted to tea-room encounters. . . .

Tearooms are popular, not because they serve as gathering places for homosexuals but because they attract a variety of men, a *minority* of whom are active in the homosexual subculture. When we consider the types of participants, it will be seen that a large group of them have no homo-sexual self-identity. For various reasons, they do not want to be seen with those who might be identified as such or to become involved with them on a "social" basis.

PRIVACY IN PUBLIC

I have mentioned that one of the distinguishing traits of an active tearoom is its isolation from other facilities in a park. The addition of four pic-nic tables close to a once popular restroom all but eliminated that facility for research purposes. This portion of a tape, made as I toured the parks in search of action one April Sunday, is indica-tive of this ecological pattern:

This [park] is really dead! The tremendous volume of picnickers in all of the parks. . . . It seems like every family in the city is out today. It is a beautiful day, very warm, very pleasant. And everyone is out with their children. . . . The one facility in this park which is most active consistently is just completely surrounded by picnickers, and this would kill any gay activity. . . .

At this stage in the development of American culture, at least, some sort of privacy is requisite for sex. Whether deviant or "normal," sexual ac-tivity demands a degree of seclusion. Even or-gies, I am told, require darkness or a minimum of light. When, as is the case with fellatio, the form of sexual engagement is prohibited, privacy de-creases risk and is even more valued.

This constitutes a dilemma for those who would engage in impersonal sex of this type: how to find a setting that is accessible and identifi-able, that will provide the necessary volume and variety of participants, while preserving at least a minimum of privacy? The trysting place must not be too available for the undesired. It must not be identifiable by the uninitiated. The potential par-ticipant passing by should be able to perceive what is taking place inside, while those playing baseball across the way should remain ignorant of the sexual game behind tearoom walls.

Ecological factors, the tearoom purlieu, that separate these facilities from other activity in the public park, have already been discussed. The presence of walls and stalls and opaque windows also help preserve the needed privacy. But there is another aspect of the tearoom encounters that is crucial to the maintenance of privacy in public settings. I refer to the silence of the interaction.

Throughout most homosexual encounters in public restrooms, nothing is spoken. One may spend many hours in these buildings and witness dozens of sexual acts without hearing a word. Of fifty encounters on which I made extensive notes,[6] only fifteen included vocal utterances. The fifteen instances of speech break down as follows: Two were encounters in which I sought to ease the strain of legitimizing myself as lookout by saying, "You go ahead—I'll watch." Four were whispered remarks between sexual partners, such as, "Not so hard!" or "Thanks." One was an exchange of greetings between friends.

The other eight verbal exchanges were in full voice and more extensive, but they reflected an attendant circumstance that was exceptional. When a group of us were locked in a restroom and attacked by several youths, we spoke for defense and out of fear. . . . This event ruptured the reserve among us and resulted in a series of conversations among those who shared this adventure for several days afterward. Gradually, this sudden unity subsided, and the encounters drifted back into silence.

Barring such unusual events, an occasionally whispered "thanks" at the conclusion of the act constitutes the bulk of even whispered communication. At first, I presumed that speech was avoided for fear of incrimination. The excuse that intentions have been misunderstood is much weaker when those proposals are expressed in words rather than signalled by body movements. As research progressed, however, it became evident that the privacy of silent interaction accomplishes much more than mere defense against exposure to a hostile world. Even when a careful lookout is maintaining the boundaries of an encounter against intrusion, the sexual participants tend to be silent. The mechanism of silence goes beyond satisfying the demand for privacy. Like all other characteristics of the tearoom setting, it serves to guarantee anonymity, to assure the impersonality of the sexual liaison.

Tearoom sex is distinctly less personal than any other form of sexual activity, with the single exception of solitary masturbation. . . . For now, let me indicate only what I mean by "less personal": simply, that there is less emotional and physical involvement in restroom fellatio—less,

even, than in the furtive action that takes place in autos and behind bushes. In those instances, at least, there is generally some verbal involvement. Often, in tearoom stalls, the only portions of the players' bodies that touch are the mouth of the insertee and the penis of the insertor; and the mouths of these partners seldom open for speech.

Only a public place, such as a park restroom, could provide the lack of personal involvement in sex that certain men desire. The setting fosters the necessary turnover in participants by its accessibility and visibility to the "right" men. In these public settings, too, there exists a sort of democracy that is endemic to impersonal sex. Men of all racial, social, educational, and physical characteristics meet in these places for sexual union. With the lack of involvement, personal preferences tend to be minimized.

If a person is going to entangle his body with another's in bed—or allow his mind to become involved with another mind—he will have certain standards of appearance, cleanliness, personality, or age that the prospective partner must meet. Age, looks, and other external variables are germane to the sexual action. As the amount of anticipated contact of body and mind in the sex act decreases, so do the standards expected of the partner. As one respondent told me:

I go to bed with gay people, too. But if I am going to bed with a gay person, I have certain standards that I prefer them to meet. And, in the tearooms, you don't have to worry about these things—because it is just a purely one-sided affair.

Participants may develop strong attachments to the settings of their adventures in impersonal sex. I have noted more than once that these men seem to acquire stronger sentimental attachments to the buildings in which they meet for sex than to the persons with whom they engage in it. One respondent tells the following story of his roommate's devotion to a particular restroom:

(We had been discussing the relative merits of various facilities, when I asked him: "Do you remember that old tearoom across from the park garage—the one they tore down last winter?")

Do I ever! That was the greatest place in the park. Do you know what my roommate did last Christmas, after they tore the place down? He took a wreath, sprayed it with black paint, and laid it on top of the snow—right where that corner stall had stood. . . . He was really broken up!

The walls and fixtures of these public facilities are provided by society at large, but much remains for the participants to provide for themselves. Silence in these settings is the product of years of interaction. It is a normative response to the demand for privacy without involvement, a rule that has been developed and taught. Except for solitary masturbation, sex necessitates joint action; and impersonal sex requires that this interaction be as unrevealing as possible. In a number of ways, the structure of tearoom encounters has been developed, refined, and communicated. The primary task of this book is to describe for the reader the social structure of impersonal sex, the mechanisms that make it possible.

How, then, does such an operation work? What rules govern it? What roles may people play in it? What sort of ritual sustains the action? What are the risks—to players and others—of such activity? What kinds of people find the tearooms inviting for sexual experience, and how do they relate this behavior to the rest of their lives? These questions remain to be answered; but, before I can reply to them, it is important for the reader to know how I found these answers. Answers become clear only when we are aware what questions were asked and how conclusions were reached.

NOTES

1. Evelyn Hooker, "Male Homosexuals and Their 'Worlds,'" in Judd Marmor, ed., *Sexual Inversion* (New York: Basic Books, 1965), p. 97.

2. Like most other words in the homosexual vocabulary, the origin of *tearoom* is unknown. British slang has used "tea" to denote "urine." Another British usage is as a verb, meaning "to engage with, encounter, go in against." See John S. Farmer and W. E. Henley, *A Dictionary of Slang and Colloquial English* (London: George Rutledge & Sons, 1921).

3. It is not possible to know how many sexual acts are performed in the various types of settings. Writers on the homosexual subculture agree, in general, on the relative popularity of these locales. For general surveys of the homosexual scene, see especially Evelyn Hooker, "The Homosexual Community," in *Personality Research* (Copenhagen: Monksgaard, 1962), pp. 40–59; and Maurice Leznoff and William A. Westley, "The Homosexual Community," *Social Problems,* Vol. 3, No. 4 (April, 1965), pp. 257–263.

4. By estimating (a) the average daily frequency of sex acts in each of twenty restrooms observed and (b) the average number of automobiles suspected of having been parked by participants near restrooms in five different parks, I have concluded that approximately 5 percent of the adult male population of the metropolitan area under study are involved in these encounters in a year's time. The imprecision of the methods used in obtaining this "guesstimate" does not warrant elaboration.

5. Alfred C. Kinsey and others, *Sexual Behavior in the Human Male* (Philadelphia: Saunders, 1948), pp. 650–651. See also William Simon and John H. Gagnon, "Homosexuality: The Formulation of a Sociological Perspective," *Journal of Health and Social Behavior,* Vol. 8, No. 3 (September, 1967), p. 180. "About one half [of the male homosexuals studied] reported that sixty percent or more of their sexual partners were persons with whom they had sex only one time. Between ten and twenty percent report that they often picked up their sexual partners in public terminals, and an even larger proportion reported similar contacts in other public or semipublic locations."

6. Although I made fifty systematic observations of tearoom encounters, fifty-three acts of fellatio were observed at those times. The sexual acts sometimes occur in such rapid succession that it is impossible to report them as involving separate encounters. . . .

CONVICTED RAPISTS' VOCABULARY OF MOTIVE
EXCUSES AND JUSTIFICATIONS*

Diana Scully and Joseph Marolla**

Psychiatry has dominated the literature on rapists since "irresistible impulse" (Glueck, 1925:323) and "disease of the mind" (Glueck, 1925:243) were introduced as the causes of rape. Research has been based on small samples of men, frequently the clinicians' own patient population. Not surprisingly, the medical model has predominated: Rape is viewed as an individualistic, idiosyncratic symptom of a disordered personality. That is, rape is assumed to be a psychopathologic problem and individual rapists are assumed to be "sick." However, advocates of this model have been unable to isolate a typical or even predictable pattern of symptoms that are causally linked to rape. Additionally, research has demonstrated that fewer than 5 percent of rapists were psychotic at the time of their rape (Abel et al., 1980).

We view rape as behavior learned socially through interaction with others; convicted rapists have learned the attitudes and actions consistent with sexual aggression against women. Learning also includes the acquisition of culturally derived vocabularies of motive, which can be used to diminish responsibility and to negotiate a non-deviant identity.

Sociologists have long noted that people can, and do, commit acts they define as wrong and, having done so, engage various techniques to disavow deviance and present themselves as normal. Through the concept of "vocabulary of motive," Mills (1940:904) was among the first to shed light on this seemingly perplexing contradiction. Wrongdoers attempt to reinterpret their actions through the use of a linguistic device by which norm-breaking conduct is socially interpreted. That is, anticipating the negative consequences of their behavior, wrongdoers attempt to present the act in terms that are both culturally appropriate and acceptable.

Following Mills, a number of sociologists have focused on the types of techniques employed by actors in problematic situations (Hall and Hewitt, 1970; Hewitt and Hall, 1973; Hewitt and Stokes, 1975; Sykes and Matza, 1957). Scott and Lyman (1968) describe excuses and justifications, linguistic "accounts" that explain and remove culpability for an untoward act after it has been committed. *Excuses* admit the act was bad or inappropriate but deny full responsibility, often through appeals to accident, or biological drive, or through scapegoating. In contrast, *justifications* accept responsibility for the act but deny that it was wrong—that is, they show in this situation the act was appropriate. *Accounts* are socially approved vocabularies that neutralize an act or its consequences and are always a manifestation of an underlying negotiation of identity.

Stokes and Hewitt (1976:837) use the term "aligning actions" to refer to those tactics and techniques used by actors when some feature of a situation is problematic. Stated simply, the concept refers to an actor's attempt, through various means, to bring his or her conduct into alignment with culture. Culture in this sense is conceptualized as a "set of cognitive constraints—objects—to which people must relate as they form lines of conduct" (1976:837), and includes physical constraints, expectations and definitions of others,

*© 1984 by The Society for the Study of Social Problems. Reprinted from *Social Problems,* 31:5 (June, 1984), pp. 530–544 by permission of the authors and the publisher.

**This research was supported by a grant (RO 1 MH33013) from the National Center For the Prevention and Control of Rape, National Institute of Mental Health. The authors thank the Virginia Department of Corrections for their cooperation and assistance in this research. Correspondence to: Department of Sociology and Anthropology, Virginia Commonwealth University, 312 Shafer Court, Richmond, VA 23284.

and personal biography. Carrying out aligning actions implies both awareness of those elements of normative culture that are applicable to the deviant act and, in addition, an actual effort to bring the act into line with this awareness. The result is that deviant behavior is legitimized.

This paper presents an analysis of interviews we conducted with a sample of 114 convicted, incarcerated rapists. We use the concept of accounts (Scott and Lyman, 1968) as a tool to organize and analyze the vocabularies of motive which this group of rapists used to explain themselves and their actions. An analysis of their accounts demonstrates how it was possible for 83 percent (n = 114)[1] of these convicted rapists to view themselves as non-rapists.

When rapists' accounts are examined, a typology emerges that consists of admitters and deniers. Admitters (n = 47) acknowledged that they had forced sexual acts on their victims and defined the behavior as rape. In contrast, deniers[2] either eschewed sexual contact or all association with the victim (n = 35),[3] or admitted to sexual acts but did not define their behavior as rape (n = 32).

The remainder of this paper is divided into two sections. In the first, we discuss the accounts which the rapists used to justify their behavior. In the second, we discuss those accounts which attempted to excuse the rape. By and large, the deniers used justifications while the admitters used excuses. In some case, both groups relied on the same themes, stereotypes, and images: some admitters, like most deniers, claimed that women enjoyed being raped. Some deniers excused their behavior by referring to alcohol or drug use, although they did so quite differently than admitters. Through these narrative accounts, we explore convicted rapists' own perceptions of their crimes.

METHODS AND VALIDITY

From September, 1980, through September, 1981, we interviewed 114 male convicted rapists who were incarcerated in seven maximum or medium security prisons in the Commonwealth of Virginia. All of the rapists had been convicted of the rape or attempted rape (n = 8) of an adult woman, although a few had teenage victims as well. Men convicted of incest, statutory rape, or sodomy of a male were omitted from the sample.

Twelve percent of the rapists had been convicted of more than one rape or attempted rape, 39 percent also had convictions for burglary or robbery, 29 percent for abduction, 25 percent for sodomy, and 11 percent for first or second degree murder. Eighty-two percent had a previous criminal history but only 23 percent had records for previous sex offenses. Their sentences for rape and accompanying crimes ranged from 10 years to an accumulation by one man of seven life sentences plus 380 years; 43 percent of the rapists were serving from 10 to 30 years and 22 percent were serving at least one life term. Forty-six percent of the rapists were white and 54 percent were black. Their ages ranged from 18 to 60 years; 88 percent were between 18 and 35 years. Forty-two percent were either married or cohabiting at the time of their offense. Only 20 percent had a high school education or better, and 85 percent came from working-class backgrounds. Despite the popular belief that rape is due to a personality disorder, only 26 percent of these rapists had any history of emotional problems. When the rapists in this study were compared to a statistical profile of felons in all Virginia prisons, prepared by the Virginia Department of Corrections, rapists who volunteered for this research were disproportionately white, somewhat better educated, and younger than the average inmate.

All participants in this study were volunteers. We sent a letter to every inmate (n = 3500) at each of the seven prisons. The letters introduced us as professors at a local university, described our research as a study of men's attitudes toward sexual behavior and women, outlined our procedures for ensuring confidentiality, and solicited volunteers from all criminal categories. Using one follow-up letter, approximately 25 percent of all inmates, including rapists, indicated their willingness to be interviewed by mailing an information sheet to us at the university. From this pool of volunteers, we constructed a sample of rapists based on age, education, race, severity of current offenses, and previous criminal records. Obviously, the sample was not random and thus may not be representative of all rapists.

Each of the authors—one woman and one man—interviewed half of the rapists. Both authors were able to establish rapport and obtain information. However, the rapists volunteered more about their feelings and emotions to the female author and her interviews lasted longer.

All rapists were given an 89-page interview, which included a general background, psychological, criminal, and sexual history, attitude scales, and 30 pages of open-ended questions intended to explore their perceptions of their crimes, their victims, and their selves. Because a voice print is an absolute source of identification, we did not use tape recorders. All interviews were hand recorded. With some practice, we found it was possible to record much of the interview verbatim. While hand recording inevitably resulted in some lost data, it did have the advantage of eliciting more confidence and candor in the men.

Interviews with the rapists lasted from three hours to seven hours; the average was about four-and-one-half hours. Most of the rapists were reluctant to end the interview. Once rapport had been established, the men wanted to talk, even though it sometimes meant, for example, missing a meal.

Because of the reputation prison inmates have for "conning," validity was a special concern in our research. Although the purpose of the research was to obtain the men's own perceptions of their acts, it was also necessary to establish the extent to which these perceptions deviated from other descriptions of their crimes. To establish validity, we used the same technique others have used in prison research: comparing factual information, including details of the crime, obtained in the interview with pre-sentence reports on file at the prisons (Athens, 1977; Luckenbill, 1977; Queen's Bench Foundation, 1976). Pre-sentence reports, written by a court worker at the time of conviction, usually include general background information, a psychological evaluation, the offender's version of the details of the crime, and the victim's or police's version of the details of the crime. Using these records allowed us to clarify two important issues: first, the amount of change that had occurred in rapists' accounts from pre-sentencing to the time when we interviewed them; and, second, the amount of discrepancy between rapists' accounts, as told to us, and the victims' and/or police versions of the crime, contained in the pre-sentence reports.

The time between pre-sentence reports and our interviews (in effect, the amount of time rapists had spent in prison before we interviewed them) ranged from less than one year to 20 years; the average was three years. Yet despite this time lapse, there were no significant changes in the way rapists explained their crimes, with the exception of 18 men who had denied their crimes at their trials but admitted them to us. There were no cases of men who admitted their crime at their trial but denied them when talking to us.

However, there were major differences between the accounts we heard of the crimes from rapists and the police's and victim's versions. Admitters (including deniers turned admitters) told us essentially the same story as the police and victim versions. However, the admitters subtly understated the force they had used and, though they used words such as *violent* to describe their acts, they also omitted reference to the more brutal aspects of their crime.

In contrast, deniers' interview accounts differed significantly from victim and police versions. According to the pre-sentence reports, 11 of the 32 deniers had been acquainted with their victim. But an additional four deniers told us they had been acquainted with their victims. In the pre-sentence reports, police or victim versions of the crime described seven rapes in which the victim had been hitchhiking or was picked up in a bar; but deniers told us this was true of 20 victims. Weapons were present in 21 of the 32 rapes according to the pre-sentence reports, yet only nine men acknowledged the presence of a weapon and only two of the nine admitted they had used it to threaten or intimidate their victim. Finally, in at least seven of the rapes, the victim had been seriously injured,[4] but only three men admitted injury. In two of the three cases, the victim had been murdered; in these cases the men denied the rape but not the murder. Indeed, deniers constructed accounts for us which, by implicating the victim, made their own conduct appear to have been more appropriate. They never used words such as *violent,* choosing instead to emphasize the sexual component of their behavior.

It should be noted that we investigated the possibility that deniers claimed their behavior was not criminal because, in contrast to admitters, their crimes resembled what research has found the public defines as a controversial rape, that is, victim an acquaintance, no injury or weapon, victim picked up hitchhiking or in a bar (Burt, 1980; Burt and Albin, 1981; Williams, 1979). However, as Table 1 indicates, the crimes committed by deniers were only slightly more likely to involve these elements.

This contrast between pre-sentence reports and interviews suggests several significant factors related to interview content validity. First, when asked to explain their behavior, our sample of convicted rapists (except deniers turned admitters) responded with accounts that had changed surprisingly little since their trials. Second, admitters' interview accounts were basically the same as others' versions of their crimes, while deniers systematically put more blame on the victims.

JUSTIFYING RAPE

Deniers attempted to justify their behavior by presenting the victim in a light that made her appear culpable, regardless of their own actions. Five themes run through attempts to justify their rapes: (1) women as seductresses; (2) women

TABLE 1 Comparison of Admitter's and Denier's Crimes Police/Victim Versions in Pre-Sentence Reports

Characteristics	Percent Admitters n = 47	Percent Deniers n = 32
White Assailant	57	41
Black Assailant	43	59
Group Rape	23	13
Multiple Rapes	43	34
Assailant a Stranger	72	66
Controversial Situation	6	22
Weapon and/or Injury Present (includes victim murdered)	74	69

mean "yes" when they say "no"; (3) most women eventually relax and enjoy it; (4) nice girls don't get raped; and (5) guilty of a minor wrongdoing.

(1) Women as Seductresses

Men who rape need not search far for cultural language which supports the premise that women provoke or are responsible for rape. In addition to common cultural stereotypes, the fields of psychiatry and criminology (particularly the subfield of victimology) have traditionally provided justifications for rape, often by portraying raped women as the victims of their own seduction (Albin, 1977; Marolla and Scully, 1979). For example, Hollander (1924:130) argues:

Considering the amount of illicit intercourse, rape of women is very rare indeed. Flirtation and provocative conduct, i.e., tacit (if not actual) consent is generally the prelude to intercourse.

Since women are supposed to be coy about their sexual availability, refusal to comply with a man's sexual demands lacks meaning and rape appears normal. The fact that violence and, often, a weapon are used to accomplish the rape is not considered. As an example, Abrahamsen (1960:61) writes:

The conscious or unconscious biological or psychological attraction between man and woman does not exist only on the part of the offender toward the woman but, also, on her part toward him, which in many instances may, to some extent, be the impetus for his sexual attack. Often a woman unconsciously wishes to be taken by force—consider the theft of the bride in Peer Gynt.

Like Peer Gynt, the deniers we interviewed tried to demonstrate that their victims were willing and, in some cases, enthusiastic participants. In these accounts, the rape became more dependent upon the victim's behavior than upon their own actions.

Thirty-one percent (n = 10) of the deniers presented an extreme view of the victim. Not only willing, she was the aggressor, a seductress who lured them, unsuspecting, into sexual action. Typical was a denier convicted of his first rape and accompanying crimes of burglary, sodomy, and abduction. According to the pre-sentence reports, he had broken into the victim's house and raped her at knife point. While he admitted to the breaking and entry, which he claimed was for altruistic purposes ("to pay for the prenatal care of a friend's girlfriend"), he also argued that when the victim discovered him, he had tried to leave but she had asked him to stay. Telling him that she cheated on her husband, she had voluntarily removed her clothes and seduced him. She was, according to him, an exemplary sex partner who "enjoyed it very much and asked for oral sex."[5] "Can I have it now?" he reported her as saying. He claimed they had spent hours in bed, after which the victim had told him he was good-looking and asked to see him again. "Who would believe I'd meet a fellow like this?" he reported her as saying.

In addition to this extreme group, 25 percent (n = 8) of the deniers said the victim was willing and had made some sexual advances. An additional 9 percent (n = 3) said the victim was willing to have sex for money or drugs. In two of these three cases, the victim had been either an acquaintance or picked up, which the rapists said led them to expect sex.

(2) Women Mean "Yes" When They Say "No"

Thirty-four percent (n = 11) of the deniers described their victim as unwilling, at least initially, indicating either that she had resisted or that she had said no. Despite this, and even though (according to pre-sentence reports) a weapon had been present in 64 percent (n = 7) of these 11 cases, the rapists justified their behavior by arguing that either the victim had not resisted enough or that her "no" had really meant "yes." For example, one denier who was serving time for a previous rape was subsequently convicted of attempting to rape a prison hospital nurse. He insisted he had actually completed the second rape, and said of his victim: "She semi-struggled but deep down inside I think she felt it was a fantasy come true." The nurse, according to him, had asked a question about his conviction for rape, which he interpreted as teasing. "It was like she was saying, 'rape me.'" Further, he stated that she had helped him along with oral sex and "from her actions, she was enjoying it." In an-

other case, a 34-year-old man convicted of abducting and raping a 15-year-old teenager at knife point as she walked on the beach, claimed it was a pickup. This rapist said women like to be overpowered before sex, but to dominate after it begins.

A man's body is like a coke bottle, shake it up, put your thumb over the opening and feel the tension. When you take a woman out, woo her, then she says "no, I'm a nice girl," you have to use force. All men do this. She said "no" but it was a societal no, she wanted to be coaxed. All women say "no" when they mean "yes" but it's a societal "no," so they won't have to feel responsible later.

Claims that the victim didn't resist or, if she did, didn't resist enough, were also used by 24 percent (n = 11) of admitters to explain why, during the incident, they believed the victim was willing and that they were not raping. These rapists didn't redefine their acts until some time after the crime. For example, an admitter who used a bayonet to threaten his victim, an employee of the store he had been robbing, stated:

At the time I didn't think it was rape. I just asked her nicely and she didn't resist. I never considered prison. I just felt like I had met a friend. It took about five years of reading and going to school to change my mind about whether it was rape. I became familiar with the subtlety of violence. But at the time, I believed that as long as I didn't hurt anyone it wasn't wrong. At the time, I didn't think I would go to prison. I thought I would beat it.

Another typical case involved a gang rape in which the victim was abducted at knife point as she walked home about midnight. According to two of the rapists, both of whom were interviewed, at the time they had thought the victim had willingly accepted a ride from the third rapist (who was not interviewed). They claimed the victim didn't resist and one reported her as saying she would do anything if they would take her home. In this rapist's view, "She acted like she enjoyed it, but maybe she was just acting. She wasn't crying, she was engaging in it." He reported that she had been friendly to the rapist who abducted her and, claiming not to have a home phone, she gave him her office number—a tactic eventually used to catch the three. In retrospect, this young man had decided, "She was scared and just relaxed and enjoyed it to avoid getting hurt." Note, however, that while he had redefined the act as rape, he continued to believe she enjoyed it.

Men who claimed to have been unaware that they were raping viewed sexual aggression as a man's prerogative at the time of the rape. Thus they regarded their act as little more than a minor wrongdoing even though most possessed or used a weapon. As long as the victim survived without major physical injury, from their perspective, a rape had not taken place. Indeed, even U.S. courts have often taken the position that physical injury is a necessary ingredient for a rape conviction.

(3) Most Women Eventually Relax and Enjoy It

Many of the rapists expected us to accept the image, drawn from cultural stereotype, that once the rape began, the victim relaxed and enjoyed it.[6] Indeed, 69 percent (n = 22) of deniers justified their behavior by claiming not only that the victim was willing, but also that she enjoyed herself, in some cases to an immense degree. Several men suggested that they had fulfilled their victims' dreams. Additionally, while most admitters used adjectives such as "dirty," "humiliated," and "disgusted," to describe how they thought rape made women feel, 20 percent (n = 9) believed that their victim enjoyed herself. For example, one denier had posed as a salesman to gain entry to his victim's house. But he claimed he had had a previous sexual relationship with the victim, that she agreed to have sex for drugs, and that the opportunity to have sex with him produced "a glow, because she was really into oral stuff and fascinated by the idea of sex with a black man. She felt satisfied, fulfilled, wanted me to stay, but I didn't want her." In another case, a denier who had broken into his victim's house but who insisted the victim was his lover and let him in voluntarily, declared "She felt good, kept kissing me and wanted me to stay the night. She felt proud after sex with me." And another denier, who had hid in his victim's closet

and later attacked her while she slept, argued that while she was scared at first, "once we got into it, she was ok." He continued to believe he hadn't committed rape because "she enjoyed it and it was like she consented."

(4) Nice Girls Don't Get Raped

The belief that "nice girls don't get raped" affects perception of fault. The victim's reputation, as well as characteristics or behavior which violate normative sex role expectations, are perceived as contributing to the commission of the crime. For example, Nelson and Amir (1975) defined hitchhike rape as a victim-precipitated offense.

In our study, 69 percent (n = 22) of deniers and 22 percent (n = 10) of admitters referred to their victims' sexual reputation, thereby evoking the stereotype that "nice girls don't get raped." They claimed that the victim was known to have been a prostitute, or a "loose" woman, or to have had a lot of affairs, or to have given birth to a child out of wedlock. For example, a denier who claimed he had picked up his victim while she was hitchhiking stated, "To be honest, we [his family] knew she was a damn whore and whether she screwed one or 50 guys didn't matter." According to pre-sentence reports this victim didn't know her attacker and he abducted her at knife point from the street. In another case, a denier who claimed to have known his victim by reputation stated:

If you wanted drugs or a quick piece of ass, she would do it. In court she said she was a virgin, but I could tell during sex [rape] that she was very experienced.

When other types of discrediting biographical information were added to these sexual slurs, a total of 78 percent (n = 25) of the deniers used the victim's reputation to substantiate their accounts. Most frequently, they referred to the victim's emotional state or drug use. For example, one denier claimed his victim had been known to be loose and, additionally, had turned state's evidence against her husband to put him in prison and save herself from a burglary conviction. Further, he asserted that she had met her current boyfriend, who was himself in and out of prison, in a drug rehabilitation center where they were both clients.

Evoking the stereotype that women provoke rape by the way they dress, a description of the victim as seductively attired appeared in the accounts of 22 percent (n = 7) of deniers and 17 percent (n = 8) of admitters. Typically, these descriptions were used to substantiate their claims about the victim's reputation. Some men went to extremes to paint a tarnished picture of the victim, describing her as dressed in tight black clothes and without a bra; in one case, the victim was portrayed as sexually provocative in dress and carriage. Not only did she wear short skirts, but she was observed to "spread her legs while getting out of cars." Not all of the men attempted to assassinate their victim's reputation with equal vengeance. Numerous times they made subtle and offhand remarks like, "She was a waitress and you know how they are."

The intent of these discrediting statements is clear. Deniers argued that the woman was a "legitimate" victim who got what she deserved. For example, one denier stated that all of his victims had been prostitutes; pre-sentence reports indicated they were not. Several times during his interview, he referred to them as "dirty sluts," and argued "anything I did to them was justified." Deniers also claimed their victim had wrongly accused them and was the type of woman who would perjure herself in court.

(5) Only a Minor Wrongdoing

The majority of deniers did not claim to be completely innocent and they also accepted some accountability for their actions. Only 16 percent (n = 5) of deniers argued that they were totally free of blame. Instead, the majority of deniers pleaded guilty to a lesser charge. That is, they obfuscated the rape by pleading guilty to a less serious, more acceptable charge. They accepted being over-sexed, accused of poor judgment or trickery, even some violence, or guilty of adultery or contributing to the delinquency of a minor, charges that are hardly the equivalent of rape.

Typical of this reasoning is a denier who met his victim in a bar when the bartender asked him if he would try to repair her stalled car. After attempting unsuccessfully, he claimed the victim drank with him and later accepted a ride. Out riding, he pulled into a deserted area "to see how my luck would go." When the victim resisted his advances, he beat her and he stated:

I did something stupid. I pulled a knife on her and I hit her as hard as I would hit a man. But I shouldn't be in prison for what I did. I shouldn't have all this time [sentence] for going to bed with a broad.

This rapist continued to believe that while the knife was wrong, his sexual behavior was justified.

In another case, the denier claimed he picked up his under-age victim at a party and that she voluntarily went with him to a motel. According to pre-sentence reports, the victim had been abducted at knife point from a party. He explained:

After I paid for a motel, she would have to have sex but I wouldn't use a weapon. I would have explained I spent money and, if she still said no, I would have forced her. If it had happened that way, it would have been rape to some people but not to my way of thinking. I've done that kind of thing before. I'm guilty of sex and contributing to the delinquency of a minor, but not rape.

In sum, deniers argued that, while their behavior may not have been completely proper, it should not have been considered rape. To accomplish this, they attempted to discredit and blame the victim while presenting their own actions as justified in the context. Not surprisingly, none of the deniers thought of himself as a rapist. A minority of the admitters attempted to lessen the impact of their crime by claiming the victim enjoyed being raped. But despite this similarity, the nature and tone of admitters' and deniers' accounts were essentially different.

EXCUSING RAPE

In stark contrast to deniers, admitters regarded their behavior as morally wrong and beyond justification. They blamed themselves rather than the victim, although some continued to cling to the belief that the victim had contributed to the crime somewhat, for example, by not resisting enough.

Several of the admitters expressed the view that rape was an act of such moral outrage that it was unforgivable. Several admitters broke into tears at intervals during their interviews. A typical sentiment was,

I equate rape with someone throwing you up against a wall and tearing your liver and guts out of you. . . . Rape is worse than murder . . . and I'm disgusting.

Another young admitter frequently referred to himself as repulsive and confided:

I'm in here for rape and in my own mind, it's the most disgusting crime, sickening. When people see me and know, I get sick.

Admitters tried to explain their crime in a way that allowed them to retain a semblance of moral integrity. Thus, in contrast to deniers' justifications, admitters used excuses to explain how they were compelled to rape. These excuses appealed to the existence of forces outside of the rapists' control. Through the use of excuses, they attempted to demonstrate that either intent was absent or responsibility was diminished. This allowed them to admit rape while reducing the threat to their identity as a moral person. Excuses also permitted them to view their behavior as idiosyncratic rather than typical and, thus, to believe they were not "really" rapists. Three themes run through these accounts: (1) the use of alcohol and drugs; (2) emotional problems; and (3) nice guy image.

(1) The Use of Alcohol and Drugs

A number of studies have noted a high incidence of alcohol and drug consumption by convicted rapists prior to their crime (Groth, 1979; Queen's Bench Foundation, 1976). However, more recent research has tentatively concluded that the connection between substance use and crime is not as direct as previously thought (Ladouceur, 1983). Another facet of alcohol and drug use mentioned in the literature is its utility in disavowing deviance. McCaghy (1968) found that child molesters used alcohol as a technique for neutralizing their deviant identity. Marolla and Scully (1979), in a review of psychiatric literature, demonstrated how alcohol consumption

is applied differently as a vocabulary of motive. Rapists can use alcohol both as an excuse for their behavior and to discredit the victim and make her more responsible. We found the former common among admitters and the latter common among deniers.

Alcohol and/or drugs were mentioned in the accounts of 77 percent (n = 30) of admitters and 84 percent (n = 21) of deniers and both groups were equally likely to have acknowledged consuming a substance—admitters, 77 percent (n = 30); deniers, 72 percent (n = 18). However, admitters said they had been affected by the substance; if not the cause of their behavior, it was at least a contributing factor. For example, an admitter who estimated his consumption to have been eight beers and four "hits of acid" reported:

Straight, I don't have the guts to rape. I could fight a man but not that. To say, "I'm going to do it to a woman," knowing it will scare and hurt her, takes guts or you have to be sick.

Another admitter believed that his alcohol and drug use

. . . brought out what was already there but in such intensity it was uncontrollable. Feelings of being dominant, powerful, using someone for my own gratification, all rose to the surface.

In contrast, deniers' justifications required that they not be substantially impaired. To say that they had been drunk or high would cast doubt on their ability to control themselves or to remember events as they actually happened. Consistent with this, when we asked if the alcohol and/or drugs had had an effect on their behavior, 69 percent (n = 27) of admitters, but only 40 percent (n = 10) of deniers, said they had been affected.

Even more interesting were references to the victim's alcohol and/or drug use. Since admitters had already relieved themselves of responsibility through claims of being drunk or high, they had nothing to gain from the assertion that the victim had used or been affected by alcohol and/or drugs. On the other hand, it was very much in the interest of deniers to declare that their victim had been intoxicated or high: That fact lessened her credibility and made her more responsible for the act. Reflecting these observations, 72 percent (n = 18) of

TABLE 2 Rapists' Accounts of Own and Victims' Alcohol and/or Drug (A/D) Use and Effect

	Admitters n = 39 %	Deniers n = 25 %
Neither Self nor Victim Used A/D	23	16
Self Used A/D	77	72
Of Self Used, No Victim Use	51	12
Self Affected by A/D	69	40
Of Self Affected, No Victim Use or Affect	54	24
Self A/D Users Who Were Affected	90	56
Victim Used A/D	26	72
Of Victim Used, No Self Use	0	0
Victim Affected by A/D	15	56
Of Victim Affected, No Self Use or Affect	0	40
Victim A/D Users Who Were Affected	60	78
Both Self and Victim Used and Affected by A/D	15	16

deniers and 26 percent (n = 10) of admitters maintained that alcohol or drugs had been consumed by the victim. Further, while 56 percent (n = 14) of deniers declared she had been affected by this use, only 15 percent (n = 6) of admitters made a similar claim. Typically, deniers argued that the alcohol and drugs had sexually aroused their victim or rendered her out of control. For example, one denier insisted that his victim had become hysterical from drugs, not from being raped, and it was because of the drugs that she had reported him to the police. In addition, 40 percent (n = 10) of deniers argued that while the victim had been drunk or high, they themselves either hadn't ingested or weren't affected by alcohol and/or drugs. None of the admitters made this claim. In fact, in all of the 15 percent (n = 6) of cases where an admitter said the victim was drunk or high, he also admitted to being similarly affected.

These data strongly suggest that whatever role alcohol and drugs play in sexual and other types of violent crime, rapists have learned the advantage to be gained from using alcohol and drugs as an account. Our sample was aware that their victim would be discredited and their own behavior excused or justified by referring to alcohol and/or drugs.

(2) Emotional Problems

Admitters frequently attributed their acts to emotional problems. Forty percent (n = 19) of admitters said they believe an emotional problem

had been at the root of their rape behavior, and 33 percent (n = 15) specifically related the problem to an unhappy, unstable childhood or a marital-domestic situation. Still others claimed to have been in a general state of unease. For example, one admitter said that at the time of the rape he had been depressed, feeling he couldn't do anything right, and that something had been missing from his life. But he also added, "being a rapist is not part of my personality." Even admitters who could locate no source for an emotional problem evoked the popular image of rapists as the product of disordered personalities to argue they also must have problems:

The fact that I'm a rapist makes me different. Rapists aren't all there. They have problems. It was wrong so there must be a reason why I did it. I must have a problem.

Our data do indicate that a precipitating event, involving an upsetting problem of everyday living, appeared in the accounts of 80 percent (n = 38) of admitters and 25 percent (n = 8) of deniers. Of those experiencing a precipitating event, including deniers, 76 percent (n = 35) involved a wife or girlfriend. Over and over, these men described themselves as having been in a rage because of an incident involving a woman with whom they believed they were in love.

Frequently, the upsetting event was related to a rigid and unrealistic double standard for sexual conduct and virtue which they applied to "their" woman but which they didn't expect from men, didn't apply to themselves, and, obviously, didn't honor in other women. To discover that the "pedestal" didn't apply to their wife or girlfriend sent them into a fury. One especially articulate and typical admitter described his feeling as follows. After serving a short prison term for auto theft, he married his "childhood sweetheart" and secured a well-paying job. Between his job and the volunteer work he was doing with an ex-offender group, he was spending long hours away from home, a situation that had bothered his wife. In response to her request, he gave up his volunteer work, though it was clearly meaningful to him. Then, one day, he discovered his wife with her former boyfriend "and my life fell apart." During the next several days, he said his anger had made him withdraw into himself and, after three days of drinking in a motel room, he abducted and raped a stranger. He stated:

My parents have been married for many years and I had high expectations about marriage. I put my wife on a pedestal. When I walked in on her, I felt like my life had been destroyed, it was such a shock. I was bitter and angry about the fact that I hadn't done anything to my wife for cheating. I didn't want to hurt her [victim], only to scare and degrade her.

It is clear that many admitters, and a minority of deniers, were under stress at the time of their rapes. However, their problems were ordinary— the types of upsetting events that everyone experiences at some point in life. The overwhelming majority of the men were not clinically defined as mentally ill in court-ordered psychiatric examinations prior to their trials. Indeed, our sample is consistent with Abel et al. (1980) who found fewer than 5 percent of rapists were psychotic at the time of their offense.

As with alcohol and drug intoxication, a claim of emotional problems works differently depending upon whether the behavior in question is being justified or excused. It would have been counterproductive for deniers to have claimed to have had emotional problems at the time of the rape. Admitters used psychological explanations to portray themselves as having been temporarily "sick" at the time of the rape. Sick people are usually blamed for neither the cause of their ill-

ness nor for acts committed while in that state of diminished capacity. Thus, adopting the sick role removed responsibility by excusing the behavior as having been beyond the ability of the individual to control. Since the rapists were not "themselves," the rape was idiosyncratic rather than typical behavior. Admitters asserted a non-deviant identity despite their self-proclaimed disgust with what they had done. Although admitters were willing to assume the sick role, they did not view their problem as a chronic condition, nor did they believe themselves to be insane or permanently impaired. Said one admitter, who believed that he needed psychological counseling: "I have a mental disorder, but I'm not crazy." Instead, admitters viewed their "problem" as mild, transient, and curable. Indeed, part of the appeal of this excuse was that not only did it relieve responsibility, but, as with alcohol and drug addiction, it allowed the rapist to "recover." Thus, at the time of their interviews, only 31 percent (n = 14) of admitters indicated that "being a rapist" was part of their self-concept. Twenty-eight percent (n = 13) of admitters stated they had never thought of themselves as rapists, 8 percent (n = 4) said they were unsure, and 33 percent (n = 16) asserted they had been a rapist at one time but now were recovered. A multiple "ex-rapist," who believed his "problem" was due to "something buried in my subconscious" that was triggered when his girlfriend broke up with him, expressed a typical opinion:

I was a rapist, but not now. I've grown up, had to live with it. I've hit the bottom of the well and it can't get worse. I feel born again to deal with my problems.

(3) Nice Guy Image

Admitters attempted to further neutralize their crime and negotiate a non-rapist identity by painting an image of themselves as a "nice guy." Admitters projected the image of someone who had made a serious mistake but, in every other respect, was a decent person. Fifty-seven percent (n = 27) expressed regret and sorrow for their victim indicating that they wished there were a way to apologize for or amend their behavior. For example, a participant in a rape-murder, who insisted his partner did the murder, confided, "I wish there was something I could do besides saying 'I'm sorry, I'm sorry.' I live with it 24 hours a day and, sometimes, I wake up crying in the middle of the night because of it."

Schlenker and Darby (1981) explain the significance of apologies beyond the obvious expression of regret. An apology allows a person to admit guilt while at the same time seeking a pardon by signalling that the event should not be considered a fair representation of what the person is really like. An apology separates the bad self from the good self, and promises more acceptable behavior in the future. When apologizing, an individual is attempting to say: "I have repented and should be forgiven," thus making it appear that no further rehabilitation is required.

The "nice guy" statements of the admitters reflected an attempt to communicate a message consistent with Schlenker's and Darby's analysis of apologies. It was an attempt to convey that rape was not a representation of their "true" self. For example,

It's different from anything else I've ever done. I feel more guilt about this. It's not consistent with me. When I talk about it, it's like being assaulted myself. I don't know why I did it, but once I started, I got into it. Armed robbery was a way of life for me, but not rape. I feel like I wasn't being myself.

Admitters also used "nice guy" statements to register their moral opposition to violence and harming women, even though, in some cases, they had seriously injured their victims. Such was the case of an admitter convicted of a gang rape:

I'm against hurting women. She should have resisted. None of us were the type of person that would use force on a woman. I never positioned myself on a woman unless she showed an interest in me. They would play to me, not me to them. My weakness is to follow. I never would have stopped, let alone pick her up without the others. I never would have let anyone beat her. I never bothered women who didn't want sex; never had a problem with sex or getting it. I loved her—like all women.

Finally, a number of admitters attempted to improve their self-image by demonstrating that, while they had raped, it could have been worse if they had not been a "nice guy." For example, one

admitter professed to being especially gentle with his victim after she told him she had just had a baby. Others claimed to have given the victim money to get home or make a phone call, or to have made sure the victim's children were not in the room. A multiple rapist, whose pattern was to break in and attack sleeping victims in their homes, stated:

I never beat any of my victims and I told them I wouldn't hurt them if they cooperated. I'm a professional thief. But I never robbed the women I raped because I felt so bad about what I had already done to them.

Even a young man, who raped his five victims at gun point and then stabbed them to death, attempted to improve his image by stating:

Physically they enjoyed the sex [rape]. Once they got involved, it would be difficult to resist. I was always gentle and kind until I started to kill them. And the killing was always sudden, so they wouldn't know it was coming.

SUMMARY AND CONCLUSIONS

Convicted rapists' accounts of their crimes include both excuses and justifications. Those who deny what they did was rape justify their actions; those who admit it was rape attempt to excuse it or themselves. This study does not address why some men admit while others deny, but future research might address this question. This paper does provide insight on how men who are sexually aggressive or violent construct reality, describing the different strategies of admitters and deniers.

Admitters expressed the belief that rape was morally reprehensible. But they explained themselves and their acts by appealing to forces beyond their control, forces which reduced their capacity to act rationally and thus compelled them to rape. Two types of excuses predominated: alcohol/drug intoxication and emotional problems. Admitters used these excuses to negotiate a moral identity for themselves by viewing rape as idiosyncratic rather than typical behavior. This allowed them to reconceptualize themselves as recovered or "ex-rapists," someone who had made a serious mistake which did not represent their "true" self.

In contrast, deniers' accounts indicate that these men raped because their value system provided no compelling reason not to do so. When sex is viewed as a male entitlement, rape is no longer seen as criminal. However, the deniers had been convicted of rape, and like the admitters, they attempted to negotiate an identity. Through justifications, they constructed a "controversial" rape and attempted to demonstrate how their behavior, even if not quite right, was appropriate in the situation. Their denials, drawn from common cultural rape stereotypes, took two forms, both of which ultimately denied the existence of a victim.

The first form of denial was buttressed by the cultural view of men as sexually masterful and women as coy but seductive. Injury was denied by portraying the victim as willing, even enthusiastic, or as politely resistant at first but eventually yielding to "relax and enjoy it." In these accounts, force appeared merely as a seductive technique. Rape was disclaimed: Rather than harm the woman, the rapist had fulfilled her dreams. In the second form of denial, the victim was portrayed as the type of woman who "got what she deserved." Through attacks on the victim's sexual reputation and, to a lesser degree, her emotional state, deniers attempted to demonstrate that since the victim wasn't a "nice girl," they were not rapists. Consistent with both forms of denial was the self-interested use of alcohol and drugs as a justification. Thus, in contrast to admitters, who accentuated their own use as an excuse, deniers emphasized the victim's consumption in an effort to both discredit her and make her appear more responsible for the rape. It is important to remember that deniers did not invent these justifications. Rather, they reflect a belief system which has historically victimized women by promulgating the myth that women both enjoy and are responsible for their own rape.

While admitters and deniers present an essentially contrasting view of men who rape, there were some shared characteristics. Justifications particularly, but also excuses, are buttressed by the cultural view of women as sexual commodities, dehumanized and devoid of autonomy and dignity. In this sense, the sexual objectification of women must be understood as an important factor contributing to an environment that trivializes, neutralizes, and, perhaps, facilitates rape.

Finally, we must comment on the consequences of allowing one perspective to dominate thought on a social problem. Rape, like any complex continuum of behavior, has multiple causes and is influenced by a number of social factors. Yet, dominated by psychiatry and the medical model, the underlying assumption that rapists are "sick" has pervaded research. Although methodologically unsound, conclusions have been based almost exclusively on small clinical populations of rapists—that extreme group of rapists who seek counseling in prison and are the most likely to exhibit psychopathology. From this small, atypical group of men, psychiatric findings have been generalized to all men who rape. Our research, however, based on volunteers from the entire prison population, indicates that some rapists, like deniers, viewed and understood their behavior from a popular cultural perspective. This strongly suggests that cultural perspectives, and not an idiosyncratic illness, motivated their behavior. Indeed, we can argue that the psychiatric perspective has contributed to the vocabulary of motive that rapists use to excuse and justify their behavior (Scully and Marolla, 1984).

Efforts to arrive at a general explanation for rape have been retarded by the narrow focus of the medical model and the preoccupation with clinical populations. The continued reduction of such complex behavior to a singular cause hinders, rather than enhances, our understanding of rape.

NOTES

1. These numbers include pretest interviews. When the analysis involves either questions that were not asked in the pretest or that were changed, they are excluded and thus the number changes.

2. There is, of course, the possibility that some of these men really were innocent of rape. However, while the U.S. criminal justice system is not without flaw, we assume that it is highly unlikely that this many men could have been unjustly convicted of rape, especially since rape is a crime with traditionally low

conviction rates. Instead, for purposes of this research, we assume that these men were guilty as charged and that their attempt to maintain an image of non-rapist springs from some psychologically or sociologically interpretable mechanism.

3. Because of their outright denial, interviews with this group of rapists did not contain the data being analyzed here and, consequently, they are not included in this paper.

4. It was sometimes difficult to determine the full extent of victim injury from the pre-sentence reports. Consequently, it is doubtful that this number accurately reflects the degree of injuries sustained by victims.

5. It is worth noting that a number of deniers specifically mentioned the victim's alleged interest in oral sex. Since our interview questions about sexual history indicated that the rapists themselves found oral sex marginally acceptable, the frequent mention is probably another attempt to discredit the victim. However, since a tape recorder could not be used for the interviews and the importance of these claims didn't emerge until the data was being coded and analyzed, it is possible that it was mentioned even more frequently but not recorded.

6. Research shows clearly that women do not enjoy rape. Holmstrom and Burgess (1978) asked 93 adult rape victims, "How did it feel sexually?" Not one said they enjoyed it. Further, the trauma of rape is so great that it disrupts sexual functioning (both frequency and satisfaction) for the overwhelming majority of victims, at least during the period immediately following the rape and, in fewer cases, for an extended period of time (Burgess and Holmstrom, 1979; Feldman-Summers et al., 1979). In addition, a number of studies have shown that rape victims experience adverse consequences prompting some to move, change jobs, or drop out of school (Burgess and Holmstrom, 1974; Kilpatrick et al., 1979; Ruch et al., 1980; Shore, 1979).

REFERENCES

ABEL, GENE, JUDITH BECKER, and LINDA SKINNER. 1980. "Aggressive behavior and sex." *Psychiatric Clinics of North America* 3(2):133–151.

ABRAHAMSEN, DAVID. 1960. *The Psychology of Crime.* New York: John Wiley.

ALBIN, ROCHELLE. 1977. "Psychological studies of rape." *Signs* 3(2):423–435.

ATHENS, LONNIE. 1977. "Violent crimes: A symbolic interactionist study." *Symbolic Interaction* 1(1): 56–71.

BURGESS, ANN WOLBERT, and LYNDA LYTLE HOLMSTROM. 1974. *Rape: Victims of Crisis.* Bowie: Robert J. Brady.

————, 1979 "Rape: Sexual disruption and recovery." *American Journal of Orthopsychiatry* 49(4): 648–657.

BURT, MARTHA. 1980. "Cultural myths and supports for rape." *Journal of Personality and Social Psychology* 38(2):217–230.

BURT, MARTHA, and ROCHELLE ALBIN. 1981. "Rape myths, rape definitions, and probability of conviction." *Journal of Applied Psychology* 11(3): 212–230.

FELDMAN-SUMMERS, SHIRLEY, PATRICIA E. GORDON, and JEANETTE R. MEAGHER. 1979. "The impact of rape on sexual satisfaction." *Journal of Abnormal Psychology* 88(1):101–105.

GLUECK, SHELDON. 1925. *Mental Disorders and the Criminal Law.* New York: Little Brown.

GROTH, NICHOLAS A. 1979. *Men Who Rape.* New York: Plenum Press.

HALL, PETER M., and JOHN P. HEWITT. 1970. "The quasi-theory of communication and the management of dissent." *Social Problems* 18(1):17–27.

HEWITT, JOHN P., and PETER M. HALL. 1973. "Social problems, problematic situations, and quasi-theories." *American Journal of Sociology* 38(3): 367–374.

HEWITT, JOHN P., and RANDALL STOKES. 1975. "Disclaimers." *American Sociological Review* 40(1): 1–11.

HOLLANDER, BERNARD. 1924. *The Psychology of Misconduct, Vice, and Crime.* New York: Macmillan.

HOLMSTROM, LYNDA LYTLE, and ANN WOLBERT BURGESS. 1978. "Sexual behavior of assailant and victim during rape." Paper presented at the annual meetings of the American Sociological Association, San Francisco, September 2–8.

KILPATRICK, DEAN G., LOIS VERONEN, and PATRICIA A. RESNICK. 1979. "The aftermath of rape: Recent empirical findings." *American Journal of Orthopsychiatry* 49(4):658–669.

LADOUCEUR, PATRICIA. 1983. "The relative impact of drugs and alcohol on serious felons." Paper presented at the annual meetings of the American Society of Criminology, Denver, November 9–12.

LUCKENBILL, DAVID. 1977. "Criminal homicide as a situated transaction." *Social Problems* 25(2): 176–187.

MAROLLA, JOSEPH, and DIANA SCULLY. 1979. "Rape and psychiatric vocabularies of motive." Pp. 301–318 in Edith S. Gomberg and Violet Franks (eds.), *Gender and Disordered Behavior: Sex Differences in Psychopathology.* New York: Brunner/Mazel.

MCCAGHY, CHARLES. 1968. "Drinking and deviance disavowal: The case of child molesters." *Social Problems* 16(1):43–49.

MILLS, C. WRIGHT. 1940. "Situated actions and vocabularies of motive." *American Sociological Review* 5(6):904–913.

NELSON, STEVE, and MENACHEM AMIR. 1975. "The hitchhike victim of rape: A research report." Pp. 47–65 in Israel Drapkin and Emilio Viano (eds.), *Victimology: A New Focus.* Lexington, KY: Lexington Books.

QUEEN'S BENCH FOUNDATION. 1976. *Rape: Prevention and Resistance.* San Francisco: Queen's Bench Foundation.

RUCH, LIBBY O., SUSAN MEYERS CHANDLER, and RICHARD A. HARTER. 1980 "Life change and rape impact." *Journal of Health and Social Behavior* 21(3):248–260.

SCHLENKER, BARRY R., and BRUCE W. DARBY. 1981. "The use of apologies in social predicaments." *Social Psychology* Quarterly 44(3):271–278.

SCOTT, MARVIN, and STANFORD LYMAN. 1968. "Accounts." *American Sociological Review* 33(1) 46–62.

SCULLY, DIANA, and JOSEPH MAROLLA. 1984. "Rape and psychiatric vocabularies of motive: Alternative perspectives." In Ann Wolbert Burgess (ed.), *Handbook on Rape and Sexual Assault.* New York: Garland Publishing.

SHORE, BARBARA K. 1979. "An examination of critical process and outcome factors in rape." Rockville, MD: National Institute of Mental Health.

STOKES, RANDALL, and JOHN P. HEWITT. 1976. "Aligning actions." *American Sociological Review* 41(5):837–849.

SYKES, GRESHAM M., and DAVID MATZA. 1957. "Techniques of neutralization." *American Sociological Review* 22(6):664–670.

WILLIAMS, JOYCE. 1979. "Sex role stereotypes, women's liberation, and rape: A cross-cultural analysis of attitude." *Sociological Symposium* 25 (Winter):61–97.

TOPLESS DANCERS
MANAGING STIGMA IN A DEVIANT OCCUPATION*

William E. Thompson and Jackie L. Harred**

A person's occupation is one of the most important elements of his or her personal and social identity, and it is common for two strangers to "break the ice" by indicating the kind of work they do" (Pavalko, 1988, p. 4). Consequently, individuals often make a number of judgments about others based on preconceived notions about particular occupations. For many (e.g.,

*From *Deviant Behavior,* 1992, Vol. 13, pp. 291–311, "Topless Dancers: Managing Stigma in a Deviant Occupation" by William E. Thompson and Jackie L. Harred. © Hemisphere Publishing Corp., NY. Reproduced with permission. All rights reserved.

**The authors wish to thank Jessie Moore for her help with some of the interviews and Dr. Joseph V. Hickey, Emporia State University, for his helpful comments on the manuscript.

doctors, judges, college professors), revealing their occupations almost immediately confers social acceptance and a certain amount of prestige. For others, especially those engaged in occupations regarded as deviant, disclosing how they make their living can be embarrassing and potentially stigmatizing. For "work provides identities as much as it provides bread for the table; . . . [it] is as much an expression of who you are as what you want" (Friedland and Robertson, 1990, p. 25).

This paper describes and analyzes how topless dancers manage the stigma related to their deviant occupation. Couched within a symbolic interactionist framework, it relies heavily on dramaturgical analysis, especially Erving Goffman's (1963) work on stigma and the management of "spoiled identities," to show how topless dancers socially and symbolically redefine their work in an effort to reduce or neutralize negative attitudes toward it and them. We also draw from social control theory, utilizing Sykes and Matza's (1957) theory of techniques of neutralization to show how dancers rationalize their actions in an effort to neutralize some of the stigma associated with their work.

METHOD

Data Collection

This study reflects approximately nine months of qualitative fieldwork including limited participant observation and ethnographic interviewing as outlined by Schatzman and Strauss (1973), Spradley (1979), and Berg (1989). Research was conducted at seven topless bars in a major metropolitan city in the Southwest with a population of approximately 1 million people. A structured interview schedule was used to collect data from over 40 topless dancers. In addition, a free-flowing interview technique was used so that dancers could provide any information they wished in addition to that obtained from the list of standardized questions. As with most ethnographic field work, some of the most insightful information was gained through casual conversation (Spradley, 1979; Berg, 1989).

All of our observations and interviews were conducted during the daytime, usually from 11:00 A.M. to approximately 6:00 P.M. because these clubs specialized in "daytime entertainment" targeted toward a business crowd. Although these bars also were open late at night, they had gained their reputations in the city as "gentlemen's clubs" that served lunch and did a substantial amount of their business during the daytime. Thus, our findings may not be generalizable to other types of topless clubs that cater primarily to a nighttime crowd. Most of the dancers we interviewed, however, also worked night shifts at these clubs and other nightclubs, so their comments regarding their work and how they managed the stigma may be generalizable beyond the scope of this particular study.

When possible, interviews were recorded on audiotape. One of the club managers permitted the researchers to interview dancers in the morning as they arrived at work before the club opened; all of these interviews (except two at the dancers' requests) were taped. Other interviews were conducted during business hours when the dancers were working. In those cases, it proved impossible to tape interviews because of the obtrusiveness of the tape recorder and interference from background noises, especially the loud music. On one occasion a female graduate student accompanied the researchers, conducted several interviews, and was allowed to go backstage to interview dancers in the dressing room as they prepared for their performances.

In addition to the structured interviews with dancers, information was obtained from unstructured interviews with at least 20 other dancers, numerous waitresses and bartenders in the clubs, two club managers, two assistant managers, and four former dancers still associated with topless clubs (as bartenders, waitresses, or door attendants).

Respondents

All of the dancers in this study were female. They ranged in age from 19 to 41 with a median age of 22. The vast majority of the dancers were white; one was black, five were Hispanic, and one was Oriental—describing herself as "half-Korean, half-American, and all woman." Approximately two-thirds (26) of the dancers had been married, but only one-third of them (13) currently lived with their spouses; the other one-third were either divorced or separated. Approximately one-third (14) of the dancers had never been married, but several of them indicated that they were either living with a boyfriend or had done so at some time in the past. Only one of the dancers interviewed was unmarried and living with a parent (her parents were divorced and she was living with her mother). Approximately one-half of the dancers (19) had at least one child, a few indicated that they had two children, and one was a mother of four.

The club managers and assistant managers were all male. One was Hispanic and in his early thirties; the other three were white and in their early to middle twenties. The waitresses and former dancers interviewed ranged in age from 21 to 43 years, with most being in their late twenties to early thirties; all were white.

Setting

All of the clubs in this study were located in the same metropolitan area (population approximately 1 million) in the Southwest. In a stratification hierarchy, these clubs represented the more elite so-called gentlemen's clubs, which were located in fairly nice areas of the city and, at least during the day, catered to middle class and upper middle class businessmen—"suits" as the dancers referred to them. The clubs had gained reputations of being "clean" and "safe," and all opened at 10:30 in the morning and served modestly priced luncheon and drink "specials" in an effort to attract businessmen from the surrounding area into the clubs over their lunch hours. In fact, two of the clubs featured well-known adult film stars and professional dancers who performed over the noon hour in addition to evening and nighttime shows.

The clubs were relatively attractive in appearance from the outside, offered plenty of free parking, and had names that, while provocative in nature, suggested that they were "high-class" clubs as opposed to "sleazy" bars. Most required customers to pay a modest cover charge for admission—in the words of two of the managers, to keep out the "riffraff" and the "gawkers." At the entrance of each of the clubs was a small entryway where the fee was paid or, if there was no cover charge, where customers were greeted by an attendant who checked coats and hats if desired, checked identification to verify age if necessary, and otherwise scrutinized customers before allowing entrance through the next set of doors into the actual club.

Although the specific layouts and decorating themes of the clubs varied, all had some common elements. There was at least one central bar (usually off to one side), and the larger clubs usually had one or two satellite bars in other areas that were used during peak business hours (the lunch hour and Friday and Saturday nights). Each also featured a main stage usually located at the front or center of the bar and from five to eight peripheral stages in various locations throughout the club. As each dancer was announced, she would dance one set[1] on the main stage and then move to one of the peripheral stages as the next dancer was introduced. Eventually, each dancer would work her way around all of the stages before she could take a "break" or be available for "table dances."[2]

All of the clubs attempted to establish a "fantasy" atmosphere. They were dark with special lights surrounding each of the stages and large spotlights focused on the main stage. Some showed videos of other dancers on the surrounding walls of the club; others used velvet draperies and other trappings to resemble early-day saloons or bordellos. All both explicitly and implicitly conveyed the message that this was a place where beautiful women were available to serve a gentleman's every whim. Conversely, all of the clubs studied had rather strict formal norms regarding customer-dancer interaction that prohibited males from mounting any of the stages (a rule that was strictly enforced), prohibited physical contact between dancers and customers (a rule that was routinely ignored if not flouted), and forbade dancers to expose the pubic area. In fact, due to some unusual zoning laws, several of the clubs required the dancers to wear clear latex over their nipples and "full-back" bottoms (equivalent to bikini underwear or bathing suit bottoms) so that at least technically the nipples and buttocks were "fully covered" at all times. These rules were attributed to city zoning laws that prohibited nudity in any club within 1000 feet of another club, a church, or a residential area. In clubs that were farther than 1000 feet from the prescribed areas, dancers were not required to cover their nipples and were allowed to wear "T-backs," which consisted of a thong-type bottom that exposes the buttocks but fully covers the pubic region.

Finally, whereas all of the clubs allowed both male and female patrons, they clearly were designed as male environments catering to male sexual fantasies. Each had a small "ladies room," but they all had large men's restrooms typically decorated with pictures of nude women and other forms of erotica. Disk jockeys always addressed the crowd as "gentlemen" regardless of whether female patrons were present, and the dancers said they were there to entertain and arouse men. Many had developed elaborate costumes and routines which they said were geared toward men's sexual fantasies (e.g., the little girl look with pigtails and baby doll pajamas or the librarian look with long hair initially drawn up in a tight bun, large-framed glasses, etc.).

Although no rules were posted, the researchers were informed that absolutely no illegal drugs were allowed on the premises and that club managers would not hesitate to call the police if either patrons or employees violated that rule. Also, although it was acknowledged that the "no-touching" rule was rarely strictly enforced, too much touching or kissing could result in a customer being asked to leave and the dancer being reprimanded. Solicitation and prostitution were strictly prohibited in all of the clubs, and all of the dancers interviewed denied that they participated in it. Interestingly, however, at each club dancers indicated that while they never engaged in prostitution, they were certain many of their fellow workers did. They had even coined the term "parking lot duty" to describe sexual encounters that supposedly occurred in the parking lots surrounding the clubs.

Within the confines of the club, topless dancing was "normalized" for both dancers and customers so that no hint of stigma or deviance was associated with the activity. Dancers used stage names[3] and customers enjoyed total anonymity if desired. As in most deviant settings, once inside the club, what typically would be viewed as deviant on the outside became the norm within.

STIGMA AND TOPLESS DANCING

Goffman (1963) defined *stigma* as any attribute that sets people apart and discredits them or disqualifies them from full social acceptance. This paper explores what happens when people are discredited (stigmatized) because of their work—in this case dancing topless—and how they attempt to reduce or eliminate the stigma.

People are most likely to be stigmatized because of their occupation if it is viewed as deviant by other members of society. Ritzer (1977) cited three criteria, any one of which can cause an occupation to be regarded as deviant: (1) if it is illegal, (2) if it is considered immoral, and (3) if it is considered improper. In the case of the topless dancers in this study, both the second and third criteria apply. Although topless dancing was legal in the city under study, it was governed by several legal statutes that set numerous restrictions on its practice, and because the city was located in the heart of what many local people refer to as the "Bible Belt," it is safe to assume that many people in the area certainly saw the behavior as "improper" and more than a few would contend that it was "immoral." In fact, a national poll conducted by *Time* magazine indicated that 52% of Americans considered topless nightclubs or bars pornographic and 38% thought they should be illegal (*Time,* 1988, p. 22). In sociological terms, topless dancing is viewed as deviant because stripping constitutes what Bryant (1977, p. 5) referred to as "sexual deviancy in symbolic context." Moreover, popular conceptions of bars portray them as settings for deviant activities (e.g., drugs, prostitution, and other illicit activities) and certainly no place for any "self-respecting lady" to work (Cavan, 1966; Detman, 1990).

Skipper and McCaghy (1970, p. 392) found that stripping or dancing nude was viewed as an unusually low-status occupation, with many believing it was "outright promiscuous." When college students were asked what kind of women they thought took their clothes off for a living, they responded, "hard women," "dumb," "stupid," "uneducated," "lower class," "can't do anything else for a living," "oversexed," "immoral," and "prostitutes" (Skipper and McCaghy 1970, p. 392). Moreover, Skipper and McCaghy (1970, p. 392) found that strippers in their study were fully cognizant of the stigma directed at them and believed that most people viewed stripping as "dirty and immoral." As a result, most of the strippers attempted to keep their occupation secret and, if asked about their jobs, said they were dancers, entertainers, or something else.

Other studies also have documented the stigma directed at strippers and topless dancers (Boles and Garbin 1974, 1977; Enck and Preston

1988). For example, Boles and Garbin (1977, pp. 118–19) discovered that a major job complaint of strippers was their "objectification" by customers and their being viewed as "just a broad in a club." A senior student who served as a participation observer for 2 1/2 months, providing the primary source of data in another study, refused to allow her name to be attached to the published article "because of the stigma associated with being a topless waitress-dancer" (Enck and Preston 1988, p. 371).

All of the dancers indicated that they felt stigmatized, at least by certain groups of people, because of their occupation. Consequently, they adopted several strategies for managing the stigma associated with their work. In some ways, how dancers handled the stigma seemed related to their initial motivation for becoming a topless dancer. Therefore, a brief discussion of the process of becoming a topless dancer is in order.

BECOMING A TOPLESS DANCER

Skipper and McCaghy (1970) described a career sequence typical for most strippers: (1) a tendency toward exhibitionistic behavior for gain, (2) an opportunity structure making stripping an accessible occupational alternative, and (3) a sudden awareness of the easy economic rewards derived from stripping. Our data indicate an almost identical process for topless dancers, with four added dimensions often being present. A large proportion of the dancers (well over one-half) indicated that the first time they danced topless was the result of a combination of being slightly or highly intoxicated and being dared or challenged to do it. Also, a large number of the dancers indicated that they desperately needed a job and could not find one that paid better than topless dancing. Finally, many acquired the job through a recruitment process involving personal networks—friends, classmates, and other acquaintances. This was accompanied by anticipatory socialization and both formal and informal on-the-job socialization into the role similar to the socialization process experienced by novice prostitutes (e.g., Heyl 1977, 1979).

A common theme was summarized by one dancer who described her first time dancing topless on stage:

My boyfriend took me to a topless bar with a couple of other friends. We were drinking and watching the girls dance, and one of my girlfriends and I started critiquing the dancers to our boyfriends. You know, we were just kind of jokin' around. I'd say, "she can't even dance," or "my tits are a lot better lookin' than hers." The next thing you know, everybody at the table was darin' me to get up on stage. Finally, I said I would, if the manager would let me. Well, one thing led to another. My boyfriend talked to the manager, and a few minutes later I was on stage. I was wearin' a pair of cut-offs and a tank top, so getting topless was simple—I just peeled off the top and started dancing. Well, guys started stuffing dollar bills into my jeans' pockets and the more I was encouraged the more I shook and danced. I was only on stage for one song, and when I counted the money in my pockets, I had made $27! Can you imagine? Twenty-seven bucks for about three minutes? I thought, hey, this ain't bad. I really needed a job, so I talked to the manager the next day and he hired me—simple as that.

Another dancer who went by the stage name of "Sheena" confided:

I broke up with my boyfriend. I had a daughter to support and no job. So, I knew a friend who danced in one of the clubs. I went to watch her one night just to see what it was like. I got "wasted," and before the night was over she had dared me to get up on stage. I borrowed one of her outfits and did—and by closing time I had danced three sets and made over $200! I thought "Wow!, this is too easy!" I've been doin' it ever since.

Another dancer, "LaFonte," described her first experience:

I had won a couple of bikini contests. One night I was in a club competing in a "best legs" contest and one of the girls took her top off! The crowd all went wild and the MC made a big deal out of it, and it was obvious she was gonna win. Well, almost every girl after her took off their tops. By the time it was my turn to go out on stage, I'd had several drinks, and I thought "What the hell?" So, I pulled off my top, strutted my stuff, and it was no big deal. I didn't win the contest, but it made applying for this job easy. I thought, "Why show your tits for free?" So, now I do it for about $400–$500 a night—you can't beat it.

Finally, one dancer expressed the pragmatism shared by many of the dancers, which combined all of the elements found by Skipper and McCaghy with the dimensions we have added. A 31-year-old mother of two explained how and why she got into the business:

I've always had a good body, and I've never been ashamed of it. My parents were pretty casual about nudity, and I adopted their philosophy. In high school I found out that short skirts, skimpy tops, and other revealing clothing really turned guys on, so I used it to my advantage. You know, give a teacher a peek, let your date have a glimpse, it was fun—and harmless.

I got my B.S. degree in business and started selling real estate. I made pretty good money, but it was long hours. And, I noticed that male clients, even with their wives in the car, were always checking me out—trying to look down my blouse, or up my skirt. My boss was always hitting on me too.

One night a friend of mine who worked in one of the clubs invited me to come watch her dance. I went and had a few drinks and watched. She kept trying to get me up on stage, but I wouldn't do it. That night she made over $500! I thought, "Wait a minute, I have to work my butt off to make $500, then with taxes and everything . . . and I've got a better body than her . . . this is crazy." I danced the next night and made $400 and didn't even know what I was doing. At first I kept my job and started dancing three nights a week. Before long, I was making a lot more dancing than selling houses. I quit the real estate job and have been dancing ever since. I figure my time is limited—after all, I'm 31, but I'm in real good shape—in fact, the dancing helps, so as long as I can make this kind of money, why not? Once the body begins to go, I can always go back to selling houses.

The common elements of "chance," "economic need," "challenge," and "intoxication" permeated the stories of how and why many of the dancers first entered the trade. It should be noted that, because of the stigma associated with the job, these stories may represent a form of rationalization and neutralization similar to those discussed later. For, as previous studies have noted, many patrons ask strippers or topless dancers about their personal lives, the most frequently asked questions being "How did you get started at *this?*" or the proverbial "What's a nice girl like you . . . ," and many of the dancers fabricate stories reminiscent of the "Perils of Pauline"

to rationalize their entrance into a deviant occupation (Boles and Garbin, 1977, p. 119).

MANAGING THE STIGMA OF BEING A TOPLESS DANCER

The topless dancers in our study used a variety of techniques to overcome the stigma associated with their occupation. For analytical purposes, we have created two "umbrella categories" under which the various techniques can be classified: (1) dividing the social world and (2) rationalization and neutralization. Most dancers employed some aspect of both of these techniques.

Dividing the Social World

Goffman (1963) indicated that information control was one of the most effective methods for managing stigma and suggested that one of the most practical ways to control information was to divide the social world. This involves establishing a relatively small group with which the discrediting information is shared, while keeping it hidden from the rest of the world. By implementing this technique, those "in the know" can help the potentially discreditable individual from being revealed to others. Dividing the social world also creates a strong sense of in-group alignments and cohesion that contributes to dancers identifying with one another and working to help conceal their stigmatizing occupational identities in other social arenas. This technique was widely employed by the dancers in this study.

When asked "What do you tell people you do for a living?" almost all of the dancers indicated that their close friends, spouses or boyfriends, and people they associated with on a regular basis knew they were "tittie dancers"[4] and had no problems with it. On the other hand, most did not tell new acquaintances, casual friends, or their parents the truth. Instead, most said they were waitresses, entertainers, or students. This technique of information control combines dividing the social world with *passing,* or trying to keep a potentially stigmatizing attribute hidden by posing as an individual who does not possess that attribute (Goffman, 1963). Many of the dancers passed as waitresses because it was the most convenient way for their friends and co-workers to help cover for them. For example, one dancer who had a child in day care indicated:

I had to tell the woman at day care where I worked because she needed the phone number. So, I just told her I was a waitress in a club. That way when she calls and they answer the phone with the club's name, she won't think anything. If she asks anybody here what I do, they'll just tell her I wait tables. It's cool.

Four of the clubs shared a common owner and many of the dancers in them indicated that they simply told people that they worked for the corporation (which was the man's name followed by the word Enterprises) and gave out the phone number of the central office rather than the number of the club.

A large number of the dancers passed as "entertainers" because, as one put it, "I'm not really lying—I *am* an entertainer, I'm just not telling the whole truth." Another dancer indicated:

I'm an entertainer—plain and simple. If I were up on stage juggling oranges, nobody would think there was anything wrong with it. Instead I stand on stage and shake my tits and ass—big deal!

Many of the dancers expressed that their parents did not know they danced topless. Various reasons were given. For example, several simply indicated that they no longer lived with their parents and believed it was none of their parents' business. Others, however, admitted that they intentionally kept their job hidden from one or both of their parents for fear of how they would react. When asked if her parents knew what she did for a living, one dancer exclaimed, "Heavens no—they'd die!" Another said, "No, I just wouldn't know how to tell them—they'd never understand." And a third dancer responded, "Are you kidding?—they'd kill me."

Some of the dancers divided their social world by telling one parent, who then helped her conceal it from the other. In every case, it was the mother who was the confidant while the father was kept in the dark. One dancer said, "I told my mom, and she was real cool about it, even kind of excited, but she warned me, 'Don't tell your dad—he just couldn't take it.' " Another responded, "I told my mom right away because we

don't keep any secrets, but we both agreed it would be a lot better if my dad didn't find out."

In some cases, dancers indicated they had attempted to keep their topless dancing secret but they were pretty sure their parents knew. In these cases, both they and their parents practiced *mutual denial.* For example, one dancer said:

They have to know. My sisters know, my brother knows, even one of our neighbors came in the club one night and recognized me. So, I just don't see how they couldn't know. Still, I've never told them and they have never acted like they know. I tell them that I'm a waitress, and that's what they tell their friends.

Similarly, two dancers indicated that their husbands did not know they danced topless. Both told their husbands they were waitresses, but one indicated that she was pretty sure her husband was suspicious because she made more money than most waitresses. She had even started hiding some of her tip money in order to reduce his suspicions but indicated that "deep down I think he knows, but this way he doesn't have to admit it."

While most of the dancers indicated that they divided their social worlds in order to help hide their deviant occupation, most also were quick to point out that they did not see anything wrong with what they were doing. Many of them used some of the techniques of neutralization outlined by Sykes and Matza (1957).

Rationalization and Neutralization

In an article on juvenile delinquency, Sykes and Matza (1957) outlined five major techniques used by youths to rationalize their law-violating behavior and neutralize the stigma associated with it: (1) denial of responsibility, (2) denial of injury, (3) denial of the victim, (4) condemnation of the condemners, and (5) appeal to higher loyalties. These techniques employed "an unrecognized extension of defenses to crimes in the form of justifications for deviance that are seen as valid by the delinquent but not by the legal system or society at large" (Sykes and Matza, 1957, p. 668). Our research shows that topless dancers employ many of these techniques to rationalize their deviant behavior—especially denial of injury, condemnation of the condemners, and, to some extent, appeal to higher loyalties.

Denial of Injury. Time and again the dancers in this study expressed bewilderment over why so many people were opposed to topless dancing and stigmatized them for doing it. One dancer complained:

Why does everybody make such a fuss over tittie dancing? It's not like we're hurting anybody or anything. . . . It's perfectly harmless, for God's sake!

Another pointed out:

People put us down like we're bad people or something. What are we doing wrong? Does it hurt anybody? These guys just want to have a few drinks and see some girls shake their tits—so what? It's not like we're dealin' drugs, or robbin' liquor stores or something.

Topless dancers not only rationalize their deviance by denying any harm but also often contend that they actually perform positive functions for society (Miller, 1978). Research on stripping and topless dancing indicates that three rationales consistently are expressed. First is the assertion that strippers and topless dancers are legitimate entertainers and, as such, provide an important and harmless release from the stresses of everyday living. Second is the notion that strip shows and topless dancing clubs provide a form of "therapy"—protecting society from rapes, sexual assaults, and other offenses that might occur if the patrons of these clubs were forced to "act out" their sexual fantasies. Third, some strippers and topless dancers contend that they provide "educational services" by displaying the female anatomy in an unabashed fashion, thus reducing the stigma associated with nudity and making both men and women more comfortable with female nudity (Salutin, 1971; Skipper and McCaghy, 1970; Boles and Garbin, 1974; Miller, 1978).

Examples of all these rationales emerged in our study. Many dancers emphasized their role as "entertainers" and accentuated the harmless "fun" and "release from the stress of everyday living" they provided for customers. Others pointed to the "public service" they performed by, as one dancer put it, "keeping these perverts off the streets." Still another summarized the so-called educational aspect when she said:

If I were a father, this is the first place I would want to bring my son when he became a teenager. Here, he could see some beautiful women, could see some tits and ass, have some fun, and not have to worry about getting in trouble, catching any diseases, or getting hurt. I think if kids 13 or 14 could come in here they'd probably develop a whole lot healthier attitude about sex.

Condemnation of the Condemners. One of the most consistent rationalization and neutralization techniques employed by topless dancers was condemnation of those who condemned them. Initially, in almost every interview, the dancers exhibited some defensiveness until they became convinced that the researchers were not making moral judgments about them or their work. When this hurdle was overcome, the entire nature of the interview usually changed, with the dancers becoming more comfortable and candid. Many confided that they enjoyed the chance to just sit and talk with somebody in the club without having to be "on" and without being "hit upon."

Virtually all of the dancers indicated that they resented the way they were treated and negatively viewed by many customers and the general public. One dancer commented:

They're a bunch of hypocrites! Even the guys who come in here and drool and hit on us wouldn't give us the time of day if they ran into us on the streets. They will come in here on Saturday nights, get drunk, and play "grab-ass," and then go to church on Sunday and condemn what we do. In general, I think we're a whole lot more honest than they are.

Other research has also found a tendency for strippers and topless dancers to condemn those who condemn them. For example, Bryant (1982, p. 153) noted:

They rationalize that what they do is no different from what all women do. All women as they see it, even wives, are really exhibitionists and prostitutes, but just charge a different kind of price, such as a dinner or marriage.

Like those in any other occupation that involves interaction with the public (e.g., sales clerks, waiters, and waitresses), topless dancers must hide their disapproval (or condemnation) from their customers. Enck and Preston (1988, p. 372) noted that a topless dancer most effectively accomplishes this goal through the use of "counterfeit intimacy" that conveys the impression she is available "for informal recreational sex while, simultaneously, she goes about the real work of the club, namely, selling alcohol. . . ." Many of the customers dramaturgically engage in their own act of "counterfeit intimacy" by telling the dancers they "love" them, proposing marriage, etc., when in reality they are happily married men who have no interest in the dancer except for voyeuristic enjoyment.

A stigma management technique employed by those in many deviant occupations is the adoption of a sophisticated name that masks or reduces the stigma associated with the work. For example, dog catchers may be called animal control officers, garbage collectors become sanitation engineers, and undertakers are now funeral directors. Presumably a similar effort could be made to reduce the stigma of topless dancing symbolically by referring to it as ecdysiastic entertainment (Bryant, 1982). The topless dancers in our study, however, not only did not attempt to use a less stigmatizing name for their work but instead used an even more stigma-laden term—"tittie dancers." In some ways this served to flaunt their deviance, especially to those who might condemn them. It basically conveyed the message "This is what I do—if you don't like it, that's too bad." In fact, some used those very words. Although, as we have indicated, many of the dancers were less than honest when people asked them what they did for a living, others were very frank about it. One dancer responded: "I tell people exactly what I do—I'm a tittie dancer—and if they don't like it, they can go to hell!"

Appeal to Higher Loyalties. A final rationalization-neutralization technique employed by topless dancers in this study was appeal to higher loyalties. This technique, as discussed by Sykes and Matza (1957), couches deviant behavior within an altruistic framework in which deviants neutralize stigma by contending they violate norms in order to benefit others. Most of the dancers in this study openly admitted they danced for the money. In the case of single mothers, wives who were attempting to support a husband and child(ren), or students who were paying their way through school, all cited the fact that they were helping others. For example, one dancer stated:

I'm not proud of what I do—but I do it for my daughter. I figure if I can make enough money doin' this and raise her right, she won't ever have to stoop to doin' the same thing.

Another said:

My parents would probably die if they knew I do this. But in a way, I do it for them. They couldn't possibly pay my way through school—so, whether they know it or not, this is making their lives a whole lot easier.

By rationalizing that others benefit from their deviance, topless dancers neutralize some of the stigma felt from external sources but, more importantly, deflect any internally generated or self-imposed stigma. By sharing these sentiments with other dancers, dancers reinforce in-group alignments, and their shared values and definition of the situation help manage stigma related to their deviant occupation while also helping to boost feelings of self-esteem associated with their work. A final quote from one of the dancers summarizes this idea:

I'm not necessarily all that proud of what I do, but I'm not a criminal, and I ain't on welfare. I've managed to take care of myself, pay all my own bills, and take care of my little boy at the same time. I don't see why anybody should be ashamed of that. In fact, I'm damn proud of it!

SUMMARY AND CONCLUSION

Topless dancing constitutes a deviant occupation that carries a great deal of social stigma for those who are engaged in it. Because so much of a person's social and personal identity is related to his or her occupation, those engaged in topless dancing practice a variety of techniques in an effort to reduce and/or manage the stigma associated with their work.

Two overriding techniques of stigma management were generally employed by the dancers in this study: dividing the social world and neutralization. Both of these stigma management strategies require a host of dramaturgical techniques on the part of the topless dancers to be effective. For the most part, by selectively allowing some people to know of their participation in topless dancing while keeping it hidden from others and by denying injury, condemning those who condemn them, and appealing to higher loyalties, the topless dancers in this study successfully manage the stigma associated with their deviant occupation.

This study raises some interesting questions for future research on topless dancing or stripping and other deviant occupations. For example, future research should compare and contrast female strippers or topless dancers with male nude and seminude dancers. Of special interest would be the issue of stigma related to the occupation. Do male dancers experience the same social stigma as female dancers? Do they feel the need to divide the social world and hide from others what they do? And are they viewed as being immoral, unintelligent, and otherwise less socially acceptable than other males?

Some studies have indicated that male strippers experience some of the same degradations from female customers as their female counterparts do from males (e.g., Peterson and Dressel, 1982), but none has addressed the issue of social stigma and whether it is as great for male dancers. Our guess is that it probably is not. The "Chippendale" dancers and now their overweight counterparts the "Chunkendales" have appeared on television talk shows and at celebrity functions, have posed for calendars and posters, and otherwise have gained national public attention that seems devoid of the stigma directed at female dancers. Their acts appear to be viewed as either humorous or entertaining and, for the most part, quite harmless. Women apparently view the men as "studs" or "hunks," and the male dancers express that type of self-concept. Consequently, although nude and seminude dancing also constitutes deviant (norm-violating) behavior for males, it appears (at least on the surface) to carry much less stigma. Research should be conducted to see if this is indeed the case. Also, research should compare male dancers who perform in gay clubs for male audiences to those who dance in clubs with predominantly or exclusively female audiences.

Moreover, since the double standards related to sex and nudity for males and females may dictate the level of stigma associated with nude dancing, it probably can be assumed that they also dramatically shape the level to which those engaged in the deviant occupation must manage the personal and social stigma experienced. Researchers might pursue this issue by using Cooley's *looking-glass self* as a theoretical framework for analyzing the extent to which both male and female dancers develop their concept of *self* as a reflection of how they interpret their audience's feelings toward them. For example, does a female dancer look out from the stage at a crowd of leering males and interpret them as viewing her as "cheap," "easy," "immoral," "stupid," and nothing more than a "bimbo" and thus internalize the stigma associated with her work and feel compelled to rationalize and neutralize it? Do male dancers, on the other hand, peer out at a group of screaming female patrons and perceive that they are being viewed as "sexy," "irresistible," and the kind of men their women customers would like to marry? Future research should explore these questions and others in an effort to better understand stigma and deviant occupations.

NOTES

1. At all of the clubs in this study each "set" involved dancing to two songs, usually one with the top on and one with the top off.

2. "Table dances" consisted of going to a customer's table for a special "personalized" performance. Most of the dancers indicated that table dances brought the highest tips, usually a minimum of $20 per table dance and often as much as $100 to $200 in a single table dance. On the other hand, some dancers refused to do table dances, claiming that they sometimes involved more intense customer interaction (e.g., touching and kissing) and made them uncomfortable.

3. All of the dancers in our study used stage names instead of their real names while dancing. Many of the names were exotic sounding, such as "Sheena," "Sabrena," "LaFonte," "Sasha," "Cheyenne," and "Angelique." This might imply that the stage names

were simply used to enhance the sensual image of the dancers on stage. However, many used very common names such as Lisa, Cindy, Tammy, or Linda, implying that at least part of the reason for using a stage name was to disguise their true identity. When we asked a dancer whose real name was Cathy why she danced by the stage name "Lisa," she responded, "If you got up on stage and shook your titties for a living would you want people to know your real name?"

4. All of the dancers referred to themselves as "tittie dancers" and punctuated their conversations with frequent reference to "titties" and "tits." When one of the authors asked a dancer why she called herself a "tittie dancer" instead of a "topless dancer," she responded, "Are you kidding, with a set of titties like these, would you call me topless?"

REFERENCES

Berg, B. L. 1989. *Qualitative Research Methods for the Social Sciences*. Boston: Allyn & Bacon.

Boles, J., and A. P. Garbin. 1974. *"Stripping for a Living: An Occupational Study of the Night Club Stripper"* (pp. 319–328). In *Deviant Behavior*, edited by Clifton D. Bryant. Chicago: Rand McNally.

———. 1977. "The Strip Club and Stripper-Customer Patterns of Interaction" (pp. 111–123). In *Sexual Deviancy in Social Context*, edited by Clifton D. Bryant. New York: New Viewpoints.

Bryant, C. D. 1977. "Sexual Deviancy in Social Context." Pp. 1–25 in *Sexual Deviancy in Social Context*, edited by Clifton D. Bryant. New York: New Viewpoints.

———. 1982. *Sexual Deviancy and Social Proscription: The Social Context of Carnal Behavior*. New York: Human Sciences Press.

Cavan, S. 1966. *Liquor License*. Chicago: Aldine.

Detman, L. A. 1990. "Women Behind Bars: The Feminization of Bartending." Pp. 241–55 in *Job Queues, Gender Queues*, edited by Barbara R. Reskin and Patricia A. Roos. Philadelphia: Temple University Press.

Enck, G. E., and J. D. Preston. 1988. "Counterfeit Intimacy: A Dramaturgical Analysis of an Erotic Performance." *Deviant Behavior* 9:369–81.

Friedland, R., and A. F. Robertson. 1990. "Beyond the Marketplace." Pp. 3–49 in *Beyond the Marketplace: Rethinking Economy and Society*, edited by Roger Friedland and A. F. Robertson. New York: Aldine de Gruyter.

Goffman, E. 1963. *Stigma: Notes on the Management of Spoiled Identity*. Englewood Cliffs, NJ: Prentice Hall.

Heyl, B. S. 1977. "The Madam as Teacher: The Training of House Prostitutes." *Social Problems* 24:545–55.

———. 1979. *The Madam as Entrepreneur: Career Management in House Prostitution*. New Brunswick, NJ: Transaction.

Miller, G. 1978. *Odd Jobs: The World of Deviant Work*. Englewood Cliffs, NJ: Prentice Hall.

Pavalko, R. M. 1988. *Sociology of Occupations and Professions* (2nd ed.). Itasca, IL: F. E. Peacock.

Peterson, D. M., & P. Dressel. 1982. "Notes on the Male Strip Show." *Urban Life and Culture* 11(July):185–208.

Ritzer, G. 1977. *Working: Conflict and Change* (2nd ed.). Englewood Cliffs, NJ: Prentice Hall.

Salutin, M. 1971. "Stripper Morality." *Transaction* 8(June):12–22.

Schatzman, L. and A. L. Strauss. 1973. *Field Research: Strategies for a Natural Society*. Englewood Cliffs, NJ: Prentice Hall.

Skipper, J. K., Jr., and C. H. McCaghy. 1970. "Stripteasers: The Anatomy and Career Contingencies of a Deviant Occupation." *Social Problems* 17(3):391–404.

Spradley, J. P. 1979. *The Ethnographic Interview*. New York: Holt, Rinehart & Winston.

Sykes, G., and D. Matza. 1957. "Techniques of Neutralization: A Theory of Delinquency." *American Sociological Review* 22(December):664–70.

Time. 1988. "Pornography: A Poll." *Time* (July 21):22.

Defining, Excusing, and Justifying Deviance: Teen Mothers' Accounts for Statutory Rape

Joanna Gregson Higginson

INTRODUCTION

In all fifty states, laws distinguish between legal and illegal sexual relations based on the age difference between the participating man and woman. These statutory rape laws vary from state to state: while most view sexual relations between an adult male (over age 18) and an "underage" female as statutory rape, the age of consent for women ranges from 11 to 18. Despite the fact that statutory rape laws exist in almost every state, they are rarely enforced, and perpetrators are infrequently prosecuted (Oberman 1994). In recent years, however, these laws have come under increased scrutiny, which means that changes may be on the horizon (Lauer 1981; Oberman 1994).

Statutory rape laws have become newsworthy in large part because of their relationship to teenage pregnancy. It is estimated that over 60 percent of the fathers of babies born to teenage mothers are not teenagers themselves, but adult men (Oberman 1994; Phoenix 1991). People concerned with ameliorating the costs of teenage pregnancy—upwards of $2 billion in annual welfare and foodstamp payments alone—have often been concerned with the role of the fathers (or absent fathers) and their financial contributions to their offspring (Maynard 1996). Studies revealing the relatively older age of the fathers are appealing because they essentially criminalize the vast majority of teenage pregnancies. Because they see criminalization as a deterrent to future teenage pregnancies, some groups have ar-

gued that the laws should be enforced with more regularity (Lauer 1981). Others want the laws to be enforced not because of their potential to deter teenage pregnancy or reduce taxpayer burden, but because of what they perceive to be the tremendous social costs of statutory rape: the victimization and exploitation of young women by older men (Lauer 1981).

While existing laws and public opinion stigmatize the older boyfriend/younger girlfriend relationship, the young women involved with these men often do not view their relationships, or themselves, in a negative light. This article concerns the following question: How do teenage girls involved with older boyfriends view their relationships? I address this question by providing a conceptual framework for understanding the different ways that teenage mothers account for their involvement with adult boyfriends.

In many ways, the issue of whether or not young women view their behavior as deviant can be conceptualized as an accounts application. Like other forms of aligning actions (Stokes and Hewitt 1976), such as Sykes and Matza's (1957) "techniques of neutralization" or Mills's (1940) "motive talk." Scott and Lyman's (1968, p. 46) "accounts" are also meant to "verbally bridge the gap between action and expectation" by offering an explanation for why the deviant engaged in behavior that was not congruent with normative expectations. Scott and Lyman distinguish between two types of accounts: justifications and excuses. They describe justifications as "accounts in which one accepts responsibility for the act in question, but denies the pejorative quality associated with it" (1968, p. 47). Excuses, in contrast, are "accounts in which one admits that the act in question is bad, wrong, or inappropriate but denies full responsibility" (1968, p. 47). Accounts, in the form of justifications or excuses, are the deviant's effort to minimize damage to

(c)1999 by Society for the Study of Symbolic Interaction. Reprinted from *Symbolic Interaction* 22: 1, pp. 25–44, by permission.

Acknowledgment: An earlier version of this paper won the 1997 Herbert Blumer Award from the Society for the Study of Symbolic Interaction.

his or her identity after the deviant act has been performed or discovered.

Researchers have used Scott and Lyman's accounts to analyze deviants' explanations for their behavior in a variety of contexts. Kalab (1987) studied accounts used by college students who did not attend class by analyzing the notes they were requested to turn in following an absence. She found that most students' explanations for their absences were excuses: they acknowledged that absence was deviant but reported that something beyond their control (such as illness) prevented them from coming to class. Ray and Simons (1987) used accounts to analyze the explanations convicted murderers gave for their crimes, and they also found a preponderance of excuses. Like Kalab, they found that most of their informants accepted the normative expectations for behavior (i.e., they agreed that what they did was deviant) and therefore felt compelled to excuse their behavior by attributing the murders to accident, intoxication, or stress. In contrast, Scully and Marolla's (1984) research on convicted rapists revealed a preponderance of justifications. They found that some rapists viewed their behavior as criminal and made excuses for their behavior, but most justified what they did on the grounds that the behavior was appropriate, acceptable, and/or deserved. Scully and Marolla noted that these accounts allowed 83 percent of their research subjects (who were incarcerated for the crime of rape) to view themselves as non-rapists.

In this article, I use Scott and Lyman's two forms of accounts as an organizing framework to conceptualize the different explanations given by teenage mothers regarding their involvement with older boyfriends. Their framework is helpful for two important reasons. First, it takes into consideration that the accounts are reactive (i.e., employed after the deviance has occurred). Second, this framework distinguishes between people who view the act as deviant and those who do not, as well as between people who assume and deny responsibility for their behavior, a source of significant variation among the teenage mothers I spoke with about statutory rape.

While this framework is helpful, it is also limiting in one major respect: this type of analysis assumes that the act in question is deviant. Many of the young women I interviewed felt that dating an older boyfriend was not deviant. For this reason, I have divided my analysis into three major sections. In the first section, I examine the justifications used by the young women who do not view having older boyfriends as deviant. In the second section, I analyze the responses of the young women who do view this behavior as deviant. Here, I look at why they define younger girlfriend/older boyfriend relationships as deviant. In the third section, I examine the excuses given by the young women to account for their involvement in behavior they define as deviant. Finally, I offer explanations as to why the young women may have different ideas about whether the act is deviant and discuss the implications of my findings for the accounts literature and for statutory rape laws.

METHODS AND SETTING

My interest in statutory rape was sparked by two separate events: an article published in the local newspaper about statutory rape (which quoted teenage mothers as saying the laws are too lenient), and a conversation I overhead between several teenage parents (during which one mother said that her older boyfriend should not be accused of statutory rape because she had lied to him about her age). That these events happened within only a few days of each other piqued my interest as to the reasons why teenage mothers get involved with older boyfriends, whether or not they view these relationships as deviant, and how necessary they perceive the existing statutory rape laws to be.

I investigated the meaning of statutory rape among teenage mothers in the context of a larger participant-observation study I was conducting at the Teen Center, a school-based program for pregnant and parenting teenagers. The Teen Center is housed in the basement of "Lakeside" High School and serves pregnant and parenting teens from the school districts junior and senior high schools. Lakeside is located in an affluent, well-educated, predominantly white university town. I had been conducting my research at the Teen Center for over 18 months at the inception of this current research paper, and had worked on maintaining rapport throughout my time there. My relations with the teen mothers were friendly; I was on speaking terms with all of the 55 young women in the program, and was particularly close (i.e., considered a good friend) with about 15. My role at the center vacillated between volunteer, intern, and nursery staff substitute throughout the course of the research (on an almost daily basis), but I was known first and foremost as someone interested in studying teenage parents. I interacted with the teens in a variety of ways over the course of three school years: during school, we carried on conversations while we watched their children in the nurseries or while I tutored them in their classes; outside of school, I took them grocery shopping, accompanied them to the doctor when their children were ill, and celebrated their children's birthdays with them.

I drew the data for this study from both casual conversations I had with teens at the Center and from formal depth-interviews I conducted with a select group of teenage mothers. I interviewed 14 teenage mothers enrolled in the program; 13 of these teenagers were White, I was Black. These mothers ranged in age from 15 to 20, and shared several common traits: they were from middle and working-class backgrounds, in the process of completing their high school education, and either parenting (12) or pregnant (2). Perhaps most important was the fact that, at one time or another, they had all been involved in a sexual relationship with someone who was 18 or over while they were still minors. This sample was essentially purposive, for I actively sought out young women who had been involved with older boyfriends. Some had revealed this to me in earlier conversations, while others were referred to me by their friends. I interviewed each of the teens once, with interviews ranging from one to two hours in length. The interviews were tape-recorded and loosely structured. I asked the teens open-ended questions about their dating histories (their first boyfriend to their most recent boyfriend) and about the nature of these different relationships (how long they dated, what they did together, why she was attracted to him, and why they broke up). I also asked about the couple's relative ages, what she thought of any age gap, what he thought, and how

significant others (i.e., parents and teachers) reacted to the age differences. Often, when I began probing for their feelings regarding age differences, the teens responded by using the phrase "statutory rape." While they were not always clear about the specific law in their state, they were all aware that the law existed and that it criminalized sexual relations between men and women of certain ages. In addition to the depth-interview data, I also recorded in my fieldnotes the conversations I participated in or observed the teens having regarding the topic of dating older boyfriends, and I have included quotes from these young women as well. I did not have to prompt these discussions; the topic of boyfriends was prevalent in their conversations, and their significantly older ages always came up when the teens described their boyfriends. Because the participant-observation portion of this research spanned three school years, I was able to see how the teens' feelings and attitudes about older boyfriends changed as dating relationships began and/or ended.

After conducting and transcribing the interviews, I coded the participants' responses according to the type(s) of account they used when describing how they felt about dating an older boyfriend (i.e., into categories of excuses and justifications). These categories were further broken down into the sub-headings described below. For those participants who viewed the act as deviant—those who used excuses—I further coded their responses according to the type of explanation they gave for defining the act as deviant, looking for similarities and differences in answers to the question of what made these relationships deviant. In addition to scanning for types of accounts, I also looked for themes regarding participant's attitudes toward statutory rape laws and relevant characteristics of their relationships (e.g., the nature and duration of their involvement and the outcome of the relationship).

JUSTIFYING DEVIANCE

Teen mothers who used justifications to account for their relationships with older men claimed responsibility for being involved with them, but denied that the relationship was deviant in any way. They used justifications to explain why dating this older person was "no big deal." The teen mothers who used justifications were either still dating their older boyfriends or had parted ways but were still on amicable terms. Because they felt that older boyfriend/younger girlfriend relationships were not deviant, and because they had come out of them unscathed, they viewed statutory rape laws as unnecessary. There was no victim, so there was no crime. Older boyfriends were simply that, boyfriends who happened to be older, and their justifications supported this belief that they were not engaging in deviant behavior.

Age Is Meaningless

Several of the teen mothers felt that the fact that their boyfriends were significantly older was of little or no importance. Because they viewed their boyfriends' ages as meaningless, they drew no distinction between dating someone who was 16 and someone who was 26; a boyfriend was a boyfriend. Tracy, the 15-year-old mother of 1-year-old Kevin, started dating her boyfriend Eddie when she was 13 and he was 18. She told me that Eddie's age was "no big deal," adding that, "It's just like you have this boyfriend and he happens to be older." Crystal, a 15-year-old mother, concurred. She explained to me that dating a 20-year-old when she was 14 "didn't bother [her] at all" because "after all, age is just a number."

Sunshine was 19 when we talked, but she had dated older men when she was younger. Her first sexual experience was with a 30-year-old man when she had just turned 16. She told me that age differences between boyfriends and girlfriends were irrelevant and that "as long as she felt good enough to be with him or liked him or whatever, then age doesn't really matter."

While Tracy, Crystal, and Sunshine told me that age was meaningless, they all qualified their answers. Tracy felt that a five to seven year age difference between a girl and her boyfriend was harmless but added, "I mean, I can understand someone freaking out if the girl was 15 and she was dating, like, a 45-year-old. That's just gross. It's like screwing your dad." Crystal also qualified her response, explaining that "a couple of

years difference is okay, but if it's like five or six, then that's just not right." Sunshine told me, "I have a thing about certain ages. I don't have like a limit, but I wouldn't be with a guy that was my dad's age because I would feel like I was with my dad, you know, and that's just gross." In qualifying their justifications, Tracy, Crystal, and Sunshine hoped to make their account sound more plausible; the differences between their ages and those of their boyfriends should be viewed as insignificant relative to what they *could* be.

Other teen mothers felt no need to qualify their answers, believing that age was meaningless no matter what the age difference. Eighteen-year-old Kelly, who had dated a high school senior when she was still in middle school, stated, "I really don't care how old a guy is." She went on to say that, "I think that you can find somebody, and whether they're 40 or not, it doesn't really matter." The justification that age was not important held true under all circumstances.

For both the "qualifiers" (like Tracy, Crystal, and Sunshine) and the "everyone is fair game" group (exemplified by Kelly) the only thing that made their relationships deviant—the age difference between themselves and their boyfriends— was discounted as an irrelevant characteristic. In that way, they claimed responsibility for their involvement yet denied partaking in anything deviant. Since the act was not defined as deviant, they felt statutory rape laws were unnecessary.

Everyone Does It, Nobody Minds

The knowledge that many of their peers at the Teen Center had older boyfriends was the source of a justification used by many of the teen mothers. Fifteen-year-old Tracy illustrated this type of justification well when she explained that none of her peers gave her a hard time for dating 20-year-old Eddie "'cause a lot of them are dating guys who are older too!" The phrase many teen mothers used to describe the prevailing attitude was that dating an older guy was "no big deal" to them or anyone else they knew at the Teen Center because "everyone does it." The young women at the Teen Center were not the only young mothers dating older men. Between 60 and 70 percent of teenage mothers in the United States become pregnant by men in their twenties (Oberman 1994; Phoenix 1991). Because so many teen mothers at the Teen Center had older boyfriends, and because it was widely approved in their teen parenting culture, it was not viewed as deviant.

Several teen mothers who had not been involved with older men themselves saw nothing wrong with their peers' decisions to date older men, supporting the justification that these relationships were not deviant because "nobody minds." Seventeen-year-old Blair was eight months pregnant when I spoke with her. Although her boyfriend was also 17, she stood up for other young women who dated older men: "If she said 'yes' then I don't think anyone should go after him because she gave in to him. In other words, I mean, if she was pressured into it, then maybe I would see something wrong with it, but if she wanted to [have sex with him], then they shouldn't get in trouble for it." Eighteen-year-old Jessica's boyfriend was five months younger than her, and she had never actually dated an older guy, but she told me that she had been interested in older guys in the past and was surprised when she found herself attracted to Patrick: "I *never* thought I would date a younger guy!" While they were not partaking in the behavior themselves, both Blair and Jessica voiced their approval of older boyfriend/younger girlfriend relationships suggesting that such behavior was acceptable in their teenage parenting subculture, regardless of whether or not one was involved in this type of relationship. Thus, when teen mothers used the justification that "nobody minds," they were correct in that it was acceptable in their peer group.

Another form of the "everyone does it, nobody minds" justification was rooted in the approval of adults, such as parents or teachers. Linda, a junior, dated an 18-year-old when she was 14. She explained to me why there was nothing deviant about their relationship: "His name was Justin. I dated him when I was in eighth grade and he was a senior in high school. But our parents were good friends, so it was cool."

In addition to her mother's approval, Linda also commented on the community sanctioning of older boyfriend/young girlfriend relationships, thereby further justifying her decision to date Justin: "Everybody knew each other in my town. I went to parties sometimes with people that were my mom's age! So everybody just kind of hung out, no matter what their age. It was no big deal to anyone." The approval of others may be rooted in mate selection norms. Until recently, it was common for women to marry "up" by choosing mates several years their senior (Atkinson and Glass 1985). While these patterns of marital age heterogamy are decreasing—that is, as men and women are increasingly likely to marry someone close to their own age (Atkinson and Glass 1985)—men are still more likely to report that they would like to marry someone younger, while women report a greater willingness to marry someone older (South 1991). Thus, the teen mothers and the people who approve of their relationships with older boyfriends may simply hold traditional values about men and women, making it not only non-deviant for the teens to date older boyfriends, but desirable. In saying that all of their peers date older men, and that nobody minds that they do, the teen mothers justified their deviance by denying the pejorative content of their behavior. Because nobody is telling them these relationships are deviant, they see no need for them to be criminalized through statutory rape laws. As Linda stated, "As long as everybody is all right with it, I don't think it should be a problem. I don't think the guy should have to serve time for it or anything."

True Love Is Never Wrong

As Christian-Smith (1995, p. 211) pointed out, most young women view romance as "the only legitimate context for sexual expression." The young women at the Teen Center subscribed to this view, qualifying their sexual relations as acceptable if the relationship was based on love. Relationships were not construed as deviant if they were serious, for a couple in love could not be doing anything wrong by simply being together. Fifteen-year-old Tracy illustrated this viewpoint when she explained that it was okay for older men to date younger women, "If there's a real emotional feeling, and not just like, 'Wow,

I like your body.'" This notion of romance as the proper context for sexual relations stands in contrast to the historical roots of romantic attachment. In colonial America, the norm was for suitable mates to be found through matchmaking, parental selection and approval of prospective mates, or compatibility between a young man and woman; the notion of romantic love and intimacy serving as the foundation for mate selection was deviant (D'Emilio and Freedman 1988). Now, love and intimacy have not only come to the fore as the normative basis for mate selection, they have totally displaced matchmaking suitability; the only deviant relationship is the relationship based solely on lust. Just as their colonial counterparts distanced themselves from the type of relationship which contemporary teens desire, these contemporary teens distance themselves from the notion of mate selection based on lust, thereby legitimating their relationships by way of contrast to what they identify as a deviant mode of attachment. For contemporary teens, romantic relationships are viewed as the only appropriate context for sexual relations.

Several teen mothers explained that they had reservations about dating someone so much older and were relieved when their boyfriends expressed serious affection. For example, Tracy remembered that, when they first started dating, she was afraid to tell 18-year-old Eddie that she was only 13. When she finally told him her real age, he alleviated her fears by telling her, "Well, it doesn't matter now because I'm already in love with you." His expression of love confirmed that their relationship was legitimate. The same was true of Crystal and her 18-year-old boyfriend, Richard. When Richard learned that Crystal was only 14, his response was, "Okay, well, it doesn't matter now." His unspoken message, Crystal thought, was that it did not matter what her age was because their relationship had developed into something serious, for she interpreted the "now" to mean "now that I'm in love with you."

Both Tracy and Crystal claimed that a mutual feeling of love was a satisfactory justification for dating older boyfriends, and this contention allowed them to avoid defining their relationships as deviant. However, Tracy and Crystal's words belied a different reality: the crucial aspect of the justification was that their boyfriends loved *them*. His expression of love provided evidence that their relationship was not deviant; the young women were not being sexually exploited if their boyfriends loved them. In this way, the young women used their boyfriends' feelings, not their own, to distinguish between acceptable and unacceptable behavior. As long as an older boyfriend truly loves his younger girlfriend, their sexual relationship should not be viewed as deviant. This account resembles Scott and Lyman's (1968) description of the self-fulfillment justification, wherein deviants justify their wrongdoing by arguing that the deviance makes them happy or complete. For the teen mothers, being in love (and being loved by somebody) was a sufficient justification on the grounds that romance (and the concomitant sexuality) was perceived as being vital to one's happiness.

Consensual Sex Is Not Rape

The young women at the Teen Center told me that sexual relationships entered into by willing partners cannot be deviant. This type of relationship was viewed by the teen mothers as consensual, and it stood in sharp contrast to the other forms of rape, which they thought of as non-consensual. Thus, consent is the key to their definition of deviance, or as Burt and Albin (1981, p. 213) pose the question, "Did she want to or did she have to?"

Fifteen-year-old Tracy explained that consensual relationships between older boyfriends and younger girlfriends are not deviant "Because the girl is willing to go with the guy. If you were raped, you wouldn't be willing." Fifteen-year-old Crystal felt that even young adolescents can make rational decisions about whether or not they want to have sex. She said sexual relations between older boyfriends and younger girlfriends should not be considered deviant "'Cause it's something that both people give consent to. Even if you're 13, you know what you're doing." Nineteen-year-old Sunshine agreed that consent made relationships legitimate, and she felt that accusing older boyfriends of statutory rape was wrong in cases where the girlfriend was a willing partner: "The laws are stupid. I mean, unless they were raped, then, you know, it takes two to tango and they agreed, so it shouldn't be any big deal. It's their life."

The teen mothers felt that their consensual involvement with their boyfriends negated any deviance. While they admitted responsibility for getting involved with older men, they denied that the relationship was deviant because it was entered into willingly by both partners. Because they did not perceive the relationships as deviant, they felt that statutory rape laws were unnecessary. Using the justification that they consented to sex reinforces the idea that no crime was committed because they wanted to have sex just as much as their boyfriends did. In addition, they would argue that they are mature enough to give informed consent. The idea that they are too young to consent suggests that they are similar to other people who cannot give informed consent—children, people who are alcohol- or drug-impaired, or people who have impaired mental capacity—a supposition that threatens their identities as mature adults who can make informed decisions. The justification that their consent makes the relationship legitimate reinforces the idea that they are mature enough to make decisions about their sexuality, that they can make decisions in their own self-interest. Their justification resembles the technique of neutralization "denial of injury," for the teen mothers reasoned that "it was permissible to do this act since no one was injured by it . . . since the act resulted in consequences that were trifling" (Scott and Lyman 1968, p. 51). Since nobody was hurt by what they did, and since nobody minded, the relationship should not be viewed as deviant. This justification is ironic, in a way, because the teens argued that no one is hurt by their involvement with older men, despite the fact that many critics of younger girlfriend/older boyfriend relationships argue the opposite: that statutory rape laws protect young girls from being sexually exploited by older men, a stance that assumes younger girlfriends (and any children resulting from the union) will end up being hurt in the long run (Oberman 1994).

DEFINING DEVIANCE

In contrast to the teens who used justifications to explain why dating older boyfriends was not deviant, another group of young women who had dated older boyfriends in the past offered specific reasons for defining these relationships as deviant. These explanations focused on specific characteristics of older boyfriends as well as an awareness of laws and societal attitudes prohibiting such relationships.

Only Dirty Old Men Date Young Girls

One of the most common explanations for why dating older boyfriends was deviant was the assertion that the kinds of men who date young girls are sick, for there must be something wrong with them if they are attracted to young girls. These boyfriends were characterized as "dirty old men" and "perverts" who exploit young, naive girls for sex because they cannot find any willing partners in their own age group. Eighteen-year-old Kristina summed up this feeling when she told me that "in a lot of cases I've heard of, the older person wants to take advantage of the younger person for sexual reasons." Amanda, a 20-year-old mother, viewed these relationships the same way, and she was furious that older men got away with this exploitation:

I was watching this talk show the other day, and they had these really old women and younger guys, you know, and I'm like, power to all of them. But there was this one guy that was like 45—maybe 57—with this 16-year-old. I'm like, *that* is not okay. And when she's 18, that's fine. But you are molesting her. She is a child. Because really, at 16, you're still just a tiny little kid; you don't know anything. There was another girl who was 13. And I was like, this is sick! This was like 13 and 39. That's way beyond sick. And actually, a 14-year-old and a 25-year-old is pretty sick, too. She is obviously a little girl and he is an older, older man.

In addition to pointing out that older men in general are "sick" for dating younger girls, Amanda was also angry that her ex-boyfriend, the father of her baby, dated her when she was younger, implying that it was his responsibility as an adult to know better:

I just think the older person . . . I think Robby's an asshole for going out with me when I was 16. I think that's horrible. Seven years difference! I was 16; he was 23. He was a total adult, I was still in my adolescent years, you know? Wanting to ditch school and get drunk all the time, and he's an adult working full-time.

He knew better, and he should have, I mean, I never came on to him, but when I wrote him poems, even with that he could have said, you know, "Come back when you're 18." The older person should do that. I would never go out with a 16-year-old, never. I couldn't do it. I think it's disgusting; I think it's sick.

LaNiece, a 16-year-old mother, also blamed her older ex-boyfriend for letting their relationship get started. She told me that she was dismayed when she found out her boyfriend's real age, for at 13, she thought she was dating a 15-year-old: "I found out [his real age], 'cause my friend, she said, 'Well, I'm just going to tell you this: he's really twenty.' And I was like, 'No he's not.' So I asked him, and he admitted it, and I didn't want him to, you know? I wanted him to lie to me." When I asked why she did not want to know his age, she offered the following explanation:

I guess 'cause I was kind of a little creeped out because he was so much older than me. I think guys who date younger girls are sick, sick, sick. For most people, it's like the guy taking advantage of the girl. It is almost every time. Or he can't get anyone his own age because there's something wrong with him.

Like Amanda, LaNiece also felt that older boyfriends were "sick" because they took advantage of young girls who do not realize they are being exploited: "I mean, if you know someone is that young, they don't know anything about *anything,* and you shouldn't even be, like, thinking about it. Thirteen and 20? That is like a man and a little girl! Seriously, like, that is so much older." Eighteen-year-old Marci, the mother of an 8-month-old boy, told me she was attracted to older men and felt like she had to be cautious to avoid being exploited in the way Amanda and LaNicce described:

Um, I have to be careful because I have to realize that a lot of times people that age, you know, it's either out there for sex or someone to make them feel like they're still attractive and desired and everything else. Nothing like a 45-or-something-year-old man being desired by an 18-year-old.

For Amanda, LaNiece, and the other girls who described older boyfriends as "sick" (or in Marci's case, potentially sick), the intentions of the older boyfriend made younger girlfriend/older boyfriend relationships deviant. While their

peers justified their relationships with older boyfriends by pointing out that their older boyfriends really loved them, these girls voiced different opinions. In their view, older boyfriends exploit naive girls who are too young to realize they are being taken advantage of, and this exploitation made the relationships deviant.

Older Boyfriends Are Abusive

Another explanation for the deviance in dating older boyfriends was based on the experiences the teens had with older boyfriends. The girls who were most adamant about the relationships being deviant were those who had been physically abused, controlled, and/or manipulated into getting pregnant.

Sixteen-year-old LaNiece told me that the typical older boyfriend/younger girlfriend scenario involved control and domination by the boyfriend: "They want to be able to tell someone what to do and when to do it. That's why they date younger girls." Her own relationship with her baby's 20-year-old father ended when "he just kept being bossy." She explained that he was controlling every part of her life and cheating on her at the same time:

He was just like, controlling everything. "Where are you going?" Or, "Why are you combing your hair like that?" I was like, "Because I want to." And he would tell me, "Oh, I know you're not wearing that to school." Or, "I know you're not doing that." So really controlling. And he was with all these other girls.

Fifteen-year-old Vanessa, the mother of a baby girl, told me her 20-year-old boyfriend cheated on her while she was pregnant and living with him, often disappearing for days at a time while he had sexual flings with other girls (and grown women). When the baby was born, he disappeared for eight months. When he eventually returned, he insulted Vanessa by repeatedly commenting on how much weight she had gained, told her that breast-feeding was disgusting and that she had to quit doing that to "any baby of mine," and chastised her for spoiling the baby. Vanessa broke up with him one week later, commenting that, "He changed. Or at least I think he changed. All he wanted to do was tell me what to do. And nothing I did was right." Like LaNiece,

Vanessa believed that the basis for his dominating personality was his age.

Several mothers told me stories about their older boyfriends "tricking" them into getting pregnant, which they saw as comparable to the other forms of abuse and domination. For example, when she was 13, Diana's 18-year-old boyfriend, Matt, told her that he had been diagnosed by his doctor as infertile, so he did not need to use a condom. Similarly, LaNiece's 20-year-old boyfriend told her that he couldn't get her pregnant:

Well, I was only 13, keep that in mind, 'cause he told me, "Oh I can't have kids, I can't have kids." And I believed him! I was like, "Oh, okay." You know, I didn't know anything about the reproductive system—I was only 13. So he said he couldn't get me pregnant and I believed him. And that was his intention, all along, to get me pregnant. 'Cause I asked him once, when I was complaining that I was all fat and my feet were all swollen, I'm like, "You probably knew you could get me pregnant. You probably just wanted to trick me so I'd get pregnant." And he got this big smile and he was like, "Well, what if I did?" And I was like, "Oh my god!" I wasn't expecting that at all. I was thinking he'd say something like, "It was an accident" or "I'm just as surprised as you are."

Both girls told me that they were tricked only because their boyfriends were older and they trusted their "judgment," but they realized later that the men used this maturity to manipulate the girls into getting pregnant.

Eighteen-year-old Kristina was physically abused by her older boyfriend. She told me that she felt like her former boyfriend duped her into thinking she was in love with him, and that his physical and sexual abuse were signs of love from him. Looking back, she was angry: "How does anybody at age 13 know they're in love? He nailed it into me that I was in love with him. He gave me all these things. He took me out to dinner. He told me this is what it means to be in love." Later, she told me what else her 18-year-old boyfriend did: he physically abused her during sexual intercourse to "prepare" her and "toughen her up" in case she was ever raped. Because she was not able to see past the dinners and the gifts at age 13, Kristina felt strongly that other young women would not either. Statutory

rape laws, she thought, could be used to intervene in relationships like hers where the girl was too young to realize she was being abused.

Dating Older Boyfriends Is Illegal

A pragmatic explanation for why dating older boyfriends was deviant was one based on the law: because the law defines these relationships as illegal, they are deviant. Even though most of the girls had only vague understandings of what the actual law was in their state, they all had an awareness that a law existed, and as a result, viewed their relationships with older boyfriends as deviant.

Twenty-year-old Amanda told me that, when she was 16, she and her 23-year-old boyfriend, Robby, were so concerned about breaking the law that they looked up the statute in the state where they lived:

That's one of the things that me and Robby were talking about before we got together, was what are people going to think, and is this okay. I went to the library and looked in the law book and saw that it was 15 and 19, you know, a 15-year-old girl/19-year-old boy is the limit. If you have a 15-year-old and a 20-year-old, it's statutory rape. But once you're 16, you can go out with someone who's any age. We made sure of that before we started really going in public and doing whatever.

Because they worked together, their primary concern was that their co-workers would think they were doing something wrong. Before they started officially "going-out," they discussed the potential problems that might arise:

The biggest problem was the age difference. It was important because . . . well, he was 23 and I was 16, and that's a huge gap in the things you do and the things you like. We were really worried about other people and what they'd think. Other people at work who would think he was a pervert, 'cause he was 23 and I was 16, and at that age—actually, at any age—that's a big difference. People were already talking about us which made it kind of weird.

Other young women did not take the initiative to look up the specific laws regarding statutory rape, but they did feel that what they were doing was deviant, if not illegal. They showed their awareness of the deviance by lying about their ages to their boyfriends—either because they knew it was illegal or they knew such relationships were socially stigmatized. Many young women began relationships with their older boyfriends under false pretenses, either blatantly lying about their ages or subtly steering the conversation away from the topic of age. Indeed, LaNiece told me that lying was very common among her peers: "I thought it was all cool because I was like in eighth grade and everything and, like, all my friends were dating older guys and we all lied about our ages. We'd be all, 'How old are you?' 'Oh, I'm 16.' 'Oh yeah, well I'm 17!' So we were all lying, you know?" Even though they lied about their ages, the girls told me that their boyfriends knew their real ages—or at least knew they were younger than they said they were—and that did not stop them from dating them or having sex with them. When she was 13, LaNiece lied about her age to her boyfriend, but she pointed out that her boyfriend, who was 20, knew her real age and should have known better than to seduce a young girl: "I told him I was 15 and he never seemed to care, so I just told him later that I was really 13 and he said, 'Yeah, I knew all along you were 13.' . . . He said, 'Yeah, I already knew how old you were, I just wanted to see how long you would wait to tell me.'" Although she went to great lengths to hide her true age—thereby showing an awareness of the deviance of dating someone so much older than herself—LaNiece found out her boyfriend knew her age all along. Thus, while she altered her behavior (or more accurately, her age) to avoid a deviant identity, he seemed to feel that there was nothing wrong with dating someone so young. Fifteen-year-old Diana told me a similar story. When she was 13, she told 18-year-old Matt that she was 15. Three weeks later (and after she became pregnant with his child), she revealed her true age only to have him tell her that he knew all along. Like LaNiece, Diana had a sense that her real age would make the relationship deviant, a feeling that was not shared by their boyfriends.

EXCUSING DEVIANCE

The young women who defined younger girlfriend/older boyfriend relationships as deviant had been involved with older boyfriends. Thus,

they had participated in an act they defined as deviant. Because they viewed these relationships as deviant, and because they did not want to lose face by assuming responsibility for the deviance, they denied responsibility for their involvement with older boyfriends. In contrast to the teens who used justifications and assumed responsibility for their involvement with older boyfriends, the young women who viewed dating older boyfriends as deviant excused their behavior as something that was beyond their immediate control. The two groups differed in another important respect as well: while the justifiers were still involved with their older boyfriends, the girls who defined that behavior as deviant (and therefore felt compelled to use excuses to account for their behavior) were no longer with their older boyfriends. The excuses they used helped them explain why they became involved with someone who turned out to be a terrible boyfriend.

I'm Only Attracted to Older Guys

Many teen mothers turned to older boyfriends because the "younger" men they knew (who were, in fact, their same age peers) were not viewed as an acceptable dating pool. The specific reasons for this perspective varied, but most had to do with the fact that the teen mother felt she was too mature to be attracted to someone her own age. Thus, older men were the only desirable dates.

Kerry, a 15-year-old, was eight months pregnant when I spoke with her. Her baby's father was 18. When asked whether she liked older guys in general, she responded that, "All of my boyfriends have been older than me." Her explanation for dating older men was that they were more mature than younger men:

[I like] somebody I don't always have to baby-sit. I get tired of being with people that look up to me. Me and my friends were talking about this. You want someone who knows exactly what you need, and a lot of them don't. Someone who can take care of himself and who's not going to look at you like a baby-sitter, which a lot of them do.

While she touted the virtues of older men, Kerry felt that statutory rape laws were necessary to protect other young women from experiencing the physical abuse she received from her baby's father. When she complained in public about the way he was treating a 3-year-old in their care, he dragged her across the room and cut her arms with a knife. Kerry felt that getting involved with this abusive boyfriend was not her fault, however, because she was not attracted to the immature men who were her own age. I spoke informally with Kerry a few months prior to the interview—when she and her boyfriend were still together—and she told me that she was against statutory rape laws because she felt they infringed on her right to make her own decisions. Once the relationship turned sour, however, she changed her account from a justification (consensual sex is not rape) to an excuse, ultimately denying responsibility for her involvement with her abusive boyfriend. This excuse resembles Scott and Lyman's (1968) "appeal to biological drives," wherein people blame their involvement in deviance on something out of their control, such as their sexual drives. For the teen mothers in this study, their sexual attraction to older boyfriends and their own level of maturity were perceived as character traits that were out of their control.

I Need A Father For My Baby

While some teen mothers explained that they were not attracted to younger men, others told me that younger men would not make good fathers for their children. Thus, they had to turn to older men. Sixteen-year-old Jennifer, the mother of a 1-year-old daughter, offered the following explanation:

People my age are too immature. And you know, obviously anybody younger than me is not going to be able to deal with my lifestyle. The people at school, I don't even think about them. You know, I think there's some guys that are cute but that's it. They're cute, but that's as far as it goes. They're immature, and I would not like to support someone else. I want it to be a mutual thing.

When she spoke of younger boys dealing with her "lifestyle," she meant handling the responsibility of dating a woman with a child, and ultimately being a father figure for her child. Sixteen-year-old Staci also told me that the boys at

the high school would not be good boyfriends, saying, "They're too immature. I think they'd all have to grow up first before I'd consider them." When I asked her what it was about older boyfriends that appealed to her, she said, "They're not worried about school. If they want to, they can take care of the kid. They're not so much into partying like in high school." These young women, then, felt compelled to date older boyfriends because there was no suitable alternative: the guys their own age were too immature to handle the responsibility of being a father. In using this excuse, the teen mothers conceded the deviance of dating older boyfriends, but blamed their involvement with them on something out of their control: the fact that younger men were too immature for them because they could not handle the demands of fatherhood. Statutory rape laws are often thought to limit hedonistic impulses—to make older men think twice before becoming involved with younger women—but these young women said that they turned to older men because the younger men they knew were too irresponsible. Seeking older men was, for them, a responsible, rational thing to do.

I Needed Something That Only He Could Give Me

While some teen mothers spoke of needing older boyfriends in a general way, others spoke of why they needed to be with a particular older boyfriend. For these young women, the men they dated fulfilled a special role—namely, that of a father-figure. Kristina, now age 18, explained why she began dating a 16-year-old when she was 12:

He and I both had a missing parent, and I think we connected really well because we knew what we wanted that we weren't getting. I was searching for something, and I found it in him. I was out for a father-figure, and that's exactly what he was. He was the dad I always wanted. I just wanted somebody to hug me and tell me they loved me and he did it. I was in love with him because he gave me what I needed.

With the benefit of hindsight, Kristina was able to speak more generally about teenagers dating people older than themselves, telling me, "I think girls who date older guys are looking for a father, or just a missing feeling or something that they're not getting from their parents at home. And it can be from a mom or dad, you know?"

Eighteen-year-old Marci only dated older men, including one who was 20 years her senior. Like Kristina, she saw the connection between her choice in men and her desire for a father-figure:

I've always been attracted to older men. You know, a lot of people say, "Oh, maybe you're looking for your father or someone to take care of you." I think it does have something to do with being taken care of, but I'm not looking for anyone like my father. I'm pretty sure about that one.

She spoke specifically about her relationship with the 37-year-old married man that began when she was 17:

He was really supportive through my pregnancy, and when my mom kicked me out, was somewhat financially supportive of me . . . until his wife found out! [laughs]. He just felt like, don't know, like somewhat of a father figure, you know? Not like my dad, but someone who gave me the advice and the caring and everything else. You know, the support that I wasn't getting anywhere else.

For Kristina and Marci, the decision to date an older man was one over which they felt little control. Thus, they distanced themselves from blame. Kristina placed the blame on her abusive father, suggesting that his violent treatment drove her to seek an older boyfriend (who also turned out to be violent) as a replacement. Likewise, Marci blamed her father, but she said that his neglect and disinterest were what forced her to seek support elsewhere. This excuse resembles two of Scott and Lyman's (1968) accounts. First, it is similar to the "self-fulfillment" excuse, in that the teen mothers were looking for a relationship they needed to make their lives complete. It also resembles the "scapegoating" excuse, for the young women blame this need for an older man on their own abusive or neglectful fathers.

CONCLUSION

Scott and Lyman (1968) accounts are valuable in understanding how teenage mothers view statutory rape. First, accounts allow the researcher to differentiate between people who view certain acts as deviant and those who do not. In the present study, this distinction allowed me to see that the women involved in abusive or unhappy relationships, viewed them as deviant because the man was older, whereas women in stable relationships with older men saw nothing wrong with their age difference. Second, they allow the researcher to distinguish between deviants who blame themselves for their wrong-doings and deviants who blame others. Here, I noted that women who felt no control over their involvement with older men perceived themselves as victims (and because of this, wanted more stringent enforcement of statutory rape laws), while women who claimed responsibility for their behavior felt like equals in their relationships (and thought statutory rape laws were unnecessary). These findings have significant implications for accounts in general because they help us to understand who uses excuses and who uses justifications.

The present study suggests that there is more difference between excuses and justifications than has been indicated in previous research. Specifically, this study shows that the people who rely on the different forms of accounts may be in relationships that are qualitatively different from one another, despite the fact that they are in seemingly similar situations. Teen mothers using justifications felt as though they had as much power in the relationship as their boyfriends, and thus as much responsibility for being involved in the deviance. This group placed as much blame on themselves as they did on anyone else. Teen mothers who relied on excuses, by contrast, felt powerless in their relationships, and thus did not claim responsibility for the deviance. Indeed, they blamed their deviance on someone else. In more general terms, this study suggests that action and responsibility will be accepted when deviants feel a sense of control over their behavior, while action and responsibility will be rejected when deviants feel as though they have no control over things that happen to them. Thus, persons engaging in the same form of deviance can have dramatically different views about their own agency and the factors that compelled them to engage in that behavior. Whether they blame themselves or others is contingent on this feeling of power or control and influences whether they will use excuses or justifications.

Perhaps the most significant contribution of this study for the accounts literature is that it posits the possibility of a sequential relationship between justifications and excuses that has not been addressed previously. Justifications and excuses may be used independently by deviant actors, but they may also follow in a sequence, as justifications give way to excuses when people become disempowered and disenchanted. In this regard, I have shown that the teen mothers who were still in relationships with older men gave justifications, and those who then broke up with their older boyfriends switched to excuses. In this way, the teen mothers demonstrated a tendency to use justifications initially, but they moved on to excuses when the relationships went bad. In essence, they demonstrated a shift from self-blame ("Even if you're thirteen, you know what you're doing") to blaming other factors beyond their control ("girls who date older guys are looking for a father"). While involved in amicable relationships, they claimed responsibility, but once things turned sour, they placed the blame elsewhere. More generally, one could hypothesize that deviants feeling a sense of power will use justifications, but they will shift to excuses when they become disempowered. Conversely, deviants who become empowered may change their accounts from excuses to justifications. Scott and Lyman (1968) proposed that deviants "phase" their accounts when rationalizing their behavior, suggesting that they go through a series of accounts as they try to negotiate a non-deviant identity with their audience. Rather than shifting accounts in the course of a conversation, as Scott and Lyman suggested, the young women in this study shifted the nature of the account over the course of their relationships, a phasing process that was distinctly sequential in nature.

Individuals engaging in a wide range of deviant behaviors utilize similar aligning actions to rationalize to themselves and others that what they are doing is not wrong, from students cheating on exams (McCabe 1992) to white-collar criminals (Benson 1985). The teenage mothers in the present study were no different, for they also were concerned with preserving a non-deviant identity, both in their minds and in the minds of others. The young women accounting for their involvement with older men are distinct from other groups of deviants, however, for they exercise justifications and excuses in an effort to minimize the damage to their own identities, even though it is their boyfriends who are legally culpable for the crime of statutory rape. In essence, the victims are accounting for the perpetrators' deviance. The fact that the young women do this suggests that while they may not be legally responsible for their involvement with older men, they are receiving messages telling them that they are deviant. They feel deviant because they are aware that they are voluntarily violating several norms at once: the norm of age homogamy in dating partners, the norm of abstaining from sexual relations at a young age, and the norm of delaying parenthood until adulthood. The fact that they are not legally liable for consenting to the sexual relationship has nothing to do with the criminal definition of the act (i.e., it is inherently deviant for the man but not the woman). Rather, it is a law based on the notion that an unmarried woman is her father's property; premarital sex damages the marriage-market value of his property, so he brings suit against the perpetrator (Oberman 1994). Today, however, women blame themselves because they have voluntarily participated in the relationship and because, in our liberated culture, women are viewed as independent actors rather than someone's property. Just as statutory rape laws are beginning to reflect the idea that women are able to give consent by excusing, for the most part, consensual acts of intercourse between minors (Oberman 1994), women have internalized the belief that giving consent means accepting blame, regardless of the circumstances surrounding the consent.

Like other persons assumed to be engaged in deviance, many of the teens reacted to the deviant label by denying that there was anything wrong with their behavior. Although some of them defined dating older men as deviant, it certainly was not a view shared by all of the teen mothers. In fact, the attitude among most members of the Teen Center was that dating older boyfriends was not deviant. In large measure, this may be because identifying the act as non-deviant makes their consent meaningful. If their consent makes the relationships acceptable, their judgment is valued and their moral independence is not questioned. On the other hand, calling the relationships deviant insults them by raising the issue of their ability to make decisions that affect their lives. An important characteristic of adolescence is the quest for autonomy—a desire to act like and be treated like adults (Smith 1962). This goal may be particularly salient for teens who are trying to justify having children at early ages. The ability to give consent is crucial if one wants to be thought of as a mature adult, which can explain why so many teens, including those not involved with older men themselves, did not view the relationships as deviant.

This perspective also paints a picture of teen mothers and their relationships with their boyfriends that we have not seen before. On the one hand, this paper corroborates the exploitation of young women that many advocates of statutory rape laws decry. Older boyfriends were described as taking advantage of younger girlfriends, and several pregnancies resulted from young women being convinced that contraception was not necessary. On the other hand, this paper also describes young women in consensual short- and long-term relationships with older boyfriends. These teen mothers wanted to make responsible choices (in choosing older men because of their potential to be responsible fathers) and they strove to be viewed as mature (in wanting their consent to be meaningful). For them, dating older boyfriends was the grown-up, mature thing to do, and the route to pregnancy was not a one-night-stand, but the consequence of a relationship they regarded as loving and committed. Like the women in Luker's (1975) study who chose not to use contraception even though the commonplace assumption was that they should, the young women at the Teen Center had compelling reasons for not abiding by statutory rape laws. For them, it made more sense to break the law, just as the women Luker interviewed provided explanations for why the costs of contraception outweighed the benefits.

These findings have important implications for public policy. This paper describes the reasons why some young women see nothing wrong with dating older men, which helps shed light on the question of whether or not current statutory rape laws are effective deterrents. This research suggests that existing laws do not deter young women from getting romantically involved with older men because the teen culture has adopted a set of justifications which make the relationships legitimate—and because their boyfriends see nothing wrong with the relationship, either. The teen mothers in this study do not view themselves as incapable of voluntarily consenting to sex, as being their fathers' property, or as being tainted by having relations with older men—the rationales underlying statutory rape laws (Oberman 1994). Thus, for the teenagers currently involved with older boyfriends, statutory rape laws were viewed as something of an anachronism. The teens do not see the necessity for these laws, do not feel that they will be caught and/or punished for violating them, and thus do not feel the need to abide by them. These findings suggest that statutory rape laws need to be modified in one of two ways. One alternative is to deter the crime of statutory rape by enforcing existing laws (thereby undermining the belief that "everyone does it and nobody minds"). A move in this direction would coincide with the strengthening of sexual harassment regulations and further emphasize the important role of power in sexual relations (in this case, the relative power older men hold over younger women) despite the fact that the young women do not always recognize the power imbalance. The move toward enforcing statutory rape laws would also reflect a notion that sexual relations between people of unequal ages are socially intolerable and detrimental. The other alternative would be to eliminate statutory rape laws altogether. Eliminating statutory rape laws would reflect the idea that these laws are inherently unequal and unfair (in criminalizing men and not women). Their removal would further liberate young women from their historically disadvantaged position—the position of needing protection from their own irrational desires. Policy makers concerned with the negative consequences of such a move (e.g., that more teenagers might become pregnant by older men) might choose to focus energy and money on sex education and contraception for adolescents rather than enforcing ineffective laws. Both of these policy modifications—either enforcing or eliminating existing laws—can result in positive consequences for women, because they transform women from being someone's property to being rational actors in command of their own lives. Either way, we would have a legal move which reflects a greater egalitarianism between men and women in all spheres of social life.

REFERENCES

ATKINSON, MAXINE P. and BECKY L. GLASS. 1985. "Marital Age Heterogamy and Homogamy, 1900 to 1980." *Journal of Marriage and the Family* 47: 685–691.

BENSON, MICHAEL L. 1985. "Denying the Guilty Mind: Accounting for Involvement in a White-Collar Crime." *Criminology* 23:583–607.

BURT, MARTHA R. and ROCHELLE S. ALBIN. 1981. "Rape Myths, Rape Definitions, and Probability of Conviction." *Journal of Applied Social Psychology* 11:212–230.

CHRISTIAN-SMITH, LINDA K. 1995. "Young Women and Their Dream Lovers." Pp. 206–227 in *Sexual Cultures and the Construction of Adolescent Identities,* edited by Janice M. Irvine. Philadelphia: Temple University Press.

D'EMILIO, JOHN and ESTELLE FREEDMAN. 1988. *Intimate Matters: A History of Sexuality in America.* New York: Harper and Row.

KALAB, KATHLEEN A. 1987. "Student Vocabularies of Motive: Accounts for Absence." *Symbolic Interaction* 10:71–83.

LAUER, REBECCA J. 1981. "Fourteenth Amendment—Statutory Rape: Protection of Minor Female and Prosecution of Minor Male." *The Journal of Criminal Law and Criminology* 72:1374–1392.

LUKER, KRISTIN. 1975. *Taking Chances: Abortion and the Decision Not to Contracept.* Berkeley: University of California Press.

MAYNARD, REBECCA (ed.). 1996. *Kids Having Kids: A Robin Hood Foundation Special Report on the Costs of Adolescent Childbearing.* New York: Robin Hood Foundation.

MCCABE, DONALD L. 1992. "The Influence of Situational Ethics on Cheating among College Students." *Sociological Inquiry* 62:365–374.

MILLS, C. WRIGHT. 1940. "Situated Actions and Vocabularies of Motive." *American Sociological Review* 5:904–913.

OBERMAN, MICHELLE. 1994. "Turning Girls into Women: Re-Evaluating Modern Statutory Rape Law." *The Journal of Criminal Law and Criminology* 85:15–79.

PHOENIX, ANN. 1991. *Young Mothers?* Oxford: Polity Press.

RAY, MELVIN C. and RONALD L. SIMONS. 1987. "Convicted Murderers' Accounts of Their Crime: A Study of Homicide in Small Communities." *Symbolic Interaction* 10:57–70.

SCOTT, MARVIN B. and STANFORD M. LYMAN. 1968. "Accounts." *American Sociological Review* 33:46–62.

SCULLY, DIANA and JOSEPH MAROLLA. 1984. "Convicted Rapists Vocabulary of Motives: Excuses and Justifications." *Social Problems* 31:530–544.

SMITH, ERNEST A. 1962. *American Youth Culture: Group Life in Teenage Society.* New York: The Free Press.

SOUTH, SCOTT J. 1991. "Sociodemographic Differentials in Mate Selection Preferences." *Journal of Marriage and the Family* 53:928–940.

STOKES, RANDALL and JOHN P. HEWITT. 1976. "Aligning Actions." *American Sociological Review* 41:839–849.

SYKES, GRESHAM M. and DAVID MATZA. 1957. "Techniques of Neutralization: A Theory of Delinquency." *American Sociological Review* 22:664–670.

Common Crime and Social Control

Drawing upon the work of Rose Coser and others, Charles Terry examines how humor functions as a survival mechanism for incarcerated individuals in his article, "The Function of Humor for Prison Inmates." His analysis uses participant observations and content analysis to examine how prisoners use humor as a principal means to negotiating and managing the gap between a normal and convict identity. Terry's novel study adds new insights to a rich body of research regarding how social control operates in total institutions.

In an excerpt from a longer article entitled, "Incarceration as a Deviant Form of Social Control," Wayne Welsh and I analyze the problems resulting from societal overincarceration, including overcrowded jails and state and federal court orders against government entities that administer them. A significant irony in crime control policy is presented. By touting incarceration as the major response to crime, the state inevitably fails to keep the "public promise" of more certain, swift, and severe punishments. Formal social control mechanisms are thwarted by the massive influx of persons brought into the criminal justice system. Given this situation, which has led to horrid jail and prison conditions in many jurisdictions, the legal system has turned on itself, labeling its own use of incarceration as "deviant"

when punishment practices become so extreme as to threaten the very legitimacy of the criminal justice system itself.

Edwin Lemert's classic work, "The Behavior of the Systematic Check Forger" examines the "behavior system" that allows persons to engage in check forging. Using Sutherland's framework developed in his research on the professional thief, Lemert studies convicted check forgers as well as those who were serving sentences for writing checks with insufficient funds. He discusses how those engaged in this form of deviance see forgery as a "regular business," how planning takes place, the required technical skills, and mobility and association issues. Unlike other forms of professional theft, the systematic forger tends to work alone, avoiding contact with other criminals whenever possible. Lemert explains how his findings are at odds with Sutherland's earlier statement that it was necessary for forgers to work in cooperative arrangements with others and concludes that check forgery is not "a professional behavior system acquired or maintained through associations with other criminals."

David Sudnow's "Normal Crimes" is a classic work in the sociology of deviance and social control. Sudnow attempts to make sense of the ways in which crimes are categorized by enforcers. He seeks to answer the question of how the penal code is employed in the everyday activity of legal administrators in order to assess the utility of the labeling perspective on deviance. "Normal crimes" are those occurrences seen as "typical" and whose perpetrators and victims have characteristics that fit common circumstances of such acts. Sudnow's examination of the "law in action" shows how the socially constructed catego-rization of crime by public defenders and prose-cutors affects legal decision making. He argues that categories of crime are not simply defined by statutes, but must be studied sociologically in order to make empirical sense of the processing of deviance by formal institutions of social con-trol. Moreover, the study suggests that the smooth operation of the criminal justice system is dependent upon such "normal crimes."

THE FUNCTION OF HUMOR FOR PRISON INMATES*

Charles M. Terry**

There's a place where you're treated like cattle. You're branded, herded and you're fed. When you come up missing somebody is sent to find you. Like a cow that strayed from the herd, you're driven back. It is known among those who share this experi-ence. But we laugh about it. Make jokes about it. If we didn't we'd probably revolt. Nobody wants to take the time to think about the conditions we find our-selves in.

A young inmate from the California Youth Authority

You know—I realized that when I'm joking around all the time with the fellas it's real cool. I mean it just seems like things are okay. But then, when I have to lay down at night, by myself, alone—it's different. You gotta have others to joke with. Otherwise it doesn't work.

An older inmate with years spent in prison

Extensive research has been done in the hopes of better understanding the mechanisms underlying socialization processes within the prison environ-ment. Particular interest has been paid to the ways prison inmates adjust to, and cope with, confinement. Various methods of survival have been studied (Clemmer, 1940; Irwin, 1970; Irwin & Cressey, 1962; McCorkle & Korn, 1954; Sykes & Messinger, 1960; Zamble & Porporino, 1988). Much of this work entails what inmates do as groups distinct from one another within the prison setting. For example, Irwin (1970) dis-cusses how inmate groups are often separated by personal characteristics.

In this exploratory study, the function of humor in prison is discussed. Male prisoners exist in a world that suppresses the expression of one's true feelings. Any exhibition of emotion relative to pain of any sort is seen as weakness and is unacceptable. Yet human feelings (for most anyway) must be displayed somehow by in-mates. This is accomplished through humor. Without humor, the prisoner value system, re-volving around the projection of invulnerability, would be difficult to accomplish.

Prison humor allows inmates to achieve con-trol in two ways: It is the only social mechanism within the prison environment that allows feel-ings to be expressed and its expression cannot be controlled by authorities. Prison inmates use humor as a reply that undermines the strength of

*From the *Journal of Contemporary Criminal Justice,* vol. 13, no. 1, February 1997, 23–40, copyright © 1997 Sage Publications, Inc. Reprinted by permission of the author and publisher.

**This study was supported by a grant from the May Co. Foundation in affiliation with the College of Letters and Sci-ences at the University of California, Santa Barbara. The au-thor gratefully acknowledges the guidance of Denise Bielby in the project's early phases, as well as the relentless assis-tance of Paul Jesilow in the preparation of this article.

the many voices of the system that continuously attempt to manage and control them. It acts as proof of their power and their release from domination.

HUMOR

Humor is a fascinating and insightful way of studying any culture. Humorous interaction has a way of exposing various aspects of social life as being different than they might appear on the surface. The good sociologist and good comedian have things in common.

> Comedians and sociologists do more than disintegrate their subject matter cognitively; they also devalue it morally. They "unmask" their subject matter by splitting it into apparent phenomenon (what most people believe is going on) and an actual noumenon (what is "really" going on). (Davis, 1993, p. 157)

Psychological studies provide ample evidence that humor acts as a stress reducer (Davidhizar & Bowen, 1992; Morreal, 1991; Overholser, 1992), is related to good health (Carroll & Shmidt, 1992), and can be instrumental in improving self-esteem (Martin, Kuiper, & Olinger, 1993). Humor also allows one a sense of superiority to the objects of the joke (Davies, 1990; Freud, 1960). "Elation is engendered when we compare ourselves favorably to others as being less stupid, less ugly, less unfortunate, or less weak" (Keith-Spiegal, 1972, p. 6). Humor can be used to defuse tension and make a situation less serious than it is initially believed to be (Coser, 1966; Ungar, 1984). Self-mockery (Ungar, 1984; Zijderveld, 1968) can neutralize stigma. By recounting past stories, or by looking at the current situation in a self-mocking manner, social bonds are strengthened and grave situations can be seen differently. Humor is a universal way of recognizing social boundaries. "Jokes . . . seek to define moral boundaries, the boundaries of values that are in conflict" (Davies, 1982, p. 387).

There are some studies of humor in institutions. Coser (1959) reported that hospital patients use it to alleviate "anxiety about self, submission to a rigid authority structure, and related to this, adjustment to rigid routine" (Coser, 1959, p. 173). She, along with Kanter (1977) and Anderson (1976), note that humor enhanced group solidarity as well as allowed people to redefine their situation. Freeman (1984) and Goffman (1961a) also mention humor in their writings on total institutions, although it is not the main focus of their work.

IDENTITY

This study focuses on identity as a concept. The notion of salient role-identity (Callero, 1985) is equated with the central self with which one identifies. Thus one might identify as being pro-choice, or a preacher first—above and beyond all other roles acted out during daily life. Consequently, all actions exhibited in other roles should reflect that central self. Although people can acquire a number of identities, it is reasonable to assume that the social interaction each person participates in will be limited relative to the number of roles made available from his or her salient role-identity.

As well as having salient role-identities, all people experience times when moving away from those identities is in order. A policeman acting sternly to a traffic violator might soften after a few moments of interaction (once he senses there will be no forthcoming resistance) and switch to a friendlier mode of communication. A composed man speaking on behalf of a lost friend at a funeral might break down and cry.

"Role distance" (Goffman, 1961b, p. 108) refers to the separateness between an individual's actions and his or her salient role-identity. It

> constitute[s] a wedge between the individual and his role, between doing and being. . . . A shorthand is involved here: the individual is actually denying not the role but the virtual self that is implied in the role for all accepting performers. (Goffman, 1961b, p. 108)

Thus the policeman, through his actions of being friendly, is denying being a policeman, and the crying man is allowing others to see his usual composure as not the real him, at least for the moment. Role distance refers to the gap between expected and actual behavior. It allows people to make "use of the 'leeway' they find in the structure to show they are not subsumed by it. 'Role distance' . . . allows individualized behavior not actually included within the realm of normative expectations" (Coser, 1966, p. 174).

Role distance as a concept is valuable in that virtually all prison humor reflects the gap between a normal (nonprison) and a convict (prison) identity. Normal refers to people holding law-abiding, mainstream values who attain a sense of worth by interacting with others similar to themselves. In normal society one might gain his or her relations of acceptance from a salient role-identity reflecting status, career, or religion.

Schmid and Jones (1991) argue that newly acquired prison identities are necessary for survival. In reference to short-term inmates, they write:

By attempting to suspend their preprison identities and constructing inauthentic prison identities through impression management, these inmates are able to forestall more radical identity change and to maintain a general sense of identity continuity for most of their prison careers. (p. 415)

Prison inmates, to acquire validation from others, develop and maintain the salient role-identity of a convict. Of significance for anyone becoming a convict is an understanding and assimilation of the informal inmate rules that govern behavior behind prison walls. Along with institutional rules all inmates are bound by an informal "inmate code" (Irwin, 1970, 1985; Mc-Corkle & Korn, 1954; Sykes & Messinger, 1960), which needs clarification before a true understanding of the culture (and the role humor plays in it) can be gained.

In the light of this inmate code or system of inmate norms, we can begin to understand the patterns of inmate behavior so frequently reported; for conformity to, or deviation from, the inmate code is the major basis for classifying and describing the social relations of prisoners. (Sykes & Messinger 1960, p. 498).

The ideal way to be in a male prison is invulnerable. Inmates project an image of fearlessness in the way they walk, talk, and socially interact. In a world where autonomy has been stripped away, these men attempt to neutralize their condition by portraying a self-image that is beyond reproach. Violation of personal boundaries is unacceptable in prison and must be dealt with according to the inmate code.

Commitment to the convict code or the identity of the convict is to a high degree a lifetime commitment to do your own time; that is to live and let live, and when you feel that someone is not letting you live, to either take it, leave, or stop him yourself, but never call for help from official agencies of control. (Irwin, 1970, p. 83)

Those who live by the inmate code and act in a manner reflecting that code as central to their self-definition have a *convict identity*.

Convicts see their world from the perspective of the code. Consequently, the rules they follow, the actions they take and the humor they use are all reflections of that outlook. In prison the relations of acceptance by others are based first and foremost on where one stands on the continuum between being a convict and being normal. Everything else follows from that. The importance of this must be emphasized. Whereas in normal society one can change roles (e.g., chaplain to Hell's Angel) and still gain respect from others, stepping outside the boundaries of the inmate code one time can shatter one's relations of acceptance in an instant.

The implicit value of the convict identity within the prison is that it acts to defuse the tension "between the home world and the institutional world" (Goffman, 1961a, p. 13). Yet there is, in nearly all inmates, a sense of what home really is. This sense of home, and what one's true identity is, can be seen by examining prison humor. Thus a convict identity, and its facilitation through humor, can be seen as nothing more than a mask that acts to keep one's normal or home identity hidden not only from the view of others but also, perhaps of even more importance, from oneself.

METHODOLOGY

Male felons with prison experience are the subject of this article. A chief resource for this project is the personal insight I have of life inside correctional facilities. Having spent roughly 12 years in county jails and state prisons in two states, I am able to depict this world from an insider perspective.

Data collection for this study began in 1994 when I was involved in a year-long sociology course. After reviewing the literature on the socialization processes of prison inmates, I realized, with the help of my adviser, that the role of humor in prison is a virtually untapped area of research. This realization, coupled with my firsthand knowledge of the importance and impact of humor in prison, was the initial cause of my decision to conduct the study.

The problem that confronted me (ironically) was that I no longer lived in prison. At this point in time I had been out more than 3 years. Nevertheless, I was still in contact with several (approximately eight) old associates who were still doing time. I also conducted weekly classes within a local county jail facility (to assist inmates in making the transition to the outside world). These two connections to the world of incarceration became my sources for data collection. Interaction with associates took place in prison visiting rooms (after which I took field notes), over the phone (conversations were taped), and through letters.

The evidence provided in this study is anecdotal and comes from a small sample of inmates. Attendance at my weekly jail classes ranged from 3 to 10 people, some of whom came on a weekly basis. Others attended two or three times, whereas some came only once. The ethnic makeup of the group varied but was, for the most part, White and Hispanic. Ages of participants ranged from the early 20s to the mid-30s. Although one regular at the meetings had served a prior prison sentence for armed robbery, most people attending the classes had relatively minor criminal backgrounds.

On average, the associates were older and had much longer histories of confinement than those attending classes. Reasons for their prison commitments ranged from murder to burglary. In addition, these inmates were housed in minimum-, medium-, and maximum-security state prison facilities. All of these individuals were Whites and Hispanics and were incarcerated in the western portion of the United States. Most important, this study deals with only the male prison culture, which, in part, reflects the male values of the socioeconomic strata from which the men were drawn. These latter items may limit the generalizability of this study.

A major value of this work is its ethnographic quality. Without having had similar experiences and a background much like those included in this study, the data would have been difficult, if not impossible, to obtain (those who share the prison experience, much like those who share a military or university background, tend to have an inherent capacity to form close bonds because of their shared experience). The communication between these inmates and me has taken place without any specific structure or format, allowing the incidents reported to unfold naturally. In many instances the humorous interactions in this project occurred as if I was actually incarcerated myself.

HUMOR AS A SECONDARY ADJUSTMENT IN PRISON

A sense of morality and decency and a need for acceptance by others are fundamental attributes of all people, including prison inmates. The need to do the right thing is inherent in being human. Failure to comply with the necessary *rules* (boundaries) of one's culture gives rise to deviance and the possibility of losing the relations of acceptance (as offered by that culture) so necessary for human survival. People are, during the course of their lifetimes, making endless adjustments relative to how they think and act, permitting a semblance of normality. The reward of being normal, in the eyes of others and, in turn, in ones own eyes, is the preservation of personal dignity.

The inmate code is the response of a population that refuses to accept society's labels. Acquisition of a convict identity lets one deny the stigma generated by the system and, instead, proclaim the worth inherent in being human. The inmate social system can be seen as a collective secondary adjustment that allows "inmates to obtain forbidden satisfactions or to obtain permitted ones by forbidden means. . . . Secondary adjustments provide the inmate with important evidence that he is still his own man, with some control of his environment" (Goffman, 1961a, pp. 54–55).

Secondary adjustments revolving around humorous social interactions in prison are instrumental in negotiating the discrepancy between normality and deviance. Specifically, they allow inmates to retain the necessary relations of acceptance essential to all people and (this of extreme significance) do so within the bounds of the inmate code.

SAD TALES AND SELF-MOCKERY

Humor functioning as a secondary adjustment to prison life tends to occur in several forms. In his study of a mental hospital, Goffman noticed that a common attribute of inmates was the *sad tale*. "The inmate tends to develop a story, a line, a sad tale—a kind of lamentation and apologia—which he constantly tells to his fellows as a means of accounting for his present low estate" (Goffman, 1961a, p. 67). Sad tales in prison are frequently told in a humorous fashion. Often, they are depicted using self-mockery. "By switching to a humorous realm individuals are seeking to effect a split between their true selves (the real) and their debased selves (the unreal) and gain absolution for the latter through laughter or ridicule" (Ungar, 1984, p. 130).

Sad tales in prison are often used to recount an inmate's sentencing. The following is a sad tale from a county jail inmate who has spent years in prison. In a letter, he wrote:

I thought I would be out right now. One of the beefs I got [crimes he was accused of] was driving on a suspended license—with five priors—but the suspension was up over four years ago—just don't have the $2000.00 it takes to get a SR-22 form from an insurance company which is what the DMV requires before re-issuing me my license. The suspension, therefore, is being mandated by my lack of funds—not any traffic violations—and upon explaining this to the judge he dismissed it out of hand as a "cop out." So I, immediately getting a little pissed off—I commenced to explain to him that if I had his politically appointed job then I would have the money to get my fucking license—but since I was just a regular type guy—not no high handed ass judge or anything—then I wasn't rolling in dough and by the way don't you know there's a depression on etc. Punk held me in contempt and gave me ninety days! Weak motherfucker should have give me six months.

The inmate's use of self mockery in this sad tale is a classic example of humor being used as a secondary adjustment to the prison environment. It is doubtful that a normal person would express himself similarly. Reference to the judge as "a weak motherfucker" for giving the inmate ninety days instead of six months in the previous tale could only be a serious statement to a lunatic.

The most fundamental attribute of the inmate's words, and one that underlies a large proportion of prison humor, is the literal denigration of the system. The entire criminal justice system, from laws on the books to police on the streets, from holding tanks inside city jails to courtrooms across the land and, finally, to the very structure of the prisons themselves, is widely known as the system. From the eyes of many prison inmates, reference to the system captures the sum of all the forces responsible for their condition of imprisonment. Understanding the underlying purpose of the humor, though, and the way in which it so obviously debases the system, provides evidence of sanity and intelligence. Through the use of humor this inmate both belittles and distances himself from the system, reinforces his convict identity and, finally, brings about a sense of solidarity with his audience.

Shared stories provide the background sound of all penal institutions. They usually revolve around some form of anger or humor. Narratives "in a jail . . . tend to be dominated by persons who are the carriers of deviant values and beliefs" (Irwin, 1985, p. 93). A large percentage of inmates are drug abusers, and though others inhabit jails, addicts and their stories are the prevailing focus of social interaction. Participation in story telling sessions has two powerful consequences. First, the individual telling a story about himself is receiving validation. Second, in the telling of the story he is reinforcing his past behavior as being okay and even admirable. Consequently, a shift in values is taking place. For example, he might tell stories of doing burglaries, which may have seemed wrong when he did them. Yet the reaction—most often laughter—he gets from the group minimizes any stigma originally attached to his deeds and validates him as being not only okay but also one of the fellas.

Drug users' stories often take the form of sad tales. During a visit, "J.D." told me about a time when he had a sizable amount of crank (methamphetamine) in his possession. He jokingly told me how he would clean his cell "four or five times a night or masturbate for hours" while looking at porno mags. He said one night he was "papering up some crank" (packaging it for distribution) when he thought he heard, "Pull the bar. Turn off the water" (which is what the guards yell out when they are going to come into your cell for a potential arrest. "Pull the bar" refers to what they do to open the cell door, and "turn off the water" means the water will be turned off so evidence (e.g., drugs) can't be flushed). He said he panicked and keystered the dope and outfit (*keystered* refers to inserting an object into the body rectally—the "outfit" is the needle and syringe). At this point, the peak of his story, in an excited tone of voice, he said, "Goddamn brother. I freaked. I dry hooped [keystered without lubrication—"the hoop" is the anus] everything and it was a bogus wire [an illusion—the guards were not coming]." By the time he got to "bogus wire" he could barely refrain from laughing. His last sentence was more or less spit out between gasps. "Ended up shittin' it back out and using it later!" By us both laughing at the telling of this story, he was able to neutralize the stigma normal people might attribute to such behavior and deny the seriousness of the situation (and his fear of getting caught). He was also able to delineate his ability to "get over on the guards" (manipulate the guards in such a way that his criminal activity remain concealed).

On another visit I heard about crack cocaine. This inmate (an addict) was convicted of robbing a bank with a note. After asking what happened to bring about his arrest, he told me he tried crack cocaine when he was "out." I asked him, "What's happening with that shit? I never tried it." He told me it was very addicting, far more addicting than heroin. Then he said, "One night on that shit and alls I needed was a pen, a notepad, and directions to the nearest bank." We both laughed. His words expressed no remorse or regret for getting caught, and, in fact, made light of the fact that he had actually robbed a bank. Being a convict and robbing banks go hand in hand. Although not all convicts are bank robbers, most bank robbers end up being prison inmates.

THE JOCULAR GRIPE

In her study of the social function of humor in a hospital setting, Coser noticed the *jocular gripe,* which she defines as "the collective expression of an individual complaint" (Coser, 1959, p. 176). The jocular gripe is the means by which personal experience, usually relative to some unpleasant situation inherent in the structure of an institution, can be humorously conveyed to others within that institution, and in doing so bring about a sense of group solidarity.

An inmate at a state prison facility writes about an event that resulted in humor being the principal agent responsible for empowering an entire cell block.

Last night we had a fog recall [forced lockdown of all men into their cells because of the security risk created by the fog]. Now, some cops took it in stride. I can see why. But, several had to use it as a forum to create an Auschwitz-like atmosphere of "comply or die." On my tier they were pouring it on heavy [attempting to maintain control] between bouts of laughter and bullshitting among themselves. So the screws [guards] were barking orders and keeping us down real good. The bimbo working our tier was straight out of a movie like "Reform School Girls"—Wendy O. Williams to the max. So since we were being treated like we were in a 1940's prison movie someone reacted. The tension was high, everybody was pissed. Bimberella starts barking some trivial shit and a guy yells "Aaahhhhhhh Shaaaaaadup!"—a perfect James Cagney, and another guy yells "Top-a-the-world-Ma!"—and everyone just started busting up. Some screw who looks like a turtle with braces on came down to "vibe" us and that just made it funnier.

Prison personnel are usually beyond attack except through the use of humor. The above tale exemplifies the jocular gripe, which "unites the group by allowing it to reinterpret together an experience that previously was individual to each" (Coser, 1959, p. 178). As each inmate sat in his cell experiencing the tension being created by the guards, he was doing so alone. The laughter that arose due to the incident was a collective response to what was, just prior to its manifestation, an individual resentment. Humor in this instance allowed the group, albeit temporarily, to be victorious over the system, and each man that laughed to regain a sense of dignity. Finally, the incident allowed the inmates to express displeasure at their treatment by the guards and do so within the domain of the convict identity by raising the specter of a genre of movies that stereotypically portrayed the inmate ideal of invulnerability.

Jocular gripes in prison help inmates maintain their dignity, although they need not be dignified. During one of my visits to a local jail I was told that during count (when inmates report to their bed areas to be counted by guards) an occurrence that commonly takes place is what I will call "insubordinate farting."[1] A standing rule exists stating all inmates must be silent until count is cleared. Violation of this requirement can result in a loss of privileges for all inmates, regardless of who breaks the rule. During count the men sit or lie on their three-tier-high bunks in silence while a guard walks up and down the dorm counting the bodies on the beds. With an expression that can be seen as nothing less than defiance, inmates will, once the guard has passed their bed area and is a safe enough distance away to insure their anonymity, fart loudly. The resulting laughter obviously mocks the guard. It also, in a safe way, attacks the system, or, in this case, the people responsible for creating the rule that all must be silent during count. It also allows the inmates to break the rules and reaffirm, at least for themselves, their own power.

The jocular gripe also confirms the convict identity. Those who understand the complaint also understand the resentment that gave rise to it, as the following example illustrates.

During phone conversations from inmates in the California Department of Corrections, which can only be made by calling collect from the prison, the accepting party is told the call is from a California state prison and may be recorded. Recently a new feature was added. Now a recording comes on the line every few minutes interrupting the conversation to, apparently, remind the person accepting the call the location of the caller. Before the recording comes on the line, you hear a few buzzing sounds. Next comes a robot-like voice exclaiming, "This is a call from a California state prison."

During one conversation, the buzzing sound came on the line (for the second or third time—both parties can hear it). As the message was about to play, my friend said, "These cocksuckers." (Now the message played. "This is a call from a California state prison.") He continued, "Bet you didn't know that til they told ya', did ya?" I answered, "No. I didn't. Gives me a feeling of intimacy though. Know what I mean? Reminds me of how I used to tell the hacks thanks everytime they came by to count me. I'd tell 'em, 'Thanks man, uh, I like motherfuckers like you checkin' on me every once in awhile makin' sure I'm okay.'" My friend responded (by now we're both laughing), "Yeah [as if he is talking to a guard], and maybe next time you come by I'll be in the middle of jackin' [masturbating]." This interchange allowed us to complain about the situation without admitting that we were powerless to change it. Further, by responding with my story about thanking the guards for checking on me, I made the difference between us (convicts) and them (guards) very clear. To top off the interaction, my friend expressed his contempt for "them" with his hypothetical story of masturbation.

Masturbation often is included in prison humor. The inability to participate in normal sexual relations can be addressed by inmates via the jocular gripe. They can subtly complain about their circumstances without harming their convict identity. In the following phone call, the inmate transforms a sign of his own vulnerability into an act of defiance.

SB: Been hot up here lately. At count time the other night I'm layin' up there on my rack [bed]. I threw all the fuckin' blankets off me down by my feet. Had a hard-on standin' straight to the sky [at this I started laughing]. Cop came by [he is holding back his laughter] to count, man, and he fuckin' did a double take, homes [we were both laughing now].
CT: You got busted, huh?
SB: Oh, shit. I don't give a fuck. Hell, I walk down the tier like that goin' to the shitter [bathroom].
CT: Well, what're ya' gonna do?
SB: What can I do? Call on Lorena Bobbitt?

This conversation glorifies fearlessness. Overcoming one's inhibitions and verbally declaring a lack of caring (especially about what a guard thinks) coincides perfectly with the salient role-identity of convict.

EXPRESSING PAIN AND MASCULINITY

Some inmates use their time in prison to prepare for the day when sex with a woman may be possible. As well as increasing an image of invulnerability and toughness, weight lifting and other physical exercises, for example, are used to improve looks and probably lessen anxiety resulting from the lack of women.

Many inmates take pride in their bodies. Those that exercise regularly are constantly bantering among themselves about their physiques, strength, and imaginary invulnerability. In a prison visiting room, I was standing in line with my friend to get to a vending machine when he said, "Feel this homeboy." He gestured toward his stomach—hard from hours of exercise. "I need all that so when Sally [fictitious name for his overweight girlfriend] gets on top I don't cave in." Another example of body pride is found in this letter from an associate for whom I had sent a photograph.

I got your picture and I see that you're still as ugly as ever. Ha! I will get a picture to you soon so that you'll see that I still look like a Greek God! I'm gonna have the bitches feinting [sic]. Ha! Well, I see the parole board next month. After going to IMU (a hole within a hole) [a segregation unit within a segregation unit, all located within a maximum security prison] for a year, a parole is doubtful. I'll probably end up doing 20. I have 16 in. Oh well. That just means I'll look like Mr. Olympia when I leave.

In a very few words, all safely made via the use of humor (his reference to being a "Greek God" and "Mr. Olympia"), this man expressed his pain as best he could ("a parole is doubtful") and reinforced his masculinity ("I'm gonna have the bitches feinting"), leaving his salient role-identity of convict firmly intact.

DISTINGUISHING BOUNDARIES AND SUPERIORITY THROUGH MOCKERY

Humor can be used to define boundaries (Davies, 1982) and establish a sense of superiority (Davies, 1990; Freud, 1960; Keith-Spiegal, 1972). In prison, mockery serves as a humorous tool whereby moral and social boundaries are defined, often at the expense of individuals or groups perceived as being lower in status by those instigating the laughter. The proper way to be in prison is seldom explicitly defined, yet the way not to be is made clear during humorous interactions. For example, during a telephone conversation, I asked an inmate who had recently been transferred to a new facility what it was like at his new home. He told me, "Over where I'm at there's a lotta weirdos—Chester lookin' motherfuckers [sex-offenders]—I don't talk to too many of them. Alls we do is laugh at those dudes. You know how it is." By understanding that "Chester lookin' motherfuckers" are suspected sex-offenders and unworthy of respect, it is obvious that sex-offenders in prison are not okay.[2]

In an attempt to collect data for this project, I asked an inmate to tell me what he and his friends laugh about. He responded, "Remember the inmate who never knew where the hell he was and didn't appear to have any hope of finding out? 'Sir, someone took my toothpaste.' 'Sir, my sweatshirt isn't in my locker anymore.'" These words are unmistakably referring to a normal person. Calling a guard "sir," let alone telling him something has been stolen, are blatant violations of the inmate code. Again, exposure to this type of humor will accentuate what is okay and what is not okay in the culture for anyone not aware of the rules. Mocking others through the use of humor strengthens social bonds, defines boundaries, allows feelings to be expressed, and acts as a weapon of attack. Mocking others allows inmates to establish superiority over out-groups and negotiate the difference in the gap between being a convict and being a normal person. Further, it helps define who has a convict identity. Those that get the joke have already learned the norms of the role. The following personal example further illustrates this point.

Recently I went to the local jail facility where I counsel a weekly group. After checking in at the desk, putting on my visitor badge, and meeting up with a couple of the guys that participate in my group, I was told by the guard to go ahead and proceed to the school room. He told me he would announce my presence to the facility. To get to the school room, it is necessary to leave one building and, after walking outside for a few yards, enter the school room. While outside, I noticed some inmates lounging in a yard. At that moment, over the P.A. system, the guard announced, "Anyone wishing to attend Chuck Terry's Transition to the Streets Class report to the front desk." To my surprise I saw the men break into laughter.

The laughter generated by the announcement of my class can be seen as a secondary adjustment that both defines boundaries and brings about a sense of superiority to those that laughed. The fact that it was made by a guard (representative of the system) caused whatever was said to be under immediate suspicion. By admitting a need to learn how to make the "transition to the streets," one would be exhibiting weakness. By hearing the announcement without laughing (when everyone else in the group laughed), or even worse, by actually attending the class, an inmate would be admitting a need for help—behavior outside the norms of the convict identity.

Humorous Language and Identity Building

Prison inmates have developed a distinct dialect[3] that contrasts the normal to the institutional world of incarceration. Typically full of profanity and slang words not understandable to outsiders, it is often communicated within a humorous context. "Language itself is used as a secondary adjustment in prison" (Goffman, 1961a, p. 316).

Many things, such as games, are renamed, redefined, and spoken of in a humorous prisonized fashion. An inmate told me how the game horseshoes is played. In normal horseshoes, a thrown shoe left leaning (a *leaner*) on the pole is worth two points. Yet this version is different. While playing "felony shoes," a person seeking credit for a leaner would be told, "the only place leaners are cool are at family picnics and family reunions." He also mentioned "felony monopoly" where humor was used to make transactions relative to the game. Inmates often refer to sports they play as, for example, five to life basketball or five to life football. The rules of such games are often changed to coincide with the culture.

In another letter, language is used in a humorous manner to criminalize or prisonize what might elsewhere be called "girl watching."

Have you watched any of the Olympics? The ice skating is pretty popular here. Nothing like a high split in a skimpy outfit. Actually, there's a couple of females [guards] here that aren't too bad in their loose county uniforms. Of course that could be time talking. I've got to be careful or I might catch a reckless eyeballing beef.

Further, prison inmates often rename themselves, as this letter illustrates.

We have pet names, usually based on what a person looks like. The Cryptkeeper from HBO's "Tales from the Crypt." Beavis from "Beavis and Butthead." Fat Albert, Shirley Temple, Opie, Barney Fife, etc. etc. We got 'em all. We have two three hundred pounders who look alike in more ways than one. They pull beanies over their faces and have Sumo wrestling matches. Wide Glide and Wide Glide Jr. Hard to tell 'em apart with beanies over their faces. Wide Glide says he has crack, but Wide Glide Jr. has San Andreas Fault. Earth shaking fun. Sometimes we laugh at the cops and sometimes with 'em, but all in all we don't play with the man [the guards] too much. We clown the skinny ones when they walk by the weight pile. Of course we have pet names for them too. Big Bird, Sweet Pea, Gomer Pyle, Barney Fife, etc.

Sometimes the names reflect the image of the convict. Often they depict personal characteristics. Of interest here is the way language is used, often with humorous connotations, to define identity and to place individuals into specific groups.

The use of language in prison, then, is instrumental in building and maintaining a convict identity. Becoming familiar with prison jargon and, in turn, exhibiting that familiarity are beneficial in creating an image that, to others, is worthy of respect. As with all social interaction among prison inmates, language, to these ends, is often expressed humorously.

There is some speculation that behavior in prison may be changing. One victim of the ever increasing number of individuals being sent to prison may be the convict identity itself. For example, older inmates often mentioned that prisoner informants (snitches) were rare in the 1950s. The situation, however, may be changing as new inmate types (e.g., addicts, white-collar criminals) are being convicted and sent to prison. In a letter from prison, an inmate uses humor to complain about ways the system is changing. He begins by answering what I had told him about how things used to be.

I had to laugh at your "buying a job," man. You must go back to the stone age when cons were cons. Nowadays its a bunch of take kindness for weakness, disrespectful, shine-the-cops-boots, punk ass inmates . . . and no one in blue [the inmates] is running jack shit. I have a few older acquaintances in here that remember it like you do . . . but its not that way anymore, especially here at this place where inmates trample each other to get to the telling office [location of where one goes to inform on others] first. But then its absolutely no different from "Crime Stoppers" and "We Tip" and all that civilian do gooder stuff out there. So, actually, its more like the streets nowadays in prison than like . . . well, like prison.

The behavior of trampling to "the telling office" (informing on others) is not okay for a convict. His analogy of those that tell on the "inside" and "Crime Stoppers" and "all that civilian do gooder stuff out there" offers insight into how humor is used to define the informal, moral boundaries of the inmate value system and how that system, at least in part, has been weakened.

DISCUSSION

During one of my many editing sessions for this article, I found myself in a room with a man who served approximately 10 months in a California Department of Corrections facility. Being roughly 50 years old, college educated, and having served time only once in his life (in his 40s), he (I'll call him Joe) was, in my view, the epitome of what I referred to in this article as a normal person. Recognizing this, I immediately thought that Joe (because of his normality) probably did not laugh much in prison. I asked, "Joe, when you were in prison, did you notice people laughing all the time?" He answered, "Oh yeah. All you ever heard was 'ha-ha this' and 'ha-ha that' all day long wherever you went. It was as if everyone in there was acting out these stupid, fake roles."

Whereas many inmates are able to use humor as a principal adaptational and coping technique, there are others who cannot. Those that are unfamiliar with the prison culture and unable to adapt to it view their prison experiences from a normal perspective. They typically look at convicts as deviant. Convicts, on the other hand, see normal inmates as deviant and often use them as the butt of their laughter. Normal inmates, although unable to experience prison as a convict does, find other normal people to associate with and, thus, retain their dignity in a manner consistent with mainstream values. Normal inmates do not accept the convict identity and therefore have no need to manage the gap common to other inmates. Consequently, they have no need to participate in the everyday humorous interaction so characteristic of convicts.

The prison environment is unique due to its strict guidelines relative to moral boundaries. The social system of male prisons revolves around the inmate code and the need to project invulnerability. This is a natural effect of the system, which, after labeling inmates deviant, treats them in a degrading and humiliating fashion. Although much of being a convict revolves around a criminal orientation, its reward is a sense of self-worth and integrity that would otherwise be impossible to attain in the prison culture.

Few prison inmates are, in reality, invulnerable. Even though a convict identity is the ideal, most men retain some normal values and, thus, fall somewhere between being normal and being a convict. Few are so fearless and beyond pain that they are incapable of experiencing uncertainty, fear, and a sense that they are in a deplorable situation. Nevertheless, such normal feelings can never be openly expressed. To do so would be inconsistent with being a convict. Yet they can and are expressed through humor.

Humor, then, is a major social instrument used by prison inmates to manage the gap between a normal and a convict identity. Prison humor is instrumental in allowing successive adjustments to take place whereby a normal role-identity can be suppressed while a convict identity can simultaneously be formed, nurtured, and played out. Humor acts to bridge the gap for convicts between the two contrasting worlds; the world outside prison walls and the world within.

NOTES

1. My thanks to Harvey Molotch for the phrase.
2. Whereas normal people are seen as deviant by convicts, they are treated well compared to those that are known violators of the inmate code (e.g., snitches,

sex-offenders). Unlike normal people, who are often able to show some degree of pride in the way they carry themselves, these cultural pariahs not only seldom laugh, they look and act miserable most of the time.

3. For an extensive listing of prison jargon, see Freeman (1984, pp. 479–543).

REFERENCES

ANDERSON, E. (1976). *A place on the corner*. Chicago: University of Chicago Pres.

CALLERO, P. L. (1985). Role-identity salience. *Social Psychology Quarterly, 48*(3),203–215.

CARROL, J. L. & SHMIDT, J. L. (1992). Correlation between humorous coping style and health. *Psychological Reports, 70*(2), 402.

CLEMMER, D. (1940). *The prison community*. Boston: Christopher.

COSER, R. L. (1959). Some social functions of laughter: A study of humor in a hospital setting. *Human Relations, 12*(2),171–182.

COSER, R. L. (1966). Role distance, sociological ambivalence, and transitional status systems. *American Journal of Sociology, 72*(2), 173–187.

DAVIDHIZAR, R., and BOWEN, M. (1992). The dynamics of laughter. *Archives of Psychiatric Nursing, 6*(2), 132–137.

DAVIES, C. (1982). Ethnic jokes, moral values and social boundaries. *The British Journal of Sociology, 33*(3), 383–403.

DAVIES, C. (1990). *Ethnic humor around the world: A comparative analysis*. Bloomington: Indiana University Press.

DAVIS, M. S. (1993). *What's so funny? The comic conception of culture and society*. Chicago: University of Chicago Press.

FREEMAN, I. C. (1984). *The joint: Language and culture in a maximum security prison*. Springfield, IL: Charles C Thomas.

FREUD, S. (1960). *Jokes and their relations to the unconscious* (Vol. 8 of *Complete psychological works*). London: Hogarth.

GOFFMAN, E. (1961a). *Asylums: Essays on the social situation of mental patients and other inmates*. New York: Doubleday.

GOFFMAN, E. (1961b). *Encounters: Two studies in the sociology of interaction*. Indianapolis: Bobbs-Merrill.

IRWIN, J. (1970). *The felon*. Englewood Cliffs, NJ: Prentice Hall.

IRWIN, J. (1985). *The jail: Managing the underclass in American society*. Berkeley: University of California Press.

IRWIN, J., & CRESSEY, D. (1962). Thieves, convicts and the inmate culture. *Social Problems, 10*,142–155.

KANTER, R. M. (1977). *Men and women of the corporation*. New York: Basic Books.

KEITH-SPIEGEL, P. (1972). Early conceptions of humor: Varieties and issues. In J. H. Goldstein & P. E. McGhee (eds.), *The psychology of humor* (pp. 3–39). New York: Academic Press.

MARTIN, R. A., KUIPER, N.A., & OLINGER, J. L. (1993). Humor, coping with stress, self-concept, and psychological well-being. *Humor International Journal of Humor Research, 6*(1), 89–104.

MCCORKLE, W. L., & KORN, R. (1954). Resocialization within prison walls. *The Annals of the American Academy of Political and Social Science, 293*, 88–98.

MORREAL, J. (1991). Humor and work. *Humor International Journal of Humor Research, 4*(3), 359–373.

OVERHOLSER, J. C. (1992). Sense of humor when coping with life stress. *Personality and Individual Differences, 13*(7), 799–804.

SCHMID, S. J., & JONES, J. S. (1991). Suspended identity: Identity transformation in a maximum security prison. *Symbolic Interaction, 14*(4),415–432.

SYKES, G. M., & MESSINGER, S. L. (1976). The inmate social system. In A. L. Guenther (Ed.), *Criminal behavior and social systems: Contributions of American sociology* (pp. 496–510). Chicago: Rand McNally.

UNGAR, S. (1984). Self-mockery: An alternative form of self-presentation. *Symbolic Interaction, 7*(1), 121–133.

ZAMBLE, E., & PORPORINO, F. (1988). *Coping, behavior, and adaptation in prison inmates*. New York: Springer-Verlag.

ZIJDERVELD, A. C. (1968). Jokes and their relation to social reality. *Social Research, 35*(2), 286–311.

INCARCERATION AS A DEVIANT FORM
OF SOCIAL CONTROL*

Henry N. Pontell and Wayne N. Welsh**

Over the past decade, the use of incarceration has increased dramatically as witnessed by population explosions in the nation's prisons and jails. The average daily jail population rose from 157,930 inmates in 1978 to 395,553 in 1989 (U.S. Department of Justice 1990), whereas the number of inmates in state and federal prisons increased from 329,821 in 1980 to 771,243 in 1990 (Associated Press 1991). Much attention typically focuses on burgeoning prison populations that house society's most serious criminals. Until their recent overcrowding problems, less attention has been given to jails, which are more numerous than prisons and more local in nature. In many jurisdictions, jails have become such brutal places to house people that judges have ordered, among other things, that they not be allowed to exceed a set population capacity. Moreover, in an effort to keep pace with what is perceived as the public's desire to equate punishment with incarceration, legislatures have approved massive funds for constructing additional facilities, despite the fact that projections show that such construction will not alleviate crowding if past trends in incarcerative policies and crime rates continue.

Overcrowded jails create a host of problems for formal social control efforts that are not easily dealt with by correctional administrators, legislators, or criminal justice officials. As Briar (1983) has pointed out:

Considered bastions of community neglect, these overcrowded, understaffed maximum security structures subject both those confined—as well as their keepers—to an array of personal indignities and life-threatening conditions unparalleled in other institutions in this country. Described as "scandalous" and "ultimate ghettos," conditions in many of these institutions are generally forced upon public purview only with the occurrence of suicides, strangulations, gang rapes, fires, escapes, and lawsuits. Yet once official assurances have been issued that crises have abated, concern subsides and previous patterns of operation may ensue. (p. 387)

A "crisis mentality" on the part of administrators and policy makers is not likely to produce effective solutions to problems in criminal justice (Feeley 1983; Sherman and Hawkins 1983). Yet the system continues its movement from one crisis to the next, and a more recent one is that of overincarceration and the resulting severe strain on penal resources.

The rise of the prisoner's rights movement in the 1970s has been accompanied by numerous court orders against prison and jail systems throughout the country. Such orders have mandated population "caps" or limits, as well as improvements in conditions of confinement, including specific changes in the internal environments of these institutions. In 1989, 31% of the nation's large jails were under court order to improve conditions of confinement (U.S. Department of Justice 1990), whereas one or more state prisons in 41 states experienced court intervention (National Prison Project 1990). These developments, coupled with scarce resources to build enough facilities have created a major roadblock for legislative efforts designed to punish with more certainty and severity. In fact it could be reasonably argued that a latent function of the "get tough

*From Henry N. Pontell and Wayne N. Welsh, *Crime and Delinquency,* vol. 40, no. 1, pp. 18–36, copyright © 1994 by Sage Publications, Inc. Reprinted by permission of Sage Publications, Inc.

**This research was supported by grants from the Committee on Research, Academic Senate, University of California, Irvine, the Guggenheim Program in Criminal Justice, Boalt Hall School of Law, University of California, Berkeley, and by a fellowship from the Social Sciences and Humanities Research Council of Canada. The authors thank Matt Leone, Patrick Kinkade, and Jack Pederson for their research assistance.

movement" (Cullen, Clark, and Wozniak 1985) has been to quicken the pace by which it becomes apparent that the capacity of the criminal justice system to punish violators is limited by a range of political, economic, social, and legal forces that cannot be easily manipulated or fully anticipated by legislative changes (Pontell 1984).

Moreover, research suggests a direct connection between prison and jail overcrowding and that progressive reforms have been used primarily as "safety-valve institutions," relieving the pressure created by legislative actions designed to enhance the severity and certainty of punishment (Rothman 1980; Sutton 1987). For example, Rothman (1980) has argued that the reforms of probation, parole, and indeterminate sentencing arose through the interplay between "conscience and convenience." Conscience was evident in the ideology of progressive reformers who believed that criminals could be rehabilitated into productive members of society. The specific reforms adopted, however, were largely a reflection of administrative convenience, as they functioned to increase official discretion in handling offenders and supplemented efficient processing and control of inmates. Similarly, as Sutton (1987) points out in his empirical study of imprisonment in the United States, incarceration rates were most closely tied to the manner in which officials used their discretionary authority to control flows of inmates through institutions. His analysis suggests that reforms were used to give authorities increased discretion to release inmates where prison and jail systems were expanding the fastest. He notes:

Jail capacities were influenced by probation legislation, which increased discretion over rates of admission, and by indeterminate sentencing, which probably encouraged faster releases. The effect of indeterminate sentencing was also strongest where jails were most expansive. It appears that reforms were used to contain explosive growth and relieve overcrowding. . . . In particular, the findings of this study imply that local jails supplemented the limited capacity of centralized prison systems, especially in urban areas. (Sutton 1987, pp. 626–27)

Research on jails has concentrated on a number of areas including the evolution of jails (Flynn 1983; Goldfarb 1975; Irwin 1985), problems such as overcrowding (Advisory Commission 1984; Flynn 1983; Pontell, Welsh, Leone, and Kinkade 1989; Welsh, Pontell, Leone, and Kinkade 1990; Welsh, Leone, Kinkade and Pontell 1991) and litigation issues (Feeley and Hanson 1986; Taft 1983; Welsh and Pontell 1991). Little systematic research exists, however, regarding the detailed accounting of the number and types of violations alleged in complaints against jail facilities and how courts have responded to them.

Overcrowded jails and subsequent court orders against them can involve broad consequences, far beyond the boundaries of these institutions themselves. For example, the large proportion of county and state budgets that needs to be devoted to corrections negatively impacts funds available for health, education, and welfare (California Legislative Analyst 1987). At the same time, the "common knowledge" that crime is increasing, or that our need to punish is increasing, is at best questionable (Clear and Harris 1987). Further, strong signals by the courts that overcrowded and inhumane conditions of incarceration will not be tolerated, combined with fiscal realities, inevitably limit the potential effectiveness of sim-ple "get tough" legislative proposals calling for harsher punishments in response to increased crime (Austin and McVey 1989). In short, court intervention in corrections may have far-reaching impacts that result in structural limits on the ability to employ punishment as a major solution to the crime problem and, more specifically, on the use of incarceration as a major form of punishment.

Jail overcrowding has already resulted in a relatively "elite" criminal being detained prior to trial, and both pretrial and sentenced-prisoner release options are extremely limited in many jurisdictions. Given the reluctance of communities to accept new jail construction in their midst (Welsh, Leone, Kinkade, and Pontell 1991), as well as severely limited local financial resources (Welsh 1990), jail administrators will be increasingly hard-pressed to regulate jail populations by simply building new facilities.

One major difficulty in fostering changes and producing less costly alternatives to overincarceration and expensive court suits is the fact that the public is not wont to support anything but victims' rights and that any support for the rights of criminals (or in the case of pretrial detainees, the rights of suspected criminals) would only be met by political disaster for legislators and other elected officials. Thus it is extraordinarily difficult to ensure decent conditions, especially under the conservative and mostly reactionary vision of the role of criminal justice and criminal punishment over the past decade (Advisory Commission 1984; Busher 1983; Cullen, Clark, and Wozniak 1985). The legislative-political process is proving itself to be impotent if not ultimately destructive, with the possible exception of approving funds for new construction.

There are, however, serious difficulties with approaches that rely on constructing new facilities, which render them extremely problematic. The costs of construction are extremely high, as are the operating costs of jails once they are built. The extremely high cost necessarily means that other social programs will suffer. There also is a long time lag between current problems and the potential opening of new facilities. There is also no guarantee, nor any body of systematic scientific evidence, that shows that when such new facilities are opened they will solve the overcrowding problem.

Nonetheless, many observers seem to agree that there is a great ability to expand the capacity to punish. Indeed, through the passage of laws that alter sentences and allocate or create new public funds, legislatures can manipulate schemes that attempt to control and to punish. It is perhaps stating the obvious, however, to say that forms of punishment are in fact limited by political, legal, economic, and cultural restraints (Newman 1978). There is some threshold at which it becomes necessary for changes to occur in forms of punishment when its use rises above manageable proportions, and when resulting crises in legitimacy require new social control practices. Foucault (1979) argues a similar idea when he notes that penal ceremonies, public tortures, and corporal punishments diminished in Europe 200 years ago because civilization had reached a point where these forms were considered too brutal to send the proper message to the public. Punishment then took on a more

ideological function, with its form changing to that of incarceration. Legislatures have not yet dropped incarceration as a major means of punishment, but their desire to expand its certainty and severity is thwarted by fiscal realities that face the state. A latent result is that selectivity in the use of incarceration increases as the state wrestles with problems associated with limited resources, and with what constitutes "legitimate punishment." As a consequence, the state inevitably fails to keep the public "promise" of more certain, swift, and severe criminal sanctions.

The manner in which this actually occurs in the criminal justice system is through the use of discretion, an institutional element that is essential to the functioning of the justice system itself. "Law" mandates that discretion exist in the criminal justice system, whereas "laws" designed to limit or do away with it, simply dislodge it to other parts of the system. For example, determinate sentencing laws aimed at reducing judicial discretion may simply result in an increase in the discretionary power of district attorneys (McCoy 1984) or move it from prison and parole authorities to judges and prosecutors (Casper, Brereton, and Neal 1981). As Sutton (1987) among others has suggested, criminal justice reforms may serve multiple manifest and latent functions. The analysis presented here has attempted to explicate the role of jails in responding to various legal changes regarding the manner in which formal social control takes place.

The "production of social control" is not a process that is merely dictated by the state. The overall ability of the state to expand its punishment capacity may vary over time, but the forms by which it attempts to accomplish this are limited by political, legal, and economic restraints. A study of the repression of ghetto riots by Balbus (1977), for example, showed that short-term expansions of local criminal justice system capacity were possible to restore public order, but that the vast majority of those arrested in police sweeps were released soon thereafter to avoid further exacerbation of already strained conditions in city courts and jails. Punishment theorists such as Rusche and Kirchheimer (1939) and Foucault (1979), as well as many legal authorities today, have viewed the "production of punishment" as a result of factors external to the legal system itself. The more we rely on the criminal justice system to control the population, the more resources it will attract, and the more unwieldy it is likely to become as it is pressured by the very social problems it was meant to control. In short, it appears that the use of imprisonment as an instrument of "normalization" is limited (Foucault 1979). That social control agents are held in contempt of court orders epitomizes the futility in responding to complex social problems through attempts to increase imprisonment. Over time, the legal system has turned on itself, labeling its own use of incarceration as "deviant" when punishment practices become so extreme as to threaten the very legitimacy of the punishment system itself.

Essential research in the area of correctional overcrowding includes much more than merely focusing on emergency plans to reduce inmate populations. In the current stampede toward nonincarcerative intermediate sanctions, policy makers have lost sight of the very factors that precipitated their widespread adoption in the first place. Such factors include an overreliance on incarceration as a means of social control, and recognition by the courts of deviant institutional conditions that resulted from short-sighted, politically motivated correctional policy. Continued failure to factor the jail overcrowding problem into valid causes and corresponding policy choices is likely to lead to more poorly planned and ineffective solutions (Welsh et al. 1990) that supplement official discretion but leave underlying social problems and their causes untouched (Irwin 1985).

As Feeley (1983) has noted in regard to court reform:

There is little incentive for those engaged in day-to-day administration of criminal courts to think about systemwide changes or, when they do, to pursue them vigorously. But when change comes, as we have seen, it is often initiated by "dramatic events" and offered as a "bold solution" that is promoted as a panacea. Such conditions do not give rise to serious thinking or realistic expectations. (p. 192)

Feeley (1983) outlines the reasons for this dilemma in what he identifies as the problems of crisis thinking, lack of historical perspective, the

inevitability of crisis thinking, and the fallacy of formalism. What Feeley notes for courts is likely to hold true for correctional institutions as well. Building more facilities and adopting a variety of intermediate sanctions have been offered as bold solutions to what has been interpreted as a major crisis in incarceration. Whether this can alter the present growth of deviant punishment systems is something that remains to be seen.

REFERENCES

Advisory Commission. 1984. *Jails: Intergovernmental Dimensions of a Local Problem.* Washington, DC: Advisory Commission on Intergovernmental Relations.

Associated Press. 1991. "U.S. Prison Population Up 8.2 Percent to 771,243." *Philadelphia Inquirer,* May 16, p. 19B.

AUSTIN, JAMES and AARON DAVID McVEY. 1989. *The 1989 NCCD Prison Population Forecast: The Impact of the War on Drugs.* San Francisco: National Council on Crime and Delinquency.

BALBUS, ISAAC D. 1977. *The Dialectics of Legal Repression: Black Rebels before the American Criminal Courts.* New York: Transaction Books.

BRIAR, KATHERINE HOOPER. 1983. "Jails: Neglected Asylums." *Social Casework* 64:387–93.

BUSHER, WALTER. 1983. *Jail Overcrowding: Identifying Causes and Planning for Solutions.* Washington, DC: Office of Justice Assistance, Research and Statistics.

California Legislative Analyst. 1987. *Analysis of the 1987–88 Budget Bill.* Report to the Joint Legislative Budget Committee. Sacramento: State of California.

CASPER, JONATHAN D., DAVID BRERETON, and DAVID NEAL. 1981. *The Implementation of the California Determinate Sentence Law.* Washington, DC: National Institute of Justice.

CLEAR, TODD R. and PATRICIA M. HARRIS. 1987 "The Costs of Incarceration." Pp. 37–55 in *America's Correctional Crisis,* edited by D. Gottfredson and S. McConville. Westport, CT: Greenwood.

CULLEN, FRANCIS T., GREGORY A. CLARK, and JOHN F. WOZNIAK. 1985. "Explaining the Get Tough Movement: Can the Public Be Blamed?" *Federal Probation* 49:16–24.

FEELEY, MALCOLM M. 1983. *Court Reform on Trial: Why Simple Solutions Fail.* New York: Basic Books.

FEELEY, MALCOLM M. and ROGER P. HANSON. 1986. "What We Know, Think We Know and Would

Like to Know about the Impact of Court Orders on Prison Conditions and Jail Crowding." Presented at the Meeting of the Working Group on Jail and Prison Crowding, Committee on Research on Law Enforcement and the Administration of Justice, National Academy of Sciences, Chicago, IL.

FLYNN, EDITH E. 1983. "Jails." Pp. 915–22 in *Encyclopedia of Crime and Justice,* edited by S. H. Kadish. New York: Macmillan.

FOUCAULT, MICHEL. 1979. *Discipline and Punish: The Birth of the Prison.* New York: Vintage.

GOLDFARB, RONALD. 1975. *Jails.* Garden City, NY: Anchor.

IRWIN, JOHN. 1985. *The Jail: Managing the Underclass in American Society.* Berkeley: University of California Press.

McCOY, CANDACE. 1984. "Determinate Sentencing, Plea Bargaining Bans, and Hydraulic Discretion in California." *Justice System Journal* 9:256–75.

National Prison Project. 1990. "Status Report: State Prisons and the Courts." *Journal of the National Prison Project* 22:7–8, 14–17, 20.

NEWMAN, GRAEME. 1978. *The Punishment Response.* Philadelphia: J. B. Lippincott.

Orange County Administrative Office. 1986. *Systems Approach to Jail Crowding in Orange County.* Prepared for the Board of Supervisors, Orange County, CA.

PONTELL, HENRY N. 1984. *A Capacity to Punish: The Ecology of Crime and Punishment.* Bloomington: Indiana University Press.

PONTELL, HENRY N., WAYNE N. WELSH, MATTHEW LEONE, and Patrick Kinkade. 1989. "Prescriptions for Punishment: Official Ideologies and Jail Overcrowding." *American Journal of Criminal Justice* 14:43–70.

ROTHMAN, DAVID J. 1980. *Conscience and Convenience: The Asylum and Its Alternatives in Progressive America.* Boston: Little, Brown.

RUSCHE, GEORG and OTTO KIRCHHEIMER. 1939. *Punishment and Social Structure.* New York: Russell and Russell.

SHERMAN, MICHAEL and GORDON HAWKINS. 1983. *Imprisonment in America.* Chicago: University of Chicago Press.

SUTTON, JOHN R. 1987. "Doing Time: The Dynamics of Imprisonment in the Reformist State." *American Sociological Review* 52:612–30.

TAFT, PHILIP B., JR. 1983. "Jail Litigation: Winning in Court Is Only Half the Battle." *Corrections Magazine* 9:22–27, 30–31.

U.S. Department of Justice, Bureau of Justice Statistics. 1990. *Jail Inmates 1989.* Bulletin NCJ-123264. Washington, DC: U.S. Department of Justice.

WELSH, WAYNE N. 1990. "The Impact of Jail Litigation on County Financial Expenditures." Paper presented at the Annual Meeting of the American Society of Criminology, November, Baltimore.

WELSH, WAYNE N., MATTHEW C. LEONE, PATRICK T. KINKADE, and HENRY N. PONTELL. 1991. "The Politics of Jail Overcrowding: Public Attitudes and Official Policies." Pp. 131–47 in *American Jails: Public Policy Issues,* edited by J. Thompson and G. L. Mays. Chicago: Nelson-Hall.

WELSH, WAYNE N. and HENRY N. PONTELL. 1991. "Counties in Court: Interorganizational Adaptations to Jail Litigation in California." *Law and Society Review* 25:73–101.

WELSH, WAYNE N., HENRY N. PONTELL, MATTHEW C. LEONE, and PATRICK T. KINKADE. 1990. "Jail Overcrowding: An Analysis of Policymaker Perceptions." *Justice Quarterly* 7:341–70.

THE BEHAVIOR OF THE SYSTEMATIC CHECK FORGER*

Edwin M. Lemert

The concept of behavior systems in crime was first approximated in this country in Hall's analysis of several types of larceny in terms of their historical, legal, and social contexts. (15) Later the concept was made explicit and formulated into a typology by Sutherland and by Sutherland and Cressey. (32, 34, 21, 26, 14, 4, pp. 579–589) Although this has hitherto inspired only a few monographic studies, there seems to be a growing consensus that focusing attention on specific orders of crime or making behavior systems the unit of study holds considerable promise for criminological research. (27, p. 134)

Because this paper proposes to assess the usefulness of Sutherland's formulation of the behavior system in analyzing or understanding the behavior of the systematic check forger, the typology outlined in his study of the professional thief will be employed. The five elements of the behavior system of the thief are as follows: (1) stealing is made a regular business; (2) every act is carefully planned, including the use of the "fix"; (3) technical skills are used, chiefly those of manipulating people; this differentiates the thief from other professional criminals; (4) the thief is migratory but uses a specific city as a headquarters; (5) the thief has criminal associations involving acquaintances, congeniality, sympathy, understandings, rules, codes of behavior, and a special language. (31, 32, 6, pp. 256–262, 27, 5, Ch. V, 10, Ch. IV, 23, 37)

Altogether seventy-two persons currently serving sentences for check forgery and writing checks with insufficient funds were studied. Three additional check offenders were contacted and interviewed outside of prison. The sample included eight women and sixty-seven men, all of whom served time in California correctional institutions.

*© 1958 by The Society for the Study of Social Problems. Reprinted from *Social Problems,* 6, (Fall, 1958), pp. 141–149 by permission of the author and the publisher.

Thirty of the seventy-five check criminals could be classified as systematic in the sense that they (1) thought of themselves as check men; (2) had worked out or regularly employed a special technique of passing checks; (3) had more or less organized their lives around the exigencies or imperatives of living by means of fraudulent checks. The remaining forty-five cases represented a wide variety of contexts in which bogus check passing was interspersed with periods of stable employment and family life, or was simply an aspect of alcoholism, gambling, or one of a series of criminal offenses having little or no consistency.

FINDINGS

Projected against the typology of professional theft, the behavior of the person falling into the systematic check forgery category qualified only in a very general way as professional crime. In other words, although it is possible to describe these forgeries as *systematic,* it is questionable whether more than a small portion of them can be subsumed as *professional* under the more general classification of professional theft. A point-by-point comparison will serve to bring out the numerous significant differences between systematic forgery and professional theft.

1. *Forgery as a "regular business."* It is questionable whether check men look upon their crimes as a "regular business" in the same way as do members of "other occupational groups" who "wish to make money in safety." (34, p. 240) In virtually all cases the motivation proved to be exceedingly complex. This fact was self-consciously recognized and expressed in different ways but all informants revealed an essential perplexity or conflict about their criminal behavior. The following statement may be taken as illustrative:

Nine out of ten check men are lone wolves. Those men who work in gangs are not real check men. They do it for money; we do it for something else. It gives us something we need. Maybe we're crazy. . . .

The conflicts expressed involved not merely the rightness or wrongness of behavior; they also disclosed a confusion and uncertainty as to the possibility of living successfully or safely by issuing false checks. All of the cases, even the few who had a history of professional thieving, admitted that arrest and imprisonment are inevitable. None knew of exceptions to this, although one case speculated that "It might be done by an otherwise respected businessman who made one big spread and then quit and retired."

The case records of the systematic check forgers gave clear testimony of this. Generally they had but short-lived periods of freedom, ranging from a few months to a year or two at the most, followed by imprisonment. Many of the cases since beginning their forgery careers had spent less total time outside prisons than within, a fact corroborated by the various law-enforcement officers queried on the point.

Many of the check men depicted their periods of check writing as continuous sprees during which they lived "fast" and luxuriously. Many spoke of experiencing considerable tension during these periods, and two cases developed stomach ulcers which caused them to "lay off at resorts." A number gambled and drank heavily, assertedly to escape their internal stress and sense of inevitable arrest. A number spoke of gradual build-up of strain and a critical point just before their arrest at which they became demoralized and after which they "just didn't care any more" or "got tired of running." The arrests of several men having a very long experience with checks resulted from blunders in technique of which they were aware at the time they made them. Some of the men gave themselves up to detectives or F. B. I. agents at this point.

In general the picture of the cool, calculating professional with prosaic, matter-of-fact attitudes towards his crimes as a trade or occupation supported by rationalizations of a subculture was not valid for the cases in question.

2. *Planning as an aspect of forgery.* In regard to the second element of professional theft—

planning—the behavior of check forgers is again divergent. Actually the present techniques of check passing either preclude precise planning or make it unnecessary. Although systematic check passers undeniably pay careful attention to such things as banking hours, the places at which checks are presented, and the kinds of "fronts" they employ, these considerations serve only as generalized guides for their crimes. Most informants held that situations have to be *exploited as they arise* with variation and flexibility being the key to success. What stands in the behavior of systematic check forgers is the rapid tempo—almost impulsiveness—with which they work.

The cases seemed to agree that check forgers seldom attempt to use the "fix" in order to escape the consequences of their crimes. The reason for this is that although one or a small number of checks might be made good, the systematic forger has too many bad checks outstanding and too many victims to mollify by offering restitution. Although the forger may be prosecuted on the basis of only one or two checks, ordinarily the prosecuting attorney will have a choice of a large number of complaints upon which to act. About the best the check forger can hope for through fixing activities is a short sentence or a sentence to jail rather than to prison.

3. *Technical skills.* Although the systematic check man relies upon technical skills—those of manipulating others—these are usually not of a high order, nor do they require a long learning period to master. From the standpoint of the appearance of the check or the behavior involved at the time of its passing, there need, of course, be no great difference between passing a bad check and passing a good check. This is particularly true of personal checks, which are at least as favored as payroll checks by check men.

When check men impersonate others or when they assume fictitious roles, acting ability is required. To the extent that elaborate impersonations are relied upon by the forger, his check passing takes on qualities of a confidence game. Most of the check men showed strong preference, however, for simple, fast-moving techniques. A number expressed definite dislike for staged arrangements, such as that of the "out of town real estate buyer" or for setting up a fictitious business in a community, then waiting several weeks or a month before making a "spread" of checks. As they put it, they "dislike the slow build-up involved."

4. *Mobility.* Like the thief, the systematic forger is migratory. Only one check man interviewed spoke of identifying himself with one community, and even he was reluctant to call it a headquarters. Generally check men are migratory within regions.

5. *Associations.* The sharpest and most categorical difference between professional theft and systematic forgery lies in the realm of associations. In contrast to pickpockets, shoplifters, and con men, whose criminal techniques are implicitly cooperative, most check men with highly developed systems work alone, carefully avoiding contacts and interaction with other criminals. Moreover, their preference for solitude and their secretiveness gives every appearance of a highly generalized reaction; they avoid not only cooperative crime but also any other kinds of association with criminals. They are equally selective and cautious in their contacts and associations with the noncriminal population, preferring not to become involved in any enduring personal relationships.

A descriptive breakdown of the thirty check forgers classified as systematic bears out this point. Only four of the thirty had worked in check passing gangs. Two of these had acted as "fences" who organized the operations. Both were close to seventy years old and had long prison records, one having been a receiver of stolen property, the other having worked as a forger. Both had turned to using gangs of passers because they were too well known to detectives either to pass checks themselves or to permit their handwriting to appear on the checks. The other two forgers who had worked in gangs were female drug addicts who had teamed up with other female addicts.[1]

Three other systematic check forgers did not work directly with other criminals but had criminal associations of a *contractual* nature. One old-time forger familiar with the now little-used methods for forging signatures and raising checks usually sold checks to passers but never

had uttered (passed) any of his own forgeries. Two men were passers who purchased either payroll checks from a "hot printer" or stolen checks from burglars. Apart from the minimal contacts necessary to sell or obtain a supply of checks, all three men were lone operators and very seclusive in their behavior.

Six of the thirty systematic forgers worked exclusively with one other person, usually a girl or "broad."[2] The check men seemed to agree that working with a girl was equivalent to working alone. These pairs ordinarily consisted of the check man and some girl not ordinarily of criminal background with whom he had struck up a living arrangement and for whom he felt genuine affection. The girl was used either to make out the checks or to pass them. In some cases she was simply used as a front to distract attention. Some men picked up girls in bars or hotels and employed them as fronts without their knowledge.

The remaining seventeen of the thirty systematic check forgers operated on a solitary basis. The majority of these argued that contact with others is unnecessary to obtain and pass a supply of checks. Most of them uttered personal checks. However, even where they made use of payroll or corporation checks they contrived to manufacture or obtain them without resorting to interaction with criminal associates or intermediaries. For example, one Nisei check man arranged with a printer to make up checks for a fraternal organization of which he represented himself as secretary-treasurer. Another man frequented business offices at noontime, and when the clerk left the office, helped himself to a supply of company checks, in one instance stealing a check writing machine for his purposes.

It was difficult to find evidence of anything more than rudimentary congeniality, sympathy, understandings, and shared rules of behavior among the check forgers, including those who had worked in gangs. Rather the opposite seemed true, suspicion and distrust marking their relationships with one another. One organizer of a gang, for example, kept careful account of all the checks he issued to his passers and made them return torn off corners of checks in case they were in danger of arrest and had to get rid of them. Only two of the thirty forgers indicated that they had at times engaged in recreational activities with other criminals. Both of these men were lone wolves in their work. One other lone wolf stated that he had on occasion had dinner with another check man he happened to know well and that he had once or twice entered into a rivalry with him to see who could pass a check in the most difficult place.

The two men who had organized gangs of check passers worked with a set of rules, but they were largely improvised and laid down by the fence rather than voluntarily recognized and obeyed by the passers. The other check men with varying degrees of explicitness recognized rules for passing checks—rules learned almost entirely on an individual trial-and-error basis. The informants insisted that "you learn as you go" and that one of the rules was "never use another man's stunt."

Such special morality as was recognized proved to be largely functional in derivation. Thus attitudes toward drinking and toward picking up women for sexual purposes were pretty much the result of individual perceptions of what was likely to facilitate or hamper the passing of checks or lead to arrest. Many of the men stated that since they were dealing primarily with business, professional, and clerical persons, their appearance and behavior had to be acceptable to these people. "Middle class" is probably the best term to describe their morality in most areas.

Careful inquiries were made to discover the extent to which the check men were familiar with and spoke an argot. Findings proved meager. Many of the men had a superficial acquaintance with general prison slang, but only four men could measurably identify and reproduce the argot of check forgery or that of thieves. Three more could be presumed to have some familiarity with it. Only one of these spoke the argot in the prison setting. Another said that he never used the argot either in prison or on the outside, except years previously when once in a great while he had "let down at a thieves' party." There were only two men who spoke of themselves as being "on the scratch."[3]

INTERPRETATION

How can these findings be reconciled with the specific statement of Sutherland's informant (31, p. 77)[4] that "laying paper" is a form of professional theft most often worked in mobs? The answer to this apparent contradiction requires that a distinction be made between forgery of *the nineteenth and early twentieth centuries and that of the present day*. In the past forgery was a much more complex procedure in which a variety of false instruments such as bank notes, drafts, bills of exchange, letters of credit, registered bonds, and post office money orders as well as checks were manufactured or altered and foisted off. A knowledge of chemicals, papers, inks, engraving, etching, lithography, and penmanship as well as detailed knowledge of bank operations were prime requisites for success. The amounts of money sought were comparatively large, and often they had to be obtained through complex monetary transactions. (7) The technological characteristics of this kind of forgery made planning, timing, specialization, differentiation of roles, morale, and organization imperative. Capital was necessary for living expenses during the period when preparations for the forgeries were being made. (24, 25, pp. 338–441, 7) Intermediates between the skilled forger and the passers were necessary so that the latter could swear that the handwriting on the false negotiable instruments was not theirs and so that the forger himself was not exposed to arrest. A "shadow" was often used for protection against the passer's temptation to abscond with the money and in order to alert the others of trouble at the bank.[5] "Fall" money was accumulated and supplied to assist the passer when arrested. Inasmuch as forgery gangs worked together for a considerable length of time, understandings, congeniality, and rules of behavior, especially with regard to the division of money, could and did develop. In short, professional forgery was based upon the technology of the period.

Although precise dating is difficult, the heyday of professional forgery in this country probably began after the Civil War and lasted through the 1920's. (29) It seems to have corresponded with the early phases of industrialization and commercial development before business and law-enforcement agencies developed methods and organization for preventing forgery and apprehending the offenders. Gradually technological developments in inks, papers, protectographs, and check-writing machines made the forging of signatures and the manufacture of false negotiable instruments more difficult. According to one source, for example, raised drafts have been virtually nonexistent since 1905. (29) Similarly, at the present time raising of checks is quite rare. The establishment of a protective committee by the American Bankers Association in 1894, related merchants' protective agencies, and improvements in police methods have made the risks of organized professional forgery exceedingly great. (24, 22)

Check gangs have always been vulnerable to arrest but this vulnerability has been multiplied many times by the large amounts of evidence left behind them in the form of countless payroll checks. Vulnerability is also heightened by the swiftness of communication today. If one person of a check-passing gang is arrested and identifies his associates, it becomes a relatively simple matter for police to secure their arrest. A sexually exploited and angered female companion may easily do the same to the check man. This goes far to explain the extreme seclusiveness of systematic check forgers and their almost abnormal fear of stool pigeons or of being "fingered." The type of persons who can be engaged as passers—unattached women, bar waitresses, drug addicts, alcoholics, petty thieves, and transient unemployed persons—also magnifies the probabilities that mistakes will be made and precludes the growth of a morale which might prevent informing to the police. These conditions also explain the fact that when the forger does work with someone it is likely to be one other person upon whom he feels he can rely with implicit confidence. Hence the man-woman teams in which the woman is in love with the man, or the case of the two homosexual girls, or of the two brothers mentioned previously.

Further evidence that organized forgery is a hazardous type of crime, difficult to professionalize under modern conditions, is indicated by the fact that the organizer or fence is apt to be an older criminal with a long record, whose handwriting methods are so well known that he has no choice other than to work through passers. Even then he does it with recognition that arrest is inevitable.

A factor of equal importance in explaining the decline of professional organized forgery has been the increasingly widespread use of business and payroll checks as well as personal checks. Whereas in the past the use of checks was confined to certain kinds of business transactions, mostly involving banks, today it is ubiquitous. Attitudes of business people and their clerical employees have undergone great change, and only the most perfunctory identification is necessary to cash many kinds of checks. Check men recognize this in frequent unsolicited comments that passing checks is "easy." Some argue that the form of the check is now relatively unimportant to passing it, that "you can pass a candy bar wrapper nowadays with the right front and story."[6] It is for this reason that the systematic check man does not have to resort to criminal associates or employ the more complex professional procedures used in decades past.

These facts may also account for the presence among lone-wolf check forgers of occasional persons with the identification, orientation, skills, codes, and argot of the thief. Case histories as well as the observations of informants show that older professional criminals in recent decades have turned to check passing because they face long sentences for additional crimes or sentencing under habitual criminal legislation. They regard checks as an "easy racket" because in many states conviction makes them subject to jail sentences rather than imprisonment. Check passing may be a last resort for the older criminal.

The presence of the occasional older professional thief in the ranks of check forgers may actually token a general decline and slow disappearance of professional thieving. One professional thief turned check passer had this to say:

I'm a thief—a burglar—but I turned to checks because it's getting too hard to operate. Police are a lot smarter now, and they have better methods. People are different nowadays too; they report things more. It's hard to trust anyone now. Once you could trust cab drivers; now you can't. We live in a different world today.[7]

THE CHECK FORGER AS AN ISOLATE

The preference of many systematic check forgers for solitary lives and their avoidance of primary-group associations among criminals may also be explicable in terms of their educational characteristics and class origins. The history of forgery reveals that in medieval times it was considered to be the special crime of the clerical class, as indeed it had to be inasmuch as the members of this class monopolized writing skills. (36, pp. 5–31) It also seems to be true from the later history of the crime that it has held a special attraction for more highly educated persons, for those of higher socioeconomic status and those of "refined" or artistic tastes.[8] The basic method of organized forgery is stated to have been invented and perfected in England, not by criminals but by a practicing barrister of established reputation in 1840. (28,8) An early gang of forgers organized by a practicing physician is also described by Felstead. (11) A number of studies directed to the differentiating characteristics of check criminals point to an "above-average" intelligence and formal education. This refers to the general population as well as to the criminal populations with which they have been compared. (3, 12, 17, p. 87, 18, p. 40)

All of this is not to say that less-educated persons do not frequently pass bad checks but rather that the persons who persist in the behavior and develop behavior systems of forgery seem much more likely than other criminals to be drawn from a segment of the population distinguished by a higher socioeconomic status. Generally this was true of the systematic forgers in this study. Eight of the thirty had completed two or more years of college. Fourteen of the thirty had fathers who were or had been in the professions and business, including a juvenile court judge, a minister, a postmaster of a large city, and three very wealthy ranch owners. One woman came from a nationally famous family of farm implement manufacturers. Four others had siblings well established in business and the professions,

one of whom was an attorney general in another state. Two of the men had been successful businessmen themselves before becoming check men.

The most important implication of these data is that systematic check forgers do not seem to have had criminal antecedents or early criminal associations. (19, 20) For this reason, as well as for technical reasons, they are not likely to seek out or to be comfortable in informal associations with other criminals who have been products of early and lengthy socialization and learning in a criminal subculture. It also follows that their morality and values remain essentially "middle" or "upper" class and that they seldom integrate these with the morality of the professional criminal. This is reflected in self-attitudes in which many refer to themselves as "black sheep" or as a kind of Dr. Jekyll-Mr. Hyde person. Further support for this interpretation comes from their status in prison where, according to observations of themselves and others, they are marginal so far as participation in the primary groups of the prison is concerned.

CONCLUSION

The cases and data presented suggest that present-day check forgery exists in systematic form but does not appear to be a professional behavior system acquired or maintained through associations with other criminals. The technical demands of contemporary check forgery preclude efficient operation on an organized, cooperative basis. In addition to these factors the class characteristics and backgrounds of systematic forgers incline them to avoid intimate association with other criminals.

NOTES

1. One may question whether they were systematic check forgers in a true sense; other informants state that "such people are not real check men; they are just supporting a habit." Their self-definitions and the organization of their lives centers around drug addiction rather than forgery.

2. One of the "pair" workers consisted of two homosexual females. The other non-man-woman pair was made up of two brothers, both of whom had sub-

stantial prison records. They worked up and down the West Coast, alternating in making out checks and playing the part of passer.

3. The attitude of the lone wolf check man toward the argot is illustrated by the following quotation:

It's just the older men in here who use argot, or some of the young guys who think they are tough. I know the argot but when I hear it I tell them to talk English. Most people on the outside know it anyway. Why call a gun a heater? What is gained by it . . . ?

These findings coincide with Maurer's. (22) He states that the argot of check forgery is relatively unspecialized and that forgers seldom have an opportunity to use it.

4. Maurer refers to check forgery as a branch of the "grift," and also speaks of professional forgers without, however, defining the term. Yet he recognizes that check forgers are usually lone wolves. (22)

5. Pinkerton enumerates the following roles of the forgery gang: (1) backer, (2) forger, (3) middleman, (4) presenter, (5) shadow; Maurer (22) without specifying the historical period to which his description applies, distinguishes the following as check forger roles: (1) connection, (2) fence, (3) passer. (24)

6. Detectives in Santa Monica, California showed the writer a collection of checks successfully passed with such signatures as: "I. M. A. Fool," "U. R. Stuck," and others not printable. For a discussion of the crudeness of bogus checks accepted by business people see (30).

7. There is evidence that there has been a sharp absolute decline in the number of pickpockets in recent years and that most of the so-called "class cannons" (highly skilled) operating now are fifty years of age or over. (23)

8. This is the thesis of Rhodes (28); two of the four participants in the famous Bank of England forgery in 1873 were college educated, one being a Harvard graduate. See Dilnot (7); forgers coming from "good" families are described by Adam (1); fourteen of the nineteen persons tried for forgery at Newgate Prison in England during the later eighteenth and early nineteenth centuries were what can be termed "middle" and "upper" class, including three army or navy officers (one who commanded the royal yacht of Queen Caroline, consort of George IV), one banker, one physician Cambridge graduate, one prosecuting attorney, two engravers (one by appointment to George III), three "gentlemen" of good connections; and three bank clerks. Two of the three men who had "poor parents" had married women of "good means." Tegg (35) and Bonger (4, pp. 429, 430, 437) give data from France and Italy which support this idea. A number of writers have commented on the fact that forgery has been quite common among the educated classes of India, particularly the "wily Brahmins." (I, 9, pp. 3–6, 16)

REFERENCES

ADAM, H. L., *Oriental Crime* (London: T. Werner Laurie, 1908).

———, *The Story of Crime* (London: T. Werner Laurie, 1908).

BERG, I., "A Comparative Study of Forgery," *Journal of Applied Psychology,* 28 (June, 1944), 232–238.

BONGER, W. A., *Criminality and Economic Conditions* (Boston: Little, Brown, 1916).

CAVAN, R. S., *Criminology* (New York: Crowell, 1948).

CLINARD, M. B., *Sociology of Deviant Behavior* (New York: Rinehart, 1957).

DILNET, G., *The Bank of England Forgery* (New York: Scribners, 1929).

———, *The Trial of Jim the Penman* (London: Geoffrey Bles, 1930).

EDWARDS, S. M., *Crime in India* (London: Oxford University Press, 1924).

ELLIOTT, M., *Crime in Modern Society* (New York: Harper and Bros., 1942).

FELSTEAD, T. S., in *Famous Criminals and Their Trials* (New York: Doran, 1926).

FOX, V., "Intelligence, Race and Age as Selective Factors in Crime," *Journal of Criminal Law and Criminology,* 37 (July–August, 1946), 141–152.

FREGIER, H. A., *Les Classes Dangereuses de la population dans les grandes villes* (Paris: Chex J. B. Balliére, 1840).

GRUHLE, H. W. and L. WETZEL, Eds. "Verbrechentype" (cited in Bonger, W. A., *op. cit.,* p. 581).

HALL, JEROME, *Theft, Law and Society,* 2nd. Ed. (Indianapolis: Bobbs-Merrill, 1952).

HARDLESS and HARDLESS, *Forgery in India* (Chunar: Sanctuary, 1920).

HOOTON, E. A., *The American Criminal,* Vol. I (Cambridge: Harvard University, 1939).

LAWES, L., *Life and Death in Sing Sing* (New York: Sun Dial Press, 1938).

LEMERT, E., "An Isolation and Closure Theory of Naive Check Forgery," *Journal of Criminal Law and Criminology,* 44 (September–October, 1953), 296–307.

———, "Generality and Specificity in Criminal Behavior: Check Forgery Considered," paper read before American Sociological Society, September, 1956.

LINDESMITH, A. R. and H. W. DUNHAM, "Some Principles of Criminal Typology," *Social Forces,* 19 (March, 1941), 307–314.

MAURER, D. W., "The Argot of Check Forgery," *American Speech,* 16 (December, 1941), 243–250.

MAURER, D. W., *Whiz Mob* (Gainesville, Florida: American Dialect Society, No. 24, 1955).

PINKERTON, W. A., "Forgery," paper read before Annual Convention of the International Association of Chiefs of Police, Washington D. C., 1905.

————, *Thirty Years a Detective* (New York: G. W. Carleton, 1884).

PUIBARAUD, L., *Les Malfaiteurs de profession* (Paris: E. Flammarion, 1893).

RECKLESS, W. C., *The Crime Problem,* 2nd Ed. (New York: Appleton Century, 1955).

RHODES, H. T. F., in *The Craft of Forgery* (London: J. Murray, 1934).

SPEARE, J. W., *Protecting the Nation's Money* (Rochester: Todd Protectograph Co., 1927).

STERNITSKY, J. L., *Forgery and Fictitious Checks* (Springfield: Charles C. Thomas, 1955).

SUTHERLAND, E. H., *The Professional Thief* (Chicago: University of Chicago, 1937).

————, "The Professional Thief," *Journal of Criminal Law and Criminology,* 28 (July–August, 1937), 161–163.

————, *Principles of Criminology,* Rev. (New York: Lippincott, 1947).

SUTHERLAND, E. H. and D. CRESSEY, *Principles of Criminology,* 5th Ed. (New York: Lippincott, 1955).

TEGG, T., *The Chronicles of Crime,* Vols. I, II (London: Camden Pelham, 1841).

TOUT, T. F., *Medieval Forgers and Forgeries,* Bulletin of the John Rylands Library, 5, 3, 4, 1919.

VON HENTIG, H., "The Pickpocket: Psychology, Tactics and Technique," *Journal of Criminal Law and Criminology,* 34 (May–June, 1943), pp. 11–16.

NORMAL CRIMES
SOCIOLOGICAL FEATURES OF THE PENAL CODE IN A PUBLIC DEFENDER OFFICE*

David Sudnow**

Two stances toward the utility of official classificatory schema for criminological research have been debated for years. One position, which might be termed that of the "revisionist" school, has it that the categories of the criminal law, e.g.,

*© 1965 by the Society for the Study of Social Problems. Reprinted from *Social Problems,* 12, (Winter, 1965) pp. 255–76 by permission of the publisher.

**This investigation is based on field observations of a Public Defender Office in a metropolitan California community. The research was conducted while the author was associated with the Center for the Study of Law and Society, University of California, Berkeley. I am grateful to the Center for financial support. Erving Goffman, Sheldon Messinger, Harvey Sacks, and Emanual Schegloff contributed valuable suggestions and criticisms to an earlier draft.

"burglary," "petty theft," "homicide," etc., are not "homogeneous in respect to causation."[1] From an inspection of penal code descriptions of crimes, it is argued that the way persons seem to be assembled under the auspices of criminal law procedure is such as to produce classes of criminals who are, at least on theoretical grounds, as dissimilar in their social backgrounds and styles of activity as they are similar. The entries in the penal code, this school argues, require revision if sociological use is to be made of categories of crime and a classificatory scheme of etiological relevance is to be developed. Common attempts at such revision have included notions such as *"white collar* crime," and *"systematic* check forger," these conceptions constituting attempts to institute sociologically meaningful specifications which the operations of criminal law procedure and statutory legislation "fail" to achieve.

The other major perspective toward the sociologist's use of official categories and the criminal statistics compiled under their heading derives less from a concern with etiologically useful schema than from an interest in understanding the actual operations of the administrative legal system. Here, the categories of the criminal law are not regarded as useful or not, as objects to be either adopted, adapted, or ignored; rather, they are seen as constituting the basic conceptual equipment with which such people as judges, lawyers, policemen, and probation workers organize their everyday activities. The study of the actual use of official classification systems by actually employed administrative personnel regards the penal code as data, to be preserved intact; its use, both in organizing the work of legal representation, accusation, adjudication, and prognostication, and in compiling tallies of legal occurrences, is to be examined as one would examine any social activity. By sociologically regarding, rather than criticizing, rates of statistics and the categories employed to assemble them, one learns, it is promised, about the "rate producing agencies" and the assembling process.[2]

While the former perspective, the "revisionist" position, has yielded several fruitful products, the latter stance (commonly identified with what is rather loosely known as the "labelling" perspective), has been on the whole more promissory than productive, more programmatic than empirical. The present report will examine the operations of a Public Defender system in an effort to assess the warrant for the continued theoretical and empirical development of the position argued by Kitsuse and Cicourel. It will address the question: what of import for the sociological analysis of legal administration can be learned by describing the actual way the penal code is employed in the daily activities of legal representation? First, I shall consider the "guilty plea" as a way of handling criminal cases, focusing on some features of the penal code as a description of a population of defendants. Then I shall describe the Public Defender operation with

special attention to the way defendants are represented. The place of the guilty plea and penal code in this representation will be examined. Lastly, I shall briefly analyze the fashion in which the Public Defender prepares and conducts a "defense." The latter section will attempt to indicate the connection between certain prominent organizational features of the Public Defender system and the penal code's place in the routine operation of that system.

GUILTY PLEAS, INCLUSION, AND NORMAL CRIMES

It is a commonly noted fact about the criminal court system generally, that the greatest proportion of cases are "settled" by a guilty plea.[3] In the county from which the following material is drawn, over 80 percent of all cases "never go to trial." To describe the method of obtaining a guilty plea disposition, essential for the discussion to follow, I must distinguish between what shall be termed "necessarily-included-lesser-offenses" and "situationally-included-lesser-offenses." Of two offenses designated in the penal code, the lesser is considered to be that for which the length of required incarceration is the shorter period of time. *Inclusion* refers to the relation between two or more offenses. The "necessarily-included-lesser-offense" is a strictly legal notion:

Whether a lesser offense is included in the crime charged is a question of law to be determined solely from the definition and corpus delicti of the offense charged and of the lesser offense. . . . If all the elements of the corpus delicti of a lesser crime can be found in a list of all the elements of the offense charged, then only is the lesser included in the greater.[4]

Stated alternatively:

The test in this state of necessarily included offenses is simply that where an offense cannot be committed without necessarily committing another offense, the latter is a necessarily included offense.[5]

The implied negative is put: Could Smith have committed A and not B? If the answer is yes, then B is not necessarily included in A. If the answer is no, B is necessarily included. While in a given case a battery might be committed in the course of a robbery, battery is not necessarily included in robbery. Petty theft is necessarily included in robbery but not in burglary. Burglary primarily involves the "intent" to acquire another's goods illegally (e.g., by breaking and entering); the consummation of the act need not occur for burglary to be committed. Theft, like robbery, requires that some item be stolen.

I shall call *lesser* offenses that are not necessarily but "only" *actually* included, "situationally-included-lesser-offenses." By statutory definition, necessarily-included offenses are "actually" included. By actual here, I refer to the "way it occurs" as irrelevant. With situational inclusion, the "way it occurs" is definitive. In the former case, no particular course of action is referred to. In the latter, the scene and progress of the criminal activity would be analyzed.

The issue of necessary inclusion has special relevance for two procedural matters:

A) A man cannot be charged and/or convicted of two or more crimes any one of which is necessarily included in the others, unless the several crimes occur on separate occasions.

If a murder occurs, the defendant cannot be charged and/or convicted of both "homicide" and "intent to commit a murder," the latter of which is necessarily included in first degree murder. If, however, a defendant "intends to commit a homicide" against one person and commits a "homicide" against another, both offenses may be properly charged. While it is an extremely complex question as to the scope and definition of "in the course of," in most instances the rule is easily applied.

B) The judge cannot instruct the jury to consider as alternative crimes of which to find a defendant guilty, crimes that are not necessarily included in the charged crime or crimes.

If a man is charged with "statutory rape" the judge may instruct the jury to consider as a possible alternative conviction "contributing to the delinquency of a minor," as this offense is necessarily included in "statutory rape." He cannot, however, suggest that the alternative "intent to commit murder" be considered and the jury cannot find the defendant guilty of this latter crime,

unless it is charged as a distinct offense in the complaint.

It is crucial to note that these restrictions apply only to (a) the relation between several charged offenses in a formal allegation, and (b) the alternatives allowable in a jury instruction. At any time before a case "goes to trial," alterations in the charging complaint may be made by the district attorney. The issue of necessary inclusion has no required bearing on (a) what offense(s) will be charged initially by the prosecutor, (b) what the relation is between the charge initially made and "what happened," or (c) what modifications may be made after the initially charged offenses and those charged in modified complaints. It is this latter operation, the modification of the complaint, that is central to the guilty plea disposition.

Complaint alterations are made when a defendant agrees to plead guilty to an offense and thereby avoid a trial. The alteration occurs in the context of a "deal" consisting of an offer from the district attorney to alter the original charge in such a fashion that a lighter sentence will be incurred with a guilty plea than would be the case if the defendant were sentenced on the original charge. In return for this manipulation, the defendant agrees to plead guilty. The arrangement is proposed in the following format: "If you plead guilty to this new lesser offense, you will get less time in prison than if you plead not guilty to the original, greater charge and lose the trial." The decision must then be made whether or not the chances of obtaining complete acquittal at trial are great enough to warrant the risk of a loss and higher sentence if found guilty on the original charge. As we shall see below, it is a major job of the Public Defender, who mediates between the district attorney and the defendant, to convince his "client" that the chances of acquittal are too slight to warrant this risk.

If a man is charged with "drunkenness" and the Public Defender and Public Prosecutor (hereafter P.D. and D.A.) prefer not to have a trial, they seek to have the defendant agree to plead guilty. While it is occasionally possible, particularly with first offenders, for the P.D. to convince the defendant to plead guilty to the originally charged offense, most often it is felt that some "exchange" or "consideration" should be offered, i.e., a lesser offense charged.

To what offense can "drunkenness" be reduced? There is no statutorily designated crime that is necessarily included in the crime of "drunkenness." That is, if any of the statutorily required components of drunk behavior (its corpus delicti) are absent, there remains no offense of which the resultant description is a definition. For drunkenness there is, however, an offense that while not necessarily included is "typically-situationally-included," i.e., "typically" occurs as a feature of the way drunk persons are seen to behave—"disturbing the peace." The range of possible sentences is such that, of the two offenses, "disturbing the peace" cannot call for as long a prison sentence as "drunkenness." If, in the course of going on a binge, a person does so in such a fashion that "disturbing the peace" may be employed to describe some of his behavior, it would be considered as an alternative offense to offer in return for a guilty plea. A central question for the following analysis will be: In what fashion would he have to behave so that disturbing the peace would be considered a suitable reduction?

If a man is charged with "molesting a minor," there are not any necessarily included lesser offenses with which to charge him. Yet an alternative charge—"loitering around a schoolyard"—is often used as a reduction. As above, and central to our analysis the question is: What would the defendant's behavior be such that "loitering around a schoolyard" would constitute an appropriate alternative?

If a person is charged with "burglary," "petty theft" is not necessarily included. Routinely, however, "petty theft" is employed for reducing the charge of burglary. Again, we shall ask: What is the relation between burglary and petty theft and the *manner in which the former occurs* that warrants this reduction?

Offenses are regularly reduced to other offenses, the latter of which are not necessarily or situationally included in the former. As I have already said, the determination of whether or not offense X was situationally included in Y involves an analysis of the course of action that constitutes the criminal behavior. I must now turn to examine this mode of behavioral analysis.

When encountering a defendant who is charged with "assault with a deadly weapon," the P.D. asks: "What can this offense be reduced to so as to arrange for a guilty plea?" As the reduction is only to be proposed by the P.D. and accepted or not by the D.A., his question becomes "what reduction will be allowable?" (As shall be seen below, the P.D. and D.A. have institutionalized a common orientation to allowable reductions.) The method of reduction involves, as a general feature, the fact that the particular case in question is scrutinized to decide its membership in a class of similar cases. But *the penal code does not provide the reference for deciding the correspondence between the instant event and the general case; that is, it does not define the classes of offense types.* To decide, for purposes of finding a suitable reduction, if the instant case involves a "burglary," reference is not made to the statutory definition of "burglary." To decide what the situationally included offenses are in the instant case, the instant case is not analyzed as a *statutorily* referable course of action; rather, reference is made to a *non-statutorily* conceived class "burglary" and offenses that are typically situationally included in it, taken as a class of behavioral events. Stated again: in searching an instant case to decide what to *reduce it to,* there is no analysis of the statutorily referable elements of the instant case; instead, its membership in a class of events, the features of which cannot be described by the penal code, must be decided. An example will be useful. If a defendant is charged with burglary and the P.D. is concerned to propose a reduction to a lesser offense, he might search the elements of the burglary at hand to decide what other offenses were committed. The other offenses he might "discover" would be of two sorts: those necessarily and those situationally included. In attempting to decide those other offenses situationally included in the instant event, the instant event might be analyzed as a statutorily referable course of action. Or, as is the case with the P.D., the instant case might be analyzed to decide if it is a "burglary" in common with other "burglaries" conceived of in terms other than those provided by the statute.

Burglaries are routinely reduced to petty theft. If we were to analyze the way burglaries typically occur, petty theft is neither situationally or necessarily included; when a burglary is committed, money or other goods are seldom illegally removed from some person's body. If we therefore analyzed burglaries, employing the penal code as our reference, and then searched the P.D.'s records to see how burglaries are reduced in the guilty plea, we could not establish a rule that would describe the transformation between the burglary cases statutorily described and the reductions routinely made (i.e., to "petty theft"). The rule must be sought elsewhere, in the character of the non-statutorily defined class of "burglaries," which I shall term *normal burglaries*.

NORMAL CRIMES

In the course of routinely encountering persons charged with "petty theft," "burglary," "assault with a deadly weapon," "rape," "possession of marijuana," etc., the P.D. gains knowledge of the typical manner in which offenses of given classes are committed, the social characteristics of the persons who regularly commit them, the features of the settings in which they occur, the types of victims often involved, and the like. He learns to speak knowledgeably of "burglars," "petty thieves," "drunks," "rapists," "narcos," etc., and to attribute to them personal biographies, modes of usual criminal activity, criminal histories, psychological characteristics, and social backgrounds. The following characterizations are illustrative:

Most ADWs (assault with deadly weapon) start with fights over some girl.

These sex fiends (child molestation cases) usually hang around parks or schoolyards. But we often get fathers charged with these crimes. Usually the old man is out of work and stays at home when the wife goes to work and he plays around with his little daughter or something. A lot of these cases start when there is some marital trouble and the woman gets mad.

I don't know why most of them don't rob the big stores. They usually break into some cheap department store and steal some crummy item like a $9.95 record player, you know.

Kids who start taking this stuff (narcotics) usually start out when some buddy gives them a cigarette and they smoke it for kicks. For some reason they always get caught in their cars, for speeding or something.

They can anticipate that point when persons are likely to get into trouble:

Dope addicts do O.K. until they lose a job or something and get back on the streets and, you know, meet the old boys. Someone tells them where to get some and there they are.

In the springtime, that's when we get all these sex crimes. You know, these kids play out in the schoolyard all day and these old men sit around and watch them jumping up and down. They get their ideas.

The P.D. learns that some kinds of offenders are likely to repeat the same offense while others are not repeat violators or, if they do commit crimes frequently, the crimes vary from occasion to occasion:

You almost never see a check man get caught for anything but checks—only an occasional drunk charge.

Burglars are usually multiple offenders, most times just burglaries or petty thefts.

Petty thefts get started for almost anything—joy riding, drinking, all kinds of little things.

These narcos are usually through after the second violation or so. After the first time some stop, but when they start on the heavy stuff, they've had it.

I shall call *normal crimes* those occurrences whose typical features, e.g., the ways they usually occur and the characteristics of persons who commit them (as well as the typical victims and typical scenes), are known and attended to by the P.D. For any of a series of offense types the P.D. can provide some form of proverbial characterization. For example, *burglary* is seen as involving regular violators, no weapons, low-priced items, little property damage, lower class establishments, largely Negro defendants, independent operators, and a non-professional orientation to the crime. *Child molesting* is seen as typically entailing middle-aged strangers or lower class, middle-aged fathers (few women), no actual physical penetration or severe tissue damage, mild fondling, petting, and stimulation, bad marriage circumstances, multiple offenders with the same offense repeatedly committed, a child complainant, via the mother, etc. *Narcotics* defendants are usually Negroes, not syndicated, persons who start by using small stuff, hostile with police officers, caught by some form of entrapment technique, etc. *Petty thefts* are about 50–50 Negro-white, unplanned offenses, generally committed on lower class persons and don't get much money, don't often employ weapons, don't make living from thievery, usually younger defendants with long juvenile assaultive records, etc. *Drunkenness* offenders are lower class white and Negro, get drunk on wine and beer, have long histories of repeated drunkenness, don't hold down jobs, are usually arrested on the streets, seldom violate other penal code sections, etc.

Some general features of the normal crime as a way of attending to a category of persons and events may be mentioned:

1. The focus, in these characterizations, is not on particular individuals, but offense types. If asked "What are burglars like?" or "How are burglaries usually committed?", the P.D. does not feel obliged to refer to particular burglars and burglaries as the material for his answer.

2. The features attributed to offenders and offenses are often not of import for the statutory conception. In burglary, it is "irrelevant" for the statutory determination whether or not much damage was done to the premises (except where, for example, explosives were employed and a new statute could be invoked). Whether a defendant breaks a window or not, destroys property within the house or not, etc., does not affect his statutory classification as a burglar. While for robbery the presence or absence of a weapon sets the degree, whether the weapon is a machine gun or pocket knife is "immaterial." Whether the residence or business establishment in a burglary is located in a higher income area of the city is of no issue for the code requirements. And, generally, the defendant's race, class position, criminal history (in most offenses), personal attributes, and particular style of committing offenses are features specifically not definitive of crimes under the auspices of the penal code. For deciding "Is this a "burglary" case I have before me" however, the P.D.'s reference to this range of non-statutorily referable personal and social at-

tributes, modes of operation, etc., is crucial for the arrangement of a guilty plea bargain.

3. The features attributed to offenders and offenses are, in their content, specific to the community in which the P.D. works. In other communities and historical periods the lists would presumably differ. Narcotics violators in certain areas, for example, are syndicated in dope rackets or engage in systematic robbery as professional criminals, features which are not commonly encountered (or, at least, evidence for which is not systematically sought) in this community. Burglary in some cities will more often occur at large industrial plants, banking establishments, warehouses, etc. The P.D. refers to the population of defendants in the county as "our defendants" and qualifies his prototypical portrayals and knowledge of the typically operative social structures, "for our county." An older P.D., remembering the "old days," commented:

We used to have a lot more rapes than we do now, and they used to be much more violent. Things are duller now in. . . .

4. Offenses whose normal features are readily attended to are those which are routinely encountered in the courtroom. This feature is related to the last point. For embezzlement, bank robbery, gambling, prostitution, murder, arson, and some other uncommon offenses, the P.D. cannot readily supply anecdotal and proverbial characterizations. While there is some change in the frequencies of offense-type convictions over time, certain offenses are continually more common and others remain stably infrequent. The troubles created for the P.D. when offenses whose features are not readily known occur, and whose typicality is not easily constructed, will be discussed in some detail below.

5. Offenses are ecologically specified and attended to as normal or not according to the locales within which they are committed. The P.D. learns that burglaries usually occur in such and such areas of the city, petty thefts around this or that park, ADWs in these bars. Ecological patterns are seen as related to socioeconomic variables and these in turn to typical modes of criminal and non-criminal activities. Knowing where an offense took place is thus, for the P.D., knowl-

edge of the likely persons involved, the kind of scene in which the offense occurred, and the pattern of activity characteristic of such a place:

Almost all of our ADWs are in the same half a dozen bars. These places are Negro bars where laborers come after hanging around the union halls trying to get some work. Nobody has any money and they drink too much. Tempers are high and almost anything can start happening.

6. One further important feature can be noted at this point. Its elaboration will be the task of a later section. As shall be seen, the P.D. office consists of a staff of twelve full-time attorneys. Knowledge of the properties of offense types of offenders, i.e, their normal, typical, or familiar attributes, constitutes the mark of any given attorney's competence. A major task in socializing the new P.D. deputy attorney consists in teaching him to recognize these attributes and to come to do so naturally. The achievement of competence as a P.D. is signalled by the gradual acquisition of professional command not simply of local penal code peculiarities and courtroom folklore, but, as importantly, of relevant features of the social structure and criminological wisdom. His grasp of that knowledge over the course of time is a key indication of his expertise.

Below, in our brief account of some relevant organizational properties of the P.D. system, we shall have occasion to re-emphasize the competence-attesting aspects of the attorney's proper use of established sociological knowledge. Let us return to the mechanics of the guilty plea procedure as an example of the operation of the notion of normal crimes.

Over the course of their interaction and repeated "bargaining" discussions, the P.D. and D.A. have developed a set of unstated recipes for reducing original charges to lesser offenses. These recipes are specifically appropriate for use in instances of normal crimes and in such instances alone. "Typical" burglaries are reduced to petty theft, "typical" ADWs to simple assault, "typical" child molestation to loitering around a schoolyard, etc. The character of these recipes deserves attention.

The specific content of any reduction, i.e., what particular offense class X offenses will be reduced to, is such that the reduced offense may bear no obvious relation (neither situationally nor necessarily included) to the originally charged offense. The reduction of burglary to petty theft is an example. The important relation between the reduced offense and the original charge is such that the reduction from one to the other is considered "reasonable." At this point we shall only state what seems to be the general principle involved in deciding this reasonableness. The underlying premises cannot be explored at the present time, as that would involve a political analysis beyond the scope of the present report.

Both P.D. and D.A. are concerned to obtain a guilty plea wherever possible and thereby avoid a trial. At the same time, each party is concerned that the defendant "receive his due." The reduction of offense X to Y must be of such a character that the new sentence will depart from the anticipated sentence for the original charge to such a degree that the defendant is likely to plea guilty to the new charge and, at the same time, not so great that the defendant does not "get his due."

In a homicide, while battery is a necessarily included offense, it will not be considered as a possible reduction. For a conviction of second degree murder a defendant could receive a life sentence in the penitentiary. For a battery conviction he would spend no more than six months in the county jail. In a homicide, however, "felony manslaughter," or "assault with a deadly weapon," whatever their relation to homicide as regards inclusion, would more closely approximate the sentence outcome that could be expected on a trial conviction of second degree murder. These alternatives would be considered. For burglary, a typical situationally included offense might be "disturbing the peace," "breaking and entering" or "destroying public property." "Petty theft," however, constitutes a reasonable lesser alternative to burglary as the sentence for petty theft will often range between six months and one year in the county jail and burglary regularly does not carry higher than two years in the state prison. "Disturbing the peace" would be a thirty-day sentence offense.

While the present purposes make the exposition of this calculus unnecessary, it can be noted and stressed that the particular content of the reduction does not necessarily correspond to a relation between the original and altered charge that could be described in either the terms of necessary or situational inclusion. Whatever the relation between the original and reduced charge, its essential feature resides in the spread between sentence likelihoods and the reasonableness of that spread, i.e., the balance it strikes between the defendant "getting his due" and at the same time "getting something less than he might so that he will plead guilty."

The procedure we want to clarify now, at the risk of some repetition, is the manner in which an instant case is examined to decide its membership in a class of "crimes such as this" (the category *normal crimes*). Let us start with an obvious case, burglary. As the typical reduction for burglary is petty theft and as petty theft is neither situationally nor necessarily included in burglary, the examination of the instant case is clearly not undertaken to decide whether petty theft is an appropriate statutory description. The concern is to establish the relation between the instant burglary and the normal category "burglaries" and, having decided a "sufficient correspondence," to now employ petty theft as the proposed reduction.

In scrutinizing the present burglary case, the P.D. seeks to establish that "this is a burglary just like any other." If that correspondence is not established, regardless of whether or not petty theft in fact was a feature of the way the crime was enacted, the reduction to petty theft would not be proposed. *The propriety of proposing petty theft as a reduction does not derive from its in-fact-existence in the present case, but is warranted or not by the relation of the present burglary to "burglaries," normally conceived.*

In a case of "child molestation" (officially called "lewd conduct with a minor"), the concern is to decide if this is a "typical child molestation case." While "loitering around a schoolyard" is frequently a feature of the way such crimes are instigated, establishing that the present defendant *did in fact loiter around a schoolyard* is secondary to the more general question "Is this a typical child molestation case?" What appears as a contradiction must be clarified by examining the status of "loitering around a schoolyard" as a

typical feature of such child molestations. The typical character of "child molesting cases" does not stand or fall on the fact that "loitering around a schoolyard" is a feature of the way they are in fact committed. It is *not* that "loitering around a schoolyard" as a *statutorily referable behavior sequence* is part of typical "child molesting cases" but that "loitering around a schoolyard" as a *socially distinct mode of committing child molestations typifies the way such offenses are enacted.* "Strictly speaking," i.e., under the auspices of the statutory *corpus delicti,* "loitering around a schoolyard," requires *loitering, around, a schoolyard;* if one loiters around a ball park or a public recreation area, he "cannot," within a proper reading of the statute, be charged with loitering around a *schoolyard.* Yet "loitering around a schoolyard," as a feature of the typical way such offenses as child molestations are committed, has the status not of a description of the way in *fact* (*fact,* statutorily decided) it occurred or typically occurs, but "the-kind-of-social-activity-typically-associated-with-such-offenses." It is not its statutorily conceived features but its socially relevant attributes that gives "loitering around a schoolyard" its status as a feature of the class "normal child molestations." Whether the defendant loitered around a schoolyard or a ball park, and whether he loitered or "was passing by," "loitering around a schoolyard" as a reduction will be made if the defendant's activity was such that "he was hanging around some public place or another" and "was the kind of guy who hangs around schoolyards." As a component of the class of normal child molestation cases (of the variety where the victim is a stranger), "loitering around a schoolyard" typifies a mode of committing such offenses, the class of "such persons who do such things as hang around schoolyards and the like." A large variety of actual offenses could thus be nonetheless reduced to "loitering" if, as kinds of social activity, "loitering," conceived of as typifying a way of life, pattern of daily activity, social psychological circumstances, etc., characterized the conduct of the defendant. The young P.D. who would object "You can't reduce it to "loitering"—he didn't really "loiter,"" would be reprimanded: "Fella, you don't know how to use that term; he might as well have "loitered"—it's the same kind of case as the others."

Having outlined the formal mechanics of the guilty plea disposition, I shall now turn to depict the routine of representation that the categories of crime, imbued with elaborate knowledge of the delinquent social structure, provide for. This will entail a brief examination of pertinent organizational features of the P.D. system.

PUBLIC "DEFENSE"

Recently, in many communities, the burden of securing counsel has been taken from the defendant.[6] As the accused is, by law, entitled to the aid of counsel, and as his pocket book is often empty, numerous cities have felt obliged to establish a public defender system. There has been little resistance to this development by private attorneys among whom it is widely felt that the less time they need spend in the criminal courts, where practice is least prestigeful and lucrative, the better.[7]

Whatever the reasons for its development, we now find, in many urban places, a public defender occupying a place alongside judge and prosecutor as a regular court employee. In the county studied, the P.D. mans a daily station, like the public prosecutor, and "defends" all who come before him. He appears in court when court begins and his "clientele," composed without regard for his preferences, consists of that residual category of persons who cannot afford to bring their own spokesmen to court. In this county, the "residual" category approximates 65 percent of the total number of criminal cases. In a given year, the twelve attorneys who comprise the P.D. Office "represent" about 3,000 defendants in the municipal and superior courts of the county.

While the courtroom encounters of private attorneys are brief, businesslike and circumscribed, interactionally and temporally, by the particular cases that bring them there, the P.D. attends to the courtroom as his regular work place and conveys in his demeanor his place as a member of its core personnel.

While private attorneys come and leave court with their clients (who are generally "on bail"), the P.D. arrives in court each morning at nine,

takes his station at the defense table, and deposits there the batch of files that he will refer to during the day. When, during morning "calendar,"[8] a private attorney's case is called, the P.D. steps back from the defense table, leaving his belongings in place there, and temporarily relinquishes his station. No private attorney has enough defendants in a given court on a given day to claim a right to make a desk of the defense table. If the P.D. needs some information from his central office, he uses the clerk's telephone, a privilege that few private lawyers feel at home enough to take. In the course of calendar work, a lawyer will often have occasion to request a delay or "continuance" of several days until the next stage of his client's proceedings. The private attorney addresses the prosecutor via the judge to request such an alteration; the P.D. talks directly over to the D.A.:

Private Attorney: "If the prosecutor finds it convenient, your Honor, my client would prefer to have his preliminary hearing on Monday, the 24th."
Judge: "Is that date suitable to the district attorney?"
Prosecutor: "Yes, your honor."
Private Attorney: "Thank you, your Honor."
Public Defender: "Bob, (D.A.), how about moving Smith's prelim up to the 16th?"
Prosecutor: "Well, Jim, we've got Jones on that afternoon."
Public Defender: "Let's see, how's the 22nd?"
Prosecutor: "That's fine, Jim, the 22nd."

If, during the course of a proceeding, the P.D. has some minor matter to tend to with the D.A., he uses the time when a private attorney is addressing the bench to walk over to the prosecutor's table and whisper his requests, suggestions, or questions. The P.D. uses the prosecutor's master calendar to check on an upcoming court date; so does the D.A. with the P.D.'s. The D.A. and P.D. are on a first-name basis and throughout the course of a routine day interact as a team of co-workers.

While the central focus of the private attorney's attention is his client, the courtroom and affairs of court constitute the locus of involvements for the P.D. The public defender and public prosecutor, each representatives of their respective offices, jointly handle the greatest bulk of the court's daily activity.

The P.D. office, rather than assign its attorneys to clients, employs the arrangement of stationing attorneys in different courts to "represent" all those who come before that station. As defendants are moved about from courtroom to courtroom throughout the course of their proceedings (both from municipal to superior courtrooms for felony cases, and from one municipal courtroom to another when there is a specialization of courts, e.g., jury, non-jury, arraignment, etc.), the P.D. sees defendants only at those places in their paths when they appear in the court he is manning. A given defendant may be "represented" by one P.D. at arraignment, another at preliminary hearing, a third at trial and a fourth when sentenced.

At the first interview with a client (initial interviews occur in the jail where attorneys go, *en masse,* to "pick up new defendants" in the afternoons), a file is prepared on the defendant. In each file is recorded the charge brought against the defendant and, among other things, his next court date. Each evening attorneys return new files to the central office where secretaries prepare court books for each courtroom that list the defendants due to appear in a given court on a given day. In the mornings, attorneys take the court books from the office and remove from the central file the files of those defendants due to appear in "their court" that day.

There is little communication between P.D. and client. After the first interview, the defendant's encounters with the P.D. are primarily in court. Only under special circumstances (to be discussed below) are there contacts between lawyers and defendants in the jail before and after appearances in court. The bulk of "preparation for court" (either trials or non-trial matters) occurs at the first interview. The attorney on station, the "attending attorney," is thus a stranger to "his client," and vice versa. Over the course of his proceedings, a defendant will have several attorneys (in one instance a man was "represented" by eight P.D.s on a charge of simple assault). Defendants who come to court find a lawyer they don't know conducting their trials, entering their motions, making their pleas, and the rest. Often there is no introduction of P.D. to defendant; defendants are prepared to expect a strange face:

Don't be surprised when you see another P.D. in court with you on Tuesday. You just do what he tells you to. He'll know all about your case.

P.D.s seldom talk about particular defendants among themselves. When they converse about trials, the facts of cases, etc., they do so not so much for briefing, e.g., "This is what I think you should do when you get him," but rather as small talk, as "What have you got going today?" The P.D. does not rely on the information about a case he receives from a previous attending attorney in order to know how to manage his "representation." Rather, the file is relied upon to furnish all the information essential for making an "appearance." These appearances range from morning calendar work (e.g., arraignments, motions, continuances, etc.) to trials on offenses from drunkenness to assault with a deadly weapon. In the course of a routine day, the P.D. will receive his batch of files in the morning and, seeing them for the first time that day, conduct numerous trials, preliminary hearings, calendar appearances, sentencing proceedings, etc. They do not study files overnight. Attorneys will often only look over a file a half hour or so before the jury trial begins.

THE FIRST INTERVIEW

As the first interview is often the only interview and as the file prepared there is central for the continuing "representation" of the defendant by other attorneys, it is important to examine these interviews and the file's contents. From the outset, the P.D. attends to establishing the typical character of the case before him and thereby instituting routinely employed reduction arrangements. The defendant's appearance, e.g., his race, demeanor, age, style of talk, way of attending to the occasion of his incarceration, etc., provides the P.D. with an initial sense of his place in the social structure. Knowing only that the defendant is charged with section 459 (Burglary) of the penal code, the P.D. employs his conception of typical burglars against which the character of the present defendant is assessed.

. . . he had me fooled for a while. With that accent of his and those Parliaments he was smoking I thought something was strange. It turned out to be just another burglary. You heard him about New York and the way he had a hold on him there that he was running away from. I just guess N.Y. is a funny place, you can never tell what kinds of people get involved in crimes there.

The initial fact of the defendant's "putting in a request to see the P.D." establishes his lower position in the class structure of the community:

We just never get wealthier people here. They usually don't stay in jail overnight and then they call a private attorney. The P.D. gets everything at the bottom of the pile.

Searching over the criminal history (past convictions and arrests) the defendant provides when preliminary face sheet data is recorded in the file, the P.D. gets a sense of the man's typical pattern of criminal activity. It is not the particular offenses for which he is charged that are crucial, but the constellation of prior offenses and the sequential pattern they take:

I could tell as soon as he told me he had four prior drunk charges that he was just another of these skid row bums. You could look at him and tell.

When you see a whole string of forgery counts in the past you pretty much know what kind of case you're dealing with. You either get those who commit an occasional forgery, or those that do nothing but . . . With a whole bunch of prior checks (prior forgery convictions) you can bet that he cashes little ones. I didn't even have to ask for the amount you know. I seldom come across one over a hundred bucks.

From the looks of him and the way he said "I wasn't doing anything, just playing with her," you know, its the usual kind of thing, just a little diddling or something. We can try to get it out on a simple assault.

When a P.D. puts questions to the defendant, he is less concerned with recording nuances of the instant event (e.g., How many feet from the bar were you when the cops came in? Did you break into the back gate or the front door?), than with establishing its similarity with "events of this sort." That similarity is established, not by discovering statutorily relevant events of the present case, but by locating the event in a sociologically constructed class of "such cases." The first questions directed to the defendant are of the character that answers to them either confirm or throw into question the assumed typicality. First questions with ADWs are of the order: "How long had you been drinking before this all started?"; with child molestation cases: "How long were you hanging around before this began?"; with forgery cases: "Was this the second or third check you cashed in the same place?"

We shall present three short excerpts from three first interviews. They all begin with the first question asked after preliminary background data is gathered. The first is with a 288 (child molestation), the second with a 459 (burglary) and the last with a 11530 (possession of marijuana). Each interview was conducted by a different Public Defender. In each case the P.D. had no information about the defendant or this particular crime other than that provided by the penal code number:

288

P.D.: O.K., why don't you start out by telling me how this thing got started?

Def: Well, I was at the park and all I did was to ask this little girl if she wanted to sit on my lap for awhile and, you know, just sit on my lap. Well, about twenty minutes later I'm walkin' down the street about a block away from the park and this cop pulls up and there the same little girl is, you know, sitting in the back seat with some dame. The cop asks me to stick my head in the back seat and he asks the kid if I was the one and she says yes. So he puts me in the car and takes a statement from me and here I am in the joint. All I was doin was playin with her a little. . . .

P.D.: (interrupting) . . . O.K. I get the story, let's see what we can do. If I can get this charge reduced to a misdemeanor, then I would advise you to plead guilty, particularly since you have a record and that wouldn't look too well in court with a jury.

(The interview proceeded for another two or three minutes and the decision to plead guilty was made.)

459

P.D.: Why don't you start by telling me where this place was that you broke into?

Def.: I don't know for sure . . . I think it was on 13th street or something like that.

P.D.: Had you ever been there before?

Def.: I hang around that neighborhood, you know, so I guess I've been in the place before, yeah.

P.D.: What were you going after?

Def.: I don't know, whatever there was so's I could get a little cash. Man, I was pretty broke that night.

P.D.: Was anyone with you?

Def.: No, I was by myself.

P.D.: How much did you break up the place?

Def.: I didn't do nothing. The back window was open a little bit, see, and I just put my hand in there and opened the door. I was just walking in when I heard police comin' so I turn around and start to run. And they saw me down the block and that was that.

P.D.: Were you drunk at the time?

Def.: I wasn't drunk, no. I maybe had a drink or two that evening but I wasn't drunk or anything like that.

11530

P.D.: Well Smith, why don't you tell me where they found it (the marijuana)?

Def.: I was driving home from the drugstore with my friend and this cop car pulls me up to the side. Two guys get out, one of them was wearing a uniform and the other was a plainclothes man. They told us to get out of the car and then they searched me and then my friend. Then this guy without the uniform he looked over into the car and picked up this thing from the back floor and said something to the other one. Then he asked me if I had any more of the stuff and I said I didn't know what he was talking about. So he wrote something down on a piece of paper and made me sign it. Then he told my friend to go home and they took me down here to the station and booked me on possession of marijuana. I swear I didn't have no marijuana.

P.D.: You told me you were convicted of possession in 1959.

Def.: Yeah, but I haven't touched any of the stuff since then. I don't know what it was doing in my car, but I haven't touched the stuff since that last time.

P.D.: You ought to know it doesn't make any difference whether or not they catch you using, just so as they find it on your possession or in a car, or your house, or something.

Def.: Man, I swear I don't know how it got there. Somebody must have planted it there.

P.D.: Look, you know as well as I do that with your prior conviction and this charge now that you could go away from here for five years or so. So just calm down a minute and let's look at this thing reason-

ably. If you go to trial and lose the trial, you're stuck. You'll be in the joint until you're 28 years old. If you plead to this one charge without the priors then we can get you into jail maybe, or a year or two at the most in the joint. If you wait until the preliminary hearing and then they charge the priors, boy you've had it, it's too late.

Def.: Well how about a trial?

(After ten minutes, the defendant decided to plead guilty to one charge of possession, before the date of the preliminary hearing.)

Let us consider, in light of the previous discussion, some of the features of these interviews.

1. In each case the information sought is not "data" for organizing the particular facts of the case for deciding proper penal code designations (or with a view toward undermining the assignment of a designation in an anticipated trial). In the 288 instance, the P.D. interrupted when he had enough information to confirm his sense of the case's typicality and construct a typifying portrayal of the present defendant. The character of the information supplied by the defendant was such that it was specifically lacking detail about the particular occurrences, e.g., the time, place, what was said to the girl, what precisely did the defendant do or not do, his "state of mind," etc. The defendant's appearance and prior record (in this case the defendant was a fifty-five year old white, unemployed, unskilled laborer, with about ten prior drunk arrests, seven convictions, and two prior sex offense violations) was relied upon to provide the sense of the present occasion. The P.D. straightforwardly approached the D.A. and arranged for a "contributing to the delinquency of a minor" reduction. In the burglary case, the question, "Had you ever been there before?", was intended to elicit what was received, e.g., that the place was a familiar one to the defendant. Knowing that the place was in the defendant's neighborhood establishes its character as a skid row area business; that the First Federal Bank was not entered has been confirmed. "What were you going after?" also irrelevant to the 459 section of the penal code, provides him with information that there was no special motive for entering this establishment. The question, "Was anyone with you?", when answered negatively, placed the event in the typical class of "burglaries" as soli-

tary, non-coordinated activities. The remaining questions were directed as well to confirming the typical character of the event, and the adequacy of the defendant's account is not decided by whether or not the P.D. can now decide whether the statutory definition of the contemplated reduction or the original charge is satisfied. Its adequacy is determined by the ability with which the P.D. can detect its normal character. The accounts provided thus may have the character of anecdotes, sketches, phrases, etc. In the first instance, with the 288, the prior record and the defendant's appearance, demeanor and style of talking about the event was enough to warrant his typical treatment.

2. The most important feature of the P.D.'s questioning is the presupposition of guilt that makes his proposed questions legitimate and answerable at the outset. To pose the question, "Why don't you start by telling me where this place was that you broke into?" as a lead question, the P.D. takes it that the defendant is guilty of a crime and that the crime for which he is charged probably describes what essentially occurred.

The P.D.'s activity is seldom geared to securing acquittals for clients. He and the D.A., as co-workers in the same courts, take it for granted that the persons who come before the courts are guilty of crimes and are to be treated accordingly:

Most of them have records as you can see. Almost all of them have been through our courts before. And the police just don't make mistakes in this town. That's one thing about __, we've got the best police force in the state.

As we shall argue below, the way defendants are "represented" (the station manning rather than assignment of counselors to clients), the way trials are conducted, the way interviews are held and the penal code employed—all of the P.D.'s work is premised on the supposition that people charged with crimes have committed crimes.

This presupposition makes such first questions as "Why don't you start by telling me where this place was . . ." reasonable questions. When the answer comes: "What place? I don't know what you are talking about," the defendant

is taken to be a phony, making an "innocent pitch." The conceivable first question: "Did you do it?" is not asked because it is felt that this gives the defendant the notion that he can try an "innocent pitch":

I never ask them, "Did you do it?" because on one hand I know they did and mainly because then they think that they can play games with us. We can always check their records and usually they have a string of offenses. You don't have to, though, because in a day or two they change their story and plead guilty. Except for the stubborn ones.

Of the possible answers to an opening question, bewilderment, the inability to answer or silence are taken to indicate that the defendant is putting the P.D. on. For defendants who refuse to admit anything, the P.D. threatens:

Look, if you don't want to talk, that's your business. I can't help you. All I can say is that if you go to trial on this beef you're going to spend a long time in the joint. When you get ready to tell me the story straight, then we can see what can be done.

If the puzzlement comes because the wrong question is asked, e.g., "There wasn't any fight— that's not the way it happened," the defendant will start to fill in the story. The P.D. awaits to see if, how far, and in what ways the instant case is deviant. If the defendant is charged with burglary and a middle class establishment was burglarized, windows shattered, a large payroll sought after and a gun used, then the reduction to petty theft, generally employed for "normal burglaries," would be more difficult to arrange.

Generally, the P.D. doesn't have to discover the atypical kinds of cases through questioning. Rather, the D.A., in writing the original complaint, provides the P.D. with clues that the typical recipe, given the way the event occurred, will not be allowable. Where the way it occurs is such that it does not resemble normal burglaries and the routinely used penalty would reduce it *too far* commensurate with the way the crime occurred, the D.A. frequently charges various situationally included offenses, indicating to the P.D. that the procedure to employ here is to suggest "dropping" some of the charges, leaving the originally charged greatest offense as it stands.

In the general case he doesn't charge all those offenses that he legally might. He might charge "child molesting" and "loitering around a schoolyard," but typically only the greater charge is made. The D.A. does so so as to provide for a later reduction that will appear particularly lenient in that it seemingly involves a *change* in the charge. Were he to charge both molesting and loitering, he would be obliged, moreover, should the case come to trial, to introduce evidence for both offenses. The D.A. is thus always constrained not to set overly high charges or not situationally included multiple offenses by the possibility that the defendant will not plead guilty to a lesser offense and the case will go to trial. Of primary importance is that he doesn't charge multiple offenses so that the P.D. will be in the best position vis-à-vis the defendant. He thus charges the first complaint so as to provide for a "setup."

The alteration of charges must be made in open court. The P.D. requests to have a new plea entered:

P.D.: Your honor, in the interests of justice, my client would like to change his plea of not guilty to the charge of burglary and enter a plea of guilty to the charge of petty theft.
Judge: Is this new plea acceptable to the prosecution?
D.A.: Yes, your honor.

The prosecutor knows beforehand that the request will be made and has agreed in advance to allow it.

I asked a P.D. how he felt about making such requests in open court, i.e., asking for a reduction from one offense to another when the latter is obviously not necessarily included and often (as is the case in burglary to petty theft) not situationally included. He summarized the office's feeling:

. . . in the old days, ten or so years ago, we didn't like to do it in front of the judge. What we used to do when we made a deal was that the D.A. would dismiss the original charge and write up a new complaint altogether. That took a lot of time. We had to re-arraign him all over again back in the muni court and everything. Besides, in the same courtroom, everyone used to know what was going on anyway. Now, we just ask for a change of plea to the lesser charge regardless of

whether it's included or not. Nobody thinks twice about asking for petty theft on burglary, or drunkenness on car theft, or something like that. It's just the way it's done.

Some restrictions are felt. Assaultive crimes (e.g., ADW, simple assault, attempted murder, etc.) will not be reduced to or from "money offenses" (burglary, robbery, theft) unless the latter involve weapons or some violence. Also, victimless crimes (narcotics, drunkenness) are not reduced to or from assaultive or "money offenses," unless there is some factual relation, e.g., drunkenness with a fight might turn out to be simple assault reduced to drunkenness.

For most cases that come before their courts, the P.D. and D.A. are able to employ reductions that are formulated for handling typical cases. While some burglaries, rapes, narcotics violations and petty thefts, are instigated in strange ways and involve atypical facts, some manipulation in the way the initial charge is made can be used to set up a procedure to replace the simple charge-alteration form of reducing.

RECALCITRANT DEFENDANTS

Most of the P.D.'s cases that "have to go to trial" are those where the P.D. is not able to sell the defendant on the "bargain." These are cases for which reductions are available, reductions that are constructed on the basis of the typicality of the offense and allowable by the D.A. These are normal crimes committed by "stubborn" defendants.

So-called "stubborn" defendants will be distinguished from a second class of offenders, those who commit *crimes which are atypical in their character (for this community, at this time, etc.) or who commit crimes which, while typical (recurrent for this community, this time, etc.), are committed atypically.* The manner in which the P.D. and D.A. must conduct the representation and prosecution of these defendants is radically different. To characterize the special problems the P.D. has with each class of defendants, it is first necessary to point out a general feature of the P.D.'s orientation to the work of the courts that has hitherto not been made explicit. This orientation will be merely sketched here.

As we noticed, the defendant's guilt is not attended to. That is to say, the presupposition of guilt, as a *presupposition,* does not say "You are guilty" with a pointing, accusatory finger, but, "You are guilty; you know it, I know it, so let's get down to the business of deciding what to do with you." When a defendant agrees to plead guilty, he is not *admitting* his guilt; when asked to plead guilty, he is not being asked, "Come on, admit it, you know you were *wrong,*" but rather, "Why don't you be sensible about this thing?" What is sought is not a *confession,* but reasonableness.

The presupposition of guilt as a way of attending to the treatment of defendants has its counterpart in the way the P.D. attends to the entire court process, prosecuting machinery, law enforcement techniques, and the community.

For P.D. and D.A. it is a routinely encountered phenomenon that persons in the community regularly commit criminal offenses, are regularly brought before the courts, and are regularly transported to the state and county penal institutions. To confront a "criminal" is, for D.A. and P.D., no special experience, nothing to tell their wives about, nothing to record as outstanding in the happenings of the day. Before "their court," scores of "criminals" pass each day.

The morality of the courts is taken for granted. The P.D. assumes that the D.A., the police, judge, the narcotics agents and others all conduct their business as it must be conducted and in a proper fashion. That the police may hide out to deceive petty violators; that narcotics agents may regularly employ illicit entrapment procedures to find suspects; that investigators may routinely arrest suspects before they have sufficient grounds and only later uncover warrantable evidence for a formal booking; that the police may beat suspects; that judges may be "tough" because they are looking to support for higher office elections; that some laws may be specifically prejudicial against certain classes of persons—whatever may be the actual course of charging and convicting defendants—all of this is taken, as one P.D. put it, "as part of the system and the way it has to be." And the P.D. is part of the team.

While it is common to overhear private attorneys call judges "bastards," policemen "hood-lums," and prosecutors "sadists," the P.D., in the presence of such talk, remains silent. When the P.D. "loses" a case—and we shall see that *losing* is an adequate description only for some circumstances—he is likely to say "I knew *he* couldn't win." Private attorneys, on the other hand, will not hesitate to remark, as one did in a recent case, "You haven't got a fucking chance in front of that son-of-a-bitch dictator." In the P.D. office, there is a total absence of such condemnation.

The P.D. takes it for granted and attends to the courts in accord with the view that "what goes on in this business is what goes on, and what goes on is the way it should be." It is rare to hear a public defender voice protest against a particular law, procedure, or official. One of the attorneys mentioned that he felt the new narcotics law (which makes it mandatory that a high minimum sentence be served for "possession or sale of narcotics") wasn't too severe "considering that they wanted to give them the chair." Another indicated that the more rigid statute "will probably cure a lot of them because they'll be in for so long." One P.D. feels that wire-tapping would be a useful adjunct to police procedure. It is generally said, by everyone in the office, that ". . . is one of the best cities in the state when it comes to police."

In the P.D.'s interviews, the defendant's guilt only becomes a topic when the defendant himself attempts to direct attention to his innocence. Such attempts are never taken seriously by the P.D., but are seen as "innocent pitches," as "being wise," as "not knowing what is good for him." Defendants who make "innocent pitches" often find themselves able to convince the P.D. to have trials. The P.D. is in a professional and organizational bind in that he requires that his "clients" agree with whatever action he takes "on their behalf":

Can you imagine what might happen if we went straight to the D.A. with a deal to which the client later refused to agree? Can you see him in court screaming how the P.D. sold him out? As it is, we get plenty of letters purporting to show why we don't do our job. Judges are swamped with letters condemning the P.D. Plenty of appeals get started this way.

Some defendants don't buy the offer of less time as constituting sufficient grounds for avoiding a trial. To others, it appears that "copping out" is worse than having a trial regardless of the consequences for the length of sentence. The following remarks, taken from P.D. files, illustrate the terms in which such "stubborn" defendants are conceived:

Def wants a trial, but he is dead. In lieu of a possible 995, DA agreed to put note in his file recommending a deal. This should be explored and encouraged as big break for Def.

Chance of successful defense negligible. Def realizes this but, says he ain't going to cop to no strong-arm. See if we can set him straight.

Dead case. Too many witnesses and . . . used in two of the transactions. However, Def is a very squirmy jailhouse lawyer and refuses to face facts.

Possibly the DA in Sup/Ct could be persuaded into cutting her loose if she took the 211 and one of the narco counts. If not, the Def, who is somewhat recalcitrant and stubborn, will probably demand a JT (jury trial).

The routine trial, generated as it is by the defendant's refusal to make a lesser plea, is the "defendant's fault":

What the hell are we supposed to do with them? If they can't listen to good reason and take a bargain, then it's their tough luck. If they go to prison, well, they're the ones who are losing the trials, not us.

When the P.D. enters the courtroom, he takes it that he is going to lose, e.g., the defendant is going to prison. When he "prepares" for trial, he doesn't prepare to "win." There is no attention given to "how am I going to construct a defense in order that I can get this defendant free of the charges against him?" In fact, he doesn't "prepare for trial" in any "ordinary" sense. (I use the term *ordinary* with hesitation; what *preparation for trial* might in fact involve with other than P.D. lawyers has not, to my knowledge, been investigated.)

For the P.D., "preparation for trial" involves, essentially, learning what "burglary cases" are like, what "rape cases" are like, what "assaults" are like. The P.D.'s main concern is to conduct his part of the proceedings in accord with complete respect for proper legal procedure. He raises objections to improper testimony; intro- duces motions whenever they seem called for; demands his "client's rights" to access to the prosecution's evidence before trial (through so-called "discovery proceedings"); cross-examines all witnesses; does not introduce evidence that he expects will not be allowable; asks all those questions of all those people that he must in order to have addressed himself to the task of insuring that the *corpus delicti* has been established; carefully summarizes the evidence that has been presented in making a closing argument. Throughout, at every point, he conducts his "defense" in such a manner that no one can say of him, "He has been negligent; there are grounds for appeal here." He systematically provides, in accord with the prescriptions of due process and the fourteenth amendment, a completely proper, "adequate legal representation."

At the same time, the district attorney, and the county which employs them both, can rely on the P.D., not to attempt to morally degrade police officers in cross examination; not to impeach the state's witnesses by trickery; not to attempt an exposition of the entrapment methods of narcotics agents; not to condemn the community for the "racial prejudice that produces our criminals" (the phrase of a private attorney during closing argument); not to challenge the prosecution of "these women who are trying to raise a family without a husband" (the statement of another private attorney during closing argument on a welfare fraud case); in sum, not to make an issue of the moral character of the administrative machinery of the local courts, the community or the police. He will not cause any serious trouble for the routine motion of the court conviction process. Laws will not be challenged, cases will not be tried to test the constitutionality of procedures and statutes, judges will not be personally degraded, police will be free from scrutiny to decide the legitimacy of their operations, and the community will not be condemned for its segregative practices against Negroes. The P.D.'s defense is completely proper, in accord with correct legal procedure, and specifically amoral in its import, manner of delivery, and perceived implications for the propriety of the prosecution enterprise.

In "return" for all this, the district attorney treats the defendant's guilt in a matter-of-fact fashion, doesn't get hostile in the course of the proceedings, doesn't insist that the jury or judge "throw the book," but rather "puts on a trial" (in their way of referring to their daily tasks) in order to, with a minimum of strain, properly place the defendant behind bars. Both prosecutor and public defender thus protect the moral character of the other's charges from exposure. Should the P.D. attend to demonstrating the innocence of his client by attempting to undermine the legitimate character of police operations, the prosecutor might feel obliged in return to employ devices to degrade the moral character of the P.D.'s client. Should the D.A attack defendants in court, by pointing to the specifically immoral character of their activities, the P.D. might feel obligated, in response, to raise into relief the moral texture of the D.A.'s and police's and community's operations. Wherever possible, each holds the other in check. But the "check" need not be continuously held in place, or even attended to self-consciously, for both P.D. and D.A. trust one another implicitly. The D.A. knows, with certainty, that the P.D. will not make a closing argument that resembles the following by a private attorney, from which I have paraphrased key excerpts:

If it hadn't been for all the publicity that this case had in our wonderful local newspapers, you wouldn't want to throw the book at these men.

If you'd clear up your problems with the Negro in . . . maybe you wouldn't have cases like this in your courts.

(after sentence was pronounced) . . . Your honor, I just would like to say one thing—that I've never heard or seen such a display of injustice as I've seen here in this court today. It's a sad commentary on the state of our community if people like yourself pay more attention to the local political machines than to the lives of our defendants. I think you are guilty of that, your Honor.

(At this last statement, one of the P.D.s who was in the courtroom turned to me and said, "He sure is looking for a contempt charge.")

The P.D. knows how to conduct his trials because he knows how to conduct "assault with deadly weapons" trials, "burglary" trials, "rape" trials, and the rest. The *corpus delicti* here provides him with a basis for asking "proper questions," making the "proper" cross examinations, and pointing out the "proper" things to jurors about "reasonable doubt." He need not extensively gather information about the specific facts of the instant case. Whatever is needed in the way of "facts of the case" arise in the course of the D.A.'s presentation. He employs the "strategy" of directing the same questions to the witness as were put by the D.A. with added emphasis on the question mark, or an inserted "Did you really see . . . ?" His "defense" consists of attempting to "bring out" slightly variant aspects of the D.A.'s story by questioning his own witnesses (whom he seldom interviews before beginning trial but who are interviewed by the Office's two "investigators") and the defendant.

With little variation, the same questions are put to all defendants charged with the same crimes. The P.D. learns with experience what to expect as the "facts of the case." These facts, in their general structure, portray social circumstances that he can anticipate by virtue of his knowledge of the normal features of offense categories and types of offenders. The "details" of the instant case are "discovered" over the course of hearing them in court. In this regard, the "information" that "comes out" is often as new to him as to the jury.

Employing a common-sense conception of what criminal lawyers behave like in cross examination and argument, and the popular portrayal of their demeanor and style of addressing adversary witnesses, the onlooker comes away with the sense of having witnessed not a trial at all, but a set of motions, a perfunctorily carried-off event. A sociological analysis of this sense would require a systematic attempt to describe the features of adversary trial conduct.

A NOTE ON SPECIAL CASES

To conduct trials with "stubborn" defendants (so-called) is no special trouble. Here trials are viewed as a "waste of time." Murders, embezzlements, multiple rape cases (several defendants with one victim), large scale robberies, dope ring operations, those cases that arouse public attention and receive special notice in the papers— these are cases whose normal features are not constructed and for which, even were a guilty plea available, both parties feel uncomfortably obliged to bring issues of moral character into the courtroom. The privacy of the P.D.-D.A. conviction machinery through the use of the guilty plea can no longer be preserved. Only "normal defendants" are accorded this privacy. The pressure for a public hearing, in the sense of "bringing the public in to see and monitor the character of the proceedings," must be allowed to culminate in a full-blown jury trial. There is a general preference in the P.D. office to handle routine cases without a jury, if it must go to trial at all. In the special case the jury must be employed and with them a large audience of onlookers, newspapermen, and daily paper coverage must be tolerated.

To put on a fight is a discomforting task for persons who regularly work together as a team. Every effort is made to bind off the event of a special case by heightened interaction outside the courtroom. In the routine case, with no jury or at least no press coverage, the whole trial can be handled as a backstage operation. With special cases there can be no byplay conversation in the courtroom between D.A. and P.D., and no leaving court together, arm in arm. Metaphorically, two persons who regularly dance together must now appear, with the lights turned on, to be fighting.

The P.D. Office reserves several of its attorneys to handle such cases. By keeping the regular personnel away from particular courtrooms, their routine interactions with the D.A. can be properly maintained. An older, more experienced attorney, from each side, comes to court to put on the show. The device of so handling the assignment of attorneys to cases serves to mark off the event as a special occasion, to set it outside the regular ordering of relationships that must resume when the special, and dreaded, case becomes a statistic in the penal institution records.

With the special cases, the client-attorney assignment procedure is instituted. The head of the P.D. Office, along with a coterie of older attorneys, goes to the first interview in the jail, and these same attorneys, or some of them, take over the case and stay with it, handling its development with kid gloves. The concern to provide "adequate legal representation" may be relegated

to a back seat. Both P.D. and D.A. must temporarily step outside their typical modes of mutual conduct and yet, at the same time, not permanently jeopardize the stability of their usual teamlike relationship.

SOME CONCLUSIONS

An examination of the use of the penal code by actually practicing attorneys has revealed that categories of crime, rather than being "unsuited" to sociological analysis, are so employed as to make their analysis crucial to empirical understanding. What categories of crime are, i.e., who is assembled under this one or that, what constitute the behaviors inspected for deciding such matters, what "etiologically significant" matters are incorporated within their scope, is not, the present findings indicate, to be decided on the basis of an *a priori* inspection of their formally available definitions. The sociologist who regards the category "theft" with penal code in hand and proposes necessary, "theoretically relevant" revisions, is constructing an imagined use of the penal code as the basis for his criticism. For in their actual use, categories of crime, as we have reiterated continuously above, are, at least for this legal establishment, the shorthand reference terms for that knowledge of the social structure and its criminal events upon which the task of practically organizing the work of "representation" is premised. That knowledge includes, embodied within what burglary, petty theft, narcotics violations, child molestation and the rest *actually stand for*, knowledge of modes of criminal activity, ecological characteristics of the community, patterns of daily slum life, psychological and social biographies of offenders, criminal histories and futures; in sum, practically tested criminological wisdom. The operations of the Public Defender system, and it is clear that upon comparative analysis with other legal "firms" it would be somewhat distinctive in character, are routinely maintained via the proper use of categories of crime for everyday decision making. The properties of that use are not described in the state criminal code, nor are the operations of reduction, detailed above.

A cautionary word is required. It will appear as obvious that the system of providing "defense" to indigent persons described above is not representative of criminal defense work generally. How the penal code is employed, i.e., how behaviors are scrutinized under its jurisdiction and dispensations made via operations performed on its categories, in other kinds of legal establishments, has not been investigated here. The present case, albeit apparently specialized, was chosen as an example only. It may well be that, in certain forms of legal work, the penal code as a statutory document is accorded a much different and more "rigorous" scrutiny. The legalistic character of some criminal prosecutions leads one to suspect that the "letter of the law" might constitute a key reference point in preparing for a criminal defense, aiming for acquittal, or changing a statutory regulation.

NOTES

1. D. R. Cressey, "Criminological Research and the Definition of Crimes," *American Journal of Sociology,* Vol. 61 (No. 6), 1951, p. 548. See also, J. Hall, *Theft, Law and Society,* second edition, Indianapolis: Bobbs-Merrill, 1952; and E. Sutherland, *Principles of Criminology,* review, New York: Lippincott, 1947, p. 218. An extensive review of "typological developments" is available in D. C. Gibbons and D. L. Garrity, "Some Suggestions for the Development of Etiological and Treatment Theory in Criminology," *Social Forces,* Vol. 38 (No. 1) 1959.

2. The most thorough statement of this position, borrowing from the writings of Harold Garfinkel, can be found in the recent critical article by J. I. Kitsuse and A. V. Cicourel, "A Note on the Official Use of Statistics," *Social Problems,* Vol. 11, No. 2 (Fall, 1963) pp. 131–139.

3. See D.J. Newman, "Pleading Guilty for Considerations," 46 J. Crim. L. C. and P. S. Also, M. Schwartz, *Cases and Materials on Professional Responsibility and the Administration of Criminal Justice,* San Francisco: Matthew Bender and Co., 1961, esp. pp. 79–105.

4. C. W. Fricke, *California Criminal Law,* Los Angeles: The Legal Book Store, 1961, p. 41.

5. People v. Greer, 30 Cal. 2d, 589.

6. For general histories of indigent defender systems in the United States, see The Association of the Bar of the City of New York, *Equal Justice for the Accused,* Garden City, New York: 1959; and E. A. Brownell, *Legal Aid in the United States,* Rochester, New York: The Lawyers Cooperative Publishing Company, 1951.

7. The experience of the Public Defender system is distinctly different in this regard from that of the Legal Aid Societies, which, I am told, have continually met very strong opposition to their establishment by local bar associations.

8. "Calendar part" consists of that portion of the court day, typically in the mornings, when all matters other than trials are heard, e.g., arraignments, motions, continuances, sentencing, probation reports, etc.

White-Collar and Corporate Crime

White-collar and corporate crime have only recently been incorporated into the general area of deviance theory, even though they account for widespread social harm. Edwin Sutherland, the progenitor of the term "white-collar crime," considers the question of whether it is really "crime" in the excerpt "Is 'White Collar Crime' Crime?" which is taken from his classic book, *White-Collar Crime*. Sutherland examines various laws relating to business practices and their differential implementation. He finds that white-collar crime fits the general criteria of criminal behavior, as contained in the legal definition of social injury and criminal punishment. He also notes that criminologists have not seen these deviant behaviors as crimes because they are treated differently by the legal system, and that lack of resentment toward such acts on the part of the public is explained by their lenient treatment by authorities.

In "Medical Criminals," which is a chapter from the book, *Prescription for Profit: How Doctors Defraud Medicaid,* Paul Jesilow, Gilbert Geis, and I describe the criminal and abusive behavior of physicians in the government health insurance program, Medicaid. Four basic categories of deviance are examined, including billing schemes, poor quality of care, illegal distribution of controlled substances, and sex with patients. Opportunities for dishonesty are dis-

cussed along with actual case histories and punishments meted out by authorities. Doctors rarely lose their licenses for Medicaid fraud, and the penalties for such acts are relatively lenient given the fiscal damage and abuse of patients involved in such cases.

Perhaps the single most costly set of white-collar crimes in history involved the savings and loan debacle in the 1980s. Fraud was responsible for a significant portion of the money lost by failed savings and loans—money that now must be paid by citizens. In "White-Collar Crime in the Savings and Loan Scandal," Kitty Calavita and I use government reports to examine fraud in the savings and loan industry and trace savings and loan crime to the perverse incentives created by government deregulation in the early 1980s. The study discusses a typology of crimes that include "unlawful risk taking, covering up, and collective embezzlement," which refers to the deliberate looting of funds by top-level bank officials. Thrift crime and the response of law enforcement are discussed in light of the government's limited capacity to deal with the sheer magnitude of the savings and loan crisis.

In "Denying the Guilty Mind," Michael Benson examines how white-collar criminals deny criminal intent when they are caught in acts of deviance. Benson studies the reactions of offenders, including anti-trust and tax violators, those violating financial trust, and those convicted of fraud and false statements. He shows how offenders attempt to deflect blame and defeat the process of status degradation during their criminal cases. "Denying the guilty mind" helps to defeat the success of the degradation ceremony and allows for minimal identity transformation of the white-collar offender.

Mark Pogrebin, Eric Poole, and Amos Martinez examine sexual intimacy between therapists and clients in their article, "Accounts of Professional Misdeeds." Recognized as one of the most serious violations of the professional-client relationship, subject to both regulatory and administrative penalties, and, in several states, criminal sanctions, the authors examine these offenses through written accounts submitted to a state grievance board by psychotherapists who had complaints filed against them by former patients.

These data are analyzed in terms of accounts and apologies and how these help structure vocabularies of motive used by these therapists to explain their deviant behavior.

In "Computer Crime," which is a chapter from the book, *Profit Without Honor: White-Collar Crime and the Looting of America,* Stephen Rosoff, Robert Tillman, and I review relatively new and technologically sophisticated forms of deviance that are enacted through the use of computers. Among the deviant behaviors presented are embezzlement and financial theft, hacking, espionage, and phone phreaking. The study employs numerous rich case histories and ties their relevant themes to theories of deviance. Among other things, we find that improved security technology is often met with better criminal technology by these sophisticated deviants, making it extraordinarily difficult to maintain effective social control mechanisms.

Is "White Collar Crime" Crime?*

Edwin H. Sutherland

[As of the writing of this chapter, which was published in 1949], 980 decisions have been made against the 70 largest industrial and mercantile corporations, with an average of 14.0 decisions per corporation. Although all of these [were] decisions that the corporations have acted unlawfully, only 158, or 16 percent, of them were made by criminal courts and were ipso facto decisions that the behavior was criminal. Since not all unlawful behavior is criminal behavior, these decisions can be used as a measure of criminal behavior only insofar as the other 822

*From *White-Collar Crime: The Uncut Version* by Edwin H. Sutherland, (New Haven: Yale University Press, 1983), pp. 45–62. (c) 1983 by Yale University Press. Reprinted by permission.

decisions can be shown to be decisions that the behavior was criminal as well as unlawful.

This is a problem in the definition of crime and involves two types of questions: First, may the word "crime" be applied to the behavior regarding which these decisions were made? Second, if so, why is it not generally applied and why have not criminologists regarded white collar crime as cognate with other crime? The first question involves semantics, the second explanation or interpretation. The following analysis will be limited almost entirely to the laws regarding restraint of trade, misrepresentation in advertising, infringements of patents and analogous rights, and unfair labor practices in violation of the National Labor Relations Law. Little attention is devoted to the other laws, in part because some of the other laws are explicit criminal laws, such as those relating to rebates or adulteration of foods and drugs, and in part because so many different laws are involved in the miscellaneous group of offenses that the analysis would be unduly extended if each of those laws was given specific attention.

The definition of crime, from the point of view of the present analysis, is important only as a means of determining whether the behavior should be included within the scope of a theory of criminal behavior. More specifically, the problem is: From the point of view of a theory of criminal behavior, are the illegal acts of corporations which have been tabulated above cognate with the burglaries, robberies, and other crimes which are customarily included within the scope of theories of criminal behavior? Some writers have argued that an act is criminal only if a criminal court has officially determined that the person accused of that act has committed a crime. This limitation in the definition of crime may be made properly if a writer is interested primarily in administrative questions. The warden of a prison would not be justified in receiving an offender in the penal institution unless that offender had been officially convicted and sentenced to serve a term of imprisonment in that institution. Similarly, public authorities would not be justified in denying civil rights to offenders who had not been convicted of crimes. In contrast, the criminologist who is interested in a theory of criminal behavior needs to know only that a certain class of acts is legally defined as crime and that a particular person has committed an act of this class. The criminologist needs to have certain knowledge on both of these points, but for this purpose a decision of a court is no more essential than it is for certain knowledge in chemistry or biology. However, . . . decisions of courts and commissions have been used as proof that prohibited acts have been committed.

The essential characteristic of crime is that it is behavior which is prohibited by the State as an injury to the State and against which the State may react, at least as a last resort, by punishment. The two abstract criteria generally regarded by legal scholars as necessary elements in a definition of crime are legal description of an act as socially harmful and legal provision of a penalty for the act.[1]

The first of these criteria—legal definition of a social harm—applies to all of the classes of acts which are included in the 980 decisions [referred to] above. This can be readily determined by the words in the statutes—"crime" or "misdemeanor" in some, and "unfair," "discrimination," or "infringement" in all the others. The person injured may be divided into two groups: first, a relatively small number of persons engaged in the same occupation as the offenders or in related occupations, and second, the general public, either as consumers or as constituents of the general social institutions which are affected by the violations of the laws.

The antitrust laws are designed to protect competitors and also to protect the institution of free competition as the regulator of the economic system and thereby to protect consumers against arbitrary prices, and to protect the institution of democracy against the dangers of great concentration of wealth in the hands of monopolies. Laws against false advertising are designed to protect competitors against unfair competition and also to protect consumers against fraud. The National Labor Relations Law is designed to protect employees against coercion by employers and also to protect the general public against interferences with commerce due to strikes and lockouts. The laws against infringements are designed to protect the owners of patents, copyrights, and trademarks against deprivation of their property and against unfair competition, and also to protect the institution of patents and copyrights which was established in order to "promote the progress of science and the useful arts." Violations of these laws are legally defined as injuries to the parties specified.

Each of these laws has a logical basis in the common law and is an adaptation of the common law to modern social organization. False advertising is related to common law fraud, and infringement to larceny. The National Labor Relations Law, as an attempt to prevent coercion, is related to the common law prohibition of restrictions on freedom in the form of assault, false imprisonment, and extortion. For at least two centuries prior to the enactment of the modern antitrust laws, the common law was moving against restraint of trade, monopoly, and unfair competition.

Each of the four types of laws under consideration, with the possible exception of the laws regarding infringements, grew primarily out of considerations of the welfare of the organized society. In this respect, they are analogous to the laws of the earliest societies, where crimes were largely limited to injuries such as treason, in which the organized society was the victim and particular persons suffered only as they were members of the organized society. Subsequent criminal laws have been concerned principally with person-to-person injuries, as in larceny, and the State has taken jurisdiction over the procedures principally in order to bring private vengeance under public control. The interest of the State in such behavior is secondary or derivative. In this sense, the four laws under consideration may properly be regarded as criminal laws in a more fundamental sense than the laws regarding larceny.

Each of the four laws provides a penal sanction and thus meets the second criterion in the definition of crime, and each of the adverse decisions under these four laws, except certain decisions under the infringement laws to be discussed later, is a decision that a crime was committed. This conclusion will be made more specific by analysis of the penal sanctions provided in the four laws.

The Sherman Antitrust Act states explicitly that a violation of the law is a misdemeanor. Three methods of enforcement of this law are provided, each of them involving procedures regarding misdemeanors. First, it may be enforced by the usual criminal prosecution, resulting in the imposition of fine or imprisonment. Second, the attorney general of the United States and the several district attorneys are given the "duty" of "repressing and preventing" violations of the law by petitions for injunctions, and violations of the injunctions are punishable as contempt of court. This method of enforcing a criminal law was an invention and, as will be described later, is the key to the interpretation of the differential implementation of the criminal law as applied to white collar criminals. Third, parties who are injured by violations of the law are authorized to sue for damages, with a mandatory provision that the damages awarded be three times the injuries suffered. These damages in excess of reparation are penalties for violation of the law. They are payable to the injured party in order to induce him to take the initiative in the enforcement of the criminal law and in this respect are similar to the earlier methods of private prosecutions under the criminal law. All three of these methods of enforcement are based on decisions that a criminal law was violated and therefore that a crime was committed; the decisions of a civil court or a court of equity as to these violations are as good evidence of criminal behavior as is the decision of a criminal court.

Judge Carpenter stated in regard to the injunctions under the antitrust law, "The Supreme Court in upholding them necessarily has determined that the things which were enjoined were crimes, as defined by one at least of the first three sections of the Act."[2]

The Sherman Antitrust Act has been supplemented by the Federal Trade Commission Law, the Clayton Law, and several other laws. Some of these supplementary laws define violations as crimes and provide the conventional penalties, but most of them do not make the criminality explicit. A large proportion of the cases which are dealt with under these supplementary laws could be dealt with, instead, under the original Sherman Act, which is explicitly a criminal law, or under the antitrust laws of the several states, which also are explicit criminal laws. In practice, the supplementary laws are generally under the jurisdiction of the Federal Trade Commission, which has authority to make official decisions as to violations. The commission has two principal sanctions under its control, namely: the stipulation and the cease and desist order. The commission may, after the violation of the law has been proved, accept a stipulation from the corporation that it will not violate the law in the future. Such stipulations are customarily restricted to the minor or technical violations. If a stipulation is violated or if no stipulation is accepted, the commission may issue a cease and desist order; this is equivalent to a court's injunction except that violation is not punishable as contempt. If the commission's desist order is violated, the commission may apply to the court for an injunction, the violation of which is punishable as contempt. By an amendment to the Federal Trade Commission Law in the Wheeler-Lea Act of 1938 an order of the commission becomes "final" if not officially questioned within a specified time and there after its violation is punishable by a civil fine. Thus, although certain interim procedures may be used in the enforcement of the laws supplementary to the Sherman Antitrust Act, fines or imprisonment for contempt is available if the interim procedures fail. In this respect the interim procedures are similar to probation in ordinary criminal cases. An unlawful act is not defined as criminal by the fact that it is punished, but by the fact that it is punishable. Larceny is as truly a crime when the thief is placed on probation as when he is committed to prison. The argument may be made that punishment for contempt of court is not punishment for violation of the original law and that, therefore, the original law does not contain a penal sanction. This reasoning is specious since the original law provides the injunction with its penalty as a part of the procedure for enforcement. Consequently, all of the decisions made under the amendments to the antitrust law are decisions that the corporations committed crimes.[3]

The laws regarding false advertising, as included in the decisions under consideration, are of two types. First, false advertising in the form of false labels is defined in the Pure Food and Drug Law as a misdemeanor and is punishable by a fine. Second, false advertising generally is defined in the Federal Trade Commission Act as unfair competition. Cases of the second type are under the jurisdiction of the Federal Trade Commission, which uses the same procedures as in antitrust cases. Penal sanctions are available in antitrust cases, as previously described, and are similarly available in these cases of false advertising. Thus, all of the decisions in false advertising cases are decisions that the corporations committed crimes.

The National Labor Relations Law of 1935 defines a violation as "unfair labor practice." The National Labor Relations Board is authorized to make official decisions as to violations of the law and, in case of violation, to issue desist orders and also to make certain remedial orders, such as reimbursement of employees who had been dismissed or demoted because of activities in col-lective bargaining. If an order is violated, the board may apply to the court for enforcement and a violation of the order of the court is punishable as contempt. Thus, all of the decisions under this law, which is enforceable by penal sanctions, are decisions that crimes were committed.[4]

The laws regarding infringements are more complex than those previously described. Infringements of a copyright or of a patented design are defined in the federal statutes as misdemeanors, punishable by fines. Decisions against the 70 corporations have been made in 7 cases under the copyright laws and in no cases, so far as discovered, on charges of infringement of patented designs. Other infringements are not explicitly defined in the federal statutes on patents and trademarks as crimes, although many states have so defined infringements of trademarks.[5] Nevertheless, these infringements may be criminal acts under federal statutes in either of two respects. First, the statutes provide that damages awarded to injured owners of patents or trademarks may be greater than the injuries actually suffered. These are punitive damages and constitute one form of punishment. Although these punitive damages are not mandatory under the Sherman Antitrust Act, they are not explicitly limited to wanton and malicious infringements. Also, the rule in federal trademark cases is that an account of profits is taken only when the infringement involves wrongful intent to defraud the original owner or deceive the public. These decisions, therefore, are equivalent to convictions in criminal trials. On these principles, 3 of the decisions against the 70 corporations in patent cases and 6 in trademark cases are classified as criminal convictions. Second, agents of the Federal Trade Commission may initiate actions against infringers as unfair competition. Infringements proceeded against in this manner may be punished in the same sense as violation of the antitrust law, namely, by stipulations, desist orders, and fines or imprisonment for violation of desist orders. Five decisions in infringement cases against the 70 corporations are classified as criminal actions in this sense. This gives a total of 21 decisions in infringement cases which may be classified as evidence of criminal behavior of the 70 corporations. Of the 222 decisions, 201 are left unaccounted for in terms of criminality. The evidence in some of these cases and in the descriptions of general practices regarding patents and trademarks justifies an estimate that a large proportion of the 201 cases—perhaps half—involved willful appropriation of the property of others and might have resulted in penalties under state or federal laws if the injured parties had approached the behavior from the point of view of crime. In spite of this estimate, the 201 decisions are not included as evidence of criminal behavior.

The laws in regard to financial manipulations, such as violations of trust, stock market manipulations, stock watering, misrepresentation in the sale of securities, are generally based on the laws of fraud or violation of trust. A poor man was recently sentenced in Indiana to serve from one to seven years in a state prison on conviction of false pretenses; he had listed with a finance company household goods which he did not own as a means of securing a loan. The same law applies to corporations but it is seldom used when corporations misrepresent their assets. The judicial decisions have tended toward higher standards of protection of stockholders and the public, and the Securities and Exchange Commission has been organized to implement these laws. Most of the regulations imposed by this commission during the last decade and a half were in accordance with some of the earlier decisions of courts.[6]

The penalties presented in the preceding section as definitive of crime were limited to fines, imprisonment, and punitive damages. In addition, the stipulation, the desist order, and the injunction without reference to penalty for contempt have the attributes of punishment. This is evident both in the fact that they result in some suffering on the part of the corporation against which they are issued, and also in the fact that they were designed by legislators and administrators to produce suffering. The suffering takes the form of public shame, which is an important aspect of all penalties. This was illustrated in extreme form in the colonial penalty of sewing the letter "T" on the clothing of a thief. In England the Bread Act of 1836 and the Adulteration of Seeds Act in 1869 provided the penalty of publication in the newspaper of the details regarding

the crimes of adulteration of these products; the Public Health Act of 1891 authorized the court to order a person twice convicted of selling meat unfit for human consumption to fix a sign on his place of business of a size to be specified by the court, stating that he had been convicted twice of violating this law. Stipulations, desist orders, and injunctions to some extent resemble these publicity penalties of England. That the publication of the stipulation in Federal Trade Commission cases is a punishment is attested by Lowell B. Mason, a member of the commission.[7]

That this suffering is designed is apparent from the sequence of sanctions used by the Federal Trade Commission. The stipulation involves the least publicity and is used for minor and technical violations. The desist order is used if the stipulation is violated and also if the violation of the law is appraised by the commission as willful and major. The desist order involves more public shame than the stipulation. The shame resulting from the stipulation and the desist order is somewhat mitigated by the argument made by corporations, in exculpation, that such orders are merely the acts of bureaucrats. Still more shameful to the corporation is an injunction issued by a court. The shame resulting from an injunction is sometimes mitigated and the corporation's face is saved by taking a consent decree, or making a plea of nolo contendere. The corporation may insist that the consent decree is not an admission that it violated the law. For instance, the meat packers took a consent decree in an antitrust case in 1921, with the explanation that they had not knowingly violated any law and were consenting to the decree without attempting to defend themselves because they wished to cooperate with the government in every possible way. This patriotic motivation appeared questionable, however, after the packers fought during the next decade and a half for a modification of the decree. The plea of nolo contendere was first used in antitrust cases in 1910 but has been used in hundreds of cases since that date. This plea at the same time saves the face of the corporation and protects the corporation against suits for damages, since the decision in a case in which the plea is nolo contendere may not be used as evidence in other cases.[8] The sequence of stipulation, desist order, and injunction indicates that the variations in public shame are designed; also, the arguments and tactics used by corporations to protect themselves against public shame in connection with these orders indicate that the corporations recognize them as punishments.

The conclusion in this semantic portion of the analysis is that 779 of the 980 decisions against the 70 large corporations are decisions that crimes were committed.

This conclusion may be questioned on the ground that the rules of proof and evidence used in reaching many of these decisions were not the same as the rules used in criminal courts. This involves, especially, the proof of criminal intent and the presumption of innocence. These rules of criminal intent and presumption of innocence, however, are not required in all prosecution in criminal courts and the number of exceptions authorized by statutes is increasing. In many states a person may be committed to prison without protection of one or both of these rules on charges of statutory rape, bigamy, adultery, passing bad checks, selling mortgaged property, defrauding a hotel keeper, and other offenses.[9] Jerome Hall and others who include *mens rea* or criminal intent as one of the essential and universal criteria of crime, justify this inclusion by the argument that exceptions such as those just listed are "bad law."[10] The important consideration here is that the criteria which have been used in defining white collar crimes are not categorically different from the criteria used in defining some other crimes. The proportion of decisions rendered against corporations without the protection of the rules of criminal intent and presumption of innocence is probably greater than the proportion rendered against other criminals, but a difference in proportions does not make the violations of law by corporations categorically different from the violations of laws by other criminals. Moreover, the difference in proportion, as the procedures actually operate, is not great. On the one hand, many of the defendants in usual criminal cases, being in relative poverty, do not get good defense and consequently secure little benefit from these rules; on the other hand, the commissions come close to observing these rules of proof and evidence although they are not re-

quired to do so. This is illustrated by the procedure of the Federal Trade Commission in regard to advertisements. Each year it examines several hundred thousand advertisements and appraises about 50,000 of them as probably false. From the 50,000 it selects about 1,500 as patently false. For instance, an advertisement of gumwood furniture as "mahogany" would seldom be an accidental error and would generally result from a state of mind which deviated from honesty by more than the natural tendency of human beings to feel proud of their handiwork.

The preceding discussion has shown that these 70 corporations committed crimes according to 779 adverse decisions, and also has shown that the criminality of their behavior was not made obvious by the conventional procedures of the criminal law, but was blurred and concealed by special procedures. This differential implementation of the law as applied to the crimes of corporations eliminates or at least minimizes the stigma of crime. This differential implementation of the law began with the Sherman Antitrust Act of 1890. As previously described, this law is explicitly a criminal law, and a violation of the law is a misdemeanor no matter what procedure is used. The customary policy would have been to rely entirely on criminal prosecution as the method of enforcement. But a clever invention was made in the provision of an injunction to enforce a criminal law; this was an invention in that it was a direct reversal of previous case law. Also, private parties were encouraged by treble damages to enforce a criminal law by suits in civil courts. In either case, the defendant did not appear in the criminal court and the fact that he had committed a crime did not appear on the face of the proceedings.

The Sherman Antitrust Act, in this respect, became the model in practically all the subsequent procedures authorized to deal with the crimes of corporations. When the Federal Trade Commission bill and the Clayton bill were introduced in Congress, they contained the conventional criminal procedures; these were eliminated in committee discussions, and other procedures which did not carry the external symbols of criminal process were substituted. The violations of these laws are crimes, as has been shown, . . . but they are treated as though they were not crimes, with the effect and probably the intention of eliminating the stigma of crime.

This policy of eliminating the stigma of crime is illustrated in the following statement by Wendell Berge, at the time assistant to the head of the antitrust division of the Department of Justice, in a plea for abandonment of the criminal prosecution under the Sherman Antitrust Act and the authorization of civil procedures with civil fines as a substitute.

While civil penalties may be as severe in their financial effects as criminal penalties, yet they do not involve the stigma that attends indictment and conviction. Most of the defendants in antitrust cases are not criminals in the usual sense. There is no inherent reason why antitrust enforcement requires branding them as such.[11]

If a civil fine were substituted for a criminal fine, a violation of the antitrust law would be as truly a crime as it is now. The thing which would be eliminated is the stigma of crime. Consequently, the stigma of crime has become a penalty in itself, which may be imposed in connection with other penalties or withheld, just as it is possible to combine imprisonment with a fine or have a fine without imprisonment. A civil fine is a financial penalty without the additional penalty of stigma, while a criminal fine is a financial penalty with the additional penalty of stigma.

When the stigma of crime is imposed as a penalty, it places the defendant within the popular stereotype of "the criminal." In primitive society "the criminal" was substantially the same as "the stranger,"[12] while in modern society the stereotype is limited largely to the lower socio-economic class. Seventy-five percent of the persons committed to state prisons are probably not, aside from their unesteemed cultural attainments, "criminals in the usual sense of the word." It may be excellent policy to eliminate the stigma of crime from violations of law by both the upper and the lower classes, but we are not here concerned with policy.

White collar crime is similar to juvenile delinquency in respect to the stigma. In both cases the procedures of the criminal law are modified so that the stigma of crime will not attach to the of-

fenders. The stigma of crime has been less completely eliminated from juvenile delinquency than from white collar crimes because the procedures for the former are a less complete departure from conventional criminal procedures, because most juvenile delinquents come from the lower class, and because the juveniles are not organized to protect their good names. Because these juvenile delinquents have not been successfully freed from the stigma of crime, they have been generally held to be within the scope of the theories of criminal behavior and in fact provide a large part of the data for criminology. Because the external symbols have been more completely eliminated from white collar crimes, white collar crimes have not generally been included within the scope of criminology. These procedural symbols, however, are not the essential elements in criminality and white collar crimes belong logically within the scope of criminology, just as do juvenile delinquencies.

Those who insist that moral culpability is a necessary element in crime may argue that criminality is lacking in the violations of laws which have eliminated the stigma from crime. This involves the general question of the relation of criminal law to the mores. The laws with which we are here concerned are not arbitrary, as is the regulation that one must drive on the right side of the street. The Sherman Antitrust Act, for instance, represents a settled tradition in favor of free competition and free enterprise. This ideology is obvious in the resentment against communism. A violation of the antitrust laws is a violation of strongly entrenched moral sentiments. The value of these laws is questioned principally by persons who believe in a more collectivistic economic system, and these persons are limited to two principal groups, namely, socialists and the leaders of Big Business. When the leaders of business, through corporate activities, violate the antitrust law, they are violating the moral sentiments of practically all parts of the American public except the socialists.

The other laws for the regulation of business are similarly rooted in moral sentiments. Violations of these laws, to be sure, do not call forth as much resentment as do murder and rape, but not all laws in the penal code involve equal resentments by the public. We divide crimes into felonies, which elicit more resentment, and misdemeanors, which elicit less resentment. Within each of these classes, again, the several statutes may be arranged in order of the degree of atrocity. White collar crimes, presumably, would be in the lower part of the range, in this respect, but not entirely out of the range. Moreover, very few of the ordinary crimes arouse much resentment in the ordinary citizen, unless the crimes are very spectacular or unless he or his immediate friends are affected. The average citizen, reading in the morning newspaper that the home of an unknown person has been burglarized by another unknown person, has no appreciable increase in blood pressure. Fear and resentment develop in the modern city principally as the result of an accumulation of crimes, as depicted in crime rates or in general descriptions. Such resentment develops under those circumstances both as to white collar crimes and other crimes. Finally, not all parts of the society react in the same manner against the violation of a particular law. It is true that one's business associates do not regard a violation of a business regulation as atrocious. It is true, also, that people in certain city slum areas do not regard larceny by their neighbors as atrocious, for they will ordinarily give assistance to these neighbors who are being pursued by the agents of criminal justice.

The differential implementation of the law as it applies to large corporations may be explained by three factors, namely, the status of the businessman, the trend away from punishment, and the relatively unorganized resentment of the public against white collar crimes. Each of these will be described.

First, the methods used in the enforcement of any law are an adaptation to the characteristics of the prospective violators of the law, as appraised by the legislators and the judicial and administrative personnel. The appraisals regarding businessmen, who are the prospective violators of the laws which are now under consideration, include a combination of fear and admiration. Those who are responsible for the system of criminal justice are afraid to antagonize businessmen; among other consequences, such antagonism may result in a reduction in contributions to the campaign funds needed to win the next election. The amendment to the Pure Food and Drug Law of 1938 explicitly excludes from the penal provisions of that law the advertising agencies and media (that is, principally, newspapers and journals) which participate in the misrepresentation. Accessories to crimes are customarily included within the scope of the criminal law, but these accessories are very powerful and influential in the determination of public opinion and they are made immune. Probably much more important than fear, however, is the cultural homogeneity of legislators, judges, and administrators with businessmen. Legislators admire and respect businessmen and cannot conceive of them as criminals; businessmen do not conform to the popular stereotype of "the criminal." The legislators are confident that these respectable gentlemen will conform to the law as the result of very mild pressures. The most powerful group in medieval society secured relative immunity by "benefit of clergy," and now our most powerful group secures relative immunity by "benefit of business," or more generally "high social status." The statement of Daniel Drew, a pious old fraud, describes the working of the criminal law with accuracy, "Law is like a cobweb: it's made for flies and the smaller kind of insects, so to speak, but lets the big bumblebee break through. When technicalities of the law stood in my way, I have always been able to brush them aside easy as anything."

This interpretation meets with considerable opposition from persons who insist that this is an egalitarian society in which all men are equal in the eyes of the law. It is not possible to give a complete demonstration of the validity of this interpretation, but four types of evidence are presented in the following paragraphs as partial demonstration.

The Department of Justice is authorized to use both criminal prosecutions and petitions in equity to enforce the Sherman Antitrust Act. The department has selected the method of criminal prosecution in a larger proportion of cases against trade unions than of cases against corporations, although the law was enacted primarily because of fear of the corporations. From 1890 to 1929 the Department of Justice initiated 438 actions under the this law with decisions favorable to the United States. Of the actions against business firms, 27 percent were criminal prosecutions, while of the actions against trade unions 71 percent were criminal prosecutions.[13] This shows that the Department of Justice has been comparatively reluctant to use a method against business firms which carries with it the stigma of crime.

The method of criminal prosecution in enforcement of the Sherman Antitrust Act has varied from one presidential administration to another. It was seldom used in the administrations of the presidents who were popularly appraised as friendly toward business, namely, McKinley, Harding, Coolidge, and Hoover.

Businessmen suffered their greatest loss of prestige in the depression which began in 1929. It was precisely in this period of low status of businessmen that the most strenuous efforts were made to enforce the old laws and enact new laws for the regulation of businessmen. The appropriations for this purpose were multiplied several times and persons were selected for their vigor in administration of the law, with the result that the number of decisions against the 70 corporations was quadrupled in the next decade.

The Federal Trade Commission Law states that a violation of the law by a corporation shall be deemed to be also a violation by the officers and directors of the corporation. Businessmen, however, are seldom convicted in criminal courts, and several cases have been reported, like the 6 percent case of the automobile industry, in which corporations were convicted and the persons who directed the corporation were all acquitted. Executives of corporations are convicted in criminal courts principally when they use methods of crime similar to the methods of the lower socioeconomic class.

A second factor in the explanation of the differential implementation of the law as applied to white collar criminals is the trend away from penal methods. This trend advanced more rapidly in the area of white collar crimes than of other crimes. The trend is seen in general in the almost complete abandonment of the extreme penalties of death and physical torture; in the supplanting of conventional penal methods by nonpenal methods such as probation and the casework methods which accompany probation; and in the supplementing of penal methods by nonpenal methods, as in the development of casework and educational policies in prisons. These decreases in penal methods are explained by a series of social changes: the increased power of the lower socioeconomic class upon which previously most of the penalties were inflicted; the inclusion within the scope of the penal laws of a large part of the upper socioeconomic class as illustrated by traffic regulations; the increased social interaction among the classes, which has resulted in increased understanding and sympathy; the failure of penal methods to make substantial reductions in crime rates; and the weakening hold on the legal profession and others of the individualistic and hedonistic psychology which had placed great emphasis on pain in the control of behavior. To some extent overlapping those just mentioned is the fact that punishment, which was previously the chief reliance for control in the home, the school, and the church, has tended to disappear from those institutions, leaving the State without cultural support for its own penal methods.[14]

The third factor in the differential implementation of the law in the area of white collar crime is the relatively unorganized resentment of the public toward white collar crimes. Three reasons for the different relation between law and mores in this area may be given. (a) The violations of law by businessmen are complex and their effects diffused. They are not simple and direct attack by one person on another person, as is assault and battery. Many of the white collar crimes can be appreciated only by persons who are experts in the occupations in which they occur. A corporation often violates a law for a decade or longer before the administrative agencies or the public becomes aware of the violation. The effects of these crimes may be diffused over a long period of time and perhaps millions of people, with no particular person suffering much at a particular time. (b) The public agencies of communication do not express the organized moral sentiments of the community as to white collar crimes, in part because the crimes are complicated and not easily presented as news, but probably in greater part because these agencies of communication are owned or controlled by businessmen and because these agencies are themselves involved in the violations of many of these laws. Public opinion in regard to picking pockets would not be well organized if most of the information regarding this crime came to the public directly from the pickpockets themselves. This failure of the public agencies of communication may be illustrated by the almost complete lack of attention by newspapers to the evidence presented in the trial of A. B. Dick and other mimeographing companies that these companies maintained a sabotage school in Chicago in which their employees were trained to sabotage the machines of rival companies, and even their own machines if the supplies of rival companies are being used.[15]

Analogous behavior of trade unions, with features as spectacular as in this case, would have been described in hundreds of newspapers with large headlines on the front page, while many newspapers did not even mention this decision, and those which did mention it placed a brief paragraph on an inner page. (c) These laws for the regulation of business belong to a relatively new and specialized part of the statues. The old common law crimes, as continued in the regular penal codes, were generally limited to person-to-person attacks, which might be committed by any person in any society. In the more complex society of the present day, legislatures have felt compelled to regulate many special occupations and other special groups. The penal code of California, for instance, contains an index of penal provisions in the statutes outside of the penal code which are designed to regulate barbers, plumbers, farmers, corporations, and many other special groups. This index occupies 46 pages, and the complete statutes to which reference is made in the index would occupy many hundreds of pages. This illustrates the great expansion of penal provisions beyond the simple requirements of the earlier societies. The teachers of criminal law, who generally confine their attention to the old penal code, are missing the larger part of the penal law of the modern state. Similarly, the general public is not generally aware of many of these specialized provisions and the resentment of the public is not organized.

For the three reasons which have been presented, the public does not have the same orga-nized resentment toward white collar crimes as toward certain of the serious felonies. The relation between the law and mores, finally, tends to be circular. The laws, to a considerable extent, are crystallizations of the mores, and each act of enforcement of the laws tends to reenforce the mores. The laws regarding white collar crimes, which conceal the criminality of the behavior, have been less effective than other criminal laws in reenforcing the mores.

The answers to the questions posed at the beginning of this chapter may be given in the following propositions: First, the white collar crimes which are discussed in this [chapter] have the general criteria of criminal behavior, namely, legal definition of social injuries and penal sanctions, and are therefore cognate with other crimes. Second, these white collar crimes have generally not been regarded by criminologists as cognate with other crimes and as within the scope of theories of criminal behavior because the administrative and judicial procedures have been different for these violations of criminal law than for other violations of criminal law. Third, this differential implementation of the criminal law as applied to businessmen is explained by the status of the businessman, the trend away from reliance on punitive methods, and the relatively unorganized resentment of the public toward white collar crimes.

Since this analysis is concerned with violations of laws by corporations, a brief description of the relation of the corporation to the criminal law is necessary. Three or four generations ago the courts with unanimity decided that corporations could not commit crimes. These decisions were based on one or more of the following principles. First, since the corporation is a legislative artifact and does not have a mind or soul, it cannot have criminal intent and therefore cannot commit a crime. Second, since a corporation is not authorized to do unlawful acts, the agents of a corporation are not authorized to do unlawful acts. If those agents commit unlawful acts, they do so in their personal capacity and not in their capacity as agents. They may be punished, therefore, as persons but not as agents. Third, with a few exceptions the only penalties that can be imposed on corporations, if found guilty of crimes, are fines. These fines are injurious to stockholders, and consequently, as a matter of policy, should not be imposed.

These principles have now been reversed by the courts and corporations are now frequently convicted of crimes. Corporations have been convicted of larceny, manslaughter, keeping disorderly houses, breaking the Sabbath, destruction of property and a great variety of other crimes.[16] Such decisions involved reversal of the three principles on which the earlier decisions were based. First, the corporation is not merely a legislative artifact. Associations of persons existed prior to the law and some of these associations have been recognized as entities by legislatures. These corporations and other associations are instrumental in influencing legislation. Consequently legislation is in part an artifact of corporations, just as corporations are in part an artifact of legislatures.[17] Second, the requirement that criminal intent be demonstrated has been eliminated from an increasing number of criminal laws, as was described above. Third, the location of responsibility has been extremely difficult in many parts of modern society, and responsibility is certainly a much more complicated concept than is ordinarily believed. The old employers' liability laws, which were based on the principle of individual responsibility, broke down because responsibility for industrial accidents could not be located. Workmen's compensation laws were substituted, with their principle that the industrial establishment should bear the cost of industrial accidents. Some attention has been given to the location of responsibility for decisions in the large corporations.[18] Although responsibility for actions of particular types may be located, power to modify such actions lies also at various other points. Due largely to the complexity of this concept, the question of individual responsibility is frequently waived and penalties are imposed on corporations. This does, to be sure, affect the stockholder who may have almost no power in making decisions as to policy, but the same thing is true of other penalties which have been suggested as substitutes for fines on corporations, namely, dissolution of the corporation, suspension of business for a specified period, restriction of sphere of action of the corporation, confiscation of goods, publicity, surety for good behavior, and supervision by the court.

Two questions may be raised regarding the responsibility of corporations from the point of view of the statistical tabulation of violations of law. The first is whether a corporation should be held responsible for the action of a special department of the corporation. The advertising department, for instance, may prepare and distribute advertising copy which violates the law. The customary plea of the executives of the corporation is that they were ignorant of and not responsible for the action of the special department. This plea is akin to the alibi of the ordinary criminal and need not to be taken seriously. The departments of a corporation know that their recognition by the executives of the corporation depends on results and that few questions will be asked if results are achieved. In the rare case in which the executives are not only unaware of but sincerely opposed to the policy of a particular department, the corporation is customarily held responsible by the court. That is the only question of interest in the present connection. Consequently, an illegal act is reported as the act of the corporation, without consideration of the location of responsibility within the corporation.

The second question is concerned with the relation between the parent corporation and the subsidiaries. This relationship varies widely from one corporation to another and even within one corporate system. When subsidiaries are prosecuted for violations of law, the parent company generally pleads ignorance of the methods which have been used. This, again, is customarily an alibi, although it may be true in some cases. For instance, the automobile corporations generally insist that the labor policy of each subsidiary is determined by that subsidiary and is not within the control of the parent company. However, when a labor controversy arose in a plant in Texas and a settlement was proposed by the labor leaders, the personnel department of that plant replied, "We must consult Detroit." They reported the following morning, "Detroit says 'No.'" For the present purpose, the corporation and its subsidiaries are treated as a unit, without regard to the location of responsibility within that unit.

NOTES

1. The most thorough analysis of crime from the point of view of the legal definition is Jerome Hall, *Principles of Criminal Law* (Indianapolis, 1947). He lists seven criteria of crime: "(1) certain external consequences ("harms"), (2) which are legally forbidden (principle of legality); (3) conduct; (4) *mens rea;* (5) the fusion, "concurrence," of *mens rea* and conduct; (6) a "causal" relationship between the legally forbidden harms and the voluntary misconduct; and (7) (legally prescribed) punishment" (p. 11). The position taken in the present chapter is in most respects consistent with Hall's definition; certain differences will be considered later.

2. *U.S. vs. Swift*, 188 F 92 (1911).

3. Some of the antitrust decisions were made against meat packers under the Packers and Stockyards Act. The penal sanctions in this act are essentially the same as in the Federal Trade Commission Act.

4. Violations of the federal Fair Labor Standards Act and of most of the state labor laws are defined as misdemeanors.

5. For a list of such states, see Walter J. Derenburg, *Trade Mark Protection and Unfair Trading* (New York, 1936), pp. 861–1012.

6. Orville C. Snyder, "Criminal Breach of Trust and Corporate Mismanagement," *Miss. Law Jour.,* 11:123–51, 262–89, 368–89, December 1938 and April 1939; A. A. Berle, "Liability for Stock Market Manipulation," *Columbia Law Rev.,* 31:264–79, February 1931; David L. Dodd, *The Judicial Valuation of Property for Stock-Issue Purposes* (New York, 1930).

7. Lowell B. Mason, "FTC Stipulation—Friend of Advertiser?" *Chicago Bar Record,* vol. 26, pp. 310 f., May 1945.

8. Paul E. Hadlick, *Criminal Prosecutions under the Sherman Antitrust Act* (Washington, 1939), pp. 131–32.

9. Livingston Hall, "Statutory Law of Crimes, 1887–1936," *Harvard Law Rev.,* 50:616–53, February 1937.

10. Hall, *Principles of Criminal Law,* ch. x.

11. Wendell Berge, "Remedies Available to the Government under the Sherman Act," *Law and Contemporary Problems,* 7:111, January 1940.

12. On the role of the stranger in punitive justice, see Ellsworth Faris, "The Origin of Punishment," *Intern. Journ. of Ethics,* 25:54–67, October 1914; George H. Mead, "The Psychology of Punitive Justice," *Amer. Journ. Sociol.,* 23:577–602, March 1918; Florian Znaniecki, *Social Actions* (New York, 1936), pp. 345–408.

13. Percentages complied from cases listed in the report of the Department of Justice "Federal Antitrust Laws, 1938."

14. The trend away from penal methods suggests that the penal sanction may not be a completely adequate criterion in the definition of crime.

15. *New York Times,* March 26, 1948, pp. 31, 37.

16. George F. Canfield, "Corporate Responsibility for Crime," *Columbia Law Rev.,* 14:469–81, June 1941; Frederic P. Lee, "Corporate Criminal Liability," ibid., 28:1–28, February 1928; Max Radin, "Endless Problem of Corporate Personality," Ibid., 32:643–67, April 1932.

17. For a summary of classical theories of corporate personality, see Frederick Hallis, *Corporate Personality* (London, 1930). See also Henri Levy-Bruhl, "Collective Personality in the Law," *Annales Sociologique,* ser. C, fasc. 3, 1938.

18. Robert A. Gordon, *Business Leadership in the Large Corporation* (Washington, D.C., 1945).

MEDICAL CRIMINALS
PHYSICIAN FRAUD IN MEDICAID*

Paul Jesilow, Henry N. Pontell, and Gilbert Geis

Organized medicine claims that it can police itself, but the record of Medicaid fraud and abuse indicates that the profession is unable to ferret out and punish errant doctors. If doctors who cheat are, as the profession's elite argue, only "the few rotten apples" in an otherwise pristine barrel, one would expect the medical associations to have an efficient control mechanism to spot and remove them quickly. However, few errant doctors are brought to enforcement's attention through professional channels. Rather, most physician offenses are uncovered by government fraud-control activities or are reported by former employees or current patients. And most of these offenses are committed by physicians in private practice, illustrating that Medicaid abuse is not exclusively the domain of doctors at work in inner-city Medicaid mills.

In this chapter we use case file material to tell the story of physicians' criminality. We also discuss the demographics of physicians sanctioned for violations of the Medicaid laws. We have removed all references to physicians' names. Our cases are drawn primarily from California and New York, because these two states have the largest number of violators and because their enforcement agents were cooperative in granting us access to files. Many states, as well as the Inspector General's Office at the Department of Health and Human Services, were unwilling to allow us access, most often because the files included the names of beneficiaries and the cost of removing the names was said to be prohibitive. On occasion, we have supplemented our case file material with professional or government reports or other reports that received attention in the press.

*(c) 1993 The Regents of the University of California. Selections from *Prescription For Profit: How Doctors Defraud Medicaid*, pp. 102–147. Reprinted by permission of University of California Press.

The apprehended doctors come from many specialties, and the details of their crimes are often shaped by their medical specialties. Some specialties seem to invite more misbehavior and easier apprehension; others may provide less room for abuse or may effectively shield malefactors from detection.

Like most statistics on lawbreakers, these cases tell us at least as much about enforcement patterns and priorities as about the actual distribution of crimes. Enforcement resources tend to be allocated to cases in which the dollar amounts are high, the aberrancies identified by computer checks are striking, the intent to commit fraud is reasonably clear, and the case seems relatively simple to prosecute successfully—all matters that recommend action to a prosecutor who has great discretion about which cases to accept. Cases involving unnecessary tests and procedures, for instance, receive much less attention than those in which bills are submitted for services never rendered, because the former are apt to involve a labyrinthine "paper chase" in which intent is extremely difficult to establish. How careful a physician is in defrauding Medicaid also influences the probability of discovery. The sloppiest and least clever crooks are most likely to be snared. Such matters influence the aggregate characteristics of physician violators who comprise the "official record" of known Medicaid fraud cases.

DEMOGRAPHICS

To obtain a general picture of physician violators and their offenses during the early years of enforcement, we obtained lists of providers suspended from participation in Medicare or Medicaid between 1977 and 1982. Federal law now requires that any physician or other health care professional convicted of a crime related to participation in Medicaid, Medicare, or other social service programs be suspended from participation in Medicare. Medicare suspension usually prompts Medicaid suspension, although a state can elect to continue to pay a provider who has been suspended from the federal program.

Of the 358 medical providers suspended during the period in question, 147 were physicians. Of the 138 physicians for whom we were able to obtain background information, 50 (36 percent) were graduates of overseas medical schools. Six of the forty-three schools mentioned had more than one graduate among the sanctioned doctors. Three physicians had graduated from the University of Havana, and two came from each of the following schools: Central University of Manila; Far Eastern Institute of Medicine, Manila; University of Innsbruck; University of Bologna; and the Medical University of Nuevo León in Mexico.

Among the eighty-eight domestically trained doctors, six had trained at Meharry Medical College, followed by the University of California, Irvine (five); Loma Linda in California (four); and the University of Louisville (three). Among the fifteen other schools that logged two graduates on the government list were such preeminent institutions as Johns Hopkins, the University of Wisconsin, UCLA, Tulane, New York University, and Columbia.

The disproportionate number of foreign graduates among the violators is striking. They constituted approximately 25 percent of doctors at work in the United States and 31 percent of the known violators. Also unexpected was the number of sanctioned doctors from Meharry Medical College, whose student body is predominantly black; black doctors made up only about 3 percent of the 400,000 physicians practicing in the United States at the time of our research. These results seem to reflect the heavier concentrations of black and foreign graduates in inner-city work, where enforcement resources are aimed against large providers and where practitioners may be most apt to feel the need—and possess the self-excusatory rationalizations—for cheating in order to compensate for the lower fees offered by Medicaid. Black physicians and foreign medical graduates may be more vulnerable to fraud detection because greater enforcement resources are focused on the communities in which they work.

Nationally, California accounted for forty-one sanctioned doctors (28 percent of the total), followed by New York with twenty-five (17 percent). Thereafter came Maryland with eight, Florida and Pennsylvania with seven each, Texas with six, and Michigan with five. These states have the largest Medicaid budgets, so their share of violators is not disproportionate.

Family or general practitioners accounted for the greatest percentage of violators (27 percent), followed by psychiatrists (18 percent), general surgeons (11 percent), internists (8 percent), and obstetricians and gynecologists (7 percent). The "other" category includes specialties with only one or two offenders. General practitioners, the largest category of sanctioned physicians, also represent the largest specialty in the profession. In contrast, psychiatrists were overrepresented among sanctioned physicians, partly because of their vulnerability to enforcement. Psychiatrists' bills are based on the time actually spent with patients. It is difficult for them to bill for extra services or interventions, but it is easy to "inflate" the time they spend with patients. The "time game" proves to be irresistible to some members of the profession, and the relative ease of catching them often induces enforcement authorities to focus resources on psychiatrists' Medicaid fraud. Anesthesiologists can also play the time game, but the time they are engaged with patients before, during, and after surgery is much more difficult to monitor. The disproportionate number of psychiatrists sanctioned for Medicaid offenses, however, cannot be laid solely at the doorstep of enforcement idiosyncrasies. Psychiatrists, as we shall see, have also been convicted of numerous other forms of illegal behavior.

We were also curious about whether women doctors were suspended from Medicaid in proportion to their presence in the profession. In the late 1970s and early 1980s about 10 percent of all physicians were women, and among the suspended doctors in our sample for whom we could ascertain gender, fourteen (about 10 percent) were women.

THE CRIMES

There are four basic categories of crimes committed by physicians caught violating Medicaid programs: (1) billing schemes, which include billing for services not rendered, charging for nonexistent office visits, or receiving or giving kickbacks; (2) poor quality of care, which includes unnecessary tests, treatments, and surgeries as well as inadequate record keeping; (3) illegal distribution of controlled substances, which includes drug prescriptions and sales; and (4) sex with patients whereby physicians, under the guise of "therapy," received payments for sexual liaisons with their patients. These categories are not mutually exclusive, and the latter two can also be regarded as subsets of poor quality of care.

Opportunities for Dishonesty

Opportunity is often the hallmark of white-collar crime by professional persons—a theme echoed by health care providers testifying before congressional committees. Two chiropractors convicted of Medicaid fraud maintained before a Senate subcommittee that the system was "so bad that it virtually invites" criminal activity.[1] A physician convicted of stealing several hundred thousand dollars from Medicaid and other government programs told a joint hearing of Senate committees that his criminal behavior was so flagrant that only a seriously flawed system could have permitted him to get away with what he did for so long. He testified that the forms he sent into the programs for payment were so "arrogant and outrageous" that the services could not possibly have been performed as he alleged they had been. He pointed out that the diagnoses he put down "didn't relate to either the services or to other diagnoses that were submitted at the same time."[2]

The fee-for-service nature of Medicaid payments provides dishonest doctors with ample opportunities to bill for services never rendered or rendered by others and to bill for unnecessary tests and procedures. At first, some Medicaid providers stumbled upon these possibilities. One physician, for example, tired of waiting for Medicaid payment, worried that the government might have lost his bills. He sent in duplicates and, in time, was paid twice. When such stories spread in the medical community, some doctors were convinced that "nobody was minding the store."

For other physicians, the opportunity to provide medical care without concern about the cost proved attractive bait for illegal behaviors. Under Medicaid's lax scrutiny, these physicians had only to convince themselves that certain services would benefit their patients, a conclusion made more appealing when the services also benefited the physicians' pocketbooks.

In the case files, we found numerous examples of reimbursements for patients who were never seen, double-billing for the same patient, billing for phantom services and lab tests, billing for fictitious visits to disguise illegal prescriptions for controlled substances, and "upgrading" services. Another scam, though one rarely treated as criminal fraud because of problems in proving intent, is billing for unnecessary services. Even surgeons who perform unneeded operations, which can be regarded as equivalent to assault, are rarely prosecuted unless the abuses are wanton, again largely because of the difficulty in second-guessing medical opinions and demonstrating recklessness or culpable intent.

Some physicians got into trouble when they billed Medicaid for services they erroneously thought were acceptable. An obstetrician, for example, was fined $5,000 and had to make restitution when he billed Medicaid for surgeries at which he was present but did not perform the operations. It had been "accepted and customary" in his private practice to charge an "appearance fee" for such services, and the doctor mistakenly thought he could bill Medicaid for his services as a "teaching physician."

Some billing schemes go undetected because government agencies fail to communicate with each other. One case involved a doctor who had graduated from Havana Institute just before Castro took power. On seven attempts she failed the Foreign Licensing Examination, so Illinois, where she was then living, decided to revoke her temporary license. Undaunted, she continued to practice and to bill Medicaid, which continued to pay her, unaware of the revocation of her license. Medicaid had reimbursed this doctor more than $180,000 before agents, investigating a pharmacy scam, discovered her because she also was involved in a scheme with the pharmacy owner. She diagnosed virtually all her patients as having an upper respiratory infection and prescribed an average of five to seven items. Most, such as soaps and shampoo, were medically unnecessary but were prescribed to benefit the pharmacy. The doctor cooperated with the Medicaid agents against the pharmacy owner and was allowed to plead guilty to one count of practicing medicine without a license. She was put on probation for a year.

Many illegal billing schemes probably go undetected because patients, other health care practitioners, and welfare workers have little to gain from reporting them; rarely do they become so incensed as to squeal on crooked providers. For example, of the 670 cases of misconduct reported in 1982 to New York State officials, only 33 came from hospitals and other health facilities, and 28 from other physicians. The officials said the overwhelming majority of cases were reported by the public, which the officials said was the least likely group to recognize a problem.[3] But some doctors were trapped after a person in the know provided the policing agency with inside information. Investigations of such cases can be planned carefully because the enforcement agents are likely to know what they are looking for before they begin. The following case is illustrative.

In November 1981 the San Diego Medi-Cal Fraud Unit received an anonymous phone call. The informant told the senior investigator that a National City physician was conspiring with welfare recipients to bilk the county's welfare program. The doctor would falsely certify individuals as medically disabled; in exchange, he would be paid cash or Medi-Cal coupons.

The investigating agent began by making a routine background check on the sixty-seven-year-old physician. It showed that his medical license was in good standing, that no malpractice suits had been brought against him, and that he was not in trouble with the California Department of Motor Vehicles. The investigator then turned to county welfare eligibility workers who might be familiar with some of the physician's patients. Agents usually interview the patients directly, but this investigator had been warned that some patients might be involved in the scheme.

The investigator found an eligibility worker who had a client who was a patient of the doctor. She described the client as "physically fit enough to play professional football." Yet each month for several years the doctor had certified this individual as disabled. The diagnosed disabilities included "angina pectoris, dislocation of the left shoulder, dislocation of the right shoulder, alcoholism, and organic brain disease."

With the assistance of an eligibility supervisor, the investigation unearthed two more social service workers who said their clients included welfare recipients whom this doctor monthly certified as disabled. What had aroused the workers' suspicion was that in each instance the doctor diagnosed the recipients as suffering from a different disability. Phone calls from the supervisor to other welfare workers then uncovered an avalanche of questionable diagnoses by the doctor. The investigator wrote:

She and her co-workers have suspected [the doctor] of wrongdoing for a long time. However, due to legal restraints they are unable to have the recipients examined by another doctor. They have based their suspicions on their observations of these recipients and numerous rumors passed on by other welfare recipients. . . . She has been told by other recipients that [the doctor] does not examine his patients and has gone as far as signing patient disability waivers in the office parking lot.

The investigator, perhaps out of civility or frustration, did not mention the eligibility workers' collective negligence in failing to report their suspicions to supervisors. Already overloaded with work, the welfare department employees were disinclined to cause trouble. But their silence cost taxpayers thousands of dollars.

The agent opened the paper-chase portion of his investigation by comparing the diagnoses listed on the welfare disability certifications with those the doctor had recorded for Medi-Cal payment. "The majority of the diagnoses differed or the dates of service were not the same," he wrote. The doctor's diagnoses for Medi-Cal billings showed some consistency. Patients with acute bronchitis in March, for example, had progressed in the doctor's diagnoses to emphysema by September. His diagnoses for the welfare department, however, varied wildly. A Medicaid "emphysema" patient was diagnosed during the same period on county welfare forms as having acute bronchitis, nervous disease, alcoholism, acute depression, infection of the right foot, and a lung infection.

Armed with this information and with the details the eligibility workers had supplied, the investigator authorized an undercover operation. On a January afternoon, an undercover agent approached the doctor's office:

She found the front door locked. The doctor answered the door and told her she had to wait outside until he could see her. Approximately one-half hour later she was allowed into the office. She found it to be extremely cluttered and filthy. She could not go in any further than the front door due to the debris. The doctor was eating tortillas he took out of the store wrapper, which he continued to eat during the duration of the visit.

She told the doctor she had been experiencing pain in her back since the end of November. She did not know the origin; however, she knew she hadn't sustained the injury from a fall. The doctor touched her back and then had her attempt a few knee bends. The examination lasted less than two minutes.

The doctor then asked her to have X rays taken and gave her a prescription for Valium. He also signed her one-month medical disability certification.

Since the visit had not turned up any criminal activity, the investigator returned to the paper chase and began studying the doctor's Medi-Cal billings for the previous summer. So far all he had were the eligibility workers' suspicions and some questionable diagnoses—not enough to indict the doctor, much less to convict him. The billing records, however, provided a nugget. During June and July the doctor had billed Medi-Cal twice a month for each of the 132 patients he claimed to have seen. It seemed very unlikely that a doctor would need to see every patient twice a month and that he would see the same number of patients from month to month.

The investigator planned another undercover operation, this time using an agent who feigned leg pain:

After a few questions concerning her leg problem, [the doctor] examined her legs and feet. The doctor filled out a form on which the agent saw two separate line entries on which the doctor had typed "examination and treatment." She signed this form in two places and observed [the doctor] place a Medi-Cal sticker on it. Less than two hours later, another operative was in the doctor's office: The doctor questioned him about his alleged condition. There was no physical examination other than the doctor held his hands. When he signed the Medi-Cal form, the doctor had only filled in the name at the top and left the remainder of the form blank. The doctor also signed the [disability certification].

Within weeks, the doctor had billed Medi-Cal for two visits by the first undercover agent. The investigator had continued to review the doctor's Medi-Cal claims and found that for two and a half years he "consistently billed and was paid two office visits per month for every recipient listed." During the period, he had collected $46,871 from Medi-Cal. Interviews with four patients who occasionally saw the doctor confirmed that he was double-billing. All denied seeing him twice in a month. Then records arrived showing that the doctor had double-billed for the final two undercover operations. That sealed his fate.

A felony complaint was filed charging eight counts of submitting fraudulent Medi-Cal claims. The physician pled not guilty, but three months later he agreed to plead guilty to a lesser charge, a misdemeanor of presenting false claims. The judge sentenced him to a $5,000 fine and ordered him to pay $30,000 restitution. In addition, he was ordered to withdraw from participation in Medicaid.

Doing Things His Way

The cases in which investigators had the easiest time demonstrating criminal intent began with personnel informing on their former employers, providing names, dates, and specifics of alleged wrongdoing and sometimes supplying records to support their allegations. The files do not show any instance of "whistle blowing"—informing on a current employer; in fact, current employees often attempted to hide or minimize their bosses' illegal activities.

The case of a Northern California physician is illustrative. Two former employees of the doctor contacted California's physician licensing board with reports of fraud less than a month after they left his employ. Both said they had attempted to cover for the doctor's crimes and to suggest to him that his actions were illegal. "It's my practice and my business, and I don't like anybody that is not submissive," the doctor had reportedly told one of the informants. Another former employee, who also provided damning testimony against the physician, told the authorities:

The doctor would not listen to her if she explained things that Medi-Cal would not permit. For example, she stated that circumcisions were not to be a paid benefit of the Medi-Cal program and that this was explained to her by Medi-Cal. She tried to explain this to the doctor, but he always wanted to do things "his way." [The employee] quit the doctor's employ after nine months. Her reasoning was that she had "been treated like a slave" and was "fed up."

Perhaps this physician risked committing criminal acts because he believed his days as a doctor were numbered. A graduate of an overseas medical school, he had not obtained a California license until he was forty-five. Within three years, the licensing board had put him on ten years' probation. One year later, as the fraud unit opened its criminal investigation, the licensing board was moving to revoke his license. Once, a former employee reported, the doctor had ordered her to bill for services a patient had refused. "Doctor," she told him, "if she complains about that, you're going to lose it altogether." The physician reportedly replied, "I don't care. I want what I can get out of it."

The doctor's criminal behavior was blatant and ubiquitous. He saw forty to fifty patients each morning at one office and then ten to twenty more at his afternoon office. Ninety percent of his practice was Medi-Cal. People might wait an hour to see him. He rarely set appointments, and he spent only a couple of minutes with a patient.

Patients, it seems, appreciated his willingness to prescribe controlled substances. According to an informant, the doctor rarely examined a patient. "[He] would sit on the examining table and ask, 'What medicine do you want today?'"

The doctor maximized his Medi-Cal receipts by prescribing only enough medication to last two weeks and having patients return for a refill. The first visit was billed as an exam and the second as a recheck. Occasionally, patients returned for a third visit within a single four-week period. Because Medi-Cal does not routinely pay for three visits in one month on the same diagnosis, the doctor or his staff changed the diagnosis for the third visit and billed Medi-Cal for a new exam. The doctor sometimes arrived at the new diagnosis by asking the patient, "What else is wrong with you?"

The doctor did not even bother billing Medi-Cal for some procedures even though they were covered. Medi-Cal, for example, allowed estrogen injections once a month, but the doctor charged patients $9 a shot for all injections. He also charged Medi-Cal more than he did his few private patients. For example, he billed the program for $47 (although he was presumably reimbursed for less) for a "procedure" for which he charged his private patients $39. When told by one of his employees that such practices were not permissible, he "said he had to do it to balance out his books because Medi-Cal didn't pay enough."

The doctor also had a method for confiscating codeine from his patients:

[The informant] stated that when patients came for codeine, the doctor would phone the pharmacy for a prescription of 3 grains. . . . The pharmacy would automatically dispense sixty tablets. The patients did not want 3 grains; they wanted 4 grains. The patients would come back to the office with the vials of medication. The vials would be given to the receptionist, who gave the vials to the informant, who put the vials on the doctor's desk. The doctor put the vials in his desk drawer. He then called the pharmacy back with a prescription for 4 grains for the patient.

The second informant corroborated these details and added that the returned medications, as well as codeine samples, were taken home to the doctor's wife, who reportedly said, "I need it."

The doctor also routinely billed for services never rendered. One of the informants reported that he told his staff, "When a patient walks through the door, whether we do anything or not, you bill an office visit." The most glaring violation occurred when the doctor went to Las Vegas and ordered his unlicensed nurse to see patients, refill their medications, and bill as if he were present. This violation was the easiest for the prosecution to prove and, unlike most cases, it went to trial. The jury deliberated three hours before finding the doctor guilty of one count of grand theft for filing sixteen false claims. The judge sentenced the doctor to make restitution of $492, fined him $15,000, and ordered him to make his records available to Medi-Cal investigators so they might make additional recoveries. He also added five years' probation and 270 days in the county jail on a work furlough program. Under this program, the doctor would spend his days at his regular employment and his nights and weekends in jail. The judge allowed the convicted physician to spend the Christmas season at home; two weekends later the doctor had to report to the county jail.

Fake Laboratory Tests

Some physicians' employees accepted their bosses' illegal conduct in order to keep their jobs. The employee, in this regard, resembles the corporate criminal whose conduct mainly benefits the company. A deputy attorney general explained how he saw one such case:

The employee's conduct was inexcusable. However, her culpability is certainly not of the same character as the doctor's. It was the doctor whose orders she followed. As a physician and her employer, he occupied a position of leadership and dominance. Since the employee's only financial gain from this conduct was the job security that came from pleasing her employer, it is likely that the doctor's dominance was a significant factor in inducing her to participate in these misrepresentations.

This doctor had directed his employee of ten years to bill Medicaid for expensive office laboratory tests, although his patients actually received inexpensive tests performed by an outside laboratory. The doctor, a graduate of Harvard Medical School, had previously been in trouble: A decade earlier the state licensing board, citing his gross negligence in the treatment of pre- and postoperative patients and nursing home patients, had placed him on two years' probation and banned him from performing any major surgical procedures. Nine years later the board once again put him on probation, charging that he was excessively prescribing amphetamines and diuretics to patients with weight-control problems. The doctor pled guilty to grand theft from the Medicaid program; he still faced trial on charges that he had bypassed his home gas meter and unlawfully obtained $4,000 in gas to heat his swimming pool and spa.

The supervising deputy attorney general who prosecuted the case clearly wanted jail time for the doctor. He argued that the doctor's blatant criminal behavior had diverted funds from needy indigents and had contributed to the public's growing lack of confidence in the medical assistance programs. He added:

There is a prevailing perception that punishment for the poor is commonly more harsh than punishment for professionals such as the defendant. A visit to courtrooms throughout California will force you to conclude that the poor in our communities are routinely sentenced to county jail for theft offenses far less serious than the premeditated swindle at issue here.

I submit that the element of deterrence should be the most important factor considered by the court in imposing sentence in this case. Persons occupying positions of public trust are intelligent and capable of weighing the risks of detection and prosecution against the financial gain to be achieved by fraudulent conduct. Anything less than one year in county jail for a crime as socially reprehensible as this would only serve to encourage other persons in positions of public trust to steal from the public. The defendant should also be required to make [full] restitution. . . . Anything less will send a message to providers of the Medi-Cal program that crime can indeed pay. On the other hand, incarceration of the defendant as recommended will become known to other persons similarly situated and will constitute a deterrence that may tend to protect the public against millions of dollars in future losses from this billion-dollar program for the poor.

The judge agreed that the doctor should make full restitution but did not fine him, instead ordering one hundred hours of community service. There also was a sixty-day jail sentence.

Blowing the Whistle on Drug Dealing

Another case began with an informant's call to the Los Angeles County central fraud reporting line, a hotline established by the county's board of supervisors to receive fraud complaints, primarily welfare illegalities. The informant's taped message was short and to the point: "He's self-employed. He's an M.D., a family doctor. I'm calling because he is committing fraud against Medi-Cal. He's been lying about dates people come there, how long the patient stayed, diagnosis, and what they have done. I could give you specific information. I would like a response."

After a six-week delay, the message was forwarded to the state's Medicaid agency. An additional six months passed before an investigator interviewed this informant, a receptionist who had been fired for questioning the physician's billing practices. She told the investigator that the doctor charged for comprehensive exams that lasted only three minutes, that he routinely wrote prescriptions without examining patients, that urine samples were commonly taken and dumped without being analyzed, that electrocardiograms were given to all new patients but never read, and that many services were often billed but never provided.

The investigator decided to randomly select two of the doctor's Medi-Cal recipients for claims review. The review led the investigator to note that the "subject appears to be billing for an excessive amount of services." Nine months after the disgruntled former employee had telephoned the hotline, the case was referred to the MFCU for further investigation.

The MFCU already had an open file on the doctor when the health department's referral arrived. A month earlier it had received a complaint from the state licensing board. A patient had called the board to complain that the doctor had billed his insurance company for services not rendered. The licensing board, in its referral, noted it had attempted to stage an undercover operation but had been unable to locate an agent who matched the physician's clientele.

The criminal investigator opened the case and requested claims information. After reviewing the claims material, he began a series of interviews. Most patients reported that they saw the doctor twice a month and received prescriptions for codeine, Valium, and Darvon; some were given vitamin B-12 injections; others purchased diet pills that the doctor sold illegally. On their initial visit, the doctor took urine and often blood, and they were given an electrocardiogram. Subsequent office visits lasted from three to five minutes.

Often the prescriptions were not for the individual the doctor saw, but for another member of the family. One beneficiary stated that the only reason she saw the doctor was to obtain "codeine pills for her husband, who was suffering from a back injury, and was unable to see the doctor in person." The doctor, however, billed the benefit program for treating both the wife and husband. When a patient complained about becoming addicted to all the drugs the doctor prescribed, he told the patient to stop seeing him.

To cover his tracks, the doctor invented diagnoses. One patient, according to the bills, suffered from an airway obstruction, heartfailure, bronchitis, neuralgia, neuritis, lumbago, and hypertension—all within a three-month span. The doctor also billed for injections he never gave, in one instance charging the government for two years of penicillin treatments for a patient who was allergic to the antibiotic.

The doctor also billed the government for "physical therapy," which lasted about five minutes and was given by his secretary. He asked some patients for two Medi-Cal stickers per visit, explaining that "one sticker is for the file and the other sticker is needed to submit to Medi-Cal for payment," and then billed Medi-Cal for two visits. The doctor's practices got patients into trouble with the health department, which restricted their Medi-Cal cards after it wrongly assumed that the "excessive visits" were their fault. The recipients, ignorant of the fake billings, never questioned the health department's decision. Most patients, however, were happy with the doctor's services; he gave them the drugs they wanted. Some traveled long distances to see him.

Twenty-two months after the former employee's telephone call, the doctor appeared in court for a preliminary hearing. Shortly thereafter, he pled guilty to three misdemeanor counts and was sentenced to five days in jail, five hundred hours of community service, and $6,000 in restitution. Two years after the initial complaint, during which time this doctor had received more than $100,000 in Medi-Cal payments, the health department put him on special claims review, which meant they would scrutinize his bills.

Another doctor prescribed controlled substances to alleged alcoholics without giving them a medical examination. He was charged with maintaining a business office for the purpose of prescribing drugs illegally. The doctor's doorman would control office traffic, screen patients to be sure they were not government agents, and collect $10 at the door before a patient would be waved in. The doctor also hired drivers to transport "patients" to his office. He was eventually convicted in a U.S. District Court jury trial for conspiracy for attempted distribution of controlled substances and for prescribing drugs without an examination. He was not charged with filing false Medicaid claims (although he had done so), but his conviction and thirty-month prison term led to his suspension from the Medicaid program.

In at least one case, a physician appears to have participated in an organized crime scheme. Five doctors and three pharmacists were among eleven persons convicted in a U.S. District Court for stealing about $20 million from the Illinois Medicaid program. They were accused of running a network of clinics, laboratories, and pharmacies that wrote and filled thousands of bogus prescriptions. The doctors had billed the Medicaid program for millions of dollars worth of unnecessary medical tests, examinations, and supplies. The fraud relied in part on the enlistment of physically and psychologically impaired doctors, some of them drug dependent. The clinics served only drug addicts, who paid cash for prescriptions in exchange for submitting to unnecessary tests and allowing a range of charges to be applied against their Medicaid cards. Whenever blood was drawn from one patient, the clinic billed the government for the taking and testing of blood from several patients. The government was also billed for items ranging from condoms to toothpaste. A government witness, a pharmacist who had pled guilty to charges of racketeering and mail fraud, was asked during the retrial of the doctor if the clinics ever treated any sick persons. "I hope not," he replied.

One of the clinic doctors had first gotten into trouble with the Illinois Medicaid program in 1969, a year after having been the program's highest-billing doctor in Chicago. He was suspended from Medicaid when it was discovered he was signing bills for care provided to Medicaid patients by another doctor who had been dropped from the program. But the ban was short-lived. Within months he was reinstated on the recommendation of the Cook County unit that managed the welfare program. In 1981, however, his name came up during an investigation of another doctor. Each of eight visits to the doctor's office by undercover agents netted prescriptions for controlled substances—all without the legally required examinations. Noncontrolled substances were also freely prescribed. At each visit Medicaid patients were advised to purchase an average of ten to twelve items. One individual received twenty-nine items on a single service date, including rubbing alcohol and Phisohex.

The doctor steered patients to a pharmacy across the hall. In one year, the pharmacy received $516,000 in Medicaid payments from the state; 80 to 90 percent of the pharmacy's prescriptions were written by the doctor. It closed its operation within days of his indictment.

Over three years, this doctor personally had collected $300,000 from Medicaid. He was sentenced to thirty months' probation and was ordered to perform sixteen hundred hours of community service. The judge rejected the prosecutor's call for a prison term, saying that the doctor's abilities would be better utilized in service to the community.

Ironically, the doctor's attorney had argued to the judge that his client should be allowed to do public service work in lieu of prison because he was schizophrenic and under psychiatric care. The attorney also claimed that the doctor was "so passive at the time he committed the crimes that he would listen to and do anything anybody told him." The Department of Registration and Education declared the doctor incapable of practicing medicine and prescribing drugs with reasonable safety and ordered his license suspended until he could prove that his medical condition had improved sufficiently for him to maintain "a minimum level of professional competency." This doctor's suspension lasted less than a year.

Medicaid and Murder

One of the most shocking Medicaid cases involved a physician living in Miami, Florida. She had arrived in the United States from Cuba in 1960 and claims to have graduated from medical school at the University of Havana. She began practicing medicine in Miami in 1967 while she completed her state licensing requirements. By 1980, five years after she began treating Medicaid patients, she had become the second largest provider of such services in Florida and was operating two clinics. According to official reports, she received $184,000 in state monies in 1980.

The doctor came to the attention of investigators when two women complained that her "acne treatments" had left them disfigured. In March 1981 the doctor was arrested on racketeering charges, which alleged that she had billed Medicaid for more than $97,000 for treatments never performed. During the jury trial, the prosecutor asked a witness if he had ever been treated by the doctor for acne, tonsillitis, viral fever, an ingrown toenail, depression, asthma, or diaper rash. The spectators and jurors laughed. The witness was a nineteen-year-old 220-pound college football player who had visited the doctor twice, complaining of a cold. But the doctor had billed the state for 51 visits and received payments of $1,885. Another of the ten witnesses testified that she had never even met the doctor, although the physician had used her Medicaid number to bill the state for 165 visits, totaling $1,638.

The jury took only one hour to convict the doctor on twenty-four counts of filing false claims and twenty-four counts of receiving payments to which she was not entitled. The judge sentenced her to twenty years in prison, saying, "This so-called white-collar crime is also stealing money allocated to the poor." A state attorney said that the money paid to the physician could have gone to treat more than ten thousand poor patients. The sentence was the most severe punishment yet given to a physician for Medicaid violations.

But the Miami doctor's story does not end here. Shortly after she was sentenced, she became a prime suspect in the murder of her former partner, who had been gunned down outside a Miami hospital a few weeks before the fraud indictment was announced. She was accused of having paid $10,000 for a contract killing to prevent her former partner from testifying against her in the fraud case.

During the murder trial, the prosecution produced a "hit list" containing the murdered partner's name and the name of the investigator heading up the case against the doctor. The doctor testified that the list was to be delivered to a *Santería* practitioner (*Santería* is a Caribbean religion) who had requested that she furnish names of people she might be involved with in future legal disputes. She did not believe in *Santería,* she said, but her accountant had recommended she try it to ease her mind.

The doctor was sentenced to life imprisonment with a twenty-five-year minimum sentence on the murder charge and another thirty years for conspiracy. The new sentences were to run consecutively with the twenty-year sentence she had already received for her Medicaid fraud conviction.

The convictions for conspiracy and murder were upheld in a district court of appeal, but on April 27, 1989, the Florida Supreme Court overturned the murder conviction and ordered a new trial. The court ruled that the circumstantial and hearsay evidence presented at the trial may have prejudiced the jury's decision.

Giving Birth to Gynecological Fraud

A California gynecologist came to the enforcement team's attention when the Surveillance and Utilization Review (SUR) unit of the state's health department routinely checked the records of the state's top two hundred providers. The files indicated that the doctor had billed Medi-Cal for analyzing Pap smears in his office when the analysis actually was done by an independent lab that charged less than half of what the government paid the gynecologist. In addition, the SUR investigators found evidence that he was double-billing the government for services.

This was not the first time the doctor had come to the attention of enforcement officials. A previous computer analysis had shown that he had billed for a variety of services with a frequency that far exceeded the average of providers of the same specialty in the same region. Health department investigators must have presumed the doctor was "upgrading" the office visits—charging for a more expensive procedure than the one actually performed—because they suggested he use a lower-paying billing code. But the doctor's billing pattern did not change.

When the SUR investigators forwarded the data they had collected to the Medi-Cal fraud unit, a criminal investigator there concluded that the doctor had altered information on billing forms "in an effort to get the claim through claims processing without being rejected. This appears to be a deliberate attempt to collect twice for the same procedures."

The investigator learned from the registered nurse who had performed the SUR investigation that the gynecologist did not have in his office the proper equipment to analyze Pap smears and that receipts in patient charts indicated the use of an outside lab a matter the doctor admitted. A phone call to the lab revealed that the lab charged $3.50 for each Pap smear, for which the doctor billed Medi-Cal $8.40.

In total, the SUR investigation of eighty-five patient charts found

billing for procedures for which there was no record in the patient's chart: thirty patients, totaling fifty-three procedures, for $733.84
double-billing: seven patients, totaling ten procedures, for $1,054.70
billing for new patients who were actually established patients: two patients, totaling two procedures, for $51.22
billing for a circumcision for a female baby: one patient, for $23.40.

On the basis of this information, a judge issued a warrant to search the doctor's office and seize patient records and files. The doctor was visibly upset when he arrived at work to find half a dozen agents on hand. An investigator tape-recorded what followed and gave the following report, starting with the doctor's expression of indignation:

"I just really don't understand the Gestapo-like tactics of this, and you're welcome to any of my records, and this is ridiculous. To encroach upon my day, and embarrassment. I just don't think this is necessary." The agent began to tell the doctor, "If you have any questions—" The doctor interrupted, turned around, and faced the agent, his face being no more than twelve inches from the agent's face, and said, "I'm just telling you what I think. You listen for a minute. See, you're on my premises, you listen." The agent replied, "Sir, I am here under a court order to search your premises." The doctor stated, "That's fine, but this could have been carried out at another time. This is just absolutely ludicrous, and I deeply, deeply resent it. I think it's most inappropriate."

As the investigation continued, the agent discovered that the double-billings had been errors by the doctor's staff and that all duplicate payments from Medi-Cal had been routinely returned. Given that the doctor was billing Medicaid for amounts in excess of $150,000 a year, mistakes were inevitable. The evaporation of his best evidence, however, did not deter the investigator, who turned his attention to interviewing patients and employees.

The employees said that the doctor kept tight control on billing. After seeing a patient, he would list for the billing clerk what he had done and the charges. In such a large office, such attentiveness to each charge is unusual; most doctors leave such matters to their clerks.

The employees admitted they charged more than they paid for Pap smears but believed this was acceptable because, "as far as they understood it, the charge was for taking the Pap smear." The employees also described the office's standard procedure for billing for births: Bill for total obstetric care, spinal anesthesia, and newborn care; if the baby was a male, bill for a circumcision. Interviews with the doctor's patients, however, indicated they did not always have spinal anesthesia, and some had no anesthesia. One patient said that the doctor had given her two shots in the cervix while she was in labor, but "it wasn't like a spinal because they went up inside for the shot, and they don't for the spinal. The doctor asked what I wanted. He said if I took a spinal, I wouldn't feel any pain. I told him, 'No, I don't want one.'" As for the "newborn care," most patients were, understandably, unsure whether the doctor had examined their newborns as required for billing. They remembered he had looked at the babies and then given them to the nurses for cleaning.

When asked about office visits, patients were able to confirm that the doctor had submitted to Medi-Cal diagnoses of phantom illnesses, such as acute gastroenteritis, when they had gone for routine prenatal checkups.

This gynecologist got into trouble in part because he followed his own whims in billing. He threw Medi-Cal update notices into the trash unread. He argued that he was entitled to higher pay for his office visits because he felt it necessary to have a nurse present during gynecological exams. He also believed he deserved the additional money he billed for Pap smears because he had to send the specimens to the laboratory and interpret the results—matters Medi-Cal deems covered by the cost of office visits.

Proving criminal intent in this case would not have been easy. The doctor was not without wile; for example, he erased a tape recording he had made of his initial meeting with the SUR investigators, probably because of telltale admissions. "I'm not as dumb as Nixon," he joked with the investigator when asked for the tape.

The government eventually chose to ignore the doctor's upgrading and billing for services not rendered and to concentrate solely on the Pap smear cases, which were the charges easiest to prove. On the billing form the doctor was supposed to check a box indicating where the Pap smear was analyzed. He usually failed to complete this item but had in some instances indicated that the work was done in his office. The prosecutors knew they had a solid case and charged the gynecologist with one count of grand theft and forty-one felony counts of filing false claims.

The doctor pled guilty to a negotiated charge of nine misdemeanor counts of filing false claims, but he maintained that "the violations were unintentional errors that occurred as a result of the complexities of the Medi-Cal billing system." The judge asked the doctor why he had pled guilty if he denied any criminal liability, and the judge then produced the Medi-Cal reimbursement form on which the doctor had indicated that the lab work was done in his office. He also pointed out that the doctor had billed for anesthesia that was never administered. The gynecologist was sentenced to repay $10,000, fined $5,000, and ordered to provide $10,000 in free obstetrical care to Medi-Cal patients at Medi-Cal rates.

Doctors in Large Clinics

The case files we reviewed included relatively few cases of doctors who used their corporate medical clinics to perpetrate fraud. The most likely explanation is that illegal billings can be hidden in a high-volume organization. Large-scale business not only provides dishonest individuals with camouflage for larceny but also allows them to place barriers between themselves and proof of their criminal culpabilities.

A Los Angeles physician who owned and operated a medical group billed Medicaid for his corporation's activities by using its Medi-Cal provider number. An investigation showed he routinely padded the bill by adding minutes to his group's charges for anesthesia services. A Los Angeles grand jury indicted the doctor on twenty counts of wrongdoing, but the prosecution ran into trouble when the district attorney's office realized that no law prohibited the doctor's behavior—a common oversight in the first decade of the benefit program. An agent wrote:

The whole case for fraud hangs on the doctor's misuse of time modifiers under the RVS [relative value scales—an insurance billing mechanism]. The problem is somewhat surprisingly that the RVS, although in common usage at the time, had never been adopted as a regulation of the Department of Health when the conduct in this case was occurring. Without undue elaborations, suffice it to say, there were serious legal problems of a due-process nature connected with penalizing anyone for breach of standards which are not a matter of written law.... If taken to trial, this case would be quite time-consuming, and the result would be difficult to predict.

Following heated pretrial arguments, the defense and prosecution struck a deal. A year and a half after the indictment, the doctor appeared in court to plead no contest to an amended charge of receiving stolen property. By agreement, his practice of medicine was put on probation for two years and he was ordered to provide 384 hours of community service during that period. In addition, the state's health department suspended him (and his corporation) from billing Medi-Cal for five years. An agent in the case wrote to the state's medical licensing board urging them to acquiesce in the agreement: "It is as tough a penalty as we would likely be able to achieve, even if we tried the case; it deters the doctor, it gives the board supervisory power over him for two years, and it will serve as a warning to other doctors."

Interjurisdictional Problems

Like many enforcement and regulatory officials, those concerned with Medicaid investigation and administration often feel frustrated by what they regard as judicial leniency and indulgence. Enforcement problems are multiplied in instances where suspect doctors move from one state to another. For example, a New York physician was convicted of stealing approximately $20,000 from the state's Medicaid program by billing for services he never performed. The court fined him $5,000, placed him on probation for three years, and ordered him to complete a one-year obligation as a VISTA volunteer. After the New York conviction, California routinely revoked this physician's license to practice medicine in that state. (Doctors frequently hold licenses in more than one state.) The doctor's request for reinstatement tried to dispel his criminal image:

He is a board-certified pediatrician, and is employed as a pediatrician on the poverty program operated in New York City by the neighborhood health services program. Throughout his medical career, the doctor has demonstrated a continuing interest in, and commitment to, the development and implementation of community health care programs. He provides medical supervision to . . . a settlement house in New York City

founded in 1889 which serves preschool children, adolescents, and senior citizens primarily from minority, low-income families living in Manhattan. He has served as a VISTA volunteer and worked with the federal Headstart Health Care Program. He also serves as a pediatrics lecturer for the Stony Brook Physician Assistant Program operated by the State University of New York. He is aware of the serious nature of his misconduct and is contrite. There is no evidence of any other criminal activity before or since the conduct in question, which occurred approximately seven years ago. The doctor appears to have rehabilitated himself. He is in compliance with all terms and conditions of the orders of probation.

One member of California's licensing board was dismayed by the doctor's dossier and commented, "He can stay in New York. I cannot believe the double standard concerning physicians. If some middle-class or poor person had committed the same crime, they would be in prison. Are the judges protecting doctors? Maybe we should do something. I realize this happened in New York, but we have had similar cases here—$20,000 stolen, $5,000 returned. Question: Is this rehabilitation?" Doctors convicted of serious offenses can often resurrect their practices elsewhere. This doctor was not relicensed in California. However, other states are not so strict in preventing errant physicians from practicing within their boundaries.

THE PUNISHMENTS

The Judicial Response

The records we reviewed do not enable us to draw definitive conclusions about judges' attitudes toward errant doctors. But it appears that judges do make an effort to tailor sentences to fit what they perceive as the special conditions of convicted doctors. For example, a psychiatrist who routinely billed the government for services either not rendered or rendered by others could have been held to account for up to $360,000—$260,000 for overcharges, $37,000 in interest, and $62,000 for government investigative costs. When the psychiatrist pleaded guilty to one felony count of grand theft, the court placed him on eight years' probation, ordered him to pay a $5,000 fine and to make restitution of $160,000, and sentenced him to six months in a county work furlough program that allowed him to work during the day but spend his nights in jail. The judge also offered the doctor the opportunity to reduce the restitution by up to $50,000 by providing a thousand hours of community service—a pay scale, $50 an hour, far higher than Medi-Cal rates at the time.

The psychiatrist probably did not deserve such special treatment. Only one month before his sentencing, he was still cheating the government. When he told a patient that "he was going to get his money one way or another," the patient complained to the government. Fifteen months later, the state Medicaid agency forwarded to the MFCU a file its agents had compiled on the doctor based on this complaint. The chief of the MFCU was shocked to find the new information unattached to the main case file. A few phone calls revealed the cause. A "computer misplaced the civil case," she was told.

Medical Mercy

Another case that illustrates the leniency accorded to high-status offenders is that of a fifty-year-old Brooklyn internist who had been paid $250,000 by Medicaid. This doctor had consistently billed for office visits, injections, and electrocardiograms he never performed. Before fraud charges could be brought, a federal grand jury indicted him on fifteen felony counts of narcotics distribution and sales. He consented to plead guilty to two counts and went to jail for four months; his medical license was revoked. When he was released from jail, the state charged him with 137 acts of Medicaid theft; he pled guilty to 3. The judge, in sentencing him to a conditional discharge, noted the doctor's recent incarceration on the unrelated offenses and his loss of license. The fact that the doctor was nearly destitute also contributed to the judge's decision to be merciful. It is unlikely that a poor person with a previous conviction for narcotics sales would have been treated so indulgently.

Revoking Licenses

It is unusual for physicians to lose their medical licenses for Medicaid violations. During the first eight years of the program, California routinely lifted the California licenses of doctors sanctioned in New York but pulled the license of only one of its own Medicaid violators. The case of that doctor, a psychiatrist, illustrates how only the most egregious violations get a doctor booted out of medicine.

The psychiatrist first ran into trouble with the Medicaid program over hundreds of bills for psychiatric treatments she never rendered. The case relied heavily on the testimony of owners and administrators of nursing homes. After a year's delay, however, some witnesses were not as sure as they originally had been about the doctor's failure to provide psychiatric care.

Because of the ambiguities in the witnesses' testimony, the state's licensing board concluded it was best to seek a negotiated penalty. An agreement was reached by which the psychiatrist received five years' probation and a nine-month suspension of her license. She also was required to provide eight hours of free community service a week for the first year and four hours a week for the remaining four years of probation. Even during the nine-month suspension, she was allowed to practice medicine as long as her work was limited to community service. The board noted, "The variation in the standard form of this condition seems justified as the public will derive some benefit from her activities. We have no evidence that she is unqualified, from a clinical standpoint, to practice medicine."

Less than a year later, the board acted to revoke the psychiatrist's license permanently. During a few morning hours over eighty days of working at a clinic in a building she and her husband owned, she had written twenty-eight hundred prescriptions, most of them for controlled substances such as Ritalin, Valium, and codeine, which she would prescribe without examinations. She also failed to fulfill most of the conditions of her probation.

In contrast to California's board, which automatically revokes the license of any doctor convicted of a crime in another state lest California become a retreat for wayward doctors, Georgia's board appears less willing to issue revocations or suspensions. A Georgia doctor convicted of twenty-three felonies for filing false claims was suspended from practice for three months and given five years' probation. In several states, including California, New York, and New Jersey, doctors can expect major license troubles if convicted of even one felony.

Georgia's judiciary also seems to be lenient with doctors who file false claims. One physician fraudulently billed the state's Medicaid program for $13,000. He was allowed to plead no contest to a misdemeanor. The court fined him $1,000 to be paid, with interest at 7.5 percent, at $85 a month. He was put on probation until he finished paying the fine. The state licensing board also placed him on probation for three months.

Judges are not inclined to send doctors to prison for billing for services never rendered. Again and again they assign probation and community service in lieu of suspended prison terms. The files we saw did not indicate the judges' sentencing criteria. The two rationales that seem most likely are that stealing funds from a government program is deemed similar to a property offense (first-time thieves are rarely sent to prison) or that physicians are too valuable a community resource to waste in prison.

Consider a New Jersey physician who pled guilty to a twenty-count indictment of Medicaid fraud. The behaviors charged represented only the tip of the doctor's criminal activities, evidenced by his repayment to the state of $60,000 in addition to a $30,500 fine. The judge sentenced the doctor to twenty years in prison but immediately suspended the prison term in favor of "two days per week gratuitous service at a hospital." The president of the New Jersey Medical Licensing Board, which revoked the doctor's license, took a firmer stand:

The illegal conduct was a systematic pattern which persisted over a three-year period. . . . Further, while letters on behalf of the doctor describe him as the only dermatologist serving a poor population in Newark, it is notable that the conduct for which he was convicted arose out of treating that same population which he now argues could benefit by his continued licensure. His crime shook public confidence in the Medicaid system as well as having attempted to divert public dollars. Despite attempts to characterize defendant's conduct as a mere digression from an otherwise virtuous life, there exists a wide gap between this individ-

ual's conduct and that which the public has a right to expect from a physician.

In another case, the New Jersey Medical Licensing Board also rejected a doctor's appeal for leniency based on his long list of good deeds: "That those anti-social activities continued concurrently with respondent's charitable work in no way lessens the breach of public trust committed by respondent under the privileged mantle of his medical licensure. Clearly, he utilized the privilege of his title to perpetrate the fraud and hoped to elude detection by the well-publicized acts of good works."

Negotiated Administrative Settlements

Sanctioned physicians face punishments from Medicaid administrators (suspensions and restitution), criminal courts (jail, fines, restitution), and physician licensing boards (license suspensions, revocations, fines). So at times physicians choose to negotiate settlements with enforcement officials and thereby possibly avoid criminal and licensure actions. Negotiations often result in voluntary, permanent suspensions from Medicaid and large restitutions. New York's Medicaid agency, for example, charged a physician with negligence and incompetence and ordered him to repay $32,000. The doctor agreed to withdraw voluntarily from the state's assistance program, and the Medicaid agency agreed to "withdraw its allegations of unacceptable practices" and to stipulate that the doctor "in no way admits to any wrongful intent or unlawful acts nor shall there be deemed such wrongful intent or unlawful acts in connection with such withdrawal from the program." After such an agreement, neither the state medical board nor a criminal court could use the administrative settlement as a basis for further action.

Such negotiated agreements between crooked doctors and the state's Medicaid agency were common in New York, probably because the agency appeared to be lenient, particularly when a physician compared the proposed administrative sanctions to the potential sentence for a criminal conviction.

New York State routinely audits its highest-billing Medicaid providers, believing that a doctor can see only so many Medicaid patients in a year and those who greatly exceed the norm are most likely to be using fraudulent tactics. Besides, only a big biller can be stealing a substantial sum; a physician who has a small Medicaid practice could not be cheating on a large scale.

For each of these high-billing doctors, the department selects a statistically valid sample of patient case files. In one instance, 100 cases were chosen from 3,327 Medicaid patients and a $157,000 billing to represent twenty-six months of a physician's practice. When this doctor was unable to produce charts for 36 of the cases, investigators discovered numerous deficiencies in his records and quality of care. Extrapolating from the sample to the doctor's full caseload, the auditors estimated that the doctor owed Medicaid $72,000 plus $6,000 interest. The agency and the doctor negotiated a settlement that included restitution of part of the estimated theft and a delayed voluntary permanent withdrawal from the state's welfare programs.

The files of negotiated settlements contain some agreements that seem unsettling given the scope and seriousness of the physicians' crimes. One audit, for example, concluded that half of one doctor's $240,000 Medicaid payments were illegally obtained. Further, it revealed:

(a) the consistent failure to provide adequate histories (e.g., presenting symptoms, complaints) to pursue diagnosis; (b) physical examinations, necessary for information indispensable to good medical care, which are incomplete, illegible or absent and are never directed by historical findings; (c) radiographs and electrocardiographs which are not interpreted or are inadequately interpreted; (d) diagnoses which are inconsistent with history, examination or lab findings, or which are not stated at all; (e) the consistent failure to record dates, treatment plans or dispositions; (f) the prescription of medications inappropriate or without regimes; and (g) the overutilization of psychotropic drugs.

Yet the state agency negotiated an agreement in which the total claim against the doctor was $77,000, and the agency agreed to accept $59,000 to be paid over two years with interest. The doctor's voluntary permanent suspension was delayed six weeks, during which time he was paid half of any Medicaid funds he earned, with the other half credited to his restitution.

Doctors who faced criminal procedures prior to Medicaid administrative actions fared worse than those who took their Medicaid lumps first. The criminal procedures usually resulted in lower restitution orders, but the doctors were suspended from Medicaid and faced licensure actions as well as adverse publicity—penalties avoided by doctors who agreed to negotiated settlements.

Some physicians convicted of crimes fight subsequent civil and administrative actions. A plea of no contest in a criminal action, for example, was later used by a doctor at an administrative hearing to try to block further action. At the hearing to bar him from Medicaid, he argued that he had no criminal intent and that his no contest plea was entered to avoid the possible adversities of going to trial. The prosecutor noted that a plea of no contest, according to court decisions, was to be accepted only when there was a "strong factual basis for the plea." The doctor also contested his permanent suspension from Medicaid on the grounds that he had cooperated with prosecutors and because "he previously enjoyed a good reputation in his community and profession." The prosecutor, in rebuttal, stated the government's position on suspension from Medicaid:

Appellant's cooperation and previous good reputation do not relieve the State of its obligation to exclude from participation in the Medical Assistance program providers whose conduct constitutes an unacceptable practice. Appellant knowingly and repeatedly defrauded the Medical Assistance program and can no longer be trusted as a provider in that program. Furthermore, it should be remembered that participation in the Medical Assistance program is voluntary and contractual in nature. No vested right is being denied the provider, as would be the case if an unacceptable practice hearing could result in a criminal conviction or in the revocation of the provider's license to practice his profession. Since the relationship between provider and government agency is a voluntary and contractual one, that government agency should have wide latitude in deciding which providers it will do business with.

Drugs, Sex, and Psychiatrists

Fraud by Psychiatrists. As noted earlier, psychiatrists were overrepresented in our sample of doctors who committed Medicaid fraud. The most common offense was inflating the amount of time spent with patients. There are also cases of billings for fictitious patients and for therapy administered by someone other than the psychiatrist. Psychiatrists have also been caught dispensing drugs to patients and charging the government for therapy time. They have also become involved sexually with patients or former patients and have billed the benefit program for such dalliances.

As discussed earlier, what is known and believed about fraud against government medical benefit programs by psychiatrists reflects particularly unfavorably on them. But there is extenuating evidence suggesting that the high rate of fraud by psychiatrists, compared with that of physicians in other specialties, may be a function of their particular susceptibility to discovery and successful prosecution. Consider, for example, the differences between psychiatrists and anesthesiologists, specialists who also bill for the time spent with patients rather than for specific procedures. Unlike the psychiatrist's patients, the anesthesiologist's patients are in no condition during treatment to remember the duration of the physician's activities. Nor do anesthesiologists have much opportunity to become familiar with patients or to exchange drugs for payment or sex. Investigators must rely almost entirely on checking hospital records concerning the times of surgeries as well as established billing norms of anesthesiologists in order to convince a prosecutor to bring charges. As a result, the behavior of an anesthesiologist who inflates his record may surface only during a routine audit and investigation—a rare occurrence.

As to the issue of billing for work done by others, one must consider that various professionals bill for services performed by their staffs. Lawyers, for instance, often charge their clients high hourly fees for work performed by low-paid clerks. Medicaid, however, views such activities by doctors as an abuse of the program. And overwhelmingly it is psychiatrists who are caught billing for others' work, although various physicians have been sanctioned for such billing. For example, two doctors got into trouble when they submitted bills for supervising hearing exams at

which they were not present, and another physician billed Medi-Cal for X rays he claimed were taken in his office under his supervision, though they were actually taken by unauthorized personnel in a different city.

When psychiatrists have had sex with patients and charged the government for therapy, the sexual misconduct has overshadowed the issue of fraud, which was usually viewed as a minor aspect of the case. All but one of the sex cases in the files we analyzed involved psychiatrists. The intense intimacy that can develop between doctor and patient is unlikely to occur nearly as readily in other specialties. A case that involved an osteopath seems almost childlike compared to the instances of psychiatric sexual abuse. The osteopath admitted to having felt the breasts of four female patients and having kissed three of the four without their consent. He pled guilty to four counts of sexual abuse in the third degree and was disqualified from the state's Medicaid program.

Psychiatrists often got into trouble with Medicaid because the autonomy they enjoy as independent providers of service runs afoul of Medicaid regulations. One clinician, for example, was suspended from Medi-Cal because he had charged the program for group psychotherapy sessions at which he was not present and that were led by his wife, a psychiatric nurse. He said the patients were told that his wife was a psychiatric nurse and not a physician, and that he and his wife discussed the cases after the sessions. Since his wife was a psychiatric nurse and provided the group psychotherapy under his supervision, he felt that he qualified as the provider for billing Medi-Cal.

Another psychiatrist was caught because his billings for the year were astronomical; he had billed for psychotherapy services rendered by nonlicensed personnel, including one individual who was a linoleum salesman when he was not delivering "psychotherapy." When the psychiatrist learned he was being investigated, he hired the former director of the state's MFCU, an attorney, to defend him. Before long, the psychiatrist skipped town and phoned another psychiatrist to persuade him to remove damaging files from his office. The colleague instead called the MFCU and told them about the files. The suspected psychiatrist eventually pled guilty.

Dishonest psychiatrists have victimized employees as well as patients and the government. One psychiatrist who charged the government for sessions provided by psychologists and nurses repeatedly promised his employees a percentage of the payments but often failed to make good. He promised a nurse 50 percent of what Medi-Cal offered, but she quit after repeated problems in collecting her salary. Another nurse left because the psychiatrist was using the payroll money for a Hawaii vacation—something he had done before. The nurse and others turned him in to the labor board and collected what was owed them. As if this were not enough, the psychiatrist was receiving a 10 percent kickback from another psychiatrist to whom he was referring cases.

Apparently, some doctors believed that even the most blatant cheating would go undetected. As early as 1969, one psychiatrist had habitually billed Medi-Cal for one-hour psychotherapy sessions that were at most half-hour visits or totally nonexistent encounters. Between May 1977 and July 1977, he billed Medi-Cal for twenty-four to twenty-eight individual one-hour sessions on each of eight separate days. On one "twenty-six-hour day," he billed an additional ten hours for private patients, producing a thirty-six-hour billing day. It was simple for the investigators to choose a couple of the doctor's more astonishing days (twenty-seven and twenty-eight hours billed) and to interview the beneficiaries the doctor claimed to have treated.

When the investigator went to the psychiatrist's office with a search warrant to seize records, the psychiatrist's lawyer was there and refused to allow the investigator to question his client. The lawyer argued that it was common for doctors to inflate time "to receive comparable payments as they receive from private patients," and he attempted to derail criminal prosecution by offering to have the doctor repay any illegal bills. "Hypothetically speaking," the lawyer offered, "if 40 percent of the total amount the doctor received from Medi-Cal were returned, would this stop any criminal action?" At his jury trial, the psychiatrist was represented by a different lawyer, but the 40 percent estimate of overpayment his first attorney had suggested came back to haunt him when the government used that figure to estimate restitution at about $125,000.

Before the trial, the doctor had removed his appointment books for prior years from his office. A search warrant for his home produced the books, which constituted the only record of the therapy sessions for the times in question. Some of the pages were missing, but these reappeared during the trial with numerous erasures, additions, and alterations in handwriting different from that of the doctor's secretary. The doctor admitted taking the appointment books but denied they had been altered. His secretary said that she could not explain the erasures. The psychiatrist denied telling a former patient, who was called to testify, to "be evasive" and to claim that some of her sessions were forty-five minutes long. The doctor maintained the witness had "hallucinated the event." He also denied telling a patient he was reducing her sessions to one-half hour because Medi-Cal would no longer pay for one-hour sessions. As justification, the doctor stated at his trial, "The traditional model of psychotherapy was put together . . . for affluent or middle-class patients. They can afford it, and they're verbal, articulate. Poor people aren't like that. They're often nonverbal. You can't have them talk for fifty minutes."

During the trial, according to the deputy attorney general, the psychiatrist continued to deny, minimize, and rationalize his guilt, blaming former secretaries for his difficulties. His attorney contended that the rules governing Medi-Cal billings were contradictory and confusing, that the errors were unintentional. The doctor's wife, who was his bookkeeper, testified that her husband worked seven days a week, got up before dawn, labored until 11 P.M. or 2 A.M., and answered telephone calls from patients at all hours of the night. Despite her testimony, her husband was convicted of one count of grand theft and eighteen counts of Medi-Cal fraud. The conviction, however, was not easily won. A second trial was ordered after the jury, following a twelve-day trial and two and a half days of deliberation, split 9–3 in favor of conviction. The second trial lasted four weeks, but this second jury took only two and a half hours to find the psychiatrist guilty. The doctor was not there to hear the verdict. The judge, rather than immediately issuing a bench warrant, as is typical when a "common" criminal fails to show, gave the psychiatrist until 9 o'clock the next morning to appear.

The prosecutor had argued for a prison term and was disappointed when the psychiatrist was sentenced to six months in jail and ordered to pay a $5,000 fine and make restitution. He was also suspended from government health programs for seven years. Although he received an unusually heavy sentence, the psychiatrist retained the real estate portfolio he had acquired—quite likely using Medi-Cal money: fifteen parcels whose tax assessment value was $1.4 million (the market value would have been much higher).

Another psychiatrist billed for patients he never saw. He would tell a mother that he needed Medi-Cal stickers for all her children even though he provided therapy for only one. He also obtained Medi-Cal stickers for canceled appointments. Investigators were tipped off by a patient who received a notification of benefits and observed that the doctor had billed for services rendered while the patient was in jail. An undercover operation and interviews with other beneficiaries quickly unearthed additional fraudulent bills. The doctor's billing clerk explained that if patients saw the doctor more than eight times in four months (Medi-Cal's limit without prior authorization), the billings were spread over a longer period to meet the legal requirement. When the investigator stated that such practices were illegal, the clerk replied that the procedure was intended only to help the patients.

In another case, a computer review revealed that a psychiatrist billed for eighteen patients in one day, all of whom he diagnosed as suffering from "anxiety neurosis." Investigator interviews with the doctor's patients indicated that he was billing for psychotherapy on patients whom he treated for general medical disorders such as diabetes and arthritis. The psychiatrist had billed Medi-Cal for scores of therapy sessions that he had not provided and that he claimed were performed in a health center where he was a salaried employee.

This doctor learned he was under investigation when one of his patients informed him that she had been interviewed by the fraud unit. He contacted a lawyer friend and asked him to intercede. The lawyer met with the fraud unit investigator and stated that the doctor wished to repay the $29,000 he had stolen. But the investigator continued his inquiries, noting that the doctor's provider number was "littered with fraud." These ongoing interviews prompted a phone call from the psychiatrist's attorney, who said he was worried that the investigation "was creating a potential problem" for the doctor with regard to his patients.

The doctor's admission of guilt and desire to repay the government probably did not work to his advantage. The government investigator had decided to end the investigation after uncovering $3,500 in fraudulent payments. The judge who sentenced the doctor, however, ordered him to make restitution of $29,000—the figure first supplied by the doctor—and fined him $5,000. The doctor's admission of guilt prior to any plea agreement made it easier for the prosecutor to obtain a ninety-day jail sentence.

The Medicaid fraud files show several other cases in which psychiatrists attempted to use the "patients' health" to deter further investigation. One psychiatrist's attorney wrote the head of the state fraud unit about the doctor's concern that "the mental health of the patient can be impaired by heavy-handed examination by your staff." The psychiatrist had informed his attorney "that the psychological condition of a number of his patients has deteriorated as a direct result of the contacts."

He suggested to the chief enforcement agent "that any further contact between his patients in your office either be supervised by [me] or be made by a board-certified psychiatrist with sufficient experience in handling chronic psychotic patients to minimize the potential for damage."

Out of Retirement and into Trouble.
The rationalizations offered by another delinquent psychiatrist illustrate a perverse form of professional jealousy. This psychiatrist had retired in his mid-sixties, when the state mental institution where he worked was closed. Friends, however, convinced him to come to work with them at a clinic in a poor neighborhood. They

would provide him with an office, free of charge, the services of the clinic's receptionists, and a steady supply of referrals. As the psychiatrist later told investigators.

A number of my friends, who were GPs and had a clinic in the ghetto area, told me to come on down. They had a need for psychiatrists. These people who lived in the ghetto area were reluctant to travel to the then state hospital outpatient treatment service or the county hospital outpatient treatment service, so they were not being treated. And, rather reluctantly, I went down and began to enlarge my practice. Like Topsy, it grew awfully fast, and it became a very busy place. . . . The practices of the GPs and the dentist in the building were conducted essentially like a county hospital outpatient spot. It was thronged. People would drop in from all over: babies crying, milk bottles strewn on the floors, kids screaming, sick people, accident cases being brought in. It was a very, very busy place. The doctors referred many of the psychiatric people to me.

The doctor's trouble began when he continued to practice after his health failed. Instead of retiring, he lessened the time he spent with patients, eventually merely renewing their prescriptions. Almost all of his patients were Medi-Cal recipients, and he always billed the program for therapy hours. He also billed for missed visits, charged for individual psychotherapy for sessions provided to a family as a group, charged office visits for prescription refills, and prescribed medications for patients who had no pathology and whom he had not examined. Among his most serious offenses was the indiscriminate prescribing of Ritalin, a drug that calms hyperactive children but acts as a strong stimulant in adults. The doctor, however, ignored the question of how to treat young adults and prescribed Ritalin for four siblings, aged nineteen, seventeen, thirteen, and twelve.

Among the numerous rationalizations this psychiatrist provided for his behavior was the complaint that he could not bill the way the general practitioners did: "I was running an outpatient clinic just as well as the other doctors in the building. Only I would stay later, and I would come in earlier because these guys could do a one-minute thing, even a new patient, and order the bronchitis medicine, or whatever, unless it

was a more serious thing. Yet, I couldn't do that sort of thing."

Inappropriate Psychiatric Treatment.
In another case, a psychiatrist was one of three responsible for treating 180 patients at a residential institution for the extremely mentally ill. Psychotherapy was not appropriate for most of the patients, whose average attention span was less than fifteen minutes, according to one nurse. Another nurse described seven of the patients in the following terms:

(1) almost a vegetable; no conversation, is dangerous; (2) curses, loses his temper easily, has a one-track mind; (3) a mute, does not talk; (4) a nonfunctioning person, asks, Where is my room? Is it smoking time? Is it time to eat?; (5) responds to conversation by saying his legs are cut off, won't let anybody touch him; (6) will not talk, walks away, pushes the doctor away when he tries to hang onto him; (7) slow-motion person, walks away.

Some of the patients could handle short therapy sessions, but only a handful received much therapy. Usually the psychiatrists simply reviewed the medical charts and adjusted medications.

When one of the psychiatrists realized that an investigation was being conducted at the institution, he approached the agent and asked about his status. The investigator, at the institution to investigate two doctors who had worked there before and had used a similar scheme, originally had not been interested in the psychiatrist, but his name had come to the agent's attention by accident while he reviewed institutional records. The agent told the psychiatrist he was being criminally investigated and read him his *Miranda* rights. The psychiatrist immediately admitted guilt and provided details of his crimes: He usually saw thirty patients in one day and billed for thirty hours of therapy, spread over several days. He also admitted that one month he became frightened and cut his billings. He hoped his cooperation would lead to a minimal punishment— the repayment of fraudulent gains.

Eventually this psychiatrist pled guilty to one count of grand theft and agreed to make restitution of $9,000. The probation officer writing the presentence report included a favorable report from the investigator regarding the doctor's co-operation. The psychiatrist was also sentenced to 30 days in jail, to be served on weekends, and 350 hours of community service.

Determining the Take.

Estimating the amount of money a doctor has stolen from Medicaid was important to investigators, who needed such figures to determine the extent of court-ordered restitution and to convince prosecutors to take a given case. Auditors often extrapolate years' worth of phony bills from average daily figures. This practice is not accepted by all criminal courts, but when it is allowed, it saves immeasurable hours of tedious work. For example, a psychiatrist who billed the government for therapy sessions conducted by a clinical psychologist and a social worker in his employ came to the government's attention because of his excessive billings. The auditor scrutinized one month of Medicaid payments made to the doctor in each of three years. He then subtracted legitimate payments from that total and divided the remainder by the number of working days in the period to establish an average daily loss. The psychiatrist was ordered to repay about $140,000 to the state. His attorney proposed he sell his half-million-dollar home and use the proceeds to pay his legal fees and part of the restitution. When the psychiatrist extended financing to the buyers, the auditor complained that the doctor stood to make a profit because the interest rate he was charging the buyers exceeded the rate the state was charging him on the balance of his restitution. So, a deal was struck by which the loan payments were sent to the probation department instead of to the psychiatrist.

Oral Copulation as Therapy.

In the case files we also found reports of psychiatrists who had sexual contact with patients. How prevalent is sexual misconduct? In a survey answered by 1,314 psychiatrists in 1986, 7 percent of the male psychiatrists and 3 percent of the female psychiatrists said they had had sexual contact with a patient. Moreover, 65 percent of these psychiatrists said they had seen at least one patient who reported sexual contact with a previous therapist; only 8 percent had reported these cases to authorities.[4]

When investigators suspect a doctor of patient abuse, they cannot rely on a paper trail that can be introduced at a trial to convince jurors of a defendant's guilt. Instead, they typically must stage an undercover operation. The following case illustrates some of the difficulties they encounter.

A psychiatrist came under investigation when a patient turned first to health administrators and then to the local police. She said she had begun to see the doctor seven years earlier because she had been depressed over her recent divorce. The doctor gave her tranquilizers and sleeping aids on the first visit. By her third session, she felt she was becoming dependent on the drugs, and she acquiesced to the doctor's request that she have oral sex with him. For the next seven years, she continued to see him on a monthly basis: she would perform fellatio, and he would write drug prescriptions for her.

The state licensing board's review unearthed two other patients who claimed similar experiences. The board assigned an investigator and an undercover operative to run a "sting" on the psychiatrist. The agent, equipped with a hidden microphone, saw the doctor and complained that she was depressed over her separation from her husband. What follows are excerpts from the investigator's report:

He repeatedly returned to the subject of conversation regarding the patient's sexual activity, asking her such questions as whether or not she masturbated or whether she has ever had a climax while she was sleeping. The doctor ultimately stated that one of her problems was that she had a cold, unemotional relationship with her father and, subsequently, married her husband subconsciously looking for a father figure. After approximately forty minutes, the doctor gave the agent a capsule which he wanted her to take. He stated the capsule would relieve the tension in her stomach. When the doctor turned his back, the agent dropped the capsule into her purse.

[At the end of the session] the psychiatrist gave her prescriptions for an antianxiety and antitension pill as well as one for an antidepressant. A week later the agent returned. The conversation, which lasted approximately one hour, dealt mainly with the agent's marital and sexual problems. The doctor stated the agent subconsciously wanted to have a sexual relationship with her father. During the conversation the doctor continually changed all subjects back to sex and, on a couple of occasions, asked the agent if she had sexual fantasies about him. The doctor stated, this feeling for a doctor by a patient does occasionally happen. The doctor persistently talked about whether or not the agent could have a sexual relationship with him and, at one point, asked if she felt that if she had sex with him it would be a gratifying experience.

Shortly thereafter, the agent returned to the office to take two personality tests, but she did not see the psychiatrist. Two days later she came back for another session.

The doctor began the conversation by asking if she had taken her medication, did she sleep better, and was she any less depressed. The agent told the doctor she had spoken to her husband on the phone the previous day and after the conversation she felt very depressed. The doctor asked if she had felt like calling him after her conversation with her husband. She told him she had just imagined talking to him. The doctor then changed the subject to a dream she had made reference to in a prior session wherein she remembered waking up and having a climax. The agent told the doctor about another dream which had nothing to do with sex. The doctor then brought the subject back to the sexual dream. He asked the agent if she would like her psychiatrist to be nice to her and if she wanted to please him. She stated she wanted him to think OK of her. He asked the agent why her husband wanted a divorce. She stated he feels she is a lousy wife, mother, and lover. She stated this was not true, she was good at all these things. The doctor asked if she liked oral sex and if her sex partners enjoyed it also. He also asked if any of her sex partners had ever stimulated her orally and, if so, could she have an orgasm this way. She advised she had, after which he made a comment relative to the fact she could have a climax orally but not with penetration. The doctor then stated, most men like oral sex and asked if she had not yet discovered that.

The doctor then changed the subject and asked the agent if she had gained any weight. She advised she had gained several pounds. He had her stand up and turn around so that he could look at her. He stated she had a nice figure. The agent sat down and picked up a book which was on the doctor's desk and advised she was nervous and he should have something in his office for people to hold on to. The doctor stated, it wasn't the book she needed to hold, but his hands instead. At that point the agent began repeating the doctor's statements because he was speaking very softly. The investigator could overhear the agent repeat that the doctor wanted her to sit on his lap. Also overheard was a statement by the agent that she could feel his penis moving. Also overheard was a statement by the agent that the doctor wanted her to kneel down in front of him. There were several minutes of unintelligible conversations after which I heard the agent say, "Why are you doing this to me?" At that point I left my vehicle and went into the office, identified myself and effected the arrest. The doctor resisted being placed in handcuffs, stating he was going to telephone his attorney before he went anywhere. The doctor was handcuffed and placed in the rear of my vehicle. At that time I advised him he was being arrested . . . and of his rights per the *Miranda* decision.

The state medical board forwarded to the county's district attorney the evidence it had collected against the psychiatrist, but the chief deputy district attorney felt there was "insufficient evidence to pursue filing charges." In his opinion, "the language of the statute prescribing conduct which is unprofessional or gross immorality is so big and uncertain that the law is probably defective." Although the investigators had compiled the testimony of former patients and a reconstruction (but not a tape recording) of the events that took place during the undercover operation, the vagueness of the statute, the doctor's subsequent strong denials of wrongdoing, and the legal difficulties of proving that the situation was not entrapment but attempted rape, all contributed to the prosecutor's reluctance to go forward.

Sexual Exploitation of the Sick. Taped confrontations involving patients did help bring about the conviction of a psychiatrist on charges of Medi-Cal fraud and his subsequent dismissal from the program. The case was initiated when two female patients reported through a university professor that the doctor billed Medi-Cal for psychotherapy sessions that in fact consisted only of sexual activity with them. Both women had been diagnosed as manic-depressive, and both were said to be suicidal. One of the women first became a patient of the psychiatrist when she was hospitalized after an attempted suicide. She reported that he became romantic with her and allowed her to leave the hospital for a day, when he had intercourse with her at his home. He released her from the hospital about a week later. She then went to his office for treatment three times a week for the first month, and once a week thereafter. The doctor billed Medi-Cal for these visits, which, according to the patient, consisted almost entirely of sexual intercourse.

The patients helped the police by secretly taping meetings with the psychiatrist in which he acknowledged his sexual involvement with them. One of the patients asked him how he felt about getting paid to have sex with her. He told her he didn't feel very good about it. He said he regretted his behavior, was depressed at the time, and was looking for intimacy. He told her that sex with her "was an expression of our being close, of getting involved emotionally, and of my not making the boundaries clear."

This psychiatrist told another patient that "the next time she was making love to imagine it was him she was having sex with." He also had sexual intercourse with her during a camping trip. According to the investigative report:

He persuaded her to go camping when he told her that a friend of his, who was also a therapist, would also be with them along with some of his patients. He reassured her that "nothing would happen." He also told her, "You have nothing to worry about, chaperons will be around." The suspect picked her up in the evening. They then drove to pick up his friend and the others. While en route he unzipped his pants and took out his penis, and said, "I don't care about Bill or anyone else, I'm going to stick this thing in you tonight." He then took her hand and tried to hold it on his penis. She kept trying to pull her hand away, but he kept pulling it back on to his penis.

They met his friend Bill in a parking lot. But he was alone, saying the others couldn't make it. While Bill drove, the doctor again unzipped his pants and removed his penis. He took her hand and put it on his penis. She told him she didn't want to do this and kept pulling back. He told her that she "owed" it to him because Medi-Cal didn't pay him enough for his services treating her.

A few days after they returned from camping, he telephoned her before a group session. He told her to be "discreet" about the camping trip, especially around his wife, who would be at the group. That night after the group meeting, she went home and attempted suicide by taking more than forty lithium pills. She said she was feeling depressed and confused by the sexual relationship. Later he advised her how to commit suicide with lithium by taking smaller doses of ten pills at a time. She was scared that she would do it and thought she had to keep receiving treatment from him. He told her that he would keep her as a patient and that sometimes they would talk and sometimes they would have sex.

In this case, the MFCU filed criminal charges against the doctor for charging Medi-Cal for his liaisons. The district attorney declined to file sexual assault charges because "the sexual conduct was not the result of force in the usual sense." At the sentencing the defendant's attorney argued that the doctor had already been punished, suffering "public humiliation and other ancillary consequences of criminal acts." The prosecutor rebutted this view: "It is important to remember that the ancillary losses suffered by a white-collar criminal are of advantages not enjoyed by many other defendants coming before the court for sentencing. Neither the legislature nor the judicial counsel in enacting the rules of court suggested that the loss of professional privileges, public humiliation, and dissolution of marriage are factors to be considered in mitigation of punishment."

The court placed the psychiatrist on three years' probation, ordered him to pay $2,000 restitution, fined him a paltry $10, and ordered a six-month jail term and continuing psychiatric counseling. The state licensing board placed the psychiatrist on ten years' probation, which allowed the doctor to practice only in a supervised setting. One of the patients sued and settled for $200,000.

More Sex as Therapy. Another psychiatrist prescribed large amounts of drugs for his wife, took drugs himself, treated patients while he was on drugs, and billed the government for psychotherapy during hours he spent having oral sex with the patient for whom he prescribed excessive drugs; he paid her $10 to $20 for each sex act.

Another case involved a "moonlighting" army psychiatrist who collected Medi-Cal payment stickers from several emotionally disturbed patients and for each of their children. He had repeatedly billed for full forty-five-minute individual psychotherapy sessions for each of the children without ever seeing them. By submitting false claims for sessions with five children and two women, he fraudulently obtained $3,852. During the same period, he maintained a sexual relationship with a Medi-Cal recipient for which he billed the program $1,184 for forty-five-minute therapy sessions that were actually sexual and social encounters, many of which lasted only a few minutes. The patient reported that the doctor had taken her to various San Francisco hotels, had sexual relations with her, and demanded her Medi-Cal card in order to deceive his wife, who was also his bookkeeper.

An investigator for the California Board of Medical Quality Assurance discovered the psychiatrist's misconduct when a patient who had borne a child by him filed a lawsuit charging the doctor with child stealing after he took the baby and fled to Hawaii. These charges were dropped when he returned the baby and agreed to pay child support. The psychiatrist pled guilty to five counts of fraud, so all other counts against him were dismissed. He was ordered to serve one year in county jail and to pay $5,036 in restitution. He was also placed on probation for three years.

All these psychiatrists who conducted sexual liaisons with patients could have been prosecuted for Medicaid fraud, in addition to suffering regulatory sanctions. But in cases of sexual misconduct, patient abuse, rather than fraud, becomes the dominant issue for the authorities. The presiding judge in the last case commented on the absence of criminal charges against the psychiatrist:

I think that the Medi-Cal fraud was circumstantial evidence that didn't bear very heavily on it [the case]. I think the thing that the medical experts stated was the biggest violation of his standard of care to a patient was that of becoming personally involved with the patient under his care, which is strictly prohibited, particularly among psychiatrists, because of the nature of the illness they're treating; and second, yes, abuse of prescription rights would be seriously frowned on by the Medi-Cal people. They frown on both the improper treatment, the psychiatric treatment, and the proper medication. Medi-Cal fraud, . . . honestly, was not so much an issue.

CONCLUSION

The judge's comments that Medicaid fraud may not be much of an issue with medical professionals may help explain the comparatively lenient punishment doctors receive. "Abuse and exploitation of patients and of prescription-writing privileges disturb colleagues, but stealing money from benefit programs lacks, for both colleagues and judges, 'the brimstone smell.'"[5] Without doctors' testimony condemning fraudulent conditions, judges are unlikely to mete out heavy sentences.

In sentencing physicians, the courts look beyond the offenses committed. As one federal judge explains:

I didn't want to send him to jail because I felt that it would deprive him and his family of the livelihood he could make as a doctor and it would deprive the neighborhood of his services. So what I was trying to accomplish was to see that to some extent he could repay society. In this particular case there was a strong enough reason to overcome whatever good would be done for society by imposing a sentence for general deterrence, which is the only justification that exists for [prison] sentences in these cases.[6]

The relative leniency expressed by judges and colleagues with respect to physician criminality most certainly contributes to the extent of the behaviors. Lacking censure, errant physicians practice without proper parameters of behavior. They are unlikely to perceive their own acts as criminal when others do not.

NOTES

1. Subcommittee on Long-Term Care, Special Committee on Aging, U.S. Senate, *Fraud and Abuse Among Practitioners Participating in the Medicaid Program* (Washington, D.C.: U.S. Government Printing Office, 1976), 81.

2. Committee on Finance and Special Committee on Aging, U.S. Senate, *Oversight of HHS Inspector General's Effort to Combat Fraud, Waste, and Abuse* (Washington, D.C.: U.S. Government Printing Office, 1982), 34–40, quote at 36.

3. Ronald Sullivan, "Health Chief for New York to Act Against Misconduct by Physicians," *New York Times,* 3 Apr. 1983.

4. Nanette Gartrell et al., "Psychiatrist-Patient Sexual Contact: Results of a National Survey, I: Prevalence," *American Journal of Psychiatry* 143 (Sept. 1986): 1126–31.

5. Edward Alsworth Ross, "The Criminaloids," *Atlantic Monthly* 99 (1907): 44–50.

6. Stanton Wheeler, Kenneth Mann, and Austin Sarat, *Sitting in Judgment: The Sentencing of White-Collar Criminals* (New Haven: Yale University Press, 1988), 155.

WHITE-COLLAR CRIME IN THE SAVINGS AND LOAN SCANDAL*

Henry N. Pontell and Kitty Calavita

The collapse of the savings and loan industry was in no small part due to what may be the costliest set of white-collar crimes in history. Accounting for the eventual cost to taxpayers is no easy task, but reports of the expenses have continued to rise dramatically since the mid-1980s. In 1989, official estimates of the bailout costs for insolvent thrifts were placed at $200 billion over the next decade, and ranged from $300 billion to $473 billion by the year 2021.[1] The General Accounting Office (GAO), revising an earlier and more conservative estimate, claimed that it "will now cost at least $325 billion and could cost as much as $500 billion over the next 30 to 40 years."[2] This new figure was "subject to significant change" depending on the general economic health of the country. A study appearing in the *Stanford Law and Policy Review* concluded that the final figure would approximate $1.4 trillion.[3]

There is abundant evidence that white-collar crime was a central factor in 70 to 80 percent of thrift failures.[4] A Resolution Trust Corporation (RTC) study estimates that about 51 percent of RTC-controlled thrifts—insolvent institutions—have had suspected criminal misconduct referred to the FBI and that "fraud and potentially criminal conduct by insiders contributed to the failure of about 41 percent of RTC thrifts."[5] In addition, the RTC reports that (1) 138 of the 392 thrifts that were under RTC conservatorship had had criminal misconduct referred to the FBI; (2) in about 50 percent of failed thrifts, insider abuse and misconduct contributed significantly to the failure; and (3) in 15 percent of the insolvencies, possible fraudulent transactions involved the participation of other financial institutions.[6]

The amount of thrift crime officially uncovered and prosecuted largely depends on the response of regulators and law enforcement officials. White-collar crimes are often well hidden by intricate paper trails and require extensive documentation before the cases can even be brought to a prosecutor. As Katz has noted, the investigative and prosecutorial functions in white-collar crimes are often one and the same.[7] Thus a central determinant of the extent of white-collar crime in the savings and loan crisis is the capacity and willingness of enforcers and other state officials to define what could be regarded as illegal behavior.

This article is organized in the following manner. First, it provides an overview of the thrift industry and the deregulation process of the early 1980s. Next, we describe the violations that pervaded the industry in the deregulated environment, arguing that some aspects of thrift fraud distinguish it from other forms of white-collar

From *Annals of the American Academy of Political and Social Science,* vol. 525, pp. 31–45, copyright © 1993 by Sage Publications, Inc. Reprinted by permission of Sage Publications, Inc.

crime. Finally, we examine the government response to the thrift debacle, delineating prevailing enforcement procedures and discussing the legislative reforms that have been triggered by the unprecedented financial losses.

INDUSTRY STRUCTURE AND ORIGINS OF THE CRISIS

The federally insured savings and loan system was put into place in the 1930s, primarily to encourage the construction and sale of new homes during the depression and to protect savings institutions from the kind of disaster that followed the 1929 depression. The Federal Home Loan Bank Act of 1932[8] established the Federal Home Loan Bank Board, designed to provide a credit system to ensure the availability of mortgage money for home financing and to oversee federally chartered savings and loans (S&Ls, also known as "thrifts"). Two years later, the National Housing Act[9] created the Federal Savings and Loan Insurance Corporation (FSLIC) to insure thrift deposits. Until the broad reforms enacted by the Financial Institutions Reform, Recovery and Enforcement Act of 1989, the Federal Home Loan Bank Board was the primary regulatory agency responsible for federally chartered savings and loans.

Economic conditions of the 1970s substantially undermined the health of the S&L industry and contributed to the dismantling of the traditional boundaries within which they had operated for decades. Perhaps most important, high interest rates and slow growth squeezed the industry at both ends. Locked into low-interest mortgages from previous eras, prohibited by regulation from paying more than 5.5 percent interest on new deposits, and with inflation reaching 13.3 percent by 1979, the industry suffered steep losses. As inflation outpaced the small return on their deposits, savings and loan institutions found it increasingly difficult to attract new funds. Compounding their problems, the development of money market mutual funds by Wall Street allowed middle-income investors to buy shares in large-denomination securities at high money-market rates, which triggered disintermediation, or massive withdrawals of deposits from savings and loans.

Along with these economic forces a new ideological era had begun. Though policymakers had been considering further loosening the restraints on savings and loans since the early 1970s, it was not until the deregulatory fervor of the early Reagan administration years that this approach gained widespread political acceptance as a solution to the rapidly escalating savings and loan crisis. Referring to the new deregulatory mentality and the conviction and enthusiasm with which deregulation was pursued, a senior thrift regulator said, "I always describe it as a freight train. I mean it was just the direction, and everybody got on board."[10] In a few bold strokes, policymakers dismantled most of the regulatory infrastructure that had kept the thrift industry together for four decades.[11] The deregulators were convinced that the free enterprise system worked best if left alone, unhampered by perhaps well-meaning but ultimately counterproductive government regulations. In 1980, the Depository Institutions Deregulation and Monetary Control Act[12] phased out restrictions on interest rates paid by savings and loans. But the move to the free-market model was incomplete and accompanied by a decisive move in the opposite direction. At the same time that the new law unleashed savings and loans to compete for new money, it bolstered the federal protection accorded these private enterprise institutions, increasing FSLIC insurance from a maximum of $40,000 to $100,000 per deposit.

In 1982, the Garn-St. Germain Depository Institutions Act[13] accelerated the phaseout on interest rate ceilings initiated in 1980. More important, however, it expanded the investment powers of thrifts, authorizing them to make consumer loans up to a total of 30 percent of their assets; make commercial, corporate, or business loans; and invest in nonresidential real estate worth up to 40 percent of their assets. In addition, the new law allowed for 100 percent financing, requiring no down payment from the borrower. At the same time, federal regulators dropped the requirement that thrifts have at least 400 stockholders, opening the door for a single entrepreneur to own and operate a federally insured savings and loan.

Federal and state governments—whose state-chartered thrifts' deposits were, by and large, insured by federal funds—had created an industry environment that was ripe for widespread law-breaking. Martin Mayer, former member of the President's Commission on Housing under the Reagan administration, describes these deregulatory years:

What happened to create the disgusting and expensive spectacle of a diseased industry was that the government, confronted with a difficult problem, found a false solution that made the problem worse. This false solution then acquired a supportive constituency that remained vigorous and effective for almost five years after everybody with the slightest expertise in the subject knew that terrible things were happening everywhere. Some of the supporters were true believers, some were simply lazy, and most were making money—lots of money—from the government's mistake.[14]

With their new-found wealth and freedom from effective regulation, thrift operators were encouraged—indeed, were impelled by their addiction to high-interest brokered deposits—to make risky investments in junk bonds, stocks, commercial real estate projects, anything that had the potential to reap windfall profits. The magic was that every deposit up to $100,000 was federally insured, and therefore these high-risk investments were, from the depositors' and bankers' perspective, essentially risk free. Some of the transactions were legitimate, if foolhardy, attempts to raise capital; others were outright scams involving insiders, borrowers, Wall Street brokers, and developers. This scenario was created by an organizational environment altered by the deregulation of the 1980s, which transformed the industry virtually overnight and precipitated its demise.

The FSLIC spent more than $2.4 billion to close or merge insolvent savings and loans in 1982, and by 1986 the federal insurance agency was itself insolvent.[15] With the number of insolvent thrifts climbing steadily, the FSLIC, knowing that it had insufficient funds to cope with the disaster, slowed the pace of closures, allowing technically insolvent institutions to stay open. Not surprisingly, the zombie thrifts continued to

hemorrhage. In the first half of 1988, the thrift industry lost an unprecedented $7.5 billion.[16]

THE VIOLATIONS

The Federal Home Loan Bank Board describes fraud as it relates to the savings and loan industry as follows:

. . . individuals in a position of trust in the institution or closely affiliated with it have, in general terms, breached their fiduciary duties; traded on inside information; usurped opportunities or profits; engaged in self-dealing; or otherwise used the institution for personal advantage. Specific examples of insider abuse include loans to insiders in excess of that allowed by regulation; high risk speculative ventures; payment of exorbitant dividends at times when the institution is at or near insolvency; payment from institution funds for personal vacations, automobiles, clothing, and art; payment of unwarranted commissions and fees to companies owned by the shareholder; payment of "consulting fees" to insiders or their companies; use of insiders' companies for association business; and putting friends and relatives on the payroll of the institutions.[17]

A GAO study of 26 of the most costly thrift failures found that every one of the institutions was a victim of fraud and abuse. Evidence presented by the FHLBB to the GAO indicates that fraud was by no means confined to these 26 thrifts; in fact, the Bank Board referred over 6000 cases for criminal investigation in 1987 and another 5000 were referred during 1988, up significantly from the 1985 and 1986 numbers—434 and 1979, respectively.[18] The common weaknesses at the 26 failed thrifts investigated by the GAO included (1) "inadequate board supervision and dominance by one or more individuals," which occurred at 73 percent of the failed thrifts; (2) "transactions not made in thrifts' best interest"; (3) "inadequate underwriting of loan administration"; (4) "appraisal deficiencies"; (5) "noncompliance with loan terms"; (6) "excessive compensation and expenditures"; (7) "high risk ADC [acquisition, development, and construction] transactions"; (8) "loans to borrowers [that] exceed legal limits"; (9) "inadequate recordkeeping"; and (10) "transactions recorded in a deceptive manner."[19]

The GAO cites one thrift that paid a chairman of its board a $500,000 bonus the same year the thrift lost almost $23 million. At another thrift, regulators told management that a bonus of more than $800,000—one-third of the institution's earnings—paid to one officer was a waste of assets; subsequently, the management paid the individual in question $350,000 to relinquish his right to future bonuses and increased his annual salary from $100,000 to $250,000. The GAO also found that extravagant expenditures were made to officers and their families for private planes, homes, and expensive parties. In one case, a majority stockholder used $2 million of thrift funds to buy a beach house and spent another $500,000 for personal household expenses.[20]

The list of frauds carried out by thrift operators and related outsiders is a long one. The misconduct can be separated into three analytically distinct categories of white-collar crime. These are (1) unlawful risk taking, (2) collective embezzlement, and (3) covering up.[21] The categories often overlap in actual cases, both because at times one individual committed several types of fraud and because the same business transaction sometimes involved more than one type.

Unlawful Risk Taking

In its study of savings and loan insolvencies, the GAO concluded, "All of the 26 failed thrifts made non-traditional, higher-risk investments and in doing so . . . violated laws and regulations and engaged in unsafe practices."[22] While deregulation made it legal for thrifts to invest in "non-traditional, higher-risk" activities, loans frequently were extended beyond permissible levels of risk—for example, by concentrating investment in one area, particularly construction loans. These high-risk levels often were accompanied by inadequate marketability studies and poor supervision of loan disbursement, both of which constitute violations of regulatory standards.

The factors that triggered this unlawful risk taking are similar in some ways to those described in other white-collar crime studies. Sutherland, Geis, Farberman, and Hagan, for example, note the importance of competition, the desire to maximize profit, and corporate subcul-

tures as major determinants of corporate crime.[23] Analyses of Medicaid fraud have documented how the conflict between government regulation and the norms of the medical profession results in an environment where fraud is likely to occur.[24]

The opportunity structure is often cited as a facilitating factor in the commission of corporate crime. Some analyses emphasize the ease with which corporate crime can be committed as a complement to the profit motive in the generation of such crime.[25] The infamous electrical company conspiracy of the 1940s and 1950s, which involved price fixing in government contract bids, provides an excellent example.[26] In that case, the small number of very large corporations that dominated the industry offered an ideal opportunity structure and facilitated the criminal conspiracy among the nation's largest electrical manufacturing companies.

The unlawful risk taking in the savings and loan industry, however, is distinct in a number of ways from such traditional corporate crimes. While successful corporate crime traditionally results in increased profits and long-term liquidity for the company, unlawful risk taking in the thrift industry is a gamble involving very bad odds. Unlike more traditional corporate and white-collar crimes in the industrial sector, S&L crimes often resulted in the bankruptcy of the institution.

Collective Embezzlement

As the Commissioner of the California Department of Savings and Loans stated in 1987, "The best way to rob a bank is to own one."[27] "Collective embezzlement," also referred to here as "looting," refers to the siphoning off of funds from a savings and loan institution for personal gain at the expense of the institution itself and with the implicit or explicit endorsement of its management. This form of illegality is estimated to have been the most costly category of thrift crime, having precipitated a significant number of the largest insolvencies to date.[28]

Discussing various forms of white-collar lawbreaking, Sutherland noted that "the ordinary case of embezzlement is a crime by a single individual in a subordinate position against a strong corporation."[29] Cressey, in his landmark study *Other People's Money,* examined the motivations of such a lone embezzler.[30] The collective embezzlement in the S&L fraud differs in important ways from this individual model. Traditional embezzlement is clearly an example of deviance in an organization, insofar as it is perpetrated by an individual stealing from the institution and thereby jeopardizing its organizational goals. Collective embezzlement, however, not only is deviance in an organization—in the sense that the misconduct harms the viability of the institution—but also constitutes deviance by the organization.[31] Not only are the perpetrators themselves in management positions, but the very goals of the institution are precisely to provide a money machine for its owners and other insiders; the S&L can be discarded after serving this purpose. This form of thrift crime utilizes what Wheeler and Rothman have called "the organization as weapon": ". . . the organization . . . is for white-collar criminals what the gun or knife is for the common criminal—a tool to obtain money from victims."[32] The principal difference between Wheeler and Rothman's profile of the organization as weapon and the collective embezzlement in the S&L industry is that the latter is an organizational crime against the organization's own best interests. That is, the organization is both weapon and victim.

Similarities exist between collective embezzlement and organized crime. Maltz has defined organized crime as "crime committed by two or more offenders who are or intend to remain associated for the purpose of committing crimes."[33] While this definition includes the dimensions of premeditation, organization, and continuity, it fails to distinguish organized crime from any other ongoing criminal conspiracy. It may be useful to reserve the term "organized crime" for conspiracies that include the facilitating factor of corruption. The organization, in other words, is not just among offenders but involves a network among offenders and local police, city hall, state officials, or other persons in a position to reduce the risk of detection and prosecution.

If organized crime is defined thus, then much of the savings and loan scandal involved organized crime. In our personal interviews with thrift regulators, FBI and Secret Service agents, and those responsible for the cleanup of the disaster, as well as our review of journalistic accounts of the thrift scandal, a recurring theme is the degree to which these crimes involved organized networks of insiders (S&L owners and officers) and outsiders (executives at other thrifts and banks, accountants, lawyers, appraisers, brokers, real estate agents, and land developers). Another consistent theme is the degree to which the financial resources of the thrift industry and individual thrift executives enabled troubled S&Ls to secure the support of influential policymakers.[34]

The most expensive S&L failure to date has been that of Charles Keating's Lincoln Savings and Loan in Irvine, California. Keating contributed heavily to political campaigns at both the state and federal levels and to both political parties. When Lincoln Savings came under fire from the Federal Home Loan Bank in 1987, five Senators intervened on Keating's behalf. The investigation of Lincoln was soon moved from the San Francisco regional office of the Federal Home Loan Bank, which was widely known for its rigorous regulatory approach, to the central office in Washington, D.C. The move is said to have postponed by two years the closing of Lincoln and the indictment of Keating, a delay that is estimated to have cost taxpayers about $2 billion.[35] While the case of the Keating Five, as the Senators who came to Keating's rescue are called, is the most well publicized instance of influence peddling to save off scrutiny of thrift activities, it is only part of a larger pattern, the repercussions of which go far beyond one or two institutions.

Covering Up

A considerable proportion of the criminal charges leveled against fraudulent savings and loans involve attempts to hide both the thrift's insolvency and the fraud that contributed to that insolvency. The cover-up is usually accomplished through a manipulation of S&L books and records; this form of fraud may be the most pervasive criminal activity of thrift operators. Of the alleged 179 violations of criminal law reported in the 26 failed thrifts studied by the GAO, 42 were for covering up, constituting the single largest category.[36] The same GAO study found that every one of the thrifts had been cited by regulatory examiners for "deficiencies in accounting."[37]

Covering up is employed for a variety of purposes by S&L operators. First, it is used to produce a misleading picture of the institution's state of health, or, more specifically, to misrepresent the thrift's capital reserves as well as its capital-to-assets ratio. Second, deals may be arranged that include covering up as part of the scheme. In cases of risky or "reciprocal" loans, for example, a reserve account may be created to pay off the first few months or years of a development loan to make it look current, whether or not the project has failed or was phony in the first place. Third, covering up may be used after the fact to disguise actual investment activity.

Regulators, in responding to the crisis in the thrift industry in the early 1980s, may have sent the wrong message to thrift operators when regulatory accounting procedures were instituted. The new procedures included a complex formula that allowed for the understating of assets and the overstating of capital in order to bolster the thrift's image of financial health. The techniques provided a gray area within which thrift operators could commit fraud with little chance of detection, and it produced a normative environment within which deceptive bookkeeping was encouraged.

In their unlawful risk taking, collective embezzlement, and covering up, thrift officers often were joined by outsiders from various occupations and professional groups, whose roles were essential for perpetrating the criminal transactions. Real estate developers and deposit brokers, among others, were coconspirators in numerous cases of thrift fraud. In some instances, innocent savings and loan institutions were victimized by less virtuous counterparts. Lewis, for example, describes how Wall Street brokerage firms enriched themselves through fraud against their clients, many of whom were thrifts which had invested in stock market schemes and related securities and junk bond deals.[38]

According to many experts, the hired guns of the industry, including appraisers, lawyers, and accountants, are among the most egregious outside offenders; their well-paid services made many of the S&L frauds possible. Perhaps most important was the role of accountants, whose audits of savings and loan records allowed many scam transactions to go unnoticed, while disguising the state of the financial institution's health. Although some of their activities technically were not criminal, a number of the largest accounting firms in the country are now being sued by government regulators for their negligence in reporting potential and actual malfeasance.

ENFORCEMENT

Cases of savings and loan malfeasance move through a complex web of enforcement jurisdictions before they are finally closed. Regulatory agencies, such as the Office of Thrift Supervision, the Resolution Trust Corporation, and the Federal Deposit Insurance Corporation (FDIC), have a number of administrative and civil remedies at their disposal. Serious cases are turned over to the FBI and the U.S. Attorney's offices for potential criminal prosecution.

As the receiver of failed institutions, the federal government, primarily through the FDIC and RTC, can become involved in civil fraud litigation. When the RTC seizes a thrift, it receives certain assets of the institution—usually real estate—and investigates the possibility of filing legal claims against former officers, directors, and outsiders. Government authorities generally do not know at the outset the precise value of legal claims assets, necessitating an examination by investigators and attorneys. These examinations focus on the validity of a potential legal claim, the chances of actual recovery, and whether or not the size of the recovery would prove sufficient to warrant a costly and time-consuming civil suit. The potential defendants usually must have either significant assets or substantial insurance coverage in order for the case to move forward.

Within the RTC, the Professional Liability Section of the Legal Division is responsible for litigating such cases. Lawsuits may target directors and officers, attorneys, accountants, commodity and securities brokers, and/or appraisers. The lawyers of this division work with RTC investigators and outside fee counsel to pursue civil recoveries for the RTC. As of July 1990, the RTC was involved in 84 civil lawsuits involving 48 thrifts; many more such cases are anticipated in the future.[39] It is estimated that in the 450 thrifts seized by July 1990, malfeasance was involved in 55 percent, or approximately 250 thrifts, with 40 percent of the cases concerning activities of accountants and lawyers.[40]

The amount of civil litigation arising from bank and thrift failures is likely to increase in the future. The extent to which the cases proliferate depends on the amount of recoverable assets and the ability of enforcement agents to locate and regain them. Preliminary RTC reports indicate that professionals may be liable for malpractice in about 20 percent of failed thrifts. Professional liability claims are important, as they can provide a source of recoverable funds through liability insurance. It must be noted, however, that the amounts recovered will be relatively small compared to the overall losses from thrift failures.

The criminal justice system becomes involved in thrift cases when a financial institution or regulator refers a suspected criminal violation to the Department of Justice. Once a criminal referral is made, the FBI or, as of January 1991, the Secret Service in the Department of the Treasury investigates to determine if criminal charges can be brought. FBI and Secret Service investigators usually work with a U.S. Attorney's office in the early stages, both to determine if the investigation should proceed and to set expectations regarding what evidence will be needed to prosecute successfully.

Prosecutorial task forces provide a useful enforcement tool in many areas of the country, bringing together a variety of agency experts to work on particularly complex financial institution fraud cases. These task forces combine the resources of the U.S. Attorney's Office, the Criminal, Tax, and Civil divisions of the Justice Department, the FBI, the Internal Revenue Service, the FDIC, the Office of Thrift Supervision, the RTC, and other agencies.

Two major legislative reforms affecting enforcement have emerged as integral parts of the Bush administration's bailout plan for the nation's thrift industry. The first, known as the Fi-

nancial Institutions Reform, Recovery and Enforcement Act of 1989 (FIRREA), went into effect in August 1989. It authorized $50 billion to be used over three years to cover the federal seizures of hundreds of insolvent savings and loan institutions and to provide funds to pay for insured deposits. The $50 billion is to be raised through the sale of bonds to be paid back over forty years.

FIRREA repeals many of the deregulatory measures instituted in the early 1980s. It limits the investments of savings and loans; restricts the purchase of junk bonds; prevents states from providing more lenient regulations for state-chartered thrifts than federal standards allow; and, perhaps most important, increases the capital requirements of thrifts, thereby restricting thrift executives' ability to gamble with taxpayer funds. One of the most important new enforcement tools provided by the law is a civil forfeiture provision for thrift-related offenses that makes it possible for enforcement agents to seize defendants' assets prior to conviction in an effort to salvage funds before they are transferred offshore, consumed, or otherwise disappear. The law also provides for increased penalties for financial institution crimes committed on or after 9 August 1989—from five to twenty years of imprisonment per offense—and extends the statute of limitations on such crimes from five to ten years. While not affecting offenses committed prior to 1984, the new statute of limitations constitutes official recognition of the large workloads of investigators and the unprecedented size of the backlog of financial fraud cases. At the same time, Congress provided substantial increases in the number of FBI agents and prosecutors to work these cases and authorized $75 million a year for three years to enhance the Justice Department's efforts to prosecute financial fraud.

The second major legislative change, enacted on 9 November 1990 as Title 25 of the Crime Control Act of 1990, is the Comprehensive Thrift and Bank Fraud Prosecution and Taxpayer Recovery Act of 1990, which strengthened some of the provisions of FIRREA and added new ones. Unlike FIRREA, which focused primarily on reforming the regulatory apparatus, the 1990 law concentrated almost entirely on law enforcement efforts and enhancing sanctions against thrift fraud. It increased penalties for concealing assets from government agencies, obstructing their functions, and placing assets beyond their reach[41] as well as for obstructing examination of a financial institution.[42] The law also increased maximum statutory penalties from twenty to thirty years' imprisonment for a range of violations, including false entries or reports, bribery, embezzlement, mail and wire fraud, and intentional misapplication of thrift funds; the law reserves the most severe sanctions for financial crime kingpins. In apparent recognition of the error of the open doors of the deregulatory period, the new legislation imposed greater restrictions on the granting of thrift charters.

Detecting and prosecuting S&L fraud constitute one of the most challenging tasks in the history of American law enforcement. First, the nature of the crimes and the complex financial transactions within which they are usually embedded make it extraordinarily difficult to detect the acts in the first place and then to uncover adequate evidence to prosecute them successfully. Second, the magnitude of the workloads resulting from this epidemic of financial fraud ensures that a substantial number of cases will fall through the cracks. In April 1990, there were 1298 inactive cases in Department of Justice files, each involving over $100,000, which under current guidelines is regarded as significant. Despite the seriousness of these significant cases, backlogs grew because of an insufficient number of FBI agents or U.S. Attorneys to keep up with the rapid pace of criminal referrals.[43] One senior FBI official noted in 1990 that he did not expect referrals to level off for at least four or five years.[44] Records of the Office of Thrift Supervision, the federal agency for thrifts since 1989, indicate that in its first two years of existence, it made 7799 criminal referrals to the Department of Justice.[45]

A recent report issued by that department to Congress documents enforcement activities for major savings and loan prosecutions for the period from 1 October 1988 to 31 May 1991. The report reveals the following: (1) 764 defendants had been charged in cases involving thrifts, with losses totaling $7.7 billion; (2) 95 of these defendants were board chairpersons, chief operating officers, or presidents, and 131 were directors or other officers; (3) 550 defendants—93 percent of those tried—were convicted, and 42 were acquitted—21 of these involved a single case in Florida; (4) 69 of those convicted were board chairpersons, chief operating officers, or presidents, and 103 were directors or other officers; (5) 326—79 percent—of the 412 defendants who have been sentenced received prison terms; and (6) fines of almost $8.1 million were imposed and restitutions of almost $271 million ordered.[46]

While these data give a general description of the results of law enforcement efforts, they cannot by themselves provide an accurate account of the full extent of fraud in the S&L crisis, nor can they be relied upon to identify the key roles played by different occupational groups and organizations in committing fraud. In the absence of other information regarding the nature of criminal referrals, investigative strategies, and enforcement resources, as well as in the face of the difficulty of detecting crime in transactions in which criminal intent can be disguised by ordinary occupational and organizational routines, such official processing data are largely ceremonial. That is, as production figures they may function to legitimate the activities of the organization reporting them.[47] The data reveal at least as much about organizational activities as they do about patterns of financial crime. For example, of the 764 defendants charged, fewer than a third—226—were directly affiliated with a thrift, and most were apparently borrowers. This may mean that more borrowers than insiders commit fraud against thrifts—after all, there are more borrowers than thrift officials; or it may simply mean that fraud by borrowers and other outsiders is easier to detect and prosecute, since the institution itself is more likely to report it and provide evidence. Despite such limitations of official data, the reported figures speak to the sheer volume of financial fraud prosecutions and to the widespread participation of insiders in the looting of their institutions.

CONCLUSION

The financial losses incurred in the savings and loan crisis are in part the result of deliberate and widespread criminal activity. The combination of deregulation, increased government deposit insurance, and the lack of effective oversight mechanisms provided a "criminogenic environment" in the thrift industry.[48] As policymakers attempt to bail out the thrifts, it is important to examine the etiology and dynamics of the crimes that played such a major role in their demise. Financial fraud of the kind described here, of course, is not new. What is new is its magnitude and scope and that it occurs at a time when the economic structure of the United States, and to a lesser extent that of other Western democracies, is increasingly focused on financial transactions rather than on the manufacturing enterprises of the industrial era. Further research, focused on the thrift and banking industries as well as other comparable financial institutions, is vital to advancing a theoretical understanding of the dynamics of white-collar crime in the postindustrial period. A clear understanding of the thrift crisis is central to enlightened decision making. This article attempts to provide the analytical base upon which such policymaking depends.

NOTES

1. U.S., Congress, House, Committee on Ways and Means, *Budget Implications and Current Tax Rules Relating to Troubled Savings and Loan Institutions: Hearings before the Committee,* 101st Cong., 1st sess., 22 Feb., 2 and 15 Mar. 1989; U.S., Congress, Senate, Committee on Banking, Housing and Urban Affairs, *Problems of the Federal Savings and Loan Insurance Corporation (FSLIC): Hearings before the Committee,* 101st Cong., 1st sess., 3 and 7–10 Mar. 1989, pt. 3.

2. Oswald Jonston, "GAO Says S&L Cost Could Rise to $500 Billion," *Los Angeles Times,* 7 Apr. 1990.

3. Christian G. Hill, "A Never Ending Story: An Introduction to the S&L Symposium," *Stanford Law and Policy Review,* 2(1):21 (Spring 1990).

4. U.S., General Accounting Office, *Failed Thrifts: Internal Control Weaknesses Create an Environment Conducive to Fraud, Insider Abuse and Related Unsafe Practices,* Statement of Frederick D. Wolf, Assistant Comptroller General, before the Subcommittee on Criminal Justice, Committee on the Judiciary, House of Representatives, GAO/T-AFMD-89-4, 22 Mar. 1989; U.S., Congress, House, Committee on Government Operations, *Combatting Fraud, Abuse and Misconduct in the Nation's Financial Institutions: Current*

Federal Reports Are Inadequate, 72d report by the Committee on Government Operations, 13 Oct. 1989.

5. Resolution Trust Corporation, Office of Investigations, Resolutions and Operations Division, *Report on Investigations to Date,* 31 Dec. 1989.

6. James R. Dudine, *The Extent of Misconduct in Insolvent Thrift Associations,* Testimony before the Commerce, Consumer and Monetary Affairs Subcommittee, Committee on Government Operations, U.S. House of Representatives, 15 Mar. 1990.

7. Jack Katz, "Legality and Equality: Plea Bargaining in the Prosecution of White-Collar and Common Crimes," *Law and Society Review,* 17(3):431 (Winter 1979).

8. 12 U.S.C. 1421 et seq.

9. 12 U.S.C. 1724 et seq.

10. Personal interview.

11. Martin Mayer, *The Greatest-Ever Bank Robbery: The Collapse of the Savings and Loan Industry* (New York: Charles Scribner's Sons, 1990).

12. Pub. L. 96-221.

13. Pub. L. 97-320.

14. Mayer, *Greatest-Ever Bank Robbery,* p. 8.

15. U.S., Congress, House, Committee on Banking, Finance and Urban Affairs, Subcommittee on Financial Institutions Supervision, Regulation and Insurance, *Financial Institution Reform, Recovery, and Enforcement Act of 1989 (H.R. 1278): Hearings before the Subcommittee,* 101st Cong., 1st sess., 8, 9, and 14 Mar. 1989.

16. Ned Eichler, *The Thrift Debacle* (Berkeley: University of California Press, 1989).

17. U.S., General Accounting Office, *Failed Thrifts: Internal Control Weaknesses,* p. 8.

18. Ibid., p. 11.

19. Ibid., pp. 13–24.

20. U.S., General Accounting Office, *Failed Thrifts: Costly Failures Resulted from Regulatory Violations and Unsafe Practices, Report to Congress,* GAO/AFMD-89-62, June 1989, p. 21.

21. Kitty Calavita and Henry N. Pontell, "'Heads I Win, Tails You Lose': Deregulation, Crime and Crisis in the Savings and Loan Industry," *Crime & Delinquency,* 36(3):309 (July 1990).

22. U.S., General Accounting Office, *Failed Thrifts: Costly Failures,* p. 17.

23. Edwin H. Sutherland, *White Collar Crime* (New York: Dryden, 1949); Gilbert Geis, "The Heavy Electrical Equipment Antitrust Cases of 1961," in *Criminal Behavior Systems: A Typology,* ed. by M. B. Clinard and R. Quinney (New York: Holt, Rinehart & Winston, 1967); Harvey A. Farberman, "A Criminogenic Market Structure: The Automobile Industry," *Sociological Quarterly* 16(4):438 (Autumn 1975);

John Hagan, *Modern Criminology: Crime, Criminal Behavior, and Its Control* (New York: McGraw-Hill, 1985).

24. Henry N. Pontell, Paul D. Jesilow, and Gilbert Geis, "Policing Physicians: Practitioner Fraud and Abuse in a Government Benefit Program," *Social Problems,* 30(1):117 (Oct. 1982); idem, "Practitioner Fraud and Abuse in Medical Benefit Programs: Government Regulation and Professional White-Collar Crime," *Law and Policy,* 6:405 (Oct. 1984); Paul Jesilow, Henry N. Pontell, and Gilbert Geis, *Prescription for Profit: How Doctors Defraud Medicaid* (Berkeley: University of California Press, 1993).

25. Stanton Wheeler and Mitchell Lewis Rothman, "The Organization as Weapon in White Collar Crime," *Michigan Law Review,* 80(7):1403 (June 1982).

26. Geis, "Heavy Electrical Equipment Antitrust Cases."

27. U.S., Congress, House, Committee on Government Operations, *Combatting Fraud, Abuse and Misconduct.*

28. Ibid.

29. Sutherland, *White Collar Crime,* p. 231.

30. Donald R. Cressey, *Other People's Money: A Study of the Social Psychology of Embezzlement* (Glencoe, IL: Free Press, 1953).

31. Lawrence Sherman, *Scandal and Reform* (Berkeley: University of California Press, 1978).

32. Wheeler and Rothman note the distinction between embezzlement and corporate crime in pointing out that "either the individual gains at the organization's expense, as in embezzlement, or the organization profits regardless of individual advantage, as in price-fixing." They argue that this separation ignores cases where both organization and individual may benefit, as when an individual's career is advanced by crime perpetrated on behalf of the organization. Wheeler and Rothman, "Organization as Weapon," p. 1405. What they neglect to note, however, is the possibility of organizational crime in which the organization is a weapon for perpetrating crime against itself.

33. Michael D. Maltz, "On Defining 'Organized Crime': The Development of a Definition and Typology," *Crime & Delinquency,* 22(3):338 (July 1976).

34. Stephen Pizzo, Mary Fricker, and Paul Muolo, *Inside Job: The Looting of America's Savings and Loans* (New York: McGraw-Hill, 1989); James Ring Adams, *The Big Fix: Inside the S&L Scandal* (New York: John Wiley, 1990); U.S., Congress, House, Committee on Standards of Official Conduct, *Report of the Special Outside Counsel in the Matter of Speaker James C. Wright, Jr.,* 101st Cong., 1st sess., 21 Feb. 1989.

35. Committee on Standards of Official Conduct, *Report in the Matter of Wright;* Mayer, *Greatest-Ever Bank Robbery.*

36. General Accounting Office, *Failed Thrifts: Costly Failures,* p. 51.

37. Ibid., p. 40.

38. Michael Lewis, *Liar's Poker* (New York: Penguin Books, 1989).

39. Resolution Trust Corporation, *Report on Fraud, Abuse and Malpractice in RTC-Controlled Thrift Associations,* Statement of James R. Dudine to the Oversight Board, 18 July 1990.

40. Ibid.

41. 18 U.S.C. 1032 et seq.

42. 18 U.S.C. 1517 et seq.

43. Robert A. Rosenblatt, "1,000 Bank, S&L Fraud Cases Go Uninvestigated, Lawmaker Says," *Los Angeles Times,* 15 Mar. 1990.

44. Personal interview.

45. Resolution Trust Corporation, "Report on Investigations to Date."

46. U.S., Department of Justice, Office of the Attorney General, *Attacking Financial Institution Fraud: A Report to the Congress of the United States,* May 1991.

47. John W. Meyer and Brian Rowan, "Institutionalized Organizations: Formal Structure as Myth and Ceremony," *American Journal of Sociology,* 83(2):340 (Sept. 1977).

48. Martin Needleman and Carolyn Needleman, "Organizational Crime: Two Models of Criminogenesis." *Sociological Quarterly,* 20(4):517 (Autumn 1979).

DENYING THE GUILTY MIND
ACCOUNTING FOR INVOLVEMENT IN A WHITE-COLLAR CRIME*

Michael L. Benson

Adjudication as a criminal is, to use Garfinkel's (1956) classic term, a degradation ceremony. The focus of this article is on how offenders attempt to defeat the success of this ceremony and deny their own criminality through the use of accounts. However, in the interest of showing in as much detail as possible all sides of the experience undergone by these offenders, it is necessary to treat first the guilt and inner anguish that is felt by many white-collar offenders even though they deny being criminals. This is best accomplished by beginning with a description of a unique feature of the prosecution of white-collar crimes.

In white-collar criminal cases, the issue is likely to be *why* something was done, rather than *who* did it (Edelhertz, 1970:47). There is often relatively little disagreement as to what happened. In the words of one Assistant U.S. Attorney interviewed for the study:

If you actually had a movie playing, neither side would dispute that a person moved in this way and handled this piece of paper, etc. What it comes down to is, did they have the criminal intent?

If the prosecution is to proceed past the investigatory stages, the prosecutor must infer from the pattern of events that conscious criminal intent was present and believe that sufficient evidence exists to convince a jury of this interpretation of the situation. As Katz (1979:445–446) has noted, making this inference can be difficult because of the way in which white-collar illegalities are integrated into ordinary occupational routines. Thus, prosecutors in conducting trials, grand jury hearings, or plea negotiations spend a great deal of effort establishing that the defendant did in-

deed have the necessary criminal intent. By concentrating on the offender's motives, the prosecutor attacks the very essence of the white-collar offender's public and personal image as an upstanding member of the community. The offender is portrayed as someone with a guilty mind.

Not surprisingly, therefore, the most consistent and recurrent pattern in the interviews, though not present in all of them, was denial of criminal intent, as opposed to the outright denial of any criminal behavior whatsoever. Most offenders acknowledged that their behavior probably could be construed as falling within the conduct proscribed by stature, but they uniformly denied that their actions were motivated by a guilty mind. This is not to say, however, that offenders *felt* no guilt or shame as a result of conviction. On the contrary, indictment, prosecution, and conviction provoke a variety of emotions among offenders.

The enormous reality of the offender's lived emotion (Denzin, 1984) in admitting guilt is perhaps best illustrated by one offender's description of his feelings during the hearing at which he pled guilty.

You know (the plea's) what really hurt. I didn't even know I had feet. I felt numb. My head was just floating. There was no feeling, except a state of suspended animation. . . . For a brief moment, I almost hesitated. I almost said not guilty. If I had been alone, I would have fought, but my family. . . .

The traumatic nature of this moment lies, in part, in the offender's feeling that only one aspect of his life is being considered. From the offender's point of view his crime represents only one small part of his life. It does not typify his inner self, and to judge him solely on the basis of this one event seems an atrocious injustice to the offender.

*Reprinted from *Criminology,* 23:4, (Nov., 1985), pp. 589–599 by permission of the author and the American Society of Criminology.

For some the memory of the event is so painful that they want to obliterate it entirely, as the two following quotations illustrate.

I want quiet. I want to forget. I want to cut with the past.

I've already divorced myself from the problem. I don't even want to hear the names of certain people ever again. It brings me pain.

For others, rage rather than embarrassment seemed to be the dominant emotion.

I never really felt any embarrassment over the whole thing. I felt rage and it wasn't false or self-serving. It was really (something) to see this thing in action and recognize what the whole legal system has come to through its development, and the abuse of the grand jury system and the abuse of the indictment system. . . .

The role of the news media in the process of punishment and stigmatization should not be overlooked. All offenders whose cases were reported on by the news media were either embarrassed or embittered or both by the public exposure.

The only one I am bitter at is the newspapers, as many people are. They are unfair because you can't get even. They can say things that are untrue, and let me say this to you. They wrote an article on me that was so blasphemous, that was so horrible. They painted me as an insidious, miserable creature, wringing out the last penny. . . .

Offenders whose cases were not reported on by the news media expressed relief at having avoided that kind of embarrassment, sometimes saying that greater publicity would have been worse than any sentence they could have received.

In court, defense lawyers are fond of presenting white-collar offenders as having suffered enough by virtue of the humiliation of public adjudication as criminals. On the other hand, prosecutors present them as cavalier individuals who arrogantly ignore the law and brush off its weak efforts to stigmatize them as criminals. Neither of these stereotypes is entirely accurate. The subjective effects of conviction on white-collar offenders are varied and complex. One suspects that this is true of all offenders, not only white-collar offenders.

The emotional responses of offenders to conviction have not been the subject of extensive research. However, insofar as an individual's emotional response to adjudication may influence the deterrent or crime-reinforcing impact of punishment on him or her, further study might reveal why some offenders stop their criminal behavior while others go on to careers in crime (Casper, 1978:80).

Although the offenders displayed a variety of different emotions with respect to their experiences, they were nearly unanimous in denying basic criminality. To see how white-collar offenders justify and excuse their crimes, we turn to their accounts. The small number of cases rules out the use of any elaborate classification techniques. Nonetheless, it is useful to group offenders by offense when presenting their interpretations.

ANTITRUST VIOLATORS

Four of the offenders had been convicted of antitrust violations, all in the same case involving the building and contracting industry. Four major themes characterized their accounts. First, antitrust offenders focused on the everyday character and historical continuity of their offenses.

It was a way of doing business before we even got into the business. So it was like why do you brush your teeth in the morning or something. . . . It was part of the everyday. . . . It was a method of survival.

The offenders argued that they were merely following established and necessary industry practices. These practices were presented as being necessary for the well-being of the industry as a whole, not to mention their own companies. Further, they argued that cooperation among competitors was either allowed or actively promoted by the government in other industries and professions.

The second theme emphasized by the offenders was the characterization of their actions as blameless. They admitted talking to competitors and admitted submitting intentionally noncompetitive bids. However, they presented these practices as being done not for the purpose of rigging prices nor to make exorbitant profits. Rather, the everyday practices of the industry required them to occasionally submit bids on projects they really did not want to have. To avoid the effort and expense of preparing full-fledged bids, they would call a competitor to get a price to use. Such a situation might arise, for example, when a company already had enough work for the time being, but was asked by a valued customer to submit a bid anyway.

All you want to do is show a bid, so that in some cases it was for as small a reason as getting your deposit back on the plans and specs. So you just simply have no interest in getting the job and just call to see if you can find someone to give you a price to use, so that you didn't have to go through the expense of an entire bid preparation. Now that is looked on very unfavorably, and it is a technical violation, but it was strictly an opportunity to keep your name in front of a desired customer. Or you may find yourself in a situation where somebody is doing work for a customer, has done work for many, many years and is totally acceptable, totally fair. There is no problem. But suddenly they (the customer) get an idea that they ought to have a few tentative figures, and you're called in, and you are in a moral dilemma. There's really no reason for you to attempt to compete in that circumstance. And so there was a way to back out.

Managed in this way, an action that appears on the surface to be a straightforward and conscious violation of antitrust regulations becomes merely a harmless business practice that happens to be a "technical violation." The offender can then refer to his personal history to verify his claim that, despite technical violations, he is in reality a law-abiding person. In the words of one offender, "Having been in the business for 33 years, you don't just automatically become a criminal overnight."

Third, offenders were very critical of the motives and tactics of prosecutors. Prosecutors were accused of being motivated solely by the opportunity for personal advancement presented by winning a big case. Further, they were accused of employing prosecution selectively and using tactics that allowed the most culpable offenders to go free. The Department of Justice was painted as using antitrust prosecutions for political purposes.

The fourth theme emphasized by the antitrust offenders involved a comparison between their crimes and the crimes of street criminals. Antitrust offenses differ in their mechanics from street crimes in that they are not committed in one place and at one time. Rather, they are spatially and temporally diffuse and are intermingled with legitimate behavior. In addition, the victims of antitrust offenses tend not to be identifiable individuals, as is the case with most street crimes. These characteristics are used by antitrust violators to contrast their own behavior with that of common stereotypes of criminality. Real crimes are pictured as discrete events that have beginnings and ends and involve individuals who directly and purposely victimize someone else in a particular place and a particular time.

It certainly wasn't a premeditated type of thing in our cases as far as I can see. . . . To me it's different than _____ and I sitting down and we plan, well, we're going to rob this bank tomorrow and premeditatedly go in there. . . . That wasn't the case at all. . . . It wasn't like sitting down and planning I'm going to rob this bank type of thing. . . . It was just a common everyday way of doing business and surviving.

A consistent thread running through all of the interviews was the necessity for antitrust-like practices, given the realities of the business world. Offenders seemed to define the situation in such a manner that two sets of rules could be seen to apply. On the one hand, there are the legislatively determined rules—laws—which govern how one is to conduct one's business affairs. On the other hand, there is a higher set of rules based on the concepts of profit and survival, which are taken to define what it means to be in business in a capitalistic society. These rules do not just regulate behavior; rather, they constitute or create the behavior in question. If one is not trying to make a profit or trying to keep one's business going, then one is not really "in business." Following Searle (1969:33–41), the former type of rule can be called a regulative rule and the latter type a constitutive rule. In certain situations, one may have to violate a regulative rule in order to conform to the more basic constitutive rule of the activity in which one is engaged.

This point can best be illustrated through the use of an analogy involving competitive games.

Trying to win is a constitutive rule of competitive games in the sense that if one is not trying to win, one is not really playing the game. In competitive games, situations may arise where a player deliberately breaks the rules even though he knows or expects he will be caught. In the game of basketball, for example, a player may deliberately foul an opponent to prevent him from making a sure basket. In this instance, one would understand that the fouler was trying to win by gambling that the opponent would not make the free throws. The player violates the rule against fouling in order to follow the higher rule of trying to win.

Trying to make a profit or survive in business can be thought of as a constitutive rule of capitalist economies. The laws that govern *how* one is allowed to make a profit are regulative rules, which can understandably be subordinated to the rules of trying to survive and profit. From the offender's point of view, he is doing what businessmen in our society are supposed to do—that is, stay in business and make a profit. Thus, an individual who violates society's laws or regulations in certain situations may actually conceive of himself as thereby acting more in accord with the central ethos of his society than if he had been a strict observer of its law. One might suggest, following Denzin (1977), that for businessmen in the building and contracting industry, an informal structure exists below the articulated legal structure, one which frequently supersedes the legal structure. The informal structure may define as moral and "legal" certain actions that the formal legal structure defines as immoral and "illegal."

TAX VIOLATORS

Six of the offenders interviewed were convicted of income tax violations. Like antitrust violators, tax violators can rely upon the complexity of the tax laws and an historical tradition in which cheating on taxes is not really criminal. Tax offenders would claim that everybody cheats somehow on their taxes and present themselves as victims of an unlucky break, because they got caught.

Everybody cheats on their income tax, 95% of the people. Even if it's for ten dollars it's the same principle. I didn't cheat. I just didn't know how to report it.

The widespread belief that cheating on taxes is endemic helps to lend credence to the offender's claim to have been singled out and to be no more guilty than most people.

Tax offenders were more likely to have acted as individuals rather than as part of a group and, as a result, were more prone to account for their offenses by referring to them as either mistakes or the product of special circumstances. Violations were presented as simple errors which resulted from ignorance and poor recordkeeping. Deliberate intention to steal from the government for personal benefit was denied.

I didn't take the money. I have no bank account to show for all this money, where all this money is at that I was supposed to have. They never found the money, ever. There is no Swiss bank account, believe me.

My records were strictly one big mess. That's all it was. If only I had an accountant, this wouldn't even of happened. No way in God's creation would this ever have happened.

Other offenders would justify their actions by admitting that they were wrong while painting their motives as altruistic rather than criminal. Criminality was denied because they did not set out to deliberately cheat the government for their own personal gain. Like the antitrust offenders discussed above, one tax violator distinguished between his own crime and the crimes of real criminals.

I'm not a criminal. That is, I'm not a criminal from the standpoint of taking a gun and doing this and that. I'm a criminal from the standpoint of making a mistake, a serious mistake. . . . The thing that really got me involved in it is my feeling for the employees here, certain employees that are my right hand. In order to save them a certain amount of taxes and things like that, I'd extend money to them in cash, and the money came from these sources that I took it from. You know, cash sales and things of that nature, but practically all of it was turned over to the employees, because of my feeling for them.

All of the tax violators pointed out that they had no intention of deliberately victimizing the government. None of them denied the legitimacy of the tax laws, nor did they claim that they cheated because the government is not representative of the people (Conklin, 1977:99). Rather, as a result of ignorance or for altruistic reasons, they made decisions which turned out to be criminal when viewed from the perspective of the law. While they acknowledged the technical criminality of their actions, they tried to show that what they did was not criminally motivated.

VIOLATIONS OF FINANCIAL TRUST

Four offenders were involved in violations of financial trust. Three were bank officers who embezzled or misapplied funds, and the fourth was a union official who embezzled from a union pension fund. Perhaps because embezzlement is one crime in this sample that can be considered *mala in se,* these offenders were much more forthright about their crimes. Like the other offenders, the embezzlers would not go so far as to say "I am a criminal," but they did say "What I did was wrong, was criminal, and I knew it was." Thus, the embezzlers were unusual in that they explicitly admitted responsibility for their crimes. Two of the offenders clearly fit Cressey's scheme as persons with financial problems who used their positions to convert other people's money to their own use.

Unlike tax evasion, which can be excused by reference to the complex nature of tax regulations or antitrust violations, which can be justified as for the good of the organization as a whole, embezzlement requires deliberate action on the part of the offender and is almost inevitably committed for personal reasons. The crime of embezzlement, therefore, cannot be accounted for by using the same techniques that tax violators or antitrust violators do. The act itself can only be explained by showing that one was under extraordinary circumstances which explain one's uncharacteristic behavior. Three of the offenders referred explicitly to extraordinary circumstances and presented the offense as an aberration in their life history. For example, one offender described his situation in this manner:

As a kid, I never even—you know kids will sometimes shoplift from the dime store—I never even did that. I had never stolen a thing in my life and that was what was so unbelievable about the whole thing, but there were some psychological and personal questions that I wasn't dealing with very well. I wasn't terribly happily

married. I was married to a very strong-willed woman and it just wasn't working out.

The offender in this instance goes on to explain how, in an effort to impress his wife, he lived beyond his means and fell into debt.

A structural characteristic of embezzlement also helps the offender demonstrate his essential lack of criminality. Embezzlement is integrated into ordinary occupational routines. The illegal action does not stand out clearly against the surrounding set of legal actions. Rather, there is a high degree of surface correspondence between legal and illegal behavior. To maintain this correspondence, the offender must exercise some restraint when committing his crime. The embezzler must be discrete in his stealing; he cannot take all of the money available to him without at the same time revealing the crime. Once exposed, the offender can point to this restraint on his part as evidence that he is not really a criminal. That is, he can compare what happened with what could have happened in order to show how much more serious the offense could have been if he was really a criminal at heart.

What I could have done if I had truly had a devious criminal mind and perhaps if I had been a little smarter—and I am not saying that with any degree of pride or any degree of modesty whatever, [as] it's being smarter in a bad, an evil way—I could have pulled this off on a grander scale and I might still be doing it.

Even though the offender is forthright about admitting his guilt, he makes a distinction between himself and someone with a truly "devious criminal mind."

Contrary to Cressey's (1953:57–66) findings, none of the embezzlers claimed that their offenses were justified because they were underpaid or badly treated by their employers. Rather, attention was focused on the unusual circumstances surrounding the offense and its atypical character when compared to the rest of the offender's life. This strategy is for the most part determined by the mechanics and organizational format of the offense itself. Embezzlement occurs within the organization but not for the organization. It cannot be committed accidentally or out of ignorance. It can be accounted for only by showing that the actor "was not himself" at the time of the offense or was under such extraordinary circumstances that embezzlement was an understandable response to an unfortunate situation. This may explain the finding that embezzlers tend to produce accounts that are viewed as more sufficient by the justice system than those produced by other offenders (Rothman and Gandossy, 1982). The only plausible option open to a convicted embezzler trying to explain his offense is to admit responsibility while justifying the action, an approach that apparently strikes a responsive chord with judges.

FRAUD AND FALSE STATEMENTS

Ten offenders were convicted of some form of fraud or false statements charge. Unlike embezzlers, tax violators, or antitrust violators, these offenders were much more likely to deny committing any crime at all. Seven of the ten claimed that they, personally, were innocent of any crime, although each admitted that fraud had occurred. Typically, they claimed to have been set up by associates and to have been wrongfully convicted by the U.S. Attorney handling the case. One might call this the scapegoat strategy. Rather than admitting technical wrong doing and then justifying or excusing it, the offender attempts to paint himself as a victim by shifting the blame entirely to another party. Prosecutors were presented as being either ignorant or politically motivated.

The outright denial of any crime whatsoever is unusual compared to the other types of offenders studied here. It may result from the nature of the crime of fraud. By definition, fraud involves a conscious attempt on the part of one or more persons to mislead others. While it is theoretically possible to accidentally violate the antitrust and tax laws, or to violate them for altruistic reasons, it is difficult to imagine how one could accidentally mislead someone else for his or her own good. Furthermore, in many instances, fraud is an aggressively acquisitive crime. The offender develops a scheme to bilk other people out of money or property, and does this not because of some personal problem but because the scheme is an easy way to get rich. Stock swindles, fraud-

ulent loan scams, and so on are often so large and complicated that they cannot possibly be excused as foolish and desperate solutions to personal problems. Thus, those involved in large-scale frauds do not have the option open to most embezzlers of presenting themselves as persons responding defensively to difficult personal circumstances.

Furthermore, because fraud involves a deliberate attempt to mislead another, the offender who fails to remove himself from the scheme runs the risk of being shown to have a guilty mind. That is, he is shown to possess the most essential element of modern conceptions of criminality: an intent to harm another. His inner self would in this case be exposed as something other than what it has been presented as, and all of his previous actions would be subject to reinterpretation in light of this new perspective. For this reason, defrauders are most prone to denying any crime at all. The cooperative and conspiratorial nature of many fraudulent schemes makes it possible to put the blame on someone else and to present oneself as a scapegoat. Typically, this is done by claiming to have been duped by others.

Two illustrations of this strategy are presented below.

I figured I wasn't guilty, so it wouldn't be that hard to disprove it, until, as I say, I went to court and all of a sudden they start bringing in these guys out of the woodwork implicating me that I never saw. Lot of it could be proved that I never saw.

Inwardly, I personally felt that the only crime that I committed was not telling on these guys. Not that I deliberately, intentionally committed a crime against the system. My only crime was that I should have had the guts to tell on these guys, what they were doing, rather than putting up with it and then trying to gradually get out of the system without hurting them or without them thinking I was going to snitch on them.

Of the three offenders who admitted committing crimes, two acted alone and the third acted with only one other person. Their accounts were similar to others presented earlier and tended to focus on either the harmless nature of their violations or on the unusual circumstances that drove them to commit their crimes. One claimed that his violations were only technical and that no one besides himself had been harmed.

First of all, no money was stolen or anything of that nature. The bank didn't lose any money. . . . What I did was a technical violation. I made a mistake. There's no question about that, but the bank lost no money.

Another offender who directly admitted his guilt was involved in a check-kiting scheme. In a manner similar to embezzlers, he argued that his actions were motivated by exceptional circumstances.

I was faced with the choice of all of a sudden, and I mean now, closing the doors or doing something else to keep that business open. . . . I'm not going to tell you that this wouldn't have happened if I'd had time to think it over, because I think it probably would have. You're sitting there with a dying patient. You are going to try to keep him alive.

In the other fraud cases more individuals were involved, and it was possible and perhaps necessary for each offender to claim that he was not really the culprit.

DISCUSSION: OFFENSES, ACCOUNTS, AND DEGRADATION CEREMONIES

The investigation, prosecution, and conviction of a white-collar offender involves him in a very undesirable status passage (Glaser and Strauss, 1971). The entire process can be viewed as a long and drawn-out degradation ceremony with the prosecutor as the chief denouncer and the offender's family and friends as the chief witnesses. The offender is moved from the status of law-abiding citizen to that of convicted felon. Accounts are developed to defeat the process of identity transformation that is the object of a degradation ceremony. They represent the offender's attempt to diminish the effect of his legal transformation and to prevent its becoming a publicly validated label. It can be suggested that the accounts developed by white-collar offenders take the forms that they do for two reasons: (1) the forms are required to defeat the suc-

cess of the degradation ceremony, and (2) the specific forms used are the ones available given the mechanics, history, and organizational context of the offenses.

Three general patterns in accounting strategies stand out in the data. Each can be characterized by the subject matter on which it focuses: the event (offense), the perpetrator (offender), or reduced. Although there are overlaps in the accounting strategies used by the various types of offenders, and while any given offender may use more than one strategy, it appears that accounting strategies and offenses correlate.

REFERENCES

CASPER, JONATHAN D. 1978. *Criminal Courts: The Defendant's Perspective*. Washington, D.C.: U.S. Department of Justice.

CONKLIN, JOHN E. 1977. *Illegal But Not Criminal: Business Crime in America*. Englewood Cliffs, N.J.: Prentice Hall.

CRESSEY, DONALD. 1953. *Other People's Money*. New York: Free Press.

DENZIN, NORMAN K. 1977. "Notes on the criminogenic hypothesis: A case study of the American liquor industry." *American Sociological Review* 42:905–920.

———. 1984. *On Understanding Emotion*. San Francisco: Jossey-Bass.

EDELHERTZ, HERBERT. 1970. *The Nature, Impact, and Prosecution of White Collar Crime*. Washington, D.C.: U.S. Government Printing Office.

GARFINKEL, HAROLD. 1956. "Conditions of successful degradation ceremonies." *American Journal of Sociology* 61:420–424.

GLASER, BARNEY G. and ANSELM L. STRAUSS. 1971. *Status Passage*. Chicago: Aldine.

KATZ, JACK. 1979. "Legality and equality: Plea bargaining," in the prosecution of white-collar crimes." *Law and Society Review* 13:431–460.

ROTHMAN, MARTIN and ROBERT F. GANDOSSY. 1982. "Sad tales: The accounts of white-collar defendants and the decision to sanction." *Pacific Sociological Review* 4:449–473.

SEARLE, JOHN R. 1969. *Speech Acts*. Cambridge: Cambridge University Press.

ACCOUNTS OF PROFESSIONAL MISDEEDS
THE SEXUAL EXPLOITATION OF CLIENTS BY PSYCHOTHERAPISTS

Mark R. Pogrebin, Eric D. Poole, and Amos Martinez

Intimate sexual relationships between mental health therapists and their clients have been increasingly reported in recent years (Akamatsu 1987). In a survey of over 1400 psychiatrists, Gartell, Herman, Olarte, Feldstein, and Localio (1987) found that 65 percent reported having treated a patient who admitted to sexual involvement with a previous therapist.[1] National self-report surveys indicate that approximately 10 percent of psychotherapists admit having had at least one sexual encounter with a client (Gartell, Herman, Olarte, Feldstein, and Localio 1986; Pope, Keith-Spiegel, and Tabachnick 1986). It is suggested that these surveys most likely underestimate the extent of actual sexual involvement with clients because some offending psychotherapists either fail to respond to the survey or fail to report their sexual indiscretions (Gartell et al. 1987). Regardless of the true prevalence rates, many mental health professional associations explicitly condemn sexual relations between a therapist and client. Such relationships represent a breach of canons of professional ethics and are subject to disciplinary action by specific licensing or regulatory bodies.

PSYCHOLOGICAL IMPACT ON CLIENT

Individuals who seek treatment for emotional or mental health problems assume a dependency role in a professional-client relationship in which direction and control are exerted by the therapist. The client's most intimate secrets, desires, and fears are revealed to the therapist. Therapeutic communication relies on the development of trust between client and therapist. In order to be successful, therapy requires the individual in

treatment to abandon the psychic defenses that shield his or her genuine self from scrutiny (Pope and Bouhoutsos 1986). The lowering of these defenses in a therapeutic relationship increases the client's emotional vulnerability. Because the potential for manipulation or exploitation of the client is heightened in such relationships, Benetin and Wilder (1989) argue that the therapist must assume a higher degree of professional responsibility to ensure that personal trust is not abused.

As Finkelhor (1984) points out, the therapeutic relationship is fundamentally asymmetrical; thus, the controlling presumption is that a client's volition under conditions of therapeutic dependency must always be considered problematic. The client cannot be considered capable of freely consenting to enter into a sexual relationship with a therapist. The therapist's sexual exploitation of a client represents an obvious violation of trust, destroying any therapeutic relationship that has been established. The client often experiences intense feelings of betrayal and anguish at having been victimized by the very person who had been trusted to help (Pope and Bouhoutsos 1986). Sexual exploitation by a therapist can result in clients' suffering emotional instability, conflicts in interpersonal relationships, and disruptions in work performance (Benetin and Wilder 1989).

THE COLORADO STATE GRIEVANCE BOARD

Historically in Colorado, grievances against licensed mental health providers were handled by two separate licensing boards: the Board of Psychologist Examiners and the Board of Social Work Examiners. During the past 20 years, the state witnessed a proliferation of practitioners in the unregulated field of psychotherapy. Individuals trained in traditional professional fields of psychology, counseling, and social work may call themselves psychotherapists, but anyone else with (or without) training in any field may refer to their practice as psychotherapy. In short, psychotherapists are not subject to mandatory licensing requirements in Colorado. Largely through the lobbying efforts of licensed mental health practitioners, the state legislature was persuaded to address some of the problems associated with the operation of a decentralized grievance process that failed to regulate unlicensed practitioners of psychotherapy. The result was the passage of the Mental Health Occupations Act, creating on July 1, 1988 the State Grievance Board within the Colorado Department of Regulatory Agencies.

The State Grievance Board has the responsibility to process complaints and undertake disciplinary proceedings against the four categories of licensed therapists and against unlicensed psychotherapists. Upon the filing of a complaint, the eight-member board (comprising four licensed therapists and four public members) initiates the following action:

1. The named therapist receives written notice and is given 20 days to respond in writing;
2. When deemed appropriate by the board, the complainant may review the therapist's response and is given 10 days to submit further information or explanation; and
3. The board reviews the available information and renders a decision about the complaint.

If the board determines that disciplinary action against a licensed therapist is warranted, the board is increased by an augmenting panel of three members, each of whom is a licensed practitioner in the same field as the psychotherapist subject to sanctioning. The board can issue a letter of admonition, place restrictions on the license or the practice, require the therapist to submit to a mental or physical examination, or seek an injunction in a state district court to limit or to stop the practice of psychotherapy. When the complaint involves an unlicensed practitioner, injunctive action is the board's only disciplinary remedy.

The governing state statute further mandates that psychotherapists provide their clients with a disclosure statement concerning their credentials (e.g., degrees and licenses) and specific client rights and information (e.g., second opinion and legal confidentiality, as well as therapeutic methods and techniques and fee structure, if requested). In the Model Disclosure Statement developed by the State Grievance Board, the impropriety of sexual relations is specifically noted:

In a professional relationship (such as ours [client and therapist]), sexual intimacy between a therapist and a client is never appropriate. If sexual intimacy occurs, it should be reported to the State Grievance Board.

During 1988 the state legislature also enacted a statute making sexual contact between therapist and client a criminal offense (Colorado Revised Statutes 18-3-405.5, Supplement 1988).

Since 1988, sexual intimacy between therapists and clients has been explicitly and formally recognized as one of the most serious violations of the professional-client relationship, subject to both regulatory or administrative and criminal penalties. Yet, between August 1, 1988 and June 30, 1990, 10 percent ($n = 33$) of the 324 complaints filed with the State Grievance Board involved allegations of sexual misconduct. Given the implications that these sexual improprieties raise for both the client as victim and the therapist as offender, we wish to examine the written accounts submitted to the board by psychotherapists who have had complaints of sexual misconduct filed against them.

THEORETICAL PERSPECTIVE

As Mills (1940, p. 904) observes, the "imputation and avowal of motives by actors are social phenomena to be explained. The differing reasons men give for their actions are not themselves without reasons." Mills draws a sharp distinction between cause and explanation or account. He focuses not on the reasons for the actions of individuals but on the reasons individuals give for their actions. Mills (1940, p. 906) views motive as "a complex of meaning, which appears to the actor himself or to the observer to be an adequate ground for his conduct." Yet, there may be another dimension: the individual's perception of how the motive will appear to others.

Mills argues that such motives express themselves in special vocabularies: first, they must satisfactorily answer questions concerning both social and lingual conduct; second, they must be accepted accounts for past, present, or future behavior. According to Scott and Lyman (1968), accounts are socially approved vocabularies that serve as explanatory mechanisms for deviance. These linguistic devices attempt to shape others' attribution about the actor's intent or motivation, turning it away from imputations that are harmful (e.g., personal devaluation, stigma, or imposition of negative sanctions).

It is no doubt true that, in many instances, being able to effectively present accounts will lessen the degree of one's moral responsibility. Moral responsibility is rarely a present-or-absent attribution. Just as there are degrees of deviation from expected conduct norms, there are probably types and degrees of accountability, as well as acceptability, to various audiences with respect to the accounts that individuals offer. "The variable is the accepted vocabulary of motives of each man's dominant group about whose opinion he cares" (Mills 1940, p. 906).

It is easy for most people to draw from a repertoire of accounts in explaining their untoward acts. This is not to suggest that their reasons are either sincere or insincere. Nor does it deny the validity of their claims; they may well have committed the disapproved behavior for the very reasons that are given. The important thing here is that they require an appropriate vocabulary of motive to guide their presentation of self. In the present study we seek to identify the meanings therapists imputed to the circumstances and events surrounding their sexual relations with clients. Of particular interest are the situated reasons or motives these individuals offer in accounting for their actions.

METHOD

To the 33 complaints of sexual misconduct filed from August 1988 through June 1990, 30 written responses from psychotherapists were submitted to the State Grievance Board.[2] Twenty-four therapists admitted to sexual involvement with clients; six denied the allegations. In the present study we examine the statements of the 24 therapists who provided accounts for their sexual relations with clients.[3] Twenty-one therapists are men; three are women.

The analytical method utilized in reviewing therapists' accounts was content analysis, which "translates frequency of occurrence of certain symbols into summary judgments and comparisons of content of the discourse" (Starosta 1984, p. 185). Content analytical techniques provide the means to document, classify, and interpret the communication of meaning, allowing for inferential judgments from objective identification of the characteristics of messages (Holsti 1969).

The 24 written responses ranged in length from 2 to 25 pages. Each response was assessed and classified according to the types of explanations invoked by therapists in accounting for their acknowledged sexual relations with clients. We employed Scott and Lyman's (1968) classic formulation of accounts (i.e., excuses and justifications) and Goffman's (1971) notion of the apology as conceptual guides in organizing the vocabularies of motive used by our group of therapists to explain their untoward behavior. Our efforts build upon the work of previous sociologists who have utilized the concept of accounts to analyze the vocabularies of motive of convicted rapists (Scully and Marolla 1984) and convicted murderers (Ray and Simons 1987) in prison interviews with researchers, as well as the vocabularies of criminal defendants in presentence interviews with probation officers (Spencer 1983) and of white-collar defendants in presentence investigation reports (Rothman and Gandossy 1982). We developed the following classification scheme consistent with the controlling themes identified in the written accounts:[4]

1. Excuse: an account in which an individual admits that an act was wrong or inappropriate, while providing a socially approved vocabulary for mitigating or relieving personal responsibility.
    (a) Appeal of defeasibility: an excuse in which an individual seeks to absolve himself or herself of responsibility by claiming to have acted on the basis of either lack of information or misinformation.
    (b) Scapegoating: an excuse in which an individual attempts to shift responsibility by asserting that

his or her behavior was a response to the actions or attitudes of others.

2. Justification: an account in which the individual acknowledges the wrongfulness of the type or category of an act but seeks to have the specific instance in question defined as an exception.

   (a) Sad tale: a highly selective portrayal of distressing biographical facts through which the individual explains his or her present act as the product of extenuating conditions.

   (b) Denial of injury: a justification in which the individual asserts that his or her act was permissible under the particular occasion since no one was harmed or the consequences were trivial (or even beneficial).

3. Apology: an account in which the individual acknowledges the wrongfulness of the act and accepts personal responsibility but seeks to portray his or her act as the product of a past self that has since been disavowed.

Excerpts from the therapists' written accounts, presented in our findings below, have been selected to illustrate the defining elements of each of the above types of accounts. Care has been taken to avoid disclosing any information that could be used to identify the source of the statements. All names are fictitious to ensure against any potential violation of anonymity.

FINDINGS

Accounts are "linguistic device[s] employed whenever an action is subjected to valuative inquiry" (Scott and Lyman 1968, p. 46). An important function of accounts is to mitigate blameworthiness by representing one's behavior in such a way as to reduce personal accountability. This involves offering accounts aimed at altering the prevailing conception of what the instant activity is, as well as one's role in the activity. Excuses, justifications, and apologies all display a common goal: giving a "good account" of oneself.

Excuses

Appeal of Defeasibility. In an appeal of defeasibility, one accounts for one's behavior by denying any intention to cause the admitted harm or by claiming a failure to foresee the unfortunate consequences of one's act, or both. As Lyman and Scott (1989, pp. 136–37) explain:

The appeal of defeasibility invokes a division in the relation between action and intent, suggesting that the latter was malfunctioning with respect to knowledge, voluntariness, or state of complete consciousness.

In the following account, the therapist claims ignorance of professional rules of conduct governing relations with clients:

I did not know that seeing clients socially outside of therapy violated hospital policy. . . . [I]f I realized it was strictly forbidden, I would have acted differently.

The next case involves a female therapist who had engaged in a long-term sexual relationship with a female client. The therapist couches her account in terms of failing to be informed by her clinical supervisors that the relationship was improper:

Both Drs. Smith and Jones had total access to and knowledge of how I terminated with her [the client] and continued our evolving relationship. Neither of them in any way inferred that I had done anything unethical or illegal. I do not understand how I can be held accountable for my actions. There were no guidelines provided by the mental health center around this issue. Both Drs. Smith and Jones knew of and approved of my relationship with her.

Other appeals of defeasibility incorporate elements of defective insight and reasoning, or just poor judgment, in an effort to deny intent. An appropriate vocabulary of motive is necessarily involved in the presentation of such appeals. For example, Scully and Marolla (1984, pp. 540–41) report that convicted rapists attempted to

. . . negotiate a non-rapist identity by painting an image of themselves as a "nice guy." Admitters projected the image of someone who had made a serious mistake but, in every other respect, was a decent person.

The deviant actor makes a bid to be seen as a person who has many of the same positive social attributes possessed by others. This individual presents the basic problem simply: "Everybody makes mistakes"; "It could happen to anyone"; or "We all do stupid things." Such fairly standard, socially approved phrases or ideas are used to sensitize others to their own mistakes, thereby reminding them of their own vulnerability and limiting their opportunity to draw lines between themselves and the individual deviant. The basic message is that the deviant act is not indicative of one's essential character (Goffman 1963). This message is supplemented by an effort to present information about the "untainted" aspects of self. In these presentational cues, deviant actors seek to bring about a softening of the moral breach in which they are involved and relieve themselves of culpability.

In the following example, a therapist admits that she simply misinterpreted her own feelings and did not consciously intend to become sexually involved with her client:

It was after a short period of time that I first experienced any sexual feelings toward her. I did excuse the feelings I had as something which I never would act on. Unfortunately, I did not understand what was happening at the time.

Similarly, another therapist seeks to diminish culpability by attributing his sexual indiscretion to a misreading of his client's emotional needs:

I experienced her expressions of affection as caring gestures of our spiritual bond, not lust. And I had no reason to suspect otherwise from her, since I had been so clear about my aversion to romantic involvement. We had sexual intercourse only once after termination. I am not promiscuous, neither sexually abusive nor seductive.

Another variant of the appeal of defeasibility involves a claim that the inappropriate behavior was an unforeseen outcome of the therapeutic process itself. This denial of responsibility requires articulating one's position in the professional argot of psychotherapy. Such professionals are able to provide rather complex and compelling accounts of themselves, attempting to convince an audience of peers of the "real" meaning or "correct" interpretation of their behavior. As Lofland (1969, p. 179) posits,

. . . since they are likely to share in the universe of understandings and cultural ideology of expert imputors, they are more likely to be aware of what kinds of reasons or explanations such imputors will buy.

The therapist in the next account focuses on the unique problems arising in the professional-client relationship that contributed to the sexual misconduct:

The two inappropriate interactions occurred when she was a practicing psychotherapist and I was seeing her as a client, supervisee, and socially. I believe that my unresolved countertransference and her transference greatly contributed to the events.

In related accounts, therapists provide a professional assessment or opinion that the therapeutic techniques utilized in treating their clients got out of hand. This approach is shown in the following:

The initial development of a change in the relationship centered around my empathetic feelings that touched on unresolved feelings of loss in my own life. One aspect of the treatment centered around a lifetime of severe feelings of abandonment and rejection that the client felt from her family. This worked powerful feelings within me and I responded by overidentifying with the client, becoming emotionally vulnerable and feeling inappropriate responsibility to ease the client's pain.

Some of these professional accounts provide lengthy and detailed descriptions of various treatment techniques utilized because of the ineffectiveness of prior intervention attempts. These therapists stress the multifarious nature of the problems encountered in treatment that warranted the use of more complex and often more risky types of treatment. The following case shows the compromising position in which the therapist placed himself in attempting to foster the client's amenability to treatment:

Because we were at an impasse in therapy I adjusted the treatment to overcome resistance. I employed several tactics, one of which was to share more of my personal life with her; another was to see her outside the usual office setting.

A slight variation of this defeasibility claim involves what Scott and Lyman (1968, p. 48) call the "gravity disclaimer," where the actor recognizes the potential risks involved in the pursuit of a particular course of action but suggests that their probability could not be predetermined.

When she came in she was very down, to the point that she was staring at the floor. I felt she was not being reached in a cognitive way, so I tried to reach her using a sensory approach. I was trying to communicate to her: caring, love, acceptance, compassion and so on. Unfortunately, with the sensory approach there is a fine line not to be crossed, and I crossed it.

The appeal of defeasibility is a form of excuse that links knowledge and intent. Actors diminish blameworthiness by defining their acts as occurring without real awareness or intent; that is, they attempt to absolve themselves of responsibility by denying having knowingly intended to cause the untoward consequences. Had they known otherwise, they would have acted differently.

Scapegoating. Scapegoating involves an attempt to blame others for one's untoward behavior. Scapegoating is available as a form of excuse in the professional-client relationship because of the contextual opportunity for the therapist to shift personal responsibility to the client. The therapist contends that his or her actions were the product of the negative attributes or will of the client, e.g., deceit, seduction, or manipulation. The therapist in the following example recognizes the wrongfulness of his behavior but deflects responsibility by holding the client culpable for her actions:

I am not denying that this sexual activity took place, nor am I trying to excuse or justify it. It was wrong. However, the woman who complained about me is a psychologist. She was counseling me as well, on some vocational issues. So if anyone had cause for complaint under the regulations, it seems it would be me.

Another example of an account where the therapist attempts to "blame the victim" for the improper sexual activity reveals the focus on his diminished personal control of the relationship:

That I became involved in a sexual relationship with her is true. While my actions were reprehensible, both morally and professionally, I did not mislead or seduce her or intend to take advantage of her. My fault, instead, was failing to adequately safeguard myself from her seductiveness, covert and overt.

Here we have a therapist recognizing the impropriety of his actions yet denying personal responsibility because of the client's overpowering

charms. The message is that the therapist may be held accountable for an inadequate "self-defense" which left him vulnerable to the client's seductive nature, but that he should not be culpable for the deviant sexual behavior since it was really he who was taken in and thus "victimized." The therapist's account for his predicament presumes a "reasonable person" theory of behavior; that is, given the same set of circumstances, any reasonable person would be expected to succumb to this persuasive client.

Justifications

Sad Tale.   The sad tale presents an array of dismal experiences or conditions that are regarded—both collectively and cumulatively—as an explanation and justification for the actor's present untoward behavior. The therapists who presented sad tales invariably focused on their own history of family problems and personal tribulations that brought them to their present state of sexual affairs with clients:

Ironically, her termination from therapy came at one of the darkest periods of my life. My father had died that year. I had met him for the first time when I was in my twenties. He was an alcoholic. Over the years we had worked hard on our relationship. At the time of his dying, we were at peace with one another. Yet, I still had my grief. At the time I had entered into individual therapy to focus on issues pertaining to my father's alcoholism and co-dependency issues. I then asked my wife to join me for marriage counseling. We were having substantial problems surrounding my powerlessness in our relationship. Therapy failed to address the balance of power. I was in the worst depression I had ever experienced in my entire life when we began our sexual involvement.

Therapists who employ sad tales admit to having sexual relations with their clients, admit that their actions were improper, and admit that ordinarily what they did would be an instance of the general category of the prohibited behavior. They claim, however, that their behavior is a special case because the power of circumstance voids the defining deviant quality of their actions. This type of account is similar to Lofland's (1969, p. 88) "special justification," where the actor views his current act as representative of some category of deviance but does not believe it to be entirely blameworthy because of extenuating circumstances. One therapist outlines the particular contextual factors that help explain his misbehavior:

The following situations are not represented as an excuse for my actions. There is no excuse for them. They are simply some of what I feel are circumstances that formed the context for what I believe is an incident that will never be repeated.
   (1) Life losses: My mother-in-law who lived with us died. My oldest son and, the next fall, my daughter had left home for college.
   (2) Overscheduling: I dealt with these losses and other concerns in my life by massive overscheduling.

Other therapists offer similar sad tales of tragic events that are seen to diminish their capacity, either physically or mentally, to cope with present circumstances. Two cases illustrate this accounting strategy:

In the summer of 1988, my wife and I separated with her taking our children to live out-of-state. This was a difficult loss for me. A divorce followed. Soon after I had a bout with phlebitis which hospitalized me for ten days.

My daughter, who lived far away with my former wife, was diagnosed with leukemia; and my mother had just died. Additional stress was caused by my ex-wife and present wife's embittered interactions.

Sad tales often incorporate a commitment to conventionality whereby one's typical behavior is depicted as conforming to generally approved rules or practices—the instant deviant act being the exception. The imputation is that "the exception proves the rule"; that is, one's normally conventional behavior is confirmed or proven by the rate untoward act.[5] The transgression may thus be viewed as an exception to the deviant classification to which it would justifiably belong if the special circumstances surrounding the enactment of the behavior in question did not exist. Given such circumstances, individuals depict themselves as more acted upon than acting. In the next case the therapist outlines the special circumstances that account for his behavior:

I had "topped out" at my job, was being given additional responsibilities to deal with, had very little skilled staff to work with, and received virtually no support from my supervisor. I was unconsciously looking for a challenging case to renew my interest in my work, and she fit that role. My finally giving into her seduction was an impulsive act based on my own hopelessness and depression.

Sad tales depict individuals acting abnormally in abnormal situations. In short, their instant deviance is neither typical nor characteristic of the type of person they really are, that is, how they would act under normal conditions. They are victims of circumstance, for if it were not for these dismal life events, their sexual improprieties would never have occurred.

Denial of Injury. Denial of injury is premised on a moral assessment of consequences; that is, the individual claims that his or her actions should be judged as wrong on the basis of the harm resulting from those acts. Again, the actor acknowledges that in general the behavior in which he or she has engaged is inappropriate but asserts that in this particular instance no real harm was done. This type of account was prevalent among the therapists who had engaged in sexual relations with clients following the termination of therapy.

A good therapy termination establishes person-to-person equality between participants. Blanket condemnations of post-therapy relationships also are founded on a belief that such relationships invariably cause harm to the former patient. I defy anyone to meet Gerry, interview her, and then maintain that any harm was done to her by me.

The issue of sexual involvement with former clients represents an unresolved ethical controversy among therapists. On the one hand, the American Psychiatric Association has no official policy which categorically bans sexual relations between a psychiatrist and a former patient; instead, there is a case-by-case analysis of such relationships conducted by an ethics committee to determine their propriety. On the other hand, some states have enacted statutes that expressly prohibit any sexual relations between psychotherapists and former clients during a specified posttherapy time period. The statutory period in Colorado is six months following the termination of therapy.
   Despite this explicit restriction, some therapists in the present study still insist that their sex-

ual relationships with former clients are neither in violation of professional standards of conduct nor in conflict with state law.

Her psychotherapy with me was successfully concluded two months prior to her seeking a social relationship with me. She herself was unequivocal in her desire for a social relationship with me, which was entirely free from any therapeutic need or motivation. . . . I expressly clarified to her that in becoming socially involved I no longer could ever again function as her therapist. With the dual relationship problem laid aside, strictly speaking, such relationships are not unethical since no ethical rule of conduct has ever been formulated against them. . . . I hope that I have convincingly demonstrated that there is no generally accepted standard of psychological practice in . . . post-termination relationships, and so I cannot have violated the statute.

In denial of injury one seeks to neutralize the untoward behavior by redefining the activity in such a way as to reduce or negate its negative quality, such as injury, harm, or wrong. To some extent this involves structuring one's accounts to alter the dominant conceptions of what the activity is. Accounts thus sometimes go beyond the "linguistic forms" that Scott and Lyman have emphasized. Deviance reduction often involves manipulation of various symbols as a basis for one's behavioral account. As seen in the preceding denials of injury, therapists sought to have their sexual relations with former clients redefined according to a professional code of conduct that is subject to individual interpretation. This ethical code may be seen as symbolically governing the therapist-client relationship, establishing the grounds on which the therapist may make autonomous moral judgments of his or her own behavior.

Apology

Scott and Lyman (1968, p. 59) assert that "every account is a manifestation of the underlying negotiation of identities." In a sense, it is probably more accurate to conceive of accounts as referring to desired outcomes rather than as negotiating techniques. They indicate a sought-after definition of the situation, one in which the focus on the deviant act and the shame attached to the individual are lessened. For example,

Goffman (1971) argues that the apology, as an account, combines an acknowledgment that one's prior actions were morally reprehensible with a repudiation of both the behavior and the former self that engaged in such activity.

Two consequences of an accused wrongdoer's action are guilt and shame. If wrongful behavior is based on internal standards, the transgressor feels guilty; if the behavior is judged on external normative comparisons, the person experiences shame. Shame results from being viewed as one who has behaved in a discrediting manner. In the following three cases, each therapist expresses his remorse and laments his moral failure:

I find myself in the shameful position that I never would have thought possible for me as I violated my own standards of personal and professional conduct.

I feel very badly for what I have done, ashamed and unprofessional. I feel unworthy of working in the noble profession of counseling.

I entered into therapy and from the first session disclosed what I had done. I talked about my shame and the devastation I had created for my family and others.

Schlenker and Darby (1981) observe that the apology incorporates not only an expression of regret but also a claim of redemption. An apology permits a transgressor the opportunity to admit guilt while simultaneously seeking forgiveness in order that the offending behavior not be thought of as a representation of what the actor is really like. One therapist expresses concern for his actions and proposes a way to avoid such conduct in the future:

I continue to feel worry and guilt about the damage that I caused. I have taken steps I felt necessary which has been to decide not to work with any client who could be very emotionally demanding, such as occurs with people who are borderline or dependent in their functioning.

This account seems to imply that one's remorse and affirmative effort to prevent future transgressions are sufficient remedies in themselves, preempting the need for others to impose additional sanctions. Self-abasement serves a dual purpose in the apology. First, it devalues the untoward behavior, thus reaffirming the moral superiority of conventional conduct. Second, it represents a form of punishment, reprimanding oneself consistent with the moral judgments of others. The message is that the actor shares the views of others, including their assessment of him or her, and both desires and deserves their acceptance. As Jones and Pittman (1982, pp. 255–56) contend,

To the extent that the threatened actor sustains his counteractive behavior or to the extent that the counteractive behavior involves effort and costly commitments, social confirmation will have the restorative power sought.

Several elements of self-management combine when an apology is offered. While confessing guilt and expressing shame, the individual directs anger at himself or herself—denouncing the act and the actor. The actor then attempts to insulate his or her identity from the stigma of the deviant act, reconfirming an allegiance to consensual values and standards of conduct. As Goffman (1971, p. 113) observes, the deviant

. . . splits himself into two parts, the part that is guilty of an offense and the part that dissociates itself from the delect and affirms a belief in the offered rule.

In the following account, the therapist accepts responsibility for his behavior but attempts to make amends by demonstrating a desire to learn from his mistakes:

I am firmly aware that my judgment at the time was both poor and impaired. I am also aware that my thinking was grandiose and immature. One cannot hold a position of public trust and violate community standards. I have incorporated that knowledge into my thoughts and acts.

The demonstration of shared understandings may also be seen as consistent with a desire to preserve self-respect; moreover, self-initiated or proactive response to one's own deviance may serve as a mechanism to lessen the actor's feelings of shame and embarrassment, to militate against negative affect, and to foster a more favorable image of self. Goffman (1971) calls this ritual attempt to repair a disturbed situation "remedial work." In the next account the therapist reveals his effort to repair his spoiled identity:

I have been grieving for Betty and the pain I have caused her. I am deeply distressed by my actions and am doing everything within my power for personal

and professional discipline and restoration. I have tried through reading, therapy, and talking with other men who had experienced similar situations to understand why I allowed this to happen.

Such impression-management strategies involving remedial work convey to others that the actor is "solicitous for the feelings of and sensibilities of others and . . . willing to acknowledge fault and accept or even execute judgment for the untoward act" (Lyman and Scott 1989, p. 143). Hewitt and Stokes (1975, p. 1) further note that actors "gear their words and deeds to the restoration and maintenance of situated and cherished identities." The vast majority of apologies were offered by therapists who sought restoration of self by immediately entering therapy themselves. In the following case, the therapist's realization of the emotional damage resulting from her homosexual affair with a client led to her self-commitment to a mental hospital:

I truly had no prior awareness of my vulnerability to a homosexual relationship before she became a client. In fact, it was such an ego dystonic experience for me that I soon ended up in the hospital myself and had two years of psychotherapy. From this therapy, as well as some follow-up therapy, I have come to understand the needs which led to such behavior. I regret the negative impact it has had on both of our lives.

Efforts to gain insight into their sexual transgressions appear critical to the therapists' transformation of self. By entering therapy, the individual becomes the object of the therapeutic process, whereby the "act" and the "actor" can be clinically separated. The very therapeutic context in which the initial deviance arose is now seen as the means by which the therapist can be redeemed through successful treatment. Through therapy individuals gain awareness of the causal processes involved in their deviant activity and are thus empowered to prevent such transgressions in the future. Introspective accounts convey a commitment both to understand and to change oneself. In this way, the therapist disavows his or her former discredited self and displays the new enlightened self.

DISCUSSION

The consequences of deviant activity are problematic, often depending on a "definition of the situation." When a particular definition of a specific situation emerges, even though its dominance may be only temporary, individuals must adjust their behavior and views to it. Alternative definitions of problematic situations routinely arise and are usually subject to negotiation. Thus, it is incumbent upon the accused therapist to have his or her situation defined in ways most favorable to maintaining or advancing his or her own interests. When "transformations of identity" are at stake, such efforts become especially consequential (Strauss 1962). The imputation of a deviant identity implies ramifications that can vitally affect the individual's personal and professional life. As noted earlier, the negotiation of accounts is a negotiation of identities. The account serves as an impression-management technique, or a "front," that minimizes the threat to identity (Goffman 1959). If the therapist can provide an acceptable account for his or her sexual impropriety—whether an excuse, justification, or apology—he or she increases the likelihood of restoring a cherished identity brought into question by the deviant behavior.

There is a close link between successfully conveying desired images to others and being able to incorporate them in one's own self-conceptions. When individuals offer accounts for their problematic actions, they are trying to ease their situation in two ways: by convincing others and by convincing themselves. An important function of accounts is to make one's transgressions not only intelligible to others but intelligible to oneself. Therapists sought to dispel the view that their deviation was a defining characteristic of who they really were; or, to put it another way, they attempted to engage the centrality or primacy of a deviant role imputation. The goal was to maintain or restore their own sense of personal and professional worth notwithstanding their sexual deviancy. In a way, laying claim to a favorable image in spite of aberrant behavior means voiding the apparent moral reality, that is, the deviance-laden definition of the situation that has been called to the attention of significant others (Grievance Board) by a victim-accuser (former client).

Goffman (1959, p. 251) maintains that individuals are not concerned with the issue of morality of their behavior as much as they are with the amoral issue of presenting a moral self:

Our activity, then is largely concerned with moral matters, but as performers we do not have a moral concern with them. As performers we are merchants of morality.

The presentation of a moral self following deviance may be interpreted as an attempt by the individual to reaffirm his commitment to consensual values and goals in order to win the acceptance of others (Tedeschi and Riorden 1981). The demonstration of shared standards of conduct may also be seen as consistent with the wish to redeem oneself in the eyes of others and to preserve self-respect. The desire for self-validating approval becomes more important when circumstances threaten an individual's identity. In these instances an actor will often make self-presentations for purposes of eliciting desired responses that will restore the perception of self by others that he or she desires. If discredited actors can offer a normal presentation of self in an abnormal situation, they may be successful in having their instant deviant behavior perceived by others as atypical, thus neutralizing a deviant characterization.

Individuals seek a "common ground" in accounts of their deviant behavior, explaining their actions in conventional terms that are acceptable to a particular audience. These accounts should not be viewed as mere rationalizations. They may genuinely be believed in. While accounts do not themselves cause one's behavior, they do provide situationally specific answers about the act in question and manifest a certain style of looking at the world.

Finally, it should be noted that, as retrospective interpretations, accounts may have little to do with the motives that existed at the time the deviance occurred. In this case accounting for one's deviant behavior requires one to dissimulate, that is, to pretend to be what one is not or not to be what one is. As Goffman (1959) asserts, social behavior involves a great deal of deliberate deception in that impressions of selves must be constantly created and managed for various others. Thus, it is not logically necessary that one agree with others' moral judgments in order to employ accounts. Even where no guilt or shame is consciously felt, one may offer accounts in the hope of lessening what could be, nonetheless, attributions of a deviant identity. When used convincingly, accounts blur the distinctions between "appearance and reality, truth and falsity, triviality and importance, accident and essence, coincidence and cause" (Garfinkel 1956, p. 420). Accounts embody a mixture of fact and fantasy. As shown in the accounts provided by therapists, what is most problematic is determining the mixture best suited for a particular situational context.

NOTES

1. Clients who suffer sexual exploitation often experience self-blame and are reluctant to disclose their victimization to others. Some are unsure what to do or to whom to report, and others simply believe it would do no good to report (Brown 1988).

2. Twenty of the 33 complaints involved unlicensed therapists. There were no discernible differences between the licensed and unlicensed therapists in type of account presented. Moreover, there was no association between type of account and disposition of the case by the Grievance Board.

3. The written statements submitted by therapists to the State Board have been obtained under provisions of Colorado's Public Records Act, which provides "any person the right of inspection of such records or any portion thereof" unless such inspection would violate any state statute or federal law or regulation or is expressly prohibited by judicial rules or court order. The first author serves as a public member on the Grievance Board. The third author is Program Administrator of the Mental Health Licensing Section in the Department of Regulatory Agencies and is directly responsible for the administration of the Grievance Board.

4. Some written explanations contained elements of more than one type of account, and we classified the response according to what we judged to be the controlling theme of the account taken in its entirety. A breakdown of the 24 cases according to their thematic account is as follows: defeasibility, $n = 8$; scapegoating, $n = 2$; sad tale, $n = 5$; denial of injury, $n = 2$; and apology, $n = 7$. It should be pointed out that our classification scheme is exhaustive of all accounts offered by therapists. The other types of accounts in Scott and Lyman's typology were not exhibited in the present data. This is not unexpected because therapists are attempting to present specific accounts that are consid-

ered appropriate to a specific type of situation. Thus, other excuses (e.g., appeal to accidents and appeal to biological drives) or justifications (e.g., denial of the victim, condemnation of condemners, and appeal to higher loyalties) were deemed either inappropriate or improper by therapists in explaining their sexual improprieties to the Grievance Board. As Scott and Lyman (1968, p. 53) argue, accounts may be regarded as illegitimate or unreasonable; consequently, "The incapacity to invoke situationally appropriate accounts, i.e., accounts that are anchored to the background expectancies of the situation," may actually exacerbate the deviant's predicament. It is thus conceivable that some therapists have simply attempted to avoid employing those types of accounts that could only make matters worse for themselves (or at last are perceived that way).

5. "The exception that proves the rule" is a form of illogical reasoning that individuals use to interpret observations that contradict their preconceived views. In the present case, however, this rationalization process may be seen as an accounting scheme used by actors to explain the apparent contradiction between their typical "normal behavior" and the "deviant exception."

REFERENCES

AKAMATSU, J. T. 1987. "Intimate Relationships with Former Clients: National Survey of Attitudes and Behavior Among Practitioners." *Professional Psychology: Research and Practice* 18:454–58.

BENETIN, J., and M. WILDER. 1989. "Sexual Exploitation and Psychotherapy." *Women's Rights Law Reporter* 11:121–35.

FINKELHOR, D. 1984. *Child Sexual Abuse: New Theory and Research.* New York: Free Press.

GARFINKEL, H. 1956. "Conditions of Successful Degradation Ceremonies." *American Journal of Sociology* 61:420–24.

GARTELL, N., J. HERMAN, S. OLARTE, M. FELDSTEIN, and R. LOCALIO. 1986. "Psychiatrist-Patient Sexual Contact: Results of a National Survey. I: Prevalence." *American Journal of Psychiatry* 143: 1126–31.

———. 1987. "Reporting Practices of Psychiatrists Who Knew of Sexual Misconduct by Colleagues." *American Journal of Orthopsychiatry* 57:287–95.

GOFFMAN, E. 1959. *The Presentation of Self in Everyday Life.* Garden City, NY: Doubleday.

———. 1963. *Stigma: Notes on the Management of Spoiled Identity.* Englewood Cliffs, NJ: Prentice-Hall.

———. 1971. *Relations in Public: Microstudies of the Public Order.* New York: Basic Books.

HEWITT, J. P., and R. STOKES. 1975. "Disclaimers." *American Sociological Review* 40:1–11.

HOLSTI, O. R. 1969. *Content Analysis for the Social Sciences and Humanities.* Reading, MA: Addison-Wesley.

JONES, E. E., and T. S. PITTMAN. 1982. "Toward a Theory of Strategic Self-Presentation." Pp. 231–62 in *Psychological Perspectives on the Self,* edited by J. M. Suls. Hillsdale, NJ: Erlbaum.

LOFLAND, J. 1969. *Deviance and Identity.* Englewood Cliffs, NJ: Prentice-Hall.

LYMAN, S. M., & M. B. SCOTT. 1989. *A Sociology of the Absurd* (2nd ed.). Dix Hills, NY: General Hall.

MILLS, C. W. 1940. "Situated Actions and Vocabularies of Motive." *American Sociological Review* 5:904–13.

POPE, K. S., and J. BOUHOUTSOS. 1986. *Sexual Intimacy Between Therapists and Patients.* New York: Praeger.

POPE, K. S., P. KEITH-SPIEGEL, and B. G. TABACHNICK. 1986. "Sexual Attraction to Clients: The Human Therapist and the (Sometimes) Inhuman Training System." *American Psychologist* 41:147–58.

RAY, M. C., and R. L. SIMONS. 1987. "Convicted Murderers' Accounts of Their Crimes: A Study of Homicide in Small Communities." *Symbolic Interaction* 10:57–70.

ROTHMAN, M. L., and R. P. GANDOSSY. 1982. "Sad Tales: The Accounts of White-Collar Defendants and the Decision to Sanction." *Pacific Sociological Review* 25:449–73.

SCHLENKER, B. R., and B. W. DARBY. 1981. "The Use of Apologies in Social Predicaments." *Social Psychology Quarterly* 44:271–78.

SCOTT, M. B., and S. M. LYMAN. 1968. "Accounts." *American Sociological Review* 33:46–62.

SCULLY, D., and J. MAROLLA. 1984. "Convicted Rapists' Vocabulary of Motive: Excuses and Justifications." *Social Problems* 31:530–44.

SPENCER, J. W. 1983. "Accounts, Attitudes, and Solutions: Probation Officer-Defendant Negotiations of Subjective Orientations." *Social Problems* 30:570–81.

STAROSTA, W. J. 1984. "Qualitative Content Analysis: A Burkean Perspective." Pp. 185–94 in *Methods for Intercultural Communication Research,* edited by W. Gudykunst and Y. Y. Kim. Beverly Hills, CA: Sage.

STRAUSS, A. 1962. "Transformations of Identity." Pp. 63–85 in *Human Behavior and Social Processes: An Interactional Approach,* edited by A. M. Rose. Boston: Houghton Mifflin.

TEDESCHI, J. T., and C. RIORDEN. 1981. "Impression Management and Prosocial Behavior Following Transgression." Pp. 223–44 in *Impression Management Theory and Social Psychological Research,* edited by J. T. Tedeschi. New York: Academic Press.

COMPUTER CRIME
HACKERS, PHREAKS, AND CYBERPUNKS*

Stephen M. Rosoff, Henry N. Pontell, and Robert Tillman

First Hacker: Wow! Richard Nixon's personal checking account is in here . . .
Second Hacker: Perfect. Now how much should he give?
First Hacker: He's a generous man. I'd say all he's got.
From *Sneakers* (1992). Screenplay by Phil Alden Robinson, Lawrence Lasker, Walter F. Parkes

*From *Profit Without Honor: White-Collar Crime and the Looting of America,* pp. 365–396, Prentice Hall, 1998.

In the late nineteenth century, the French social theorist Gabriel Tarde constructed his *law of insertion,* which noted how newer criminal modes are superimposed on older ones through a process of imitative learning and technological innovation.[1] Thus, for example, the European highwayman of the eighteenth century prepared the way for the American stagecoach bandit of the nineteenth century. Likewise, the train robber of the nineteenth century was the progenitor of the twentieth-century truck hijacker. As the twenty-first century looms, Tarde's insight is being validated again—this time in ways Tarde himself scarcely could have imagined.

Today, the falsified ledger, long the traditional instrument of the embezzler is being replaced by corrupted software programs. The classic weapons of the bank robber, as well, can now be drawn from a far more sophisticated arsenal containing such modern tools as automatic teller machines and electronic fund transfers. In short, white-collar crime has entered the computer age.

Computer crime has been defined broadly as "the destruction, theft, or unauthorized or illegal use, modification, or copying of information, programs, services, equipment, or communication networks."[2] Donn B. Parker, one of the country's leading computer crime researchers, offers a less formal definition of computer crime as any intentional act associated with computers where a victim suffers a loss and a perpetrator makes a gain.[3] Under these definitional guidelines, the following offenses all could be classified as computer crimes: (1) electronic embezzlement and financial theft; (2) computer hacking and malicious sabotage, including the creation, installation, or dissemination of computer viruses; (3) utilization of computers and computer networks for purposes of espionage; (4) use of electronic devices and computer codes for making unauthorized long-distance telephone calls. Each of these offenses will be examined in this chapter; however, it would be helpful to consider first just how big this problem has become and how fast it has grown.

For obvious reasons, computer crime has a short history. Its most immediate precursor was probably the invention of the so-called blue box in the early 1960s. The blue box was an illegal electronic device capable of duplicating the multifrequency dialing system developed by AT&T. The telephone company had described its new direct-dialing technology in its technical journals, apparently confident that no one in the general public would ever read or at least understand such esoteric information. How wrong they were. "Ma Bell" became the first casualty of the first law of electronic crime: *If it can be done, someone will do it.* Motivated by a curious blend of mischievousness and greed, a cadre of young wizards tape-recorded piccolos and other high-pitched sounds, and thus created the blue box, which gave them unauthorized access to the entire Bell network. They called themselves "phone phreaks." One ingenious phreak even discovered that a giveaway whistle packaged in Cap'n Crunch cereal produced a perfect 2,600-cycle tone that allowed him to place overseas telephone calls without paying charges.

Although occasional arrests were made, phone phreaking was more or less hidden from the public—both by the phreaks themselves who feared exposure *and* by the telephone company which feared an epidemic. But in 1971, a popular magazine "blew the whistle" (appropriately enough!) with the publication of an explosive article entitled "Secrets of the Little Blue Box."[4]

At about this same time, the fledgling computer industry had graduated from the self-contained mainframe to interactive linkage and primitive networks. Once again, the first law of electronic crime was activated, as computer buffs now could use terminals to explore powerful mainframes previously off-limits.

A new term entered the public lexicon—*hacker.* In the 1970s, the early hackers began using school computers for a variety of misdeeds—most notably the alteration of grades. However, since few schools even had computers then, hacking was still a relatively minor nuisance.

However, by the end of the decade, modems (devices linking computers with telephones) and computerized bulletin board systems (BBSs) appeared. By the early 1980s, the home PC (personal computer) had become increasingly common. To the hackers this was the missing ingredient—a high-tech skeleton key that could open a myriad of locked doors. For example, in 1985 twenty-three teenagers broke into a Chase Manhattan Bank computer by telephone, destroying accounting records and changing passwords. No money was stolen, but customers effectively were denied access to their own files.[5]

Predictably, the first generation of hackers, for all their mischief, were only setting the stage for far more insidious types of computer crime; for what may have begun as a questionable hobby shared by a network of adolescent social misfits has been co-opted by a more insidious class of white-collar criminal. Some individuals began employing the basic hacker methodology to break into systems, not as a vandalic prank or simply to do it, but to steal. "Computers have created opportunities for career criminals, an increasing number of whom are becoming computer literate."[6] An early (and ongoing) example involves the planting of an unauthorized program—known as a Trojan horse. A Trojan horse program can transfer money automatically to an illegal account whenever a legal transaction is made.[7] To many skilled thieves and embezzlers, this was akin to striking the mother lode.

How common and how costly has computer crime become? A 1993 survey reports that 70 percent of the more than four hundred companies responding admitted to at least one security infringement in the previous twelve months; 24 percent put the loss per incident at more than $100,000.[8] The head of the group which conducted the survey noted: "The problem is much more serious than expected."[9]

Moreover, computer crime is no longer just an American problem. It has been uncovered in both Canada[10] and Mexico,[11] as well as Western European nations such as the United Kingdom,[12] Sweden,[13] The Netherlands,[14] Germany,[15] and Italy.[16] Viruses have been created in such distant places as Bulgaria and South Africa.[17] Hackers reportedly have proliferated in France and Israel,[18] India and Singapore,[19] as well as the former Soviet Union (where they are called *chackers*).[20] Likewise, computer security has become a major concern in Japan[21] and Australia.[22] And in one especially malignant use of computer technology, an Argentine kidnapping ring illegally accessed financial records to determine how much ransom money potential victims could afford to pay.[23]

Regarding cost, estimates of annual losses due to computer crime range from $550 million (National Center for Computer Crime Data) to $15 billion (Inter-Pact computer security organization)[24] or even more. This remarkably wide range of estimates no doubt reflects the substantial variation which exists in defining what qualifies as computer crime. For instance, about 14 million federal tax returns are now filed electroni-

cally. A 1993 report by the General Accounting Office warns the IRS of its potential vulnerability to a number of new fraud schemes.[25] Should this be classified as tax evasion or computer crime? Dealers in child pornography now use private computer bulletin board services to advertise materials and exchange information.[26] Can this really be considered computer crime? Organized crime syndicates and illegal drug cartels routinely employ computers to launder money. Since the computer has become an indispensable tool of money-laundering, should all those billions of dollars be considered part of the cost of computer crime? The truth is that there is little consensus in these matters. In fact, some experts have adopted a so-called "agnostic" position that the true cost is unknowable. To further complicate estimation, it has been suggested that by the year 2000 virtually *all* business crime will conform to what now is considered computer crime.[27]

Another gray area is that of software piracy. No one knows the total cost of this offense, but it is certainly in the billions. Based on their 1985 survey of forty-five thousand households, McGraw-Hill Information Systems conservatively estimates that there is one pirated copy of software for every authorized copy.[28] An overseas dealer, for example, was selling pirated copies of the popular *Lotus 1-2-3* spreadsheet software (which usually retails for around $200) for $1.50![29] To put it in perspective, this means that for every $100 in pirated Lotus sales generated by this dealer, MicroPro, the manufacturer of Lotus, lost nearly $15,000 in legitimate sales.

There is in addition surely a huge "dark figure" of unreported computer crimes. "Because of public humiliation, liability issues, and security inadequacies, many corporations do not report computer crime losses, especially large ones."[30] The fear of "copycat" incidents also probably discourages the reporting of security breaches.[31] Furthermore, when it is information that is stolen, rather than money, the loss may be incalculable in terms of dollars. Finally, the estimation of computer crime losses perhaps is most complicated by the clandestine nature of the crimes themselves. The most talented electronic thieves are able to cover up all traces that a crime has been committed. As the president of a major computer security consulting firm has noted: "We only read about the failed computer criminals. The really successful ones are never detected in the first place."[32]

However, even if the actual computer crime loss figure can only be guessed, no one questions that the losses are enormous. A survey by ComSec, an organization of computer security professionals, reports that 36 of 300 companies responding (12 percent) acknowledged losses of $100,000 or more in just the first three months of 1993, with another 42 (14 percent) losing between $10,000 and $100,000. For the preceding year, 69 percent of respondents admitted security problems, with 53 percent of those problems resulting in losses of at least $10,000.[33] Once more, the findings far exceeded the predictions of the startled investigators.

But survey data and raw numbers, however powerful, are an undramatic way to tell a dramatic story. To understand the dimensions and the dangers of computer crime, we must examine the crimes themselves. So let us now consider in more detail the four categories of computer crime suggested earlier.

EMBEZZLEMENT AND FINANCIAL THEFT

According to recent FBI statistics, the average armed bank robbery nets $3,177.[34] The Data Processing Management Association reports that the average computer crime loss may be as high as $500,000.[35] This great disparity reveals that while there are physical limitations to the potential payoff available to the blue-collar robber— large amounts of money have weight and take up space—the white-collar thief who can access the appropriate computer can steal a fortune without moving anything heavier than some decimal points. As if to demonstrate this lack of physical limitations, a gang of rogue employees in a major railroad's computerized inventory center once stole two hundred boxcars by permanently keeping them under repair.[36] As a 1991 report by the National Research Council warns: "The modern thief can steal more with a computer than with a gun."[37] In addition, bank robbers must face the

prospect of getting shot at; not so the computer criminal. Dillinger never had it so good.

One of the most famous bank-related computer crimes, however, did involve the physical movement of hard cash. For three years, beginning in 1970, the chief teller at the Park Avenue branch of New York's Union Dime Savings Bank embezzled over $1.5 million from hundreds of accounts. Despite having no formal computer training, he was able to shift nonexistent money around from account to account, falsifying quarterly interest payments and satisfying visiting auditors with remarkable ease. So slick were his manipulations that reportedly, he had difficulty explaining the intricacies of his crime to the bank's executives after his arrest.[38] He eventually served fifteen months of a twenty-month sentence. At last report, he was driving a taxicab in New Jersey. None of his pilfered funds has ever been recovered.

His eventual downfall happened almost by accident—as a by-product of an entirely different case. A routine police raid on a "bookie joint" revealed that he had been betting as much as $30,000 a day on sporting events. "If his indiscreet bookmakers had not kept his name in their files, he might well have kept up his embezzlement for quite a while longer than he did."[39]

It is interesting to note that the Union Dime Savings case serves as a perfect model of Donald Cressey's earlier research on the social psychology of embezzlement. According to Cressey, embezzlers typically go through a three-stage process. In stage 1, they are faced with what they perceive to be an unshareable financial problem, that is, a need for money which they cannot share with spouses, relatives, or friends. A $30,000-a-day gambling habit on an $11,000 a year salary[40] would certainly seem to qualify in this regard. In stage 2, they recognize an opportunity to solve their problem secretly. This opportunity rests in the positions of trust which they hold. A position of chief teller, of course, would provide just such an opportunity. Finally, in stage 3, they manage to avoid internalizing a criminal identity by rationalizing their acts as borrowing rather than stealing.[41] It is the curse of compulsive gamblers like the Union Dime teller to continue expecting a financial recovery, even as the debts keep mounting. As we shall see, such labored rationalization is a recurring theme among computer criminals.

In 1991, someone, believed to be an employee, used the computer in the payroll department of a prestigious New York bank to steal $25 million without leaving a trace. As of this writing, the case remains unsolved—not because there are no suspects, but because there are too many. "[H]undreds of employees had access to the same data that appear to have made at least one of them very rich."[42]

But not all electronic embezzlers work for banks. An employee in the computer center of a big-city welfare department once stole $2.75 million, over a nine-month period, by entering fraudulent data into the computerized payroll system and thereby creating a phantom work force complete with fake social security numbers. He would intercept the weekly paychecks "earned" by the fictitious crew, endorse and cash them, and dream of early retirement. He was uncovered only when a police officer found a fistful of phony checks in his illegally parked rental car.[43]

As we have already noted, some embezzlers have employed a Trojan horse—the "bad" program concealed inside the "good" program—as a means of diverting cash into fraudulent accounts. A common variation on this method involves a practice known as the *salami* technique. This type of fraud has been around for many years and was known in the precomputer era as "rounding down."[44] Salami techniques divert (or, in keeping with the metaphor, "slice off") very small amounts of assets from very large numbers of private accounts. The stolen assets are so small, sometimes a few cents or even just a fraction of a cent per transaction, that they do not make a noticeable dent in any single account.[45]

How many people, after all, will bother to stoop down to retrieve a dropped penny? But when multiplied over a million or so bank transactions at computer speed, these "dropped pennies" can turn into tens or hundreds of thousands of dollars—well worth stooping for. For example, in the 1980s an employee at an investment firm used a computer to set up false accounts and filled them by diverting three-tenths of a cent interest from actual accounts.[46]

One of the more spectacular salami-type embezzlements took place in California at around the same time as the Union Dime Savings case. Over a six-year period, the chief accountant for a large produce company siphoned more than $1.5 million from his employers. While studying computer technology, he developed a program able to add small sums to disbursement accounts in payment of phony produce orders.[47] He later claimed that his motivation was simply to receive a promised annual bonus of which he felt he had been cheated. He decided he was entitled to three-quarters of 1 percent of the company's gross, and he began looting the company at exactly that rate. "He did this by devising a special algorithm—a set of rules for making calculations—which he used as a master program to alter the company's accounting data in the computer."[48] Because this firm grossed $30 million a year, pennies became dollars and dollars became a fortune.

When he eventually was arrested and tried, he pleaded *nolo contendere* (no contest), perhaps expecting the same sort of typically light sentence his counterpart at Union Dime Savings was to receive. Instead, he was sentenced to ten years in San Quentin and served just over five. Upon release, he became—what else?—a computer consultant.

The stark difference in the punitive sanctions meted out in these two roughly equivalent embezzlement cases underscores how confused the general public often is about computer crime. Depending upon how a prosecutor chooses to present a case, a jury is apt to perceive a computer criminal as anything from a pathetic "nerd" gone bad to an electronic terrorist threatening the very foundation of the American way of life.

Sometimes embezzlers are not low- or mid-level employees of a company, but those at the very top. This certainly would apply to the notorious Equity Funding scandal. This case well illustrates the lack of definitional consensus regarding computer crime. Because the Equity Funding case is considered by some to be mainly one of securities fraud, rather than true computer fraud, many analyses of computer crime never mention Equity Funding—although it is arguably one of the most costly frauds ever perpetrated.

In the 1970s, the Los Angeles-based insurance firm and mutual fund company programmed its computer to issue insurance policies on people who did not exist and then sell those fake policies to other companies, through a system of reinsurance customarily employed in that business to spread actuarial risk and increase cash flow.[49] This was done to inflate the price of Equity Funding stock which had begun to fall after a spectacular run-up in the early 1960s. The scheme grew over time to epic proportions. Fictitious policy holders, or persons already dead, were carrying $3.2 billion in life insurance. Some of the conspirators were skimming from the resale proceeds, and other conspirators were skimming from the skimmers.

It has been observed that as computer crimes go, the Equity Funding fraud was not a particularly sophisticated one and would have been uncovered sooner or later, if only because there were just too many people involved.[50] The most effective computer crimes probably are the work of a single individual or at most a small gang. Moreover, because the fraud was conducted by management itself, there was little incentive to conceal the misuse of the computer from company officials. In the final analysis, Equity Funding was simply a gigantic "pyramid scam" run amok.[51]

When the computer fraud is committed by someone from outside the victimized organization, embezzlement becomes theft. Here again, banks are a frequent target. In 1980, for example, the Wells Fargo bank of San Francisco lost $21 million allegedly to two boxing promoters who used a computer for illegal EFTs (Electronic Fund Transfers).[52] In 1988, the First National Bank in Chicago lost $55 million through a fraudulent wire transfer.[53] In absolute terms, this is a great deal of money; but, in relative terms, it hardly makes a ripple in the more than $1 trillion that is transferred electronically by American banks each day.[54]

Probably the best-known EFT case is that of Stanley Mark Rifkin, who stole $10.2 million from California's Security National Bank in less than an hour.[55] Rifkin was a computer programmer who was creating a back-up system for Security National's wire room—the bank's commu-

nication center from where between $2 billion and $4 billion are transferred every day. The purpose of the back-up system was to allow the bank to continue making EFTs even if the primary system crashed.[56] Rifkin, of course, had to learn the system intimately, and, as his education continued, he began to think about robbing the bank. On October 25, 1978, he stole an employee access code from the wall of the wire room, walked to a nearby telephone booth, and transferred the $10.2 million to a New York bank and then to Switzerland. The next day, the cash was converted into diamonds.[57]

Rifkin may have been a brilliant computer programmer, but he turned out to be an inept criminal. He was arrested ten days later after attempting to sell some diamonds in Beverly Hills. He was convicted in March, 1979, and received a sentence of eight years in federal prison.

More recently, beginning in the mid-1980s, officials in several states began uncovering a simple but alarmingly effective form of electronic bank robbery. An individual would open an account and eventually receive computer-coded deposit slips. Near the beginning of a month, he or she then would place some of those deposit slips on the counter where blank deposit slips normally would be. When customers unknowingly used them, the money would be deposited in the criminal's account. By the time the irate customers questioned their monthly bank statements, the thieves had emptied their accounts and were nowhere to be found.[58]

Another form of electronic larceny came to light in 1987, when nine Pittsburgh teenagers were arrested for computer fraud. They had made thousands of dollars in purchases using stolen credit card numbers. They had obtained these numbers by using their PCs to break into the files of a West Coast credit card authorization service, which provided them with a lengthy list of valid credit card numbers and expiration dates.[59]

In 1993, one of the most brazen computer crimes in memory occurred in Connecticut. Two ex-convicts built a homemade automatic teller machine, wheeled it into a shopping mall, and planted it there for sixteen days. The bogus machine even contained money for its users, thus enhancing its seeming legitimacy. But despite its clever masquerade, it was yet another species of Trojan horse, designed to copy secret access codes from customers' ATM cards. This allowed the criminals to withdraw more than $100,000 from banks in six states.[60] They were arrested two months later on a variety of fraud, theft, and conspiracy charges.

HACKING

The pioneer hackers of the 1960s and 1970s probably exemplified Edwin Lemert's classic concept of primary deviance,[61] that is, their conduct would have been described by observers as norm violating. Of course, computers were so new then, there may have been few clear norms to violate. If their intent was not to destroy private files, could they be considered vandals? If their intent was not to steal data, could they be considered thieves? Perhaps the least ambiguous way to characterize them was as trespassers.

On the other hand, there was likely little, if any, of Lemert's notion of secondary deviance,[62] that is, no deviant self-identity on the parts of the hackers themselves. Indeed, their mastery of skills that may have seemed more magic than science to the general public endowed them with a sense of intellectual elitism. As one author, commenting on the first generation of hackers, has observed: "[T]o be a computer hacker was to wear a badge of honor."[63]

Hackers, particularly those of the nondestructive, nonlarcenous ilk, might be thought of as a deviant subculture. They ascribe to a set of norms, which apparently they take very seriously, but which often conflicts with the norms of the dominant society. They have their own peculiar code of ethics. For instance, they believe computerized data are public property and that passwords and other security features are only hurdles to be jumped in pursuit of these communal data.[64] They even appear to adhere to an ultimate proscription: "Hackers will do just about anything to break into a computer except crashing a system. That's the only taboo."[65]

Another way of looking at young hackers is from the perspective of Sykes and Matza's well-known "drift" theory of delinquency.[66] Hackers might be viewed in this manner as fundamentally conforming youths who drift into occasionally deviant behavior through the use of such "neutralizations" as the claim that they are only trying to expose lax security systems[67] or merely learn more about computers.[68] These may seem like weak rationalizations, but more than one young hacker has justified his misconduct on those very grounds.

Furthermore, even the most benign intentions can go terribly awry. A group of seven Milwaukee high school students, devoted electronic joy riders who called themselves the "414" gang, learned this lesson in 1983. They were from all accounts nice young men—Eagle Scouts, exemplary students. But, in the name of fun-and-games, they managed to break into a file at the Los Alamos, New Mexico, nuclear weapons facility and also erase a file at New York's Memorial Sloan-Kettering Cancer Center.[69] When they were apprehended, they denied any illegality in their actions. Their public statements seemed to be drawn directly from Sykes and Matza's inventory of neutralization techniques: "[I]t's not our fault" (denial of responsibility); "We didn't intend harm" (denial of injury); "There was no security" (denial of victim).[70]

Like the fabled sorcerer's apprentice, the 414s became intoxicated with their inordinate power and failed to contemplate maturely the consequences of their actions. This sort of irresponsibility has been the hackers' bane from the very beginning. If there is such a construct as "white-collar delinquency," teenage hackers are its embodiment.

Beyond the fun-and-games, however, there is a dark side to hacking, personified by a second generation of hackers whose intentions are undeniably malicious. One such hacker revealed this dark side in an article he wrote under the ominous pen name Mr. X:

I can turn off your electricity or phone, destroy your credit rating—even take money out of your bank account—without ever leaving the keyboard of my home computer. And you would never know I was the one ruining your life![71]

If one doubts the plausibility of Mr. X's frightening boast, consider that in 1985 seven New Jersey teenagers were arrested for stealing

$30,000 worth of computer equipment, which they had billed to total strangers on "hacked" credit card numbers.[72] Hackers have also invaded credit files[73]—including those at TRW, the nation's largest credit information storage system.[74] Anyone who has ever been victimized in this manner has experienced the living hell of the credit pariah. If one's credit rating is sabotaged, one can no longer apply for a mortgage or loans of any kind. Even renting an apartment may become impossible.[75]

The infamous case of Kevin Mitnick is a good example of how a hacker can degenerate from prankster to public enemy. Like many computer wizards, he began his criminal career in high school by breaking into the school's main computer system. Later, he managed to hack into the central computer of the entire Los Angeles Unified School District. After dropping out of school in 1981, at the age of seventeen, he was arrested as part of a hacker ring that had stolen key manuals from Pacific Telephone. Mitnick was prosecuted as a juvenile and placed on probation. The following year, he was in trouble again. This time he used publicly available computers at the University of Southern California to break into numerous systems—including some at the U.S. Department of Defense. His probation was revoked, and he spent six months in a California Youth Authority facility.[76]

Up to this point, Mitnick arguably was still more aging "brat" than criminal. He had not yet stolen money or damaged data; but a manifest pattern of escalation already was emerging. In 1988, Mitnick, now twenty-five, was arrested for repeatedly breaking into a computer software system at the Digital Equipment Corporation in Massachusetts. He copied the software, which had cost DEC more than $1 million to develop. He further cost DEC more than $4 million in downtime. And if this were not enough, Mitnick had also broken into the computer system at Leeds University in England by telephone, using the sixteen unauthorized MCI long-distance telephone account numbers in his possession.[77]

A notable aspect to this case is the way Mitnick was portrayed both by the government and the media. He became the symbol of computer crime and the future-shock paranoia it generates

in society. Mitnick has been labeled "the Willie Horton of computer crime"[78]—a reference to the notorious rapist who was made the symbol of violent crime during the 1988 presidential election. Even a former hacking cohort of Mitnick, known as Susie Thunder, once declared: "He's really crazy . . . He's dangerous."[79] He was denied bail and spent seven and one-half months in jail awaiting trial—a very unusual fate for a white-collar criminal. So frightened were the authorities of Mitnick's skills and potential for electronic vengeance that all his telephone calls had to be dialed by others. Finally, Mitnick entered into a plea bargain and, in 1989, received a one-year sentence to be followed by entry into a rehabilitation program for computer addiction.

More recently, a group of young hackers, ranging in age from eighteen to twenty-two and calling themselves by such exotic names as Phiber Optik, Acid Phreak, Outlaw, and Scorpion,[80] were arrested in 1992 for corrupting the databases of some of the largest corporations in America. The MOD, alternately known as the Masters of Destruction[81] or the Masters of Deception,[82] allegedly stole passwords and technical data from Pacific Bell, NYNEX, and other telephone companies, Martin Marietta, ITT, and other Fortune 500 companies, several big credit agencies, two major universities, and the Educational Broadcasting Network.[83] The damage caused by these hackers was extensive. One company alone, Southwestern Bell, suffered losses of $370,000.[84]

In what resembles a high-tech parody of urban gang warfare, the MOD apparently were motivated by a fierce competition with a rival "gang," the Legion of Doom.[85] Donn B. Parker, who once interviewed Phiber Optik,[86] has noted the importance of one-upmanship in the hacker subculture: "Computer hacking is a meritocracy. You rise in the culture depending on the information you can supply to other hackers."[87]

One of the most disturbing aspects of malicious hacking involves the area of national security. In 1983, for example, a nineteen-year-old UCLA student used his PC to break into a Defense Department international communications system.[88] In 1991, a gang of Dutch hackers managed to crack Pacific Fleet computers during the

Persian Gulf War.[89] More recently still, two young hackers broke into computers at the Boeing Corporation—a major defense contractor[90]—and later used their home PCs to examine confidential government agency files.[91] A 1993 report from the American military's inspector-general found "serious deficiencies in the integrity and security" of a Pentagon computer used to make $67 billion a year in payments.[92] Members of Congress have expressed great concern over such stories, calling for tougher sanctions and the federalization of all computer crime.

Another reason for so much congressional anxiety is the threat of pernicious computer viruses—once a rare phenomenon, now, some claim, approaching epidemic proportions. A virus is an instructional code lodged in a computer's disk operating system that is designed to copy itself over and over. When the infected computer comes in contact with an uninfected piece of software, the virus is transmitted. "In today's computer culture, in which everybody from video gamesters to businessmen trade computer disks like baseball cards, the potential for widespread contagion is enormous."[93]

For example, in 1988, a previously unknown virus infected over one hundred thousand PC disks across the United States, including about ten thousand at George Washington University alone. Embedded in the virus was the cryptic message, WELCOME TO THE DUNGEON.[94] It turned out to be the creation of two brothers operating a computer store in Pakistan. Under a bizarre retailing philosophy that might best be described as schizoid vigilantism, they were selling pirated software, then punishing their customers for buying it.[95]

Some viruses are relatively innocuous, such as the so-called Peace virus. Designed by a twenty-three-year-old Arizona programmer, it showed up on the screens of thousands of Macintosh computers in 1987, flashed a single peace message, then erased itself and disappeared.[96]

Certain viruses might even be described as playful:

A rogue program that made the rounds of Ivy League schools featured a creature inspired by *Sesame Street* called the Cookie Monster. Students trying to do useful work would be interrupted by persistent messages saying: "I want a cookie." In one variation, the message would be repeated with greater and greater frequency until users typed the letters C-O-O-K-I-E on their terminal keyboards.[97]

Far less playful, however, is the Rock Video virus that entertains unsuspecting users with an animated image of Madonna—then erases all their files and displays the ignominious taunt, YOU'RE STUPID.[98]

Sadly, most viruses wreak havoc without even offering glimpses of glamorous rock stars as compensation. In 1988, Robert Morris, a Cornell University graduate student, planted the infamous Internet virus which infected a vast network of six thousand computers stretching from Berkeley to Princeton to M.I.T. and caused at least a quarter of a million dollars in damage.[99] Morris was sentenced to three years probation, fined $10,000, and ordered to perform four hundred hours of community service.[100] This comparatively light sentence was received with hostility by some members of both the computer community and the general public. Sanctioning renegade hackers remains a controversial topic, since they are characteristically so far removed from any popular criminal stereotype.

On the other hand, Morris's offense was hardly trivial. It has been reported that when the Internet virus entered the computers at the Army's Ballistic Research laboratory in Maryland, system managers feared the United States had been invaded.[101]

Some other viruses appear deceptively benign. In December, 1987, a seemingly harmless "Christmas Tree" virus, designed by a German student, was loosed on a worldwide IBM network. Instructions to type the word "Christmas" would flash on a terminal screen. Users who complied with this innocent-sounding request tripped a virus that ultimately infected 350,000 terminals in 130 countries. IBM had to shut down its entire electronic mail system for two days to contain the spread.[102]

Viruses are sometimes placed in so-called "time bombs." In other words, the virus program contains delayed instructions to go off at some future date. An early example was the Jerusalem virus, so named because it was discovered at

Hebrew University. This virus, which had the potential to cause a computer to lose all its files instantly, was set to go off on the fortieth anniversary of the State of Israel. Fortunately, the virus was eradicated well before that date.[103] Additional examples are the Joshi virus, which instructed the user to type "Happy Birthday Joshi" and was set to activate on January 5, 1993, and the Casino virus, set to activate on January 15, April 15, and August 15, 1993. Casino is a particularly odd virus which challenges the user to a slot-machine game and damages files if the user loses.[104]

Probably the best-known prosecution involving a computer virus was that of Donald Burleson in Texas. He worked in the computer room of a Fort Worth securities-trading firm and was responsible for assuring that the company's password system operated properly. Burleson, a man of unconventional political beliefs, was a member of a fanatical tax protest movement. He argued frequently with his employers over the issue of federal withholding tax, which he insisted not be deducted from his paycheck. In 1985, when his employers learned he was planning to sue them to force them to stop withholding his taxes, he was fired. Before turning in his keys, the enraged Burleson planted a "worm." A worm is similar to a virus, except it is not contagious and only infects its host computer.

A few days later, the director of accounting discovered to his horror that "168,000 commission records no longer existed on the computer—they had been deleted from the system!"[105] This, of course, would make the month's payroll impossible to calculate. Burleson was arrested and became the first person ever tried for sabotage by virus.[106] He was convicted in 1988, fined $12,000, and placed on seven years probation.[107]

Except for precipitating the first "virus trial," the Burleson case does not seem, upon reflection, especially remarkable. Yet it was a media sensation. This may be explained in part simply by its timing. Just a few months earlier, "the Christmas Tree virus had embarrassed IBM and introduced readers to the concept of viruses as a type of computer crime."[108] For whatever reason, computer viruses subsequently have captured the public's imagination. Perhaps the term itself,

with its mad scientist imagery and plague like connotation, has generated a strange blend of fright and titillation. In any event, the media seldom underplay a virus story. Studies reveal that the level of public interest in viruses is a direct function of increasing or decreasing media attention.[109]

Critics of the media have argued that the virus "epidemic" has been overblown; that there are more problematic computer crime issues worthier of public concern. They cite as an example of alleged "media hype" the Michelangelo virus, which was supposed to infect millions of computers worldwide on March 6, 1992 (Michelangelo's birthday), and erase everything it touched. "In the end, scattered copies of Michelangelo were found—but nowhere near the millions predicted."[110]

ESPIONAGE

While computer viruses generally receive substantial media attention, statistics reveal that the misuse of computers as tools for industrial, political, and international espionage may be a cause for greater concern. Industrial espionage exploded during the 1980s, perhaps increasing by an estimated 75 percent or more.[111] A data loss protection consultant in Houston has observed that the percentage of his firm's jobs in which electronic eavesdropping devices turned up quadrupled (5 percent to 20 percent) in the single year 1983.[112] In a sensational representation of that "golden age" of computer espionage, a major FBI sting operation in 1982 targeted more than twenty employees of the Hitachi and Mitsubishi corporations of Japan, who were suspected of stealing data from IBM.[113]

In 1992 American companies suffered losses from computer-related industrial espionage exceeding $1 billion. It is estimated that more than 85 percent of these crimes were committed or aided by employees—sometimes to settle a grudge, sometimes simply to make some money.[114] For example, employees with access to equipment and passwords can download strategic data or client lists and sell them to unscrupulous competitors. Because of the number of company insiders with such access, as well as the number of predatory outsiders capable of breaking through passwords and cracking data encryption, many computer networks have proven vulnerable to spying and data theft.[115]

A Canadian-based computer company filed a $5 million lawsuit in 1992 against a former employee, alleging that he copied the firm's entire customer database and used it to establish his own competing business.[116] At about that same time, computerized trade-secret data were stolen from a California technology company.[117] Six months later, the head of a rival firm and a former employee of the victimized firm were indicted on charges of conspiracy and data theft.[118] These criminal indictments were considered precedent-setting because electronic industrial espionage cases traditionally had been fought in the civil court arena.[119]

Occasionally, industrial espionage and virus infection are melded into a single computer crime. Consider the plight of the head of a British technology company whose latest product was sabotaged with a software virus by a rival exhibitor during a 1993 trade show for potential customers. In an open letter to an industry journal, this embittered executive talks about his experience with white-collar crime in a tone more suggestive of a street crime victim:

There is a fair chance that whoever planted the virus is reading this. So to him I have a private message. Whoever you are, I understand why your bosses told you to do it. Nevertheless, it was vandalism, you tried to wreck something which is very valuable to me, and I won't stand for it. I'm going to pursue this with the full weight of the law, and if I ever find out who you are, may God help you.[120]

A dramatic example of political espionage occurred in New York in 1992. The confidential medical records of a congressional candidate were hacked from a hospital computer by an unknown party and sent to a tabloid newspaper. Those records revealed that the candidate once had attempted suicide, and this information soon was published in a front-page story. The candidate won the election, despite the publicity regarding her medical history, but the personal aftermath of this electronic invasion of her privacy serves as a reminder of why this book is as much

about victims as villains. "It caused me a lot of pain," she would later say, "especially since my parents didn't know."[121]

Computer crime in the area of international espionage is more difficult to assess. Since by definition this brand of white-collar crime often involves material classified as secret by the government, details of certain cases probably have been concealed from public scrutiny. A few stories, however, have been reported by the media.

The most widely chronicled computer espionage case is that of the so-called "Hanover Hackers" in 1989. A group of young West German men were arrested for selling American military data to the Soviet KGB in exchange for cash and cocaine. This spy ring consisted of five members of West Germany's notorious Chaos Computer Club, which had achieved European hacking stardom in 1987 by breaking into two NASA computers.[122] The most proficient member of the Hanover group, twenty-four-year-old Markus Hess, had illegally accessed a computer at the Lawrence Berkeley Laboratory on the University of California campus and had used that computer as a launch pad to access U.S. military computers at sites such as the Pentagon, the White Sands Missile Range, and the Redstone Missile Base.[123]

Of the five original Hanover Hackers, the youngest one was not charged in exchange for testifying; another was burned to death in what was either a hideous suicide or a brutal murder. The remaining three who stood trial were convicted in 1990. Germany was reuniting, the cold war was winding down, and no one seemed particularly anxious to lock the defendants up and throw away the key. That they sold classified computer data to the Russians was undeniable; but just how valuable those data were was not at all clear. For one thing, the relatively small payments they received did not seem commensurate with a major espionage success. When the U.S. National Security Agency assessed the damage, one of their scientists observed in a memo: "Looks like the Russians got rooked."[124] In one of those truth-is-stranger-than-fiction twists, that scientist was Robert Morris, Sr., whose son had released the Internet virus eighteen months earlier.

The sentences handed down ranged from one year and eight months to two months. All the defendants were put on probation, because their drug problems had, in the opinion of the judges, clouded their judgment and mitigated their responsibility.[125]

International computer espionage in the United States appears to be taken more seriously than in Europe. Indeed, it has been called the single most important security issue of the 1990s.[126] This concern may have originated in the early 1980s, when the Reagan administration withdrew funding for an international research center in Vienna, because its computers were tied in to other research centers in both the United States and the Soviet Union. A fear was expressed that this connection might have allowed the Russians to log in to American computers and scan for classified data.[127]

Under the Computer Fraud and Abuse Act of 1986, it is illegal to tamper with any computer system used by the federal government or by government contractors. The act empowers the FBI to investigate the damage, destruction, or alteration of any data stored in such systems.[128] A representative case occurred in 1990 when personal computers at NASA and the EPA were infected with the SCORES virus, although the FBI ultimately turned this case over to local police because of difficulty in proving the suspect's intent to contaminate government computers.[129]

The first indictment of an American hacker on espionage charges occurred in 1992. The accused spy was a computer programmer from California. He allegedly stole secret Air Force flight orders for a military exercise at Fort Bragg, North Carolina.[130] Although the value of this material to the international intelligence community is dubious, the illegal possession of classified computer data is considered espionage, "even if no attempt is made to pass it to a foreign government."[131]

PHONE PHREAKING

As noted earlier in this chapter, phreaking is one of the oldest and most durable forms of electronic crime. Among the first generation of phone phreaks, some achieved legendary status: Jerry Schneider, the shameless self-promoter who appeared on the *60 Minutes* television program in 1976 and used his telephone to raise the overdraw limit on Dan Rather's personal checking account from $500 to $10,000, as millions of viewers looked on—including a stunned Rather;[132] Joe the Whistler, blind since birth but possessing perfect musical pitch and an uncanny ability to call anywhere in the world by whistling into a receiver;[133] the six-member gang—dubbed the "Gay Phone Phreaks" by the tabloid press— who placed an untraceable $19,000 twelve-hour call to Indonesia;[134] and rising above them all was the king of the phreakers—Captain Crunch.

Captain Crunch took his pseudonym, of course, from the breakfast cereal with the direct-dialing whistle. At the time of the famous *Esquire* article,[135] Captain Crunch was a twenty-eight-year-old walking encyclopedia of telephony. Despite three later convictions, he never considered himself a criminal and utilized the same neutralization techniques as his hacker brethren, claiming he was performing a valuable public service by exposing weaknesses in communication systems (denial of injury again). Captain Crunch's foremost ambition in those days was to phreak legally in the employ of the phone company. Reportedly, he was quite dismayed when AT&T hired his old friend Joe the Whistler, but not him.[136]

As a devoted member of the sixties counterculture, Captain Crunch's favorite activity was spying electronically on the government. In an ironic role reversal, he may be the only criminal ever to eavesdrop electronically on FBI phone calls. While he was serving a four-month prison sentence in 1977, "He tweaked the coil of an FM radio with a nail file to listen in on guards' [telephone] conversations."[137]

It is not difficult to find a perverse charm in the exploits of Captain Crunch, or those of his co-legends. Even the austere Donn Parker acknowledges personal affection for the Captain.[138] But the blend of social immaturity and grand egotism that gave the pioneer phone phreaks their "Robin Hood" images also gave them the potential to teach their special knowledge (intentionally or otherwise) to career criminals. Thus, Parker argues, despite their individual charms, Captain Crunch and his crew are "dangerous."[139]

Furthermore, there now exists a second generation of phone phreaks, more dangerous—and less charming—than the first. A 1993 survey by TAI (Telecommunications Advisors, Inc.) reveals that 70 percent of respondents report that they have been victims of telephone toll fraud.[140] TAI interprets this finding as an indication that toll fraud may be a greater risk than previously believed. As the report observes: "[I]n 1990, 70 percent of respondents probably did not even know what toll fraud was, but it is now a thriving underground business."[141]

A 1992 published interview with a young phone phreak reveals once more that the familiar litany of neutralization techniques continues to be recited by members of the hacker subculture. This phreak insists that fraudulent calls are of no consequence to multi-million-dollar corporations[142] (denial of victim again). He further asserts that his actions express his anticapitalist political beliefs. This latter claim seems to flirt with hypocrisy, since he admittedly is making a considerable profit from his crimes.

And how much money can an ambitious anticapitalist make? A 1992 congressional committee, chaired by Representative Edward Markey, estimated that toll fraud costs $2.3 billion annually.[143] In 1993, the International Communications Association complained to the FCC that over a five-year period 550 incidents of toll fraud had cost its members alone $73.5 million.[144]

The fast-growing cellular telephone industry has been hit particularly hard by illegally accessed calls; losses industrywide are now at $300 million a year and climbing.[145] The weakness of cellular phones is that they can be scanned easily by using an inexpensive Radio Shack scanner.[146] Cordless telephones are also considered easy prey.[147]

Here are a few examples of recent toll fraud cases:

NASA (a perennial target of hackers and phreakers) reportedly lost $12 million in unauthorized calls over a two-year period as a result of computer tampering at its Johnson Space Center in Houston.[148]

The chief of police of St. Croix in the U.S. Virgin Islands was convicted in 1992 of long-distance telephone fraud. He stole and used access codes from Caribbean Automated Long-Line Services (CALLS).

CALLS claimed its losses may have been as high as $185,000.[149]

Also in 1992, the Christian Broadcast Network lost $40,000 to a phone phreak who had hacked into its system and regularly placed calls to Pakistan.[150]

One of the problematic aspects of toll fraud is the assessment of responsibility for illegally accessed codes. In a battle of titans worthy of Greek mythology, Japan's Mitsubishi Corporation and AT&T counter-sued in 1991 over AT&T's alleged failure to warn its customers of the potential for unauthorized use of phone systems and Mitsubishi's failure to pay a $430,000 bill accumulated by 30,000 unauthorized calls allegedly placed by phreaks who had cracked their system.[151] The two companies eventually settled out of court in 1992.

In response to the issue of liability, a number of American insurance firms and long-distance carriers now are providing coverage against toll fraud.[152] In 1992, for example, The Travelers Corporation offered $1 million in protection for $49,000 with a $100,000 deductible. At the lowest end, a $50,000 policy was available for $2,500 with a $5,000 deductible.[153] These premiums illustrate some of the substantial indirect costs of phone phreaking.

Another cause for concern is the movement of phone phreaks into the area of industrial espionage. The proliferation of fax machines has created one of the easiest ways to steal corporate information. Computer criminals can now break into a phone line and produce a "shadow" version of the faxes received.[154] According to security experts, most corporations currently are vulnerable to data leaks resulting from telephone espionage.[155]

Finally, a common toll fraud scheme involves "call-sell operators," who buy stolen outdialing access codes and use them to make or sell long-distance calls, often overseas. The charges for these calls, which can run into huge sums of money, later show up on the victimized party's telephone bill.[156]

Antifraud systems, such as voice-recognition devices, now are appearing on the market.[157] But computer criminals, as Gabriel Tarde might well have predicted, consistently have responded to improved security technology with improved criminal technology, and they will no doubt in time find a way to keep apace. This, in turn, will encourage still more advances in security and continue a never-ending cycle of thrust and parry.

NOTES

1. Tarde, Gabriel. *The Laws of Imitation.* Gloucester, Massachusetts: Peter Smith, 1962. This book was published originally in 1903.

2. Perry, Robert L. *Computer Crime.* New York: Franklin Watts, 1986.

3. Parker, Donn B. *Fighting Computer Crime.* New York: Scribners, 1983.

4. Rosenbaum, Ron. "Secrets of the Little Blue Box." *Esquire* 76, October, 1979: 222–226.

5. Francis, Dorothy B. *Computer Crime.* New York: Dutton, 1987.

6. Parker, Donn B. "Computer Crimes, Viruses, and Other Crimoids." *Executive Speeches* 3, 1989: 15–19.

7. Perry, op. cit.

8. *PC User.* "Security Survey Reveals Huge Financial Losses," April 21, 1993: p. 20.

9. Ibid.

10. Wood, Chris. "Crime in the Computer Age," *Maclean's* 101, January 25, 1988: 28–30.

11. Sherizen, Sanford. "The Globalization of Computer Crime and Information Security." *Computer Security Journal* 8, 1992: 13–19.

12. Sykes, John. "Computer Crime: A Spanner in the Works." *Management Accounting* 70, 1992: p. 55. This article notes the exploits of England's "Mad Hacker."

13. Saari, Juhani. "Computer Crime—Numbers Lie." *Computers & Security* 6, 1987: 111–117.

14. Norman, Adrian R. D. *Computer Insecurity.* London: Chapman and Hall, 1989.

15. Hafner, Katie, and Markoff, John. *Cyberpunk.* New York: Touchstone, 1991.

16. Rockwell, Robin. "The Advent of Computer Related Crimes." *Secured Lender* 46, 1990: pp. 40, 42.

17. Sherizen, op. cit.

18. Major, Michael J. "Taking the Byte out of Crime: Computer Crime Statistics Vary as Much as the Types of Offenses Committed." *Midrange Systems* 6, 1993: 25–28.

19. Gold, Steve. "Two Hackers Get Six Months Jail in UK." *Newsbytes,* May 24, 1993: 1–2.

20. Sherizen, op. cit.

21. Ibid.

22. Hooper, Narelle. "Tackling the Techno-Crims." *Rydge's,* September, 1987: 112–119.

23. Sherizen, op. cit.

24. Major, op. cit.

25. Quindlen, Terry H. "IRS Computer Systems Are Catching More Fishy Tax Returns: GAO Praises Agency for Reeling in Electronic Cheaters But Urges Tighter Controls." *Government Computer News* 12, 1993: p. 67.

26. Torres, Vicki. "New Puzzle: High-Tech Peophilia." *Los Angeles Times,* March 5, 1993: p. B3.

27. Major, op. cit.

28. Francis, op. cit.

29. Elmer-DeWitt, Phillip. "Invasion of the Data Snatchers." *Time* 132, September 26, 1988: 62–67.

30. Ibid., p. 25.

31. Didio, Laura. "Security Deteriorates as LAN Usage Grows." *LAN Times* 7, 1993: 1–2.

32. Quoted in Schuyten, Peter J. "Computers and Criminals." *New York Times,* September 27, 1979: p. D2.

33. Didio, op. cit.

34. U.S. Department of Justice. "FBI Uniform Crime Reports 1991" in *Crime in the United States 1991,* 1992: p. 13.

35. Nawrocki, Jay. "There Are too Many Loopholes: Current Computer Crime Laws Require Clearer Definition." *Data Management* 25, 1987: 14–15.

36. Brandt, Allen. "Embezzler's Guide to the Computer." *Harvard Business Review* 53, 1975: 79–89.

37. Bass, Frank. "Potential for Computerized Fraud Growing, Say Experts." *Houston Post,* August 14, 1991: pp. A1, A8.

38. Whiteside, Thomas. *Computer Capers: Tales of Electronic Thievery, Embezzlement, and Fraud.* New York: Thomas Y. Crowell, 1978.

39. Ibid.

40. Conklin, John E. *"Illegal But Not Criminal": Business Crime in America.* Englewood Cliffs, New Jersey: Prentice Hall, 1977.

41. Cressey, Donald R. *Other People's Money: A Study in the Social Psychology of Embezzlement.* Belmont, California: Wadsworth, 1971.

42. Violino, Bob. "Are Your Networks Secure?" *Information Week,* April 12, 1993: p. 30.

43. Brandt, op. cit.

44. Francis, op. cit.

45. Ibid.

46. Ibid.

47. Whiteside, op. cit.

48. Ibid., p. 93.

49. Seidler, Lee. *The Equity Funding Papers: The Anatomy of a Fraud.* New York: Wiley, 1977.

50. Whiteside, op. cit.

51. Ibid.

52. Thornton, Mary. "Age of Electronic Convenience Spawning Inventive Thieves." *Washington Post,* May 20, 1984: A1, A8–A9.

53. Violino, op. cit., 30–33.

54. Adam, John A. "Data Security." *IEEE Spectrum* 29, 1992: 18–20. See also Sherizen, Sanford. "Future Bank Crimes." *Bank Systems & Technology* 26: 60, 62.

55. Schuyten, op. cit.

56. Bloombecker, Buck. *Spectacular Computer Crimes.* Homewood, Illinois: Dow Jones-Irwin, 1990.

57. Ibid.

58. Thornton, op. cit.

59. Roberts, Ralph, and Kane, Pamela. *Computer Security.* Greensboro, North Carolina: Compute! Books, 1989.

60. *Houston Chronicle.* "Duo Arrested in Phony Teller Machine Scheme." June 30, 1993: p. 6A.

61. Lemert, Edwin M. *Human Deviance, Social Problems, and Social Control.* Englewood Cliffs, New Jersey: Prentice Hall, 1967.

62. Ibid.

63. Hafner and Markoff, op. cit., p. 11.

64. McEwen, J. Thomas. "Computer Ethics." *National Institute of Justice Reports,* January/February 1991: 8–11.

65. Ibid., p. 9

66. Sykes, Gresham M., and Matza, David. "Techniques of Neutralization: A Theory of Delinquency." *American Sociological Review* 22, 1957: 664–666.

67. Kabay, Mich. "Computer Hackers Are No Vigilantes." *Computing Canada* 18, 1992: p. 36.

68. Keefe, Patricia. "Portraits of Hackers as Young Adventurers Not Convincing." *Computerworld* 26, 1992: p. 33.

69. O'Driscoll, Patrick. "At 17, a Pro at Testifying on Computers." *USA Today,* September 26, 1983: p. 2A.

70. Quoted in Francis, op. cit., p. 28.

71. Quoted in Francis, op. cit., p. 35.

72. Ibid.

73. Van Brussel, Carolyn. "Arrest of N.Y.C. Hackers Hailed as 'Breakthrough.' " *Computing Canada* 18, 1992: p. 1.

74. Benedetto, Richard. "Computer Crooks Spy on Our Credit." *USA Today,* July 22–24, 1984: p. 1A.

75. Kirvan, Paul. "Is a Hacker Hovering in Your Horoscope?" *Communications News* 29, 1992: p. 48.

76. Rebello, Kathy. "'Sensitive Kid' Faces Trial." *USA Today,* February 28, 1989: 1B–2B.

77. Ibid.

78. Bloombecker, op. cit., p. iv.

79. Ibid., p. 142.

80. Brown, Bob. "Indictment Handed Down on 'Masters of Disaster.' " *Network World* 29, 1992: p. 34.

81. Moses, Jonathan M. "Wiretap Inquiry Spurs Computer Hacker Charges." *Wall Street Journal,* July 9, 1992: p. B8.

82. Thyfault, Mary E. "Feds Tap into Major Hacker Ring." *Information Week,* July 13, 1992: p. 15.

83. Schwartau, Winn. "Hackers Indicted for Infiltrating Corporate Networks." *Infoworld* 14, 1992: p. 56. See also Daly, James. "Frustrated Hackers May Have Helped Feds in MOD Sting." *Computerworld* 26, 1992: p. 6.

84. Schwartau, op. cit. See also *Wall Street Journal.* "Hackers Plead Guilty." March 22, 1993: p. B2; and *Wall Street Journal.* "Hacker is Sentenced." June 7, 1993: p. B2.

85. Tabor, Mary B. W. "Urban Hackers Charged in High-Tech Crime." *New York Times,* July 23, 1992: p. A1. For a detailed account of the rivalry between the Masters of Destruction and the Legion of Doom see Sterling, Bruce. *The Hacker Crackdown.* New York: Bantam Books, 1992.

86. Littman, Jonathan. "Cyberpunk Meets Mr. Security." *PC-Computing* 5, 1992: 288–293.

87. Quoted in Francis, op. cit., p. 25.

88. Meddis, Sam. "Lawmakers: Pull Plug on Hackers." *USA Today,* November 4, 1983: p. 3A.

89. *USA Today.* "Blabbermouth Computers." July 27, 1993: p. 8A.

90. *New York Times.* "US Charges Young Hackers." November 15, 1992: p. 40.

91. *Government Computer News.* "Feds Charge 2 in Computer Break-in." November 23, 1992: p. 8.

92. Collins, Chris. "Hackers' Paradise." *USA Today,* July 6, 1993: p. 5A.

93. Elmer-DeWitt, Phillip. "Invasion of the Data Snatchers." *Time* 132, September 26, 1988: p. 63.

94. Ibid., 62–67.

95. Ibid.

96. Ibid.

97. Ibid., p. 66.

98. Ibid.

99. Bloombecker, op. cit.

100. Hafner and Markoff, op. cit.

101. Ibid.

102. Bloombecker, op. cit.

103. Elmer-DeWitt, op. cit.

104. Daly, James. "Viruses Ringing in the New Year." *Computerworld* 27, 1992: p. 79.

105. Bloombecker, op. cit.

106. Lewyn, Mark. "First 'Computer Virus' Trial Starts Today." *USA Today,* September 6, 1988: p. 3B.

107. Lewyn, Mark. "Computer Verdict Sets 'Precedent.' " *USA Today,* September 27, 1988: p. 1A.

108. Bloombecker, op. cit., p. 104.

109. Zalud, Bill. "Doing the Virus Hustle." *Security* 27, 1990: 42–44.

110. Burgess, John. "Viruses: An Overblown Epidemic?" *Washington Post,* December 30, 1992; F1, F3.

111. Friedman, Jon, and Meddis, Sam. "White-Collar Crime Cuts into Companies' Profits." *USA Today,* August 30, 1984: p. 3B.

112. Ibid.

113. Parker, 1983, op. cit.

114. Rothfeder, Jeffrey. "Holes in the Net." *Corporate Computing* 2, 1993: 114–118.

115. Violino, op. cit.

116. Buchok, James. "$5M Suit Filed Over Database Copying Claim." *Computing Canada* 18, 1992:1–2.

117. O'Connor, Rory J. "High-Tech Cops Wade Through Digital Dump of Information." *San Jose Mercury News,* October 24, 1992: 10D–11D.

118. Groves, Martha. "2 Indicted on Trade-Secret Theft Charges." *Los Angeles Times,* March 5, 1993: p. D1.

119. Ratcliffe, Mitch. "Symantec Execs Face Felony Rap in Borland Case." *MacWEEK* 7, 1993: 1–2.

120. "Jules." "On the Use of Weapons." *EXE* 10, 1993: 52–53.

121. Hasson, Judi. "Access to Medical Files Reform Issue." *USA Today,* July 27, 1993: 1A–2A.

122. Hafner and Markoff, op. cit.

123. Stoll, Clifford. *The Cuckoo's Egg.* New York: Doubleday, 1989.

124. Hafner and Markoff, op. cit.

125. Stoll, op. cit.

126. Ibid.

127. Hafner and Markoff, op. cit.

128. Belts, Mitch. "Recovering From Hacker Invasion." *Computerworld* 27, 1993: p. 45.

129. *Houston Post.* "Dallas Police Investigate Suspect in Spreading of Computer Virus." December 29, 1990: p. 19.

130. Markoff, John. "Hacker Indicted on Spy Charges." *New York Times,* December 8, 1992: p. 13.

131. Ibid., p. 13.

132. Bloombecker, op. cit.

133. Parker, 1983, op. cit.

134. Ibid.

135. Rosenbaum, op. cit.

136. Parker, 1983, op. cit.

137. Ibid.

138. Ibid.

139. Ibid., p. 180.

140. Daly, James. "Toll Fraud Growing." *Computerworld* 27, 1993: 47–48.

141. Ibid., p. 47.

142. Herman, Barbara. "Yacking with a Hack: Phone Phreaking for Fun, Profit, & Politics." *Teleconnect* 10, 1992: 60–62.

143. Quinn, Brian. "$ 2.3 Billion: That's About How Much Toll Fraud is Costing Us a Year (Maybe More)." *Teleconnect* 10, 1992: 47–49. See also Taff, Anita. "Users Call for Toll Fraud Laws to Distribute Losses." *Network World* 9, 1992: 27–28.

144. Dodd, Annabel. "When Going the Extra Mile Is Not Enough." *Network World* 10, 1993: 49–50.

145. McMenamin, Brigid. "Why Cybercrooks Love Cellular." *Forbes* 150, 1993: p. 189.

146. Panettieri, Joseph C. "Weak Links: For Corporate Spies, Low-Tech Communications Are Easy Marks." *Information Week,* August 10, 1992: 26–29.

147. Ibid.

148. Rill, Derick. "Hackers Reach Out and Touch NASA." *Houston Post,* December 6, 1990: p. A22.

149. Luxner, Larry. "V.I. Official Convicted in Fraud Case." *Telephony* 222, 1992: 20–22.

150. Lewyn, Mark. "Phone Sleuths Are Cutting Off the Hackers: Corporations and Phone Companies Join to End Long-Distance Fraud." *Business Week,* July 13, 1992: p. 134.

151. *Washington Post.* "AT&T, Mitsubishi Settle Phone Suit." October 13, 1992: p. C3.

152. Daly, James. "Get Thee Some Security." *Computerworld* 27, 1993: 31–32. See also Daly, James. "Out to Get You." *Computerworld* 27, 1993: 77–79.

153. Brown, Bob. "Insurer Adds Phone Fraud Protection." *Network World* 9, 1992: 1–2.

154. Panettieri, op. cit.

155. Ibid.

156. Urbois, Jeff. "Saving Your Company From Telephone Fraud." *MacWEEK* 6, 1992: p. 22.

157. Quinn, op. cit.

Mental Disorder

In his classic work, "On Being Sane in Insane Places," D.L. Rosenhan explores the question of how sanity exists by having people pose as "pseudopatients" in twelve different hospitals. The experiment raises questions as to the definitions of what is considered "normal" and "abnormal," but does not challenge the notion that some behaviors may be odd or deviant. The study finds that diagnoses of sanity and insanity are less substantive and more subjective than previously realized. Rosenhan concludes that given the special environment of psychiatric hospitals, which he describes in detail, it is not possible to distinguish the sane from the insane.

Along similar lines of thought, Erving Goffman presents the path leading to institutionalization, and the changes in identity that occur once one is admitted, in his work, "The Moral Career of the Mental Patient." Goffman describes the ways in which persons are admitted to hospitals ("prepatient phase"), and the "betrayal funnel" that can be part of this process. The "inpatient phase" of the patient career involves a full range of mortifying experiences that involve the transformation of self in response to the hospital environment. In time, the patient's views become discredited, and he or she is forced to actually take, or pretend to take, the hospital's view in order to best survive his or her institutionalization.

Ronny Turner and Charles Edgley's work, "From Witchcraft to Drugcraft," questions the biochemical etiology of mental illness. The authors argue that explanations of deviant behavior focusing on the witch, the curse, and the sin, have been supplanted by the terminology of medicine, psychiatry, and biochemistry. Evidence is presented to show that diagnoses of mental illness are not and cannot be based on chemical analyses, but rather are social judgments that result in the labeling of deviance.

ON BEING SANE IN INSANE PLACES*

D. L. Rosenhan**

If sanity and insanity exist, how shall we know them?

The question is neither capricious nor itself insane. However much we may be personally convinced that we can tell the normal from the abnormal, the evidence is simply not compelling. It is commonplace, for example, to read about murder trials wherein eminent psychiatrists for the defense are contradicted by equally eminent psychiatrists for the prosecution on the matter of the defendant's sanity. More generally, there are a great deal of conflicting data on the reliability, utility, and meaning of such terms as "sanity," "insanity," "mental illness," and "schizophrenia".[1] Finally, as early as 1934, Benedict suggested that normality and abnormality are not universal.[2] What is viewed as normal in one culture may be seen as quite aberrant in another. Thus, notions of normality and abnormality may not be quite as accurate as people believe they are.

To raise questions regarding normality and abnormality is in no way to question the fact that some behaviors are deviant or odd. Murder is deviant. So, too, are hallucinations. Nor does raising such questions deny the existence of the personal anguish that is often associated with "mental illness." Anxiety and depression exist. Psychological suffering exists. But normality and abnormality, sanity and insanity, and the diagnoses that flow from them may be less substantive than many believe them to be.

At its heart, the question of whether the sane can be distinguished from the insane (and whether degrees of insanity can be distinguished from each other) is a simple matter: Do the salient characteristics that lead to diagnoses reside in the patients themselves or in the environments and contexts in which observers find them? From Bleuler, through Kretchmer, through the formulators of the recently revised *Diagnostic and Statistical Manual* of the American Psychiatric Association, the belief has been strong that patients present symptoms, that those symptoms can be categorized, and, implicitly, that the sane are distinguishable from the insane. More recently, however, this belief has been questioned. Based in part on theoretical and anthropological considerations, but also on philosophical, legal, and therapeutic ones, the view has grown that psychological categorization of mental illness is useless at best and downright harmful, misleading, and pejorative at worst. Psychiatric diagnoses, in this view, are in the minds of the observers and are not valid summaries of characteristics displayed by the observed.[3-5]

Gains can be made in deciding which of these is more nearly accurate by getting normal people (that is, people who do not have, and have never suffered, symptoms of serious psychiatric disorders) admitted to psychiatric hospitals and then determining whether they were discovered to be sane and, if so, how. If the sanity of such pseudopatients were always detected, there would be prima facie evidence that a sane individual can be distinguished from the insane context in which he is found. Normality (and presumably abnormality) is distinct enough that it can be recognized wherever it occurs, for it is carried within the person. If, on the other hand, the sanity of the pseudopatients were never discovered, serious difficulties would arise for those who support traditional modes of psychiatric diagnosis. Given that the hospital staff was not incompetent, that the pseudopatient had been behaving as sanely as he had been outside of the hospital, and that it had never been previously suggested that he belonged in a psychiatric hos-

*Reprinted from *Science,* Vol. 179, 4070, (Jan. 19, 1973), pp. 250–258, by permission of the American Association for the Advancement of Science, Copyright © 1973 by the AAAS.

**Portions of these data were presented to colloquiums of the psychology departments at the University of California at Berkeley and at Santa Barbara; University of Arizona, Tucson; and Harvard University, Cambridge, Massachusetts.

pital, such an unlikely outcome would support the view that psychiatric diagnosis betrays little about the patient but much about the environment in which an observer finds him.

This article describes such an experiment. Eight sane people gained secret admission to 12 different hospitals.[6] Their diagnostic experiences constitute the data of the first part of this article; the remainder is devoted to a description of their experiences in psychiatric institutions. Too few psychiatrists and psychologists, even those who have worked in such hospitals, know what the experience is like. They rarely talk about it with former patients, perhaps because they distrust information coming from the previously insane. Those who have worked in psychiatric hospitals are likely to have adapted so thoroughly to the settings that they are insensitive to the impact of that experience. And while there have been occasional reports of researchers who submitted themselves to psychiatric hospitalization,[7] these researchers have commonly remained in the hospitals for short periods of time, often with the knowledge of the hospital staff. It is difficult to know the extent to which they were treated like patients or like research colleagues. Nevertheless, their reports about the inside of the psychiatric hospital have been valuable. This article extends those efforts.

PSEUDOPATIENTS AND THEIR SETTINGS

The eight pseudopatients were a varied group. One was a psychology graduate student in his twenties. The remaining seven were older and "established." Among them were three psychologists, a pediatrician, a psychiatrist, a painter, and a housewife. Three pseudopatients were women, five were men. All of them employed pseudonyms, lest their alleged diagnoses embarrass them later. Those who were in mental health professions alleged another occupation in order to avoid the special attentions that might be accorded by staff, as a matter of courtesy or caution, to ailing colleagues.[8] With the exception of myself (I was the first pseudopatient and my presence was known to the hospital administrator and chief psychologist and, so far as I can tell, to them alone), the presence of pseudopatients and

the nature of the research program was not known to the hospital staffs.[9]

The settings were similarly varied. In order to generalize the findings, admission into a variety of hospitals was sought. The 12 hospitals in the sample were located in five different states on the East and West Coasts. Some were old and shabby, some were quite new. Some were research-oriented, others not. Some had good staff-patient ratios, others were quite understaffed. Only one was a strictly private hospital. All of the others were supported by state or federal funds or, in one instance, by university funds.

After calling the hospital for an appointment, the pseudopatient arrived at the admissions office complaining that he had been hearing voices. Asked what the voices said, he replied that they were often unclear, but as far as he could tell they said "empty," "hollow," and "thud." The voices were unfamiliar and were of the same sex as the pseudopatient. The choice of these symptoms was occasioned by their apparent similarity to existential symptoms. Such symptoms are alleged to arise from painful concerns about the perceived meaninglessness of one's life. It is as if the hallucinating person were saying, "My life is empty and hollow." The choice of these symptoms was also determined by the *absence* of a single report of existential psychoses in the literature.

Beyond alleging the symptoms and falsifying name, vocation, and employment, no further alterations of person, history, or circumstances were made. The significant events of the pseudopatient's life history were presented as they had actually occurred. Relationships with parents and siblings, with spouse and children, with people at work and in school, consistent with the aforementioned exceptions, were described as they were or had been. Frustrations and upsets were described along with joys and satisfactions. These facts are important to remember. If anything, they strongly biased the subsequent results in favor of detecting sanity, since none of their histories or current behaviors were seriously pathological in any way.

Immediately upon admission to the psychiatric ward, the pseudopatient ceased simulating *any* symptoms of abnormality. In some cases, there was a brief period of mild nervousness and anxiety, since none of the pseudopatients really believed that they would be admitted so easily. Indeed, their shared fear was that they would be immediately exposed as frauds and greatly embarrassed. Moreover, many of them had never visited a psychiatric ward; even those who had, nevertheless had some genuine fears about what might happen to them. Their nervousness, then, was quite appropriate to the novelty of the hospital setting, and it abated rapidly.

Apart from that short-lived nervousness, the pseudopatient behaved on the ward as he "normally" behaved. The pseudopatient spoke to patients and staff as he might ordinarily. Because there is uncommonly little to do on a psychiatric ward, he attempted to engage others in conversation. When asked by staff how he was feeling, he indicated that he was fine, that he no longer experienced symptoms. He responded to instructions from attendants, to calls for medication (which was not swallowed), and to dining-hall instructions. Beyond such activities as were available to him on the admissions ward, he spent his time writing down his observations about the ward, its patients, and the staff. Initially these notes were written "secretly," but as it soon became clear that no one much cared, they were subsequently written on standard tablets of paper in such public places as the dayroom. No secret was made of these activities.

The pseudopatient, very much as a true psychiatric patient, entered a hospital with no foreknowledge of when he would be discharged. Each was told that he would have to get out by his own devices, essentially by convincing the staff that he was sane. The psychological stresses associated with hospitalization were considerable, and all but one of the pseudopatients desired to be discharged almost immediately after being admitted. They were, therefore, motivated not only to behave sanely, but to be paragons of cooperation. That their behavior was in no way disruptive is confirmed by nursing reports, which have been obtained on most of the patients. These reports uniformly indicate that the patients were "friendly," "cooperative," and "exhibited no abnormal indications."

THE NORMAL ARE NOT DETECTABLY SANE

Despite their public "show" of sanity, the pseudopatients were never detected. Admitted, except in one case, with a diagnosis of schizophrenia,[10] each was discharged with a diagnosis of schizophrenia "in remission." The label "in remission" should in no way be dismissed as a formality, for at no time during any hospitalization had any question been raised about any pseudopatient's simulation. Nor are there any indications in the hospital records that the pseudopatient's status was suspect. Rather the evidence is strong that, once labeled schizophrenic, the pseudopatient was stuck with that label. If the pseudopatient was to be discharged, he must naturally be "in remission"; but he was not sane, nor, in the institution's view, had he ever been sane.

The uniform failure to recognize sanity cannot be attributed to the quality of the hospitals, for, although there were considerable variations among them, several are considered excellent. Nor can it be alleged that there was simply not enough time to observe the pseudopatients. Length of hospitalization ranged from 7 to 52 days, with an average of 19 days. The pseudopatients were not, in fact, carefully observed, but this failure clearly speaks more to traditions within psychiatric hospitals than to lack of opportunity.

Finally, it cannot be said that the failure to recognize the pseudopatients' sanity was due to the fact that they were not behaving sanely. While there was clearly some tension present in all of them, their daily visitors could detect no serious behavioral consequences—nor, indeed, could other patients. It was quite common for the patients to "detect" the pseudopatients' sanity. During the first three hospitalizations, when accurate counts were kept, 35 of a total of 118 patients on the admissions ward voiced their suspicions, some vigorously. "You're not crazy. You're a journalist, or a professor [referring to the continual note-taking]. You're checking up on the hospital." While most of the patients were reassured by the pseudopatient's insistence that he had been sick before he came in but was fine now, some continued to believe that the pseudopatient was sane throughout his hospitalization.[11] The fact that the patients often recognized normality when staff did not raises important questions.

Failure to detect sanity during the course of hospitalization may be due to the fact that physicians operate with a strong bias toward what statisticians call the type 2 error.[5] This is to say that physicians are more inclined to call a healthy person sick (a false positive, type 2) than a sick person healthy (a false negative, type 1). The reasons for this are not hard to find: It is clearly more dangerous to misdiagnose illness than health. Better to err on the side of caution, to suspect illness even among the healthy.

But what holds for medicine does not hold equally well for psychiatry. Medical illnesses, while unfortunate, are not commonly pejorative. Psychiatric diagnoses, on the contrary, carry with them personal, legal, and social stigmas.[12] It was therefore important to see whether the tendency toward diagnosing the sane insane could be reversed. The following experiment was arranged at a research and teaching hospital whose staff had heard these findings but doubted that such an error could occur in their hospital. The staff was informed that at some time during the following 3 months, one or more pseudopatients would attempt to be admitted into the psychiatric hospital. Each staff member was asked to rate each patient who presented himself at admissions or on the ward according to the likelihood that the patient was a pseudopatient. A 10-point scale was used, with a 1 and 2 reflecting high confidence that the patient was a pseudopatient.

Judgments were obtained on 193 patients who were admitted for psychiatric treatment. All staff who had had sustained contact with or primary responsibility for the patient—attendants, nurses, psychiatrists, physicians, and psychologists— were asked to make judgments. Forty-one patients were alleged, with high confidence, to be pseudopatients by at least one member of the staff. Twenty-three were considered suspect by at least one psychiatrist. Nineteen were suspected by one psychiatrist *and* one other staff member. Actually, no genuine pseudopatient (at least from my group) presented himself during this period.

The experiment is instructive. It indicates that the tendency to designate sane people as insane can be reversed when the stakes (in this case, prestige and diagnostic acumen) are high. But what can be said of the 19 people who were suspected of being "sane" by one psychiatrist and another staff member? Were these people truly "sane," or was it rather the case that in the course of avoiding the type 2 error the staff tended to make more errors of the first sort—calling the crazy "sane"? There is no way of knowing. But one thing is certain: Any diagnostic process that lends itself so readily to massive errors of this sort cannot be a very reliable one.

THE STICKINESS OF PSYCHODIAGNOSTIC LABELS

Beyond the tendency to call the healthy sick—a tendency that accounts better for diagnostic behavior on admission than it does for such behavior after a lengthy period of exposure—the data speak to the massive role of labeling in psychiatric assessment. Having once been labeled schizophrenic, there is nothing the pseudopatient can do to overcome the tag. The tag profoundly colors others' perceptions of him and his behavior.

From one viewpoint, these data are hardly surprising, for it has long been known that elements are given meaning by the context in which they occur. Gestalt psychology made this point vigorously, and Asch[13] demonstrated that there are "central" personality traits (such as "warm" versus "cold") which are so powerful that they markedly color the meaning of other information in forming an impression of a given personality.[14] "Insane," "schizophrenic," "manic-depressive," and "crazy" are probably among the most powerful of such central traits. Once a person is designated abnormal, all of his other behaviors and characteristics are colored by that label. Indeed, that label is so powerful that many of the pseudopatients' normal behaviors were overlooked entirely or profoundly misinterpreted. Some examples may clarify this issue.

Earlier I indicated that there were no changes in the pseudopatient's personal history and current status beyond those of name, employment, and, where necessary, vocation. Otherwise, a veridical description of personal history and circumstances was offered. Those circumstances were not psychotic. How were they made consonant with the diagnosis of psychosis? Or were those diagnoses modified in such a way as to bring them into accord with the circumstances of the pseudopatient's life, as described by him?

✗ As far as I can determine, diagnoses were in no way affected by the relative health of the circumstances of a pseudopatient's life. Rather, the reverse occurred: The perception of his circumstances was shaped entirely by the diagnosis. A clear example of such translation is found in the case of a pseudopatient who had had a close relationship with his mother but was rather remote from his father during his early childhood. During adolescence and beyond, however, his father became a close friend, while his relationship with his mother cooled. His present relationship with his wife was characteristically close and warm. Apart from occasional angry exchanges, friction was minimal. The children had rarely been spanked. Surely there is nothing especially pathological about such a history. Indeed, many readers may see a similar pattern in their own experiences, with no markedly deleterious consequences. Observe, however, how such a history was translated in the psychopathological context, this from the case summary prepared after the patient was discharged.

This white 39-year-old male . . . manifests a long history of considerable ambivalence in close relationships, which begins in early childhood. A warm relationship with his mother cools during his adolescence. A distant relationship to his father is described as becoming very intense. Affective stability is absent. His attempts to control emotionality with his wife and children are punctuated by angry outbursts and, in the case of the children, spankings. And while he says that he has several good friends, one senses considerable ambivalence embedded in those relationships also. . . .

The facts of the case were unintentionally distorted by the staff to achieve consistency with a popular theory of the dynamics of a schizophrenic reaction.[15] Nothing of an ambivalent nature had been described in relations with parents, spouse, or friends. To the extent that ambivalence could be inferred, it was probably not greater than is found in all human relationships. It is true the pseudopatient's relationships with his parents changed over time, but in the ordinary context that would hardly be remarkable—indeed, it might very well be expected. Clearly, the meaning ascribed to his verbalizations (that is, ambivalence, affective instability) was determined by the diagnosis: schizophrenia. An entirely different meaning would have been ascribed if it were known that the man was "normal."

All pseudopatients took extensive notes publicly. Under ordinary circumstances, such behavior would have raised questions in the minds of observers, as, in fact, it did among patients. Indeed, it seemed so certain that the notes would elicit suspicion that elaborate precautions were taken to remove them from the ward each day. But the precautions proved needless. The closest any staff member came to questioning these notes occurred when one pseudopatient asked his physician what kind of medication he was receiving and began to write down the response. "You needn't write it," he was told gently. "If you have trouble remembering, just ask me again."

If no questions were asked of the pseudopatients, how was their writing interpreted? Nursing records for three patients indicate that the writing was seen as an aspect of their pathological behavior. "Patient engages in writing behavior" was the daily nursing comment on one of the pseudopatients who was never questioned about his writing. Given that the patient is in the hospital, he must be psychologically disturbed. And given that he is a disturbed, continuous writing must be a behavioral manifestation of that disturbance, perhaps a subset of the compulsive behaviors that are sometimes correlated with schizophrenia.

One tacit characteristic of psychiatric diagnosis is that it locates the sources of aberration within the individual and only rarely within the complex of stimuli that surrounds him. Consequently, behaviors that are stimulated by the environment are commonly misattributed to the patient's disorder. For example, one kindly nurse found a pseudopatient pacing the long hospital corridors. "Nervous, Mr. X?" she asked. "No, bored," he said.

The notes kept by pseudopatients are full of patient behaviors that were misinterpreted by well-intentioned staff. Often enough, a patient would go "berserk" because he had, wittingly or unwittingly, been mistreated by, say, an attendant. A nurse coming upon the scene would rarely inquire even cursorily into the environmental stimuli of the patient's behavior. Rather, she assumed that his upset derived from his pathology, not from his present interactions with other staff members. Occasionally, the staff might assume that the patient's family (especially when they had recently visited) or other patients had stimulated the outburst. But never were the staff found to assume that one of themselves or the structure of the hospital had anything to do with a patient's behavior. One psychiatrist pointed to a group of patients who were sitting outside the cafeteria entrance half an hour before lunchtime. To a group of young residents he indicated that such behavior was characteristic of the oral-acquisitive nature of the syndrome. It seemed not to occur to him that there were very few things to anticipate in a psychiatric hospital besides eating.

A psychiatric label has a life and an influence of its own. Once the impression has been formed that the patient is schizophrenic, the expectation is that he will continue to be schizophrenic. When a sufficient amount of time has passed, during which the patient has done nothing bizarre, he is considered to be in remission and available for discharge. But the label endures beyond discharge, with the unconfirmed expectation that he will behave as a schizophrenic again. Such labels, conferred by mental health professionals, are as influential on the patient as they are on his relatives and friends, and it should not surprise anyone that the diagnosis acts on all of them as a self-fulfilling prophecy. Eventually, the patient himself accepts the diagnosis, with all of its surplus meanings and expectations, and behaves accordingly.[5]

The inferences to be made from these matters are quite simple. Much as Zigler and Phillips have demonstrated that there is enormous overlap in the symptoms presented by patients who have been variously diagnosed,[16] so there is enormous overlap in the behaviors of the sane and the

insane. The sane are not "sane" all of the time. We lose our tempers "for no good reason." We are occasionally depressed or anxious, again for no good reason. And we may find it difficult to get along with one or another person—again for no reason that we can specify. Similarly, the insane are not always insane. Indeed, it was the impression of the pseudopatients while living with them that they were sane for long periods of time—that the bizarre behaviors upon which their diagnoses were allegedly predicated constituted only a small fraction of their total behavior. If it makes no sense to label ourselves permanently depressed on the basis of an occasional depression, then it takes better evidence than is presently available to label all patients insane or schizophrenic on the basis of bizarre behaviors or cognitions. It seems more useful, as Mischel[17] has pointed out, to limit our discussions to *behaviors,* the stimuli that provoke them, and their correlates.

It is not known why powerful impressions of personality traits, such as "crazy" or "insane," arise. Conceivably, when the origins of and stimuli that give rise to a behavior are remote or unknown, or when the behavior strikes us as immutable, trait labels regarding the *behaver* arise. When, on the other hand, the origins and stimuli are known and available, discourse is limited to the behavior itself. Thus, I may hallucinate because I am sleeping, or I may hallucinate because I have ingested a peculiar drug. These are termed sleep-induced hallucinations, or dreams, and drug-induced hallucinations, respectively. But when the stimuli to my hallucinations are unknown, that is called craziness, or schizophrenia—as if that inference were somehow as illuminating as the others.

THE EXPERIENCE OF PSYCHIATRIC HOSPITALIZATION

The term "mental illness" is of recent origin. It was coined by people who were humane in their inclinations and who wanted very much to raise the station of (and the public's sympathies toward) the psychologically disturbed from that of witches and "crazies" to one that was akin to the physically ill. And they were at least partially successful, for the treatment of the mentally ill *has* improved considerably over the years. But while treatment has improved, it is doubtful that people really regard the mentally ill in the same way that they view the physically ill. A broken leg is something one recovers from, but mental illness allegedly endures forever.[18] A broken leg does not threaten the observer, but a crazy schizophrenic? There is by now a host of evidence that attitudes toward the mentally ill are characterized by fear, hostility, aloofness, suspicion, and dread.[19] The mentally ill are society's lepers.

That such attitudes infect the general population is perhaps not surprising, only upsetting. But that they affect the professionals—attendants, nurses, physicians, psychologists, and social workers—who treat and deal with the mentally ill is more disconcerting, both because such attitudes are self-evidently pernicious and because they are unwitting. Most mental health professionals would insist that they are sympathetic toward the mentally ill, that they are neither avoidant nor hostile. But it is more likely that an exquisite ambivalence characterizes their relations with psychiatric patients, such that their avowed impulses are only part of their entire attitude. Negative attitudes are there too and can easily be detected. Such attitudes should not surprise us. They are the natural offspring of the labels patients wear and the places in which they are found.

Consider the structure of the typical psychiatric hospital. Staff and patients are strictly segregated. Staff have their own living space, including their dining facilities, bathrooms, and assembly places. The glassed quarters that contain the professional staff, which the pseudopatients came to call "the cage," sit out on every dayroom. The staff emerge primarily for caretaking purposes—to give medication, to conduct a therapy or group meeting, to instruct or reprimand a patient. Otherwise, staff keep to themselves, almost as if the disorder that afflicts their charges is somehow catching.

So much is patient-staff segregation the rule that, for four public hospitals in which an attempt was made to measure the degree to which staff and patients mingle, it was necessary to use "time out of the staff cage" as the operational measure. While it was not the case that all time spent out of the cage was spent mingling with patients (attendants, for example, would occasionally emerge to watch television in the dayroom), it was the only way in which one could gather reliable data on time for measuring.

The average amount of time spent by attendants outside of the cage was 11.3 percent (range, 3 to 52 percent). This figure does not represent only time spent mingling with patients, but also includes time spent on such chores as folding laundry, supervising patients while they shave, directing ward clean-up, and sending patients to off-ward activities. It was the relatively rare attendant who spent time talking with patients or playing games with them. It proved impossible to obtain a "percent mingling time" for nurses, since the amount of time they spent out of the cage was too brief. Rather, we counted instances of emergence from the cage. On the average, daytime nurses emerged from the cage 11.5 times per shift, including instances when they left the ward entirely (range, 4 to 39 times). Late afternoon and night nurses were even less available, emerging on the average 9.4 times per shift (range, 4 to 41 times). Data on early morning nurses, who arrived usually after midnight and departed at 8 a.m., are not available because patients were asleep during most of this period.

Physicians, especially psychiatrists, were even less available. They were rarely seen on the wards. Quite commonly, they would be seen only when they arrived and departed, with the remaining time being spent in their offices or in the cage. On the average, physicians emerged on the ward 6.7 times per day (range, 1 to 17 times). It proved difficult to make an accurate estimate in this regard, since physicians often maintained hours that allowed them to come and go at different times.

The hierarchical organization of the psychiatric hospital has been commented on before,[20] but the latent meaning of that kind of organization is worth noting again. Those with the most power have least to do with patients, and those with the least power are most involved with them. Recall, however, that the acquisition of role-appropriate behaviors occurs mainly through the observation of others, with the most powerful having the most influence. Consequently, it is understandable that attendants not only spend more time with patients than do any other members of the staff—that is required by their station in the hierarchy—but also, insofar as they learn from their superiors' behavior, spend as little time with patients as they can. Attendants are seen mainly in the cage, which is where the models, the action, and the power are.

I turn now to a different set of studies, these dealing with staff response to patient-initiated contact. It has long been known that the amount of time a person spends with you can be an index of your significance to him. If he initiates and maintains eye contact, there is reason to believe that he is considering your requests and needs. If he pauses to chat or actually stops and talks, there is added reason to infer that he is individuating you. In four hospitals, the pseudopatient approached the staff member with a request which took the following form: "Pardon me, Mr. [or Dr. or Mrs.] X, could you tell me when I will be eligible for grounds privileges?" (or ". . . when I will be presented at the staff meeting?" or ". . . when I am likely to be discharged?"). While the content of the question varied according to the appropriateness of the target and the pseudopatient's (apparent) current needs, the form was al-

ways a courteous and relevant request for information. Care was taken never to approach a particular member of the staff more than once a day, lest the staff member become suspicious or irritated. In examining these data, remember that the behavior of the pseudopatients was neither bizarre nor disruptive. One could indeed engage in good conversation with them.

The data for these experiments are shown in Table 1, separately for physicians (column 1) and for nurses and attendants (column 2). Minor differences between these four institutions were overwhelmed by the degree to which staff avoided continuing contacts that patients had initiated. By far, their most common response consisted of either a brief response to the question, offered while they were "on the move" and with head averted, or no response at all.

The encounter frequently took the following bizarre form: (pseudopatient) "Pardon me, Dr. X. Could you tell me when I am eligible for grounds privileges?" (physician) "Good morning, Dave. How are you today?" (Moves off without waiting for a response.)

It is instructive to compare these data with data recently obtained at Stanford University. It has been alleged that large and eminent universities are characterized by faculty who are so busy that

TABLE 1 Self-Initiated Contact by Pseudopatients with Psychiatrists and Nurses and Attendants, Compared to Contact with Other Groups

Contact	Psychiatric Hospitals		University Campus (nonmedical)	University Medical Center Physicians		
	(1) Psychiatrists	*(2)* Nurses and Attendants	*(3)* Faculty	*(4)* "Looking for a Psychiatrist"	*(5)* "Looking for an Internist"	*(6)* No Additional Comment
Responses						
Moves on, head averted (%)	71	88	0	0	0	0
Makes eye contact (%)	23	10	0	11	0	0
Pauses and chats (%)	2	2	0	11	0	10
Stops and talks (%)	4	0.5	100	78	100	90
Mean number of questions answered (out of 6)	*	*	6	3.8	4.8	4.5
Respondents (No.)	13	47	14	18	15	10
Attempts (No.)	185	1283	14	18	15	10

*Not applicable

they have no time for students. For this comparison, a young lady approached individual faculty members who seemed to be walking purposefully to some meeting or teaching engagement and asked them the following six questions.

1. "Pardon me, could you direct me to Encina Hall?" (at the medical school: ". . . to the Clinical Research Center?").
2. "Do you know where Fish Annex is?" (there is no Fish Annex at Stanford).
3. "Do you teach here?"
4. "How does one apply for admission to the college?" (at the medical school: ". . . to the medical school?").
5. "Is it difficult to get in?"
6. "Is there financial aid?"

Without exception, as can be seen in Table 1 (column 3), all of the questions were answered. No matter how rushed they were, all respondents not only maintained eye contact, but stopped to talk. Indeed, many of the respondents went out of their way to direct or take the questioner to the office she was seeking, to try to locate "Fish Annex," or to discuss with her the possibilities of being admitted to the university.

Similar data, also shown in Table 1 (columns 4, 5, and 6), were obtained in the hospital. Here too, the young lady came prepared with six questions. After the first question, however, she remarked to 18 of her respondents (column 4), "I'm looking for a psychiatrist," and to 15 others (column 6), "I'm looking for an internist." Ten other respondents received no inserted comment (column 6). The general degree of cooperative responses is considerably higher for these university groups than it was for pseudopatients in psychiatric hospitals. Even so, differences are apparent within the medical school setting. Once having indicated that she was looking for a psychiatrist, the degree of cooperation elicited was less than when she sought an internist.

POWERLESSNESS AND DEPERSONALIZATION

Eye contact and verbal contact reflect concern and individuation; their absence, avoidance and depersonalization. The data I have presented do not do justice to the rich daily encounters that grew up around matters of depersonalization and avoidance. I have records of patients who were beaten by staff for the sin of having initiated verbal contact. During my own experience, for example, one patient was beaten in the presence of other patients for having approached an attendant and told him, "I like you." Occasionally, punishment meted out to patients for misdemeanors seemed so excessive that it could not be justified by the most radical interpretations of psychiatric canon. Nevertheless, they appeared to go unquestioned. Tempers were often short. A patient who had not heard a call for medication would be roundly excoriated, and the morning attendants would often wake patients with, "Come on, you m - - - - - f - - - - - s, out of bed!"

Neither anecdotal nor "hard" data can convey the overwhelming sense of powerlessness which invades the individual as he is continually exposed to the depersonalization of the psychiatric hospital. It hardly matters *which* psychiatric hospital—the excellent public ones and the very plush private hospital were better than the rural and shabby ones in this regard, but, again, the features that psychiatric hospitals had in common overwhelmed by far their apparent differences.

Powerlessness was evident everywhere. The patient is deprived of many of his legal rights by dint of his psychiatric commitment.[21] He is shorn of credibility by virtue of his psychiatric label. His freedom of movement is restricted. He cannot initiate contact with the staff, but may only respond to such overtures as they make. Personal privacy is minimal. Patient quarters and possessions can be entered and examined by any staff member, for whatever reason. His personal history and anguish is available to any staff member (often including the "gray lady" and "candy striper" volunteer) who chooses to read his folder, regardless of their therapeutic relationship to him. His personal hygiene and waste evacuation are often monitored. The water closets may have no doors.

At times, depersonalization reached such proportions that pseudopatients had the sense that they were invisible, or at least unworthy of account. Upon being admitted, I and other pseudopatients took the initial physical examinations in a semipublic room, where staff members went about their own business as if we were not there.

On the ward, attendants delivered verbal and occasionally serious physical abuse to patients in the presence of other observing patients, some of whom (the pseudopatients) were writing it all down. Abusive behavior, on the other hand, terminated quite abruptly when other staff members were known to be coming. Staff are credible witnesses. Patients are not.

A nurse unbuttoned her uniform to adjust her brassiere in the presence of an entire ward of viewing men. One did not have the sense that she was being seductive. Rather, she didn't notice us. A group of staff persons might point to a patient in the dayroom and discuss him animatedly, as if he were not there.

One illuminating instance of depersonalization and invisibility occurred with regard to medications. All told, the pseudopatients were administered nearly 2,100 pills, including Elavil, Stelazine, Compazine, and Thorazine, to name but a few. (That such a variety of medications should have been administered to patients presenting identical symptoms is itself worthy of note.) Only two were swallowed. The rest were either pocketed or deposited in the toilet. The pseudopatients were not alone in this. Although I have no precise records on how many patients rejected their medications, the pseudopatients frequently found the medications of other patients in the toilet before they deposited their own. As long as they were cooperative, their behavior and the pseudopatients' own in this matter, as in other important matters, went unnoticed throughout.

Reactions to such depersonalization among pseudopatients were intense. Although they had come to the hospital as participant observers and were fully aware that they did not "belong," they nevertheless found themselves caught up in and fighting the process of depersonalization. Some examples: A graduate student in psychology asked his wife to bring his textbooks to the hospital so he could "catch up on his homework"—this despite the elaborate precautions taken to conceal his professional association. The same student, who had trained for quite some time to get into the hospital, and who had looked for-

ward to the experience, "remembered" some drag races that he had wanted to see on the weekend and insisted that he be discharged by that time. Another pseudopatient attempted a romance with a nurse. Subsequently, he informed the staff that he was applying for admission to graduate school in psychology and was very likely to be admitted, since a graduate professor was one of his regular hospital visitors. The same person began to engage in psychotherapy with other patients—all of this as a way of becoming a person in an impersonal environment.

THE SOURCES OF DEPERSONALIZATION

What are the origins of depersonalization? I have already mentioned two. First are attitudes held by all of us toward the mentally ill—including those who treat them—attitudes characterized by fear, distrust, and horrible expectations on the one hand, and benevolent intentions on the other. Our ambivalence leads, in this instance as in others, to avoidance.

Second, and not entirely separate, the hierarchical structure of the psychiatric hospital facilitates depersonalization. Those who are at the top have least to do with patients, and their behavior inspires the rest of the staff. Average daily contact with psychiatrists, psychologists, residents, and physicians combined ranged from 3.9 to 25.1 minutes, with an overall mean of 6.8 (six pseudopatients over a total of 129 days of hospitalization). Included in this average are time spent in the admissions interview, ward meetings in the presence of a senior staff member, group and individual psychotherapy contacts, case presentation conferences, and discharge meetings. Clearly, patients do not spend much time in interpersonal contact with doctoral staff. And doctoral staff serve as models for nurses and attendants.

There are probably other sources. Psychiatric installations are presently in serious financial straits. Staff shortages are pervasive, staff time at a premium. Something has to give, and that something is patient contact. Yet, while financial stresses are realities, too much can be made of them. I have the impression that the psychological forces that result in depersonalization are much stronger than the fiscal ones and that the addition of more staff would not correspondingly improve patient care in this regard. The incidence of staff meetings and the enormous amount of record-keeping on patients, for example, have not been as substantially reduced as has patient contact. Priorities exist, even during hard times. Patient contact is not a significant priority in the traditional psychiatric hospital, and fiscal pressures do not account for this. Avoidance and depersonalization may.

Heavy reliance upon psychotropic medication tacitly contributes to depersonalization by convincing staff that treatment is indeed being conducted and that further patient contact may not be necessary. Even here, however, caution needs to be exercised in understanding the role of psychotropic drugs. If patients were powerful rather than powerless, if they were viewed as interesting individuals rather than diagnostic entities, if they were socially significant rather than social lepers, if their anguish truly and wholly compelled our sympathies and concerns, would we not *seek* contact with them, despite the availability of medications? Perhaps for the pleasure of it all?

THE CONSEQUENCES OF LABELING AND DEPERSONALIZATION

Whenever the ratio of what is known to what needs to be known approaches zero, we tend to invent "knowledge" and assume that we understand more than we actually do. We seem unable to acknowledge that we simply don't know. The needs for diagnosis and remediation of behavioral and emotional problems are enormous. But rather than acknowledge that we are just embarking on understanding, we continue to label patients "schizophrenic," "manic-depressive," and "insane," as if in those words we had captured the essence of understanding. The facts of the matter are that we have known for a long time that diagnoses are often not useful or reliable, but we have nevertheless continued to use them. We now know that we cannot distinguish insanity from sanity. It is depressing to consider how that information will be used.

Not merely depressing, but frightening. How many people, one wonders, are sane but not recognized as such in our psychiatric institutions? How many have been needlessly stripped of their privileges of citizenship, from the right to vote and drive to that of handling their own accounts? How many have feigned insanity in order to avoid the criminal consequences of their behavior, and, conversely, how many would rather stand trial than live interminably in a psychiatric hospital—but are wrongly thought to be mentally ill? How many have been stigmatized by well-intentioned, but nevertheless erroneous, diagnoses? On the last point, recall again that a "type 2 error" in psychiatric diagnosis does not have the same consequences it does in medical diagnosis. A diagnosis of cancer that has been found to be in error is cause for celebration. But psychiatric diagnoses are rarely found to be in error. The label sticks, a mark of inadequacy forever.

Finally, how many patients might be "sane" outside the psychiatric hospital but seem insane in it—not because craziness resides in them, as it were, but because they are responding to a bizarre setting, one that may be unique to institutions which harbor nether people? Goffman[4] calls the process of socialization to such institutions "mortification"—an apt metaphor that includes the processes of depersonalization that have been described here. And while it is impossible to know whether the pseudopatients' responses to these processes are characteristic of all inmates—they were, after all, not real patients—it is difficult to believe that these processes of socialization to a psychiatric hospital provide useful attitudes or habits of response for living in the "real world."

SUMMARY AND CONCLUSIONS

It is clear that we cannot distinguish the sane from the insane in psychiatric hospitals. The hospital itself imposes a special environment in which the meanings of behavior can easily be misunderstood. The consequences to patients hospitalized in such an environment—the powerlessness, depersonalization, segregation, mortification, and self-labeling—seem undoubtedly counter-therapeutic.

I do not, even now, understand this problem well enough to perceive solutions. But two matters seem to have some promise. The first concerns the proliferation of community mental health facilities, of crisis intervention centers, of the human potential movement, and of behavior therapies that, for all of their own problems, tend to avoid psychiatric labels, to focus on specific problems and behaviors, and to retain the individual in a relatively non-perjorative environment. Clearly, to the extent that we refrain from sending the distressed to insane places, our impressions of them are less likely to be distorted. (The risk of distorted perceptions, it seems to me, is always present, since we are much more sensitive to an individual's behaviors and verbalizations than we are to the subtle contextual stimuli that often promote them. At issue here is a matter of magnitude. And, as I have shown, the magnitude of distortion is exceedingly high in the extreme context that is a psychiatric hospital.)

The second matter that might prove promising speaks to the need to increase the sensitivity of mental health workers and researchers to the *Catch-22* position of psychiatric patients. Simply reading materials in this area will be of help to some such workers and researchers. For others, directly experiencing the impact of psychiatric hospitalization will be of enormous use. Clearly, further research into the social psychology of such total institutions will both facilitate treatment and deepen understanding.

I and the other pseudopatients in the psychiatric setting had distinctly negative reactions. We do not pretend to describe the subjective experiences of true patients. Theirs may be different from ours, particularly with the passage of time and the necessary process of adaptation to one's environment. But we can and do speak to the relatively more objective indices of treatment within the hospital. It could be a mistake, and a very unfortunate one, to consider that what happened to us derived from malice or stupidity on the part of the staff. Quite the contrary, our overwhelming impression of them was of people who really cared, who were committed and who were uncommonly intelligent. Where they failed, as they sometimes did painfully, it would be more accurate to attribute those failures to the environment in which they, too, found themselves than to personal callousness. Their perceptions and

behavior were controlled by the situation, rather than being motivated by a malicious disposition. In a more benign environment, one that was less attached to global diagnosis, their behaviors and judgments might have been more benign and effective.

NOTES

1. P. Ash, *J. Abnorm. Soc. Psychol.* 44, 272 (1949); A. T. Beck, *Amer. J. Psychiat.* 119, 210 (1962); A. T. Boisen, *Psychiatry* 2, 233 (1938); N. Kreitman, *J. Ment. Sci.* 107, 876 (1961); N. Kreitman, P. Sainsbury, J. Morrisey, J. Towers, J. Scrivener, *ibid.*, p. 887; H. O. Schmitt and C. P. Fonda, *J. Abnorm. Soc. Psychol.* 52, 262 (1956); W. Seeman, *J. Nerv. Ment. Dis.* 118, 541 (1953). For an analysis of these artifacts and summaries of the disputes, see J. Zubin, *Annu. Rev. Psychol.* 18, 373 (1967); L. Phillips and J. G. Draguns, *ibid.* 22, 447 (1971).

2. R. Benedict, *J. Gen. Psychol.* 10, 59 (1934).

3. See in this regard H. Becker, *Outsiders: Studies in the Sociology of Deviance* (Free Press, New York, 1963); B. M. Braginsky, D. D. Braginsky, K. Ring, *Methods of Madness: The Mental Hospital as a Last Resort* (Holt, Rinehart & Winston, New York, 1969); G. M. Crocetti and P. V. Lemkau, *Amer. Sociol. Rev.* 30, 577 (1965); E. Goffman, *Behavior in Public Places* (Free Press, New York, 1964); R. D. Laing, *The Divided Self: A Study of Sanity and Madness* (Quadrangle, Chicago, 1960); D. L. Phillips, *Amer. Sociol. Rev.* 28, (1963); T. R. Sarbin, *Psychol. Today* 6, 18 (1972); E. Schur, *Amer. J. Sociol.* 75, 309 (1969); T. Szasz, *Law, Liberty and Psychiatry* (Macmillan, New York, 1963); *The Myth of Mental Illness: Foundations of a Theory of Mental Illness* (Hoeber-Harper, New York, 1963). For a critique of some of these views, see W. R. Gove, *Amer. Sociol. Rev.* 35, 873 (1970).

4. E. Goffman, *Asylums* (Doubleday, Garden City, N. Y., 1961).

5. T. J. Scheff, *Being Mentally Ill: A Sociological Theory* (Aldine, Chicago, 1966).

6. Data from a ninth pseudopatient are not incorporated in this report because, although his sanity went undetected, he falsified aspects of his personal history, including his marital status and parental relationships. His experimental behaviors therefore were not identical to those of the other pseudopatients.

7. A. Barry, *Bellevue Is a State of Mind* (Harcourt Brace Jovanovich, New York, 1971); I. Belknap, *Human Problems of a State Mental Hospital*

(McGraw-Hill, New York, 1956); W. Caudill, F. C. Redlich, H. R. Gilmore, E. B. Brody, *Amer. J. Orthopsychiat.* 22, 314 (1952); A. R. Goldman, R. H. Bohr, T. A. Steinberg, *Prof. Psychol.* 1, 427 (1970); unauthored, *Roche Report* 1 (No. 13), 8 (1971).

8. Beyond the personal difficulties that the pseudopatient is likely to experience in the hospital, there are legal and social ones that, combined, require considerable attention before entry. For example, once admitted to a psychiatric institution, it is difficult, if not impossible, to be discharged on short notice, state law to the contrary notwithstanding. I was not sensitive to these difficulties at the outset of the project, nor to the personal and situational emergencies that can arise, but later a writ of habeas corpus was prepared for each of the entering pseudopatients and an attorney was kept "on call" during every hospitalization. I am grateful to John Kaplan and Robert Bartels for legal advice and assistance in these matters.

9. However distasteful such concealment is, it was a necessary first step to examining these questions. Without concealment, there would have been no way to know how valid these experiences were; nor was there any way of knowing whether whatever detections occurred were a tribute to the diagnostic acumen of the staff or to the hospital's rumor network. Obviously, since my concerns are general ones that cut across individual hospitals and staffs, I have respected their anonymity and have eliminated clues that might lead to their dentification.

10. Interestingly, of the 12 admissions, 11 were diagnosed as schizophrenic and one, with the identical symptomatology, as manic-depressive psychosis. This diagnosis has a more favorable prognosis, and it was given by the only private hospital in our sample. On the relations between social class and psychiatric diagnosis, see A. deB. Hollingshead and F. C. Redlich, *Social Class and Mental Illness: A Community Study* (Wiley, New York, 1958).

11. It is possible, of course, that patients have quite broad latitudes in diagnosis and therefore are inclined to call many people sane, even those whose behavior is patently aberrant. However, although we have no hard data on this matter, it was our distinct impression that this was not the case. In many instances, patients not only singled us out for attention, but came to imitate our behaviors and styles.

12. J. Cumming and E. Cumming, *Community Ment. Health* 1, 135 (1965); A. Farina and K. Ring, *J. Abnorm. Psychol.* 70, 47 (1965); H. E. Freeman and O. G. Simmons, *The Mental Patient Comes Home* (Wiley, New York, 1963); W. J. Johannsen, *Ment. Hygiene* 53, 218 (1969); A. S. Linsky, *Soc. Psychiat.* 5, 166 (1970).

13. S. E. Asch, *J. Abnorm. Soc. Psychol.* 41, 258 (1946); *Social Psychology* (Prentice Hall, New York, 1952).

14. See also I. N. Mensh and J. Wishner, *J. Personality* 16, 188 (1947); J. Wishner, *Psychol. Rev.* 67, 96 (1960); J. S. Bruner and R. Tagiuri, in *Handbook of Social Psychology,* G. Lindzey, Ed. (Addison-Wesley, Cambridge, Mass., 1954), vol. 2, pp. 634–654; J. S. Bruner, D. Shapiro, R. Tagiuri, in *Person Perception and Interpersonal Behavior,* R. Tagiuri and L. Petrullo, Eds. (Stanford Univ. Press, Stanford, Calif., 1958), pp. 277–288.

15. For an example of a similar self-fulfilling prophecy, in this instance dealing with the "central" trait of intelligence, see R. Rosenthal and L. Jacobson, *Pygmalion in the Classroom* (Holt, Rinehart & Winston, New York, 1968).

16. E. Zigler and L. Phillips, *J. Abnorm. Soc. Psychol.* 63, 69 (1961). See also R. K. Freudenberg and J. P. Robertson, *A.M.A. Arch. Neurol. Psychiatr.* 76, 14 (1956).

17. W. Mischel, *Personality and Assessment* (Wiley, New York, 1968).

18. The most recent and unfortunate instance of this tenet is that of Senator Thomas Eagleton.

19. T. R. Sarbin and J. C. Mancuso, *J. Clin. Consult. Psychol.* 35, 159 (1970); T. R. Sarbin, *ibid.* 31, 447 (1967); J. C. Nunnally, Jr., *Popular conceptions of Mental Health* (Holt, Rinehart & Winston, New York, 1961).

20. A. H. Stanton and M. S. Schwartz, *The Mental Hospital: A Study of Institutional Participation in Psychiatric Illness and Treatment* (Basic, New York, 1954).

21. D. B. Wexler and S. E. Scoville, *Ariz. Law Rev.* 13, 1 (1971).

*I thank W. Mischel, E. Orne, and M. S. Rosenhan for comments on an earlier draft of this manuscript.

THE MORAL CAREER OF THE MENTAL PATIENT*

Erving Goffman

Traditionally the term *career* has been reserved for those who expect to enjoy the rises laid out within a respectable profession. The term is coming to be used, however, in a broadened sense to refer to any social strand of any person's course through life. The perspective of natural history is taken: Unique outcomes are neglected in favor of such changes over time as are basic and common to the members of a social category, although occurring independently to each of them. Such a career is not a thing that can be brilliant or disappointing; it can no more be a success than a failure. In this light, I want to consider the mental patient, drawing mainly upon data collected during a year's participant observation of patient social life in a public mental hospital,[1] wherein an attempt was made to take the patient's point of view.

One value of the concept of career is its two-sidedness. One side is linked to internal matters held dearly and closely, such as image of self and felt identity; the other side concerns official position, jural relations, and style of life, and is part of a publicly accessible institutional complex. The concept of career, then, allows one to move back and forth between the personal and the public, between the self and its significant society, without having overly to rely for data upon what the person says he thinks he imagines himself to be.

This paper, then, is an exercise in the institutional approach to the study of self. The main concern will be with the *moral* aspects of career—that is, the regular sequence of changes that career entails in the person's self and in his framework of imagery for judging himself and others.[2]

The category "mental patient" itself will be understood in one strictly sociological sense. In this perspective, the psychiatric view of a person becomes significant only in so far as this view itself alters his social fate—an alteration which seems to become fundamental in our society when, and only when, the person is put through the process of hospitalization.[3] I therefore exclude certain neighboring categories: the undiscovered candidates who would be judged "sick" by psychiatric standards but who never come to be viewed as such by themselves or others, although they may cause everyone a great deal of trouble;[4] the office patient whom a psychiatrist feels he can handle with drugs or shock on the outside; the mental client who engages in psychotherapeutic relationships. And I include anyone, however robust in temperament, who somehow gets caught up in the heavy machinery of mental hospital servicing. In this way the effects of being treated as a mental patient can be kept quite distinct from the effects upon a person's life of traits a clinician would view as psychopathological.[5] Persons who become mental hospital patients vary widely in the kind and degree of illness that a psychiatrist would impute to them, and in the attributes by which laymen would describe them. But once started on the way, they are confronted by some importantly similar circumstances and respond to these in some importantly similar ways. Since these similarities do not come from mental illness, they would seem to occur in spite of it. It is thus a tribute to the power of social forces that the uniform status of mental patient cannot only assure an aggregate of persons a common fate and eventually, because of this, a common character, but that this social reworking can be done upon what is perhaps the most obstinate diversity of human materials that can be brought together by society. Here there lacks only the frequent forming of a protective group-life by ex-patients to illustrate in full the classic cycle of response by which deviant subgroupings are psychodynamically formed in society.

*From *Psychiatry, 22* (1959), pp. 123–142. Used by permission of William Alanson White Psychiatric Foundation, Inc., © 1959. Copyright renewed 1987.

This general sociological perspective is heavily reinforced by one key finding of sociologically oriented students in mental hospital research. As has been repeatedly shown in the study of nonliterate societies, the awesomeness, distastefulness, and barbarity of a foreign culture can decrease in the degree that the student becomes familiar with the point of view to life that is taken by his subjects. Similarly, the student of mental hospitals can discover that the craziness or "sick behavior" claimed for the mental patient is by and large a product of the claimant's social distance from the situation that the patient is in, and is not primarily a product of mental illness. Whatever the refinements of the various patients' psychiatric diagnoses, and whatever the special ways in which social life on the "inside" is unique, the researcher can find that he is participating in a community not significantly different from any other he has studied.[6] Of course, while restricting himself to the off-ward grounds community of paroled patients, he may feel, as some patients do, that life in the locked wards is bizarre; and while on a locked admissions or convalescent ward, he may feel that chronic "back" wards are socially crazy places. But he need only move his sphere of sympathetic participation to the "worst" ward in the hospital, and this too can come into social focus as a place with a livable and continuously meaningful social world. This in no way denies that he will find a minority in any ward or patient group that continues to seem quite beyond the capacity to follow rules of social organization, or that the orderly fulfillment of normative expectations in patient society is partly made possible by strategic measures that have somehow come to be institutionalized in mental hospitals.

The career of the mental patient falls popularly and naturalistically into three main phases: the period prior to entering the hospital, which I shall call the *prepatient phase;* the period in the hospital, the *inpatient phase;* the period after discharge from the hospital, should this occur, namely, the *ex-patient phase.*[7] This paper will deal only with the first two phases.

THE PREPATIENT PHASE

A relatively small group of prepatients come into the mental hospital willingly, because of their own idea of what will be good for them, or because of wholehearted agreement with the relevant members of their family. Presumably these recruits have found themselves acting in a way which is evidence to them that they are losing their minds or losing control of themselves. This view of oneself would seem to be one of the most pervasively threatening things that can happen to the self in our society, especially since it is likely to occur at a time when the person is in any case sufficiently troubled to exhibit the kind of symptom which he himself can see. As Sullivan described it,

What we discover in the self-system of a person undergoing schizophrenic changes or schizophrenic processes, is then, in its simplest form, an extremely fear-marked puzzlement, consisting of the use of rather generalized and anything but exquisitely refined referential processes in an attempt to cope with what is essentially a failure at being human—a failure at being anything that one could respect as worth being.[8]

Coupled with the person's disintegrative re-evaluation of himself will be the new, almost equally pervasive circumstance of attempting to conceal from others what he takes to be the new fundamental facts about himself, and attempting to discover whether others too have discovered them.[9] Here I want to stress that perception of losing one's mind is based on culturally derived and socially engrained stereotypes as to the significance of symptoms such as hearing voices, losing temporal and spatial orientation, and sensing that one is being followed, and that many of the most spectacular and convincing of these symptoms in some instances psychiatrically signify merely a temporary emotional upset in a stressful situation, however terrifying to the person at the time. Similarly, the anxiety consequent upon this perception of oneself, and the strategies devised to reduce this anxiety, are not a product of abnormal psychology, but would be exhibited by any person socialized into our culture who came to conceive of himself as someone losing his mind. Interestingly, subcultures in American society apparently differ in the amount of ready imagery and encouragement they supply for such self views, leading to differential rates of *self-referral;* the capacity to take this disintegrative view of oneself without psychiatric prompting seems to be one of the questionable cultural privileges of the upper classes.[10]

For the person who has come to see himself—with whatever justification—as mentally unbalanced, entrance to the mental hospital can sometimes bring relief, perhaps in part because of the sudden transformation in the structure of his basic social situations; instead of being to himself a questionable person trying to maintain a role as a full one, he can become an officially questioned person known to himself to be not so questionable as that. In other cases, hospitalization can make matters worse for the willing patient, confirming by the objective situation what has theretofore been a matter of the private experience of self.

Once the willing prepatient enters the hospital, he may go through the same routine of experiences as do those who enter unwillingly. In any case, it is the latter that I mainly want to consider, since in America at present these are by far the more numerous kind.[11] Their approach to the institution takes one of three classic forms: They come because they have been implored by their family or threatened with the abrogation of family ties unless they go "willingly"; they come by force under police escort; they come under misapprehension purposely induced by others, this last restricted mainly to youthful prepatients.

The prepatient's career may be seen in terms of an extrusory model; he starts out with relationships and rights, and ends up, at the beginning of his hospital stay, with hardly any of either. The moral aspects of this career, then, typically begin with the experience of abandonment, disloyalty, and embitterment. This is the case even though to others it may be obvious that he was in need of treatment, and even though in the hospital he may soon come to agree.

The case histories of most mental patients document offense against some arrangement for face-to-face living—a domestic establishment, a workplace, a semipublic organization such as a church or store, a public region such as a street or park. Often there is also a record of some *complainant,* some figure who takes that action against the offender which eventually leads to his hospitalization. This may not be the person who makes the first move, but it is the person who makes what turns out to be the first effective move. Here is the *social* beginning of the patient's career, regardless of where one might locate the psychological beginning of his mental illness.

The kinds of offenses which lead to hospitalization are felt to differ in nature from those which lead to other extrusory consequences—to imprisonment, divorce, loss of job, disownment, regional exile, noninstitutional psychiatric treatment, and so forth. But little seems known about these differentiating factors; and when one studies actual commitments, alternate outcomes frequently appear to have been possible. It seems true, moreover, that for every offense that leads to an effective complaint, there are many psychiatrically similar ones that never do. No action is taken; or action is taken which leads to other extrusory outcomes; or ineffective action is taken, leading to the mere pacifying or putting off of the person who complains. Thus, as Clausen and Yarrow have nicely shown, even offenders who are eventually hospitalized are likely to have had a long series of ineffective actions taken against them.[12]

Separating those offenses which could have been used as grounds for hospitalizing the offender from those that are so used, one finds a vast number of what students of occupation call career contingencies.[13] Some of these contingencies in the mental patient's career have been suggested, if not explored, such as socio-economic status, visibility of the offense, proximity to a mental hospital, amount of treatment facilities available, community regard for the type of treatment given in available hospitals, and so on.[14] For information about other contingencies one must rely on atrocity tales: A psychotic man is tolerated by his wife until she finds herself a boyfriend, or by his adult children until they move from a house to an apartment; an alcoholic is sent to a mental hospital because the jail is full, and a drug addict because he declines to avail himself of psychiatric treatment on the outside; a rebellious adolescent daughter can no longer be managed at home because she now threatens to have an open affair with an unsuitable companion; and so on. Correspondingly there is an equally important set of contingencies causing the person to bypass this fate. And should the person enter the hospital, still another set of contingencies will help determine when he is to obtain a discharge—such as the desire of his family for his return, the availability of a "manageable" job, and so on. The society's official view is that inmates of mental hospitals are there primarily because they are suffering from mental illness. However, in the degree that the "mentally ill" outside hospitals numerically approach or surpass those inside hospitals, one could say that mental patients *distinctively* suffer not from mental illness, but from contingencies.

Career contingencies occur in conjunction with a second feature of the prepatient's career— the *circuit of agents*—and agencies—that participate fatefully in his passage from civilian to patient status.[15] Here is an instance of that increasingly important class of social system whose elements are agents and agencies, which are brought into systemic connection through having to take up and send on the same persons. Some of these agent-roles will be cited now, with the understanding that in any concrete circuit a role may be filled more than once, and a single person may fill more than one of them.

First is the *next-of-relation*—the person whom the prepatient sees as the most available of those upon whom he should be able to most depend in times of trouble; in this instance the last to doubt his sanity and the first to have done everything to save him from the fate which, it transpires, he has been approaching. The patient's next-of-relation is usually his next of kin; the special term is introduced because he need not be. Second is the *complainant,* the person who retrospectively appears to have started the person on his way to the hospital. Third are the *mediators*—the sequence of agents and agencies to which the prepatient is referred and through which he is relayed and processed on his way to the hospital. Here are included police, clergy, general medical practitioners, office psychiatrists, personnel in public clinics, lawyers, social service workers, school teachers, and so on. One of these agents will have the legal mandate to sanction commitment and will exercise it, and so those agents who precede him in the process will be involved in something whose outcome is not yet settled. When the me-

diators retire from the scene, the prepatient has become an inpatient, and the significant agent has become the hospital administrator.

While the complainant usually takes action in a lay capacity as a citizen, an employer, a neighbor, or a kinsman, mediators tend to be specialists and differ from those they serve in significant ways. They have experience in handling trouble, and some professional distance from what they handle. Except in the case of policemen, and perhaps some clergy, they tend to be more psychiatrically oriented than the lay public, and will see the need for treatment at times when the public does not.[16]

An interesting feature of these roles is the functional effects of their interdigitation. For example, the feelings of the patient will be influenced by whether or not the person who fills the role of complainant also has the role of next-of-relation—an embarassing combination more prevalent, apparently, in the higher classes than in the lower.[17] Some of these emergent effects will be considered now.[18]

In the prepatient's progress from home to the hospital he may participate as a third person in what he may come to experience as a kind of *alienative coalition.* His next-of-relation presses him into coming to "talk things over" with a medical practitioner, an office psychiatrist, or some other counselor. Disinclination on his part may be met by threatening him with desertion, disownment, or other legal action, or by stressing the joint and explorative nature of the interview. But typically the next-of-relation will have set the interview up, in the sense of selecting the professional, arranging for time, telling the professional something about the case, and so on. This move effectively tends to establish the next-of-relation as the responsible person to whom pertinent findings can be divulged, while effectively establishing the other as the patient. The prepatient often goes to the interview with the understanding that he is going as an equal of someone who is so bound together with him that a third person could not come between them in fundamental matters; this, after all, is one way in which close relationships are defined in our society. Upon arrival at the office the prepatient suddenly finds that he and his next-of-relation have not been accorded the same roles, and apparently that a prior understanding between the professional and the next-of-relation has been put in operation against him. In the extreme but common case the professional first sees the prepatient alone, in the role of examiner and diagnostician, and then sees the next-of-relation alone, in the role of advisor, while carefully avoiding talking things over seriously with them both together.[19] And even in those nonconsultative cases where public officials must forcibly extract a person from a family that wants to tolerate him, the next-of-relation is likely to be induced to "go along" with the official action, so that even here the prepatient may feel that an alienative coalition has been formed against him.

The moral experience of being third man in such a coalition is likely to embitter the prepatient, especially since his troubles have already probably led to some estrangement from his next-of-relation. After he enters the hospital, continued visits by his next-of-relation can give the patient the "insight" that his own best interests were being served. But the initial visits may temporarily strengthen his feeling of abandonment; he is likely to beg his visitor to get him out or at least to get him more privileges and to sympathize with the monstrousness of his plight—to which the visitor ordinarily can respond only by trying to maintain a hopeful note, by not "hearing" the requests, or by assuring the patient that the medical authorities know about these things and are doing what is medically best. The visitor then nonchalantly goes back into a world that the patient has learned is incredibly thick with freedom and privileges, causing the patient to feel that his next-of-relation is merely adding a pious gloss to a clear case of traitorous desertion.

The depth to which the patient may feel betrayed by his next-of-relation seems to be increased by the fact that another witnesses his betrayal—a factor which is apparently significant in many three-party situations. An offended person may well act forbearantly and accommodatively toward an offender when the two are alone, choosing peace ahead of justice. The presence of a witness, however, seems to add something to the implications of the offense. For then it is beyond the power of the offended and of-

fender to forget about, erase, or suppress what has happened; the offense has become a public social fact.[20] When the witness is a mental health commission, as is sometimes the case, the witnessed betrayal can verge on a "degradation ceremony."[21] In such circumstances, the offended patient may feel that some kind of extensive reparative action is required before witnesses, if his honor and social weight are to be restored.

Two other aspects of sensed betrayal should be mentioned. First, those who suggest the possibility of another's entering a mental hospital are not likely to provide a realistic picture of how in fact it may strike him when he arrives. Often he is told that he will get required medical treatment and a rest, and may well be out in a few months or so. In some cases they may thus be concealing what they know, but I think, in general, they will be telling what they see as the truth. For here there is a quite relevant difference between patients and mediating professionals; mediators, more so than the public at large, may conceive of mental hospitals as short-term medical establishments where required rest and attention can be voluntarily obtained, and not as places of coerced exile. When the prepatient finally arrives he is likely to learn quite quickly, quite differently. He then finds that the information given him about life in the hospital has had the effect of his having put up less resistance to entering than he now sees he would have put up had he known the facts. Whatever the intentions of those who participated in his transition from person to patient, he may sense they have in effect "conned" him into his present predicament.

I am suggesting that the prepatient starts out with at least a portion of the rights, liberties, and satisfactions of the civilian and ends up on a psychiatric ward stripped of almost everything. The question here is *how* this stripping is managed. This is the second aspect of betrayal I want to consider.

As the prepatient may see it, the circuit of significant figures can function as a kind of *betrayal funnel*. Passage from person to patient may be effected through a series of linked stages, each managed by a different agent. While each stage tends to bring a sharp decrease in adult free status, each agent may try to maintain the fiction that no further decrease will occur. He may even manage to turn the prepatient over to the next agent while sustaining this note. Further, through words, cues, and gestures, the prepatient is implicitly asked by the current agent to join with him in sustaining a running line of polite small talk that tactfully avoids the administrative facts of the situation, becoming, with each stage, progressively more at odds with these facts. The spouse would rather not have to cry to get the prepatient to visit a psychiatrist; psychiatrists would rather not have a scene when the prepatient learns that he and his spouse are being seen separately and in different ways; the police infrequently bring a prepatient to the hospital in a straitjacket, finding it much easier all around to give him a cigarette, some kindly words, and freedom to relax in the back seat of the patrol car; and finally, the admitting psychiatrist finds he can do his work better in the relative quiet and luxury of the "admission suite" where, as an incidental consequence, the notion can survive that a mental hospital is indeed a comforting place. If the prepatient heeds all of these implied requests and is reasonably decent about the whole thing, he can travel the whole circuit from home to hospital without forcing anyone to look directly at what is happening or to deal with the raw emotion that his situation might well cause him to express. His showing consideration for those who are moving him toward the hospital allows them to show consideration for him, with the joint result that these interactions can be sustained with some of the protective harmony characteristic of ordinary face-to-face dealings. But should the new patient cast his mind back over the sequence of steps leading to hospitalization, he may feel that everyone's *current* comfort was being busily sustained while his long-range welfare was being undermined. This realization may constitute a moral experience that further separates him for the time from the people on the outside.[22]

I would now like to look at the circuit of career agents from the point of view of the agents themselves. Mediators in the person's transition from civil to patient status—as well as his keepers, once he is in the hospital—have an interest in establishing a responsible next-of-relation as the patient's deputy or *guardian;* should there be no

obvious candidate for the role, someone may be sought out and pressed into it. Thus while a person is gradually being transformed into a patient, a next-of-relation is gradually being transformed into a guardian. With a guardian on the scene, the whole transition process can be kept tidy. He is likely to be familiar with the prepatient's civil involvements and business, and can tie up loose ends that might otherwise be left to entangle the hospital. Some of the prepatient's abrogated civil rights can be transferred to him, thus helping to sustain the legal fiction that while the prepatient does not actually have his rights he somehow actually has not lost them.

Inpatients commonly sense, at least for a time, that hospitalization is a massive unjust deprivation, and sometimes succeed in convincing a few persons on the outside that this is the case. It often turns out to be useful, then, for those identified with inflicting these deprivations, however justifiably, to be able to point to the cooperation and agreement of someone whose relationship to the patient places him above suspicion, firmly defining him as the person most likely to have the patient's personal interest at heart. If the guardian is satisfied with what is happening to the new inpatient, the world ought to be.[23]

Now it would seem that the greater the legitimate personal stake one party has in another, the better he can take the role of guardian to the other. But the structural arrangements in society which lead to the acknowledged merging of two persons' interests lead to additional consequences. For the person to whom the patient turns for help—for protection against such threats as involuntary commitment—is just the person to whom the mediators and hospital administrators logically turn for authorization. It is understandable, then, that some patients will come to sense, at least for a time, that the closeness of a relationship tells nothing of its trustworthiness.

There are still other functional effects emerging from this complement of roles. If and when the next-of-relation appeals to mediators for help in the trouble he is having with the prepatient, hospitalization may not, in fact, be in his mind. He may not even perceive the prepatient as mentally sick, or, if he does, he may not consistently hold to this view.[24] It is the circuit of mediators, with their greater psychiatric sophistication and their belief in the medical character of mental hospitals, that will often define the situation for the next-of-relation, assuring him that hospitalization is a possible solution and a good one, that it involves no betrayal, but is rather a medical action taken in the best interests of the prepatient. Here the next-of-relation may learn that doing his duty to the prepatient may cause the prepatient to distrust and even hate him for the time. But the fact that this course of action may have had to be pointed out and prescribed by professionals, and be defined by them as a moral duty, relieves the next-of-relation of some of the guilt he may feel.[25] It is a poignant fact that an adult son or daughter may be pressed into the role of mediator, so that the hostility that might otherwise be directed against the spouse is passed on to the child.[26]

Once the prepatient is in the hospital, the same guilt-carrying function may become a significant part of the staff's job in regard to the next-of-relation.[27] These reasons for feeling that he himself has not betrayed the patient, even though the patient may then think so, can later provide the next-of-relation with a defensible line to take when visiting the patient in the hospital and a basis for hoping that the relationship can be reestablished after its hospital moratorium. And of course this position, when sensed by the patient, can provide him with excuses for the next-of-relation, when and if he comes to look for them.[28]

Thus while the next-of-relation can perform important functions for the mediators and hospital administrators, they in turn can perform important functions for him. One finds, then, an emergent unintended exchange or reciprocation of functions, these functions themselves being often unintended.

The final point I want to consider about the prepatient's moral career is its peculiarly *retroactive* character. Until a person actually arrives at the hospital there usually seems no way of knowing for sure that he is destined to do so, given the determinative role of career contingencies. And until the point of hospitalization is reached, he or others may not conceive of him as a person who is becoming a mental patient. However, since he will be held against his will in the hospital, his next-of-relation and the hospital staff will be in great need of a rationale for the hardships they are sponsoring. The medical elements of the staff will also need evidence that they are still in the trade they were trained for. These problems are eased, no doubt unintentionally, by the case-history construction that is placed on the patient's past life, this having the effect of demonstrating that all along he had been becoming sick, that he finally became very sick, and that if he had not been hospitalized much worse things would have happened to him—all of which, of course, may be true. Incidentally, if the patient wants to make sense out of his stay in the hospital, and, as already suggested, keep alive the possibility of once again conceiving of his next-of-relation as a decent, well-meaning person, then he too will have reason to believe some of this psychiatric work-up of his past.

Here is a very ticklish point for the sociology of careers. An important aspect of every career is the view the person constructs when he looks backward over his progress; in a sense, however, the whole of the prepatient career derives from this reconstruction. The fact of having had a prepatient career, starting with an effective complaint, becomes an important part of the mental patient's orientation, but this part can begin to be played only after hospitalization proves that what he had been having, but no longer has, is a career as a prepatient.

THE INPATIENT PHASE

The last step in the prepatient's career can involve his realization—justified or not—that he has been deserted by society and turned out of relationships by those closest to him. Interestingly enough, the patient, especially a first admission, may manage to keep himself from coming to the end of this trail, even though in fact he is now in a locked mental hospital ward. On entering the hospital, he may very strongly feel the desire not to be known to anyone as a person who could possibly be reduced to these present circumstances, or as a person who conducted himself in the way he did prior to commitment.

Consequently, he may avoid talking to anyone, may stay by himself when possible, and may even be "out of contact" or "manic" so as to avoid ratifying any interaction that presses a politely reciprocal role upon him and opens him up to what he has become in the eyes of others. When the next-of-relation makes an effort to visit, he may be rejected by mutism, or by the patient's refusal to enter the visiting room, these strategies sometimes suggesting that the patient still clings to a remnant of relatedness to those who made up his past, and is protecting this remnant from the final destructiveness of dealing with the new people that they have become.[29]

Usually the patient comes to give up his taxing effort at anonymity, at not-hereness, and begins to present himself for conventional social interaction to the hospital community. Thereafter he withdraws only in special ways—by always using his nickname, by signing his contribution to the patient weekly with his initial only, or by using the innocuous "cover" address tactfully provided by some hospitals; or he withdraws only at special times, when, say, a flock of nursing students makes a passing tour of the ward, or when, paroled to the hospital grounds, he suddenly sees he is about to cross the path of a civilian he happens to know from home. Sometimes this making of oneself available is called "settling down" by the attendants. It marks a new stand openly taken and supported by the patient, and resembles the "coming out" process that occurs in other groupings.[30]

Once the prepatient begins to settle down, the main outlines of his fate tend to follow those of a whole class of segregated establishments—jails, concentration camps, monasteries, work camps, and so on—in which the inmate spends the whole round of life on the grounds, and marches through his regimented day in the immediate company of a group of persons of his own institutional status.[31]

Like the neophyte in many of these "total institutions," the new inpatient finds himself cleanly stripped of many of his accustomed affirmations, satisfactions, and defenses, and is subjected to a rather full set of mortifying experiences: restriction of free movement; communal living; diffuse authority of a whole echelon of people; and so on. Here one begins to learn about the limited extent to which a conception of oneself can be sustained when the usual setting of supports for it are suddenly removed.

While undergoing these humbling moral experiences, the inpatient learns to orient himself in terms of the "ward system."[32] In public mental hospitals this usually consists of a series of graded living arrangements built around wards, administrative units called services, and parole statuses. The "worst" level involves often nothing but wooden benches to sit on, some quite indifferent food, and a small piece of room to sleep in. The "best" level may involve a room of one's own, ground and town privileges, contacts with staff that are relatively undamaging, and what is seen as good food and ample recreational facilities. For disobeying the pervasive house rules, the inmate will receive stringent punishments expressed in terms of loss of privileges; for obedience he will eventually be allowed to reacquire some of the minor satisfactions he took for granted on the outside.

The institutionalization of these radically different levels of living throws light on the implications for self of social settings. And this in turn affirms that the self arises not merely out of its possessor's interactions with significant others, but also out of the arrangements that are evolved in an organization for its members.

There are some settings which the person easily discounts as an expression or extension of him. When a tourist goes slumming, he may take pleasure in the situation not because it is a reflection of him but because it so assuredly is not. There are other settings, such as living rooms, which the person manages on his own and employs to influence in a favorable direction other persons' views of him. And there are still other settings, such as a workplace, which express the employee's occupational status, but over which he has no final control, this being exerted, however tactfully, by his employer. Mental hospitals provide an extreme instance of this latter possibility. And this is due not merely to their uniquely degraded living levels, but also to the unique way in which significance for self is made explicit to the patient, piercingly, persistently, and thoroughly. Once lodged on a given ward, the patient is firmly instructed that the restrictions and deprivations he encounters are not due to such things as tradition or economy—and hence dissociable from self—but are intentional parts of his treatment, part of his need at the time, and therefore an expression of the state that his self has fallen to. Having every reason to initiate requests for better conditions, he is told that when the staff feels he is "able to manage" or will be "comfortable with" a higher ward level, then appropriate action will be taken. In short, assignment to a given ward is presented not as a reward or punishment, but as an expression of his general level of social functioning, his status as a person. Given the fact that the worst ward levels provide a round of life that inpatients with organic brain damage can easily manage, and that these quite limited human beings are present to prove it, one can appreciate some of the mirroring effects of the hospital.[33]

The ward system, then, is an extreme instance of how the physical facts of an establishment can be explicitly employed to frame the conception a person takes of himself. In addition, the official psychiatric mandate of mental hospitals gives rise to even more direct, even more blatant, attacks upon the inmate's view of himself. The more "medical" and the more progressive a mental hospital is—the more it attempts to be therapeutic and not merely custodial—the more he may be confronted by high-ranking staff arguing that his past has been a failure, that the cause of this has been within himself, that his attitude to life is wrong, and that if he wants to be a person he will have to change his way of dealing with people and his conceptions of himself. Often the moral value of these verbal assaults will be brought home to him by requiring him to practice taking this psychiatric view of himself in arranged confessional periods, whether in private sessions or group psychotherapy.

Now a general point may be made about the moral career of inpatients which has bearing on many moral careers. Given the stage that any person has reached in a career, one typically finds that he constructs an image of his life course—past, present, and future—which selects, abstracts, and distorts in such a way as to provide him with a view of himself that he can usefully

expound in current situations. Quite generally, the person's line concerning self defensively brings him into appropriate alignment with the basic values of his society, and so may be called an *apologia*. If the person can manage to present a view of his current situation which shows the operation of favorable personal qualities in the past and a favorable destiny awaiting him, it may be called a *success story*. If the facts of a person's past and present are extremely dismal, then about the best he can do is to show that he is not responsible for what has become of him, and the term *sad tale* is appropriate. Interestingly enough, the more the person's past forces him out of apparent alignment with central moral values, the more often he seems compelled to tell his sad tale in any company in which he finds himself. Perhaps he partly responds to the need he feels in others of not having their sense of proper life courses affronted. In any case, it is among convicts, "winos," and prostitutes that one seems to obtain sad tales the most readily.[34] It is the vicissitudes of the mental patient's sad tale that I want to consider now.

In the mental hospital, the setting and the house rules press home to the patient that he is, after all, a mental case who has suffered some kind of social collapse on the outside, having failed in some overall way, and that here he is of little social weight, being hardly capable of acting like a full-fledged person at all. These humiliations are likely to be most keenly felt by middle-class patients, since their previous condition of life little immunizes them against such affronts; but all patients feel some downgrading. Just as any normal member of his outside subculture would do, the patient often responds to this situation by attempting to assert a sad tale proving that he is not "sick," that the "little trouble" he did get into was really somebody else's fault, that his past life course had some honor and rectitude, and that the hospital is therefore unjust in forcing the status of mental patient upon him. This self-respecting tendency is heavily institutionalized within the patient society where opening social contacts typically involve the participants' volunteering information about their current ward location and length of stay so far, but not the reasons for their stay—such interaction being conducted in the manner of small talk on the outside.[35] With greater familiarity, each patient usually volunteers relatively acceptable reasons for his hospitalization, at the same time accepting without open immediate question the lines offered by other patients. Such stories as the following are given and overtly accepted.

I was going to night school to get a M.A. degree, and holding down a job in addition, and the load got too much for me.

The others here are sick mentally but I'm suffering from a bad nervous system and that is what is giving me these phobias.

I got here by mistake because of a diabetes diagnosis, and I'll leave in a couple of days. [The patient had been in seven weeks.]

I failed as a child, and later with my wife I reached out for dependency.

My trouble is that I can't work. That's what I'm in for. I had two jobs with a good home and all the money I wanted.[36]

The patient sometimes reinforces these stories by an optimistic definition of his occupational status: A man who managed to obtain an audition as a radio announcer styles himself a radio announcer; another who worked for some months as a copy boy and was then given a job as a reporter on a large trade journal, but fired after three weeks, defines himself as a reporter.

A whole social role in the patient community may be constructed on the basis of these reciprocally sustained fictions. For these face-to-face niceties tend to be qualified by behind-the-back gossip that comes only a degree closer to the "objective" facts. Here, of course, one can see a classic social function of informal networks of equals: They serve as one another's audience for self-supporting tales—tales that are somewhat more solid than pure fantasy and somewhat thinner than the facts.

But the patient's *apologia* is called forth in a unique setting, for few settings could be so destructive of self-stories except, of course, those stories already constructed along psychiatric lines. And this destructiveness rests on more than the official sheet of paper which attests that the patient is of unsound mind, a danger to himself and others—an attestation, incidentally, which seems to cut deeply into the patient's pride, and into the possibility of his having any.

Certainly the degrading conditions of the hospital setting belie many of the self-stories that are presented by patients; and the very fact of being in the mental hospital is evidence against these tales. And of course, there is not always sufficient patient solidarity to prevent patient discrediting patient, just as there is not always a sufficient number of "professionalized" attendants to prevent attendant discrediting patient. As one patient informant repeatedly suggested to a fellow patient:

If you're so smart, how come you got your ass in here?

The mental hospital setting, however, is more treacherous still. Staff has much to gain through discreditings of the patient's story—whatever the felt reason for such discreditings. If the custodial faction in the hospital is to succeed in managing his daily round without complaint or trouble from him, then it will prove useful to be able to point out to him that the claims about himself upon which he rationalizes his demands are false, that he is not what he is claiming to be, and that in fact he is a failure as a person. If the psychiatric faction is to impress upon him its views about his personal make-up, then they must be able to show in detail how their version of his past and their version of his character hold up much better than his own.[37] If both the custodial and psychiatric factions are to get him to cooperate in the various psychiatric treatments, then it will prove useful to disabuse him of *his* view of their purposes, and cause him to appreciate that they know what they are doing, and are doing what is best for him. In brief, the difficulties caused by a patient are closely tied to his version of what has been happening to him, and if cooperation is to be secured, it helps if this version is discredited. The patient must "insightfully" come to take, or affect to take, the hospital's view of himself.

NOTES

1. The study was conducted during 1955–56 under the auspices of the Laboratory of Socio-environmental

Studies of the National Institute of Mental Health. I am grateful to the Laboratory Chief, John A. Clausen, and to Dr. Winfred Overholser, Superintendent, and the late Dr. Jay Hoffman, then First Assistant Physician of Saint Elizabeth's Hospital, Washington, D.C., for the ideal cooperation they freely provided. A preliminary report is contained in Goffman, "Interpersonal Persuasion," pp. 117–193; in *Group Processes: Transactions of the Third Conference,* edited by Bertram Schaffner: New York, Josiah Macy, Jr. Foundation, 1957. A shorter version of this paper was presented at the Annual Meeting of the American Sociological Society, Washington, D.C., August 1957.

2. Material on moral career can be found in early social anthropological work on ceremonies of status transition, and in classic social psychological descriptions of those spectacular changes in one's view of self that can accompany participation in social movements and sects. Recently new kinds of relevant data have been suggested by psychiatric interest in the problem of "identity" and sociological studies of work careers and "adult socialization."

3. This point has recently been made by Elaine and John Cumming, *Closed Ranks;* Cambridge, Commonwealth Fund, Harvard Univ. Press, 1957; pp. 101–102. "Clinical experience supports the impression that many people define mental illness as 'That condition for which a person is treated in a mental hospital.' . . . Mental illness, it seems, is a condition which afflicts people who must go to a mental institution, but until they do almost anything they do is normal." Leila Deasy has pointed out to me the correspondence here with the situation in white collar crime. Of those who are detected in this activity, only the ones who do not manage to avoid going to prison find themselves accorded the social role of the criminal.

4. Case records in mental hospitals are just now coming to be exploited to show the incredible amount of trouble a person may cause for himself and others before anyone begins to think about him psychiatrically, let alone take psychiatric action against him. See John A. Clausen and Marian Radke Yarrow, "Paths to the Mental Hospital," *J. Social Issues* (1955) 11:25–32; August B. Hollingshead and Fredrick C. Redlich, *Social Class and Mental Illness;* New York, Wiley, 1958: pp. 173–174.

5. An illustration of how this perspective may be taken to all forms of deviancy may be found in Edwin Lemert, *Social Pathology;* New York, McGraw-Hill, 1951; see especially pp. 74–76. A specific application to mental defectives may be found in Stewart E. Perry, "Some Theoretic Problems of Mental Deficiency and Their Action Implications," *Psychiatry* (1954) 17: 45–73; see especially p. 68.

6. Conscientious objectors who voluntarily went to jail sometimes arrived at the same conclusion regarding criminal inmates. See, for example, Alfred Hassler, *Diary of a Self-made Convict;* Chicago, Regnery, 1954; p. 74.

7. This simple picture is complicated by the somewhat special experience of roughly a third of ex-patients—namely, readmission to the hospital, this being the recidivist or "repatient" phase.

8. Harry Stack Sullivan, *Clinical Studies in Psychiatry;* edited by Helen Swick Perry, Mary Ladd Gawel, and Martha Gibbon; New York, Norton, 1956; pp. 184–185.

9. This moral experience can be contrasted with that of a person learning to become a marihuana addict, whose discovery that he can be "high" and still "op" effectively without being detected apparently leads to a new level of use. See Howard S. Becker, "Marihuana Use and Social Control." *Social Problems* (1955) 3:35–44; see especially pp. 40–41.

10. See footnote 4: Hollingshead and Redlich, p. 187, Table 6, where relative frequency is given of self-referral by social class grouping.

11. The distinction employed here between willing and unwilling patients cuts across the legal one, of voluntary and committed, since some persons who are glad to come to the mental hospital may be legally committed, and of those who come only because of strong familial pressure, some may sign themselves in as voluntary patients.

12. Clausen and Yarrow; see footnote 4.

13. An explicit application of this notion to the field of mental health may be found in Edwin M. Lemert, "Legal Commitment and Social Control," *Sociology and Social Research* (1946) 30:370–378.

14. For example, Jerome K. Meyers and Leslie Schaffer, "Social Stratification and Psychiatric Practice: A Study of an Outpatient Clinic," *Amer. Sociological Rev.* (1954) 19:307–310. Lemert, see footnote 5; pp. 402–403. *Patients in Mental Institutions,* 1941; Washington, D.C., Department of Commerce, Bureau of Census, 1941; p. 2.

15. For one circuit of agents and its bearing on career contingencies, see Oswald Hall, "The Stages of a Medical Career," *Amer. J. Sociology* (1948) 53:227–336.

16. See Cumming, footnote 3; p. 92.

17. Hollingshead and Redlich, footnote 4; p. 187.

18. For an analysis of some of these circuit implications for the inpatient, see Leila C. Deasy and Olive W. Quinn, "The Wife of the Mental Patient and the Hospital Psychiatrist." *J. Social Issues* (1955) 11:49–60. An interesting illustration of this kind of analysis may also be found in Alan G. Gowman,

"Blindness and the Role of Companion," *Social Problems* (1956) 4:68–75. A general statement may be found in Robert Merton, "The Role Set: Problems in Sociological Theory," *British J. Sociology* (1957) 8:106–120.

19. I have one case record of a man who claims he thought *he* was taking his wife to see the psychiatrist, not realizing until too late that his wife had made the arrangements.

20. A paraphrase from Kurt Riezler, "The Social Psychology of Shame," *Amer. J. Sociology* (1943) 48:458.

21. See Harold Garfinkel, "Conditions of Successful Degradation Ceremonies," *Amer. J. Sociology* (1956) 61:420–424.

22. Concentration camp practices provide a good example of the function of the betrayal funnel in inducing cooperation and reducing struggle and fuss, although here the mediators could not be said to be acting in the best interests of the inmates. Police picking up persons from their homes would sometimes joke good-naturedly and offer to wait while coffee was being served. Gas chambers were fitted out like delousing rooms, and victims taking off their clothes were told to note where they were leaving them. The sick, aged, weak, or insane who were selected for extermination were sometimes driven away in Red Cross ambulances to camps referred to by terms such as "observation hospital." See David Boder, *I Did Not Interview the Dead;* Urbana, Univ. of Illinois Press, 1949; p. 81; and Elie A. Cohen, *Human Behavior in the Concentration Camp;* London, Cape, 1954; pp. 32, 37, 107.

23. Interviews collected by the Clausen group at NIMH suggest that when a wife comes to be a guardian, the responsibility may disrupt previous distance from in-laws, leading either to a new supportive coalition with them or to a marked withdrawal from them.

24. For an analysis of these nonpsychiatric kinds of perception, see Marian Radke Yarrow, Charlotte Green Schwartz, Harriet S. Murphy, and Leila Calhoun Deasy, "The Psychological Meaning of Mental Illness in the Family," *J. Social Issues* (1955) 11:12–24; Charlotte Green Schwartz, "Perspectives on Deviance: Wives' Definitions of their Husbands' Mental Illness," *Psychiatry* (1957) 20:275–291.

25. This guilt-carrying function is found, of course, in other role-complexes. Thus, when a middle-class couple engages in the process of legal separation or divorce, each of their lawyers usually takes the position that his job is to acquaint his client with all of the potential claims and rights, pressing his client into demanding these, in spite of any nicety of feelings about

the rights and honorableness of the ex-partner. The client, in all good faith, can then say to self and to the ex-partner that the demands are being made only because the lawyer insists it is best to do so.

26. Recorded in the Clausen data.

27. This point is made by Cumming, see footnote 3; p. 129.

28. There is an interesting contrast here with the moral career of the tuberculosis patient. I am told by Julius Roth that tuberculosis patients are likely to come to the hospital willingly, agreeing with their next-of-relation about treatment. Later in their hospital career, when they learn how long they yet have to stay and how depriving and irrational some of the hospital rulings are, they may seek to leave, be advised against this by the staff and by relatives, and only then begin to feel betrayed.

29. The inmate's initial strategy of holding himself aloof from ratifying contact may partly account for the relative lack of group-formation among inmates in public mental hospitals, a connection that has been suggested to me by William R. Smith. The desire to avoid personal bonds that would give license to the asking of biographical questions could also be a factor. In mental hospitals, of course, as in prisoner camps, the staff may consciously break up incipient group-formation in order to avoid collective rebellious action and other ward disturbances.

30. A comparable coming out occurs in the homosexual world, when a person finally comes frankly to present himself to a "gay" gathering not as a tourist but as someone who is "available." See Evelyn Hooker, "A Preliminary Examination of Group Behavior of Homosexuals," *J. Psychology* (1956) 42:217–225; especially p. 221. A good fictionalized treatment may be found in James Baldwin's *Giovanni's Room;* New York, Dial, 1956; pp. 41–63. A familiar instance of the coming out process is no doubt to be found among prepubertal children at the moment one of these actors sidles *back* into a room that had been left in an angered huff and injured *amour-propre*. The phrase itself presumably derives from a *rite-de-passage* ceremony once arranged by upper-class mothers for their daughters. Interestingly enough, in large mental hospitals the patient sometimes symbolizes a complete coming out by his first active participation in the hospital-wide patient dance.

31. See Goffman, "Characteristics of Total Institutions," pp. 43–84; in *Proceedings of the Symposium of Preventive and Social Psychiatry;* Washington, D.C., Walter Reed Army Institute of Research, 1958.

32. A good description of the ward system may be found in Ivan Belknap, *Human Problems of a State Mental Hospital;* New York, McGraw-Hill, 1956; see especially p. 164.

33. Here is one way in which mental hospitals can be worse than concentration camps and prisons as places in which to "do" time; in the latter, self-insulation from the symbolic implications of the settings may be easier. In fact, self-insulation from hospital settings may be so difficult that patients have to employ devices for this which staff interpret as psychotic symptoms.

34. In regard to convicts, see Anthony Heckstall-Smith, *Eighteen Months;* London, Wingate, 1954; pp. 52–53. For " wino's" see the discussion in Howard G. Bain, "A Sociological Analysis of the Chicago Skid-Row Lifeway" unpublished M.A. thesis, Dept. of Sociology, Univ. of Chicago, Sept., 1950; especially "The Rationale of the Skid-Row Drinking Group," pp. 141–146. Bain's neglected thesis is a useful source of material on moral careers.

Apparently one of the occupational hazards of prostitution is that clients and other professional contacts sometimes persist in expressing sympathy by asking for a defensible dramatic explanation for the fall from grace. In having to bother to have a sad tale ready, perhaps the prostitute is more to be pitied than damned. Good examples of prostitute sad tales may be found in Sir Henry Mayhew, "Those that Will Not Work," pp. 210–272; in his *London Labour and the London Poor,* Vol. 4, London, Griffin, Bohn, and Cox, 1862. For a contemporary source, see *Women of the Streets,* edited by C. H. Rolph; London, Zecker and Warburg, 1955; especially p. 6. "Almost always, however, after a few comments on the police, the girl would begin to explain how it was that she was in the life, usually in terms of self-justification." Lately, of course, the psychological expert has helped out the profession in the construction of wholly remarkable sad tales. See, for example, Harold Greenwald, *Call Girl;* New York, Ballantine, 1958.

35. A similar self-protecting rule has been observed in prisons. Thus, Hassler, see footnote 6, in describing a conversation with a fellow-prisoner; "He didn't say much about why he was sentenced, and I didn't ask him, that being the accepted behavior in prison" (p. 76). A novelistic version for the mental hospital may be found in J. Kerkhoff, *How Thin the Veil: A Newspaperman's Story of His Own Mental Crack-up and Recovery;* New York, Greenberg, 1952; p. 27.

36. From the writer's field notes of informal interaction with patients, transcribed as near verbatim as he was able.

37. The process of examining a person psychiatrically and then altering or reducing his status in consequence is known in hospital and prison parlance as *bugging,* the assumption being that once you come to the attention of the testers you either will automatically be labeled crazy or the process of testing itself will make you crazy. Thus psychiatric staff are sometimes seen not as *discovering* whether you are sick, but as *making* you sick; and "Don't bug me, man," can mean, "Don't pester me to the point where I'll get upset." Sheldom Messenger has suggested to me that this meaning of bugging is related to the other colloquial meaning, of wiring a room with a secret microphone to collect information usable for discrediting the speaker.

From Witchcraft to Drugcraft
Biochemistry as Mythology*

Ronny E. Turner and Charles Edgley**

From the fourteenth through the seventeenth century continental Europeans executed more than 500,000 witches. This ideology or theodicy enabled and justified inquisitors (witchprickers) to persecute thousands of people over a longer period of time than the centuries mentioned above. Witchcraft was the legitimized and acceptable explanation for deviance, therapeutic welfare, and exploitation; it was the "cause" of the black plague, heresy, crime, poor harvests, women stepping out of traditional roles, and any or all maladies affecting the individual or society.[1]

Likewise, the nineteenth century saw another problem, masturbation, so ubiquitous as to cause virtually every form of deviance. Masturbation caused masturbatory insanity which produced more masturbation in a continuous confusion of concepts of cause and effect. This "self abuse" of the nineteenth century, which has become a therapy in today's medical nomenclature, was seen as the etiology of suicide, neurasthenia, dementia, brain damage, neuroses, homosexuality, hypochondria, and epilepsy; it led to physical, mental, moral, and intellectual degeneracy. Like witchcraft earlier, masturbation threatened to destroy society.[2]

The condition, craft, and curse of the witch, used by humanity for centuries to explain aberrant behavior, no longer hold sway in the Western world. They have been replaced by the languages of medicine, psychiatry, and biochemistry. With the increasing medicalization of our rhetoric[3] the witch, the curse, sin, and the devil have all given way to the errant chemical—a chemical pathology of the brain. The primary political implication of this shift, of course, has been to cast chemotherapy into the role of preserver of the status quo of social conduct, now called "mental health," by curing or mitigating deviance in its various forms by subsuming it under the rubric of "mental illness." The biochemical specialist, psychobiologist, psychiatrist dispensing antipsychotic drugs, medical doctors prescribing a vast chemical arsenal—these representatives of science have replaced the witchpricker. In short, drugcraft has replaced witchcraft.

THE BRAIN AS A CHEMICAL FACTORY

That there are chemical and neurological processes and components involved in all of the activities of the brain goes without saying; the brain is in large measure a chemical machine that functions with an infinitely complex interplay of chemical processes. Chemicals transmit impulses among the brain cells; dopamine, secreted by nerve cells, crosses synapses as neurotransmitters "communicate" to neuroreceptors. Through this process it is believed that thought, mood, and behavior are either created or activated.

Organic-biochemical theories assume that imbalances in these chemical processes are responsible for a wide variety of mental illnesses—especially schizophrenia and chronic depression. Stein's description of the matter is typical:

Serious emotional problems, such as depression, result more from the breakdown of the good feeling system (in the brain) than from lack of environmental inputs. The normal brain . . . finds ways to produce good feelings one way or another . . . the abnormal brain of a depressive must be quite abnormal indeed when a successful businessman who has a nice family and everything going for him walks out of a window one day—that's bad chemistry.[4]

Many other eminent scientists could be cited to show the current unanimity of this view.[5]

*Reprinted from *Social Science Journal,* 20:4 (October 1983), pp. 1–12, by permission of JAI Press, Inc.

**Revised version of a paper originally presented at the meetings of the Western Social Science Association, Denver, Colorado, April 1982.

Frederick Goodwin, Chief of Clinical Psychobiology at the National Institute of Mental Health, for example, says:

There appears to be a chemical basis to variations in people which may directly produce illness, but may also *interact* with illness. . . . Depression may have a totally different chemical base . . . depression is an inability of the brain to produce a good feeling.[6]

How does all of this work? In acute schizophrenia, the receptors are believed to be too sensitive to an excessive amount of released dopamine or else the neurotransmitters reabsorb their manufactured dopamine too slowly after transmission. The problem of a surplus of dopamine or overly sensitive receptors is addressed by administering antischizophrenic drugs to either block or blunt the absorption of the dopamine receptors.[7] Harvard neurophysiologist Seymore Kety, the most persistent spokesman for this point of view, foresees the day when "it may be possible to get a treatment that is so specific it eradicates the *cause*—then you have a 'cure' which leads to the prevention of emotional disabilities."[8]

Although none of these claims has ever been demonstrated to be true and the biochemical mechanisms postulated are not well understood even by their advocates, a veritable parade of chemical substances have been used in the attempt to find what Don Jackson once derisively called a "Salk Vaccine for the mind."[9] Introduced over a quarter of a century ago, Chlorpromazine was believed to be an effective drug in reversing the symptoms of schizophrenia by biochemically blocking the release of dopamine from certain submicroscopic sacs in the brain cells. Nevertheless, "there are over 330,000 institutionalized psychotics (many of whom are diagnosed as schizophrenic) who have proven wholly unresponsive to dopamine blockage therapies."[10] Similarly, a host of antidepressant drugs such as Elavil, Tofranil, Sinequan, Marplan, and Nardil have been pumped into the systems of depressives, the most common category of mental patient, because they are believed somehow to increase or inhibit neurotransmitter action. Hyperactive children, adolescents with extreme fluctuations in mood, and adults facing the anxieties of everyday life are among others who have been served this chemical pharmacopoeia.[11]

Furthermore, the futures market in drugs looks bright, at least judging from the statements of those who speculate on such matters. Drugs are seen in the not-too-distant future as improving the performance of "normal" people by increasing memory and intellectual acuity. The need for sleep could be lessened, thereby allowing more waking hours for other activities. Although drugcraft has been developing rapidly since World War II, research in brain chemistry is in its infancy. "We're on the verge of a new era."[12] Some neuroscientists even foresee the day when it "would become possible to diagnose mental illness from a simple blood, urine, or spinal fluid sample."[13] Doctors would then give appropriate drugs "once the imbalances in blood chemistry are determined."[14]

THE TAUTOLOGY OF BRAIN-MIND-BEHAVIOR ARGUMENTS

What are we to make of these dreams and claims? There can be little doubt that such promises fall on receptive ears. The public, overburdened with moral and value conflicts already, would love to think that the ubiquitous problem of deviant behavior could be resolved via vaccination. But despite the claims, promises, and dreams, underlying modern drugcraft is an epistemological problem that simply will not go away. The problem, simply stated, is this: because the brain is involved in human conduct, just as every other part of the body is, does not make deviant behavior a problem in medicine any more than the fact that nuclear physics may be used in building a bomb makes international conflicts problems in physics. To transform badness into madness reclassifies the problem, but contributes nothing to its solution and is a concrete impediment to its understanding.[15] While there are chemical and neurological components to "paranoid" or "schizophrenic" personalities, just as there are to any other kind, this does not make paranoia or schizophrenia a disease.[16] Literally speaking, a mind can be no more sick than a joke can be. "Mental illness" is a misuse of language—a metaphor masquerading as a literal truth because the "as if" character of the metaphor has been dropped.[17]

Treated throughout organic/biochemical theories of deviance is the largely taken-for-granted assumption that a person's social acts are governed (or at least affected) by the neurochemical functioning of the brain. Conversely, these arguments assert that a person's conduct, the social context of his acts, and many other factors affect the chemical composition of the brain. "Many schizophrenic patients are under extreme emotional stress which is known to cause profound biochemical changes in man."[18] An environment loaded with stress might "trigger" chemical reactions which produce mental illness in certain persons. In other words, the organic assumption at work here is that brains secrete mental illness just as the kidneys secrete urine.

This line of reasoning flounders at several crucial points. First, it is difficult, if not impossible, to differentiate between a person's internal brain chemistry and his or her external conduct in terms of which precedes the other, since persons are inherently active.[19] If we do not know which comes first, causal relationships are impossible to determine. In fact, the connection between these "internal" and "external" variables[20] is ordinarily assigned by linguistic convention. Second, in the absence of an exclusive differentiation between cause and effect, a haunting tautology lurks in the wings of the biochemical arguments. The brain is construed as an independent variable at one time and a dependent one the next. Aberrations in brain chemistry are seen to cause mental illness at one time and to be the result of it at another. What is symptom and what is disease is virtually never defined with anything approaching conceptual exclusiveness.[21]

Without resolving this inherent tautology, this paper will show that biochemical theories of deviance do and must by necessity rely on social judgments in the determination of mental illness. Distinguishing the mentally healthy from the mentally ill is part of a social process of defining who is deviant and who is normal; the identification of chemical compositions in the brain *is not* and *cannot* be *prima facie* evidence for the diagnosis of mental illness.

THE MYTHS OF CHEMICAL MENTAL ILLNESS

By considering several "mental illnesses," we will show that it is not possible to distinguish either medically or chemically socially acceptable from socially unacceptable behavior; nor could one diagnose endogenously or exogenously "caused" chemical differences in the brain. The problems, diagnoses, and processes leading to the identification of a person as deviant, as well as the help, "solution," or therapy, reside in a social arena and are social questions.[22]

The decision to identify a person as mentally ill is obviously not now based on chemical or blood analysis. The promise of drugcraft is that this procedure could some day be used to diagnose mental illness and lead to chemical cures. But how can this happen if the physical "symptoms" are not systematically differentiated from the meaningful behavior out of which the symptomatic inference is drawn? Moreover, the prior symptomotology on which patients might be differentiated for chemical analysis and research is inexact, unsystematic, ambiguous, and lacks a creditable consensus even among psychiatrists. How could such a chaotic nosology be a basis for establishing variables in the testing of brain chemistry? Even if one conceded that the mentally ill could somehow be differentiated from the mentally healthy by using some measure of social consensus (not an easy task either), the identification of chemical differences in the brain (if they *were* ever substantiated) would rest on prior social labeling anyway.

Depression

Two cases will help us understand the problem of where and what draws the line between mental illness and "normal" behavior. Consider the case of two people exhibiting an incapacitating depression in which they display the "same" symptoms and are unable to carry on their customary roles in life. Assuming that a chemical configuration could be isolated and identified as the medical condition of depression, they should both have the same essential brain chemistry. All parties to person A's situation agree that he is depressed because his spouse recently died and the grief is overwhelming. In addition, person A is unemployed, the bills are piling up, and he[23] sees little likelihood of changing his circumstances.

Person B, on the other hand, shows all the same behavioral characteristics as A, but no one can figure out why. Person B has not experienced a traumatic death, has a good job, was recently promoted, and has all the accouterments of the American Dream. What he is lacking seems to be an understandable rationale for being depressed! In the absence of a vocabulary of motives[24] that places B's actions in some kind of comprehensible and acceptable framework, he is very likely to be labeled mentally ill while person A is not.

Would it be possible to distinguish between A and B solely on a chemical basis? Are both mentally ill? Let us further suppose that a year has passed and person A now has a good job, has solved his financial problems, but still is severely depressed because he misses his wife. Generally in our society (and it differs from place to place and from situation to situation) a person is allowed a certain period of time for such emotional wounds to heal. But beyond this period (usually less than a year) if a person still grieves in ways that affect others, he or she still may be regarded as sick. How can chemistry distinguish between grief of two weeks (socially acceptable, normal conduct) and grief of a year and a half (unacceptable, abnormal, sick)?

Clearly, person A was not regarded as mentally ill initially, not because of his chemistry, but because he is entitled to be depressed given his problems, while person B was regarded as sick because his social circumstances do not explain or justify his conduct. Obviously, then, the diagnoses of mental illness and mental health are dependent upon a series of social processes with their own contingencies, not on distinguishable chemical differences. Surely, the implication of biochemical explanations of mental illness is that there is some kind of chemical difference in the brains of persons A and B. But the problem seems to be tantamount to distinguishing between spit and saliva. While both have the same chemical composition, socially they are defined in vastly different ways. Spit is saliva in an inap-

propriate place. Chemistry *qua* chemistry cannot differentiate between spit and saliva, nor tell us how or when a certain type of moisture in the mouth comes to be regarded as spit. Mental illness, then, is behavioral spit. Szasz says correctly that if depression is a chemically induced disease, then so is happiness.[25]

Paranoid Schizophrenia

If schizophrenia is a "disorder in thinking," to whom is the thinking incomprehensible? What chemical evidence distinguishes ordered from disordered thinking? It would seem quite inconceivable that chemical analysis of two different brains could, in a double-blind experiment, distinguish normal thinking and conceptions of reality from abnormal and unrealistic ones.

Our hypothetical person A says someone is out to get him. Likewise, person B believes he has good reasons to protect his vulnerable self from social or even physical assaults. Given that both actors in this scenario *believe* someone is out to get them, would not they both register the same chemical readouts if their brain chemistry were deciphered (assuming there *is* a causative chemical component to paranoia)? Both A and B have fears, occasionally break out in cold sweats, are sick at their stomachs, talk constantly of enemies, and are suffering from their experience as they perceive it. Both have described their threatened feelings to others.

But let us suppose that person A, in fact, does have someone out to get him. His boss wants him fired, a younger executive is bucking for his job, and his wife is having an affair with his best friend. Does this person possess a mental disease called "paranoid schizophrenia" or is he accurately interpreting the social situation in which he finds himself? Once we understand his situation, few people would claim that he is mentally sick.

Person B, on the other hand, is considered mentally ill by almost everyone because they do not accept his assertion that someone is out to get him. Others see his behavior as a fundamental misinterpretation of his social situation and no one can talk him out of it. Paranoia, by definition, means the person sees threats that do not exist. Is it chemistry that befogs the mind in this way? Is it chemistry that enables person A to read his situation correctly while forcing person B to misinterpret his so radically? What if person A blithely ignored the threats his situation posed? We might call him stupid or naive, but almost never would we call him "sick."

Lemert[26] has demonstrated that those persons diagnosed as paranoid schizophrenics *do* have people out to get them. The "dynamics of exclusion" that often result from paranoid performances are quite real so that eventually, if not initially, the paranoid comes to have enemies. Labeling a person as paranoid, with all the implications of that designation, obviously reinforces the person's paranoia. Could chemistry distinguish unwarranted paranoia from the warranted variety? Original paranoia from the socially reinforced kind?

Questions such as these pose problems similar to trying to distinguish tap water from Holy Water. There is a real difference, but the difference that exists exists solely by social definition. To understand the difference necessitates an understanding of the Catholic Church, not chemical processes. Are there chemical differences in the brains of Republicans, Democrats, and anarchists? Or is Thomas Szasz's rendering of the problem more to the point?

If you believe that you are Jesus, or have discovered a cure for cancer (and you have not), or the Communists are after you (and they are not)—then your beliefs are likely to be regarded as symptoms of schizophrenia. But if you believe that the Jews are the Chosen People, or that Jesus was the Son of God, or that Communism is the only scientifically and morally correct form of government—then your beliefs are likely to be regarded as a reflection of who you are: Jew, Christian, Communist. This is why we will discover the chemical cause of schizophrenia when we discover the chemical cause of Judaism, Christianity, and Communism. No sooner and no later.[27]

There is probably as much chemical difference in diagnosed schizophrenics and normal people as between liberals and conservatives, though in the latter case the definitions are sharper and the behavior more predictable.

The Delusional Schizophrenic

Supposedly, the neurochemical analysis could differentiate between the person who hears legitimate, nonexistent voices from those who hear illegitimate, nonexistent voices. Again, Thomas Szasz states, "If you talk to God, you are praying; if God talks to you, you have schizophrenia. If the dead talk to you, you are a spiritualist; if God talks to you, you are schizophrenic."[28]

Even setting aside Szasz's acerbic sarcasm, we can still appreciate his point. Many Christians talk to God daily, yet they are not usually seen as schizophrenic.[29] Even if God talks to you, the right identity and vocabulary of motives can be mobilized to legitimize the experience. For example, the Reverend Jerry Falwell, spokesman for the Moral Majority, claims that God told him to oppose the Equal Rights Amendment. Evangelist Oral Roberts claims to have seen Christ standing 900 feet tall, and talked with him personally one evening. Christ assured him that his new hospital in Tulsa, Oklahoma, delayed by debt and politics, would be completed. After Roberts reported this experience, an extra $5 million was received in contributions. Are the brains of Falwell and Roberts the chemical equivalent of a dopamine disordered schizophrenic who claims to have conversed with Plato?

Person A converses daily with God and hears voices from a deity. These voices are nonexistent by scientific standards. If he is Pentecostal, he may claim to be a vessel through which the Holy Spirit speaks to others in "tongues." If one follows the logic of neurochemistry, would not person A have a similar brain chemistry to person B who claims to hear voices from some being residing in another galaxy?

These rhetorical questions show a highly relative and heavily nuanced social process in which persons in society have defined normal and abnormal from the standpoint of their own values. It is not *hearing* voices that constitutes psychiatric disease, it is *whose* voices are being heard. Given these examples, it is difficult to see how chemistry could address itself to deviance because of its socially constructed nature. "If Christianity or Communism[30] were called diseases, would they [neurochemists] then look for the chemical and genetic 'causes' of these 'conditions'?"

Extending the arguments of the psychobiologists: If Christianity were considered a disease and research done on the brains of Christians as is now done with schizophrenics, should we not expect to find the chemical complex that makes Christians Christian? Furthermore, if these substances could be identified and extracted or manufactured, could not the recruitment of potential Christians be medicalized? Injections of this "Christian chemical complex" could then be given producing "chemo-Christians," thereby considerably reducing the workload of the clergy. Presumably there would be slightly different chemical formulas to produce Christians of various denominations: Baptists, Methodists, and Catholics. Backsliders might be cured with a booster shot. Would we differentiate chemo-Christians from a "social" Christian, one who accepted the theology in the traditional fashion? Indeed, had the promises of modern neurochemistry been available in the 1930s, the holocaust might have been avoided. Eradicating Jews would have been unnecessary; they could have been "cured" instead.

OTHER CURIOSITIES IN THE BIOCHEMICAL ARGUMENTS

That persons of different ages engage in different kinds of conduct is an observation accepted by everyone. A three-year-old child may play with imaginary friends and converse with them regularly. Such behavior is taken to be evidence of a "vivid" and "active" imagination—not psychopathology. An adult, however, who continues a relationship with an imaginary friend and makes it public would most likely be regarded as deranged.[31] Children, in other words, are afforded modes of pretense denied to adults, and an adult who engaged in such behavior would, at the very least, be regarded as "malingering" or faking a mental illness. But faking a mental illness is also a mental illness in psychiatric nomenclature. Are there chemical differences in the acceptable pretending of the child and the unacceptable pretending of the adult? Between pretending and malingering? It is difficult to see how neuro-

chemistry could make such distinctions—it is easy to see how society does.

Equally curious are the research studies that show the incidence of schizophrenia to be much greater in the lower socioeconomic classes than in the upper and middle classes.[32] Moreover, why would a chemical malady surface three times more often among the single than among the married?[33] Does marriage alter biochemistry, thereby providing a measure of immunity? Why are kleptomaniacs invariably found among the upper classes? Why is it that most of the mentally ill (as was true of witches in the sixteenth century) are women over 40 years of age? It seems clear to a number of observers that neurochemical explanations of complex social phenomena are cases of scientific reductionism run amok. For example, Drummond asserts:

Whatever schizophrenia is, it amounts to the breaking of certain largely unstated rules of social behavior. Rule-breaking, like rules themselves, exists in a broader context than neurophysiology. The biochemical approach to mental illness assumes that sharp lines can be drawn through the cloudy residue of rule-breaking, and that the microscopic analysis of those lines will yield the etiology of diseases similar to diabetes or pneumococcal pneumonia. This is reductionist stupidity similar to trying to understand capital punishment by analyzing the chemical transformations in the muscles of the executioner.[34]

The biochemical theories of deviance are somewhat analogous "to finding runners (people who have been observed to run) and trying to determine what running is and what *causes* it by blood tests . . ."[35] The blood chemistry of runners is found to differ from nonrunners. Convinced that running lies in the blood, chemicals are given to the runners and scientists observe that running is altered beneficially or deleteriously, depending on the various drugs injected; this observation that runners and running are affected by drugs is used as "evidence" that running is caused by chemical elements in the blood. From a social perspective the running is explained in various ways: the person was late for work, exercising for cardiovascular fitness, training for the hundred meter dash, or avoiding a mugger.[36]

J. S. Mill warned that there always has been a tendency "to believe that whatever receives a name must be an entity or being, having an independent existence of its own."[37] Witchcraft was the name given to deviance in earlier centuries; the rhetoric was reified and hypostatized into tautological, causal relationships. An ontological entity or condition of witchcraft was believed to exist; after all, witches both black and white were empirically observed to be "real."

CONCLUSION: THE TWO MEANINGS OF BIOCHEMISTRY AS MYTHOLOGY

Our inquiry into the mythologies of biochemistry has been conducted primarily along one line in this paper. By showing how biochemistry fails to account for what it purports to explain, much of the paper has had a debunking and satiric tone. In other words, we have explored the mythology of biochemistry according to the common sense view of myth as "falsehood." However, there is another meaning of the term "myth" which must be explored. This is the more intellectually traditional view, born in anthropology and folklore, that a myth is a narrative tale conducted for certain social purposes. Since myths are usually associated with primitive cultures, the dominant mythologies of our own time and place, especially scientific ones, are often overlooked either because they blatantly bill themselves as the "truth," or because our immersion in them obscures our vision; it is most difficult to question the myths by which we live. The medicalization of deviance may be viewed in this second context as a change in the narrative tales of our society. It is this second meaning of mythology—a story told for social purposes—with which we wish to conclude our analysis.

Science has been able to replace other forms of explanation primarily by producing and claiming certain "facts" as its own. Just as witchcraft claimed to account for certain aberrations in human conduct, drugcraft makes such claims today. But neither, strictly speaking, deals with "facts," because all facts are paradigm dependent and therefore integrally tied to interpretation.[38] Drugcraft is an attempt, like many before it, to provide objective, value-free standards for assessing social conduct. The medicalization of illness implies that factors not primarily related to social ones be the unit of analysis. However, "illness, by its very nature is a socially determinable, and hence variable notion, and further, it is an evaluative rather than a factual one."[39] The logic of science tears everything from its social, cultural, and situational context in an effort to produce pure and universal truth. But since nothing can truly be separated from such meaningful contexts, the attempt has merely lead to a systematic obscuring of the mythological uses of science itself.[40]

The critique of biochemical explanations of mental disorder we have launched in this paper is reasonably well known in the psychiatric community. Volumes of research have shown the unreliability of the psychiatric account of mental disorder.[41] Yet it is these very diagnostic categories that are the basis of biochemical arguments. If the categories and explanations are known to be faulty, why do we continue to use them? This is a question that leads directly to the second meaning of mythology.

The best single analytical variant of mythology for sociological purposes is the idea of "vocabularies of motive."[42] This powerful concept reminds us that human relationships on this planet have always been possible because of constructed understandings concerning why people do the things they do. A vocabulary of motives is a communicated rationale, excuse, or justification for conduct in question. It puts action into an understandable context, thereby allaying what has always been the one thing human beings cannot deal with: mystification. Aberrant behavior, is, of course, particularly troublesome, and especially likely to create social contexts in which explanations are desperately sought. In the past, humors, phrenology, demons, fate, God, the unconscious, and a host of other notions have been invoked and have "worked" as a rationale for bizarre or unusual conduct. Each of these "explanations" gives people a sense that the behavior of another can be placed within a context of meaning—a story with a point. In this sense, modern drugcraft may be seen as a sophisticated reemergence of the "bad-blood" arguments of the nineteenth century. Such biochemical explanations of deviant behavior have in common with those previously mentioned the ostensible virtue of taking responsibility away from the actor and the context of his acts and placing them in the body—a convenience made possible because the body is always present but not always accounted for; therefore, always available to be invoked as a rationale for conduct in question.[43]

The extraordinary success of biological science in establishing itself as the dominant vocabulary of motives of the twentieth century should not divert us from a close examination of the problems to which such explanations inevitably lead. Every mythology has social consequences (indeed, that is what myths are for). But the biochemical version is fraught with some very negative ones,[44] not the least of which is that it diverts our attention away from the existential burdens that we all share as human and social beings. In all these things we must resist the compelling temptation to look for lost possessions (in this case the meanings of a person's life) under lamp posts simply because the light is better there.

NOTES

1. See Nachman Ben-Yehuda, "The European Witch Craze of the 14th to 17th Centuries," *American Journal of Sociology,* vol. 86, no. 1 (July 1980), pp. 1–31 for an extensive sociological analysis of variables related to the development of witchcraft.

2. A concise and succinct statement of how badness became madness is insightfully presented in Peter Conrad and Joseph Schneider, *Deviance and Medicalization* (St. Louis: C. V. Mosby, 1980).

3. Thomas Szasz, *The Myth of Mental Illness* (New York: Perennial Library, 1961); Paul Chalfant, "Sinners, Suckers and Sickees: The Medicalization of Practically Everything," in H. Paul Chalfant (ed.), *Sociological Stuff* (Dubuque: Kendall-Hunt Publishing Co., 1977), pp. 239–245; Peter Conrad, "Implications of Changing Social Policy for the Medicalization of Deviance," *Contemporary Crises*, vol. 4 (1982), pp. 195–205; Eliot Friedson, *Profession of Medicine* (New York: Dodd Mead, 1970).

4. Joel Greenberg, "Memory Research: An Era of Good Feeling," *Science News*, vol. 114, no. 22 (November 25, 1978), p. 365.

5. Richard Haier, "The Diagnosis of Schizophrenia: A Review of Recent Developments," *Schizophrenia 1980* (Washington, D.C.: National Institute of Mental

Health, 1981), pp. 2–13; Malcolm Bowers, "Biochemical Process in Schizophrenia: An Update," *Schizophrenia 1980* (Washington, D.C.: National Institute of Mental Health, 1981), pp. 27–37.

6. Greenberg, *op. cit.*, p. 365.

7. Bowers, *op. cit.*, pp. 27–37. We are well aware of the intricacies of the mind/brain debate; it is not our purpose to enter into such a discussion here. Our inquiry centers instead on the claim that the social conduct called "mental illness" can be accounted for biochemically as well as the meaning and significance of such claims. Those who wish to immerse themselves in a full treatment of the complexity of the mind/brain problem should consult C.V. Borst, *The Mind/Brain Identity Theory* (London: St. Martin's Press, 1973).

8. Joel Greenberg, "The Brain: Holding the Secrets of Behavior," *Science News*, vol. 114, no. 22 (November 25, 1978), p. 366.

9. Don Jackson, *Myths of Madness* (New York: Macmillan, 1964).

10. Barbara Villet, "Opiates of the Mind," *Atlantic Monthly* (June 1978), p. 83.

11. Peter Conrad, "The Discovery of Hyperkinesis: Notes on the Medicalization of Deviant Behavior," *Social Problems*, vol. 23 (October 1975), pp. 12–25.

12. Matt Clark, et al., "Drugs and Psychiatry: A New Era," *Newsweek* (November 12, 1979), p. 104.

13. Hedley Donovan, "Psychiatry on the Couch," *Time*, vol. 113, no. 14 (April 2, 1979), p. 77.

14. *Ibid.*, p. 77.

15. Thomas Szasz, *Ceremonial Chemistry* (Garden City: Anchor Press, 1974).

16. E. Fuller Torrey, *The Death of Psychiatry* (New York: Penguin Books, 1974), p. 39.

17. Ronny E. Turner and Charles Edgley, "Sociological Semanticide: On Reification, Tautology, and the Destruction of Language," *Sociological Quarterly*, vol. 21, no. 4 (Autumn 1980), pp. 595–605.

18. Amerigo Farina, *Schizophrenia* (Morristown, NJ: General Learning Press, 1972).

19. John Dewey, *Human Nature and Conduct* (New York: Henry Holt and Co., 1922), pp. 112–113.

20. Herbert Blumer's cautions about "variable" analysis were never more pertinent than here. See his "Sociological Analysis and the 'Variable,'" in Herbert Blumer, *Symbolic Interaction: Perspective and Method* (Englewood Cliffs: Prentice Hall, 1969), pp. 127–139.

21. Torrey, *op. cit.*

22. See Howard Becker, *Outsiders* (New York: The Free Press, 1963); Edwin Schur, *Labeling Deviant Behavior* (New York: Harper and Row, 1971); Thomas Scheff, *Being Mentally Ill* (Chicago: Aldine, 1966); Thomas Szasz, *Schizophrenia* (New York: Basic

Books, 1976); and D. L. Rosenhan, "On Being Sane in Insane Places," *Science*, vol. 179 (January 1973), pp. 250–258.

23. The term "paranoia" is a good illustration of the contorted logic of medical psychiatry. The word comes from the Greek *para* and *nous* and literally means "beside the mind." Never has a problem in living been so inaccurately named. For paranoia, as Ernest Becker has shown so well, is actually the most intense and focused functioning of the mind. It is the mind acting alone, trying to make sense out of experience for a person who is impoverished, weak, and frightened. Furthermore, paranoia seems to come easier to those who are most open to the subtleties of experience, the unfairness of the world, the miscarriage of human events, and the general hopelessness of the human condition—hardly "beside the mind." For a full discussion of the interpersonal and dramaturgical bases of paranoia, see Ernest Becker, *Angel in Armor* (New York: George Braziller, 1969), pp. 123–155.

24. For an analysis of the vocabulary of motives perspective see R. S. Peters, *The Concept of Motivation* (London: Routledge and Kegan Paul, 1958); C. W. Mills, "Situated Actions and Vocabularies of Motive," *American Sociological Review* (December 1940), pp. 904–913; Marvin Scott and Stanford Lyman, "Accounts," *American Sociological Review,* vol. 33, no. 1 (1968), pp. 46–62; and Charles Edgley and Ronny E. Turner, "Masks and Social Relations: An Essay on the Sources and Assumptions of Dramaturgical Social Psychology," *Humboldt Journal of Social Relations,* vol. 3 (Fall/Winter 1975), pp. 3–12.

25. Szasz, *op. cit.,* p. 34.

26. Edwin Lemert, "Paranoia and the Dynamics of Exclusion," *Sociometry,* vol. 25, no. 1 (March 1962), pp. 2–20.

27. Thomas Szasz, *The Second Sin* (Garden City: Anchor, 1974), pp. 113–114.

28. *Ibid.,* p. 113.

29. We must be careful here. Psychiatric nosology has made suspect many conventional religious interpretations, especially those which literally interpret spiritual relationships, and it is quite possible that there are psychiatrists, as well as many educated lay persons, who regard such practices as evidence of mental illness.

30. Should such a blatantly political view as "communism" seem a far-fetched example of the lengths to which the rhetoric of organic psychiatry could be extended, one only has to look to the conservative use of such arguments in the so-called "Twinkie" defense constructed for San Francisco policeman Dan White after he killed Mayor George Moscone and Supervisor Harvey Milk in a fit of antihomosexual rage. For a full

account of the trial and the role played by biochemical arguments in it, see Thomas Szasz, "How Dan White Got Away with Murder and How American Psychiatry Helped Him Do It," *Inquiry* (August 6 and 20, 1979).

31. See James Stewart in the Hollywood classic, "Harvey."

32. A. Hollingshead and F. Redlich, *Social Class and Mental Illness* (New York: Wiley and Sons, 1958).

33. O. Odegaard, "The Incidence of Psychosis in Various Occupations," *International Journal of Social Psychiatry,* vol. 2 (1956), pp. 85–104.

34. Hugh Drummond, "Dr. D. is Mad as Hell," *Mother Jones* (December 1979), p. 61.

35. Farino, *op. cit.,* p. 11.

36. *Ibid.,* p. 11.

37. Turner and Edgley, "Sociological Semanticide," *op. cit.,* p. 595.

38. Thomas Kuhn, *The Structure of Scientific Revolution* (Chicago: University of Chicago Press, 1962); and Harold Garfinkel, *Studies in Ethnomethodology* (Englewood Cliffs: Prentice Hall, 1967).

39. Bernard Rollin, "On the Nature of Illness," *Man and Medicine,* vol. 4, no. 3 (1979), p. 161.

40. Theodore Roszak, *The Making of a Counter-Culture* (New York: Anchor, 1969), pp. 205–238.

41. E. Zigler and L. Phillips, "Psychiatric Diagnosis: A Critique," *Journal of Abnormal and Social Psychology,* vol. 63 (1961), pp. 607–618; David Mechanic, *Medical Sociology* (New York: Free Press, 1978); D. L. Rosenhan, "On Being Sane in Insane Places," *Science,* vol. 179 (January 1973), pp. 250–258; and Erving Goffman, *Asylums* (Garden City: Anchor, 1961).

42. C. W. Mills, *op. cit.;* Kenneth Burke, *A Rhetoric of Motives* (Berkeley: University of California Press, 1950); and Edgley and Turner, "Masks and Social Relations," *op. cit.*

43. Scott and Lyman, *op. cit.*

44. The liabilities of the drug revolution have only begun to surface. See George E. Crane, "Clinical Psychopharmacology in the Twentieth Century," *Science,* vol. 181 (July 13, 1973), pp. 124–128; D. F. Klein and J. M. David, *Diagnosis and Drug Treatment of Psychiatric Disorders* (Baltimore: Williams and Wilkins, 1969); and L. A. Scrouffe and M. A. Stewart, "Treating Problem Children with Stimulant Drugs," *New England Journal of Medicine,* vol. 289 (August 23, 1973), pp. 407–412. The "side effects" of therapeutic drugs have been downplayed by the pharmaceutical industry; there is little discussion of the 40–50 percent of schizophrenics who develop tartive dyskinesia after long-term use of drugs analogized as insulin for the diabetic. Furthermore, well-designed research studies

have shown "no quantitative correlation between the percentage of patients receiving drug therapy . . . and the amount of improvement or releases." Andrew Scull, *Decarceration* (Englewood Cliffs, N.J.: Prentice Hall, 1977), p. 84. Compared to placebo patients, schizophrenics treated with Chlorpromazine were more susceptible to deterioration when released from the hospital. See Maurice Rappaport, et al., *Schizophrenics for Whom Phenothiazines May Be Contraindicated or Unnecessary* (University of California: Langley Porter Neuropsychiatric Institute, 1975). Although in some cases there were temporary improvements, in the long run the patients not receiving the drugs did better. The touting of drugs as causative agents in reducing staff loads in mental hospitals or the deinstitutionalization of the mentally ill now seems at best fiction, perhaps designed to justify massive uses of psychotropic chemicals. There are simply too many social correlates of discharge to regard it as a purely clinical phenomenon. See G. W. Brown, "Length of Hospital Stay and Schizophrenia," *Acta Psychiatrica et Neurologica Scandinavia,* vol. 35 (1960), pp. 414–430; J. R. Greenly, "Exit from a Mental Hospital," Ph.D. dissertation, Yale University, 1970; Greenly, "Alternative Views of the Psychiatrist's Role," *Social Problems,* vol. 20 (1972), pp. 252–262; and D. Watt and D. Buglass, "The Effects of Clinic and Social Factors on the Discharge of Chronic Psychiatric Patients," *Social Psychiatry,* vol. 1 (1966), pp. 57–63.